WORLD ENCYCLOPEDIA OF ENTREPRENEURSHIP

This book is dedicated to Naomï Josephine Dana

World Encyclopedia of Entrepreneurship

Edited by

Léo-Paul Dana

Adjunct Professor, GSCM – Montpellier Business School, France, on study leave from the University of Canterbury, New Zealand and Founding Editor, Journal of International Entrepreneurship *and* Journal of Enterprising Communities

Edward Elgar

Cheltenham, UK • Northampton, MA, USA

Published by
Edward Elgar Publishing Limited
The Lypiatts
15 Lansdown Road
Cheltenham
Glos GL50 2JA
UK

Edward Elgar Publishing, Inc.
William Pratt House
9 Dewey Court
Northampton
Massachusetts 01060
USA

A catalogue record for this book
is available from the British Library

Library of Congress Control Number: 2010929024

ISBN 978 1 84542 479 4 (cased)

Typeset by Servis Filmsetting Ltd, Stockport, Cheshire
Printed and bound by MPG Books Group, UK

Contents

Contributors

Acs, Zoltan J., George Mason University, USA

Althoff, Kai, University of Siegen, Germany

Anderson, Robert Brent, University of Regina, Canada

Atherton, Andrew, University of Lincoln, UK

Audretsch, David B., Max Planck Institute of Economics, Germany

Backes-Gellner, Uschi, University of Zurich, Switzerland

Baldacchino, Godfrey, University of Prince Edward Island, Canada

Baumol, William J., New York University and Princeton University (Emeritus), USA

Bögenhold, Dieter, Free University of Bolzano, Italy

Bonnet, Jean, Université de Caen, France

Bradley, Raymond Trevor, Institute for Whole Social Science, USA

Brau, Thomas, Université de Caen, France

Casson, Mark, University of Reading, UK

Cussy, Pascal, Université de Caen, France

Dana, Léo-Paul, University of Canterbury, New Zealand

Dana, Teresa E., University of Canterbury, New Zealand

Degen, A. Allan, Ben Gurion University of the Negev, Israel

Down, Simon, University of Newcastle, UK

Fachinger, Uwe, University of Vechta, Germany

Fayolle, Alain, EMLYON Business School, France

Ferguson, Lynn, Canada

Filion, Louis Jacques, HEC Montréal, Canada

Frith, Kirk, University of Lincoln, UK

Gasse, Yvon, Université Laval, Canada

Ghoul, Wafica Ali, Lebanese International University, Lebanon

Gottschalk, Petter, Norwegian School of Management, Norway

Hamilton, Robert T., University of Canterbury, New Zealand

Han, Mary, Ryerson University, Canada

Harms, Rainer, Twente University, The Netherlands

Hawver, Thomas H., Virginia Commonwealth University, USA

Huebscher, Jutta, Passau University, Germany

Julien, Pierre-André, Université de Québec à Trois-Rivières, Canada

Kao, Kenneth R., Memorial University of Newfoundland, Canada

Kao, Raymond W.Y., Ryerson University, Canada

Kao, Rowland R., Oxford University, UK

Kautonen, Teemu, University of Turku, Finland

Kilby, Peter, Wesleyan University, USA

Kleinbaum, Adam M., Harvard Business School, USA

Koch, Andreas, Institute for Applied Economic Research, Germany

Kolb, Susanne, University of Siegen, Germany

Kraus, Sascha, University of Liechtenstein and Utrecht University, The Netherlands

Kyrö, P., Helsinki School of Economics, Finland

Lendner, Christian, University of Applied Sciences Deggendorf, Germany

Leong, David, Nanyang Technological University, Singapore

Light, Ivan H., University of California, Los Angeles, USA

Maksimov, Vladislav R., Georgia State University, USA

Mason, Colin M., University of Strathclyde, UK

McDougall, Patricia P., Indiana University, USA

McElwee, Gerard, Nottingham Trent University, UK

Morris, Michael, Oklahoma State University, USA

Niemi, M., University of Tampere, Finland

Obrecht, Jean J., EM Strasbourg Business School, France

Oviatt, Benjamin M., University of New South Wales, Australia and Georgia State University, USA

Palmroos, Jenni, University of Vaasa, Finland

Peredo, Ana Maria, University of Victoria, Canada

Pollack, Jeffrey M., University of Richmond, USA

Ratten, Vanessa, Duquesne University, USA

Schaper, Michael T., Curtin University, Australia

Schjoedt, Leon, Illinois State University, USA

Singer, Alan E., Appalachian State University, USA

Staber, Udo, University of Canterbury, New Zealand

Storey, David, University of Warwick, UK

Terjesen, Siri, Indiana University, USA

Tomasino, Dana, Institute for Whole Social Science, USA

Vainio, Pekka, University of Vaasa, Finland

Weber, Paull C., Curtin University, Australia

Welpe, Isa, Munich University of Technology, Germany

Welter, Friederike, Jönköping International Business School, Sweden

Wennberg, Karl, Stockholm School of Economics, Sweden

Werner, Arndt, IfM Bonn, Germany

Foreword

Entrepreneurship is not a new phenomenon but it is certainly dynamic. Indeed, writers as far back as the seventeenth century started to develop the concept and identify its underpinning elements. With time, the concept has flourished, to the extent that it is central to ideologies in societies and economies worldwide. However, pinning down the concept of entrepreneurship is challenging, not least because of the mercurial nature of the object itself, the permeability of the field and the range of paradigmatic positions adopted by scholars. Whilst there is no universal readily accepted definition of the concept of entrepreneurship, it is fair to say that it is multi-dimensional. It involves analysing people and their actions together with the ways in which they interact within their environments, be these social, economic or political, as well as the institutional, policy and legal frameworks which help define and legitimize human activities.

The vibrancy of the academic field of entrepreneurship and its pace of development is unequivocal. Worldwide it is estimated that there are over twenty learned journals and innumerable research-based books on the subject. As well as possessing a well-developed corpus of literature and theories, based upon the foundation stones of the social sciences including economics, psychology and sociology, the field has also challenged orthodox thinking and contributed to the development of modern business and management theories. For example, entrepreneurship is integral to most theories of innovation and has also been highly influential in the field of strategic management. In other words, as well as drawing upon the intellectual pillars of the social sciences, entrepreneurship scholars and their works are now influencing and helping to redefine the academic mainstream and its boundaries.

However, the concept of entrepreneurship and its constituent parts remain contested terrain. Hence, more thinking, data collection and theorizing remains to be done. This is what makes the field attractive, challenging and vigorous at the same time. Indeed, the entries in this *Encyclopedia* illustrate the 'boundary-free' nature of the field and its attraction to scholars from a range of disciplines. Yet, if we are to move forward and continue to develop the subject and its conceptual foundations, it is important that we develop shared understandings and attempt to define some of its constituent parts. The entries in the *Encyclopedia* help in this process. The contributions are extensive and authoritative, providing rigorously argued positions on the key elements and subjects of entrepreneurship. The *Encyclopedia* illuminates the variety of subject areas and concepts within the field, the differing paradigmatic lenses of scholars, as well as the most and least developed areas of research. These contributions reflect a deep analysis of underpinning concepts in the literature, such as the *entrepreneurial process*, and the significance of supportive structures and institutions central to entrepreneurship as an activity, such as *venture capital*. There are also aspects of the field which are closer to achieving a consensus conceptually, such as *business angels*, through to those which have a long-standing tradition for research, such as *family business*, and more controversial areas such as *criminal entrepreneurship*, which is relatively fluid and a more recent area of study. These 'state-of-the-art' contributions provide important reference points for scholars and interested parties, as well as a platform for further intellectual endeavour.

I am both proud and delighted to provide this Foreword. Professor Léo-Paul Dana is one of the leading world academics in the field of entrepreneurship and it is fitting that he is the editor of this *World Encyclopedia of Entrepreneurship*. He has assembled a world-class set of contributors, which is both a testimony to his influence in the field, as well as demonstrating that entrepreneurship is very much a worldwide phenomenon. I do hope that the entries in this landmark publication help stimulate further thinking on, and subsequent understanding of, the important field of entrepreneurship.

Professor Robert Blackburn
Director, Small Business Research Centre
Kingston Business School
Kingston University
Kingston-upon-Thames, UK

Preface

I felt greatly honoured when Francine O'Sullivan, Commissioning Editor for Edward Elgar, suggested that I organize this interdisciplinary *World Encyclopedia of Entrepreneurship.* The project was launched in February 2005, and after years of invitations, submissions and revisions, here is the result. I truly believe that it will be an asset to countless researchers.

I would like to take this opportunity to thank the many world-class authors who contributed to this encyclopedia. Their entries are presented in alphabetical order, by subject. Here I shall mention just a few. Among the themes on the following pages, Louis Jacques Filion (holder of the Rogers–J.A. Bombardier Chair of Entrepreneurship) discusses issues related to defining the entrepreneur. Economist William Baumol focuses on economics and the entrepreneur. David Audretsch (Distinguished Professor and the Ameritech Chair of Economic Development) discusses entrepreneurship policy. French Professor Emeritus Jean-Jacques Obrecht (former President of the European affiliate of the International Council for Small Business) discusses the environment for entrepreneurship. Alan Singer (James Holshouser Distinguished Professor of Ethics) writes about ethics. University of California, Los Angeles sociologist Professor Emeritus Ivan H. Light addresses global entrepreneurship and transnationalism. University of Reading Professor Mark Casson (Director, Centre for Institutional Performance) reports on the historical context of entrepreneurship.

Among the entries that follow, some are firm-specific including write-ups about entrepreneur Conrad Hilton, founder of the world's first international hotel chain, and serial entrepreneur Howard Hughes and the entrepreneurial Hudson's Bay Company that once controlled much of what later became the Dominion of Canada.

The entry about interdependent innovation is presented by Adam M. Kleinbaum of Harvard Business School. Research-based entries include Ben Oviatt's contribution about international entrepreneurship, and an entry about island entrepreneurship, by Godfrey Baldacchino, who holds the Canada Research Chair in Island Studies. A. Allan Degen, Professor at the Jacob Blaustein Institute for Desert Research, discusses pastoralism as a form of entrepreneurship. In her entry, Ana Maria Peredo outlines a proposed definition of social entrepreneurship and the history of discussion surrounding its definition. Particular attention is paid to what makes social entrepreneurship entrepreneurial, and the distinction between being a social entrepreneur and being the founder or manager of a social enterprise.

Among the entries that follow, Ivan H. Light presents a sociological perspective of entrepreneurship, focusing on the ethnic ownership economy. Professor David Storey reports on the fastest growing companies, in his entry entitled, 'Ten percenters'. The topic of territorial entrepreneurship is presented by Professor Emeritus Pierre-André Julien. Third world entrepreneurs are the subject of Economics Professor Emeritus Peter Kilby, editor of the famous 1971 collection *Entrepreneurship and Economic Development.*

I am very grateful to entrepreneur Edward Elgar and to Francine O'Sullivan for giving me this opportunity. I would also like to thank the 105 experts who submitted entries and the referees who helped with the decision of which to accept.

Léo-Paul Dana
Montpellier, France
2011

1 Business angels

Colin M. Mason

INTRODUCTION

Business angels are conventionally defined as *high net worth individuals who invest their own money, along with their time and expertise, directly in unquoted companies in which they have no family connection, in the hope of financial gain*. The term *angel* was coined by Broadway insiders in the early 1900s to describe wealthy theatre-goers who made high-risk investments in theatrical productions. Angels invested in these shows primarily for the privilege of rubbing shoulders with the theatre personalities that they admired. The term *business angel* was given to those individuals who perform essentially the same function in a business context (Benjamin and Margulis, 2000: 5). There is a long tradition of angel investing in businesses (Sohl, 2003). Moreover, angel investing is now an international phenomenon, found in all developed economies and now diffusing to emerging economies such as China (Lui Tingchi and Chen Po Chang, 2007). However, it has only attracted the attention of researchers since the 1980s.

Several aspects of this definition need to be highlighted in order to emphasize the distinctiveness of business angels as a type of investor.

High Net Worth

Having wealth is a prerequisite for becoming a business angel. Business angels invest upwards of £10 000 per deal (sometimes in excess of £100 000) and typically have a portfolio of two to five investments (some angels have more). However, they are not investing their entire savings in this way. Because of the high risk of investing in unquoted companies, most angels allocate just 5 per cent to 15 per cent of their overall investment portfolio to such investments. Thus, if these investments fail, as they often do, the losses will not affect their lifestyle. Some rather dated evidence on the wealth of angels suggests that they tend to be 'comfortably' off rather than super-rich. Gaston (1989a) reported that one in three business angels in the USA had a net worth (excluding principal residence) in excess of $1 million. Mason and Harrison (1994) noted that only 19 per cent of UK business angels were (sterling) millionaires.

Investing their Own Money

The fact that angels are investing their own money distinguishes them from institutional venture capital funds whose investment funds come from such sources as pension funds, banks and foundations and, as a result, have a legal duty of care for how they invest such funds. This has several implications. First, business angels do not have to invest if they do not find appropriate investments whereas venture capital funds have a fixed life, typically ten years, over which the fund must invest and exit. Second, business angels can make quicker investment decisions (Freear et al., 1995). Third, they have less need for specialist financial and legal due diligence, so the costs for the investee business are lower. Fourth, business angels can adopt idiosyncratic investment criteria whereas venture capital funds have raised their investment funds to invest in specific types of businesses and so must follow these investment criteria when investing.

Direct

Business angels make their own investment decisions as opposed to investing in some form of pooled investment vehicle in which the investment decisions are made by fund managers. This implies that those people who become business angels have both the personal networks that will provide a flow of investment opportunities and the competence to undertake the appraisal of new and young entrepreneurial companies. Indeed, a consistent theme in the literature is that the majority of business angels are successful, cashed-out entrepreneurs,[1] while the remainder either have senior management experience in large businesses or have specialist business expertise (for example, accountants). On account of such backgrounds these individuals have access to deal flow and, at least in theory, the competence to make investment decisions. However, angels report in surveys (for example, Sørheim, 2003a) that their initial investments involved a steep learning curve.

Time and Expertise

Part of the investment approach of business angels involves the support they give their investee businesses through a variety of hands-on roles, including mentoring, the provision of strategic advice, networking and, in some cases, direct involvement in a specific functional capacity. The opportunity to be involved with a business start-up is a significant motive for business angels. Involvement also reduces information asymmetries and moral hazard and so is a means of risk reduction.

Unquoted Companies

Business angels are investing in unquoted companies as opposed to companies that are listed on a stock market. Although angels invest in all sorts of situations, including management buyouts and buy-ins and rescue/turnaround situations, their typical investment is in a new or recently started business. The key point here is that business angels want to be active investors in the companies in which they invest, helping them to grow, whereas stock-market investing is passive.

Financial Gain

Business angels are investing in the hope of achieving a financial return, typically in the form of a capital gain that is accomplished through some form of harvest event such as an acquisition of the investee company or an initial public offering (IPO). However, psychic income is also an important motivation. Studies are consistent in identifying that the fun and enjoyment that is derived from such investments is an important subsidiary reason for becoming a business angel. This links back to an earlier point: business angels are also characterized as being *hands-on investors*. The ability to provide support to investee companies reinforces the tendency for business angels to have a business background. Some angels also express altruistic motives. Evidence in the USA indicates that most business angels would be willing to forego *some* financial return either to invest in businesses that were seen as socially beneficial (Sullivan, 1994) or simply to support new entrepreneurs (Wetzel, 1981). Evidence of altruistic motives is much weaker in other countries.

CHARACTERISTICS OF BUSINESS ANGELS

One of the striking features in the literature is the remarkable consistency in the characteristics of business angels across countries. Japan is the only country where research suggests that angels have a distinctively different profile (Tashiro, 1999). The profile of the *typical* business angel is characterized as follows:

- *Male.* Studies in various countries are consistent in finding that upwards of 95 per cent of business angels are male. This can be attributed to the relatively small numbers of women who have built successful entrepreneurial companies or hold senior positions in large companies. However, the small minority of women who are business angels have similar characteristics to those of their male counterparts (Harrison and Mason, 2007).
- *In the 45–65 year age group.* This reflects the length of time required to build significant personal net worth, the greater amount of discretionary wealth of this age group as their children cease to become financially dependent on them, and the age at which people with a successful business career might choose, or be forced, to disengage. Becoming a business angel is often a way in which such individuals try to remain economically active. For example, cashed-out entrepreneurs in their forties or fifties often report that they became business angels because they quickly became bored by a life of leisure.
- *Successful cashed-out entrepreneurs*. Most business angels have had experience of business start-up, growth and harvest. In the process this has given them the kind of experience necessary to become an investor. The remainder are typically either people who have held senior positions in large companies or have specialist commercial skills and are involved in working with entrepreneurial companies (for example, accountants, consultants, lawyers) and whose wealth is derived from high income. It is also important to emphasize that non-business professionals (for example, doctors, dentists) and public sector employees are conspicuous by their absence from the ranks of business angels (Gaston, 1989a).
- *Well educated.* Economic success is underpinned by a high level of education. Business angels typically have a university degree and/or professional qualifications. However, angels with PhDs are rare. This reflects other research that suggests that the relationship between education and entrepreneurship is an inverted U-shape (that is, both too little and too much education is a hindrance to entrepreneurial behaviour) (Reynolds, 1997).

There have been surprisingly few attempts to compare business angels with non-investors. Lindsay (2004) finds that angels score more highly on measures of entrepreneurial orientation which, in turn, suggests that they act in an entrepreneurial manner in undertaking their investment activities. However, this might simply reflect the entrepreneurial background of most business angels. Duxbury et al. (1996) suggest that angels are distinctive from non-investors in terms of their psychological traits, with an internal locus of control, very high need for achievement (nAch), a moderately high need for affiliation and autonomy, and are intrinsically motivated. But again, these are also entrepreneurial traits.

This profile masks considerable heterogeneity in the business angel population, not so much in terms of their demographics but rather in their motivation and investment focus. The most basic distinction is between *active angels*, those individuals with experience of investing and who are continuing to look for investments, *latent angels*, inactive investors who have made investments in the past, and *virgin angels*, individuals who are looking to invest but have yet to make their first investment (Coveney and Moore, 1998).

There are several classifications of active investors. Gaston (1989a) identifies ten distinct types of business angel but without elaborating on the methodological basis for the classification. Coveney and Moore (1998) identify three types of business angel based on their level of entrepreneurial activity and intensity of investment activity: entrepreneur angel, income seeking angels and wealth maximizing angels. Sørheim and Landström (2001) use cluster analysis to differentiate Norwegian business angels in terms of their competence and investment activity. This produces four distinct types of business angel:

- *Lotto investors* (30 per cent): low investment activity level and limited experience of starting and running businesses. They make very few investments and have limited ability to add value to their investments.
- *Traders* (24 per cent): high investment activity but limited experience of starting and running entrepreneurial businesses. They are keen to invest but have limited ability to add value.
- *Analytical investors* (21 per cent): low level of investment activity but possess fairly high competence.
- *Business angels* (25 per cent): very high level of investment activity and high competence.

ECONOMIC SIGNIFICANCE OF BUSINESS ANGELS

Business angels are recognized as playing a vital role in economic development at both national and local/regional scales. There are three aspects of the informal venture capital market which are significant from an economic development perspective. First, the amount of finance that business angels have invested, or have available to invest, is significant. It is impossible to be precise about the number of business angels, the number of investments made and the amount invested because they have no obligation to identify themselves or register their investments. Indeed, the vast majority of business angels strive to preserve their anonymity and are secretive about their investment activity, not least to avoid being inundated by entrepreneurs and other individuals seeking to persuade them to invest or provide financial support for other causes (Benjamin and Margulis, 2000). Thus, all measures of the size of the informal venture capital market are fairly crude estimates. Gaston (1989b) has estimated that in the USA business angels invest 13 times more dollars than venture capital funds and make 40 times more investments. A more up-to-date estimate by Sohl (2003) suggests that there are 300000 to 350000 business angels in the USA, investing approximately $30 billion per annum in close to 50000 ventures. Venture capital funds, in contrast, invest $30–$35 billion in fewer than 3000 entrepreneurial ventures. The equivalent estimate for the UK is 20000 to 40000 business angels investing £0.5 billion to £1 billion per annum in 3000 to 6000 companies. They make eight times as many investments in start-up companies as venture capital funds (Mason and Harrison, 2000). However, these calculations of the amounts invested by business angels are an underestimate of the size of the informal venture capital market. First, most business angels have further funds available to invest (Coveney and Moore, 1998; Mason and Harrison, 1994; 2002a) but cannot identify appropriate investment opportunities. This uncommitted capital is substantial: one study reported that it exceeded the amount invested by the respondents in the three years prior to the survey (Mason and Harrison, 2002a). Second, there is a substantial pool of potential, or virgin, business angels who share the characteristics of active angels but have not entered the market (Coveney and Moore, 1998; Freear et al., 1994a). However, with appropriate forms of support – such as help with deal flow and with the technical aspects of investing – they could be encouraged to enter the market (Freear et al., 1994a; Mason and Harrison, 1993). Sohl (1999) has estimated that these potential angels exceed the number of active investors by a factor of five to one.

The economic significance of business angels stems from where this capital is invested. Finance from business angels occupies a crucial place in the spectrum of finance available to growing businesses. In terms of *size of investment*, business angels invest in what is often termed (at least in Europe) the 'equity gap', providing amounts of finance that are beyond the ability of entrepreneurs to raise from their own resources and from family and below the minimum investment threshold of venture capital funds[2] – currently in excess of £1million in the UK and $5 million in the USA (Sohl, 2003). Business angels, investing on their own or in small ad hoc groups, will typically invest up to £100000, while the larger angel syndicates (see below) can make investments of £250000 and above. This is usually provided in the form of equity or a combination of equity plus loans. In terms of *stage of business development*, investments by business angels are skewed towards the seed, start-up and early growth stages whereas venture capital funds focus on later stage deals. The role of business angels in seeding new ventures has become even more critical in recent years as institutional venture capital funds in North America and Europe have raised their minimum investment size and continued to shift their investment focus to later stage investments.

A second factor which underpins the economic significance of angel investing is the hands-on involvement of business angels in their investee businesses, with the nature of this involvement ranging from informal coaching, mentoring and advice, to board participation. Demand-side studies indicate that many entrepreneurs are seeking 'smart money' and for this reason business angels are valued ahead of other funding sources (Cressy and Olofsson, 1997; Lindström and Olofsson, 2001; Sætre, 2003). Business angels typically invest in industries and markets with which they are familiar. As a consequence, the entrepreneurs who are funded by business angels derive considerable value from the expertise, knowledge and experience that their investors pass on through this hands-on involvement. This, in turn, increases the prospects for the success of their businesses. Indeed, entrepreneurs often report that the hands-on involvement of business angels is more valuable than the capital that they have received. However, hard evidence on the impact of this involvement on business performance remains elusive.

Taken together these points highlight the complementary roles of business angels and institutional venture capital funds in supporting entrepreneurial activity. This is evident in terms of the size and stage of investments made by business angels and venture capital funds (Freear and Wetzel, 1990). Harrison and Mason (2000) have highlighted other forms of complementarity in the form of information sharing, co-investing and sequential investing, and note significant collaboration in these areas between business angels and venture capital funds in the UK. However, they also highlight the frequent tensions that arise from the different motives and expectations of angels and fund managers, the bureaucracy of venture capital funds and the unequal power relationship between angels and funds. The importance of business angels in providing a deal flow for venture capital funds is highlighted by Madill et al. (2005) who note that 57 per cent of technology firms in Ottawa who had received funding from angels went on to raise institutional venture capital, compared with only 10 per cent of firms which did not raise any angel investment.

The third contribution of business angels to economic development arises from its geographical characteristics. This has two dimensions. First, 'angels live everywhere' (Gaston, 1989a: 273). According to Gaston's US research the proportion of business angels in the adult population is fairly constant at about four per 1000 adults. This contrasts with investments by institutional venture capital which are geographically concentrated (Mason, 2007). Second, the majority of investments by business angels are local. This reflects both the localized nature of their business and personal networks through which they identify most of their investments (see below) and their hands-on investment style and consequent need for frequent contact with their investee businesses. Business angel investment is therefore an important mechanism for retaining and recycling wealth within the region in which it was created.

THE INVESTMENT PROCESS OF BUSINESS ANGELS

A number of discrete stages can be identified in the investment process of business angels:

- deal origination
- deal evaluation; this can, in turn, be subdivided into at least two sub-stages:
  - initial screening
  - detailed investigation
- negotiation and contracting
- post-investment involvement
- harvesting.

This sequence is similar in most respects to the investment decision-making model of institutional venture capital funds. However, the approach of business angels is less sophisticated.

Deal Origination

The evidence is consistent in suggesting that business angels adopt a relatively ad hoc and unscientific approach to identifying investment opportunities. Atkin and Esiri (1993) emphasize that most investments arise from chance encounters. In some cases – especially in the case of occasional investors – the entrepreneur is not a stranger but a business associate who is known to the angel (for example, client, supplier) (Atkin and Esiri, 1993). Most of the deals that business angels receive are referred by individual and institutional sources in their extensive and longstanding networks of relationships. Professional contacts are much less significant than friends: of these, accountants are the most frequent sources, whereas few business angels receive deal flow from lawyers, bankers and stockbrokers. Those angels who are known in their communities also receive approaches from entrepreneurs. Information in the media is another source of deal flow for a significant minority of business angels. Some business angels also undertake their own searches for investment opportunities. Kelly and Hay (2000) observe that the most active investors place less reliance than occasional investors on 'public' sources (for example, accountants, lawyers) for their deal flow and put more emphasis on 'private' sources.

Calculating yield rates for various sources of deal flow (that is, comparing investments made against deals referred for each information source) indicates that informal personal sources of information – business associates, friends and approaches from entrepreneurs – have the highest probability of leading to investments whereas non-personal sources such as accountants, lawyers and banks have a low likelihood of generating investments (Freear et al., 1994b; Mason and Harrison, 1994). Investing in businesses that are referred by trusted business associates and friends is an obvious way in which business angels can minimize adverse selection problems.

Deal Evaluation

The process of evaluating investment opportunities involves at least two distinct stages – initial screening and detailed investigation (or due diligence) (Riding et al., 1993). The initial step of business angels is to assess investment opportunities for their 'fit' with their own personal investment criteria. The investment opportunity will also be considered in terms of its location (how close to home?), the nature of the business and the amount needed and any other personal investment criteria (Mason and Rogers, 1997). The business angel will also typically ask themself two further critical questions: first, 'Do I know anything about this industry, market or technology?' and, second, 'Can I add any value to this business?' Clearly, the ability to add value is very often a function of whether the angel is familiar with the industry. If the answer to either question is negative then the opportunity will be rejected at this point.

Angels then undertake a quick review of those opportunities that fall within their investment criteria to derive some initial impressions. Although most business angels expect a business plan, they are unlikely to read it in detail at this stage. Their aim at this point in the decision-making process is simply to assess whether the proposal has sufficient merit to justify the investment of time to undertake a detailed assessment. The market and the entrepreneur are the key considerations at this stage. Less significant are the product/service and financial factors. Indeed, angels exhibit considerable scepticism about the value of financial information in the business plan of start-ups (Mason and Rogers, 1997). Nevertheless, investors want to see that there is the potential for significant financial return, that the principals are financially committed and what the money that is invested will be used for.

The purpose of the initial screen is to filter out 'no hopers' in order to focus their time on those opportunities that appear to have potential. These are subject to more detailed appraisal. The investor will read the business plan in detail, go over the financial information, visit the premises, do some personal research to gather additional information on market potential, competition and so on, and assess the principals. Indeed, getting to know the principals personally (by a series of formal and informal meetings) is the most vital part of the process (May and Simmons, 2001). However, it would appear that most angels emphasize their intuition and gut feeling rather than performing formal analysis (Haines et al., 2003) – although more experienced angels, and angel groups adopt more sophisticated approaches (for example, see Blair, 1996).

Once the opportunity has passed from the initial screen to detailed investigation the importance of 'people' factors becomes critical (Riding et al., 1995), with investors emphasizing management abilities, an understanding of what is required to be successful, a strong work ethic, integrity, honesty, openness and personal chemistry (Haines et al., 2003; Landström, 1998; Mason and Stark, 2004). This reflects the long-lasting and personal nature of the angel–entrepreneur relationship.

This stage ends when the investor has decided whether or not to negotiate a deal with the investor. In their Canadian study, Riding et al. (1993) found that 72.6 per cent of opportunities were rejected at the initial impressions stage, a further 15.9 per cent were rejected following more detailed evaluation, and as this stage proceeded another 6.3 per cent were eliminated, a cumulative rejection rate of 94.8 per cent. Thus, business angels proceed to the negotiation stage with only 5 per cent of the investment opportunities that they receive.

The key role of the entrepreneur/management team in the decision whether or not to invest is emphasized by Feeney et al. (1999). Their approach was to ask business angels 'What are the most common shortcomings of business opportunities that you have reviewed recently?' This highlighted shortcomings in both the management (lack of management knowledge, lack of realistic expectations, personal qualities) and the business (poor management team, poor profit potential for the level of risk, poor fit, undercapitalized/lack of liquidity, insufficient information provided). Asking investors 'What are the essential factors that prompted you to invest in the firms that you have chosen?' (Feeney et al., 1999) highlighted three management attributes – track record, realism, integrity and openness – and four attributes of the business – potential for high profit, an exit plan, security on their investment and involvement of the investor. However, while the primary deal killer is the perception of poor management, the decision to invest in an opportunity involves a consideration of management ability, growth and profit potential. In other words, angels are looking for businesses that show growth potential and have an entrepreneurial team with the capability to realize that potential (Feeney et al., 1999).

Negotiation and Contracting

Having decided, in principle, to invest, the business angel must negotiate terms and conditions of the investment that are acceptable both to themselves and to the entrepreneur. There are three main issues: valuation, structuring of the deal (share price, type of shares, size of shareholding, timing) and the terms and conditions of the investment, including the investor's role.

In the study by Riding et al. (1993) half of the investment opportunities that reached this stage were not consummated. The most frequent reason for not making an investment was associated with valuation, notably:

> inappropriate views by entrepreneurs (in the opinion of the investors) regarding the value of the firm as a whole and, within the firm, the value of an idea compared to the overall value of a business. Most investors note that potential entrepreneurs overvalue the idea and undervalue the potential contributions (both financial and non-financial) that are required to grow and develop a business. (Haines et al., 2003: 24)

Putting a value on the 'sweat equity' of the entrepreneurs is also problematic.

There is no universally agreed method of valuing a small company. Market-based valuations are inappropriate because small businesses are not continually valued by the market and appropriate comparator stocks are unlikely to be available. Asset-based valuations are more commonly used, although finance theory prefers earnings or cash-flow based valuations because they value the business in terms of the future stream of earnings that shareholders might expect from the business. However, these approaches are complex. Valuation of new and early stage businesses adds further complications because they may only have intangible assets (for example, intellectual property). It is therefore not surprising, especially since most angel investments are concentrated at start-up and early stage, that methods of pricing and calculating the size of shareholdings are remarkably imprecise and subjective (Mason and Harrison, 1996), based on rough rules of thumb or gut feeling. May and Simmons (2001: 129), who are themselves investors, note that 'the truth about valuing a start-up is that it's often a guess'.

Angels draw up contracts as a matter of course to safeguard their investment, although their degree of sophistication varies. Contracts specify the rights and obligations of both parties and what will by done, by whom and over what time frame. Their objective is to align the incentives of the entrepreneur and the investor by means of performance incentives and direct control measures. Kelly and Hay (2003) note that certain issues are non-negotiable: veto rights over acquisitions/divestments, prior approval for strategic plans and budgets, restrictions on the ability of management to issue share options, non-compete contracts required by entrepreneurs on the termination of their employment in the business, and restrictions on the ability to raise additional debt or equity finance. These issues give investors a say in material decisions that could impact the nature of the business or the level of equity holding. However, there are also a number of contractual provisions to which angels attach low importance, and which might be considered to be negotiable.

Investors recognize that the investment agreement must be fair to both sides (May and Simmons, 2001): contracts that favour the investor will be detrimental to the entrepreneur's motivation. In Mason and Harrison's (1996) study, two-thirds of investors and entrepreneurs considered that the investment agreement was equally favourable to both sides, and half of the investors reported that this was their objective. Indeed, a significant minority of investors believed that the agreement actually favoured the entrepreneur. Thus, the available evidence suggests that in most cases entrepreneurs are not exploited by investors when raising finance.

The inclusion of contractual safeguards does not indicate whether investors will be willing to invoke them to protect their interests. Moreover, contracts are, of necessity, incomplete by their very nature. There are three reasons for this: it is costly to write complete contracts; it is impossible to foresee all contingencies; and on account of asymmetric information (van Osnabrugge, 2000). Thus, in practice investors place a heavy reliance on their relationship with the entrepreneur to deal with any problems that arise (Kelly and Hay, 2003; van Osnabrugge, 2000). Indeed, Landström et al. (1998) argue that one of the purposes of establishing a contractual framework at the outset is to provide a basis for a relationship between the parties to develop. In other words, the contract is less a protection mechanism per se; rather, it is a means by which mutual behaviour expectations of all parties in the transaction can be clarified.

Most angel investments involve input from professional advisers. For example, lawyers would normally review, and might draw up, the investment agreement, but would not be involved in the negotiations. Similarly, accountants may be consulted for advice but would rarely play a more prominent role. Thus, transactions costs are low (Mason and Harrison, 1996). In Lengyel and Gulliford's (1997) study the entrepreneur's costs amounted to an average of 5.1 per cent of the funds raised (and 29 per cent reported no costs) while for the investor the average costs were 2.8 per cent of the amount invested (and 57 per cent reported no costs).

The time taken by business angels to make investments is much quicker than that of venture capital funds (Freear et al., 1995). Mason and Harrison (1996) report that in their study the entire investment process rarely extended over more than three months, and often took less than a month. Most negotiations took less than a week to complete whereas the evaluation could take up to three months or more. Thus, in nearly half of the investments less than a month elapsed between the entrepreneur's first meeting with the investor and the decision to invest; in 85 per cent of cases the elapsed time was under three months.

Post-investment Involvement

Most business angels play an active role in their investee businesses. There is a spectrum of involvement: at one extreme are passive investors who are content to receive occasional information to monitor the performance of their investment, while at the other extreme are investors who use their investment to buy themselves a job. However, most angels do not want day-to-day involvement, hence the typical involvement ranges from a day a week (or its equivalent) to less than a day a month (Mason and Harrison, 1996). Nevertheless, Sætre (2003) emphasizes that some angels are so involved, and involved so early, that they are indistinguishable from the entrepreneurs, and are seen by the entrepreneurs as being part of the entrepreneurial team. In similar vein, Politis and Landström (2002) see angel investing as simply a continuation of an entrepreneurial career.

Madill et al. (2005) identify a number of roles that business angels play in their investee businesses: advice about the management of the business, contacts, hands-on assistance (for example, legal advice, accountancy advice, provision of resources), providing business and marketing intelligence, serving on the board of directors or advisory board, preparing firms to raise venture capital and providing credibility and validation. Sørheim (2003b) also emphasizes the role of business angels in helping their investee businesses to raise additional finance. The nature and level of involvement is influenced by geography. Landström (1992) notes that frequency of contact between angels and their investee companies is inversely related to the geographical distance that separates them. It is also influenced by the age and performance of the business, with angels more involved at particular stages of business development and in crisis situations.

However, in contrast to what agency theory would suggest, the involvement of angels in their investee businesses is not motivated by monitoring considerations. First, as noted earlier, angels derive psychic income from their involvement in their investee businesses in the form of fun and satisfaction from being involved with new and growing businesses and their belief that their experience, know-how and insights can 'make a difference'. Second, angels see themselves as 'offering help' rather than 'checking up' on their investee businesses by acting as mentors, providing contacts, guidance and hands-on assistance (Haines et al., 2003).

A majority of entrepreneurs and angels regard their relationship as productive and consensual – although entrepreneurs have a more favourable view of its productiveness than angels (Freear et al., 1995; Mason and Harrison, 1996). One study reported that half of the entrepreneurs who had raised finance from business angels regarded their contributions as being helpful or very helpful (Mason and Harrison, 1996). Another study reported that entrepreneurs considered that the most valuable contribution of their business angel has been as a sounding board (Harrison and Mason, 1992). There is a suggestion that entrepreneurs want their investors to be more involved in certain areas, especially financial management (Ehrlich et al., 1994). Criticisms by entrepreneurs who have raised finance from angels are mainly concerned with those who lack knowledge of the product or market (Lengyel and Gulliford, 1997). However, there has been no rigorous attempt to assess whether this involvement of business angels has a favourable impact on the performance of their investee businesses.

Harvesting

Returns from angel investing are highly skewed. A UK study reported that 40 per cent of investments made a loss (34 per cent a total loss), and another 13 per cent only achieved break-even or generating bank account-level returns. However, there was a significant subset of investments, some 23 per cent in total, which generated internal rates of return (IRRs) in excess of 50 per cent (Mason and Harrison, 2002b). Research in the USA has reported that the average investment returned 2.6 times the investment, 48 per cent returned more cash than was invested and 7 per cent returned more than ten times the amount invested (Wiltbank and Broeker, 2007).

The UK study identified large investments, large deal sizes and deals involving multiple investors as being more likely to be high-performing investments (Mason and Harrison, 2002b). A separate analysis of the returns distribution of technology and non-technology investments found no significant differences in the returns profile (Mason and Harrison,

2004). The US study reported that high returns were associated with the length of due diligence, industry experience and participation, while low returns were associated with follow-on investments (Wiltbank and Broeker, 2007).

The median time to exit in the UK is four years for high-performing investments and six years for moderately performing investments, while failures appear, on average, after two years (Mason and Harrison, 2002b). In Finland investments that had a positive outcome were five years old at harvest whereas those which failed had an average holding time of 2.8 years (Lumme et al., 1998). In the USA the average holding period is 3.5 years (Wiltbank and Broeker, 2007). A trade sale (that is, sale of the company to another company) is the most common exit route for successful investments, with an IPO accounting for only a small minority of cases. Trade sales, along with sale to existing shareholders, are the most common exit routes for investments with little or no value (Lumme et al., 1998; Mason and Harrison, 2002b).

THE CHANGING NATURE OF THE ANGEL MARKET

The angel marketplace is evolving from a largely invisible, atomistic market dominated by individual and small ad hoc groups of investors who strive to keep a low profile and rely on word-of-mouth for their investment opportunities, to a more organized marketplace in which angel syndicates (sometimes termed 'structured angel groups') are becoming increasingly significant. As a result, the angel marketplace is in the process of being transformed from a 'hobby' activity to one that is now increasingly professional in its operation, with published routines for accessing deals, screening deals, undertaking due diligence, negotiating and investing (May, 2002). Nevertheless, solo investors still dominate the market.

There are currently estimated to be over 250 angel syndicates located throughout the USA and growing evidence of specialization by industry sector (for example, health-care angel syndicates) and type of investor (for example, women-only angel syndicates). A national body to bring angel groups together for the purposes of transferring best practice, lobbying and data collection was created in 2003 (the Angel Capital Association). The same trend is also clearly evident in the UK, although at an earlier stage.

Angel syndicates emerged because individual angels found advantages of working together, notably in terms of better deal flow, superior evaluation and due diligence of investment opportunities, and the ability to make more and bigger investments, as well as social attractions. They operate by aggregating the investment capacity of individual high net worth individuals (HNWIs). Groups typically range from 25 to 75 members. Syndicates take various forms but in the most common model a manager or a core group of members will screen the deal flow and select the companies which are invited to pitch to members. Members then vote whether to pursue their interest in the business. If the vote is in favour a sub-group will be appointed to undertake the due diligence and report back to the full membership. If the recommendation is positive, individual members make their own decisions whether or not to invest (there is likely to be a minimum investment threshold for each deal) and the syndicate will combine all of the member dollars into a single investment. Some of the larger and longer established US syndicates have also established sidecar funds – that is, committed sources of capital that invest alongside the angel group. The investors in such funds are normally the syndicate members but may also include other HNWIs or institutions. These funds give the syndicate additional capital to invest in deals to avoid dilution and enables syndicate members to achieve greater diversification by exposing them to more investments than they can make directly through the syndicate (May, 2002; May and Simmons 2001).

The emergence of angel syndicates is of enormous significance for the development and maintenance of an entrepreneurial economy:

- They reduce sources of inefficiency in the angel market. The angel market has traditionally been characterized by inefficiency on account of the fragmented and invisible nature of angels, whereas angel syndicates are generally visible and are therefore easier for entrepreneurs to approach.
- They have stimulated the supply-side of the market. Syndicates offer considerable attractions for HNWIs who want to invest in emerging companies, particularly those who lack the time, referral sources, investment skills or the ability to add value. Other attractions of syndicates are that they enable individual angels to invest in particular opportunities that they could never have invested in as individuals, achieve diversification, and offer the opportunity to learn from more experienced investors.
- They are helping to fill the 'new' equity gap. Venture capital funds have consistently raised their minimum size of investment and are increasingly abandoning the early stage market. This has resulted in the emergence of a new equity gap which covers amounts that are too large for typical '3F' money (founder, family, friends) but too small for most venture capital funds. Angel syndicates are now increasingly the only source for venture capital in this range.
- They have the ability to provide follow-on funding. With the withdrawal of many venture capital funds from the small end of the market, individual angels and their investee businesses have increasingly been faced with the problem of the absence of follow-on investors. However, because angel syndicates have greater financial firepower than individual angels or ad hoc angel groups they are able to provide follow-on financing, making it more efficient for the entrepreneur who avoids the need to start the search for finance anew each time a new round of funding is required.
- The ability of angel groups to add value to their investments is much greater. The range of business expertise that is found among angel syndicate members means that in most circumstances they are able to contribute much greater value-added to investee businesses than an individual business angel, or even most early stage venture capital funds.
- Angel syndicates have greater credibility with venture capitalists. Venture capital funds often have a negative view of business angels and may therefore avoid investing in deals in which angels are involved (Harrison and Mason, 2000). However, because of the professionalism and quality of the membership of angel syndicates venture capital funds hold them in much higher esteem. Accordingly, the increasing prominence of angel syndicates results in much greater complimentarity between the angel market and venture capital funds, to the benefit of

fast-growing companies that raised their initial funding from angel syndicates but now need access to the amounts of finance that venture capital funds can provide.

The tantalizing issue is whether the essence of angel investing will be lost with the growth of professional angel groups as they take on more and more of the hallmarks of venture capital funds.

WEB RESOURCES

Angel Capital Association: North America's professional alliance of angel groups which brings together many of the 265 angel organizations in the USA and Canada to share best practices, network, and help develop data about the field of angel investing. www.angelcapitalassociation.org/

British Business Angel Association (BBAA) is the National Trade Association for the UK's Business Angel Networks and the early stage investment market and is backed by the Department for Business, Enterprise and Regulatory Reform (formally the Department of Trade and Industry). www.bbaa.org.uk/

European Business Angel Network (EBAN) comprises national federations of BANs, networks with a national, regional and local coverage and other interested entities having a direct involvement in promoting informal investment in Europe. www.eban.org/

NOTES

1. 'Cashed-out' entrepreneurs are entrepreneurs who have sold and exited from a business that they have started and developed; that is, entrepreneurs who have had a harvest event.
2. For a venture capital fund the transactions costs involved in making investments – the time involved in undertaking the evaluation and negotiation of a deal, professional costs and the provision of post-investment support – are both substantial and largely fixed regardless of the size of the investment. In 'small' investments these transaction costs represent a significant proportion of the overall investment, making them uneconomic. Business angels are able to make small investments because they do not cost their time in the same way as a venture capital fund managers and their requirement for professional support, for example from lawyers and accountants, is minimal.

REFERENCES

Atkin, R. and M. Esiri (1993), 'Informal investment – investor and investee relationships', paper presented to the sixteenth National Small Firms Policy and Research Conference, Nottingham, 17–19 November.

Benjamin, G.A. and J.B. Margulis (2000), *Angel Financing: How to Find and Invest in Private Equity*, New York: Wiley.

Blair, A. (1996), 'Creating an informal investor syndicate: personal experiences of a seasoned informal investor', in R.T. Harrison and C.M. Mason (eds), *Informal Venture Capital: Evaluating the Impact of Business Introduction Services*, Hemel Hempstead: Prentice Hall, pp. 156–96.

Coveney, P. and K. Moore (1998), *Business Angels: Securing Start-Up Finance*, Chichester: Wiley.

Cressy, R. and C. Olofsson (1997), 'The financial conditions for Swedish SMEs: survey and research agenda', *Small Business Economics*, **9**, 179–94.

Duxbury, L., G. Haines and A. Riding (1996), 'A personality profile of Canadian informal investors', *Journal of Small Business Management*, **24** (2), 44–55.

Ehrlich, S.B., A.F. De Noble, T. Moore and R.R. Weaver (1994), 'After the cash arrives: a comparative study of venture capital and private investor involvement in entrepreneurial firms', *Journal of Business Venturing*, **9** (1), 67–82.

Feeney, L., G.H. Haines and A.L. Riding (1999), 'Private investors' investment criteria: insights from qualitative data', *Venture Capital: An International Journal of Entrepreneurial Finance*, **1**, 121–45.

Freear, J. and W.E. Wetzel (1990), 'Who bankrolls high-tech entrepreneurs?', *Journal of Business Venturing*, **5**, 77–89.

Freear, J., J.E. Sohl and W.E. Wetzel Jr (1994a), 'Angels and non-angels: are there differences?', *Journal of Business Venturing*, **9**, 109–23.

Freear, J., J.E. Sohl and W.E. Wetzel Jr (1994b), 'The private investor market for venture capital', *The Financier*, **1** (2): 7–15.

Freear, J., J.E. Sohl and W.E. Wetzel Jr (1995), 'Angels: personal investors in the venture capital market', *Entrepreneurship and Regional Development*, **7**, 85–94.

Gaston R.J. (1989a), *Finding Venture Capital for Your Firm: A Complete Guide*, New York: John Wiley & Sons.

Gaston, R.J. (1989b), 'The scale of informal capital markets', *Small Business Economics*, **1**, 223–30.

Haines, G.H. Jr, J.J. Madill and A.L Riding (2003), 'Informal investment in Canada: financing small business growth', *Journal of Small Business and Entrepreneurship*, **16** (3/4), 13–40.

Harrison, R.T and C.M. Mason (1992), 'The roles of investors in entrepreneurial companies: a comparison of informal investors venture capitalists', in N.C. Churchill, S. Birley, W.D. Bygrave, D.F. Muzyka, C. Wahlbin and W.E. Wetzel Jr (eds), *Frontiers of Entrepreneurship Research 1992*, Babson Park, MA: Babson College, pp. 388–404.

Harrison, R.T. and C.M. Mason (2000), 'Venture capital market complementarities: the links between business angels and venture capital funds in the UK', *Venture Capital: An International Journal of Entrepreneurial Finance*, **2**, 223–42.

Harrison, R.T. and C.M. Mason (2007), 'Does gender matter? Women business angels and the supply of entrepreneurial finance', *Entrepreneurship Theory and Practice*, **31**, 447–74.

Kelly, P. and M. Hay (2000), '"Deal-makers": reputation attracts quality', *Venture Capital: An International Journal of Entrepreneurial Finance*, **2**, 183–202.

Kelly, P. and M. Hay (2003), 'Business angel contracts: the influence of context', *Venture Capital: An International Journal of Entrepreneurial Finance*, **5**, 287–312.

Landström, H. (1992), 'The relationship between private investors and small firms: an agency theory approach', *Entrepreneurship and Regional Development*, **4**, 199–223.

Landström, H. (1998), 'Informal investors as entrepreneurs', *Technovation*, **18**, 321–33.

Landström, H., S. Manigart, C. Mason and H. Sapienza (1998), 'Contracts between entrepreneurs and investors: terms and negotiation process', in P.D. Reynolds, W.D. Bygrave, N.M. Carter, S. Manigart, C.M. Mason, G.D. Meyer and K.G. Shaver (eds), *Frontiers of Entrepreneurship Research 1998*, Babson Park MA: Babson College, pp. 571–85.

Lengyel, Z. and J. Gulliford (1997), *The Informal Venture Capital Experience*, London: Local Investment Networking Company.

Lindsay, N.J. (2004), 'Do business angels have entrepreneurial orientation?', *Venture Capital: An International Journal of Entrepreneurial Finance*, **6**, 197–210.

Lindström, G. and C. Olofsson (2001), 'Early stage financing of NTBFs: an analysis of contributions from support actors', *Venture Capital: An International Journal of Entrepreneurial Finance*, **3**, 151–68.

Lui Tingchi, M. and B. Chen Po Chang (2007), 'Business angel in investment in the China market', *Singapore Management Review*, **29**, 89–101.

Lumme, A., C. Mason and M. Suomi (1998), *Informal Venture Capital: Investors, Investments and Policy Issues in Finland*, Dordrecht: Kluwer Academic Publishers.

Madill, J.J., G.H. Haines Jr and A.L. Riding (2005), 'The role of angels in technology SMEs: a link to venture capital', *Venture Capital: An International Journal of Entrepreneurial Finance*, **7**, 107–29.

Mason, C.M. (2007), 'Venture capital: a geographical perspective', in H. Landström (ed.), *Handbook of Research on Venture Capital*, Cheltenham, UK and Northampton, MA, USA: Edward Elgar, pp. 86–112.

Mason, C.M. and R.T. Harrison (1993), 'Strategies for expanding the informal venture capital market', *International Small Business Journal*, **11** (4), 23–38.

Mason, C.M. and R.T. Harrison (1994), 'The informal venture capital market in the UK', in A. Hughes and D.J. Storey (eds), *Financing Small Firms*, London: Routledge pp. 64–111.

Mason, C.M. and R.T. Harrison (1996), 'Informal venture capital: a study of the investment process and post-investment experience', *Entrepreneurship and Regional Development*, **8**, 105–26.

Mason, C.M. and R.T. Harrison (2000), 'The size of the informal venture capital market in the United Kingdom', *Small Business Economics*, **15**, 137–48.

Mason, C.M. and R.T. Harrison (2002a), 'Barriers to investment in the informal venture capital sector', *Entrepreneurship and Regional Development*, **14**, 271–87.

Mason, C.M. and R.T. Harrison (2002b), 'Is it worth it? The rates of return from informal venture capital investments', *Journal of Business Venturing*, **17**, 211–36.

Mason, C.M. and R.T. Harrison (2004), 'Does investing in technology-based firms involve higher risk? An exploratory study of the performance of technology and non-technology investments by business angels', *Venture Capital: An International Journal of Entrepreneurial Finance*, **6**, 313–32.

Mason, C.M. and A. Rogers (1997), 'The business angel's investment decision: an exploratory analysis', in D. Deakins, P. Jennings and C.M. Mason (eds), *Entrepreneurship in the 1990s*, London: Paul Chapman Publishing, pp. 29–46.

Mason, C.M. and M. Stark (2004), 'What do investors look for in a business plan? A comparison of the investment criteria of bankers, venture capitalists and venture capitalists', *International Small Business Journal*, **22**, 227–48.

May, J. (2002), 'Structured angel groups in the USA: the dinner club experience', *Venture Capital: An International Journal of Entrepreneurial Finance*, **4**: 337–42.

May, J. and C. Simmons (2001), *Every Business Needs an Angel: Getting the Money You Need to Make Your Business Grow*, New York: Crown Business.

Politis, D. and H. Landström (2002), 'Informal investors as entrepreneurs – the development of an entrepreneurial career', *Venture Capital: An International Journal of Entrepreneurial Finance*, **4**, 77–101.

Reynolds, P.D. (1997), 'Who starts new firms? Preliminary exploration of firms-in-gestation', *Small Business Economics*, **9**, 449–62.

Riding, A.L., P. Dal Cin, L. Duxbury, G. Haines and R. Safrata (1993), *Informal Investors in Canada: The Identification of Salient Characteristics*, Ottawa: Carleton University.

Riding, A.L., L. Duxbury and G. Haines Jr (1995), *Financing Enterprise Development: Decision-Making by Canadian Angels*, Ottawa: School of Business, Carleton University.

Sætre, A.S. (2003), 'Entrepreneurial perspectives on informal venture capital', *Venture Capital: An International Journal of Entrepreneurial Finance*, **5**, 71–94.

Sohl, J.E. (1999), 'The early stage equity market in the United States', *Venture Capital: An International Journal of Entrepreneurial Finance*, **1**, 101–20.

Sohl, J.E. (2003), 'The private equity market in the USA: lessons from volatility', *Venture Capital: An International Journal of Entrepreneurial Finance*, **5**, 29–46.

Sørheim, R. (2003a), 'The pre-investment behaviour of business angels: a social capital approach', *Venture Capital: An International Journal of Entrepreneurial Finance*, **5**, 337–64.

Sørheim, R. (2003b), 'Business angels as facilitators for further finance: an exploratory study', *Journal of Small Business and Enterprise Development*, **12**, 178–91.

Sørheim, R. and H. Landström (2001), 'Informal investors – a categorisation with policy implications', *Entrepreneurship and Regional Development*, **13**, 351–70.

Sullivan, M.K. (1994), 'Altruism and entrepreneurship', in W.D. Bygrave, S. Birley, N.C. Churchill, E. Gatewood, F. Hoy, R.H. Keeley and W.E. Wetzel Jr (eds), *Frontiers of Entrepreneurship Research*, Babson Park, MA: Babson College, pp. 373–80.

Tashiro, Y. (1999), 'Business angels in Japan', *Venture Capital: An International Journal of Entrepreneurial Finance*, **1**, 259–73.

Van Osnabrugge, M. (2000), 'A comparison of business angel and venture capitalist investment procedures: an agency theory-based analysis', *Venture Capital: An International Journal of Entrepreneurial Finance*, **2**, 91–109.

Wetzel, W.E. (1981), 'Informal risk capital in New England', in K.H. Vesper (eds), *Frontiers of Entrepreneurship Research 1981*, Wellesley, MA: Babson College, pp. 217–45.

Wiltbank, R. and W. Broeker (2007), *Returns to Angel Investors in Groups*, Kansas City, KS: Kauffman Foundation.

2 Chinese clan entrepreneurship

David Leong

When early immigrants arrived at Singapore from China, clan associations provided them with social contacts, training, business ideas, market information, business concepts, start-up capital and technical assistance. This web of ethnic networks played an important role in facilitating the development of entrepreneurship in Singapore. Since different dialect groups had their own associations, this resulted in industry clustering. The Hakka entrepreneurs, for instance, dominated the city's medical halls. More recently, clan associations in Singapore have been linking up with similar associations overseas, resulting in impressive networks of international entrepreneurs. This chapter presents an account of the evolution of Chinese clan associations into vehicles for international entrepreneurship.

Dollinger (1985) explains that entrepreneurs are hardly isolated in their decisions. They are influenced by networks of significant others. Networking involves calling upon a web of contacts for information, support and assistance. The literature on networks is rich. Aldrich and Whetten (1981), Baker (1990), Donckels and Lambrecht (1997), Holt (1987), Johannisson (1986), Mitchell (1973) and others, discuss social ties, which are all explanatory variables for network structures. Aldrich and Zimmer (1986) integrated network theory into the study of entrepreneurship. Carsrud et al. (1986) found networks to be important in understanding new venture development. Aldrich et al. (1987) found network accessibility to be significant in predicting new venture creation. Dubini and Aldrich (1991) found networks central to entrepreneurship. Birley et al. (1991) looked at networks in different geographic contexts.

In a study of Korean entrepreneurs in Atlanta, Min and Jaret (1985) found family networks to be a source of manpower. In their investigation of Surinamese entrepreneurs in Amsterdam, Boissevain and Grotenbreg (1987), found that ethnic networks can provide introductions to wholesalers, and warnings of government inspections. Dana (1993) found a similar network among Italians in Canada. Also, Dunung (1995) noted that an ethnic network contributed to the success of Chinese entrepreneurs in Thailand. However, ethnic networks are not exclusive to minority groups.

This entry is about ethnic Chinese networks in Singapore, where the ethnic Chinese comprise three-quarters of the population. Here, the ethnic networks were institutionalized as clan associations. Each dialect group established its own clan network, and these were instrumental in the development of entrepreneurship in Singapore. Each association became a networking resource and a marketing research organization. In addition to providing potential and existing entrepreneurs with opportunities for networking and gathering market information, clan associations supported schools to propagate entrepreneurial spirit.

The methodology for this study relied extensively on archival research. In addition to clan documents, interviews with entrepreneurs and retired entrepreneurs were very useful.

HISTORICAL BACKGROUND

In 1819, Sir Thomas Stamford Raffles, Lieutenant-Governor of Bencoolen, landed in Singapore with the intention of establishing a trading post for the East India Company. The indigenous people, at the time, were Malay fishermen.

Raffles bought the rights to establish a trading post, and with the objective of attracting entrepreneurs from abroad, he made Singapore a free port. Within a few months, thousands of Chinese immigrants settled in Singapore. By 1824, there were 10 683 people in Singapore of which 31 per cent were Chinese (Saw, 1970). Yen (1986) documented that a famine in 1826 prompted 4000 men to leave China and seek opportunities in Singapore.

During the following decades, thousands more came from Fujian province and from Guangdong. By 1840, half of Singapore's population was Chinese (Saw, 1970). At the time, most worked on plantations. Then, the decline of agriculture in Singapore prompted urbanization. Telok Ayer Street became the economic heart of the Chinese community, and the home of several clan associations.

The inauguration of the Suez Canal, in 1869, made Singapore a major node along the England to Australia route. This created countless opportunities for Singapore. Immigrants from China left their rural homes in Singapore and moved to the city. There, they became cargo-carriers, cart-pullers, dock labourers and traders. Many worked with the dream of becoming entrepreneurs, and they did. They built and operated go-downs (warehouses), and developed the support industries of the port.

By 1901, there were 164 041 Chinese people in Singapore (Leung, 1988). This was almost three-quarters of the population. For linguistic reasons, the Chinese in Singapore tended to live among and work with others who spoke the same dialect. The dominant dialect groups in Singapore are listed in Table 2.1. When new immigrants arrived, they joined established people who spoke the same dialect. (The segregation of dialect groups was a policy set by Raffles.) Newcomers worked for entrepreneurs, and learned specific trades. It was a tradition that an employee learned from an employer how to become an entrepreneur. This led to considerable occupational clustering. Many Hokkiens lived on China Street, where they sold sundry items along with fresh greens. Telok Ayer Street was home to larger-scale Hokkien entrepreneurs, importing rice and other goods from neighbouring countries. On Chin Chew Street, Teochew entrepreneurs traded spices. On Chulia Street, Teochew merchants sold bird's nests and shark's fins. Regarded as a lower

Table 2.1 Chinese dialect groups in Singapore

Dialect group	Dialect spoken	Origin in China
Cantonese/Guangzhouren	Guangzhouhua	Guangdong Province
Foochow/Fuzhouren	Fuzhouhua	Fujian Province
Hainanese/Hainanren	Hainanhua	Hainan Island
Hakka/Kejiaren	Kehua	Guangdong Province (mainly)
Henghua/Xinghuahren	Xinghuahua	Fujian Province
Hokchia/Fuqinren	Fuqinhua	Fujian Province
Hokkien/Minnanren	Minnanhua	Fujian Province
Teochew/Chaozhouren	Chaozhouhua	Guangdong Province

class on the social echelon, the Cantonese were clustered in the district around Kreta Ayer. Many of them sold cloth. Some sold furniture, musical instruments, tobacco and silk, which they imported from China. By 1947, there were 939 144 Chinese in Singapore (Saw, 1970).

Chiang and Chan (1994) found that three socio-cultural features explained the success of Chinese entrepreneurs in Singapore:

1. personal qualities including hard work ethic, commitments, perseverance, determination and realism;
2. family and central values associated with it, including loyalty, commitment, protection, welfare, paternalism and mutual obligations; and
3. the ability of Chinese entrepreneurs to organize themselves by creating relations embedded in the structure of trade and clan associations.

CLAN ASSOCIATIONS

Clan associations (*hui kuan* in Mandarin, *wui kun* in Cantonese, and *huay kwan* in Fujian) were established for the purpose of fostering friendship among immigrants sharing the same dialect, and to promote commercial and industrial development, while upholding cultural traditions. From conversations with members, one could understand the latest trends in product development and price fluctuations. Also, the clan provided (and still provides) a centre where entrepreneurs could discuss partnerships, or obtain financing. A clan usually established several associations.

Unpublished records indicate that the Hakkas formed at least 29 clan associations in Singapore. Eleven of these were organized to bring together individuals from specific counties in China. In seven other cases, membership was based on family names. Four were co-operative societies. Seven others were professional, social and recreational associations. As a whole, they were crucial to the development of entrepreneurs among new immigrants from various villages in China.

The first Hakka clan associations in Singapore were the Wui Chiu Hui Kuan (established in 1822), and the Ying Foh Fui Kuan (founded in 1823). The Char Yong Association was formed in 1857, followed by the Singapore Char Yong Association, in 1858. The Fui Chew Association was set up in 1870. Situated on Beach Road, the Foong Shoon Fui Kuan was established in 1873.

In 1929, eight[1] existing Hakka associations pooled their resources to create the Nanyang Khek Community Guild, an umbrella organization. Its founding president was Mr Aw Boon Haw, the well-known philanthropist made famous by his tiger balm enterprise. The early stages of his business had depended on the participation and assistance of established Hakka entrepreneurs in Singapore. Collective planning and efforts helped his firm develop, and through association networking it was possible for Mr Aw to invite clansmen to share his vision and work as a team at his Wing On Tong Pharmaceutical Factory. Tiger balm needed distribution channels, and this prompted Hakka clansmen to start medicine halls – a sector in which they became dominant thanks to Mr Aw. Over time, his success served as a motivating factor for Hakka people, who adopted him as a role model. Finally, he led the Nanyang Khek Community Guild.

Table 2.2 Small and medium enterprises operated by Hakka people in British Singapore

Sectors	Sole proprietorships	Partnerships	Limited companies	Total
Chinese medical halls	142	23	2	167
Imported goods/clothing materials	70	27	1	98
Importers and exporters/grocery shops	47	23		70
Tailors	60	3		63
Metal goods/ironmongery	50	7		57
Leather goods/shoes	44	7		51
Watches/opticals/goldsmith	40	9		49
Apparels	29	11		40
Pawnshops	10	14		24
Furniture	15			15
Hotels	8			8
Others (cinemas, newspapers, etc.)	43	3		46

Source: *Hakka Association Annual Report* (1965).

The purpose of creating such a network was to improve relationships among members of different Hakka associations. The long-term goal was to promote commercial and industrial development, and to organize charity events, educational institutions and welfare projects – all for the benefit of Hakka people. Committee members included representatives from Indonesia, Malaya, North Borneo, Sarawak and Thailand, as well as Singapore.

Eventually, Hakka entrepreneurs became dominant in certain small business sectors. Hakka entrepreneurs owned two major newspapers, dozens of pawnshops, 56 import shops, 70 grocery stores and 167 medical halls. Although some business entities were partnerships, most were sole proprietorships, as indicated in Table 2.2.

The specific objectives of the Nanyang Khek Community Guild are 'to foster better relationships among members of the Khek community to promote industrial and commercial development, and to organize charitable, educational welfare projects' (Nanyang Khek Community Guild, n.d.: 13).

The guild has four categories of members: (1) the fundamental members, which are the eight founding clan associations; (2) the ordinary association members, which are other associations belonging to the Khek community, in Singapore or abroad; (3) corporate members, which are commercial or industrial establishments that are owned by a member of the Khek community; and (4) individual members, who belong to the Khek community or family members thereof.

Membership of the guild involves obligations and privileges. There are prohibitions on gambling, lotteries and interference with prices or trade. An internal policing system allows the Management Committee to investigate allegations of wrongdoings. Members found guilty are deprived of guild privileges.

The structure of the guild is such that different sections have assigned responsibilities. The 'Organisation Section' initiates research about the economic standing of community members, and deals with commercial and industrial matters of members. The Culture and Education Section is responsible for educational matters such as publications. The Welfare Section attends to financial matters. The Social Section is responsible for networking activities.

Like the Hakkas, other dialect groups also created clan associations. During the nineteenth century, the Hokkiens (from Fujian) established the Hokkien Huay Kuan. The Teochews (from Guangdong) set up the Ngee Ann Kongsi. The Hainanese formed the Singapore Kiung Chou Hwee Kuan in 1857. Henghua immigrants from Kang Tau (in the Fuquing district of Fujian's old Fuzhou prefecture) and who shared the surname 'Ong' created the Singapore Kang-Tau Ong Clansmen Association; among themselves they spoke Xinghuahua dialect. People from the south of Fujian province and who shared the name 'Ong' joined the Singapore Hokkien Ong Clansmen General Association; there, Minnanhua was the dialect spoken. Of 298 surnames which are common in Singapore, Chen is among the most popular with over a dozen clan associations (Cheng, 1990).

The Gan Clan Association was established on Bukit Pasoh Road. The Wong Clan of Toishan established itself on Jink Chuan Road. Although each clan used a different dialect and represented different geographic origins, clan associations all had something in common. They all encouraged networking. Clan associations could provide market knowledge, technical training, entrepreneurship education, a workforce, market contacts, suppliers, credit, consumers and successful role models. This facilitated their task of propagating Confucian values, which reinforced a propensity for entrepreneurship. Figure 2.1 illustrates the interaction of forces.

ENTREPRENEURS IN CHINESE TRADITION

According to Confucianism, ignorance is an obstacle and education is valued. The traditional cultural beliefs of the Hakka people emphasize several related values. Among these are persistence and perseverance, qualities that may improve an individual's chances as an entrepreneur. Also crucial are notions such as respect for order, status and authority. Again, this may help in management of a business. The Hakka people also believe in the virtue of thrift. Weber (1904–05) argued that thrift was a cultural value linked to entrepreneurship. Finally, the Hakka people place emphasis on having a sense of shame. It was argued that a sense of shame would help individuals maintain honesty and long-term interpersonal relationships.

To propagate these values, the Hakka associations built several private schools. While other schools emphasized learning to read and write, the schools of the Hakka associations had ulterior motives. Their objective was not limited to teaching reading and writing. Also, Hakka children were taught social etiquette and Hakka cultural values. The youth were encouraged to lead their lives such as to make future contributions to their people. These schools were to create entrepreneurs.

The first of these Hakka schools was the Yin Sin School, consisting of six classrooms. Located on Telok Ayer Street, it opened in 1905. A year later, the 20-classroom Kee Fatt School was established at 30 Cainhill Road. Several other schools were built and supported by Hakka associations. These are shown in Table 2.3. For the past 50 years, however, the Hakka people have opened no new schools.

A clan association of the Teochews, the Singapore Teo Chew Poit Ip Huay Kuan,

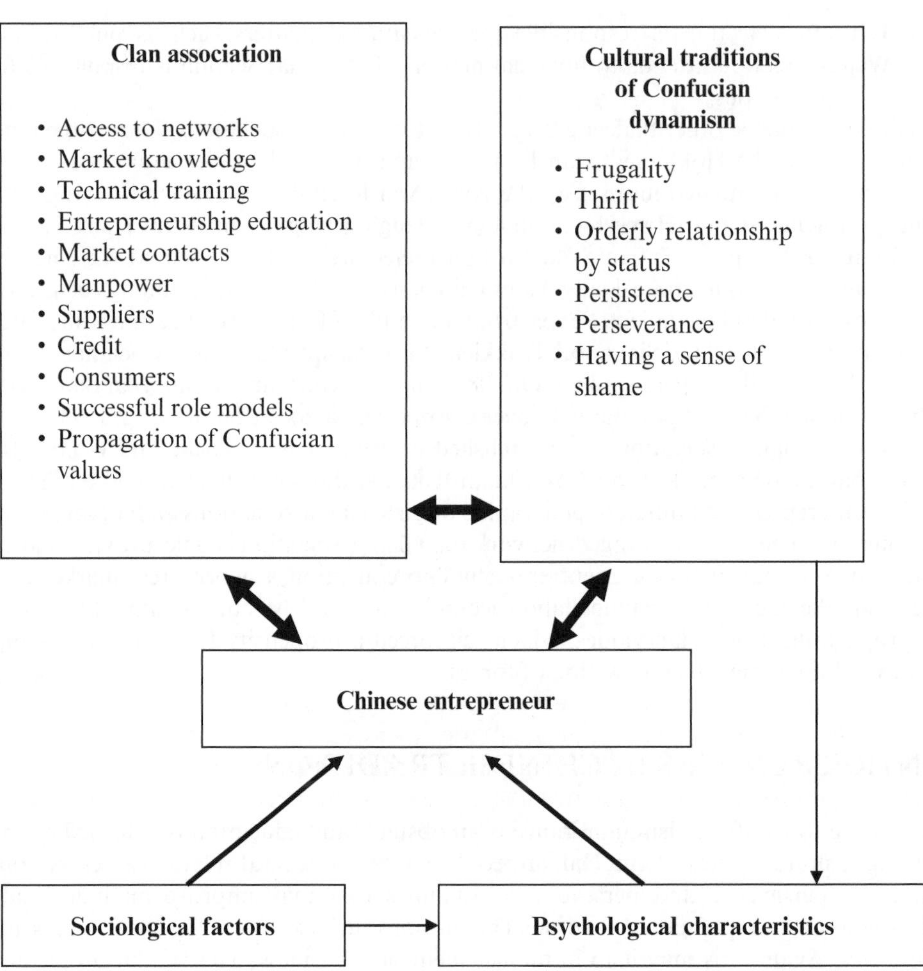

Figure 2.1 Forces contributing to entrepreneurship among Singaporean Chinese

Table 2.3 Schools producing Hakka entrepreneurs

Institution	Year opened	Number of classrooms	Address
Yin Sin School	1905	6	Telok Ayer Street
Kee Fatt School	1906	20	30 Cainhill Street
Nam Thung Public School	1927	3	7½ mi. Holland Road
Tong Fah School	1933	6	53 Craig Road
Tai Keow Public School	1936	8	288 Q Lorong Tai Seng
Lee Chee Public School	1938	8	3 Mataban Street
Sam Foh School	1946	3	467 Beach Road
Wen Shien Public School	1949	7	160 Neil Road

Source: Nanyang Khek Community Guild.

established the Ngee Ann College, in 1959. This was a Chinese-medium college, which provided tertiary education to students who graduated from Chinese high schools. It eventually evolved into Ngee Ann Polytechnic.

The Hokkien Hui Kuan (Hokkien Clan Association) donated land to build Nanyang University, which opened in 1958. This was the first Chinese-language university outside China. Eventually, Nanyang University became home to the Nanyang Technological Institute, and in 1991 to Nanyang Technological University.

THE CHANGING ROLE OF CLAN ASSOCIATIONS

Independence changed demographics and this had a great impact on clan associations. Under British colonial rule, the associations were central to the success of entrepreneurship in Singapore. Members of the Chinese community tended to interact mostly with others from the same dialect group. These were people who shared a strong identity with their geographic roots, and with whom there were no communication barriers. This arrangement also allowed them to rely on *guanxi* relationships. The Singapore Chinese Chamber of Commerce and Industry (established in 1906) was the supreme economic institution of the Chinese community.

The creation of the Republic of Singapore gave rise to a new nationalism that transcended dialect groups. The redistribution of population, to new housing estates, resulted in heterogeneous neighbourhoods; clan associations were not allowed to follow. During the 1960s, only 39 new clan associations were established (Cheng, 1985).

In the new housing estates, the Singapore government set up a variety of new institutions including Citizen Consultative Committees, Community 'Centres' and Residents' Committees. In 1978, the state launched an annual campaign aimed at encouraging Singaporeans to speak Mandarin in lieu of dialects. Social interaction across clan lines resulted in intermarriage, and the decline in the use of dialects in homes. Clan associations – in the traditional sense – were losing their economic importance. Although they still offered opportunities for business networking, it was possible to succeed without joining them.

The year 1981 witnessed a new type of clan association, when the Hakkas, originating from Jiexi established the Hepo Corporation. This was not a *hui kuan*; rather, the term 'corporation' was used to emphasize its commercial purpose as an instrument for investment.

Thus, the role of clan associations evolved. During the 1980s, the Singapore government took initiatives to stimulate entrepreneurship in the republic. The traditional role of clan associations waned. Whereas the associations were formally the principal vehicles fostering local entrepreneurship in Singapore, governmental bodies took over this role. These are the Economic Development Board, the National Productivity Board and the Trade Development Board.

Yet, this did not make the clan associations obsolete. Instead, they embarked on a plan of far greater proportions. As discussed by Cheng (1990), in 1984, Mr Chua Gim Siong sought government endorsement and support for clan associations. His success led to a national seminar on clan associations in December 1984. Nine associations, representing seven dialect groups, organized this event, the purpose of which was to

Table 2.4 Founding members of the Singapore Federation of Chinese Clan Associations

Clan association	Dialect group
Sam Kiang Huay Kuan	Sanjiangren
Singapore Foochew Association	Fuzhouren
Singapore Hokkien Huay Kuan	Minnanren
Singapore Kiung Chow Hwee Kuan	Hainanren
Singapore Kwangtung Hui Kuan	Guangzhouren
Singapore Nanyang Khek Community Guild	Kejiaren
Singapore Teo Chew Poit Ip Huay Kuan	Chaozhouren

examine how clan associations could contribute to the future. The event was attended by several hundred delegates, representing 185 clan associations, and led to the creation of an umbrella organization. Thus, in 1986, the Singapore Federation of Chinese Clan Associations was established, to promote a Singapore-wide network of clan associations. The founding members are listed in Table 2.4.

Together with the Singapore Chinese Chamber of Commerce, the federation contributes to the success of ethnic Chinese entrepreneurship in Singapore. While the Singapore Chamber of Commerce concentrates on economic and business matters at large, the Federation focuses on promoting, fostering and encouraging relationships and co-operation. It coordinates activities among different clan associations, and contributes to the propagation of cultural traditions which are relevant to Confucian dynamism and entrepreneurship, factors illustrated in Figure 2.1.

Most recently, clans in Singapore have been networking not only amongst themselves, but also with their counterparts overseas. Eight clan groups have linked up with international associations of like clans. This has resulted in several worldwide networks of Chinese entrepreneurs, who are forging global economic links.

Some clan associations have formed holding companies to invest overseas. Foong Shoon Holdings Limited, for example, was established by members of the Foong Shoon Fui Kuan. Already, some international networks of clans are operating in China. Their activities include manufacturing, trading, property development, infrastructure development, hotel management and medical care.

CONCLUSION

The role of clan associations, and the nature of their importance, has changed over time. During colonial rule, they enhanced networking relationships of local entrepreneurs who spoke the same dialect. During the early years of independence, the Singapore government provided services similar to those that the clan associations had pioneered. Simultaneously, the spread of English, as Singapore's language of business, facilitated interaction among people of dialect groups. For a period, clan associations were actually discouraged, because they were deemed contradictory to efforts that focused on creating a feeling of Singaporean identity across clan lines. More recently, the Singapore government has been encouraging the establishment of international networks among fellow clan associations. These institutions, which pioneered local entrepreneurship in colonial Singapore, have become instruments of international entrepreneurship.

NOTE

1. These were the Char Yong Association, the Fong Yun Thai Association, Foong Shoon Fui Kuan, Sam Foh Whai Kuan, the Singapore Eng Teng Association, the Singapore Nanyang Shang Hang Thung Hsiang Hui, Wui Chiu Fui Kung and Ying Foh Fui Kun.

REFERENCES

Aldrich, Howard E. and David A. Whetten (1981), 'Organizational sets, action sets and networks', in Paul C. Nystrom and William H. Starbuk (eds), *Handbook of Organisational Design*, vol. 2, Oxford: Oxford University Press, pp. 385–408.

Aldrich, Howard E. and Catherine Zimmer (1986), 'Entrepreneurship through social networks', in Donald L. Sexton and Raymond W. Smilor (eds), *The Art and Science of Entrepreneurship*, Cambridge, MA: Ballinger, pp. 3–24.

Aldrich, Howard E., Ben Rosen and William Woodward (1987), 'The impact of social networks on business foundings and profit in a longitudinal study', *Frontiers of Entrepreneurship Research*, Wellesley, MA: Babson College, pp. 154–68.

Baker, W.E. (1990), 'Market networks and corporate behavior', *American Journal of Sociology*, **3**, 589–625.

Birley, Sue, Stan Cromie and Andrew Myers (1991), 'Entrepreneurial networks: their emergence in Ireland and overseas', *International Small Business Journal*, **4** (July–September), 56–74.

Boissevain, Jeremy and Hanneke Grotenbreg (1987), 'Ethnic enterprise in the Netherlands: the Surinamese of Amsterdam', in Robert Goffee and Robert Scase (eds), *Entrepreneurship in Europe: The Social Process*, London: Croom Helm, pp. 105–30.

Carsrud, Alan L., Connie Marie Gaglio and Kenneth W. Olm (1986), 'Entrepreneurs – mentors, networks and successful new venture development: an exploratory study', *Frontiers of Entrepreneurship Research*, Wellesley, MA: Babson College, pp. 229–43.

Cheng, Lim Keak (1985), *Social Change and the Chinese in Singapore*, Singapore: Singapore University Press.

Cheng, Lim Keak (1990), 'Reflections on the changing roles of Chinese clan associations in Singapore', *Asian Culture*, **14** (April), 57–71.

Chiang, Claire and Chan Kwok Bun (1994), *Stepping Out: The Making of Chinese Entrepreneurs*, Singapore: Prentice Hall.

Dana, Léo-Paul (1993), 'An inquiry into culture and entrepreneurship', *Journal of Small Business and Entrepreneurship*, **10** (4), 16–31.

Dollinger, Marc J. (1985), 'Environmental contact and financial performance of the small firm', *Journal of Small Business Management*, **23** (1), 24–30.

Donckels, Rik and Johan Lambrecht (1997), 'The network position of small business: an explanatory model', *Journal of Small Business Management*, **35** (2), 13–25.

Dubini, Paola and Howard E. Aldrich (1991), 'Personal and extended networks are central to the entrepreneurship process', *Journal of Business Venturing*, **6** (5), 305–13.

Dunung, Sanjyot P. (1995), *Doing Business in Asia*, New York: Lexington Books.

Hakka Association Annual Report (1965), Jubilee Celebration edn, October, Singapore: Nanyang Khek Community Guild.

Holt, David H. (1987), 'Network support systems', in Neil C. Churchill, John A. Hornaday, Bruce A. Kirchoft, O.J. Krasner and Karl H. Vesper (eds), *Frontiers of Entrepreneurship Research*, Wellesley, MA: Babson College, pp. 45–56.

Johannisson, Bengt (1986), 'The network strategies: management technology for entrepreneurship and change', *International Small Business Journal*, **1** (Autumn), 19–30.

Leung, Yuen Sang (1988), 'The economic life of the Chinese in the late nineteenth century Singapore', in Lee Lai To (ed.), *Early Chinese Immigrant Societies*, Singapore: Heinemann Asia.

Min, Pyong Gap and Charles Jaret (1985), 'Ethnic business success: the case of Korean small business in Atlanta', *Sociology and Social Research*, **69** (3), 412–35.

Mitchell, J. Clyde (1973), 'Networks, norms and institutions', in Jeremy Boissevan and J. Clyde Mitchell (eds), *Network Analysis: Studies in Human Interaction*, The Hague: Mouton, pp. 2–35.

Nanyang Khek Community Guild (n.d.), *Rules and Regulations of Nanyang Khek Community Guild*, Singapore: Nanyang Khek Community Guild.

Saw Swee Hock (1970), *Singapore Population in Transition*, Philadelphia, PA: University of Pennsylvania Press.

Weber, Max (1904–05), 'Die protestantische Ethik und der Geist des Kapitalismus', *Archiv fur Sozialwissenschaft und Sozialpolitik* (20–21); translated (in 1930) by Talcott Parsons, *The Protestant Ethic and the Spirit of Capitalism*, New York: George Allen & Unwin.

Yen, Ching-Hwang (1986), *A Social History of the Chinese in Singapore and Malaya 1800–1911*, Singapore: Oxford University Press.

3 Configuration approach in entrepreneurship research

Rainer Harms and Sascha Kraus

The configuration approach is an approach to analyse (new) venture development and change. A configuration is 'any multidimensional constellation of conceptually distinct characteristics that commonly occur together' (Fiss, 2007: 1). Under a configuration perspective, organizations can be described as complex systems whose development and performance is influenced by interrelations between factors from the domains of environment, structure, strategy, and leadership (Miller, 1987). As a result of forces that select in factors that 'fit' within the context of a firm's current position, and select out elements that do not, the configuration approach posits that there will be a limited number of empirically observable firm types (Miller et al., 1984). Following this perspective, Miller (1996: 507) describes a research programme for configuration research: 'Since configurations are about organizational wholes, more should be done to discover their thematic and systemic aspects – to probe into just why and how their elements interrelate and complement each other to produce the driving character of an enterprise.'

This perspective can be applied to the context of entrepreneurship, as research has acknowledged that there are different types of new ventures. For instance, high-technology start-ups in the information technology (IT) sector might be very different along various domains compared to a newly founded coffee store. Since the relationships between the domains that constitute these new venture 'types' may be very different, research ought to take these differences into account. Gartner et al. (1989) argue that entrepreneurship research can benefit from an explicit study of diversity among new ventures. In the remainder of the chapter, we outline the configuration approach and discuss it along the lines of content, static and dynamic approaches, and methodology, before highlighting its benefits and challenges.

OUTLINING THE CONFIGURATION APPROACH

The configuration approach was introduced to business studies by Miller et al. (1984), whose key study *Organizations: A Quantum View* influenced a stream of research in strategic management and entrepreneurship. The configuration approach has been studied under many names including 'Gestalt approach', 'enhanced contingency approach' or 'multiple-domain studies'. A comparison of the configuration approach with the universal effects approach (analysing one domain) and the contingency approach (analysing two domains) serves to outline the contingency approach.

A key topic in entrepreneurship research is the analysis of new venture performance (NVP) and change. In single domain studies, factors that are hypothesized to impact on NVP are treated as if they were independent from another. A formal expression for this

Table 3.1 Single versus multiple domain studies in entrepreneurship research: benefits and limitations

	Benefits	Limitations
Single domain	• Simple methods may be used • Fine-grained analysis of constructs possible	• Little explanation of variance • Does not detect interactive relationships • Little normative value
Two domains	• Analyses performance implications of fit between two constructs	• Bivariate contingencies may be too general
Multiple domains	• Allows examination of multivariate relationships • May enhance predictive relevance	• Complex methods required

Source: Adapted from Dess et al. (1993: 780).

relationship is provided by Sandberg and Hofer (1987), who posit that NVP = f(E; S; I), that is, NVP is a function of characteristics of the entrepreneur (E), strategy (S) and industry (I). However, in reality, these factors may not be independent from another. The personality of the entrepreneur, the strategy, and the environment simultaneously influence new venture creation, performance, and change (Gartner, 1985).

For example, such a dependent's contingent relationship occurs when the performance impact of a certain strategy S_x will be different when applied in industry I_y or in industry I_z. This type of contingency is acknowledged in two-domain studies. For example, Lumpkin and Dess (2001) show that the performance impact of proactiveness and competitive aggressiveness (which are elements of an entrepreneurial strategy) impact differently on performance, contingent on industry dynamism, hostility or the industry life-cycle stage.

While the consideration of bivariate contingencies may better explain variance of NVP, proponents of the multiple-domain (configuration) approach posit that bivariate contingencies may be too general, and that interactions between a larger set of variables need to be considered. In addition, the configuration approach acknowledges non-linear and complex relationships. Dess et al. (1993) have summarized the benefits and limitations of the different approaches (see Table 3.1).

To carry out studies based on the configuration approach, the issue of variable selection needs to be addressed. As outlined, variables from multiple domains ought to be selected. A 'domain' can be understood as a superordinate term that encompasses variables that are contextually related. Miller (1987: 686) specifies the nature of domains: They ought to have proven to play a key role in widely accepted paradigms in business studies and analyses and they have to been shown empirically to relate to other domains. Generally, the domains of 'environment', 'structure', 'leadership' and 'strategy' ought to be considered. Pertaining to entrepreneurship research, the domains of 'person' and 'environment' could be emphasized to capture the specific characteristics of new ventures (Harms et al., 2009). In case the analysis of entrepreneurial strategies is the focus of research, the strategy domain might be stressed to provide more detail for this particular domain.

THE CONFIGURATION APPROACH IN ENTREPRENEURSHIP RESEARCH

Interpretations of 'Entrepreneurship'

In entrepreneurship research, two streams of literature in which the configuration is applied can be identified. While both research streams focus on the analysis of the interaction of configuration domains, they differ with respect to the underlying interpretation of 'entrepreneurship'.

In the first stream of research, entrepreneurship is understood as a discipline that studies new venture creation and the development of new ventures. Based on this interpretation of entrepreneurship, researchers try to identify, empirically or conceptually, distinct types of new ventures along the lines of the configuration domains. One of the first studies in that direction was undertaken by Gartner et al. (1989) who identified new venture taxonomies based on personal (for example, work experience), organizational (for example, partnership), environmental (for example, importance of suppliers) and process (for example, time spent on specified start-up activities) characteristics. They identified eight distinct types of new ventures, labelled them according to their main characteristics ('Escaping to something new', 'Putting the deal together', 'Roll over skills/ contacts', 'Purchasing a firm', 'Leveraging expertise', 'Aggressive service', 'Pursuing the unique idea' and 'Methodical organizing'), and described how the domains interact to form a particular type of new venture.

In the second stream of literature, entrepreneurship can best be understood as a firm-level strategic approach that is positively associated with a firm's proclivity to act entrepreneurially. Under this perspective, Miller (1983; 2006), Covin and Slevin (1986) and Stevenson and Jarillo (1990) deal with 'entrepreneurial archetypes' in the sense that they seek to identify varieties of entrepreneurship and their personal, structural, and environmental correlates. For example, Miller (1983) identified different sources of entrepreneurship in different types of firms. In the 'simple-firm' configuration, which are small and dominated by the owner, personal characteristics of the owner strongly impact firm-level entrepreneurship. 'Organic firms' are highly adaptive and characteristics of the environment impact on the degree of entrepreneurship. Organic firms in dynamic or hostile markets exhibit a higher degree of entrepreneurship. 'Planning firms' tend to be larger and more formalized and the explicitness of strategy is positively correlated with entrepreneurship

Static and Dynamism

A second way to structure research based on the configuration approach is along the lines of static versus dynamic approaches. In entrepreneurship research, most studies seek to identify new venture types and establish links to NVP. Since these approaches do not consider intra-configuration dynamics or the development from one configuration to another, these approaches can be termed static.

The dynamic approach to configuration analysis explicitly takes configuration development and change into account. Configuration change is argued to be fundamental rather than evolutionary. Since the costs of fundamental changes might be huge, change is often delayed until the costs of a 'misfit' become larger than the costs of fundamental change. Thus, a (new) venture might hold on to its current style of leadership, its current strategy or its current market for as long as it can. The concept of revolutionary change can be illustrated by Greiners life-cycle concept (Greiner 1972): In a start-up, leadership is centralized and informal, based on the strong position of the founder. When a firm grows, centralized and informal leadership may not suffice anymore to coordinate the firm. However, founders tend to be reluctant to change their status, which then may lead to a crisis in firm development. This crisis can be solved by 'revolutionary' changes.

In entrepreneurship research, to date there have been no published studies that track the development of new venture configurations over time. However, studies that are based on the life cycle-approach do consider change, although these studies focus on structural variables and neglect other domains. Thus, a dynamic configuration analysis in entrepreneurship research is still missing. However, as the imprinting hypothesis states that the conditions of new venture creation have a significant impact on venture development, an analysis of start-up configurations would be a natural starting point for other configuration analyses.

Methodology

Configurations can be derived analytically, by developing ideal types, respectively typologies created via theoretical reasoning. Typologies are created based on theoretical explanations of the interaction between its elements. While typologies can foster imaginative thinking about configurations, they ought to be empirically tested lest they be regarded as speculations. In that respect, Hambrick (1984: 28) criticizes pure typologies 'since they are largely the product of rather personal insight [and] may not accurately reflect reality'. Therefore, only limited explanatory or predictive power can be ascribed to typologies.

A second way to derive configurations is empirically, by detecting real types, or taxonomies, via quantitative and qualitative methods (Scherer and Beyer, 1998). A survey of taxonomic studies in entrepreneurship research (Harms et al., 2007) identified more than 30 studies that deal with the empirical identification of new and small venture types using multiple domains. However, unless theoretically grounded, taxonomies may contain statistical artefacts and may therefore be of limited value for researchers and practitioners.

Therefore, the literature proposes to test typologies empirically (Doty and Glick, 1994), and to provide a theory-based interpretation of taxonomies (Miller, 1987). A recent example of quantitative testing of a qualitative entrepreneurship typology is the analysis by Hill and Birkinshaw (2007). Hill and Birkinshaw (2007) created a typology based a venture's relative emphasis on exploration versus exploitation and the internal versus external locus of opportunity they pursue, which they tested on a sample of corporate venture units.

A number of empirical methods have been used to identify configurations, namely clustering algorithms, analysis of interaction effects, and deviation score approaches (Fiss, 2007). Since these approaches might not be sufficient to model complex and non-linear relationships that are characteristic of configurations, Fiss (2007) proposes set-theoretic methods. These methods allow for the distinction between necessary and sufficient conditions for performance, and thereby enable the analysis of the structure between the configuration domains.

BENEFITS AND CHALLENGES

There are a number of benefits for practitioners and researchers that might result from the application of the configuration approach in entrepreneurship research. First, nascent entrepreneurs can use configurations as role models for their own start-up activities (Unger and Frese, 2005). Second, configurations can be a tool for self-assessment for existing entrepreneurs, who might compare their firm to successful archetypes. Third, configurations can be used to give tailored advice to entrepreneurs, in line with the affiliation to a specific new venture types.

Through future research, the configuration approach may go beyond single-domain or two-domain studies to analyse complex interactions between the domains in particular configurations. In that respect, Doty and Glick (1994) argue that the configuration approach may be a specific approach to theory building. Statements about the relationships between the domains may be regarded as theories of the middle range. These theories may be less generalizable (that is, they apply to a certain taxonomy, but not to others), but may be more precise that general theories of NVP and change.

However, there are also challenges for researchers who wish to apply the configuration approach. First, it is methodologically and theoretically demanding. For example, to analyse configuration dynamics, longitudinal data-sets are needed. Second, on a theoretical level, the issue of incommensurability between the theoretic approaches that impact on a configuration needs to be addressed (Scherer and Beyer, 1998).

The configuration approach has already begun to contribute to entrepreneurship research by highlighting the diversity of new ventures and by providing a tool by which to grasp the complexity of the variables that pertain to new venture performance and change. If the aforementioned challenges can be dealt with, and refined tools for analysis will become widely available, even more configuration studies will appear and contribute to the field.

REFERENCES

Covin, Jeffrey G. and Dennis P. Slevin (1986), 'The development and testing of an organizational-level entrepreneurship scale', in R. Ronstad, J.A. Hornaday, R. Peterson and K.H. Vesper (eds), *Frontiers of Entrepreneurship Research*, Wellesley, MA.: Babson College, pp. 628–39.

Dess, G., S. Newport, and A.M.A. Rasheed (1993), 'Configuration research in strategic management: key issues and suggestions', *Journal of Management*, **19** (4), 775–95.

Doty, D.H. and W.H. Glick (1994), 'Typologies as a unique form of theory building: toward improved understanding and modeling', *Academy of Management Review*, **19** (2), 230–51.

Fiss, P.C. (2007), 'A set-theoretic approach to organizational configurations', *Academy of Management Review*, **32** (4), 1180–98.

Gartner, W.B. (1985), 'A conceptual framework for describing the phenomenon of new venture creation', *Academy of Management Journal*, **10** (4), 696–706.

Gartner, W.B., T.R. Mitchell and K.H. Vesper (1989), 'A taxonomy of new business ventures', *Journal of Business Venturing*, **4** (3), 169–86.

Greiner, L.E. (1972), 'Evolution and revolution as organizations grow', *Harvard Business Review*, **50** (4), 37–46.

Hambrick, D.C. (1984), 'Taxonomic approaches to studying strategy: some conceptual and methodological issues', *Journal of Management*, **10** (1), 27–41.
Harms, R., S. Kraus and C.H. Reschke (2007), 'Configurations of new ventures in entrepreneurship research – contributions and research gaps', *Management Research News*, **30** (9), 661–73.
Harms, R., S. Kraus and E.J. Schwarz (2009), 'The suitability of the configuration approach in entrepreneurship research', *Entrepreneurship and Regional Development*, **21** (1), 25–49.
Hill, S. and J. Birkinshaw (2007), 'Strategy-organization configurations in corporate venture units: impact on performance and survival', *Journal of Business Venturing*, **23** (4), 423–44.
Lumpkin, G.T. and G.G. Dess (2001), 'Linking two dimensions of entrepreneurial orientation to firm performance: the moderating role of environment and industry life cycle', *Journal of Business Venturing*, **16** (5), 429–52.
Miller, D. (1983), 'The correlates of entrepreneurship in three types of firms', *Management Science*, **29** (7), 770–91.
Miller, D. (1987), 'The genesis of configuration', *Academy of Management Journal*, **12** (1), 686–701.
Miller, D. (1996), 'Configurations revisited', *Strategic Management Journal*, **17** (7), 505–12.
Miller, Danny (2006), 'Entrepreneurial archetypes', in Michael A. Hitt and Duane R. Ireland (eds), *The Blackwell Encyclopedia of Management – Entrepreneurship*, Malden: Blackwell, pp. 66–9.
Miller, Danny, Peter H. Friesen and Henry Mintzberg (1984), *Organizations: A Quantum View*, Englewood Cliffs, NJ: Prentice-Hall.
Sandberg, W. and C.W. Hofer (1987), 'Improving new venture performance: the role of strategy, industry structure and the entrepreneur', *Journal of Business Venturing*, **2** (1), 5–28.
Scherer, A.G. and R. Beyer (1998), 'Der Konfigurationsansatz im Strategischen Management – Rekonstruktion und Kritik', *Die Betriebswirtschaft*, **58** (3), 332–47.
Stevenson, H.H. and J.C. Jarillo (1990), 'A paradigm of entrepreneurship: entrepreneurial management', *Strategic Management Journal*, **11** (special issue), 17–27.
Unger, Jens M. and M. Frese (2005), 'Configuration of small and micro businesses and success: strategies, firm, and environment', Academy of Management Conference, Honolulu, Hawaii, 5–10 August.

4 Criminal entrepreneurship

Petter Gottschalk

Opportunity discovery is about valuable goods and services for which there is a market. The criminal entrepreneur's task is to discover and exploit opportunities, defined most simply as situations in which there is a profit to be made in criminal activity. In turn, criminal entrepreneurship yields opportunities for other entrepreneurs such as private investigators (see Figure 4.1). Opportunity discovery relates to the generation of value, where the entrepreneur determines or influences the set of resource choices required to create value.

Opportunities to create new economic value exist because of demand for goods and services in illegal markets. Entering an illegal market as an entrepreneur is based on the assumption that there are competitive imperfections reflecting changes in technology, demand or other factors that individuals or groups in an economy attempt to exploit. For example, *Ismael Zambada-Garcia* is a Mexican drug lord. He is capo (captain) and

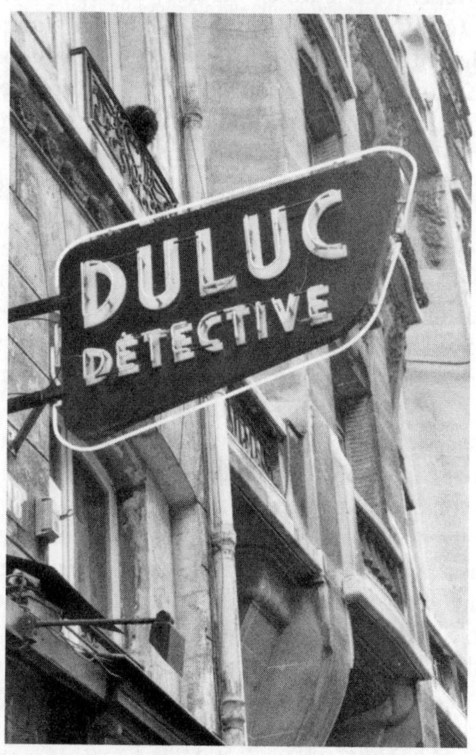

Figure 4.1 Office of Duluc, established in 1913, Paris, France; photograph by Léo-Paul Dana

head of the Sinaloa cartel in Mexico. He is 'El Mayo', Mexico's number one drug dealer. He climbed to the top by eliminating rivals and victory over Columbian cocaine producers. Zambada-Garcia got indirect help from the police, because police in Mazatlan shot and killed his most powerful rival Ramon Arellano Felix in 2002. The Tijuana cartel by Felix was weakened, while the Sinaloa cartel of Zambada-Garcia was strengthened. Competitive imperfections were created by the purposeful actions of Zambada-Garcia.

Terrence 'Terry' Adams is the head of Britain's most enterprising, and feared, organized crime gang. He has an imaginative mind capable of sophisticated, complex and dishonest financial manipulation. When moving into new territories and new businesses, his integrative thinking helped build up links with other groups and cocaine cartels.

Curtis 'Cocky' Warren was one of Britain's biggest and richest drug traffickers. Unlike most other drug traffickers, Warren is a highly intelligent force. Warren does not drink, smoke or use drugs. He has a photographic memory for telephone and bank account numbers. His organization had contacts with the Colombian Cali Cartel, Moroccan and Turkish criminal organizations.

Tam 'The Licensee' McGraw is head of a criminal organization in Glasgow. His integrative thinking enabled him to balance and integrate law enforcement officials and competitors into his organized crime. When one of the criminals in McGraw's organization phoned Margaret McGraw (his wife) late at night with the news that her husband had been arrested, her reply left the caller stunned. 'It's okay', she said, 'the boys have been on to me already to say that it's okay, they have it in hand, not to worry, he'll be home tomorrow, you have to just sit tight.' The boys that Margaret McGraw had been referring to were the Serious Crime Squad police unit who investigated crimes of the type committed by organized crime gangs and bank robbers. Tam McGraw was a police informer.

Jamal Ahmidan was doing well in the narcotics trade. He was caught and put in jail, where he converted to Islam. When he was released from prison, he had planned terror attacks together with other inmates. To finance the intended terrorism, he continued to head the narcotics trade. At the same time he planned the train station explosions in Madrid. With money from drug dealing he bought explosive material, which was used in the subway system in Madrid. Hence, Ahmidan was involved in both criminal business and terrorism. The terror bombing in Madrid in 2004 hit commuter trains to Spain's capital in the morning of 11 March. One hundred and ninety one people were killed and 1460 injured. The attack was carried out by an Islamic group. The attack consisted of a coordinated series of ten explosions onboard four commuter trains in the rush hour. A total of 13 bombs were placed, but three did not explode.

Victor Bout is claimed to be the world's largest weapons dealer. He was born in Tajikistan. He has Russian military training and speaks six languages fluently. He has supplied Afghan groups with weapons and ammunition. His headquarters are in the Arab Emirates, first in Sharjah and later Ajman. In the summer of 2004 one of Bout's transport planes landed in Liberia, containing helicopters, armoured vehicles and firearms.

Edoardo Contini is chief executive of the Camorra Mafia in Napoli in Italy. He is currently managing the mafia from his prison cell. Napoli is the home town for the Camorra mafia, which is successful in narcotics and blackmail.

Lo Hsing Han is the narcotics baron of Burma. He contributes to the finances of the military junta in Burma, which holds the peace prize laureate Aung San Suu Kyi under house arrest. Lo Hsing Han is mostly doing business from Singapore, where he manages his narcotics empire. He started opium trading in the 1950s. He was arrested and sentenced to death in 1973, but was released from prison again in 1980. In 1992 he founded Asia World Company, which is the legal branch of his narcotics empire. He now controls the economy in Burma together with the spider man Tay Za. In 2006, Han arranged the wedding for the daughter of the junta leader Tan Shwe. Tan Shwe is the military dictator in Myanmar (Burma) by being the chief commander in the military junta.

Ahjed Wali Karzai is the opium baron of Afghanistan. He is the younger brother of president Hamid Karzai in the country. Sixty members of parliament in Kabul are assumed to be involved in opium production. Karzai's family is not only the wealthy owner of the Afghan Helmand restaurants in the USA, the family is also very influencial in the Helmand and Kandahar provinces with 62 per cent of Afghanistan's opium production and more than half of the global production.

Bernardo Provenzano is the chief executive of Cosa Nostra on Sicily. His calling name is 'the tractor', because early in his mafia career he ploughed down people by shooting them. He was jailed in 2006, but is probably still in charge of the organization. Another calling name is 'the bookkeeper', because in recent years he has led the operations of his criminal empire in a discrete and careful way.

Shinobu Tsukasa is the sixth generation boss (*kumicho*) in the criminal organization Yamaguchi Gumi in Japan. The organization consists of 750 clans with 17 500 members. The organization is involved in almost all kinds of criminal business.

CRIMINAL BUSINESS ENTERPRISE

Why does a criminal entrepreneur choose to organize a criminal business enterprise in order to exploit a market opportunity? Entrepreneurial opportunities can be exploited in a variety of ways, and we seek to understand the conditions under which organizing an enterprise is the most efficient way of exploiting a particular opportunity.

Whatever the source of competitive imperfections causing a criminal entrepreneur to enter an illegal market, their existence, per se, often only holds the potential for creating new economic value. The realization of this potential tends to require additional economic activities – activities that sometimes require the organization of an enterprise.

If a particular individual possesses all the resources – whether tangible or intangible – necessary to create economic wealth associated with a market opportunity, no additional economic organization is required to exploit this opportunity. The individual is said to be engaging in arbitrage if he or she possesses all the resources necessary to exploit a market opportunity, and thus no additional coordination through economic organization is required to create economic value.

If an individual does not possess all the resources required to exploit an opportunity, access to those resources will need to be obtained by the entrepreneur. This can be done in a variety of ways. For example, the entrepreneur can recruit the owners of these resources into a hierarchical structure to gain access required to exploit an opportunity. Alternatively, the entrepreneur might form an alliance with the owners of these resources in a network structure to gain access.

ENTREPRENEURIAL LEADERSHIP

Entrepreneurial leadership is characterized by judgement in decision-making. Judgement is where individuals take decisions without access to any generally agreed rule that could be implemented using publicly available information known to be true. A drug dealer who buys before he or she knows the price at which it can be resold must make a judgement about what the future price will be, for instance. Judgement refers primarily to business decision-making when the range of possible future outcomes is generally unknown. Judgement is required when no obviously correct model or decision rule is available or when relevant data is unreliable or incomplete.

Entrepreneurial judgement is ultimately judgement about the control of resources. As an innovator, a leader, a creator, a discoverer and an equilibrator, the entrepreneur exercises judgement in terms of resource acquisition and allocation to prosper from criminal business opportunities. As founder and developer of the business enterprise, the entrepreneur must exercise judgemental decision-making under conditions of uncertainty.

ENTREPRENEURIAL CRIME STRATEGY

Entrepreneurial strategy is based on entrepreneurial vision. Entrepreneurial vision is a tacit perception of business opportunities for the criminal business organization. To successfully reorganize resources into the envisioned business opportunities, 'resource owners must be coordinated on the entrepreneur's conception of the business and be motivated to perform properly'. An essential part of the entrepreneurial role of restructuring resources (knowledge, weapons, money, cars, and so on) is the provision of a clear image of why and how the business needs to change to sustain the crime business over time.

Strategy is both a plan for the future and pattern from the past, it is the match an organization makes between its internal resources and skills (sometimes collectively called competencies) and the opportunities and risks created by its external environment. Strategy is the long-term direction of an organization. Strategy is the course of action for achieving an organization's purpose. Strategy is the direction and scope of an organization over the long term, which achieves advantage for the organization through its configuration of resources within a changing environment and to fulfil stakeholders' expectations (Johnson and Scholes, 2002).

Given an entrepreneurial strategy, strategic management is important in a criminal business enterprise. Strategic management includes understanding the strategic position of an organization, strategic choices for the future, and turning strategy into action. Understanding the strategic position is concerned with the impact on strategy of the external environment, internal resources and competences, and the expectations and influence of stakeholders. Strategic choices involve understanding the underlying bases for future strategy at both higher and lower unit levels and the options for developing strategy in terms of both the directions in which strategy might move and the methods of development. Translating strategy into action is concerned with ensuring that strategies are working in practice. A strategy is not just a good idea, a statement or a plan. It is only meaningful when it is actually being carried out (Johnson and Scholes, 2002).

In entrepreneurial criminal businesses, strategic management must stimulate entrepreneurship in the whole organization. Entrepreneurial employees can provide a wide range of entrepreneurial services to their organization including generating and evaluating innovative ideas related to potential crimes (for example, money laundering, trafficking, fraud, corruption). An entrepreneurial strategy pays attention to entrepreneurship that focuses on individuals, their knowledge, resources and skills, and the processes of discovery and creativity, which constitute the heart of entrepreneurship.

ENTREPRENEURIAL CRIME MANAGEMENT

The emergence of criminal business enterprises is strongly associated with entrepreneurial innovation rather than an extension of managerial routine. It occurs at times of great volatility. Volatility reflects the fact that the economic, competitive and law enforcement environment is continually subjected to shocks. Shocks are extremely varied: they include disruptions because of police actions, fads and fashions in consumer tastes, and rivalry among competitors.

The dominant theoretical explanation of the creation of criminal business enterprises and managerial hierarchies remains transaction cost economics. According to transaction cost theory, internalization of resources is prompted under behavioural norms of bounded rationality and opportunism. Therefore, managing the crime business is not only attributed to great acts of entrepreneurial endeavour, but also as the linear outcome of incremental cost and risk-minimizing decisions by a far-seeing professional management pursuing optimal decisions. Vertical integration is here viewed as a managerial process focused on contractual change, rather than entrepreneurial innovation.

While the entrepreneur is the agent of development, the criminal business enterprise is the means of coordination and the agent of growth. As the agent of development, the entrepreneur creates change. Major changes include new goods and services, new methods of smuggling, new markets, new sources of supply and new ways of organizing the business. As the means of coordination, the enterprise allows deployment of resources according to market opportunities. As the agent of growth, the enterprise is a structured arrangement of capabilities, which can produce economic development.

Entrepreneurial management manifests itself in a regime in the organization. A regime is the set of rules, both formal and informal, that regulate the operation of organized crime and its interaction with society. Regime change is sometimes needed to take advantage of new criminal business opportunities. One dimension of a regime is employment, where employment regime is dependent on the employees' major work motivation, the mode of coordinating and controlling employees, and the standard for selecting staff.

WOMEN IN ORGANIZED CRIME

Often, women are considered victims of organized crime. A typical example is trafficking in women, where women are exploited in prostitution by criminal organizations. However, there are examples of women playing a quite different role in organized crime.

For example, someone has told the story of Arlete, who was the daughter of Jose

Baptista da Costa in Brazil. He was killed in 1981. This crime remains unsolved – like most other homicides involving the cupola – despite the fact that suspicion fell on a former policeman and aspiring competitor. Arlete took over her father's business to protect the territory. Arlete was dissatisfied, claiming that she should receive half the monthly proceeds from her territory. She decided to use violence to resolve the question. She contacted three policemen – all of them later killed in crimes that have also remained unsolved – known for their violent dealings in the criminal underworld. Arlete and her three bodyguards also attacked competitors.

Another example of daughter takeover in Brazil is Suely Correia de Mello. Her father was murdered in Rio de Janeiro over a territory dispute for the 'jogo dos bichos'. According to an interview given to a major national newspaper, Suely, a lawyer, had ambitions to become a public prosecutor, but was tried and found guilty of murder. She was one of the richest bankers and owned a real estate company created solely to manage the innumerable properties she had acquired during her lifetime.

Sicilian mafia women are perceived as loyal and subordinate wives who do not interfere with their husband's criminal projects and decisions. In contrast, Camorra women have always been much more involved and aware of their men's activities. They are not passive onlookers, but are the active backbone of this criminal organization, and have become increasingly involved, sometimes out of necessity, and sometimes because of a specific criminal intent.

Women in the Neapolitan criminal underworld of the Camorra mafia take on active, formal roles as directors of legal companies, which represent the front-end of the organization. They also take on leadership positions internally, making strategic decisions regarding the clan's activities, taking matters into their own hands, and even killing. For example, in May 2002, in Lauro, a town in the province of Avellino, a shoot-out between women from the Graziano clan and women from the Cavas clan left three women dead and six injured. This suggests that Camorra women are now definitely taking centre stage as major players.

As directors of front-end companies, Camorra women received public contracts, as was the case of Maria Orlando, mother of Lorenzo Nuvoletta of the Nuvoletta clan, or Antonietta Di Costanzo, wife of Antonio Orlando, the uncle of Lorenzo Nuvoletta.

Anna Mazza in Napoli became involved in Camorra activities when rival gangs murdered her husband, Gennaro Moccia, capo and boss of Afragola. She became known as 'the Black Widow'. She supported her sons in avenging their father's murder and became the leader of the gang, directing its activities and influencing its ideology. She became a capo in her own right – one of the most dangerous and most bloody. She led the group while her sons were in prison. When her eldest son, Angelo, became a leader of the Alfieri confederation, her leadership role grew less important, although she still managed local criminal activities, as well as relationships with politicians, while her sons were involved in regional Camorra warfare. Today, it appears that she still runs the clan, directs its activities and visits her sons in prison.

Successful women entrepreneurs in organized crime are hard to find. It is somewhat easier to find successful women entrepreneurs in legal businesses. For example, someone conducted a five-country analysis of self-reported determinants of success. They studied female entrepreneurs in Canada, Ireland, the Czech Republic, Poland and Japan. The women became entrepreneurs because they felt rejected – a phenomenon sometimes labelled the 'push factor'. While some women defined success in terms of profits, many used non-financial factors such as number of clients, number of employees, years in business or because 'my peers say so'. The most important factor identified in the study was networking. Business education and training was second.

The contribution of female entrepreneurs is seldom acknowledged in either legal nor criminal business. For example, in a study of female immigrant entrepreneurs, it was found that female immigrant entrepreneurs made a significant contribution to the Australian economy. The study examined the economic contributions of a group of Asian-born women entrepreneurs in Sydney. The empirical study showed that they make significant economic contributions to the creation of new businesses and jobs in addition to other non-quantifiable economic benefits to Australia.

In the USA, Georgia Durante saw the local mafia as her way out of boredom and poverty. In Rochester, New York, Durante started running errands for local mafioso Sammy Gingello. These errands involved taking packages into New York City, and she claims that she once delivered a letter directly to the powerful New York boss Carlo Gambino. She was also instructed to keep an eye on local comings and goings and to keep Gingello informed – a traditional female role in organized crime: when men's movements are restricted or attract more attention, it is often easier for women to pick up information.

Georgia Durante's principle role was as a driver: she started driving for mafia associates who collected extortion money from premises including building sites. Sometimes these shakedowns involved violence, and she became an expert at getting away fast from the scene of the crime. Durante's mafia career was in some way similar to a man's: she was attracted to local mafia figures by their money and the strange fascination that violence exerts; she saw her way out of a dreary existence by associating with them. As they got to know her, they began to give her more demanding tasks. She always accepted these commissions, feeling they gave her status and enjoying the trust that was invested in her. It gave her a sort of fascination to be trusted at this level. She felt connected to fear, but the thought never crossed her mind that she might be in any kind of danger. She was too engrossed in the intrigue.

LONDON'S FIRST ORGANIZED CRIME LORD

According to the BBC, Jonathan Wild was London's first organized crime lord. His story illustrates many of the points we want to make in this chapter. First, illegal and legal activities are combined and benefit from each other in Wild's organization. Next, political and other official contacts are useful in criminal entrepreneurship.

'Thief-takers' were the men and women who operated in England in the days before there was an established police force and a public prosecutor. Effectively created by the laws of the time – specifically the 1697 Act of Parliament, which offered rewards for the capture and successful prosecution of highwaymen – they captured those who had committed crimes, and either handed them over to the authorities or prosecuted them themselves. There have been women thief-takers, but the majority were men, and they worked for the cash rewards offered as a very good living could be made this way. Highwaymen, coiners and burglars were worth £40 reward each (plus any equipment the criminal may have been using), with an additional £100 if robbery was committed within 5 miles of Charing Cross. This kind of sum would normally take three to four years to earn for the ordinary man. The reward also carried a free pardon for any offences the thief-taker may have committed. If the thief-taker died, any reward would be passed on to his descendents.

Jonathan Wild was the most famous thief-taker of the time. In the early eighteenth century he captured and brought to justice many London criminals. What was slow to come to the attention of the law was that he was at the same time involved in many criminal activities of his own.

Wild set up an office in Newtoner's Lane and invited victims of crime to come to him with details of any stolen goods, and promised them that he would recover them. His popularity as a receiver of stolen goods meant that he often either had the goods in his possession already, or knew who had stolen them. One of his scams was to order the theft of specific goods so that he could return them to their grateful owners. He managed to please the thieves by paying for their goods, and please the victims, by reuniting them with their property (at a fee, of course). The thieves were also happy because it was a lot easier to steal small goods of sentimental value for which a good reward would be offered, than have to try to steal more valuable property that could be heavily protected.

Wild began to expand his empire – he divided London into districts, and set up gangs in each district, screening them from justice. He arranged for 'specialist' gangs, that robbed churches, or followed the various country fairs, gangs of conmen, gangs who ruled the prostitutes, gangs who collected protection money, to name but a few. He did not lead any gangs – he merely organized and advised them.

CONCLUSION

This chapter was based on the enterprise paradigm of organized crime. The business enterprise model of organized crime focuses on how economic considerations, rather than hierarchical or ethnic considerations, lie at the base of the formation and success of organized crime groups. Regardless of ethnicity or hierarchy, the enterprise model labels economic concerns as the primary cause of organized criminal behaviour. The enterprise paradigm is an approach to studying the problem of organized crime, grounded in the structural-functional school of sociology, general systems theory and the theories of formal legal organizations.

REFERENCE

Johnson, G. and K. Scholes (2002), *Exploring Corporate Strategy*, Harlow, UK: Pearson Education, Prentice Hall.

5 Defining the entrepreneur

Louis Jacques Filion

INTRODUCTION

This chapter reflects on the notion of defining the entrepreneur. After presenting some background information on the various meanings associated with the term 'entrepreneur', we introduce the three main pioneers who dealt with this subject: Cantillon, Say and Schumpeter. Fifteen of the most frequently mentioned elements from definitions found in the literature were retained, along with 12 of the activities that best characterize what entrepreneurs do. Six main components are proposed for inclusion in a definition of the entrepreneur: (1) innovation, (2) opportunity recognition, (3) risk management, (4) action, (5) use of resources and (6) added value. Some sample definitions are proposed, and the conclusion suggests that there are different levels of innovation and of entrepreneurial expression.

What is an entrepreneur? What characterizes entrepreneurs and distinguishes them from other organizational and social actors? How can the entrepreneur be defined? These are typical questions that most new entrepreneurship researchers ask, and to which a variety of answers can be found in the literature. As for why there is such a broad range of perspectives, the answer is far from simple.

First, the range of entrepreneurial roles is increasing steadily, and now includes venture creators, technopreneurs, intrapreneurs, extrapreneurs, social entrepreneurs, the self-employed and many others. In this chapter, the term 'entrepreneur' is used to refer to all these entrepreneurial actors.

Observation reveals that entrepreneurship is a complex phenomenon involving a set of activities with technical, human, managerial and entrepreneurial characteristics, the performance of which requires a diverse set of skills. Generally, entrepreneurial actors play additional roles (mainly managerial) when they carry their entrepreneurial activities, and this, too, must be taken into account. Clearly, the range of roles begs the question as to what constitutes the common core activities for all these actors and what sets the entrepreneurial aspect of their activities apart from the other aspects.

Given the many different categories and types of entrepreneurs, it is reasonable to wonder whether there can possibly be elements that are common to them all. Why are there so many definitions of the entrepreneur? In fact, there are several reasons, including the range of disciplines, research fields and paradigms through which actors and situations can be studied. The humanities differ from physics and the other 'hard' sciences, in that specialists can study and define phenomena from widely different standpoints.

In our own graduate research courses in entrepreneurship, we discuss and define the entrepreneur using several different analysis grids, including that devised by Burrell and Morgan (1979), based on two vectors: subjectivist-objectivist and radical-regulation. The grid can be used to classify the humanities literature into four categories:

1. Functionalist: objective view of reality and a regulatory view of society.
2. Interpretativist: subjective view of reality and a regulatory view of society.
3. Radical structuralist: objective view of reality and focus on radical change.
4. Radical humanist: subjective view of reality and focus on radical change (Burrell and Morgan, 1979; Howorth et al., 2005).

Definitions of the entrepreneur will obviously differ according to the authors' paradigms. Other entrepreneurship researchers have also proposed the Burrell and Morgan grid as a means of understanding the different standpoints for definitions of the term *entrepreneur* (Howorth et al., 2005). There are many reasons for the broad range of perspectives, but one in particular stands out, namely, the prism through which the author of the definition observes and understands reality. This is the first element that should be considered in any definition. Morgan (1997) also suggested nine metaphors for looking at organizational life. They also offer rich perspectives for examining entrepreneurship.

Researchers have always been interested in defining the entrepreneur, but the literature on the subject was most abundant in the 1970s, 1980s and 1990s. This was the time when growing numbers of researchers from a host of different disciplines, including many emerging disciplines in the humanities and administrative sciences, began to take an interest in entrepreneurs: Kilby (1971); Wortman (1987); Low and MacMillan (1988); Bygrave (1989; 1993); Gartner (1990); Cunningham and Lischeron (1991); Reynold (1991); Bull and Willard (1993); Brazeal and Herbert (1999) and Sharma and Chrisman (1999). Even after the 1990s the subject remained a real concern for researchers: Davidsson et al. (2001); Busenitz et al. (2003); Sarasvathy (2004); Gartner et al. (2006); Grégoire et al. (2006); and Ireland and Webb (2007).

A BRIEF HISTORY OF THE ORIGIN AND MEANING OF THE TERM 'ENTREPRENEUR'

The term 'entrepreneur' is a French word derived from the verb 'entreprendre', which means to do or to undertake. It can be divided into two parts, 'entre', meaning 'between', and 'preneur' meaning 'taker'. Literally, then, an *entre-preneur* is a 'between-taker', or 'go-between'.

The term 'entrepreneur' first appeared in the literature in 1253, when it was used in different forms (for example, 'empreneur'). It appears to have taken on its present, definitive spelling in 1433 (Rey, 1994: 700). We know it was used commonly in the 1500s and 1600s. For example, Champlain, speaking of his first voyage to explore the St Lawrence River in 1603, wrote that he had been invited to make the trip 'to see the country and what entrepreneurs would do there' (Champlain, 1632, in Giguère, 1973, vol. 2: 702, free translation from the French).

Hélène Vérin (1982) wrote a doctoral thesis in literature in which she discusses the shades of meaning of the terms 'entrepreneur' and 'enterprise' through history. She notes that the ancestor of the term 'enterprise' – 'emprise' (from the Latin imprisia) – referred to something bold, firm and daring (Vérin, 1982: 31–3). She also examined variations in meaning over the centuries, and especially between the thirteenth and eighteenth centuries. The current meaning that also refers to an *enterprise leader* first appeared in the early nineteenth century (Rey, 1994: 700).

THREE PIONEERS IN THE FIELD OF ENTREPRENEURSHIP

Three authors in particular were among the first to reflect extensively on what entrepreneurs do. The concept of entrepreneur can be understood more easily through the writings of these main pioneers.

Richard Cantillon

The first, Cantillon, was what we would now call a venture capitalist looking for investment opportunities with better than average yields. His perspective as an investor meant that the *element of risk* was a core aspect of how he viewed entrepreneurial projects and defined what he considered to be an entrepreneur (Cantillon, 1755). As Schumpeter pointed out: 'Cantillon had a clear conception of the function of the entrepreneur . . . This, of course, is scholastic doctrine. But nobody before Cantillon had formulated it so fully. And it may be due to him that French economists . . . never lost sight of the entrepreneurial function and its central importance' (1954: 222). Cantillon described the entrepreneur as a person who purchases a raw material at a known price in order to sell it at an unknown price (Cantillon, 1755). In Cantillon's definition, an entrepreneur's role lies between that of two or more other actors. He or she is an intermediary (or go-between) who instigates a transformation.

Jean-Baptiste Say

After Cantillon, the author who had the greatest impact on the field of entrepreneurship as it is today was Jean-Baptiste Say, nearly a century later. Say was himself an entrepreneur, and came from an entrepreneurial family. He was also a prolific writer, and wrote from the standpoint of someone preparing others to become entrepreneurs and hoping to convince them of the importance of entrepreneurs in economic development. He identified the *element of innovation* as being most characteristic of the entrepreneur; in other words, he regarded entrepreneurs as being people who could do new things, people who could do more with less, and people who would obtain more by doing something in a new or different way (Say, 1815; 1996). Therefore, Say saw the entrepreneur as an economic actor whose activities generated an *added value.* In his monumental work on the history of economics, Schumpeter pointed out that Say was the first to draw a clear distinction between the role of the entrepreneur and the role of the capitalist (Schumpeter, 1954: 555).

Joseph Alois Schumpeter

Joseph Alois Schumpeter is the author to whom the association between entrepreneurs and innovation is most often attributed by experts. In fact, as Schumpeter himself pointed out, he simply took over the definition presented by Jean-Baptiste Say (Schumpeter, 1954). He went further, however, postulating that 'the essence of entrepreneurship lies in the perception and exploitation of new opportunities' (Schumpeter, 1928). When he went into politics in an Austrian-Hungarian empire that needed to become more dynamic, Schumpeter identified entrepreneurs as being the people most needed to revitalize the economy and the organizations. Writing one century after Say, his thinking appears to be more complex and more complete. He associated innovation by entrepreneurs with five elements:

1. The introduction of a new good.
2. The introduction of a new method of production.
3. The opening of a new market.
4. The conquest of a new source of supply of raw material.
5. The carrying out of the new organization of any industry (Schumpeter, 1934: 66).

It is interesting to note that none of the combinations proposed by Schumpeter to define innovation included new venture creation as such. In his writings, Schumpeter often mentioned the concept of *creative destruction* to refer to the contribution of innovation by entrepreneurs (Schumpeter, 1954). It is to remember that he used the term *entrepreneur* to refer, to what we now call *intrapreneurs* as well, since the term was not coined during Schumpeter's lifetime.

Clearly, then, the standpoint from which an author approaches the concept of entrepreneurship influences the key elements he or she will use to define that concept. The humanities involve a certain amount of subjectivity, in that there is not necessarily a clear-cut answer to a question as is the case in the hard sciences. Definitions depend on the original standpoint – often the disciplinary field – that determines the prism through which human beings see and understand reality, and express their subjectivity.

An interesting element to consider here is the database on which the three pioneers, Richard Cantillon, Jean-Baptiste Say and Joseph Alois Schumpeter, based their reflections on entrepreneurs, their characteristics and their roles. Today, many authors and publications ascribe a great deal of importance to the samples used, in order to classify the research as being reliable and valid, and therefore in compliance with scientific criteria. However, the three pioneers in the field of entrepreneurship were not researchers as we understand the term today. Their point of reference, far from being a 'representative sample', was in fact composed simply of people they knew who had played entrepreneurial roles. In the case of Say and Schumpeter, these were more socially oriented roles that they wished to develop.

THE MOST COMMON ELEMENTS USED IN DEFINITIONS OF THE ENTREPRENEUR

There are many ways to define an entrepreneur. For most people, an entrepreneur is a person who owns and leads a business. However, specialists increasingly use a larger number of elements in their definitions of and references to entrepreneurs (Julien, 1998). Ultimately, virtually every author has a different definition of the term, depending on the specific entrepreneurs or entrepreneurial category studied. We have identified 15 elements (Table 5.1) mentioned most frequently in the definitions from the entrepreneurship

Table 5.1 The elements mentioned most frequently in definitions of the term 'entrepreneur'

Elements defining the entrepreneur	Authors
1. Innovation	Schumpeter (1947); Cochran (1968); Drucker (1985); Julien (1989; 1998)
2. Risk	Cantillon (1755); Knight (1921); Palmer (1971); Reuters Ltd (1982); Rosenberg (1983)
3. Coordination of resources for production; organizing factor of production or of the management of resources	Ely and Hess (1893); Cole (1942; and in Aitken 1965); Belshaw (1955); Chandler (1962); Leibenstein (1968); Wilken (1979); Pearce (1981); Casson (1982).
4. Value creation	Say (1815; 1996); Bruyat and Julien (2001); Fayolle (2008)
5. Projective and visionary thinking	Longenecker and Schoen (1975); Filion (1991; 2004).
6. Focus on action	Baty (1981)
7. Leadership	Hornaday and Aboud (1971)
8. Dynamo of the economic system	Weber (1947); Baumol (1968); Storey (1982); Moffat (1983)
9. Venture creation	Collins et al. (1964); Smith (1967); Collins and Moore (1970); Brereton (1974); Komives (1974); Mancuso (1979); Schwartz (1982); Carland et al. (1984); Vesper (1990)
10. Opportunity recognition	Smith (1967); Meredith et al. (1982); Kirzner (1983); Stevenson and Gumpert (1985); Timmons (1989); Dana (1995); Shane and Venkataraman (2000); Bygrave and Zacharakis (2004); Timmons and Spinelli (2004)
11. Creativity	Zaleznik and Kets de Vries (1976); Pinchot (1985)
12. Anxiety	Lynn (1969); Kets de Vries (1977; 1985)
13. Control	McClelland (1961)
14. Introduction of change	Mintzberg (1973); Shapero (1975)
15. Rebellion/delinquency	Hagen (1960)

literature that we believe are most relevant (Filion, 1987; 1988). Many authors include different elements in their definitions, or present different definitions during their careers. In such cases we have selected the concept the author in question appears to regard as being most important. We chose a selection of authors dealing with the subject over the centuries, and especially over recent decades because the use of the recent literature alone does not provide a true overview of the different perspectives from which the subject was examined in the shaping of what is in the process of becoming the field of study of entrepreneurship.

Table 5.1 does not present the shades of meaning that authors included in their definitions of the entrepreneur. For instance, Dana (1995) found that people of unlike cultural origins relate to opportunity in different ways, and argued that entrepreneurship should therefore not be viewed simply as a function of opportunity recognition, but rather as a function of cultural perceptions of opportunity.

TOWARDS A DEFINITION OF THE ENTREPRENEUR

To define what entrepreneurs are, we can first look at what they do – that is, at their activity systems. We have observed entrepreneurs repeatedly, in the course of many research projects, and one aspect that stands out is their ability to act independently. Therefore, we can say that one of the primary characteristics of an entrepreneur is the ability to conceive and implement an activity system. In other words, entrepreneurs are people who are able to translate thoughts into action; they are dreamers and thinkers who do.

Our observations have also shown that entrepreneurs are people who engage in activities they themselves have designed. But not just any activity – these are activities that were defined as a result of recognizing an entrepreneurial opportunity (Table 5.2). In many cases, the opportunity involved doing something differently and therefore adding value to what existed previously. Generally speaking, entrepreneurs initiate, implement and develop their projects trying to use a limited number of resources in order to generate surpluses and profits which can then be reinvested to achieve further development. Their motivation is to innovate or introduce something new while minimizing the risk.

We will not comment in detail on every element of Table 5.2. What we will say, however, is that it is not possible to define the entrepreneur based solely on the

Table 5.2 Activities and characteristics often attributed to entrepreneurs

Activities	Characteristics
1. Learning	Experience of a sector; memorized information; use of feedback
2. Choosing a sector	Interest; motivation; assessment of potential added value for the future
3. Identifying a niche	Care; analytical capacities; precision; target
4. Recognizing and developing an entrepreneurial opportunity	Originality; differentiation; creativity; intuition; initiative; culture that value innovation
5. Visualizing projectively	Ability to dream realistically; conceptual skills; systemic thinking; anticipation; foresight; ability to set goals and objectives; visioning
6. Managing risk	Thriftiness; security; conservatism; moderate risk-taker; ability to tolerate uncertainty and ambiguity; independence
7. Designing (products, services, organizations)	Imagination; problem-solving skills
8. Committing to action	Self-confidence related to clearly defined identity; long-term commitment; hard worker; energy; result orientation; decision-making; passion; locus-of-control; determination; perseverance; tenacity
9. Using resources	Resourcefulness; coordination; control
10. Building relations systems	Networking skills; flexibility; empathy; listening and communication skills; use of mentors; vision
11. Managing – sales; negotiations; people – and delegating	Versatility; adaptability; capacity to design tasks; ability to trust
12. Developing	Leadership; seeks challenges

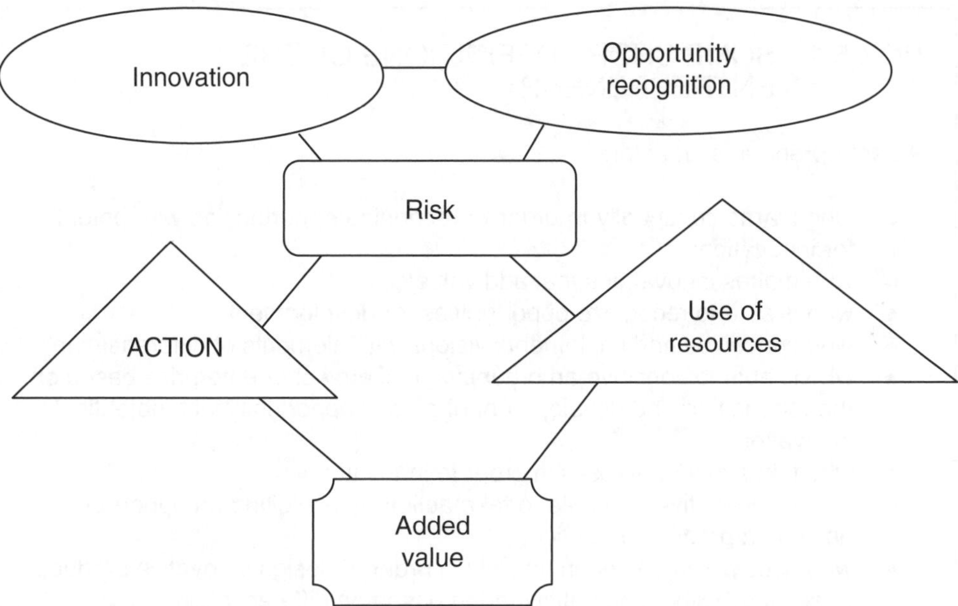

Figure 5.1 Main elements used to define the term 'entrepreneur'

characteristics of people who play entrepreneurial roles. Characteristics can be used to refine and clarify certain aspects of a definition, but cannot be regarded as constituting its core. Table 5.2 presents the activities mentioned most frequently in the entrepreneurship literature, which we felt were most relevant in achieving a definition (left-hand column). However, it is important to establish the relative importance of each activity.

It can be useful to consider activities when defining a research subject or structuring a research project. Activities are easily identifiable and can be delimited. Some can even be measured. Nevertheless, care is needed when observing the activities of entrepreneurs, because many are management activities that complement or add to entrepreneurial activities, rather than purely entrepreneurial activities as such. This is the case, for example, of the management activities listed under point 11 of Table 5.2.

It is our contention that there are levels in entrepreneurial expression, meaning that the elements used to define the entrepreneur can be ranked in importance. A distinction must be drawn between 'essential' elements, that is, those that entrepreneurs perform when doing what they do as entrepreneurs, and other elements that, although partly explaining the entrepreneur's success, are more managerial in nature. For a definition of the entrepreneur, we therefore suggest focusing on the 'essential' entrepreneurial act, in the sense of that which constitutes the essence of the entrepreneur's activity, that is, the act of recognizing and developing entrepreneurial opportunities. The definition should also include at least the six components set out in Figure 5.1.

Therefore, a definition of entrepreneurs should include at least these six elements: an entrepreneur is an actor who *innovates* by *recognizing opportunities*; he or she makes moderately *risky* decisions that leads into *actions* requiring the efficient *use of resources* and contributing an *added value*.

BOX 5.1 SOME SHORT DEFINITIONS OF THE ENTREPRENEUR

An entrepreneur is an actor:

- who learns continually in order to recognize opportunities with potential for innovation;
- who makes innovations that add value;
- who is able to recognize opportunities for development;
- who conceives and implements visions with elements of differentiation;
- who is able to conceive an organizational project or enterprise based on the recognition and development of a risky opportunity with potential for innovation;
- who takes moderate risks in order to innovate;
- who is innovative and able to take action by exploiting an opportunity to develop a product or service;
- who uses resources economically in order to design innovative products or services with a competitive edge based on differentiation;
- who is focused on the recognition of risky opportunities with a potential for innovation in order to fulfil a social or market need;
- who is imaginative and able to move away from the beaten track by carrying out innovative activities with added value.

In our view, however, there is no single, absolute definition of what an entrepreneur is and does, just like there is no 'one best way' (Taylor, 1947). Everything depends on the standpoint or perspective of the person creating the definition, and the aspects and elements on which that person decides to focus in his or her research. Some definitions of entrepreneurs can be very short; examples would include: 'Entrepreneurs are dreamers who do' or 'Entrepreneurs are doers who get results'. Box 5.1 suggests some simple definitions of the entrepreneur.

All these definitions present at least one aspect of what an entrepreneur is and does. The next step is to devise a definition that reflects the six main elements and additional dimensions of the entrepreneur's activity system. Box 5.2 lists some more complete suggested definitions of what an entrepreneur is and does.

Entrepreneurship is the field that studies entrepreneurs, entrepreneurial actors and entrepreneurial environments.

CONCLUSION

We share the opinion of Mark Casson, who wrote that 'The most difficult part of studying entrepreneurship is to define who and what an entrepreneur is' (Casson, 1982: 1). There are many dimensions that can be considered in a definition of what an entrepreneur is, based on what entrepreneurs do. An important dimension to remember is

BOX 5.2 SAMPLE DEFINITIONS

An entrepreneur is:

- An imaginative actor who recognizes entrepreneurial opportunities, makes moderately risky decisions with a view to innovating, and takes action by using resources to implement a differentiated vision that contributes an added value.
- An intuitive, resourceful, tenacious actor who is able to recognize and develop risky opportunities with potential for innovation, and who adds value to what already exists by setting up activities that involve a scarce use of resources.
- A results-oriented designer of innovations who is able to develop risky opportunities, who learns to be creative and resourceful, takes action by making practical use of limited resources and a network of contacts, and who is able to structure organizational activities to form a client satisfaction system that contributes an added value.
- A results-oriented actor who maintains a high level of sensitivity in order to recognize and develop entrepreneurial opportunities. This actor makes moderately risky decisions and is discerning in the use of resources. As long as this actor continues to take action by designing and implementing value-added innovations, he or she will continue to play an entrepreneurial role that contributes development.

that there are different levels of entrepreneurial expression. Ultimately, each discipline could have its own definition of the entrepreneur. However, every definition must reflect the contingency elements on which it is based. Questions concerning the definition of the entrepreneur will continue as long as researchers devise new disciplinary sets and metaphors to explore the different facets of human behaviour. Fully integrated, more complete definitions of the entrepreneur will become possible once a science of action has been developed. Even then, it may well be that entrepreneurs will continue to be misunderstood not only by others, but by themselves as well.

REFERENCES

Aitken, H.G.J. (1965), *Explorations in Enterprise*, Cambridge, MA: Harvard University Press.

Baty, G. (1981), *Entrepreneurship in the Eighties*, Reston, VA: Reston Publishing.

Baumol, W.J. (1968), 'Entrepreneurship in economic theory', *The American Economic Review*, **58** (2), 64–71.

Belshaw, C.S. (1955), 'The cultural milieu of the entrepreneur', *Explorations in Entrepreneurial History*, **7**, 146–63.

Brazeal, D.V. and T.T. Herbert (1999), 'The genesis of entrepreneurship', *Entrepreneurship Theory and Practice*, **23** (1), 29–45.

Brereton, P.R. (1974), 'The qualification for entrepreneurship', *Journal of Small Business Management*, **12** (4), 1–3.

Bruyat, C. and P.A. Julien (2001), 'Defining the field of research in entrepreneurship', *Journal of Business Venturing*, **16** (2), 39–56.
Bull, I. and G.E. Willard (1993), 'Towards a theory of entrepreneurship', *Journal of Business Venturing*, **8** (3), 183–95.
Burrell, G. and G. Morgan (1979), *Sociological Paradigms and Organisational Analysis*, London: Heinemann Educational Books.
Busenitz, L.W. III, D. Shepherd, T. Nelson, G.N. Chandler and A. Zacharakis (2003), 'Entrepreneurship research in emergence: past trends and future directions', *Journal of Management*, **29** (3), 285–308.
Bygrave, W. (1989), 'The entrepreneurship paradigm (1): a philosophical look at its research methodologies', *Entrepreneurship Theory and Practice*, **14** (1), 7–26.
Bygrave, W. (1993), 'Theory building in the entrepreneur paradigm', *Journal of Business Venturing*, **8** (3), 255–80.
Bygrave, W.D. and A. Zacharakis (eds) (2004), *The Portable MBA in Entrepreneurship*, 2nd edn, Hoboken, NJ: Wiley.
Cantillon, R. (1755), *Essai sur la nature du commerce en général*, London: Fetcher Gyler. Also: edited with an English translation by Henry Higgs, London: Macmillan (1931). The manuscript was probably written around 1720 and was published after Cantillon was murdered in 1734. It is believed that he himself wrote the French and English versions.
Carland, J.W., F. Hoy, W.R. Boulton and J.A.C. Carland (1984), 'Differentiating entrepreneurs from small business owners: a conceptualization', *Academy of Management Review*, **9** (2), 354–9.
Casson, M. (1982), *The Entrepreneur: An Economic Theory*, Oxford: Martin Robertson.
Champlain, S. (1632), in G.E. Giguère (ed.) (1973), *Oeuvres complètes de Champlain* (*Complete Works of Champlain*) 3 vols, Montreal: Éditions du jour.
Chandler, A.D. Jr (1962), *Strategy and structure: Chapters in the History of the American Industrial Enterprise*, Cambridge, MA and London: MIT Press.
Cochran, T.C. (1968), 'Entrepreneurship', in D.L. Sills (ed.), *International Encyclopedia of the Social Sciences*, London and New York: Macmillan and The Free Press, vol. 5, pp. 87–91.
Cole, A.H. (1942), 'Entrepreneurship as an area of research, the tasks of economic history', *Supplement to Journal of Economic History*, **2**, 118–26.
Collins, O. and D.G. Moore (1970), *The Organization Makers: A Behavioral Study of Independent Entrepreneurs*, New York: Appleton-Century-Crofts (Meredith Corp.).
Collins, O. and D.G. Moore with D.B. Unwalla (1964), 'The enterprising man', *MSU Business Studies*, Bureau of Business and Economic Research, Graduate School of Business Administration, Michigan State University, East Lansing, Michigan.
Cunningham, J.B. and J. Lischeron (1991), 'Defining entrepreneurship', *Journal of Small Business Management*, **29** (1), 45–61.
Dana, L.-P. (1995), 'Entrepreneurship in a remote Sub-Arctic community: Nome, Alaska', *Entrepreneurship: Theory and Practice*, **20** (1), 55–72. Reprinted in Norris Krueger (ed.) (2002) *Entrepreneurship: Critical Perspectives on Business and Management*, vol. 4, London: Routledge, pp. 255–75.
Davidsson, P., M.B. Low and M. Wright (2001), 'Editors' introduction: Low and MacMillan ten years on – achievements and future directions for entrepreneurship research', *Entrepreneurship Theory and Practice*, **25** (4), 5–16.
Drucker, P.F. (1985), *Innovation and Entrepreneurship: Practice and Principles*, London: Heinemann.
Ely, R. and R.H. Hess (1893), *Outline of Economics*, New York: Macmillan.
Fayolle, A. (2008), *Entrepreneurship and New Value Creation – The Dynamic of the Entrepreneurial Process*, London: Cambridge University Press.
Filion, L.J. (1987), 'Entrepreneur and entrepreneurship: a survey of the essential literature on the subject', unpublished working paper, *GREPME*, Université du Québec à Trois-Rivières.
Filion, L.J. (1988), 'The strategy of successful entrepreneurs in small business: vision, relationships and anticipatory learning', doctoral thesis, Lancaster University, (UMI 8919064) (About the definition of entrepreneur, see vol. 1, ch. 2, pp. 7–92).
Filion, L.J. (1991), 'Vision and relations: elements for an entrepreneurial metamodel', *International Small Business Journal*, **9** (2), 26–40.
Filion, L.J. (2004), 'Operators and visionaries: differences in the entrepreneurial and managerial systems of two types of entrepreneurs', *International Journal of Entrepreneurship and Small Business*, **1** (1/2), 35–55.
Gartner, W.B. (1990), 'What are we talking about when we talk about entrepreneurship?', *Journal of Business Venturing*, **5** (1), 15–28.
Gartner, W.B., P. Davidsson and S.A. Zahra (2006), 'Are you talking to me? The nature of community in entrepreneurship scholarship', *Entrepreneurship Theory and Practice*, **30** (3), 321–31.
Grégoire, D.A., M.X. Noël, R. Déry and J.P. Béchard (2006), 'Is there conceptual convergence in

entrepreneurship research? A co-citation analysis of the Frontiers of Entrepreneurship Research 1981–2004', *Entrepreneurship Theory and Practice*, **30** (3), 333–74.

Hagen, E. (1960), 'The entrepreneurs as rebel against traditional society', *Human Organization*, **19** (4), 185–7.

Hornaday, J.A. and J. Aboud (1971), 'Characteristics of successful entrepreneurs', *Personnel Psychology*, **24** (2), 141–53.

Howorth, C., S. Tempest and C. Coupland (2005), 'Rethinking entrepreneurship methodology and definitions of the entrepreneur', *Journal of Small Business and Enterprise Development*, **12** (1), 24–40.

Ireland, R.D. and J.W. Webb (2007), 'A cross-disciplinary exploration of entrepreneurship research', *Journal of Management*, **33** (6), 891–927.

Julien, P.A. (1989), 'The entrepreneur and economic theory', *International Small Business Journal*, **7** (3), 29–39.

Julien, P.A. (ed.) (1998), *The State of the Art in Small Business and Entrepreneurship*, Aldershot and Brookfield, VT: Ashgate.

Kets de Vries, M. (1977), 'The entrepreneurial personality: a person at the cross-roads', *Journal of Management Studies*, **14** (1), 34–47.

Kets de Vries, M.F.R. (1985), 'The dark side of entrepreneurship', *Harvard Business Review*, Nov–Dec. 160–67.

Kilby, P. (ed.) (1971), 'Hunting the heffalump', *Entrepreneurship and Economic Development*, New York: The Free Press.

Kirzner, I. (1983), *Perception, Opportunity and Profit: Studies in the Theory of Entrepreneurship*, Chicago, IL: University of Chicago Press. First published 1979.

Knight, F.H. (1921), *Risk, Uncertainty and Profit*, Boston, MA and New-York: Houghton Mifflin. Also Chicago, IL: University of Chicago Press.

Komives, J.L. (1974), 'What are entrepreneurs made of?', *Chemtech*, Dec., 716–21.

Leibenstein, H. (1968), 'Entrepreneurship and development', *American Economic Review*, **58** (2), 72–83.

Longenecker, J.G. and J.E. Schoen (1975), 'The essence of entrepreneurship', *Journal of Small Business Management*, **13** (3), 26–32.

Low, M.B. and I.C. MacMillan (1988), 'Entrepreneurship: past research and future challenges', *Journal of Management*, **14**: 139–61.

Lynn, R. (1969), 'Personality characteristics of a group of entrepreneurs', *Occupational Psychology*, **43**, 151–2.

Mancuso, J.R. (1979), 'Who is the entrepreneur?', *Business Graduate*, **9** (2), 32–3.

McClelland, D.C. (1961), *The Achieving Society*, Princeton, NJ: Van Nostrand. (See also the New Introduction to this book: New York: Irvington Publishers, 1976.)

Meredith, G.G., R.E. Nelson and P.A. Neck (1982), *The Practice of Entrepreneurship*, Geneva: International Labour Organization.

Mintzberg, H. (1973), *The Nature of Managerial Work*, New York: Harper and Row.

Moffat, D.W. (1983), *Economics Dictionary*, 2nd edn, New York: Elsevier.

Morgan, G. (1997), *Images of Organization*, Thousand Oaks, CA: Sage.

Palmer, M. (1971), 'The application of psychological testing to entrepreneurial potential', *California Management Review*, **13** (3), 32–8.

Pearce, D.W. (1981), *The Macmillan Dictionary of Modern Economics*, London: Macmillan Press.

Pinchot, G. III (1985), *Intrapreneuring*, New York: Harper & Row.

Reuters Ltd (1982), *Reuter's Glossary of Economic and Financial Terms*, London: Heinemann.

Rey, A. (ed.) (1994), *Le Robert, Dictionnaire historique de la langue française*, Paris: Dictionnaires Le Robert.

Reynold, P. (1991), 'Sociology and entrepreneurship: concepts and contributions', *Entrepreneurship Theory and Practice*, **16** (2), 47–70.

Rosenberg, J.M. (1983), *Dictionary of Business and Management*, 2nd edn, Chichester, UK and New York: Wiley.

Sarasvathy, S.D. (2004), 'The questions we ask and the questions we care about: reformulating some problems in entrepreneurship research', *Journal of Business Venturing*, **19**: 707–17.

Say, J.B. (1815), *Cathéchisme d'économie politique*, Maison Mame (1972); also translation: (1816), *Catechism of Political Economy: On Familiar Conversations on the Manner in Which Wealth Is Produced, Distributed and Consumed by Society*, London: Sherwood.

Say, J.B. (1996), *Cours d'économie politique et autres essais*, Paris: GF-Flammarion.

Schumpeter, J.A. (1928), 'Des Unternehmer', in Ludwig Elster et al. (eds), *Handworterbuch der Staatsvissenschaften*, (4th edn, Jena); in H. Hartmann (1959), 'Managers and entrepreneurs: a useful distinction', *Administrative Science Quarterly*, **3** (3), 429–51.

Schumpeter, J.A. (1934), *The Theory of Economic Development*, Cambridge, MA: Harvard University Press. First edition in German published in 1912.

Schumpeter, J.A. (1947), 'The creative response in economic history', *Journal of Economic History*, **7** (Nov), 149–59.

Schumpeter, J.A. (1954), *History of Economic Analysis*, ed. Elizabeth Boody Schumpeter, New York: Oxford University Press.

Schwartz, R. (1982), 'The entrepreneur: an artist masquerading as a businessman?', *International Management*, Feb., 21–32.
Shane, S. and S. Venkataraman (2000), 'The promise of entrepreneurship as a field of research', *Academy of Management Review*, **25** (1), 217–26.
Shapero, A. (1975), 'The displaced uncomfortable entrepreneur', *Psychology Today*, **7** (11), 83–89.
Sharma, P. and J.J. Chrisman (1999), 'Toward a reconciliation of the definitional issues in the field of corporate entrepreneurship', *Entrepreneurship Theory and Practice*, **23** (3), 11–27.
Smith, N.R. (1967), *The Entrepreneur and His Firm: The Relationship Between Type of Man and Type Of Company*, East Lansing, MI: Bureau of Business Research, Michigan State University.
Stevenson, H.H. and D.E. Gumpert (1985), 'The heart of entrepreneurship', *Harvard Business Review*, Mar.–Apr., 85–94.
Storey, D. (1982), *The New Firm*, New York: Praeger.
Taylor, F.W. (1947), *Scientific Management. Comprising: Shop Management; The Principles of Scientific Management; Testimony Before the Special House Committee*, New York and London: Harper & Brothers.
Timmons , J.A. (1989), *The Entrepreneurial Mind*, Andover, MA: Brick House.
Timmons, J.A. and S. Spinelli (2004), *New Venture Creation*, 6th edn, New York: Irwin/McGraw-Hill.
Vérin, H. (1982), *Entrepreneurs, entreprise: histoire d'une idée*, Paris: Presses Universitaires de France.
Vesper, K.H. (1990), *New venture strategies*, 2nd edn, Englewood Cliffs, NJ: Prentice Hall.
Weber, M. (1947), *The Theory of Social and Economic Organization*, New York: Free Press.
Wilken, P.H. (1979), *Entrepreneurship: A Comparative and Historical Study,* Norwood, NJ: Ablex Publications.
Wortman, M. (1987), 'Entrepreneurship: an integrating typology and evaluation of empirical research in the field', *Journal of Management*, **13** (2), 259–79.
Zaleznik, A. and M.F.R. Kets de Vries (1976), 'What makes entrepreneurs entrepreneurial?', *Business and Society Review*, **17**, 18–23.

6 Economics and entrepreneurship

William J. Baumol

Economists first began writing on the subject of entrepreneurship in the eighteenth century. The entrepreneur is most often defined to be an individual who founds and organizes a new business firm, though both narrower and broader interpretations have been employed, with significant implications (see below). The term is often ascribed to the Anglo-Irish writer, Richard Cantillon (1730), though any contemporary copy of his book, which was written in English, has survived only in French translation that he may or may not have carried out himself. The manuscript was lost in the fire set by a servant who first robbed and murdered the author. Before that, and for a considerable time after his death, the terms in usage in the English literature were 'adventurer' (as in merchant adventurer) or 'undertaker' (a direct translation of the French term or its German counterpart: *unternehmer*).

The place of this topic in the economic literature is curious. There is widespread acknowledgement of its importance, notably for economic growth, accompanied by its virtual absence from the writings of most economists for more than half a century. Many textbooks write of four 'factors of production': labour, land, capital and entrepreneurship, and provide at least one chapter for each of the first three, while the fourth, often acknowledged as the leader of the activities of the others, is confined to a few brief remarks or even nothing beyond its initial listing. This has begun to change. There is now a rich empirical literature on topics such as the personal characteristics of the entrepreneurs, their activities, their financial needs, their psychological propensities and their earnings. However, they are still all but absent from formal theory, for reasons that will be discussed presently, along with a description of some recent theoretical excursions at the microeconomic level.

1 A BIT OF CLASSIFICATION

Before delving into the literature it is useful to point out several lines along which entrepreneurship can be studied. First, there is diversity in the connotation that is assigned to the term. From its beginnings in the work of Richard Cantillon, many of the writings referred to anyone who organized and launched a firm as an entrepreneur. This individual's task was to bring together the requisite quantities and qualities of land, labour and capital, to assign a role to each of them and ensure that it was carried out efficiently. This entrepreneur, then, was captain of the ship. But the firm organized in the process could well be just another one of the thousands that had been founded earlier, offering the same products as its predecessors and providing those outputs in the traditional way. Such a *replicative entrepreneur* clearly plays a significant role in the economy, as creator of many of the enterprises that underlie its activities. Entrepreneurship of this sort is important also as an attractive route for exit from poverty, because when unemployment is rife the only way to acquire an income may be as the founder of a tiny enterprise, for example, as no more than an itinerant peddler, with no employees. And the number of such firms in which the entrepreneur hires no one is impressive. 'Census Bureau figures indicate that there are over 18 million nonemployer firms in the United States – roughly three times the number of employer firms' (National Research Council, Committee on National Statistics, 2007: 78). But the data suggest that there is little correlation between the number of such replicative firms and the rate of growth of the economy. Indeed, it is plausible that a relatively stagnant economy will drive more people into this sort of occupation, and the data seem to support this hypothesis.

Growth, rather, is to be expected from the other type of entrepreneur, the *innovative entrepreneur*, whose firms are characterized by the supply of new products, the employment of new production methods, the discovery and exploitation of promising new market opportunities and the creation of novel forms of organization. This is the type of entrepreneur upon whom J.-B Say (1819) focused his discussion and who was the central character in the writings of Joseph Schumpeter. There seems to be little evidence indicating their number, but it seems clear that this number is far smaller than that of the replicative entrepreneurs. Moreover, as will be discussed presently, there seems to be little statistical evidence indicating the magnitude of the contribution of the innovative entrepreneurs to the growth of their economy, though there is a good deal of historical evidence suggesting strongly that this contribution is substantial and may well be critical.

Besides distinguishing between replicative and innovative entrepreneurs, the literature differentiates 'innovation' from invention. The former term is used to represent the entire process from the emergence of a novelty (invention) to its improvement to a state sufficient to make it marketable, its introduction into the producing firm and its entry into the marketplace. Though the inventor may or not be an entrepreneur, the innovation process generally requires entrepreneurial activity to bring the novelty out from the drawing boards and into the workings of the economy.

The literature also proceeds in two directions in its position on the risk entailed in entrepreneurship. Both Cantillon and Frank Knight (1921) took the position that a primary role of the entrepreneur is that of risk-bearer or, even more extreme, of uncertainty, defined as subjection to prospects so unpredictable that they even preclude any evaluation in terms of probabilities. In contrast, Schumpeter (1911) held the position that the entrepreneurs, in their role as entrepreneurs, undertake no risk at all, because they work with other people's money – that of the investing capitalists. It will be argued below that neither of these positions is quite right, and that while, in reality, entrepreneurs are subject to risks that are far from negligible, there is a great deal more to their activity than risk-bearing alone.

2 SOME EMPIRICAL INVESTIGATIONS OF THE ENTREPRENEUR

As noted, there is now a profusion of careful and illuminating empirical investigations of entrepreneurship, much of it contributed by sociologists and psychologists as well as economists. Here only the work of the last of these will be considered. The writings on several significant topics will be discussed.

Specialization of Small Entrepreneurial Firms in the Innovation Process

Albeit unsystematic, there is an abundance of suggestive evidence indicating that there is a division of labour between small and large enterprises, with the former responsible for a disproportionate share of the revolutionary breakthroughs, such as the electric light, the aeroplane, the internal combustion engine, while the giant corporations (which account for the bulk of private research and development expenditure) focus on cumulative incremental improvements, such as are entailed in the evolution of the Wright brothers' flying machine to the Boeing 777. Research and development (R&D) in the large business enterprise tends characteristically to be bureaucratically organized, with management deciding the R&D budget, staffing and even the projects to which the R&D division should be devoting its efforts. The inherent conservatism of the process naturally leads to the expectation that these firms will tend to specialize in the incremental improvements and tend to avoid the risks of the unknown that the revolutionary breakthrough entails. The latter, rather, is left most often to small or newly founded enterprises, guided by their enterprising creators. The US Small Business Administration has prepared a chart listing breakthrough innovations of the twentieth century for which small firms are responsible and its menu of inventions literally spans the range from A to Z, from the aeroplane to the zipper. This remarkable list includes a strikingly substantial share of the technical breakthroughs of the twentieth century. For example, it lists FM radio, the helicopter, the personal computer, and the pacemaker, among a host of others, many of enormous significance for our economy (US Small Business Administration, 1995). A more recent study, also sponsored by the US Small Business Administration (2003), provides systematic evidence with similar implications.[1] Perhaps most notably, the study finds that 'a small firm patent is more likely than a large firm patent to be among the top 1 percent of most frequently cited patents'. Among other conclusions, in the words of its authors, this study also reports that 'Small firms represent one-third of the most prolific patenting companies that have 15 or more U.S. patents . . . Small patenting firms are roughly 13 times more innovative per employee than large patenting firms' (ibid.: 2).

This leads to the conjecture that most of the revolutionary new ideas of the past two centuries have been, and are likely to continue to be, provided more heavily by independent innovative entrepreneurs who operate small business enterprises. These small entrepreneurial firms appear to have come close to monopolizing the portion of R&D activity that is engaged in the search for revolutionary breakthroughs.

Earnings

It is clear that the most successful and most noted of entrepreneurs are rewarded handsomely. Indeed, this group includes the world's wealthiest person. But, on average, the compensation of this activity is remarkably low. Freeman (1978) and Benz and Frey (2004) show that the average earnings of self-employed individuals are significantly lower than those of employees with similar qualifications, and the same is presumably true, in particular, of the self-employed innovative entrepreneurs. There are at least two studies that support this hypothesis for innovative entrepreneurs. Thomas Astebro (2003) reports on the basis of a sample of 1091 inventions that:

> The average IRR [internal rate of return] on a portfolio investment in these inventions is 11.4 percent. This is higher than the risk-free rate but lower than the long-run return on high-risk securities and the long-run return on early-stage venture capital funds . . . the distribution of return is skew; only between 7–9 percent reach the market. Of the 75 inventions that did, six received returns above 1400 percent, 60 percent obtained negative returns and the median was negative. (Astebro, 2003: 226)

Perhaps even more striking is the recent work of Nordhaus (2004), whose calculations show how little of the efficiency rent goes to the innovator:

> Using data from the U.S. non-farm business section, I estimate that innovators are able to capture about 2.2 percent of the total surplus from innovation. This number results from a low rate of initial appropriability (estimated to be around 7 percent) along with a high rate of depreciation of Schumpeterian profits (judged to be around 20 percent per year) . . . the rate of profit on the replacement cost of capital over the 1948–2001 period is estimated to be 0.19 percent per year. (Nordhaus, 2004: 34)

Attitudes toward Risk

There are a number of studies investigating whether entrepreneurs tend to be more willing than the general population to undertake risks. Parker (2006) provides an admirable summary of the findings from which the following is excerpted:

> The available evidence certainly supports the notion that entrepreneurs are unrealistically optimistic. 68% of respondents to Cooper et al.'s (1988) survey of American entrepreneurs thought the odds of their business succeeding were better than for others in the same sector while only 5% thought that they were worse . . . Arabsheibani et al (2000) compare expectations of future prosperity with actual outcomes using British panel data, and find that while employees and self-employed Britons both held systematically over-optimistic expectations about future incomes, the self-employed are consistently and substantially the most over-optimistic.
>
> . . . optimism . . . is the enemy of the rational [input] buyer . . . optimistic entrepreneurs will drive out realistic entrepreneurs from product markets [by bidding input prices to excessive levels]. Realists would make positive profits in the absence of the over-optimists, but may be unable to do so when optimists are present because optimists produce excess output that reduces prices below the break even price in the industry.
>
> On the other hand, optimism can convey some advantages. [for example] Bernardo and Welch (2001) claim that over-optimistic entrepreneurs are less likely to imitate their peers and are more likely to explore their environment. This generates valuable informational benefits to the entrepreneurial group, enabling it to thrive in spite of the costs incurred by the particular group members who obtained the information. (See Parker, 2006: 3–7 for the full discussion.)

In short, there is an abundance of evidence that entrepreneurs, as a group are characterized by a markedly excessive view of their prospects. This may help to account for their willingness to enter an occupation whose earnings prospects are significantly lower than what they could have earned by accepting a position in an established firm. But it also helps to explain their relative propensity to undertake innovations that are radical breakthroughs. For that reason, society may be heavily indebted to this group. For they seem to be the contributors, on a disproportionate scale, of the effective adoption of those breakthrough inventions that arguably underlie the unprecedented growth rates of per capita gross domestic product (GDP) in the world's most successful economies of recent centuries.

Education and Innovative Entrepreneurship

It is again convenient to return to Parker (2006) for a clear summary of the current state of the discussion of the education of entrepreneurs. As a group, are they highly educated or is the opposite true?

It is commonly observed that some of the most successful entrepreneurs have relatively low levels of education. For example, Bill Gates and Michael Dell dropped out of Harvard and the University of Texas respectively, while Richard Branson dropped out of school. Bhide (2000) claims that informal skills, especially the ability to satisfy customers' fuzzy wants, is more important for promoting entrepreneurial success than human capital. Pursuing this theme, Orzach and Tauman (2005) suggest that gifted entrepreneurs may optimally acquire less education than wage and salary workers if this conveys a signal of strength about their own innate abilities in entrepreneurship. Thus if ability in entrepreneurship matters more for business success than formal education does, financiers will reward the more able by offering them favourable credit contracts; other individuals will not find it in their interests to emulate the gifted individuals because with their lower entrepreneurial abilities they benefit more by taking more schooling. The prediction that entrepreneurs are on average more educated than employees also accords with recent evidence from several countries, including the USA (Flota and Mora, 2001; Lofstrom, 2002), Great Britain (Cowling et al., 2004; Henley, 2004), the Netherlands (Bosma et al., 2004) and Sweden (Davidsson and Honig, 2003). When using years of schooling as a measure of education, Garcia-Mainar and Montuenga-Gomez (2005) report a higher return to education in paid employment than in self-employment. This finding has not been observed in other countries, however. For example, Van der Sluis et al. (2004) apply instrumental variable (IV) methods to US National Longitudinal Survey of Youth (NLSY) data and estimate a higher rate of return to education for entrepreneurs (14 per cent) than for employees (10 per cent) (see Parker, 2006: 14–17).

The data assembled in a recent study of a large sample of noted inventors and entrepreneurs, by Baumol et al. (2009), as compiled from a substantial set of published lists, indicate that inventors are better educated than entrepreneurs in terms of the share who earned a college degree. The differential holds in all three time periods into which the data were divided, before 1800, 1800–1899, and 1900–1985. But the results indicate that, in the USA at least, both inventors and entrepreneurs are better educated than the set of all adults. The difference is particularly striking for those with a college degree, and the difference widens over time. In 1950, only 7 per cent of the US adult population had graduated from college, compared with 67 per cent of US inventors born between 1900 and 1910 and 44 per cent of US entrepreneurs. According to our data, 100 per cent of US inventors and 75 per cent of US entrepreneurs born between 1951 and 1985 graduated from college, compared with 25 per cent of the corresponding US population.

The educational attainment of inventors and entrepreneurs can also be compared with that of R&D personnel generally, using data from the National Science Foundation's *Science and Engineering Indicators* (National Science Board, 2006), and the US Bureau of Labor Statistics (BLS). The NSF data describe individuals who report R&D as a major work activity. Of this group, 59 per cent hold a bachelors degree as their highest degree, with 28 per cent holding master's degrees, 4 per cent holding professional degrees and 9 per cent holding doctorates. The results indicate that inventors are far more likely to have an advanced degree than the average person working in R&D, but that entrepreneurs have similar levels of education to R&D workers.

Disappearance of the Entrepreneur from Modern Mainstream Economics

Societies with a record of non-military invention that is respectable or even extraordinary have repeatedly failed to put those inventions to substantial use. This is strikingly true of ancient Rome, with its working steam engine created by Heron of Alexandria, of medieval China with its innovative printing press, great ships, its clocks, its umbrella and its spinning wheel, as well as the Soviet Union with the many contributions of its well-educated scientists and engineers. It is at least plausible that a significant part of the explanation was the absence of a cadre of innovative entrepreneurs who could improve their status in society by promotion of such useful products. And with the absence of such entrepreneurs the growth of these societies was severely handicapped.

Given the acknowledged importance of the entrepreneur's role, it might be expected that modern theoretical investigation would have produced an extensive entrepreneurship analysis. Instead, the entrepreneurs virtually vanished from mainstream theory and, along with that, they were virtually banished from the textbooks. This is probably not the result of a distaste for the subject or scepticism about its significance, but a consequence of the absence of an obvious way to capture entrepreneurial activity in the way the literature has produced its analyses of land, labour and capital. There are at least two reasons for this. First, the most advanced and powerful microeconomic models predominately are designed to study timeless static equilibria. But, for the entrepreneur, the intertemporal transition process is the heart of the story. Schumpeter (1911) shows the entrepreneur as destroyer of equilibria by constant innovation, while Israel Kirzner (1979) tells how the alert entrepreneur seeks out the arbitrage opportunities presented by disequilibria, thereby moving the economy back toward equilibrium. Such a relentless attack upon both equilibria and disequilibria does not fit a stationary model from which firm creation and invention are excluded.

The second reason for the entrepreneur's disappearance from mainstream theory is the indispensably essential attribute of an invention: it necessarily is something that was never available before. It follows that invention must be the ultimate heterogeneous product. This impedes the optimality analysis that underlies most microeconomic theory. An optimality calculation entails at least an implicit comparison among the available choices for the decision at issue, while the innovating entrepreneurs normally deal with no set of well-defined substitutes among which they may choose on the basis of their attributes that are quantifiable and comparable. In contrast, standard firm theory analyses well-defined choices of management among comparable options in fully operational enterprises where the entrepreneur has already completed his job and left to create other firms.

Thus, neoclassical theory is justified in excluding the entrepreneurs, because it deals with subjects for which they are irrelevant. That does not mean that no theory of entrepreneurship is needed, or that such a theory is lacking, but it means that a theory of entrepreneurship must be sought elsewhere than in static mainstream microeconomics, and that is what Schumpeter succeeded in doing.

Schumpeter's Model and Beyond: Supply and Earnings of Entrepreneurial Activity

The basic Schumpeterian model (1911) asserts that the successful innovative entrepreneur's reward is profit that temporarily exceeds what is obtainable under a regime of perfect competition. This attracts rivals, who seek to share those profits by imitating the innovation, and thereby erode its super-competitive earnings. To prevent termination of these rewards, the entrepreneur can never desist from further innovation and cannot rest on his laurels.

In this way, the Schumpeterian analysis shows how the entrepreneur is driven to work without let-up in promotion of economic growth. Thus, it clearly reveals the tight association between innovative entrepreneurship and growth.

This work should also serve as the foundation for further theoretical analysis, and there are, indeed, some beginnings of efforts in that direction, a good deal of it the work of the present author (see, for example Baumol, 2002). The first of these deviations stems from the empirical work that finds the rewards of entrepreneurs as a group to fall short of the earnings of employees with similar education and experience. In standard economic terms this means that the average entrepreneur receives *negative* economic profits, that is, she loses out by earning less than she could by accepting employment in an established enterprise. This is in conflict with Schumpeter's premise that the innovative entrepreneur earns positive monopoly profits soon after the initial introduction of an invention, profits that are gradually driven down to the competitive level, thus yielding a surplus over the entire life cycle of the product. But if entry into the innovation process is unrestricted, and if over-optimism leads entrepreneurs to embark on enterprises that are not really promising, then standard theory of entry into markets and its effects on prices easily enables us to understand why in reality the innovative entrepreneurs' average economic profits are negative.

But can we say more about the resulting prices and earnings, as imposed by market forces? The answer is that this can easily be done, using the standard model of the determination of discriminatory prices, that is, prices for identical products that differ from one customer to another, or even from one sale to another (Baumol, 2007). A moment's thought indicates that this is exactly what happens in Schumpeter's story but in which the prices differ not between customers but between time periods. That is, there is intertemporal price discrimination. Moreover, the formulas that determine the discriminatory prices in the two cases are identical. So, if we are informed about costs, supply and demand, we can determine exactly what those prices will be because the competition of rival entrepreneurs will drive those prices down to the sub-competitive level that is just sufficient to induce entry. For if prices were any higher than this, more entry would be induced and the expanded production would force those prices down, while the reverse would occur if prices were below those levels. Thus, the standard and well-explored microanalysis of discriminatory prices enables us to determine to exactly what levels the prices and rewards of the entrepreneur's products will be driven by competitive market forces, depending on the state of competition and the resulting demand elasticities in the different pertinent periods. So a micro-theoretic model of the entrepreneur can now be claimed to exist, on a par with the theories of land, labour and capital.

Social Institutions and Allocation of Entrepreneurial Activity

The rest of the story contains material on the supply and allocation of entrepreneurship among its available uses, and the key role here is played by evolving institutions. This part of the story is of critical importance for growth and the general welfare, because both of these depend on the activities upon which entrepreneurs choose to focus. For example, do they choose to promote a new source of energy or, instead, a new type of military equipment?

In the economic growth literature, it has often been asserted that an expanded supply of entrepreneurs effectively stimulates growth, while shrinkage in the supply undermines it. But an explanation of the entrepreneurs' appearance and disappearance is shrouded in mystery, with hints about cultural developments and vague psychological and sociological changes. The historical evidence suggests a more mundane explanation – that entrepreneurs are always present but, as institutions and the associated structure of rewards in the economy change, entrepreneurs switch their activities, moving where pay-offs become more attractive. In doing so, they move in and out of the activities usually recognized as entrepreneurial, exchanging them for other activities that also require enterprising talent but are often distant from production of goods and services. The generals of ancient Rome, the Mandarins of the Tang, Sung, and Ming Chinese empires, the captains of late medieval private and mercenary armies, the rent-seeking contemporary lawyers, and the Mafia dons – all are clearly enterprising and often successful. And when institutions have changed so as to modify profoundly the relative payoffs offered by the different enterprising activities, the supply of entrepreneurs shifts accordingly. We may divide entrepreneurs into two categories, the productive and the unproductive, with the latter, in turn, divided into subgroups such as rent-seeking entrepreneurs and destructive entrepreneurs, including the organizers of private armies or criminal groups. Once there is a pertinent change in the institutions that govern the relative rewards, the entrepreneurs will shift their activities between productive and unproductive occupations, so the set of productive entrepreneurs will appear to expand or contract autonomously. For example, when institutional change prevents the formation of private armies, entrepreneurs are forced to look elsewhere to realize their financial ambitions. If, simultaneously, rules against confiscation of private property and for patent protection of inventions are adopted, entrepreneurial talent will shift into productive, innovative directions.

NOTE

1. Quoting the press release describing the study, 'A total of 1,071 firms with 15 or more patents issued between 1996 and 2000 were examined. A total of 193,976 patents were analyzed. CHI [the firm that carried out the study] created a data-base of these firms and their patents. This list excluded foreign-owned firms, universities, government laboratories and nonprofit institutions' (US Small Business Administration, 2003: 2). This report examines technical change through patenting and it defines small firms as 'businesses with fewer than 500 employees'.

REFERENCES

Arabsheibani, G., D. De Meza, J. Maloney and B. Pearson (2000), 'And a vision appeared unto them of a great profit: evidence of self-deception among the self-employed', *Economics Letters*, **67**, 35–41.

Astebro, T. (2003), 'The return to independent invention: evidence of unrealistic optimism, risk seeking or skewness loving', *Economic Journal*, **113**, 226–38.

Baumol, W.J. (2002), *The Free-Market Innovation Machine: Analyzing the Growth Miracle of Capitalism*, Princeton, NJ: Princeton University Press.

Baumol, W.J. (2007), 'Entrepreneurship and innovation: the (micro) theory of price and profit', paper presented at the American Economic Association annual conference 2008, available at: http://www.aeaweb.org/annual_mtg_papers/2008/2008_345.pdf.

Baumol, W.J., M. Schilling and E. Wolff (2009), 'The superstar inventors and entrepreneurs: how were they educated?', *Journal of Economics and Management Strategy*, **18** (3), 711–28.

Benz, M. and B. Frey, (2004), 'Being independent raises happiness at work', *Swedish Economic Policy Review*, **11**, 95–134.

Bernardo, A.E. and I. Welch (2001), 'On the evolution of overconfidence and entrepreneurs', *Journal of Economics & Management Strategy*, **10**, 301–30.

Bhide, A.V. (2000), *The Origin and Evolution of New Businesses*, Oxford: Oxford University Press.

Bosma, N., M. van Praag, R. Thurik and G. de Wit (2004), 'The value of human and social capital investments for the business performance of startups', *Small Business Economics*, **23**, 227–36.

Cantillon, R. (1730), *Essai Sur la Nature de Commerce en Général*, trans. H. Higgs, London: Macmillan, 1931 edn.

Cooper, A.C., C.Y. Woo and W.C. Dunkelberg (1988), 'Entrepreneurs perceived chances for success', *Journal of Business Venturing*, **3**, 97–108.

Cowling, M., P. Mitchell and M. Taylor (2004), 'Job creators', *Manchester School*, **72**, 601–17.

Davidsson, P. and B. Honig (2003), 'The role of social and human capital among nascent entrepreneurs', *Journal of Business Venturing*, **18**, 301–33.

Flota, C. and M.T. Mora (2001), 'The earnings of self-employed Mexican-Americans along the US–Mexico border', *Annals of Regional Science*, **35**, 483–99.

Freeman, R. (1978), 'Job satisfaction as an economic variable', *American Economic Review*, **68**, 135–41.

Garcia-Mainar, I. and V.M. Montuenga-Gomez (2005), 'Education returns of wage earners and self-employed workers: Portugal vs. Spain', *Economics of Education Review*, **24**, 161–70.

Henley, A. (2004), 'Self-employment status: the role of state dependence and initial circumstances', *Small Business Economics*, **22**, 67–82.

Kirzner, I. (1979), *Perception, Opportunity and Profit*, Chicago, IL: University of Chicago Press.

Knight, F. (1921), *Risk, Uncertainty and Profit*, Boston, MA and New York: Houghton Mifflin.

Lofstrom, M. (2002), 'Labour market assimilation and the self-employment decision of immigrant entrepreneurs', *Journal of Population Economics*, **15**, 83–114.

National Research Council, Committee on National Statistics (2007), *Understanding Business Dynamics: An Integrated Data System for America's Future*, Washington, DC: National Academies Press.

National Science Board (2006), *Science and Engineering Indicators 2006*, 2 vols, Arlington, VA: National Science Foundation (volume 1, NSB 06-01; volume 2, NSB 06-01A).

Nordhaus, W.D. (2004), 'Schumpeterian profits in the American economy: theory and measurement', National Bureau of Economics Research Working Paper No. 10433.

Orzach, R. and Y. Tauman (2005), 'Strategic dropouts', *Games & Economic Behaviour*, **50**, 79–88.

Parker, S.C. (2006), 'New agendas in the economics of entrepreneurship: optimism, education, wealth and entrepreneurship', paper presented at the American Economic Association Special Session on Entrepreneurship, Boston, MA, 8 January.

Say, J.-B. (1819), *Traite d'économie politique*, 4th edn, trans. C. Prinsep, Boston, MA: Wells and Lilly, 1821 edn.

Schumpeter, J. (1911), *The Theory of Economic Development*, trans. R. Opie, Cambridge, MA: Harvard University Press, 1934 edn.

US Small Business Administration (1995), *The State of Small Business: A Report of the President, 1994*, Washington, DC: US Government Printing Office.

US Small Business Administration (2003), *Small Serial Innovators: The Small Firm Contribution to Technical Change*, CHI Research Inc. for SBA Office of Advocacy, 27 February, Contract no. SBAHQ-01-C-0149.

Van der Sluis, J., M. van Praag and A. van Witteloostuijn (2004), 'Comparing the returns to education for entrepreneurs and employees', mimeo, University of Amsterdam.

7 Employee start-ups

Andreas Koch

Generally, an employee start-up is defined as a new firm founded by an individual which has been employed by another private firm within the same industry prior to the foundation. With respect to the terminology, there has been some fuzziness in the past years which mainly results from the usage of the term 'spin-off'.[1] In some context, this term is used synonymously to what we call an 'employee start-up' (for example, by Erikson and Kuhn, 2006; Klepper, 2001). However, this can be misleading and provoke misunderstandings, as the term 'spin-off' is also used in management, financial and jurisprudential research. In these contexts, the term does not refer to (independent) start-ups, but mostly to divestments (corporate venturing) as a strategy of existing firms, which remain under the control of the divesting firm (also called 'corporate spin-offs', for example Cusatis et al., 1994; Parhankangas, 1999; Schnee et al., 1998). Some authors also have used the term 'spin-out' (Agarwal et al., 2004; Koster, 2006; for an overview and discussions of terminology see, for example, Parhankangas and Arenius, 2003; Koster, 2006; Tübke et al., 2004). Due to this ambiguous use of the term 'spin-off', more authors have recently begun to use the term 'employee start-ups' (for example Franco, 2005; Klepper, 2001; Shah et al., 2006), which I would strongly endorse in order to avoid further misunderstanding.

To get back to the subject, an employee start-up combines the transfer of an individual with the transfer of some kind of industry-specific knowledge, experience – or, in some cases, even existing products, services or technologies – from an existing firm to a new firm (see Figure 7.1).

This implies that routines are embodied in the individual moving from dependent employment to self-employment which may have an impact on the structure and the dynamics of the start-ups. This transfer of routines, sometimes also described as 'heritage' or in so-called 'parenting models' (Agarwal et al., 2004; Dahl and Reichstein, 2006; Klepper, 2001; Portugal Ferreira et al., 2006) is a central element and motivation for research on employee start-ups, as it is of crucial interest how existing knowledge and experience can be employed for further development of new competences and

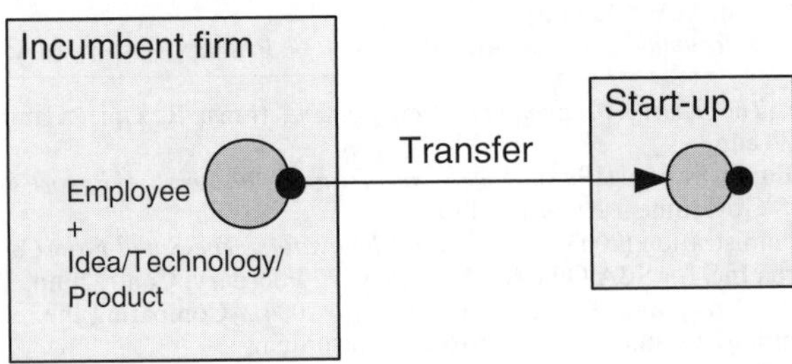

Figure 7.1 Basic elements of employee start-ups

innovations. In an evolutionary view, the existing structure (knowledge, products, firms, and so on) forms the base for what can be developed in the future. Research on employee start-ups can be a very promising field in order to further understand the mechanisms of evolutionary technological and economic change.

NOTE

1. The term 'spin-offs' originated in the USA in the 1940s when it was increasingly recognized that – particularly in large-scale governmental research programmes (for example, space technology, defence industry) – there were a series of by-products that had the potential to be exploited for themselves (for example, Danilov, 1969; Olken, 1966). These by-products or unintended inventions were frequently exploited in new firms founded by former employees of the research programmes or bigger firms (famous examples for spin-offs are the TEFLON®, a material first explored in space technology, or, on the firm side, the German SAP GmbH, founded by IBM-employees, or several spin-offs from Fairchild Semiconductors, also referred to as 'Fairchildren' (Martin, 1984). Further examples can be found in Klepper (2001) or Hellmann (2004).

REFERENCES

Agarwal, Rajshree, Raj Echambadi, April M. Franco and M.B. Sarkar (2004), 'Knowledge transfer through congenital learning. Spin-out generation, development and survival', *Academy of Management Journal*, **47** (4), 501–22.

Cusatis, Patrick J., James A. Miles and J. Randall Woolridge (1994), 'Some new evidence that corporate spin-offs create value', *Journal of Applied Corporate Finance*, **7** (1), 100–107.

Dahl, Michael S. and Toke Reichstein (2006), 'Heritage and survival of spin-offs: quality of parents and parent-tenure of founders', paper presented at the Academy of Management Annual Meeting, Atlanta, 12–16 August.

Danilov, Victor J. (1969), 'The spin-off-phenomenon', *Industrial Research*, **11** (5), 54–8.

Eriksson, Tor and Johan M. Kuhn, (2006), 'Firm spin-offs in Denmark 1981–2000 – patterns of entry and exit', *International Journal of Industrial Organization*, **24**, 1021–40.

Franco, April M. (2005), 'Employee entrepreneurship: recent research and future directions', in Sharon A. Alvarez, Rajshree Agarwal and Olav Sorenson (eds), *Handbook of Entrepreneurship, Vol. 1: Interdisciplinary Perspectives*, International Handbook Series on Entrepreneurship, New York: Springer, pp. 81–96.

Hellmann, Thomas (2004), 'When do employees become entrepreneurs?', working paper 1770, Stanford Graduate School of Business.

Klepper, Steven (2001), 'Employee startups in high-tech industries', *Industrial and Corporate Change*, **10** (3), 639–74.

Koster, Sierdjan (2006), 'Whose child? How existing firms foster new firm formation: individual start-ups, spinouts and spin-offs', dissertation, Groningen University.

Martin, Michael J.C. (1984), *Managing Technological Innovation & Entrepreneurship*, Reston, VA: Reston Publishing.

Olken, Hyman (1966), 'Spin-offs, a business pay-off', *California Management Review*, **9** (2), 17–24.

Parhankangas, Annaleena (1999), *Disintegration of Technological Competencies: An Empirical Study of Divestments through Spin-off Arrangements*, Acta Polytecnica Scandinavica. Mathematics, Computing and Management in Engineering Series 99, Espoo: Finnish Academy of Technology.

Parhankangas, Annaleena and Pia Arenius (2003), 'From a corporate venture to an independent company: a base for a taxonomy for corporate spin-off firms', *Research Policy*, **32** (3), 463–81.

Portugal Ferreira, Manuel, Ana T. Tavares, William Hesterly and Sungu Armagan (2006), 'Network and firm antecedents of spin-offs: motherhooding spin-offs', FEP working papers no. 201, February, University of Porto.

Schnee, Edward J., Lee G. Knight and Ray A. Knight (1998), 'Corporate spin-offs', *Journal of Accountancy*, **185** (6), 47–54.

Shah, Sonali K., Rajshree Agarwal and David B. Audretsch (2006), 'The knowledge context & the entrepreneurial process: academic, user & employee entrepreneurship', University of Illinois working paper no. 06-0118, University of Illinois, Urbana Champaign.

Tübke, Alexander, Pablo Á. de Toledo Saavedra and José-Luis Galán Gonzalez (2004), 'Towards a first spin-off typology and a new concept for corporate spin-off research', *International Journal of Technology Transfer and Commercialisation*, **3** (3), 263–90.

8 Entrepreneurial decision-making

Jean Bonnet, Pascal Cussy and Thomas Brau

In economic theory, decision-making is supposed to result from an optimization calculation that any economic agent performs under the essential hypotheses of rationality. It means that agents seek to maximize their utility function (if households) or to maximize their profit (if businesses) using efficiently the available resources to achieve these objectives within the constraints they face (budget constraint for households, costs constraints for businesses[1]). There is therefore no waste of resources. Tastes and preferences are the first elements of choice in economics. In daily life it enables us to understand the specialization of some economies since in their research of the maximal satisfaction, consumers adapt their budget to their hierarchy of taste. For instance, the history and culture of French emphasis on the quality of life have developed a taste for 'eating well' and 'good drinking' in the French population. French consumers then have a share of spending on food which remains higher than the American share (also due to the fact that the standard of living is higher in the USA). Nevertheless the smaller share of the American is more devoted to eating out (Jany-Catrice, 2004)[2] and includes mainly franchisees restaurants. Because of the French culinary tradition, one finds that catering activity in France is more than in the USA, the result of individual independent small entrepreneurs. However, the choice of becoming an entrepreneur in the catering sector is not a simple choice. We can identify the steps that will constitute an illustration of decision-making in economics. One must have a taste for this job compared to salaried jobs. For example, one needs to be able to manage a team. It is also necessary to identify which kind of restaurants and in which area opportunities for profit for this type of activity exist. This is a problem of information (identification of needs, unmet demand), which requires, according to Kirzner (1973), a key ability – alertness. Becoming an entrepreneur also requires committing individual resources like specific managerial abilities (Lucas, 1978) or financial resources. Each individual is not similarly endowed with these resources, which could explain why some are prevented from embarking on entrepreneurial venture. Entrepreneurial decision-making always involves individuals and their resources in a risky process, since one anticipates on the basis of current information the future development of the activity but a large number of uncertainties can intervene (economic conjuncture, attractiveness of the restaurant, and so on). Then the choice to be an entrepreneur also depends on the risk attitude of the individual. Moreover the optimizing calculation refers to complex methods that only few people are able to carry out (Simon, 1955). Profit opportunities are thus partly built by entrepreneurs according to their perceptions. For example it is often argued that entrepreneurs show an excessive confidence in the success of their businesses due to patterns of simplified decision-making. In this way non-economic factors such as personal characteristics of the new entrepreneur have an influence both on the propensity and the success of the new firm. The 'need for achievement' and the 'locus of control' are the psychological characteristics that resulted in a large number of studies in the population of managers or entrepreneurs

(Hansemark, 2003). Because setting up a firm is also creating his own job, one can argue that the decision to set up a new firm can be viewed as a self-employment choice. In such a case, it is necessary to link entrepreneurship with some individual characteristics (such as human capital level or psychological traits) but also with some characteristics on the labour market (nature of rigidities, level of unemployment) and, more globally, on the structure of rewards of the economy (Baumol, 1990).

Overall it appears that the choice to become an entrepreneur is complex and takes into account tastes of individuals, imperfect information on both opportunities for profit but also on the skills of individuals, different access to some initial resources, attitudes towards risk, patterns of simplified decision-making, change in the situation of individuals and search for personal achievement.

1 THE STANDARD MODEL OF CHOICE (CHOICE IN A MODEL OF COMPETITION WITH PERFECT INFORMATION AND WITHOUT UNCERTAINTY)

The entrepreneurial choice in a competitive economy without uncertainty and with perfect information may be interpreted like any economic choice, for example, a consumer choice. In the standard model each individual is supposed to express coherent choices and so to rank all the considered baskets of goods. His preferences are then represented by a utility function that depends on the quantity of each consumed good. The utility function is a mathematical function which describes the preferences of an individual between different choices (for example, for a consumer, between various baskets of goods). It assigns a value which generally has no interpretation but expresses the ranking of the different options by the individual. The rational consumer chooses, among all the baskets that he is able to buy taking into account his budget constraint, his preferred basket of foods, the one that maximizes his utility. A set of properties about demand of goods may then be deduced from this analysis.

This reasoning can be applied in the entrepreneurial choice without uncertainty. Suppose that in society there are only two job situations – being employed or being an entrepreneur – and that these situations can be distinguished by four characteristics (management, accountability, independence, sociability). The job of the entrepreneur is characterized by high levels of management, accountability, independence and sociability, and vice versa for the employee. In this case, the agents must make a discrete choice between both options depending on their preferences, that is, how they value characteristics of each of these options. If the occupational choice (being self-employed or an employee) was along a continuum, then individuals would have to reason at the margin. An optimal decision would be such that a small variation would not add anything more. Typically each status presents an opportunity cost which depends on the preferences of agents, that is, how they value each of these attributes. A person who values the four characteristics of the entrepreneur prefers the situation of the entrepreneur because he will get more utility from the entrepreneur status than from the employee status. In this case, the choice is easily done but it is nevertheless extraordinary that such situations arise because there are actually many more features than in our simplified example. One can imagine people who dislike the task of management, but who appreciate the sense of responsibility and independence. Some will choose to become entrepreneurs because, consistent with their preferences, the cost for them (to bear the management responsibilities) is less than the benefits they obtain from responsibility and independence. Another way to express it is to say that the opportunity cost of giving up independence and responsibility is greater than the benefit of employee status that does not have to bear the responsibilities of management. Other people with different tastes will prefer the opposite employee status. For them the benefits of non-management will more than offset the disadvantages of the loss of independence and responsibility.

Among different type of firms, it is possible to choose between different baskets of characteristics. For example, being a franchisee enables the entrepreneur to relax the characteristics of independence and responsibility. To have a partner in the firm is also a way to share out responsibility. Being on piecework relaxes the characteristic of sociability and accounting; some individuals like independence but dislike dealing with clients and accounting work.

Evans and Leighton (1989) state that individuals who prefer autonomy are more likely to become self-employed. Lazear (2005) shows that students who will become entrepreneurs have chosen to acquire a diversity of skills in their education programme because it is the minimum level of the required skills that determines the earnings of the entrepreneur. For instance Lazear (2005) writes that the creation of a restaurant requires mobilization of numerous different skills; the entrepreneur must certainly cook well, but also must have a taste for decoration, must like to welcome guests, must be able to keep the books. However, if the entrepreneur cannot perform all these skills he needs to know how to hire the right people in the labour market.

Yet the choice of setting up a firm does not come down to the choice of the characteristics of a certain status, but deals with having a project and achieving it in a complex and risky world where information is not perfect. One of the first problems is to identify a project, that is, to seize market opportunities.

2 THE ENTREPRENEUR AND THE MARKET: MAINLY A PROBLEM OF INFORMATION AND ADJUSTMENT

Schumpeter in his seminal work (1911) has noted the predominant role of the innovative entrepreneur that drives the growth and that breaks the economic circuit otherwise reproducible indefinitely. For that purpose bank loans are necessary to divert intermediate and investment goods in order to realize the innovation (at the end the added value created by innovation exceeds the increase in prices (inflation) due to bank loans). Yet the role of the entrepreneur is so linked with growth that he appears to be more driven by personal traits (see below) and all the explanation is embedded in the innovation characteristic without any more explanation about the functioning of the market. A great deal of debate around market equilibrium and planned versus market functioning of economies arose in the 1920s and 1930s.

According to the market hypothesis of pure and perfect competition, which constitutes the general framework of analysis in economics, all information is available at no cost nor any delay for every firm or consumer so that: 'For a society, then, we can speak of a state of equilibrium at a point of time – but it means only that the different plans which the individuals composing it have made for action in time are mutually compatible' (Hayek, 1937: 41). But the view of the market is obviously more complex. According to Hayek's notable works on the role of information and the discovery process in the market (1937; 1945; 1948; 1978), the market is a process in perpetual adjustment where the building of the needs, preferences and production plans are themselves inseparable from interaction, demonstration and learning effects (Heertje, 1982).

For example, businesses adjust, over time, the features of their products according to the information that they obtain about customers' satisfaction (restaurants and cafés fill their slack periods thanks to happy hours, usually they renew their menu in order to adapt themselves to fashion and to stimulate a new interest among their clients). The entrepreneur has therefore an important place, but his role does not predominate over the customer's view.

Kirzner (1979; 1985) retains the ability of alertness for defining the entrepreneurial function; the ability to perceive opportunities for profit for new needs or to offer products best suited to the tastes of consumers.[3] These opportunities are seized by entrepreneurs because: 'If one has become sufficiently alerted to the existence of an opportunity – that is, one has become sufficiently convinced regarding the facts of a situation – it becomes virtually impossible to imagine not taking advantage of the opportunity so discovered' (Kirzner, 1985: 22). This alertness acts positively on the coordination of plans of supply and demand in the market.

'In the course of this entrepreneurial process, new products may be introduced, new qualities of existing products may be developed, new methods of production may be ventured, new forms of industrial organization, financing, marketing or tackling risk may be developed' (Kirzner, 1985: 30). As a result the entrepreneur generates knowledge shared by economics agents and therefore reduces their ignorance. Entrepreneurial profit is a pure profit that is not to be related to the use of any factor of production. It follows a simultaneous decision to buy and sell in the wake of discoveries of advantageous price differences whose existence is based on the ignorance of agents about accurate supply and demand. According to Kirzner, discovering profit opportunities so far ignored by economic agents would therefore require no specific investment.

This is an extreme position on the entrepreneurial function theorization which will be built upon by Casson (1982) in a more applied way. Individuals differ not only in their tastes, but also in access to information for various reasons related to their characteristics (social environment, education, occupation, and so on). The entrepreneur believes that the totality of the information available to him is unique; he then takes his decision alone and expects a profit by taking positions vis-à-vis others. It is only because he is the one to start the project that he can expect a profit. His dilemma is to convince finance providers that he is right while revealing partial information, because the others are also potential competitors and thus profit reducers.

Research (Fairlie and Robb, 2006) shows that the capture of market opportunities is not independent of a kind of 'entrepreneurial human capital'. This latter, linked to relatives' environment may explain a larger propensity of entrepreneurship in families of business owners. Yet successful entrepreneurship is nevertheless ensured only if these new entrepreneurs have acquired management experience in the enterprise of their parents. This management experience allows them probably to move easily in a risky environment. This leads us to consider the initial financial and managerial attributes that the entrepreneur must have if he wants to launch a project with great chances of success.

3 ENTREPRENEURIAL ABILITIES AND RESOURCES ACCESS

Decision-making in economics commits resources in order to achieve a single goal (maximizing the usefulness of the consumer, profit maximization of the company). In some cases the non-availability of certain resources even prevents the project from happening.

The firm has theoretically no entrepreneur, as it makes choices among alternative values for a small number of well-defined variables – price, production, advertising expenses – according to repetitive codified mathematical processes of maximization.

Nevertheless Baumol (1968) noted that there is room for clever ruses, ingenious schemes, brilliant innovations, charisma that differentiate the entrepreneurs. There is therefore some skill to entrepreneurship. In this regard Lucas (1978) challenges the standard theory for which the U-shape curve of production costs determines both the size, the number of companies and entry and exit of the firms to and from the market.[4] It is more appropriate to suggest that there are individuals with various managerial capacities and that the distribution of managerial capacity explains the various sizes of companies. A few individuals have a high level of managerial leadership that allows them to launch and conduct large companies (recent examples are Bill Gates with Microsoft and Richard Branson with Virgin).

In low developed countries the actual wage is low and a great proportion of individuals are self-employed because they cannot find a salaried position providing them with better earnings. With economic development, many small individual entrepreneurs will prefer to take a job in an existing business rather than to engage in an entrepreneurial venture. As real wages increase, a number of entrepreneurs with less managerial ability will prefer to work as employees. The fact remains that this relationship is not linear, as we find that the development of the economy has created new opportunities for enhancing entrepreneurship (Audretsch, 2006). That is what demonstrates the high level of entrepreneurial activity observed in North America.

Some authors put forward access to financial capital as a prerequisite for any entrepreneurial and especially any innovative commitment. A set of theoretical articles show that new entrepreneurs are financially constrained (Jaffee and Russell, 1976; Stiglitz and Weiss, 1981). However, there is no empirical consensus on the existence of credit rationing. For instance, Evans and Jovanovic (1989), Evans and Leighton (1989) and Holtz-Eakin et al. (1994) show a significant positive relationship between individuals' wealth and their probability of becoming self-employed. They conclude that start-ups suffer from a capital gap. Nevertheless financial capital could be correlated with unobservable factors such as managerial skills or, more generally, human capital of the entrepreneur. Hence the introduction in some work (Blanchflower and Oswald, 1998; Lindh and Ohlsson, 1996) of exogenous events such as inheritances, gifts or income from the lottery, confirms the positive influence of wealth on entrepreneurial commitment. Financial constraints would exist and would tend to exclude those who have insufficient funds. According to Parker (2004: 181) this leads to the endogeneity problem, 'Whereby the self-employed are wealthy because of previous success in self-employment'. Parker shed light on several alternative explanations also consistent with the previous results on financial constraints. Berger and Udell (1992) adopt an intermediate position: they argue that while the macro effects of credit rationing may be small, there is evidence to suggest that when credit is rationed for some firms it may be more readily available for others.

Cressy (1996: 1253), for his part, finds, using British data, 'that human capital in the true determinant of survival of new firms and that the correlation between financial capital and survival is spurious'. In the French survey Sine (information system on new firms) we have found that a majority of new firms are not facing credit rationing, but that a significant share is 'self-constrained' (Bonnet et al., 2005). Yet the study refers to entrepreneurial projects that are concretized in new firms. General entrepreneurial intentions in the French population that are aborted due to financial constraints are not reported. The result given by Cressy concerning British new firms is: 'We conclude that firms self-select for finance (rather than being selected by the banks), those with greater human capital being more likely to take up the bank's offer. Thus, there is no credit rationing of start-ups' (Cressy, 1996: 1254). In a recent report, the OECD (2006: 11) supports the idea that 'in a mumber of high-income OECD countries, there is little evidence of an overall scarcity of financing for SMEs'. Although there is no empirical consensus on the existence of credit rationing, it is acknowledged that one of the main weaknesses for the development of European incubators is the lack and underdevelopment of seed financing and business angel networks (Aernoudt, 2004). This situation is in contrast with the US, where a financial system supporting business formation and growth has been created (Acs and Szerb, 2007). Hurst and Lusardi (2004) show in the USA that there is no relationship between wealth and entrepreneurship for much of the distribution of wealth. The rate of entry is almost constant between the 1st and 9th decile and significantly increases for individuals only at the 95th percentile or below the 5th percentile because of a low opportunity cost.

Of course these results, especially the French results, shed light on the lack of entrepreneurship spirit and opportunities (see below) that have more to do with the functioning of a 'wage society' than with the availability of financing. Specifically this accounts for the low development of venture capital in France.[5] The choice to become an entrepreneur can also be analysed as an arbitrage between a wage occupation and a firm's risky project. The project is risky because the future earnings that can be negative or positive are not known in advance.

4 ENTREPRENEURSHIP: DECISION-MAKING IN UNCERTAINTY

Indeed, the economy is continually affected by shocks that play a role in the enterprise's performance. For example our individual who opens his restaurant engages his personal assets in order to obtain, in the future, a profit that is uncertain and depends on different probabilities in the state of the world (economic events, attractiveness of the restaurant, new law about value added tax, new rules about smoking/no smoking areas, and so on). Knight (1921) is considered one of the first to justify the existence of the firm by uncertainty. It distinguishes the risk that is measurable from the uncertainty that is not measurable. The entrepreneur is then the one who endorses this uncertainty, makes decisions (hierarchical position) and controls (he assumes the role of responsibility in particular in giving a fixed return to the factors of production). The entrepreneur earns profit as a counterpart of his management of uncertainty. Yet according to Knight the risk is not the source of profit because the firm can avoid it by an insurance mechanism. It represents only a cost.

Nowadays the choice to entrepreneur or wage earner is often analysed in the frame of the standard analysis of choice in uncertainty. This analysis considers the preferences of individuals represented by a function of expected utility, known as the Von Neumann and Morgenstern function (1944 [1947]), based on objectives probabilities. Savage (1954) also showed that under a number of assumptions, preferences can be represented by a function of expected utility based on subjective probabilities. As a result, the distinction between risk and uncertainty then presents little interest.

Kihlstrom and Laffont (1979) apply this analysis to the choice of individuals between working as an employee in a competitive job market or becoming an entrepreneur. The second choice is viewed as more risky. While an employee may lose his job, his salary is at least partly independent of the results of the firm in which he is working.

The gain from entrepreneurship can be measured by the certain equivalent income that the individuals assigned to this activity. This is the monetary valuation of possible future gains. It depends on their attitude to risk and decreases when individuals show risk aversion. It is sufficient then to compare this equivalent with the salary that some people perceive to understand their decision, assuming that the wage is perceived as certain. The authors show that, at the equilibrium, the individuals demonstrating the greatest risk aversion become employed, while those who are less averse become entrepreneurs. In addition, among the entrepreneurs, those who have the least amount of risk aversion lead larger companies.[6]

Stewart and Roth (2001), in a meta-analysis, show that entrepreneurs have a greater level of risk-propensity. Yet this result is challenge by Miner and Raju (2004) who claim that the result is not so clear because some relevant studies have not been taken into account. Moreover the latter authors think that it is necessary to control for some variables, as Brockhaus (1987) in a previous study has already recognized, like gender, cultural background, stage of business development and type of business owned.

Liles (1974) has identified four main negative occurrences of risk-taking in cases of failure. The financial difficulties that could lead to a significant reduction in living standards, the psychological well-being of the person who committed himself to the new firm, the professional career which can be compromised and the familial risk that could also exist if the firm survives because being an entrepreneur requires investing a lot of time.

It has also been observed that, in most cases, a greater propensity for risk (for entrepreneurs) is tempered by a deep judgement that prevents them from taking extreme risks (Mueller and Thomas, 2000).

The representation of the behavior of individuals with an expected utility function is nevertheless contested, partly as a result of the complexity of the environment in which decisions must be taken or because experience shows that individuals do not always act rationally but rely on their intuition.

5 THE LIMIT OF RATIONALITY IN DECISION-MAKING

The complexity refers to situations in which the decision-maker is not sure what the probability distribution of a future event will be because of very complex interactions. In fact the decision is often taken with the help of simplified mechanisms (with deformation of probabilities by the agents). Herbert Simon (1955; 1956) highlighted the bounded rationality of decision-makers who are limited in both knowledge and the capacity to calculate. The implementation of the means to achieve the ends and its consequences are poorly understood.

Compared with the optimal decision, alternatives choices are found. The opportunities for profit are partly built by entrepreneurs based on their perceptions (mental constructs in a repetitive non-optimizing cognitive process). Entrepreneurs have a strong tendency to consider the opportunity as unique and that the situation decision could not be replicated. They resort to heuristics simplifying assumptions (Kahneman, 2003) and are subject to bias decision because: 'People rely on a limited number of heuristics principles which reduce the complex tasks of assessing probabilities and predicting values to simpler judgmental operations' (Tversky and Kahneman, 1974: 1124). For instance, two individuals will attribute a different success probability to a typical restaurant (restaurant with Cuban food and Cuban musical entertainment) according to their perception of the reality. One of them will attribute a higher probability than the other because such an establishment is opened and works close to his home. His estimation does not rely on a rational calculus but more on a subjective perception.

Kahneman and Tversky have also shown that economic agents do not behave consistently with regard to risk. More precisely, the same individual manifests less risk-aversion when he has to choose between losses than when he has to choose between gains (reflection effect). This lower risk-aversion in the field of losses may then conduct some long-term unemployed people to entrepreneurship (self-employment). In effect unemployment that lasts may be analysed as a situation of a certain loss of wealth and then decreases the degree of risk-aversion of individuals.

Moreover, in the standard analysis, the entrepreneur is considered a passive game player who considers the success or failure probabilities as exogenous. Yet the entrepreneur plays a more important role. The essential difference is that the game player cannot exercise any control on the gain, while the entrepreneur may influence by his acts the making of his decision. According to Byers et al. (1998) the entrepreneurs often estimate that their decisions are based on facts and that their returns rely more on their perspicacity judgement than on their luck. They have a tendency to overestimate the influence of their competences. Then another bias that is documented in some studies is entrepreneurial overconfidence (the fact that in participating himself in the action the entrepreneur overestimates his chance of success).

According to Cooper et al. (1988), 68 per cent of entrepreneurs estimate their own probabilities of success to be more important than for similar enterprises directed by others. Thirty-three per cent of them even think that their probability of success is 100 per cent. For De Meza and Southey (1996), the population of new entrepreneurs has a tendency to overestimate the occurrence of future favourable events. Then the entrepreneurial overconfidence intervenes in the level of indebtedness if the wealth of the entrepreneur is insufficient to cover the initial investment project. Camerer and Lovallo (1999) have built an experiment where subjects have choice to entry on the market. In the case of subjects that self-select (the returns of their risky decisions depend on their competencies) they have observed more entrants on the market. Self-selection reinforces overconfidence because participants think they can beat the odds. This optimistic behaviour tends to persist even in the event of bad results (Ross and Anderson, 1982), because individuals have some difficulty in accepting they have made errors. Carrillo and Mariotti (2000) show that this behaviour leads to a preference for ignorance. At best the revision process of the probabilities is incomplete according to Bénabou and Tirole (2002). This capability to shoulder true uncertainty needs a high degree of self-confidence, the belief in his effective control, and in his good fortune that relies on some personality traits.

6 THE INCLUSION OF NON-ECONOMIC FACTORS: THE EXAMPLE OF THE ENTREPRENEUR PERSONALITY

The classic utility function does not include a number of psychological characteristics or personal enjoyment that drives the economic agent in his decision-making. The importance of psychological variables has been sustained for a long time by numerous research works (Koh, 1996; Shapero, 1975; McClelland, 1961).

Among psychological variables the locus of control (Mueller and Thomas, 2000) and the need of achievement (Johnson 1990) are key variables. The locus of control (Rotter 1971) reflects the disposition to act for an individual, that is, the degree with which he thinks that he can have an influence on his environment. Some individuals are then said to be external because they are inclined to think that the awards they received in their life are outside their own control and they rely on luck, on the benevolence of a mentor or the control of a powerful person. Others think that they can modify for good or bad the course of these events. This latter psychological characteristic, qualifies as internal locus of control, has been found in the entrepreneurial involvement and in the opportunity to exploit some effective abilities of leadership (Shapero, 1975). It expresses one thing we often find in the surveys on the motives to set up or to take over a new firm as the notion of 'willingness to control his destiny'. Van Praag et al. (2004) have demonstrated that a positive link exists between this characteristic and the earnings of two populations (employees and entrepreneurs) from the National Longitudinal Survey of Youth (NLSY). They find that the coefficient is stronger for entrepreneurs (compared with salaried people).

McClelland (1961) has resumed the concept of achievement motivation defined in Murray (1938) in his personality system. Along this latter a need is 'strength in the spirit region which organizes the perception, the intellectual activity and the action'; the specific need of achievement is then defined as the accomplishment of something difficult in fields as large as managing, operating or organizing the physical objects, but also human behaviours and ideas. An individual responding to a need of achievement motive is going to try to achieve his goal as quickly and independently as possible. He is going to try to excel in the clearing of obstacles and he is especially going to try to go into competition with other individuals to try to outdo them, in order to increase his satisfaction in the setting up of his successful talent. The entrepreneur field is then a field of excellence of the exercise of the need of achievement. Collins et al. (2004) in the frame of a meta-analysis show the link between the need of achievement and the choice to follow an entrepreneurial orientation but also the level of performance of the entrepreneur.

Lee and Tsang (2001) have demonstrated that a positive link exists between the need of achievement and venture growth. Like the need of achievement, the internal locus of control shows the same result for larger firms in their sample.

These traits of personal characteristics, and moral attitudes, have been recognized historically by the greatest economists as being favourable to entrepreneurial decision-making and success of the new company. Van Praag (2006) provides an admirable summary of the findings, to which we are indebted, in the following paragraph.

For Say (1971, first published in 1803) a successful entrepreneur must demonstrate prudence, probity and regularity. Marshall (1890) defined general ability for a successful entrepreneur as: 'To be able to bear in mind many things at a time, to have everything ready when wanted, to act promptly and show resource when anything goes wrong, to accommodate oneself quickly to changes, to be steady and trustworthy, to have always a reserve of force' (Marshall, 1930: 206–7).

According to Schumpeter, the entrepreneur should not feel reluctant to do something new (Van Praag, 2006). 'This mental freedom . . . is something peculiar and by nature rare' (Schumpeter, [1911] 1934: 86). The entrepreneur should 'be strong enough to swim against the tide of the society in which he is living' (Heertje, 1982: 86). He must have leadership skills, a special interest in creativity 'the joy of creation', 'a taste for the competition', the will to win 'and wants to achieve a certain social distinction'.

For Knight (1921) the ability to deal with uncertainty requires a high degree of self-confidence, a disposition to act on one's own opinion and belief in his good fortune. Kirzner (1973: 68) puts forward the concept of alertness which is the only character trait that the entrepreneur needs: 'The kind of knowledge required for entrepreneurship is knowing where to look for knowledge . . . The word, which captures most closely this kind of "knowledge", seems to be alertness'.

Baumol (1968) thinks it is not possible to integrate all these qualities in a formalized theory. It may, however be possible to examine what can be done to encourage this activity, which is essential for economic development (Leibenstein, 1968). To do that requires putting more interest in the pay-off of the activity of entrepreneurs, that is, looking for occupational choices.

7 ENTREPRENEURIAL DECISION-MAKING: ALSO A DECISION TO CREATE HIS OWN JOB

The decision to become an entrepreneur is to a large extent a microeconomic decision about the proper allocation of one's human capital, balancing an opportunity cost of entrepreneurship with a reward expectation (monetary, symbolic, social or psychological). According to Moskowitz and Vissing-Jorgensen (2002), the returns of the financial initial investment of the entrepreneur are no higher than he would obtain on the financial markets, while the risk (due to non-diversification) is high: 'About 75 percent of all private equity is owned by households for whom it constitutes at least half of their total net worth. Furthermore, households with entrepreneurial equity invest on average more than 70 percent of their private holdings in a single private company in which they have an active management interest' (Moskowitz and Vissing-Jorgensen, 2002: 745).

The decision to start a business is most of the time associated with a decision to become self-employed. Two main individual motives drive the decision to set up a firm:

- A constrained motive (or push motive): new entrepreneurs are motivated by a low opportunity cost of entrepreneurship. This may be due to an individual's failure in the labour market (unemployment or employed in an unsuitable job) or to perceived dissatisfactions in a salaried position (insufficient independence, not satisfying his need of achievement, only partial control of his own fate).[7]

- An opportunity motive (or pull motive): new entrepreneurs are positively drawn to entrepreneurship. It corresponds to a strategy for an individual to obtain better rewards on his human capital, which may be undervalued by the labour market due to information asymmetries or work incentive considerations.[8] It can also result from the individual's ability to perceive and seize market opportunities, to transform an idea into an innovative project.

Both reasons are not independent. An economy that creates a lack of jobs (low growth rate) and that suffers from the malfunctioning of the labour market – for example, a high average period of unemployment – strengthens entrepreneurship for negative reasons and especially discourages entrepreneurial venture for positive reasons. In France the share of unemployed new entrepreneurs is high because the propensity to set up a firm when employed or a student is low.

At the European level, Wennekers (2006) shows that there is a negative relationship between the unemployment rate and the propensity to set up a firm. This result confirms the fact that labour market considerations have an influence on the total entrepreneurial activity.

Many macroeconomic and institutional causes can explain the differences in entrepreneurial intensity between countries and areas. They include economic growth, rate of unemployment, the development and the operation of the financial system, the intensity of the administrative barriers, specificities of the labour market, legal consequences of the failure of the firm, the entrepreneurship spirit and the collective perception of the failure of the firm. This set of causes refer to what Baumol names, in a notable 1990 article, the rules of the game – that is, the structure of reward in the economy. He notes that certain societies historically favoured rather unfavourable structures of reward for the development of entrepreneurship. These structures divert the national or local elites from the entrepreneurial function and prove indirectly harmful to the diffusion of technical progress (ancient Rome with the valorization of the political office, medieval China with the mandarin system). More recently, they enable us to understand the 'unhooking' of certain European countries in reference to the difference which exists between an entrepreneurial society, which develops private initiative, and a wage society, which increases the opportunity cost to undertake. In an entrepreneurial society, being a wage earner does not ensure stable employment because of the ability of the employers to lay off workers. On the other hand, the flexibility of the labour market can more easily encourage individuals to become an entrepreneur insofar as this action constitutes a positive signal for the future employers even if the company fails.

8 CONCLUSION

The entrepreneurial commitment can be considered decision-making by excellence in economics. Indeed, it implies uncertainty and risk-taking because the entrepreneur is fully responsible for the development of the new company, and in general he has committed a significant part of his personal savings to the firm. Also, from a microeconomic point of view, entrepreneurial involvement is complex. It refers to the desire for better recognition (valuation of his human capital) but also for some personal aspirations to address professional dissatisfaction or in search of work more suited to the entrepreneur. From a macroeconomic point of view, labour market rigidities combined with institutional inefficiencies may lead, in some European countries, to strong entrepreneurship for low opportunity costs motives (push motives) but, globally, to a weak propensity of setting up a firm for innovative motives – valuation of a new idea – (pull motives). Too rigid a labour market and the stigmatization of the entrepreneurial failure discourages some qualified and experienced employees from the entrepreneurial option. In most European countries, the unemployed population is very much overrepresented in the population of new entrepreneurs. Some cultural aspects may also be put forward. For example Hofstede (2001) notices that uncertainty-avoidance is not equally distributed among the cultures. It is in countries where uncertainty-avoidance is higher that we find the lower levels of self-employment. In these countries individuals like to follow rules and procedures, and prefer the administrated organization. A recent study from Noorderhaven et al. (2004) show that the level of self-employment in 15 European countries is partly explained by dissatisfactions with life and the way democracy works. These two dissatisfactions, according to the authors, are close to professional dissatisfaction.

The insufficient pull motives for entrepreneurship in Europe refer to what Audretsch (2007) calls the European paradox. The lack of entrepreneurship capital in Europe leads to a high level of knowledge investment for a poor result in terms of growth and reduction of unemployment.

> Barriers to entrepreneurship can impede knowledge spillover entrepreneurship. Such barriers range from legal restrictions and impediments to the existence and availability of early stage finance, or to social and institutional tradition discouraging entrepreneurship and a stigma associated with failed attempts as entrepreneurship. The capacity of an economy to generate entrepreneurial behaviour is shaped by the extent of its underlying entrepreneurship capital. (Audretsch, 2007: 69)

NOTES

1. For each possible level of production, the company will seek the optimal amount of each factor to be used, that is, the quantities that can minimize the total cost.
2. About 50 per cent of total spending on food against 28 per cent in the case of France in 1997.
3. It can also be the implementation of new, more efficient, production techniques.
4. The motivations of his work is based on the fact that companies are often multi-product and external growth strategies are complex and not only axed in the pursuit of the optimum size.
5. However, in the Third World the financial constraints are often binding. For instance it has been noticed that it is often too risky in these countries to change one's way of life. One cannot transfer the minimum financial provision in order to engage in a production detour. This effect is counterbalanced thanks to microfinance and small business lending which allow people to become entrepreneurs.
6. Some also define the risk premium of entrepreneurship (entrepreneurship premium). This is the difference between the evaluation of future profits (certain equivalent) by a given individual and an individual who is risk neutral.
7. Professional dissatisfaction of the entrepreneur in respect of jobs held prior to the establishment of his company are wider than simple wage claims. They cover such considerations as more autonomy (Cromie, 1987) problems with co-workers or the hierarchy (Brockhaus, 1980; Greenbank, 2006) and career prospects (Dyer, 1994).

8. This imperfect valuation of human capital in the labour market can result from an insufficient functioning of the internal labour market in the enterprise for different reasons (small size of firm, lack of recognition of the individual's productivity, or the firm's strategy to restrict wage increases in order to preserve social cohesion).

REFERENCES

Acs, Z.J. and L. Szerb (2007), 'Entrepreneurship, economic growth and public policy', *Small Business Economics*, **28**, 109–22.

Aernoudt, R. (2004), 'Incubators: tool for entrepreneurship', *Small Business Economics*, **23**, 127–35.

Audretsch, D. (2006), 'L'émergence de l'économie entrepreneuriale', *Reflets et Perspectives de la vie économique*, **45** (1), 43–70.

Audretsch, D. (2007), 'Entrepreneurship capital and economic growth', *Oxford Review of Economic Policy*, **23** (1), 63–78.

Baumol, William J. (1968), 'Entrepreneurship in economic theory', *American Economic Review*, **58** (Mar.), 64–71.

Baumol, William J. (1990), 'Entrepreneurship, productive, unproductive and destructive', *Journal of Political Economy*, **98** (Oct.), 893–921.

Berger, Allen and Gregory Udell (1992), 'Some evidence on the empirical significance of credit rationing', *Journal of Political Economy*, **100**, 1047–77.

Bénabou, R. and J. Tirole (2002), 'Self-confidence and personal motivation', *Quarterly Journal of Economics*, **117** (Aug.), 871–915.

Blanchflower, D.G. and A.J. Oswald, (1998), 'What makes an entrepreneur?', *Journal of Labor Economics*, **16** (1), 26–60.

Bonnet, J., S. Cieply and M. Dejardin (2005), 'Financial constraints on new firms: looking for regional disparities', *Brussels Economic Review*, 3 (Autumn), 217–46.

Brockhaus, R.H. (1980), 'The effect of job dissatisfaction on the decision to start a business', *Journal of Small Business Management*, **18**, 37–43.

Brockhaus, R.H. (1987), 'Entrepreneurial folklore', *Journal of Small Business Management*, **25**, 1–6.

Byers, T.H., H. Kist and R.I. Sutton (1998), 'Characteristics of the entrepreneur: social creatures, not solo heroes', in R.C. Dorf (ed.), *The Handbook of Technology Management*, Boca Raton, FL: CRC Press, pp. 1–5.

Camerer, C.F. and D. Lovallo (1999), 'Overconfidence and excess entry: an experimental approach', *American Economic Review*, **89** (1), 306–18.

Carrillo, J.D. and T. Mariotti (2000), 'Strategic ignorance as a self-disciplining device', *Review of Economic Studies*, **67** (3), 529–44.

Casson, M. (1982), *The Entrepreneur: An Economic Theory*, Aldershot, UK and Brookfield, VT, USA: Edward Elgar.

Collins, C.J., P.J. Hanges and E.A. Locke (2004), 'The relationship of achievement motivation to entrepreneurial behavior: a meta-analysis', *Human Performance*, **17** (1), 95–117.

Cooper, A.C., C.Y. Woo and W.C. Dunkelberg (1988), 'Entrepreneurs. Perceived chances for success', *Journal of Business Venturing*, **3**, 97–108.

Cressy, R. (1996), 'Are business startups debt-rationed?', *The Economic Journal*, **106** (438), 1253–70.

Cromie, S. (1987), 'Motivations of aspiring male and female entrepreneurs', *Journal of Occupational Behaviour*, **8**, 251–61.

De Meza, D. and C. Southey (1996), 'The borrower's curse: optimism, finance and entrepreneurship', *The Economic Journal*, **106**, 375–86.

Dyer, W.G. (1994), 'Toward a theory of entrepreneurial careers', *Entrepreneurship Theory and Practice*, **19** (2), 7–21.

Evans D.S. and Linda S. Leighton (1989), 'Some empirical aspects of entrepreneurship', *American Economic Review*, **79** (3), 519–35.

Evans D.S. and B. Jovanovic (1989), 'An estimated model of entrepreneurship choice under liquidity constraints', *Journal of Political Economy*, **97** (4), 808–27.

Fairlie R.W. and A. Robb (2006), 'Families, human capital, and small business: evidence from the characteristics of business owners survey', in Mirjam Van Praag (ed.), *Entrepreneurship and Human Capital*, Amsterdam: Amsterdam Center for Entrepreneurship Faculty of Economics and Business, University of Amsterdam, pp. 5–11.

Greenbank, P. (2006), 'Starting up in business, an examination of the decision-making process', *Entrepreneurship and Innovation*, **7** (3), 149–59.

Hansemark, O.C. (2003), 'Need for achievement, locus of control and the prediction of business start-ups: a longitudinal study', *Journal of Economic Psychology*, **24**, 301–19.
Hayek, F. von (1937), 'Economics and knowledge', *Economica*, New Series, **4** (13), 33–54.
Hayek, F. von (1945), 'The use of knowledge in society', *American Economic Review*, **35** (4), 519–30.
Hayek, F. von (1948), 'The meaning of competition', in *Individualism and Economic Order*, Chicago, IL: University of Chicago Press, pp. 92–106.
Hayek, F. von (1978), 'Competition as a Discovery Procedure', in *New Studies in Philosophy, Politics, Economics and the History of Ideas*, Chicago, IL: University of Chicago Press, pp. 179–90.
Heertje, A. (1982), 'Schumpeter's model of the decay of capitalism', in H. Frisch (ed.), *Schumpeterian Economics*, Eastbourne, UK: Praeger, Chapter 5.
Hofstede, G. (2001), *Cultures' Consequences*, 2nd edn, Thousand Oaks, CA: Sage.
Holtz-Eakin, D., D. Joulfaian and H. Rosen (1994), 'Entrepreneurial decisions and liquidity constraints', *Rand Journal of Economics*, **25**, 334–47.
Hurst, E. and A. Lusardi (2004), 'Liquidity constraints, household wealth, and entrepreneurship', *Journal of Political Economy*, **112**, 319–47.
Jaffee, D.W. and T. Russell (1976), 'Imperfect information, uncertainty and credit rationing', *The Quarterly Journal of Economics*, **90**, 651–66.
Jany-Catrice, F. (2004), 'Une analyse socioéconomique de l'emploi dans l'hôtellerie-restauration en France et aux Etats-Unis', Economie et Sociétés, série 'Socio-économie du travail', AB, no. 23, 1/2004, 147–71.
Johnson, B.R. (1990), 'Toward a multidimensional model of entrepreneurship: the case of achievement motivation and the entrepreneur', *Entrepreneurship Theory and Practice*, **14**, 39–54.
Kahneman, D. (2003), 'Maps of bounded rationality: psychology for behavioral economy', *American Economic Review*, **93** (5), 1449–75.
Kihlstrom, R. and J.J. Laffont (1979), 'A general equilibrium entrepreneurial theory of firm formation based on risk aversion', *Journal of Political Economy*, **87** (4), August, 719–48.
Kirzner, I.M. (1973), *Competition and Entrepreneurship*, Chicago: University of Chicago Press.
Kirzner, I.M. (1979), *Perception, Opportunity, and Profit*, Chicago, IL: University of Chicago Press.
Kirzner, I.M. (1985), *Discovery and the Capitalist Process*, Chicago, IL: University of Chicago Press.
Knight, F.H. (1921), *Risk, Uncertainty and Profit*, Boston, MA: Houghton Mifflin.
Koh, H.C. (1996), 'Testing hypotheses of entrepreneurial characteristics', *Journal of Managerial Psychology*, **11** (3), 12–25.
Lazear, E.P. (2005), 'Entrepreneurship', *Journal of Labor Economics*, **23** (4), 649.
Lee, D.Y and E.W.K. Tsang (2001), 'The effects of entrepreneurial personality, background and network activities on venture growth', *Journal of Management Studies*, **38**, 583–602.
Leibenstein, H. (1968), 'Entrepreneurship and development', *American Economic Review*, **58** (2), 72–83.
Liles, P.R. (1974), *New Business Ventures and the Entrepreneur*, Homewood, IL: Irwin.
Lindh, T. and H. Ohlsson (1996), 'Self-employment and windfall gains: evidence from the Swedish lottery', *Economic Journal*, **106** (Nov.), 1515–26.
Lucas, R.E. (1978), 'On the size distribution of business firms', *Bell Journal of Economics*, **9** (Autumn), 508–23.
Marshall, A. (1930), *Principles of Economics*, London: Macmillan (first edition 1890).
McClelland, David D. (1961), 'Entrepreneurship behavior' and 'Characteristics of entrepreneurs', in *The Achieving Society*, Princeton, NJ: D. Van Nostrand, pp. 205–58, 259–300.
Miner, J.B and N.S. Raju (2004), 'Risk propensity differences between managers and entrepreneurs and between low-and high-growth entrepreneurs: a reply in a more conservative vein', *Journal of Applied Psychology*, **89** (1), 3–13.
Moskowitz, T. and A. Vissing-Jorgensen (2002), 'The returns to entrepreneurial investment: a private equity premium puzzle?', *American Economic Review*, **4** (Sep.), 745–78.
Mueller, S.L. and A.S. Thomas, (2000), 'Culture and entrepreneurial potential: a nine country study of locus of control and innovativeness', *Journal of Business Venturing*, **16** (1), 51–75.
Murray, Y.H. (1938), *Explorations in Personality*, New York: Oxford University Press.
Noorderhaven, N., R. Thurik, S. Wennekers and A.V. Stel (2004), 'The role of dissatisfaction and per capita income in explaining self-employment across 15 European countries', *Entrepreneurship, Theory and Practice*, **28**, 447–66.
OECD (2006), *The SME Financing Gap: Theory and Evidence*, Vol.1, Paris: OECD.
Parker, S.C. (2004), *The Economics of Self-Employed and Entrepreneurship*, Cambridge: Cambridge University Press.
Ross, Lee and Craig A. Anderson (1982), 'Shortcomings in the attribution process: on the origins and maintenance of erroneous social assessments', in Daniel Kahneman, Paul Slovic and Amos Tversky (eds), *Judgment under Uncertainty: Heuristics and Biases*, Cambridge: Cambridge University Press, pp. 129–52.
Rotter, J.B. (1971), 'External control and internal control', *Psychology Today*, **5**, 37–42, 58–9.
Savage, L.J. (1954), *The Foundations of Statistics*, New York: John Wiley & Sons.

Say, J. (1971), *A Treatise on Political Economy or the Production, Distribution and Consumption of Wealth*, New York: A.M. Kelley. (First published in 1803.)
Schumpeter, J. ([1911] 1934), *The Theory of Economic Development*, English trans. R. Opie, London: Oxford University Press, 1980.
Shapero, A. (1975), 'The displaced, uncomfortable entrepreneur', *Psychology Today*, **9** (6), 83–8.
Simon, Herbert A. (1955), 'A behavioral model of rational choice', *Quarterly Journal of Economics*, **69** (1), 99–118.
Simon, Herbert A. (1956), 'Rational choice and the structure of the environment', *Psychological Review*, **63** (2), 129–38.
Stewart, W.H and P.L. Roth (2001), 'Risk propensity differences between entrepreneurs and managers: a meta-analytic review', *Journal of Applied Psychology*, **86** (1), 145–53.
Stiglitz, J.E., and A. Weiss (1981), 'Credit rationing in markets with imperfect information', *American Economic Review*, **3**, 349–410.
Tversky, A. and D. Kahneman (1974), 'Judgement under uncertainty: heuristics and biaises', *Science*, September 1974, 185(4157), pp.1124–31.
Van Praag, C.M. (2006), *Successful Entrepreneurship: Confronting Economic Theory with Empirical Practice*, Cheltenham, UK and Northampton, MA, USA: Edward Elgar.
Van Praag, C.M., J. van der Sluis and Arjen van Wittelloostuijn (2004), 'The impact of the locus-of-control personality trait on the earnings of employees vis-à-vis entrepreneurs', Tinbergen Institute Discussion Paper No. TI 04-130/3, November.
Von Neumann, J. and O. Morgenstern (1944), *Theory of Games and Economic Behavior*, Princeton, NJ: Princeton University Press, 2nd edn 1947.
Wennekers, S. (2006), 'Entrepreneurship at country level: economic and non-economic determinants', Erasmus Research Institute of Management (ERIM), http://repub.eur.nl/publications/eco_man/erim/erim3/957613528/.

9 Entrepreneurial desirability

Yvon Gasse

Since entrepreneurship is above all a way of life and a lifestyle it is important to obtain a better understanding of the immediate factors that may influence its attractiveness or, even better, its desirability. Personal, social and cultural factors have a direct impact on the perceived desirability of a particular form of behaviour or action. Thus, when the community strongly values business creation, the result will be a positive perception of this activity among the people forming the community. Desirability includes two factors: first, the perception that the spin-offs of entrepreneurial behaviour will be personally desirable and the view that they will also be socially desirable. The most commonly observed elements in the community that may impact on desirability are described briefly below.

FAMILY AND FRIENDS

It seems that entrepreneurs usually come from families in which the parents or other members work in business or are self-employed; a number of studies indicates that this is the case for 50 per cent of entrepreneurs (Gasse and D'Amours, 2000). It may be thought that a young person growing up in a family or in surroundings like this will regard his or her parents or friends as models to be imitated. The same finding was made by Diochon and her colleagues (Diochon et al., 2001) in a Canadian study of entrepreneurs actively involved in business creation (nascent entrepreneurs), where 46 per cent of them had parents who were entrepreneurs or business owners.

IMMEDIATE ENVIRONMENT

According to Peter Drucker (1985), the emergence of an entrepreneurial economy is as much a cultural and psychological event as it is an economic and technological event. Thus, some societies, communities or groups adopt entrepreneurial values more easily than others. In Quebec, for example, the Beauce region has shown that, where there is a social network, a lack of job opportunities outside the area or in major organizations and a climate favourable to local investment, the latent cultural forces could be mobilized and furnish the values that underlie an entrepreneurial economy (Granmaison, 2000). Thus, Reynolds et al. (1994) found that the presence of several small and medium-sized enterprises (SMEs) in a given industry and an urban location had an impact on the creation of new businesses. These influences can also be found in a number of countries (the USA, France, the UK, Sweden, Germany and Italy).

LEVELS OF EDUCATION AND SKILL

Almost all the recent studies (Gasse and D'Amours, 2000) in Canada and elsewhere indicate that the level of education among entrepreneurs is higher than that in the population as a whole. This is particularly true of creators of high-technology businesses or those with high growth potential. Since these businesses base their competitive advantages on their founders' knowledge, good training is necessary. In a study of the management skills and practices of SME managers (Gasse, 1998), it can be seen that on average these managers had completed 13 years of education and that almost 75 per cent of them had attended university. The level of skill can determine personal effectiveness in performing required tasks. As a rule, perceptions of skill can strongly influence a person's view as to whether it is possible to master a particular situation. If this person views him or herself as skilled, then he or she will tend to consider an action such as the creation of a business to be feasible (Krueger, 2000).

PSYCHOLOGICAL PROFILE

The authors are generally agreed in recognizing that entrepreneurs usually display a great deal of motivation and perseverance in their efforts. They are capable of maintaining a high work pace for relatively lengthy periods. Idleness makes them tense and impatient. Entrepreneurs who establish businesses with strong growth potential embark on a process that demands their creativity and their complete and utter involvement. An entrepreneur who succeeds in launching a business shows a high level of determination and constancy in resolving various problems and difficulties encountered. He or she does not allow him or herself to be intimidated by complex situations. An entrepreneur is strongly convinced of and committed to his or her actions (Gasse and D'Amours, 2000). Several recent studies of nascent entrepreneurs (for example, Menzies et al., 2002) have confirmed the importance of psychological and social dynamics in the creation of new businesses. These people are seeking autonomy and independence, want to become their own bosses and take the initiative in order to achieve this.

SUMMARY

A typical entrepreneur has a deep need for personal achievement, he or she is self-confident, likes a moderate level of risk and is full of energy and motivation. It is certainly clear that these characteristics are not all found to a high degree in any entrepreneur in particular. Even though these dimensions combine to produce a total effect and may appear to complement one another, it is a fact that every human being is a complex creature with a unique personality. In order to be successful, it is not essential to have all these characteristics, although it is desirable to encourage their emergence and development in potential entrepreneurs (if it is felt that they have been identified among successful entrepreneurs). The combined effect of these characteristics may influence not only the desirability of being an entrepreneur but also the speed and intensity with which entrepreneurial initiatives are undertaken.

The experience and age of the founder when he or she is interested in launching a business also come into play. People of all ages venture into business but in Canada and the USA, approximately two-thirds of these individuals are between 25 and 40 years old when they start out (Reynolds, 1997). Those who are younger are often lacking in experience, contacts and financing, while those who are older are subject to family and professional constraints. In a recent study of nascent entrepreneurs in Canada (Gasse et al., 2002), we see that 57 per cent of them are between 25 and 44 years old and have up to ten years' experience in the field in which the new business will be active.

These observations indicate therefore that certain people are more likely to create businesses than others. Once again, this does not mean that those whose training and profile are different cannot establish a business or do not do so. However, certain backgrounds and characteristics seems to prepare individuals better for making a decision geared toward entrepreneurship when the opportunity arises, although the decision may also depend on other factors.

REFERENCES

Diochon, M., Y. Gasse, T.V. Menzies and D. Garand (2001), 'From conception to inception: initial findings from the Canadian study on entrepreneurial emergence', Proceedings of the Administrative Sciences Association of Canada, London, Ontario, 27–29 May, pp. 41–51.

Drucker, P.F. (1985), *Innovation and Entrepreneurship*, New York: Harper & Row.

Gasse, Y. (1998), 'Les compétences et les pratiques de gestion des dirigeants de PME', working paper, Centre d'Entrepreneuriat et de PME, Université Laval.

Gasse, Y. and A. D'Amours (2000), *Profession: Entrepreneur*, Montréal: Les Éditions Transcontinentales.

Gasse, Y., M. Diochon and T.V. Menzies (2002), 'Les entrepreneurs naissants et la poursuite de leur projet d'entreprise: une étude longitudinale', Actes du 6ième Congrès International Francophone de la PME, Montréal, Canada, 30 October.

Granmaison, J. (2000) *Les pionniers de l'entrepreneurship beauceron*, Québec: Les Éditions de la Fondation de l'Entrepreneurship.

Krueger, N. (2000), 'The cognitive infrastructure of opportunity emergence', *Entrepreneurship Theory and Practice*, **24**, 5–23.

Menzies, T.V., Y. Gasse, M. Diochon and D. Garand (2002), 'Nascent entrepreneurs in Canada: an empirical study', paper presented at the ICSB 47th World Conference, San Juan, Puerto Rico, June.

Reynolds, P. (1997), 'Who starts new firms?', *Small Business Economics*, **9**(1), 550–64.

Reynolds, P.D., D.J. Storey and P. Westhead (1994), 'Regional characteristics affecting entrepreneurship: a cross-national comparison', paper presented at the Frontiers of Entrepreneurship Research, Wellesley, MA.

10 Entrepreneurial orientation

Thomas H. Hawver and Jeffrey M. Pollack

Entrepreneurial orientation (EO), introduced in the literature by Khandwalla (1977), is defined as reflecting 'the organizational processes, methods, and styles that firms use to act entrepreneurially' (Lumpkin and Dess, 1996: 139). Originally this concept grew from research that centered on corporate entrepreneurship but has grown to include new, smaller firms. The majority of the research on EO has been conducted at the firm level in the hope of better predicting firm performance through strategic components of the firm. The interest stems from how the behavior of the firm coalesces with the specific marketplace and how the firm participates in activities designed for firm survival, renewal, or innovation (Covin and Slevin, 1986; Davidsson, 2007; Lumpkin and Dess, 1996).

For both new and existing firms, participating in activities to generate revenues is a crucial element for business survival. Activities such as new product development, product improvement and strategic planning all aid the survival and growth of businesses. Though these elements are common in most firms, the degree to which they are capitalized on varies from firm to firm. For example, a fast-food franchise may focus more on existing product improvement, while a firm entering the commercial printing industry may place their efforts in new product development. The mature firm, alternatively, in either of these industries may focus their efforts on strategic planning. Clearly, the efforts toward survival may differ depending on several factors such as industry and stage of growth, though all of these firms have a degree of entrepreneurial orientation.

The construct of EO is comprised of five dimensions: (1) autonomy, (2) innovativeness, (3) risk-taking, (4) proactiveness and (5) competitive aggressiveness (Lumpkin and Dess, 1996). Originally, Covin and Slevin (1986) proposed three dimensions (that is, proactiveness, innovativeness and risk-taking), and Lumpkin and Dess (1996) added two more (that is, autonomy and competitive aggressiveness). Autonomy and innovativeness illustrate the internal actions of the firm and their impact on individuals and teams within it. Specifically, the dimension of autonomy refers to the degree of freedom a team or individual has to work independently to put forward ideas and take actions necessary to make entrepreneurship occur. Whether within an existing firm or a new venture, autonomy becomes a necessary antecedent for any entrepreneurial activity to occur. Like autonomy, innovativeness must exist to some degree for entrepreneurship to occur. In terms of the EO dimension, innovativeness refers to the degree of support a team or individual receives from the firm to engage in activities that lead to novel ideas, products or services.

The remaining three dimensions reflect the external actions of a firm. The dimension of risk-taking has a less rigid definition than the other dimensions with respect to EO. While the definition of risk is often context specific, Lumpkin and Dess (1996: 144) define risk-taking as 'incurring heavy debt or making large resource commitments, in the interest of obtaining high returns by seizing opportunities in the marketplace'. In other words, the risk-taking dimension of EO refers to the frequency of behaviors of a firm with the intention of exploiting available resources for potential future gain. The proactiveness dimension of EO refers to a firm's behavior related to acting in anticipation of potential opportunities, changes, pitfalls, and 'seeking new opportunities which may or may not be related to the present line of operations, introduction of new products and brands ahead of competition, strategically eliminating operations which are in the mature or declining stages of life cycle' (Venkatraman, 1989: 949). Finally, competitive aggressiveness looks at the degree to which a firm attempts to outperform competitors within the same market. This dimension can be viewed as the effort a firm puts forth to enter a new market or to be the leader in an existing one.

The extant research on EO is substantial. Some of the more recent studies conducted on EO are highlighted in this section. Stam and Elfring (2008) found that the centrality of firms that did not have many bridging ties weakened the EO and performance relationship. Moreno and Casillas (2008) illustrated the complexity that exists in the relationship between EO and growth, strategy, environment and resources. Though the authors do not find a significant relationship between EO and firm growth, they do find that the higher the EO the more apt a firm is to use strategies targeted for expansion. Keh et al. (2007) found that EO affects how a firm acquires and utilizes marketing information. Contrary to Moreno and Casillas (2008), Keh et al. (2007) did find a direct relation between EO and firm performance (as measured by firm growth). Building on the finding that firms higher on EO perform better, Covin et al. (2006) found that higher EO had a positive effect on sales growth rate.

The majority of the research conducted on EO has been at the firm level, but other potential levels of analysis exist. Those levels, either side of the firm level, are the individual and the field level. At the field, or industry, level EO has examined the emergence of overall innovations that emerge (Reynolds et al., 2004). At the individual level, an increasing number of researchers have adapted the construct to study entrepreneurially oriented individuals. Around the world, roughly 10 per cent of people old enough to work are involved in entrepreneurship and recent estimates show that about 300 million people are involved in the venture creation process (Hisrich et al., 2007; Reynolds et al., 2004). Traditionally, these individuals are ignored within the literature because results regarding individual-level characteristics of entrepreneurs have been mixed and generally disappointing (for example, Begley and Boyd, 1987; Lumpkin and Dess, 1996; Sadler-Smith et al., 2003).

However, a growing literature exists that suggests entrepreneurs do think differently from everyone else and that individual-level cognitive processing research could be promising (for example, Baron, 1998). Additionally, there is a very small, but growing body of literature on entrepreneurs, emotions and responses to failures (for example, Goss, 2005a; 2005b; Cross and Travaglione, 2003; Shepherd, 2004). As the number of individual entrepreneurs grows it is becoming increasingly important to recognize that individual-level characteristics detailing how entrepreneurs think, feel and act are important to study. The common practice of studying EO at the firm level leaves a gap in the literature, and future research would be well served to explore how an individual's entrepreneurial orientation affects firm performance.

REFERENCES

Baron, R. (1998), 'Cognitive mechanisms in entrepreneurship: why and when entrepreneurs think differently than other people', *Journal of Business Venturing*, **13**, 275–94.

Begley, T.M. and D.P. Boyd (1987), 'Psychological characteristics associated with performance in entrepreneurial firms and small businesses', *Journal of Business Venturing*, **2**, 79–94.

Covin, J.G. and D.P. Slevin (1986), 'The development and testing of an organizational-level entrepreneurship scale', in R. Ronstadt, J.A Hornaday, R. Peterson and K.H. Vesper (eds), *Frontiers of Entrepreneurship Research 1986*, Wellesley, MA: Babson College, pp. 628–39.

Covin, J.G., K.M. Green and D.P. Slevin (2006), 'Strategic process effects on the entrepreneurial orientation-sales growth rate relationship', *Entrepreneurship Theory and Practice*, **20**, 57–81.

Cross, B. and A. Travaglione (2003), 'The untold story: is the entrepreneur of the 21st century defined by emotional intelligence?', *International Journal of Organizational Analysis*, **11**, 221–8.

Davidsson, P. (2007), 'Method challenges and opportunities in the psychological study of entrepreneurship', in J.R. Baum, M. Frese and R.A. Baron (eds), *The Psychology of Entrepreneurship*, Mahwah, NJ: Erlbaum, pp. 287–323.

Goss, D. (2005a), 'Entrepreneurship and "the social": towards a deference-emotion theory', *Human Relations*, **58**, 617–36.

Goss, D. (2005b), 'Schumpeter's legacy? Interaction and emotions in the sociology of entrepreneurship', *Entrepreneurship Theory and Practice*, **29**, 205–18.

Hisrich, R., J. Langan-Fox and S. Grant (2007), 'Entrepreneurship research and practice: a call to action for psychology', *American Psychologist*, **62**, 575–89.

Keh, H.T., T.T.M. Nguyen and H.P. Ng (2007), 'The effects of entrepreneurial orientation and marketing information on the performance of SMEs', *Journal of Business Venturing*, **22**, 592–611.

Khandwalla, P. (1977), *The Design of Organizations*, New York: Harcourt Brace Jovanovich.

Lumpkin, G.T. and G.G. Dess (1996), 'Clarifying the entrepreneurial orientation construct and linking it to performance', *Academy of Management Review*, **21**, 135–72.

Moreno, A.M. and J.C. Casillas (2008), 'Entrepreneurial orientation and growth of SMEs: a causal model', *Entrepreneurship Theory and Practice*, **32**, 507–28.

Reynolds, P.D., W.D. Bygrave and E. Autio (2004), *Global Entrepreneurship Monitor 2003 Executive Report*, Babson Park, MA: Babson College.

Sadler-Smith, E., Y. Hampson, A. Chaston and B. Badger (2003), 'Managerial behavior, entrepreneurial style, and small firm performance', *Journal of Small Business Management*, **41**, 47–67.

Shepherd, D.A. (2004), 'Educating entrepreneurship students about emotion and learning from failure', *Academy of Management Learning & Education*, **3**, 274–87.

Stam, W. and T. Elfring, (2008), 'Entrepreneurial orientation and new venture performance: the moderating role of intra- and extraindustry social capital', *Academy of Management Journal*, **51**, 97–111.

Venkatraman, N. (1989), 'Strategic orientation of business enterprises: the construct, dimensionality, and measurement', *Management Science*, **35**, 942–62.

11 Entrepreneurship education[1]

Alain Fayolle

1 INTRODUCTION

Entrepreneurship has become an important economic and social phenomenon as well as a popular research subject. It has also become an academic and teaching field, considering the fast-increasing number of universities worldwide which offer entrepreneurship programmes and courses. However, there is nothing further from the truth and numerous epistemological, theoretical, pedagogical and practical challenges remain. As previously stated by numerous researchers, there is no consensus regarding what entrepreneurship is. As a consequence, how could there be a consensus regarding what entrepreneurship stands for as a teaching subject? In this context, the objective of this chapter is to contribute to turn the current conceptual weaknesses into strengths. We aim at offering a generic 'teaching model', a coherent framework, in terms of perspectives, objectives, content and pedagogical methods, towards a renewed and more mature approach to entrepreneurship education. The basis of our approach is to accept the diversity of contexts, points of view, definitions and methods found in entrepreneurship courses and programmes, and to leverage them as opportunities for the participants. Such a framework should indeed be very helpful for entrepreneurship educators and teachers when designing entrepreneurship teaching programmes and fostering effective learning processes in entrepreneurship education.

As stated by researchers in entrepreneurship worldwide, the field is very young, emergent and in adolescence (or infancy) phase (Brazeal and Herbert, 1999; Low, 2001). Entrepreneurship as a human behaviour still seems somewhat mysterious and to a certain extent magical. Numerous researchers have stressed this lack of accepted paradigms or theories in entrepreneurship education (Béchard and Grégoire, 2005a; Fiet, 2000a; 2000b; Hills, 1988; Katz, 2003; Kuratko, 2005; McMullan and Long, 1990; Sexton and Bowman, 1984; Vesper, 1982).

As a consequence, old ideas and old questions come and go regarding entrepreneurship education.[2] For instance, a lot of politicians, practitioners and educators still believe that entrepreneurship education should only be concerned about the creation of new ventures and new jobs. The same people, inspired by the 'role model' school of thought, believe that entrepreneurs are always more credible and more effective that 'traditional' professors to teach entrepreneurship.

The most recurrent old question is probably: 'Can entrepreneurship be taught?' The idea of the 'born entrepreneur' has not totally disappeared (Cunningham and Lischeron, 1991) and is regularly revived by the media, the politicians and sometimes by the business world itself. Fiet (2000a: 2) stated that 'There is an ongoing debate in the entrepreneurship academy about whether we can actually teach students to become entrepreneurs'. Some people still argue that it is not possible to teach entrepreneurship. For them, entrepreneurship is a matter of personality and psychological characteristics. One of the arguments that has been advanced is that talent and temperament cannot be taught (Thompson, 2004). But one could argue that this is true for many professions and professional situations. Nobody will dispute the fact that medicine, law or engineering can be taught and yet there are doctors, lawyers and engineers who are talented and others who are not (Hindle, 2007). A similar argument can be made for entrepreneurship and entrepreneurs.

Hence we argue that there is no doubt that it is possible to educate people in entrepreneurship. However, as in any discipline, it is impossible to tell whether these professionals will be talented or not, just as it is impossible to guarantee a priori the success of many courses of action. Transmitting to entrepreneurs knowledge which is useful to better manage their development and overcome difficulties during the preparation and start-up phases of their project *is* teaching. Helping entrepreneurs to develop their aptitudes, attitudes and personality is less obvious (Fayolle, 1997). This analysis is confirmed in Peter Drucker's words quoted by Kuratko (2005: 580): 'It is becoming clear that entrepreneurship, or certain facets of it, can be taught. Business educators and professionals have evolved beyond the myth that entrepreneurs are born not made.' So, it is quite easy to argue that 'Can entrepreneurship be taught?' is no longer a relevant question.

We believe that old ideas and questions remain in entrepreneurship education because the main stakeholders, practitioners, politicians, researchers and educators tend to think and act in separated worlds, without strong and regular connections. As stated in particular by Davidsson (2003) and Fayolle (2004; 2007a), entrepreneurship is simultaneously an economic and social phenomenon, a research object and a subject of teaching. Bouchikhi (2003) shares the same view and states that entrepreneurship professors are at the crossroads of three spheres: public policy, business practice and academic community. Those three spheres work largely in isolation from each other and most entrepreneurship professors come from or are pulled into one sphere or another, so standing firmly at the centre of the network is difficult.

Old ideas and questions also remain in entrepreneurship education because numerous epistemological, theoretical, pedagogical and practical challenges do exist. As previously stated by numerous researchers, there is no consensus regarding what entrepreneurship is. As a consequence, how could there be a consensus regarding what entrepreneurship stands for as a teaching subject? Two articles (Katz, 2003; Kuratko, 2005) published in leading journals in the field propose, each in their own way, a comprehensive literature review of the subject aimed at defining the characteristics of this development as well as its main limitations and key challenges. As underlined by Béchard and Grégoire (2005a), entrepreneurship teaching activities remain in many cases closer to craft than science, driven by experience more than by systematic teaching approaches.

In this context, the objective of this chapter is to contribute to turn these conceptual and social weaknesses into strengths. We aim at offering a coherent framework, in terms of perspectives, objectives, content and pedagogical methods, towards a renewed and more mature approach to entrepreneurship education. Drawing from the literature in education sciences, we propose a 'teaching model' framework, developed both at the ontological and didactical levels. In particular, the question of the definition of entrepreneurship education is discussed and then the objectives, contents, pedagogical methods, evaluation issues useful in entrepreneurship courses and programmes are developed. Building upon the literature in education sciences, Béchard and Grégoire (2005b; 2007) have proposed and illustrated different teaching models in entrepreneurship. The concept of 'teaching model' is well known in education science (see, for instance, Anderson, 1995, or Joyce and Weil, 1996) but rarely used in the entrepreneurship field, where there are no common framework or agreed good practices regarding how to teach or educate (Brockhaus et al., 2001; Fiet, 2000a; 2000b). Quoting Legendre (1993), Béchard and Grégoire (2005b: 107) define a teaching model as 'the representation of a certain type of setting designed to deal with a pedagogical situation in function of particular goals and objectives, that integrates a theoretical framework justifying this design and giving it an exemplary character'. From these authors, 'the relevance of teaching models is that the concept focuses on the link connecting the conceptions that scholars and educators have about teaching and their actual teaching behaviour' (Béchard and Grégoire, 2005b: 108). In this light, the concept of a teaching model integrates a number of dimensions related to both the ontological and educational levels. In order to define our 'teaching model' for entrepreneurship education we will consequently discuss those two levels in two separate sections.

2 THE ONTOLOGICAL LEVEL OF A 'TEACHING MODEL' FOR ENTREPRENEURSHIP EDUCATION

The ontological level of the teaching model we propose includes two dimensions: on the one hand, an explicit definition and acknowledgement of what entrepreneurship is (and is not) as a teaching field and, on the other, a definition of what 'education' implies for educators and for students within the entrepreneurship context.

2.1 Definition of Entrepreneurship as a Teaching Field

For the vast majority of people, the idea or the concept of entrepreneurship is not clear. The word 'entrepreneurship' is polysemous: it may designate attitudes such as autonomy, creativity, innovation, risk-taking or the act of venture creation. In this light, entrepreneurship education can, for example, open people's minds and/or extend their knowledge.

Some recent works (Fayolle, 2007b; 2007c; Fayolle and Klandt, 2006a; 2006b), with contributions from leading international specialists on the questions and issues raised by entrepreneurship education, propose several definitions and new perspectives regarding entrepreneurship education. Fayolle and Klandt (2006b), for example, distinguish three areas of learning, related to mindsets (or culture), behaviours and situations.

The definitions used in the political and business spheres refer particularly to specific needs and objectives which can be integrated or addressed through teaching and educating initiatives. A recent work conducted by a European group of experts representing all European Union (EU) member countries proposed a common definition. A consensus was reached regarding the inclusion of two distinct elements:

- a broader concept of entrepreneurship education which should include the development of entrepreneurial attitudes and skills as well as personal qualities and which should not be directly focused on the creation of new ventures; and

- a more specific concept of new venture creation-oriented training (Commission Européenne, 2002).

As a refinement of this general distinction, Hindle (2007) proposes to articulate the definition of entrepreneurship education around that of the research object. In this light, if we define the field of entrepreneurship as the 'examination of how, by whom, and with what effects, opportunities to create future goods and services are discovered, evaluated and exploited' (Shane and Venkataraman, 2000: 120) then entrepreneurship education should be defined as 'knowledge transfer regarding how, by whom, and with what effects, opportunities to create future goods and services are discovered, evaluated and exploited' (Hindle, 2007). This definition echoes the works of some Austrian economists, notably Schumpeter's (1934) and Kirzner's (1979), those of March (1991) about the exploration and exploitation dimensions (respectively entrepreneurial and resource management functions), and those of Stevenson and Gumpert (1985). Existing knowledge may be transferred without major difficulties based on this first 'layer' of knowledge, but research based on this definition of the object should produce complementary transferable knowledge. In the same vein, and as they are identified by Davidsson et al. (2006), from others definitions of entrepreneurship proposed by researchers focusing on other aspects such as the pursuit of opportunities, the emergence processes or the creation of new enterprises (Bruyat and Julien, 2001; Gartner, 1988; Low and MacMillan, 1988; Stevenson and Jarillo, 1990),[3] different conceptions of entrepreneurship education could be derived.

The variety of possible definitions comes both from the coexistence of the various spheres which have interests in the field (academic, political and business) and from the diversity of approaches within each sphere. As stated previously it is important that these different spheres learn how to better communicate and understand each other (Bouchikhi, 2003).

In summary, there are various definitions of entrepreneurship that have been proposed in the context of entrepreneurship education, in various settings. This is not per se an issue, as long as one of those definitions is explicitly selected and considered when designing an entrepreneurship education programme. A major concern is therefore more the absence of a precise definition of entrepreneurship as a teaching field than the significant number of existing definitions. As in the words of Lewin: 'There is nothing as practical as a good definition'.[4]

2.2 Definition of Education in the Context of Entrepreneurship

Defining what entrepreneurship education is (as a generic notion) obliges one to refine at least the definitions of 'to teach' and 'to educate', as more precise and not substitutable notions.

> *To teach* – To impart knowledge or skill to; to provide knowledge of; instruct in; to condition to a certain action or frame of mind; to cause to learn by example or experience; [. . .]
>
> *To educate* – To develop the innate capacities of, especially by schooling or instruction; to stimulate or develop the mental or moral growth of; to develop or refine (one's taste or appreciation, for example). [. . .][5]

Table 11.1 Didactical and entrepreneurial models of learning

Didactical model	Entrepreneurial model
Teaching by the teacher exclusively	Mutual learning
Passive student, listener	Learning by doing
Learning by reading	Learning through interpersonal exchanges, debates and discussions
Learning through teacher's feedback	Learning through feedback from different and numerous people
Learning in a scheduled and organized environment	Learning in a flexible, informal environment
Learning without pressure of immediate objectives	Learning under pressure: objectives must be reached
Others' input is not encouraged	Learning by borrowing from others
Fear of mistakes and failure	Learning through trials and errors
Learning by taking notes	Learning by solving problems
Learning through a network of expert teachers	Learning through guided discovery

Source: Gibb (1993).

Given that entrepreneurship rather refers to individual initiative, creativity and sometimes innovation, it appears inadequate to favour the emergence of entrepreneurs or make a society more entrepreneurial by only giving lessons or 'imparting knowledge'. In the definition proposed above, teaching appears to imply a certain passivity from the learner. The word 'educate' seems therefore more appropriate. Indeed, entrepreneurship education relates to the evolution of learning processes and methods from a didactical mode towards an entrepreneurial mode, as demonstrated by Allan Gibb (1996). The main differences between both learning modes are presented in Table 11.1.

Hence teaching and educating have different meanings and do not necessarily meet the same objectives. The notion of education seems more appropriate to situations intended for developing learners' minds, raising people's awareness of the entrepreneurial phenomenon, giving them keys to their personal development and professional orientation, and giving them incentives to act entrepreneurially. The notion of 'teaching' appears more appropriate to contexts related to knowledge transfer of entrepreneurial themes and dimensions. Both notions of 'teaching' and 'educating' must therefore be combined in entrepreneurship courses and programmes. Opposing these two notions, separating them or favouring one at the expense of the other would no doubt be detrimental to the field.

Moreover, drawing mainly from Kember (1997), Ramsden (2003) and Robertson (1999), Grégoire and Béchard see educator's conceptions as 'conceptions that an educator has about a series of elements relevant to education' (Béchard and Grégoire, 2005b: 109). These conceptions relate to the meaning and focus of teaching, the knowledge to be taught and the roles of both teacher and students. Béchard and Grégoire (2005b) underline three different types of conceptions:

> *To teach is* a) to impart information; b) to ensure the appropriation of knowledge; c) to converse with the students about knowledge.

> *A teacher is* a) a presenter; b) a facilitator and tutor; c) a coach/developer.
> *Students are* a) passive recipients; b) participants; c) active participants in the co-construction of their knowledge.

The 'a' conceptions are relevant with an objectivist philosophical paradigm whereas the 'b' conceptions are in line with a subjectivist philosophical paradigm and the 'c' conceptions derive from an interactionist philosophical paradigm (Béchard and Grégoire, 2005b).

Clarifying their philosophical positions seems essential for entrepreneurship educators because as underlined by Merriam (1982: 90–91):[6]

> Philosophy contributes to professionalism. Having a philosophic orientation separates the professional educator from the paraprofessional in that professionals are aware of what they are doing and why they are doing it. A philosophy offers goals, values and attitudes to strive for. It thus can be motivating, inspiring, energizing to the practitioner.

Having outlined the two dimensions of our teaching model at the ontological level, we in the next section outline the various dimensions at the educational level.

3 THE EDUCATIONAL LEVEL OF A 'TEACHING MODEL' FOR ENTREPRENEURSHIP EDUCATION

Entrepreneurship education covers a wide variety of audiences, objectives, contents and pedagogical methods. The educational level relates to the design and the architecture of a programme around five specific interrelated questions:

- Why (objectives, goals)?
- What (contents, theories)?
- For whom (targets, audiences)?
- How (methods, pedagogies)?
- For which results (evaluation, assessment)?

In what follows, we expose and discuss the diversity of answers to those five questions that have been provided in the context of entrepreneurship education, following a basic framework derived from the sciences of education (Mialaret, 2005).

3.1 The 'Why' Dimension

The objectives and goals of entrepreneurship education should be connected to social needs. The sources of those needs are multiple and concern governments, institutions (such as universities, engineering and business schools, and public agencies), firms (large firms, small and medium-sized enterprises) and individuals (students, would-be entrepreneurs, and so on). Social expectations and benefits expected from entrepreneurship education are therefore multiple, implying a broad variety of goals relating to personal objectives or to socio-economic objectives (Fayolle, 2000). Those two dimensions are detailed hereafter.[7]

Personal objectives can relate to personal development, awareness and mindset, or culture. Entrepreneurship enables individuals to develop their talents and creativity, to realize their dreams, to acquire more independence and a certain feeling of freedom. Even if acting entrepreneurially is often difficult (many are called, but few are chosen), venture creation in itself implies a learning process which can be useful for the individual's personal development (Gibb, 2002). In this light, entrepreneurship education should aim at developing a taste for entrepreneurship in its broadest sense and stimulating a spirit of enterprise and value creation. Raising students' awareness may be done in different ways, by emphasizing what entrepreneurs bring to our economies and societies for example. Entrepreneurs' motivations, values and attitudes can also be presented and discussed, for example, through testimonies or case studies.

Moreover, entrepreneurship education can help students see in new venture creation a possible career option, develop in them positive and favourable attitudes towards entrepreneurial situations and go beyond the common binary point of view of civil servant versus. employee (Matlay and Mitra, 2002). Hence entrepreneurship education also entails proposing new career perspectives for part or all of one's professional life.

Finally the entrepreneur, as the central element of the entrepreneurial process, should be always in search of opportunities to organize and use appropriate resources in order to turn these opportunities into economic or social activities. In doing so, the entrepreneur activates the 'creative destruction' process, to borrow Schumpeter's imagery: he or she creates an enterprise which produces innovations which, in turn, will force existing companies to either adapt or disappear. The various levels of development and economic growth of different regions at a given point in time or of one single region over different periods of time can indeed be directly linked to the intensity of their entrepreneurial activity. Entrepreneurship education can therefore constitute an essential tool in developing the entrepreneurial culture of a region (Gray, 1998; Keats and Abercrombie, 1991). Beyond the development of an entrepreneurial spirit and taste for entrepreneurship, entrepreneurship education can also contribute to improve the image and highlight the role of entrepreneurs in society. This is all the more important since some regions, as is the case in France for instance, are not particularly open to such issues.

On the other hand, *socio-economic objectives* relate to the transmission of techniques, tools and ways to handle situations in order to increase the chances of new venture creation, survival and success. In this case the objectives are articulated around the transfer and development of knowledge, specific techniques and skills in order to increase the learners' entrepreneurial potential. The objective is therefore to prepare them to better think, analyse and act as entrepreneurs in specific situations and in various contexts. This can concern creation, takeover or intrapreneurship situations. Some of the themes that can be developed cover creativity and individual alertness, the capability to make judgements and take decisions regarding specific strategies, the ability to manage innovation and deal with the liabilities of newness or the ability to acquire and manage scarce resources such as intellectual property.

In particular, entrepreneurship education constitutes an excellent way to help people discover what business is, the way it works, to develop a systemic approach and to learn how to think of a firm in a more global and less compartmentalized perspective. It can, for example, help students or participants actually engaged in venture creation projects (prospective entrepreneurs, nascent or experienced) by facilitating individual learning processes, putting individuals in touch with potential partners, gaining access to and acquiring key resources, and, finally, providing coaching.

3.2 The 'What' Dimension

Drawing on Hindle's findings (2007) and Johannisson's levels of learning (1991), we can distinguish three main dimensions which orient and structure the contents of entrepreneurship education: the professional dimension, the spiritual dimension and the theoretical dimension.

The professional dimension of entrepreneurship education relates more specifically to practical knowledge, or know-how, and secondarily to theoretical knowledge. Specifically, this dimension relies on three kinds of knowledge:

- *Know-what*: what one has to do in order to decide and act in any given situation. For example, what one must do in order to create a technological company, to validate an opportunity, to conduct a market study, and so on.
- *Know-how*: how to deal with any given situation. For example, how to check the adequacy between a given project and one's personal profile taking into account accumulated experience, how to identify the risks and deal with them, and so on.
- *Know-who*: who are the useful people and which are the useful networks in a given context. For example, being able to identify the generic actors of new venture creation in the biotechnology sector, locating those who may be interested in or concerned by a project, identifying relevant venture capital agencies and business angels, and so on.

The spiritual dimension should enable individuals to position themselves in space and time as regards the entrepreneurial phenomenon. Positioning oneself in space consists in identifying the entrepreneurial situation(s) which are consistent with one's profile. Positioning oneself in time implies recognizing the moments in one's life when it is both possible and desirable to engage oneself in an entrepreneurial project. Contents should focus therefore mainly on two aspects:

- *Know-why*: what determines human behaviour and actions, entrepreneurs' attitudes, values and motivation. What leads ordinary human beings do what entrepreneurs do. Testimonies of entrepreneurs in various situations with varying degrees of performance may, along with debates with teachers and feedback, constitute appropriate and interesting modes of learning for this type of content.
- *Know-when*: when is the right time to go ahead? What is the best situation given my profile? Is this a good project for me? These are some of the key questions students are confronted with. Case studies, interviews with experts and professionals can constitute good ways to address these points.

Finally, *the theoretical dimension* relates to theories and scientific knowledge that is useful to understand the entrepreneurial phenomenon, completing and strengthening the contents related to the professional and spiritual dimensions. The contents taught along that dimension could concern the effects and impacts of entrepreneurship or any other question related to the phenomenon and process. Fiet (2000a) demonstrates the importance of the theoretical dimension of entrepreneurship education and underlines the need to use relevant theories in entrepreneurship classrooms.

3.3 The 'For Whom' Dimension

There are significant differences between courses intended, for example, for graduate management students and courses intended for students with a scientific, technical or literary background[8] or for teachers and PhD students. Similarly, teaching entrepreneurship to individuals who are strongly committed to their venture creation project, to professionals and other practitioners committed to the field of entrepreneurship or to students who have neither intention nor concrete project is very different in nature.

The variety of audiences of entrepreneurship education programmes therefore includes students with various socio-demographic characteristics and various levels of involvement and aspirations in the entrepreneurial process. It represents incontestably a source of difficult questions and raises problems regarding the design and implementation of entrepreneurship education.[9] Educators particularly in the design phase have to understand their audience and gather knowledge regarding the general psychological characteristics, the background and the social environment of the participants (Béchard and Grégoire, 2005b).

3.4 The 'How' Dimension

The teaching methods used in an entrepreneurship education programme relate to the 'how' question of our framework, which follows the 'why' (objectives) and the 'what' (contents). Although some teachers tend to overemphasize it, pedagogy is not per se an end. Pedagogy is a means to achieve objectives. As soon as objectives have been set and specific constraints have been identified, methods can be selected.

In the field of entrepreneurship education, there is a wide range of pedagogical methods, approaches and modalities which have been tested and used (Carrier, 2007; Hindle, 2007). Those include the use of real-life or virtual cases, role plays and problems, for example, through the elaboration or evaluation of business plans, the development of a new venture creation project or behavioural simulations and computer simulations. It might also involve traditional or interactive approaches, such as interviews with entrepreneurs or the guidance of young entrepreneurs through support missions to help them in their project. Those approaches can be supported by oral or multimedia communication tools such as videos or films. In entrepreneurship as in almost disciplines, the growing use of information and communication technologies (ICT) in particular tend to develop and offer to a certain extent more autonomous ways of learning, outside of the classroom and far from the more traditional and dependent methods of learning.

There appears to be no universal pedagogical recipe regarding how to teach entrepreneurship. The choice of techniques and modalities depends mainly on the objectives, contents and constraints imposed by the institutional context. 'Learning by doing', a good example of an active method which is often praised by teachers in the field, is well suited to some pedagogical situations, while it may be particularly inappropriate in others. The watchword here is to be cautious, especially when considering that little research has been conducted regarding the assessment of entrepreneurship education (Fayolle, 2005). It remains to be proved that a given pedagogical approach is better than another, which provides interesting challenges for researchers in the next few years.

3.5 The 'For Which Results' Dimension

The literature in education sciences highlights the fact that the evaluation question has to be risen as soon as a teaching programme is designed (Mialaret, 2005). So evaluation is a key dimension of the framework, of the same level of importance as the other dimensions. We learn from education sciences that at least six general approaches[10] to educational evaluation can be identified (Eseryel, 2002). Among them, goal-based and systems-based approaches are predominantly used in the evaluation of training (Phillips, 1991). For the former, the framework of Kirkpatrick (1959) remains the most influential and, for the latter, several models can be used such as the Context, Input, Process, Product model (Worthen and Sanders, 1987), the Training Validation System model (Fitz-Enz, 1994) and the Input, Process, Output, Outcome model (Bushnell, 1990).

Several researchers have underlined a deep lack of studies and research regarding the outcomes and effectiveness of entrepreneurship education (Garavan and O'Cinnéide, 1994a; 1994b; Hindle and Cutting, 2002; Honig, 2004). The issues and challenges regarding the assessment of entrepreneurship education programmes include the selection of evaluation criteria and their effective measurement.

The selection of evaluation criteria has to deal with the great diversity of objectives promoted by entrepreneurship teaching programmes (Gartner and Vesper, 1994). On top of this diversity, evaluation criteria can be related to specific knowledge, specific skills and tools, level of interest or awareness or intention, degree of participation in the classroom or motivation, and so on, based on what the programme's organisers want and are able to measure.

The effective measurement. As stated in the entrepreneurship literature, the measurement of the impact of an entrepreneurship education programme has to be considered as regards the effect of time and contextual variables. Block and Stumpf (1992) proposes a framework for measurement during, shortly after, between nil and five years after and over five years after participants have attended a programme, showing in each case the criteria which could be used. Regarding the contextual variables, numerous research (Fayolle et al., 2006a; 2006b; Krueger, 1993; Peterman and Kennedy, 2003; Tkachev and Kolvereid, 1999) have demonstrated the influence of personal and environmental factors such as the social status of entrepreneurial activities and situations, the parental role models, the prior entrepreneurial exposure or experience and, finally, the preference for a self-employment career.

4 CONCLUSION

As stated in numerous studies, entrepreneurship education is becoming increasingly more important everywhere in the world. At the same time research works in entrepreneurship are growing and getting increasing legitimacy within the scientific community. However, limited research addresses educational or pedagogical issues in the field of

Table 11.2 Key dimensions of teaching models for entrepreneurship education

Dimensions	Alternatives
Ontological dimensions	
Entrepreneurship	Broad concept (development of entrepreneurial attitudes and skills as well as personal qualities) or narrow concept (new venture creation) Focus on exploration and exploitation, the pursuit of opportunities, emergence processes, the creation of new enterprises, the dialogic individual/new value creation
Education	Didactical versus entrepreneurial models of learning Educator's philosophical paradigm (objectivist, subjectivist, interactionist)
Educational dimensions	
Why (objectives, goals)	Personal objectives (personal development, awareness and mindset, culture) Socio-economic objectives (transmitting techniques, tools regarding how to handle situations in order to increase the chances of new venture creation, survival or success)
What (contents, theories)	Professional dimension (know what, know how, know who) Spiritual dimension (know why, know when) Theoretical dimension
For whom (targets, audiences)	Socio-demographic segments (age, background, social categories, . . .) Level of involvement and aspirations (general population, prospective or experienced entrepreneurs)
How (methods, pedagogies)	Real-life versus virtual roles, cases and problems Traditional versus interactive approaches Oral versus multimedia communication tools
For which results (evaluation, assessment)	Educational evaluation approach (goal-based, system-based . . .) Selection and effective measurements of evaluation criteria

entrepreneurship. Only a few researchers are focusing their energy and resources on the sub-field of entrepreneurship education.

This situation is problematic and detrimental to entrepreneurship both as a research object and as a teaching domain. In this chapter we attempt to offer in entrepreneurship education a conceptual framework largely inspired by education sciences and a discussion around its two main levels, the ontological and educational levels. The various dimensions of our teaching model for entrepreneurship education are summarized in the Table 11.2.

The practical implications of this research concern mainly educators, trainers and teachers in the field of entrepreneurship. They suggest thinking from a new perspective the design of entrepreneurship teaching programmes. They also underline the fact that to make progress in entrepreneurship education practices it is necessary to acquire some knowledge coming from education sciences. It is useful for any educator or teacher in the conception phase of entrepreneurship teaching programmes to be more explicit about the teaching model he or she is using. To do that, one must clarify the ontological dimension by defining the teaching domain and highlighting the main conceptions as entrepreneurship educator. One also must think about and build around the key educational questions: 'Why?' objectives, 'What?' (contents), 'How?' (methods), 'For whom?' (targets, audiences) and 'For which?' results (evaluation).

The theoretical implications are mainly about the concept of a 'teaching model' in entrepreneurship education. It suggests that there is no successful entrepreneurship teaching programme without a good design strongly rooted in a scientific knowledge. This chapter is also bringing a theoretical contribution to this key notion. It proposes a general framework of a 'teaching model' in entrepreneurship. This framework is a bridge between education sciences and the field of entrepreneurship. It gives to entrepreneurship education its first scientific legitimacy. From our knowledge of entrepreneurship literature, only Béchard and Grégoire (2005b; 2007) have proposed such 'teaching models' in entrepreneurship but in a specific way. Our own approach is less specific and much more generic.

The practical and theoretical implications underline the importance and the interest for such topic. Numerous future research can be considered. Some could address research questions in relation to the notion of a 'teaching model' and its application in entrepreneurship. What are the main (the most used) configurations of a 'teaching model' in entrepreneurship? What are the most successful configurations of a 'teaching model' in entrepreneurship? Do educators use similar configurations to teach experts and entrepreneurs? Finally, entrepreneurship researchers interested in education issues could also explore other domains, other theories, other concepts of education sciences in order to feed the entrepreneurship field and help to formulate new questions or bring new answers.

NOTES

1. I would like to warmly thank my colleague Benoit Gailly from the université catholique de Louvain (Belgium) for his help at different steps of this work.
2. The notion of entrepreneurship education is, in this chapter, a generic notion which covers a wide diversity of learning and teaching situations and institutional settings.
3. To summarize the thoughts of these authors, entrepreneurship is 'The process of organising which leads to the creation of new organisations' (Gartner), 'The creation of new enterprise' (Low and MacMillan), 'The process by which individuals either on their own or inside organisations pursue opportunities without regard to the resources they currently control' (Stevenson and Jarillo) and 'The dialogic individual – new value creation in a change dynamic both for the individual and the concerned environment' (Bruyat and Julien).
4. Kurt Lewin exactly said: 'There is nothing practical as a good theory'.
5. *The American Heritage Dictionary of the English Language* (2000), 4th edn, Houghton Mifflin.
6. Cited in Hiemstra (1988).
7. But other categorizations are possible. For example, Kirby (2007) identifies the following goals for entrepreneurship education: 'For some, it is concerned with raising awareness of entrepreneurship – with teaching students *about* entrepreneurs and, in particular, their roles and functions in the economy and society (Carter and Jones-Evans, 2000; Glancey and McQuaid, 2000; Swedberg, 2000). For others it is more than this. For them it is about developing in their students the attributes of the successful entrepreneur (Kirby, 2003; Rae, 1997). This is education *for* enterprise. In contrast, others (perhaps a small minority) are more concerned with education *through* enterprise – with using the new venture creation process to help students acquire a range of both business understanding and transferable skills or competences.' We could add a fourth goal to Kirby's list, talking about education *in* an entrepreneurial environment.

8. See for instance Brand et al. (2007).
9. We can also teach children, adolescents, young adults, adults, seniors, and so on.
10. Goal-based evaluation, goal-free evaluation, responsive evaluation, systems evaluation, professional review and quasi-legal.

REFERENCES

Anderson, L.W., (1995), *International Encyclopaedia of Teaching and Teacher Education*, 2nd edn, Oxford: Pergamon Press.

Béchard, J.P. and D. Grégoire (2005a), 'Entrepreneurship education research revisited: the case of higher education', *Academy of Management, Learning & Education*, **4** (1), p.22–43.

Béchard, J.P. and D. Grégoire (2005b), 'Understanding teaching models in entrepreneurship for higher education', in P. Kÿro and C. Carrier (eds), *The Dynamics of Learning Entrepreneurship in a Cross-Cultural University Context*, Tampere: University of Tampere, Faculty of Education, pp.104–34.

Béchard, J.P. and D. Grégoire (2007), 'Archetypes of pedagogical innovation for entrepreneurship education: model and illustrations', in A. Fayolle (ed.) *Handbook of Research in Entrepreneurship Education*, vol 1, Cheltenham, UK and Northampton, MA, USA: Edward Elgar Publishing.

Block, Z. and S.A. Stumpf (1992), 'Entrepreneurship education research: experience and challenge', in D.L. Sexton and J.M. Kasarda (eds), *The State of the Art of Entrepreneurship*, Boston, MA: PWS-Kent, pp. 17–45.

Bouchikhi, H. (2003), 'Entrepreneurship professors and their constituencies: manifesto for a plural professional identity', IntEnt Conference 2003, Grenoble, 5–7 September.

Brand, M., I. Wakkee and M. Van Der Veen (2007), 'Teaching entrepreneurship to non-business students: insights from two Dutch universities', in A. Fayolle (ed.), *Handbook of Research in Entrepreneurship Education*, vol 2, Cheltenham, UK and Northampton, MA, USA: Edward Elgar Publishing.

Brazeal, D.V. and T.T. Herbert (1999), 'The genesis of entrepreneurship', *Entrepreneurship Theory and Practice*, **23** (3) 29–45.

Brockhaus, R.H., G.E. Hills, H. Klandt and H.P. Welsch (2001), *Entrepreneurship Education: A Global View*, Aldershot: Ashgate.

Bruyat, C. and P.A. Julien (2001), 'Defining the field of research in entrepreneurship', *Journal of Business Venturing*, **16** (2), 165–80.

Bushnell, D.S. (1990), 'Input, process, output: a model for evaluating training', *Training and Development Journal*, **44** (7), 41–3.

Carrier, C. (2007), 'Strategies for teaching entrepreneurship: what else beyond lectures, case studies and business plan?', in A. Fayolle (ed.), *Handbook of Research in Entrepreneurship Education*, vol. 1, Cheltenham, UK and Northampton, MA, USA: Edward Elgar Publishing.

Carter, S. and D. Jones-Evans (2000), *Enterprise and Small Business: Principles, Practice and Policy*. Harlow: Prentice Hall.

Commission Européenne (2002), 'Making progress in promoting entrepreneurial attitudes and skills through primary and secondary education', report from the expert group on entrepreneurship education.

Cunningham, J.B. and J. Lischeron (1991), 'Defining entrepreneurship', *Journal of Small Business Management*, **29** (1), 45–61.

Davidsson, P. (2003), 'The domain of entrepreneurship research: some suggestions', in J. Katz and S. Shepherd (eds), *Cognitive Approaches to Entrepreneurship Research – Advances in Entrepreneurship, Firm Emergence and Growth*, vol. 6, Maryland Heights, MO: Elsevier Science, pp. 315–72.

Davidsson, P., F. Delmar and J. Wicklund (2006), *Entrepreneurship and the Growth of the Firms*, Cheltenham, UK and Northampton, MA, USA: Edward Elgar Publishing.

Eseryel, D. (2002), 'Approaches to evaluation of training: theory & practice', *Educational Technology & Society*, **5** (2), 93–8.

Fayolle, A., (1997), 'L'enseignement de l'entrepreneuriat: réflexions autour d'une expérience', *Cahiers de recherche, EM Lyon*, no. 9705.

Fayolle, A. (2000), 'L'enseignement de l'entrepreneuriat dans le système éducatif supérieur français: un regard sur la situation actuelle', *Revue Gestion 2000*, mars-avril, 133–54.

Fayolle, A. (2004), 'Entrepreneuriat, de quoi parlons-nous?', *L'Expansion Management Review*, no. 114, Septembre, 67–74.

Fayolle, A. (2005), 'Evaluation of entrepreneurship education: behaviour performing or intention increasing', *International Journal of Entrepreneurship and Small Business*, **2** (1), 89–98.

Fayolle, A. (2007a) *Entrepreneurial Process Dynamics*, Cambridge: Cambridge University Press.

Fayolle, A. (2007b) *Handbook of Research in Entrepreneurship Education – A General Perspective*, vol. 1, Cheltenham, UK and Northampton, MA, USA: Edward Elgar Publishing.
Fayolle, A. (2007c) *Handbook of Research in Entrepreneurship Education – A Contextual Perspective*, vol. 2, Cheltenham, UK and Northampton, MA, USA: Edward Elgar Publishing.
Fayolle, A. and H. Klandt (2006a), *International Entrepreneurship Education. Issues and Newness*, Cheltenham, UK and Northampton, MA, USA: Edward Elgar Publishing.
Fayolle, A. and H. Klandt (2006b), 'Issues and newness in the field of entrepreneurship education: new lenses for new practical and academic questions', in A. Fayolle and H. Klandt (eds), *International Entrepreneurship Education*, Cheltenham UK and Northampton, MA, USA: Edward Elgar Publishing, pp. 1–17.
Fayolle, A., B. Gailly and N. Lassas-Clerc (2006a), 'Effect and counter-effect of entrepreneurship education and social context on student's intentions', *Estudios de Economica Applicada*, **24**, 509–23.
Fayolle, A., B. Gailly and N. Lassas-Clerc (2006b), 'Assessing the impact of entrepreneurship education programmes: a new methodology', *Journal of European Industrial Training*, **30** (9), 701–20.
Fiet, J.O. (2000a), 'The theoretical side of teaching entrepreneurship', *Journal of Business Venturing*, **16** (1), 1–24.
Fiet, J.O. (2000b), 'The pedagogical side of teaching entrepreneurship', *Journal of Business Venturing*, **16** (2), 1–17.
Fitz-Enz, J. (1994), 'Yes . . . you can weigh training's value', *Training*, **31** (7), 54–8.
Garavan, T. and B. O'Cinnéide (1994a), 'Entrepreneurship education and training programmes: a review and evaluation', *Journal of European Industrial Training*, part I, **18** (8), 3–12.
Garavan, T. and B. O'Cinnéide (1994b), 'Entrepreneurship education and training programmes: a review and evaluation', *Journal of European Industrial Training*, part II, **18** (11), 13–21.
Gartner, W.B. (1988), 'Who is an entrepreneur? Is the wrong question', *American Journal of Small Business*, **12** (2), 11–31.
Gartner, W.B. and K.H. Vesper (1994), 'Experiments in entrepreneurship education: successes and failures', *Journal of Business Venturing*, **9** (2), 179–87.
Gibb, A.A. (1993), 'The enterprise culture and education. Understanding enterprise education and its links with small business, entrepreneurship and wider educational goals', *International Small Business Journal*, **11** (3), 11–37.
Gibb, A.A. (1996), 'Entrepreneurship and small business management: can we afford to neglect them in the twenty-first century business school?', *British Journal of Management*, **7** (4), 309–24.
Gibb, A.A. (2002), 'In pursuit of a new enterprise and entrepreneurship paradigm for learning: creative destruction, new values, new ways of doing things and new combinations of knowledge', *International Journal of Management Reviews*, **4** (3), 233–69.
Glancey, K.S. and R.W. McQuaid (2000), *Entrepreneurial Economics*, London: macMillan.
Gray, C. (1998), *Enterprise and Culture*, London: Routledge.
Hiemstra, R. (1988), 'Translating personal values and philosophy into practical actions', in R.G. Brockett (ed.), *Ethical Issues in Adult Education*, New York: Teachers College, Columbia University.
Hills, G.E. (1988), 'Variations in university entrepreneurship education: an empirical study in an evolving field', *Journal of Business Venturing*, **3**, 109–22.
Hindle, K. (2007), 'Teaching entrepreneurship at the university: from the wrong building to the right philosophy', in A. Fayolle (ed.), *Handbook of Research in Entrepreneurship Education*, vol. 1 Cheltenham, UK and Northampton, MA, USA: Edward Elgar Publishing.
Hindle, K. and N. Cutting (2002), 'Can applied entrepreneurship education enhance job satisfaction and financial performance? An empirical investigation in the Australian pharmacy profession', *Journal of Small Business Management*, **40** (2), 162–7.
Honig, B. (2004), 'Contingency model of business planning', *Academy of Management Learning and Education*, **3** (3), 258–73.
Johannisson, B. (1991), 'University training for entrepreneurship: a Swedish approach', *Entrepreneurship and Regional Development*, **3** (1), 67–82.
Joyce, B.R. and M. Weil (1996), *Models of Teaching*, 5th edn., Boston, MA: Allyn and Bacon.
Katz, J.A. (2003), 'The chronology and intellectual trajectory of American entrepreneurship education', *Journal of Business Venturing*, **18** (3), 283–300.
Keats, R. and N. Abercrombie (1991), *Enterprise Culture*, London: Routledge.
Kember, D. (1997), 'A reconceptualization of the research into university academics' conceptions of teaching', *Learning and Instruction*, **7** (3), 255–75.
Kirby, D.A. (2003) *Entrepreneurship.* Maidenhead: McGraw-Hill.
Kirby, D.A. (2007), 'Changing the entrepreneurship education paradigim', in A. Fayolle (ed.), *Handbook of Research in Entrepreneurship Education*, vol 1 Cheltenham, UK and Northampton, MA, USA: Edward Elgar Publishing.
Kirkpatrick, D.L. (1959), 'Techniques for evaluating training programs', *Journal of the American Society of Training Directors*, **13**, 3–26.

Kirzner, I.M. (1979), *Perception, Opportunities and Profit*, Chicago, IL: University of Chicago Press.
Krueger, N.F. (1993), 'The impact of prior entrepreneurial exposure on perceptions of new venture feasibility and desirability', *Entrepreneurship Theory and Practice*, Fall, 5–21.
Kuratko, D.F. (2005), 'The emergence of entrepreneurship education: development, trends and challenges', *Entrepreneurship Theory and Practice*, September, 577–97.
Legendre, R. (1993), *Dictionnaire Actuel de l'Education*, 2nd edn, Montréal: Guérin.
Low, M.B. (2001), 'The adolescence of entrepreneurship research: specification of purpose', *Entrepreneurship Theory and Practice*, **25** (4), 17–26.
Low, M.B. and I.C. MacMillan (1988), 'Entrepreneurship: past research and future challenges', *Journal of Management*, **14** (2), 139–61.
March, J.G. (1991), 'Exploration and exploitation in organisational learning', *Organization Science*, **2** (1), 71–87.
Matlay, H. and J. Mitra (2002), 'Entrepreneurship and learning: the double act in triple helix', *International Journal of Entrepreneurship and Innovation*, **3** (1), 7–16.
McMullan, W.E. and W.A. Long (1990), *Developing New Ventures: The Entrepreneurial Option*, New York: Harcourt Brace Jovanovitch.
Mialaret, G. (2005), *Les sciences de l'éducation*, 10th edn, Paris: PUF.
Peterman, N.E. and J. Kennedy (2003), 'Enterprise education: perceptions of entrepreneurship', *Entrepreneurship Theory and Practice*, **28** (2), 129–44.
Phillips, J.J. (1991), *Handbook of Training Evaluation and Measurement Methods*, 2nd edn, Houston, TX: Gulf.
Rae, D.M. (1997), 'Teaching entrepreneurship in Asia: impact of a pedagogical innovation', *Entrepreneurship, Innovation and Change*, **6** (3), 193–227.
Ramsden, P. (2003), *Learning to Teach in Higher Education*, 2nd edn, London: Routledge.
Robertson, D.L. (1999), 'Professors perspectives on their teaching: a new construct and developmental model', *Innovative Higher Education*, **23** (4), 271–94.
Schumpeter, J.A. (1934), *The Theory of Economic Development*, Cambridge, MA: Harvard University Press.
Sexton, D.L. and N.B. Bowman (1984), 'Entrepreneurship education suggestions for increasing effectiveness', *Journal of Small Business Management*, **22** (2), 18–25.
Shane, S. and S. Venkataraman (2000), 'The promise of entrepreneurship as a field of research', *Academy of Management Review*, **25** (1), 217–26.
Stevenson, H.H. and D.E. Gumpert (1985), 'The heart of entrepreneurship', *Harvard Business Review*, March–April, 85–92.
Stevenson H.H. and J.C. Jarillo (1990), 'A paradigm of entrepreneurship: entrepreneurial management', *Strategic Management Journal*, **11**, 17–27.
Swedberg, R. (2000), *Entrepreneurship: The Social Science View*, Oxford: Oxford University Press.
Tkachev, A. and L. Kolvereid (1999), ' Self-employment intentions among Russian students', *Enterpreneurship & Regional Development*, **11** (3), 269–80.
Thompson, J.L. (2004), 'The facets of the entrepreneur: identifying entrepreneurial potential', *Management Decision*, **42** (2), 243–58.
Vesper, K.H. (1982), 'Research on education in entrepreneurship', in C.A. Kent, D.L. Sexton and K.H. Vesper (eds), *Encyclopedia of Entrepreneurship*, New York: Prentice Hall, pp. 321–43.
Worthen, B.R. and J.R. Sanders (1987), *Educational Evaluation*, New York: Longman.

12 Entrepreneurship in the ethnic ownership economy

Ivan H. Light

The ethnic ownership economy encompasses self-employed people, their unpaid family workers, and their co-ethnic employees. The ethnic ownership economy has three sectors: formal, informal and illegal. Access to these sectors importantly depends upon prior access to four capital resources: financial capital, social capital, human capital and cultural capital. In turn, young people obtain access to these economic resources through the class system and/or through the ethnic/religious groups to which they belong. The resources obtained influence the extent to which young people enter the formal, informal or informal sector of their group's ethnic ownership economy. Middleman minorities are well endowed in these resources so their self-employment rates are recurrently high.

Although descended from middleman minority theory, which Max Weber (1981: ch. 16C) initiated, the ethnic economy literature now more broadly addresses the economic independence of immigrants and ethnic minorities in general, not just of middleman minorities. This expansion releases the ethnic economy from narrow focus upon historical trading minorities, and opens a discussion of the entire range of immigrant and ethnic minority self-help and self-defense through business ownership. Business ownership represents a ubiquitous self-defense of immigrants and ethnic minorities, but especially of any who confront disadvantage in labor markets. Business ownership permits immigrants and ethnic minorities to reduce their employment disadvantage, renegotiating their participation in the general labor market from a position of greater strength. Unable to find work in the general labor market, or unwilling to accept the work that the general labor market offers, or just reluctant to mix with foreigners, immigrants and ethnic minorities have the option of self-employment in the ethnic economy of their group or of working for a co-ethnic. Although ethnic and immigrant groups differ in how well and how much they avail themselves of independent business, none ever lacks an ethnic economy.

Light and Karageorgis (1994: 648) defined an ethnic economy as, 'the ethnic self-employed and employers, their unpaid family workers, and their co-ethnic employees'. Somewhat later, this definition of ethnic economy became the *ethnic ownership economy*, now only a co-equal *component* of an ethnic economy, not the whole of it. As currently understood, an *ethnic economy* consists of two sectors: the ethnic-controlled economy and the ethnic ownership economy (Light, 2005; Light and Gold, 2000).[1] An *ethnic ownership economy* is still defined by business ownership. As before, an ethnic ownership economy still includes the self-employed, their unpaid family workers and co-ethnic employees. In contrast, an *ethnic-controlled economy* requires ethnic control, not ownership, and addresses employees who collectively influence hiring and wages in their workplaces. Such employees may *control* a business without actually owning it. This chapter is not about the ethnic-controlled economy. Rather, it explores how members of ethnic minorities become entrepreneurs in the ethnic ownership economy of their group.

Ethnic ownership economies have three sectors: formal, informal and illegal

Table 12.1 Ethnic ownership economy and sectors

Sector	Ethnic ownership economy		
	Formal	Informal	Illegal
	1	2	3

Examples
1 Owners of dry-cleaning retail store, their unpaid family workers, and their co-ethnic employees
2 Owners of unlicensed garment factory, their unpaid family workers and their co-ethnic employees
3 Owners of illegal lottery, their unpaid family workers, and their co-ethnic employees

Source: Light (2005: 652).

(Table 12.1). The formal sector consists of ethnic or immigrant-owned firms that pay taxes and are enumerated by public authorities. If co-ethnics own these firms, then both the owners and their co-ethnic employees work in the formal sector of the ethnic ownership economy. The ethnic ownership economy's informal sector contains ethnic minority or immigrant owned firms that, producing legal commodities, produce them without paying taxes and/or obtaining requisite licenses. The size of the ethnic economy's informal sector is hard to measure so research studies often ignore it. If the existence of informal sectors is not recognized, awareness will be restricted to the formal sector, resulting in underestimation of the extent of ethnic minority or immigrant self-employment. The illegal sector of an ethnic ownership economy consists of co-ethnic-owned firms that produce illegal goods and services such as narcotic drugs, prostitution and gambling. The illegal sector does not include predatory crimes that yield victims rather than customers. The illegal sector is usually relegated to criminologists as if the pariah sector existed in shameful isolation. This treatment obscures the organic relationship of the illegal sector to the other two sectors of the ethnic ownership economy. The result is underestimation of immigrant and ethnic minority employment and economic influence, and mystification of the movements of personnel and capital between and among the sectors (Nee et al., 1994).

Whether employees or owners, all co-ethnics working in any ethnic ownership sector belong to the ethnic economy of their group. The size of ethnic economies varies historically and among ethno-cultural groups (Fairlie and Meyer, 1996; Li, 2001). Sometimes most co-ethnics find employment in the ethnic ownership economy; sometimes, few do. Sometimes ethnic minorities and immigrants congregate most heavily in the formal sector, sometimes in the informal and sometimes in the illegal. Mapping the absolute and relative size and distribution of ethnic ownership sectors is of great importance to understanding the economic prospects of immigrants and ethnic minorities as well as to making intelligent policy choices. As matters stand, however, only the ethnic ownership economies of the formal sector can be estimated from official data sources. Ethnic ownership economies in the informal sector and the illegal sector are inaccessible from official sources, and must be estimated from social science research (Fairlie, 1999). Accordingly, just improving and debating the adequacy of size estimates is a continuing methodological concern of research in this area.

As one result, researchers have developed quantitative methods that permit them to estimate the size of ethnic ownership economies from public data sources. These methodologies permit analysts to estimate the size and sectoral distribution of ethnic ownership economies of a multiplicity of ethnoracial groups in multiple locations whereas previous methodology relied upon case studies of one group in a single location. Estimates indicate that ethnic ownership economies are surprisingly large. Light and Gold (2000: 34) found that just the formal sector's ethnic ownership economies contained 11 per cent of the labor force of all foreign born persons in 1990. They estimated that 10 per cent of the average American ethnic group's workers found employment in the informal sector of the ethnic ownership economy; using somewhat different definitions. Of course, constituent groups had higher and lower ethnic ownership economies than the statistical average. Among Hispanics, the percentage was 9.9 per cent; among African Americans, 5.6 per cent; Asians, 19.2 per cent and Koreans more than 50 per cent. Specific groups fall above and below this average, which also varies from city to city and country to country. In the most comprehensive and serious effort to measure informal sector self-employment using a case study, Tienda and Raijman (2000) found that 38 per cent of Mexican immigrant households in Chicago worked in the informal economy. Adding the informal and formal sectors, Light and Gold (2000: 52) estimated that about 20 per cent of the average ethno racial group works in ethnic ownership economies.

SINGLE AND DOUBLE DISADVANTAGE

Immigrant and ethnic minority workers often turn to self-employment because of disadvantage in the labor force. Unable to find a job, they start their own business. Disadvantage increases self-employment in the informal and illegal as well as in the formal sector of the ethnic ownership economy. Racial, ethnic and religious discrimination are major causes of disadvantage, but lack of language skill and unaccredited human capital are also important. Disadvantage is not a simple or unitary concept. Current thinking distinguishes labor market disadvantage from resource disadvantage. *Labor market disadvantage* occurs when workers cannot obtain wage or salary employment that reaches the prevailing market return on their productivity (Light and Rosenstein, 1995: 153–5). The most extreme labor market disadvantage is long-term unemployment, which one expects to last forever. In such a case, all earnings prospects depend on self-employment. Groups experience *resource disadvantage* when, as a result of some current or past historical experience, such as slavery or peonage, members enter the labor market with fewer resources than others. Resources include all attributes that improve the productivity of employees, notably human capital, but also social capital, cultural capital and financial capital (Jenssen, 2001; Morris, 2001). Even if resource-disadvantaged employees earn the expected wage, fully equivalent to what equivalently disadvantaged non-co-ethnics earn, their wages will be low because resource-disadvantaged workers exhibit low productivity. Less productive workers receive lower pay than more productive workers. In this case, they experience only one disadvantage, resource disadvantage. They are singly disadvantaged.

However, when labor force disadvantage and resource disadvantage combine, those subjected to discrimination in the labor market are low-productivity employees as well. Because subject to discrimination *and* being less productive, the doubly disadvantaged typically lack the human, cultural, social and financial capital that support self-employment in the formal sector. As a result, their multiple disadvantages impel the doubly disadvantaged into the ethnic economy's informal or illegal sectors. These sectors do not require the same abundance or type of resources, as does the formal sector. On the other hand, when immigrants or ethnic minorities have strong resources of human, social, cultural and financial capital, and when they suffer only discrimination in the labor force, the disadvantaged have resources that empower their self-employment in the formal sector. Subjected to disadvantage in the labor force, they turn easily to self-employment in the formal sector, thus tending to mitigate or even overcome their earnings disadvantage in the labor market.

This *resource constraint version* of disadvantage theory explains puzzling anomalies that arise from the highly unequal rates of self-employment among immigrants and ethnic minorities. The basic conundrum has been to explain unequal rates and unequal sectoral distribution of self-employment among disadvantaged groups. Why do some preponderate in the formal sector whereas others preponderate in the informal or illegal sectors? Resource constraint theory proposes that doubly disadvantaged groups usually have the expected motive to undertake self-employment in the formal sector, but they *lack appropriate* capital resources. They want to start their own business, but they do not know how, and would lack the other resources even if they did know how. As a result, the self-employment of the doubly disadvantaged develops in the informal sector or in the illegal sector rather than in the formal sector. The formal sector requires the most resources of the kind the doubly disadvantaged least command. Conversely, well-educated and affluent groups have the capital resources to undertake self-employment in the formal sector when they face disadvantage in the labor market.

By treating the formal, the informal, and the illegal sectors as organic parts of the same ethnic ownership economy, the ethnic economy literature exposes movements of personnel and money among the sectors. These movements signal changes in the social location of ethnic groups. When successful in the informal sector, immigrant and ethnic minority firms and their owners may migrate into the formal sector. In these cases, business owners who were initially doubly disadvantaged, and who went to work in the informal sector, overcome their initial disadvantage. By working in the informal sector, the doubly disadvantaged *acquired new capital resources* that fueled their transition from informal to formal sector business ownership and from social marginality to respectability. The same progression can take initially disadvantaged immigrants and ethnic minorities out of illegal business into the legal sectors. The transition of American Chinatowns from sordid vice districts in the nineteenth century to tourist attractions in the twentieth century reflects this kind of transition. So does the Cinderella story of racketeer capital invested in Las Vegas thanks to which a generation of Jewish and Italian American gangsters became respectable business owners.

Of course, if the frequency of life history transitions from informal sector to formal sector or from illegal sector to formal sector were much higher than it is, the frequent transitions would wipe out any association between ethno-racial origins and the preponderant sector of entrepreneurship. Starting in the informal sector or in the illegal sector would not reduce anyone's likelihood of winding up in the formal sector. Conversely, entrepreneurs who started in the formal sector, like Donald Trump, would frequently wind up as lunch-stand operators. In fact, these inter-sectoral transitions are infrequent. The advantaged hang on to their advantages, and the disadvantaged hang onto their disadvantages. Among the disadvantaged, those doubly disadvantaged preponderantly occupy the informal and illegal sector while those only labor market disadvantaged occupy the formal sector. This association shows that double disadvantage is only infrequently overcome by entrepreneurial success. That said, when disadvantage is overcome, and graduation to the formal sector is achieved on a wholesale basis, then an ethnic group has improved its social position.

FOUR CAPITAL RESOURCES

The ethnic economy literature has clarified and classified the resources people actually use to start and operate business firms as well as the social sources of these resources (Morris, 2001). Current thinking identifies four resources that emanate from two locations in the social order. The four resources are all different forms of capital, which is defined narrowly as any resource hoard that facilitates entrepreneurship (Johannisson, 2000; Sequeira and Rasheed, 2004). Obviously, financial capital accomplishes this goal, and, in the past, financial capital was regarded as the key resource. Currently, researchers add three other forms of capital to this list while retaining financial capital. The other three are human capital, social capital and cultural capital. Human capital refers to skills acquired in classrooms and on the job. Since the acquisition of these skills requires that their owner invest time and money in learning them, the ownership of hard skills represents an investment in personal productivity. Students invest in the expectation of long-run gain. For example, a four-year college degree now costs more than $100 000, but the college graduate has skills that render him or her more productive and, therefore, able to command a higher salary. Since the self-employed as a group have more years of education than do wage and salary workers as a group, human capital appears empirically to contribute to self-employment.

Social capital means access to formal and informal social networks that facilitate and support entrepreneurship (Rušinović, 2006: ch. 4). Weak and strong social ties to others constitute these networks. The strength or weakness of a social tie depends upon its intensity and duration. Networks are a scarce resource that requires effort to build and maintain. Participants must invest time, energy and money in building and maintaining their social network. That done, their social network yields vocationally relevant information and help. Strong social ties yield help; weak social ties yield information so both strong and weak ties are desirable components of entrepreneurial networks. Help means loans of money and equipment, referrals, preferential buying, selling, and servicing, memberships and the like. Information includes technical assistance, timely advice, market tips, gossip, news, email and so forth. Entrepreneurs' networks work best when social relationships are reciprocal. Reciprocal relationships are those in which the firm expectation exists that a favor done will be reciprocated. Reciprocal relationships require trust. For example, if Joe has a computer and Ann has a truck, Joe can borrow Ann's truck today because Ann believes that when she needs a computer later, Joe will return her favor. Ann exhibits a trust-based expectation of reciprocity that, when present, enables both Joe and Ann to avoid having to buy or rent infrequently used capital equipment. Lacking comparable reciprocity, Joe's and Ann's competitors must rent computers and trucks, and the rental cost will increase the price of their commodity. Similarly, social capital can be embodied or hidden in other forms of capital.

Cultural capital is the fourth form of entrepreneurial capital (Light, 2004). Cultural capital refers to aptitudes, interests, beliefs, habits, lifestyles and customs that facilitate entrepreneurship. Much cultural capital is inherited or passed down in the course of primary socialization to adulthood; some is acquired. Max Weber's (1958) celebrated theory of the Protestant work ethic exemplifies and illustrates cultural capital. As is very well known, Weber taught that the Protestant Reformation of the sixteenth century encouraged traditional European peasants to save their money and work harder than their parents had been accustomed to doing. Early modern Protestants valued hard work, punctuality, thrift and temperance a lot more than Catholics. These traits still support entrepreneurship, and all such vocationally relevant character traits (as well as social institutions such as the family) are still cultural in origin whether they emanate from Protestantism or from some other ethno-religious tradition. For reasons like this, cultural capital supports the entrepreneurship of those who have the most and the right kind.

SOURCES OF ENTREPRENEURIAL CAPITAL

Where do entrepreneurs acquire capital resources? The ethnic economy literature does not investigate individual differences in personality as a source of motives or capabilities. This is a valid inquiry, but the ethnic economy literature does not undertake this line of inquiry. The ethnic economy literature is agnostic about individual differences, and cannot, in most cases, explain why of two members of the same ethno-religious or ethno-cultural group, one becomes an entrepreneur and the other does not. This incapacity arises from the structure of explanation that the ethnic economy literature deploys. Capabilities are traced to group memberships. Individuals who are members of the same group are presumed to have the same capabilities. If, having the same capabilities, they diverge in their behavior, then something other than shared capabilities must explain the divergence. Fully assimilated members of a society's dominant ethnic group are just as ethnic as immigrants. To be ethnic is just to have a culture. But, the ethnic economy cannot offer an ethnic reason why some Germans in Germany become entrepreneurs and others do not, or why some Malays in Malaysia become entrepreneurs and others do not. Class must be the source of that internal explanation. However, when comparing Germans and Malays in Portugal, the ethnic economy approach may find ethno-cultural differences that would explain why one group has a higher self-employment rate than another.

Eschewing explanation of individual difference, the ethnic economy literature proceeds like an actuary, *predicting rates of self-employment* among groups with different amounts and different kinds of capital resources. To this end, the ethnic economy literature distinguishes ethnic resources and class resources depending upon a resource's provenance. Class resources derive from an entrepreneur's placement within the class structure of society. Resources possessed thanks to one's class placement are one's class resources. Generally speaking, the class system of society bestows more entrepreneurial capital upon rich people than upon poor people so the rich are expected to exhibit higher rates of formal sector self-employment. Rich people inherit wealth and influential social networks. They can afford expensive educations. They are likely to have entrepreneur parents or relatives, who teach them the entrepreneurial way of thinking and acting. In sum, rich people have superior access to financial capital, human capital, social capital and cultural capital that supports their entrepreneurship. For example, Donald Trump's father was a construction entrepreneur who took his adolescent son to job sites and introduced him to real estate promoters. Donald Trump later attended Wharton School of Finance. As a young man, Donald Trump inherited $5 million that staked his initial ventures in real estate development. In contrast, back in east Los Angeles, Antonio Lopez had only five years of schooling in Guadalajara, started work at 11, knew only working-class people like his parents, and inherited only a guitar from his father. Is it any wonder that Trump became the real estate mega-tycoon and Lopez the owner of a taco stand, rather than the reverse?

However, the contribution of the class system to entrepreneurial resources, while still true, is old knowledge. There is no need to belabor this well understood point. The ethnic economy literature builds on this received wisdom, but adds new. The ethnic economy literature has contributed awareness that a second major source of entrepreneurial resources exists. This source is the ethno-cultural and the ethno-religious group structure of societies. Quite independent of the class system, ethno-cultural and ethno-religious groups may confer financial capital, human capital, social capital and cultural capital upon members who are not rich. For example, poor people can borrow financial capital from kin and friends if they have a large extended family that consists of people who normatively endorse lending money to family members. The Amish, the Chinese and the Hindustanis have both extended families and the belief that one should lend money to extended kin. Therefore, poor entrepreneurs who are Amish, Chinese or Hindustani have superior chances to borrow start-up capital thanks to their ethno-cultural provenance. In contrast, white Americans have a hyper-nuclear family system that strips away the extended kin who might otherwise be available to lend them start-up money. Moreover, white Americans generally believe that it is *inadvisable* to lend money to kin. 'Don't mix family and business' is their cultural belief. Again, Asians, Latin Americans and Africans utilize rotating savings and credit associations to support saving and lending. These informal institutions make capital available to people on the strength of their social standing in a large community. Even poor communities utilize these informal financial institutions. However, white Americans have no such informal institutions in their cultural repertoire. White Americans have neither rotating savings and credit associations nor extended kin from whom to borrow. If banks refuse loans, and they are not rich, then white Americans have no alternative source of loan capital, as do Amish, Chinese and Hindustanis.

Comparable cases can be made for the contribution of the ethno-religious and ethno-cultural structure of society to the availability of social capital, cultural capital and, even, human capital. Ethnic groups that value human capital a lot will invest heavily in it even when the expected money rewards are low. They thus endow their young adults with productive skills than enable their entrepreneurship. The economic development of South Korea in the late twentieth century benefited immensely from the vast respect of the Korean people for education, and their willingness to acquire it even when the expected return was lower than the cost. Conversely, of course, the Amish reject education beyond the eighth grade so Amish youth fail to acquire the schoolroom's human capital even when the market economy generously rewards human capital. In both these cases, group-level attitudes toward education affect human capital acquisition net of that capital's expected money return. These attitudes are cultural in origin. In this manner, ethnic cultures and class cultures become alternative sources from which entrepreneurs may derive vocationally relevant human capital. Everyone participates simultaneously in a class culture and an ethnic culture. Fully assimilated members of the ethnic majority also have an ethnic culture in which they participate and from which they derive such capital resources as their group membership affords them.

Country clubs, luxury resorts, and college fraternities are sources of class-derived social capital, but Methodists, vegetarians, housewives and farmers also have social capital. The social networks of humble persons will not include as many powerful or rich people as do the social networks of the rich and wellborn. As a result, the humble people cannot obtain equivalent help and information from their social networks as do the rich and wellborn from theirs. However, for all that, the humble people still have access to social networks through which help and information may flow in abundance. If so, well-connected people of modest class origins can still have access to social capital that supports a modest entrepreneurship. Antonio Lopez drew on his social network of Guadalajara *paisanos* to obtain help and information that enabled him to open a taco stand in Los Angeles. Donald Trump drew on his social network of tycoons and millionaires to obtain the help and information that enabled him to rebuild Atlantic City. Rebuilding a resort city is a bigger enterprise than opening a taco stand. The difference in enterprise scale is a product of class origins. However, *both* Trump and Lopez made use of social networks to support their entrepreneurship. The example illustrates the availability of entrepreneurial social capital to many more people than only those who are rich and wellborn (Halpern, 2005: 48).

Social capital is the telephone connection that permits people to communicate; but cultural capital is what they say once connected. Since adults who understand business rise to the top of the class system, the cultural capital of the rich and wellborn accurately refracts the values, attitudes, practices and habits that enabled entrepreneurship in the older generation. Just being born into this class conveys its entrepreneurship-supporting cultural capital. That birthright advantage increases the likelihood that the children of the rich and wellborn will become important formal sector entrepreneurs. But this conclusion cannot be the whole truth. If entrepreneurship were just for the rich, why do some non-rich people own taco stands and dry cleaning establishments? Evidently, the rich and wellborn do not monopolize what Nobel Prize winner Edmund S. Phelps (2007) called, 'entrepreneurial culture'. Stigmatized middleman minorities also transmit an entrepreneurship-supporting cultural capital, handing it along to their young people. This cultural capital enables middleman minorities (such as Armenians in the Levant, Jews in Europe, the overseas Chinese) to generate more entrepreneurs than do other ethno-religious or ethno-cultural groups. Sometimes ethnic or religious groups acquire the cultural capital that supports entrepreneurship. The Quakers of England accomplished this acquisition in the eighteenth century, and the Gurage of Ethiopia in the twentieth (Nida, 2006). Ethnic cultures may contain or replicate the entrepreneurship-supporting cultural capital of the rich and wellborn. When they do, people of modest class background have access to some or all the cultural capital of entrepreneurship even though they are neither rich nor wellborn.

CONCLUSION

Ethnic minorities and immigrant groups often face disadvantage in the labor market. Ethnic ownership economies are a basic and ubiquitous source of economic self-defense in this situation. All ethnic and immigrant minorities control and transmit social capital, financial capital, human capital and cultural capital that supports the entrepreneurship of their youth. Some have more than others, but all have some. Therefore, young people of modest class background and outsider ethnic status may acquire the basic resources of entrepreneurship thanks to their ethnic or religious affiliation in addition to whatever their class background provided, if anything. Just looking at classic middleman minorities, we see that rich Jews, Armenians and Chinese derive resources of entrepreneurship from their class background as well as from their ethnic background. Because they are rich, they have class resources; because they are Jewish, Armenian or Chinese, they have ethnic resources of entrepreneurship in abundance. However, poor Jews, Armenians or Chinese still acquire cultural capital of entrepreneurship from their ethnic culture. Even without supporting class resources, this cultural capital increases the likelihood that poor Jews, poor Armenians or poor Chinese will become self-employed. When they do, they strengthen the ethnic ownership economy of their group and therewith that group's ability to defend itself against disadvantage in the labor force. It is no wonder then that middleman minorities like these demonstrate high rates of self-employment in the formal sector. Conversely, if we consider ethnic groups that are not middleman minorities, which encompasses most of humanity, their children acquire entrepreneurship that supports entrepreneurship in the formal sector principally when born into the rich class. Children of the working class do not obtain entrepreneurship-supporting capitals from either their class culture or from their ethnic culture; hence, their access to formal sector self-employment is less likely. They may achieve access only into informal sector self-employment for this reason because the informal sector requires lesser resources of entrants.

On the other hand, wayward youth, with no chance for legitimate business ownership, may have access to a cultural capital that supports entrepreneurship in the illegal sector of their group's ethnic ownership economy. They have the wisdom of the street, not the wisdom of the business school. For this reason, the working-class youth are better endowed with the requisite capital for self-employment in the illegal sector than are MBAs. This conclusion need not mean that some steal and others earn an honest living. Playing *The Godfather*, Marlon Brando remarked that one could steal more with a briefcase than with a machine gun. Prisons are the entrepreneurship academies of the lower working class. When the working-class youth succeed in illegal enterprise, they or their descendants can relocate the business into the formal sector, which upgrades their own status but also the average status of the members of their ethnic group.

NOTE

1. One must differentiate an ethnic ownership economy from an ethnic enclave economy. The terms are not synonyms although they are often carelessly treated as if they were. An ethnic enclave economy is an ethnic ownership economy that is geographically clustered around a high-density residential core. Ethnic enclave economies are a special case of an ethnic ownership economy.

REFERENCES

Fairlie, Robert W. (1999), 'Drugs and legitimate self-employment', Department of Economics University of California, Santa Cruz.

Fairlie, Robert W. and Bruce D. Meyer (1996), 'Ethnic and racial self-employment differences and possible explanations', *The Journal of Human Resources*, **31**: 757–93.

Halpern, David (2005), *Social Capital*, Cambridge: Polity Press.

Jenssen, Jenifer I. (2001), 'Social networks, resources, and entrepreneurship', *The International Journal of Entrepreneurship and Innovation*, **2**: 103–9.

Johannisson, Bengt (2000), 'Networking and entrepreneurial growth', in Donald L. Sexton, and Hans Landström (eds), *The Blackwell Handbook of Entrepreneurship*, Oxford: Blackwell, pp. 368–86.

Li, Peter S. (2001), 'Immigrants' propensity to self-employment: evidence from Canada', *International Migration Review*, **35**: 1106–28.

Light, Ivan (2004), 'Cultural capital', in Maryanne Cline Horwitz (ed.), *New Dictionary of the History of Ideas*, New York: Scribner's.

Light, Ivan (2005), 'Ethnic economies', in Neil Smelser and Richard Swedberg (eds), *Handbook of Economic Sociology*, 2nd edn, New York: Russell Sage Foundation, ch. 26.

Light, Ivan and Steven Gold (2000), *Ethnic Economies*, San Diego, CA: Academic Press.

Light, Ivan and Stavros Karageorgis (1994), 'The ethnic economy', in Neil Smelser and Richard Swedberg (eds), *Handbook of Economic Sociology*, New York: Russell Sage Foundation, ch. 26.

Light, Ivan and Carolyn Rosenstein (1995), *Race, Ethnicity, and Entrepreneurship in Urban America*, Hawthorne, NY: Aldine de Gruyter.

Morris, Michael (2001), 'The critical role of resources', *Journal of Developmental Entrepreneurship*, **6**: 5–7.

Nee, Victor, Jimy Sanders and Scott Sernau (1994), 'Job transitions in an immigrant metropolis: ethnic boundaries and the mixed economy', *American Sociological Review*, **59**: 849–72.

Nida, Worku (2006), 'Entrepreneurship as a social movement: how the Gurage became successful entrepreneurs and what it says about identity in Ethiopia', PhD dissertation, University of California, Los Angeles.

Phelps, Edmund S. (2007), 'Entrepreneurial culture', *Wall Street Journal*, 12 February, A15.

Rušinović, Katja (2006), *Dynamic Entrepreneurship: First and Second-Generation Immigrant in Dutch Cities*, Amsterdam: Amsterdam University Press.

Sequeira, Jenifer M. and Abdul A. Rasheed (2004), 'The role of social and human capital in the start-up and growth of immigrant businesses', in Curt H. Stiles and Craig S. Galbraith (eds), *Ethnic Entrepreneurship: Structure and Process*, Amsterdam: Eslevier, pp. 77–94.

Tienda, Marta and Rebeca Raijman (2000), 'Immigrants' income packaging and invisible labor force activity', *Social Science Quarterly*, **81**: 291–310.

Weber, Max (1958), *The Protestant Ethic and the Spirit of Capitalism*, Upper Saddle River, NJ: Prentice-Hall. First published 1906.

Weber, Max (1981), *The General Economic History*, New Brunswick NJ: Transactions. First published 1927.

13 Entrepreneurship policy

David B. Audretsch

1 INTRODUCTION

A generation of management and economics scholars such as Chandler (1977; 1990) concluded that there was little room for entrepreneurship in the context of starting a new firm, to generate efficiency and ultimately business and managerial success. Schumpeter (1942: 132) similarly concluded that, due to scale economies in the production of new economic knowledge, large corporations would not only have the innovative advantage over small and new enterprises, but that ultimately the economic landscape would consist only of giant corporations: 'Innovation itself is being reduced to routine. Technological progress is increasingly becoming the business of teams of trained specialists who turn out what is required and make it work in predictable ways.'

Accordingly, a generation of scholars suggested that public policy should focus exclusively on the large corporation. For example, Galbraith (1979: 93–94) argued that entrepreneurship was disappearing in the contemporary economy, where the great entrepreneurs of the Industrial Revolution were replaced by the hierarchical large corporation: 'The great entrepreneur must, in fact, be compared in life with the male *Alpis mellifera*. He accomplishes his act of conception at the price of his own extinction.' Thus, according to Galbraith (1979: 61), the entrepreneur 'is a diminishing figure in the planning system. Apart from access to capital, his principal qualifications were imagination, capacity for decision and courage in risking money, including, not infrequently, his own. None of these qualifications is especially important for organizing intelligence or effective in competing with it.'

By contrast, it was argued that public policy needed to focus on the large corporation. According to Schumpeter (1942: 106): 'What we have got to accept is that (the large-scale establishment or unit of control) has come to be the most powerful engine of . . . progress and in particular of the long-run expansion of output not only in spite of, but to a considerable extent through, this strategy which looks so restrictive.' Galbraith (1958 [1976]: 86–7) echoed this view:

> There is no more pleasant fiction than that technical change is the product of the matchless ingenuity of the small man forced by competition to employ his wits to better his neighbor. Unhappily, it is a fiction. Technical development has long since become the preserve of the scientist and engineer. Most of the cheap and simple inventions have, to put in bluntly and unpersuasively, been made.

However, as entrepreneurship has become recognized as an engine of economic growth, employment creation and competitiveness in global markets (Audretsch et al. 2006), public policy has shifted its priorty to promote entrepreneurship. For example, Romano Prodi (2002: 1), who at the time served as President of the European Commission, proclaimed that the promotion of entrepreneurship was a central cornerstone of European economic growth policy: 'Our lacunae in the field of entrepreneurship needs to be taken seriously because there is mounting evidence that the key to economic growth and productivity improvements lies in the entrepreneurial capacity of an economy.' With the 2000 Lisbon Proclamation, the European Council made a commitment to becoming not just the leader in knowledge but also the entrepreneurship leader in the world in order to ensure prosperity and a high standard of living throughout the continent.

Europe was not alone in focusing on entrepreneurship as a key factor generating economic growth. From the other side of the Atlantic, Mowery (2005: 1) observes:

> During the 1990s, the era of the 'New Economy,' numerous observers (including some who less than 10 years earlier had written off the U.S. economy as doomed to economic decline in the face of competition from such economic powerhouses as Japan) hailed the resurgent economy in the united States as an illustration of the power of high-technology entrepreneurship. The new firms that a decade earlier had been criticized by such authorities as the MIT Commission on Industrial Productivity (Dertouzos et al., 1989) for their failure to sustain competition against large non-U.S. firms were seen as important sources of economic dynamism and employment growth. Indeed, the transformation in U.S. economic performance between the 1980s and 1990s is only slightly less remarkable than the failure of most experts in academia, government, and industry, to predict it.

The purpose of this chapter is to explain the emergence of entrepreneurship, not as a business strategy, but rather as a bona fide strategy and priority of public policy. The following section explains the emergence of a mandate for entrepreneurship policy. The economic rationale providing an intellectual and theoretical basis for public policy intervention to promote entrepreneurship is explained in the third section. The fourth section explains what exactly constitutes entrepreneurship policy the instruments used to implement entrepreneurship policy, and the locus of entrepreneurship policy. Finally, conclusions and a summary are provided. In particular, just as entrepreneurship has become a bona fide area for the management of business, it has also emerged as a bona fide strategy for public policy.

2 THE MANDATE FOR ENTREPRENEURSHIP POLICY

Between the 1950s and 1980s public policy to promote economic growth, employment and international competitiveness focused largely on promoting the factor of physical capital, which placed large corporations in manufacturing industries at the focal point of policy. This policy approach, which Audretsch and Thurik (2001) and Audretsch (2007a, 2007b) term the managed economy, reflected the insights generated by the Nobel Prize-winning Solow model, which linked economic growth and productivity explicitly to the factor of physical capital.

Globalization has shifted the comparative advantage of Organisation for Economic Co-operation and Development (OECD) countries away from physical capital towards knowledge capital. The endogenous growth theory (Romer, 1986) provided an intellectual framework which correspondingly shifted the focus of public policy towards instruments which would promote investments in knowledge, such as research and development (R&D), patents, human capital and universities.

Even as the comparative advantage in (physical) capital in OECD countries was beginning to fade, scholars and policy-makers began to recognize the primacy of a very different factor of production – knowledge capital, which is based not just on technological and scientific knowledge, but also in a broader sense of ideas, creativity, originality and novelty. The recognition by Romer (1986) and Lucas (1993), among others, that knowledge was not only endogenous, but that it also spilled over for commercialization by firms and individuals other than the firm or university actually creating that knowledge in the first place, shifted the policy debate and focus away from instruments inducing investments in physical capital, towards instruments generating knowledge and ideas, such as university research, education and training, R&D and patents.

Thus, even as the OECD countries began losing the comparativeness advantage in physical capital, they seemed to be at least as well poised to thrive with a knowledge-based economy. In particularly, the Nordic countries, but also Northern Europe more generally, ranked among the world's leaders in terms of the most common measures of knowledge. Thus, the inability of countries which were knowledge leaders, such as Sweden, to prosper in the global economy was so striking that it was referred to as the Swedish Paradox. However, it was not just Sweden that exhibited surprising low growth rates and rising unemployment, while at the same time have high rates of investment in research, human capital and culture. The European Union adapted the label to describe what it termed *the European Paradox*. While the prescriptions of investments in knowledge generated economic models of scholars, the experience of Sweden, and much of Europe, was suggesting that the links between knowledge and growth are, in fact, more nuanced and complicated.

The conditions inherent in knowledge – high uncertainty, asymmetries and transactions cost – can result in decision-making hierarchies in companies reaching the decision not to pursue and try to commercialize new ideas that individual economic agents, or groups or teams of economic agents think are potentially valuable and should be pursued. The characteristics of knowledge distinguishing it from information, a high degree of uncertainty combined with non-trivial asymmetries, combined with a broad spectrum of institutions, rules and regulations impose what Audretsch and Keilbach (2007), Audretsch et al. (2006) and Braunerhjelm et al. (2010) term *the knowledge filter*. The knowledge filter is the gap between knowledge that has a potential commercial value and knowledge that is actually commercialized. The greater is the knowledge filter, the more pronounced is the gap between new knowledge and commercialized knowledge.

It is the knowledge filter that impedes investments in knowledge from spilling over for commercialization that leads to the so-called Swedish Paradox and European Paradox. Europe was not alone in having investments in knowledge choked off from generating economic growth by the knowledge filter.

Confronted with what is termed the knowledge filter impeding the spillover of knowledge from the firm or organization where it was originally generated, for commercialization by third-party firms, public policy instruments to promote investment in knowledge, such as human capital, R&D, and university research may not adequately generate economic growth. One interpretation of the *European Paradox*, where such investments in new knowledge have certainly been substantial and sustained, but vigorous growth and reduction of unemployment have remained elusive, is that the presence of such an imposing knowledge filter chokes off the commercialization of those new knowledge investments, resulting in diminished innovative activity and, ultimately, stagnant growth.

By choking off the spillover and commercialization of knowledge and new ideas, the knowledge filter at the same time presents opportunities for individuals, or teams of individuals, that might place a high valuation on the potential of that knowledge, to become entrepreneurs. If someone is not able to pursue and implement their vision within the context of an incumbent firm or organization, in order to appropriate the value of her knowledge and ideas, they would need to start a new firm, that is, become an entrepreneur.

The start-up of a new firm reflects knowledge spillover entrepreneurship because the ideas serving as the basis for the start-up were obtained, typically for little or no cost, from a different, incumbent firm or organization. Thus, knowledge spillover entrepreneurship serves as a conduit for the spillover new ideas generated by an incumbent organization but left uncommercialized.

The knowledge spillover theory of entrepreneurship (Braunerhjelm et al., 2010; Audretsch, 1995; Audretsch and Keilbach, 2007; Audretsch et al., 2006), suggests that contexts which are rich in knowledge will tend to generate more entrepreneurial opportunities. By contrast, those contexts that have less knowledge will generate fewer entrepreneurial opportunities. A consequence of globalization, which has shifted the comparative advantage of developed countries from physical capital to knowledge capital, is that entrepreneurial opportunities become more pervasive (Audretsch, 2007a).

From the end of the Second World War into the 1980s, public policy to promote economic growth, employment and competitiveness focused extensively on an approach to foster investments in physical capital and nurturing institutions that facilitated the most effective development and utilization of the labor force deployed to work with that capital. Small business was seen as generally being peripheral to even detracting from the efficient organization of capital in large corporations.

As globalization shifted the comparative advantage in the OECD countries towards knowledge, ideas and creativity, the policy emphasis accordingly shifted towards promoting investments in knowledge, such as research and development, universities, human capital and education. Little emphasis was placed on small and medium-sized enterprises, since research and development, along with patenting and investments in human capital were generally perceived to lie in the domain of large corporations.

However, along with the recognition that entrepreneurship provides a crucial role by providing a conduit for knowledge spillovers, has come the emergence of a new policy approach – entrepreneurship policy. The focus of entrepreneurship policy is to encourage and promote not just investments in knowledge, but also their commercialization through the start-up of a new firm. Thus, the focus is on policies that enable people, particularly in knowledge-based and creative industries, to start new business and to facilitate the growth of such new ventures.

Recent literature has identified the emergence of a new public policy approach (Audretsch, 2007a; 2007b), with a focus on generating entrepreneurship capital, or the capacity of an economy to generate entrepreneurial activity. Investments in knowledge and ideas may not automatically spill over for commercialization, which would trigger innovation and growth. Rather, as is explained above, the knowledge filter impedes the spillover and commercialization of knowledge. By commercializing ideas and knowledge that might otherwise not have been commercialized, the start-up of a new firm serves as an important conduit for the spillover of knowledge. Thus, in an effort to appropriate the returns in terms of economic growth, employment, and international competitiveness from costly investments in knowledge, such as public research, education, and universities, a mandate for public policy and institutions to shift away from the managed economy towards an entrepreneurial society has emerged in the OECD countries (Audretsch, 2007a; 2007b).

3 THE ECONOMIC RATIONALE UNDERLYING POLICY INTERVENTION FOR ENTREPRENEURSHIP

Besides a mandate for entrepreneurship policy, there is also an economic rationale for public policy intervention to create an entrepreneurial economy. Linking entrepreneurship to economic growth is not an automatic justification for public policy intervention. In fact, Bresnahan and Gambardella (2004: 5) argue that the emergence of the most prominent contemporary region, Silicon Valley, that has set the standard for an entrepreneurial economy rich in entrepreneurship capital, did not result from public policy intervention: 'Our overall research design took seriously the proposition government policy leading and directing cluster formation might be an important part of the cluster formation story . . . we ultimately reject that proposition.'

Rather, for an economic rationale to justify public policy intervention, a reason must exist why the good or service in question, in this case entrepreneurship, will not be adequately provided by the private market. The economic rationale for public policy intervention to support entrepreneurship is based on market failure. There are four types of market failure – network externalities, knowledge externalities, failure externalities and demonstration externalities – providing an economic rationale for policy intervention. Entrepreneurial activity will tend to be suppressed as a result of these four types of market failure (Audretsch and Keilbach, 2007).

Network Externalities

When the value of an individual's or firm's capabilities and knowledge is conditional upon complementary firms and individuals, network externalities exist. Such network externalities frequently have a strong spatial component. In this case geographic proximity will facilitate accessing these complementary inputs. Thus, the value of an entrepreneurial firm and individual will be greater in the (local) presence of other entrepreneurial firms and individuals. The value of any individual's or firm's capabilities is therefore conditional upon the existence of partners in a network. Regions with an entrepreneurial cluster will tend to be more attractive to firms and knowledge workers. By contrast, regions with a paucity of entrepreneurship and knowledge will be less attractive to firms and workers.

Thus, this source of market failure involves the geographic context which provides the (potential) platform for interactions and networks. Contexts, or regions, that do not enjoy a rich density of entrepreneurial networks will be burdened with more significant barriers to entrepreneurship, because the expected value of any recognized opportunity will be correspondingly lower in the absence of such networks, resulting in a lower propensity for economic agents to make the decision to become an entrepreneur.

Knowledge Externalities

The high propensity for knowledge to be associated with externalities is the second source of market failure. As Arrow (1962) suggested and Audretsch and Feldman (1996) show, knowledge generates externalities and can spill over for commercialization and innovation by third-party firms and individuals. However, as Audretsch and Feldman (1996) suggest, close geographic proximity to knowledge sources will facilitate the spillover of knowledge.

Audretsch and Feldman (1996) and Audretsch et al. (2006) provide compelling empirical evidence that knowledge-spillover entrepreneurship has a strong propensity to spatially cluster within close geographic proximity to knowledge sources. Similarly, Gilbert et al. (2008) provide empirical evidence that those entrepreneurial start-ups locating within a geographic cluster exhibit a superior performance vis-à-vis their counterparts that do not locate within a geographic cluster. Thus, location can influence the access of entrepreneurial start-ups to external knowledge spillovers. Public policy can compensate for the lack of an entrepreneurial cluster in a particular region by trying to facilitate an environment that is favourable to the formation of entrepreneurial clusters.

Failure Externalities

The third source of market failure emanates from the positive economic value created by entrepreneurial firms that fail. Entrepreneurial firms have a significantly greater propensity to failure within a few years subsequent to start-up (Caves, 1998). The failure rate for start-ups is even greater for knowledge-based and high-technology entrepreneurship. The higher failure rate of entrepreneurship in general and knowledge-based and high-technology entrepreneurship in particular is attributable to a greater degree of uncertainty. Entrepreneurial failure may generate significant positive value for other, third-party firms and entrepreneurs that can use these ideas.

Valuation of a potential new enterprise by private financiers does not include failure externalities. A private investor can only appropriate her investment if the entrepreneurial venture succeeds. The external value created by a failed firm for use by other third-party firms is not considered or valued by private investors. In the event of entrepreneurial failure, the private investor will not appropriate anything from the original investment, regardless of how great the externalities are.

However, from the perspective of public policy, which firm actually succeeds and subsequently generates growth and employment for the region is of less concern than that it is generated at all. After all, the public policy goal is typically growth for the overall region but not necessarily for any particular enterprise.

Demonstration Externalities

The fourth source of market failure is the demonstration effect associated with entrepreneurial activity. The demonstration effect refers to the learning undertaken by (potential) entrepreneurs and firms about the viability of entrepreneurship from observing incidents of entrepreneurial activity. The decision to commercialize ideas and enter into entrepreneurship can be influenced by observing the outcomes and consequences when others enter into entrepreneurship. The demonstration effect may be especially valuable for a region burdened with an impoverished amount of entrepreneurship capital.

As a result of the market failures inherent in the externalities involved in knowledge spillover entrepreneurship – which stem from networks, knowledge, failure and demonstration – a gap is created in the valuation of potential entrepreneurial activities between private parties and the local public policy-makers. Thus, the constraints for obtaining early stage finance for entrepreneurial start-ups and nascent entrepreneurs tend to be even greater outside of a successful entrepreneurial cluster than within an entrepreneurial cluster.

The four sources of market failure associated with entrepreneurship contribute to significant barriers to entrepreneurship at least in some contexts. The economic rationale for entrepreneurship policy is to mitigate these four sources of market failure. The role that entrepreneurship plays in permeating the knowledge filter and serving as a conduit of knowledge spillovers, combined with the strong propensity for those knowledge spillovers to be geographically bounded and remain localized, suggests a key role for public policy to promote entrepreneurship. By compensating for market failure, public policy can create a virtuous entrepreneurial circle, where entrepreneurs become networked and linked to each other, and provide strong role models of knowledge spillover entrepreneurship for other individuals to emulate.

4 INSTRUMENTS OF ENTREPRENEURSHIP POLICY

With both a mandate and rationale for undertaking entrepreneurship policy, two important issues remain. The first revolves around what exactly constitutes entrepreneurship policy and a bona fide entrepreneurship policy instrument. The second involves the mechanisms and policy channels for implementing entrepreneurship policy.

A broad spectrum of diverse policy approaches to promote entrepreneurship exist across countries and context. Still an important feature distinguishing entrepreneurship policy from more traditional approaches towards business characteristic of the managed economy (Audretsch and Thurik, 2001) is a shift away from the focus on the traditional triad of policy instruments essentially constraining the freedom of firms to contract – regulation, competition policy or antitrust in the USA and public ownership of business.

Instead, as a result of globalization, a new policy approach has emerged with a focus on enabling the creation and commercialization of knowledge. Along with this shift in policy approach has emerged a distinction between entrepreneurship policy from the traditional small business policies. This distinction involves reconsidering the role of small and new firms. In the managed economy public policy generally took the stance of trying to preserve small businesses that were widely perceived to be burdened with an inherent cost disadvantage due to operating at a suboptimal scale of output. Thus, small business policy was essentially preservationist in the managed economy.

For example, in light of the fact that small firms constituted an ever-decreasing share of the US economy during the first half of the twentieth century, Congress passed the Small Business Act of 1953, which established the US Small Business Administration (SBA), with an explicit mandate to 'aid, counsel, assist and protect . . . the interests of small business concerns'. The agency was directed to help small businesses obtain government contracts and loans, along with management and technical assistance. The Act tried to protect small firms from exposure to a hostile economic environment, to at least mitigate the continued disappearance of small business and to preserve the role of small business in the US economy.

By contrast, entrepreneurship public policy views new ventures as serving as a conduit for knowledge spillovers and thus serving as an engine of growth, employment generation and competitiveness in global markets. The focus of entrepreneurship is on the promotion of facilitating entrepreneurs to start new firms and on new and small firms involved in the commercialization of knowledge, or knowledge-based entrepreneurship.

Small business policy typically refers to policies implemented by governmental agencies charged with the mandate to promote small business. The actual definition of a small business varies considerably across countries, ranging from enterprises with fewer than 500 employees in the USA and Canada, to fewer than 250 employees in the European Union, to 50 employees in many developing countries.

Small business policy typically takes the existing enterprises within the appropriate size class as exogenous, or given, and then develops instruments to promote the continued viability of those enterprises. Thus, small business policy is almost exclusively targeted on the existing stock of enterprises and virtually all of the instruments included in the policy portfolio are designed to promote the viability of these small businesses.

By contrast, entrepreneurship policy has a much broader focus. The definition, introduced by Stevenson and Lundström (2005: 19) for OECD countries, is 'Entrepreneurship policy consists of measures taken to stimulate more entrepreneurial behaviour in a region or country . . . We define entrepreneurship policy as those measures intended to directly influence the level of entrepreneurial vitality in a country or a region.'

There are at least two important ways that distinguish entrepreneurship policy from small business policy (Stevenson and Lundström, 2005). The first is the breadth of policy orientation and instruments. While small business policy focuses on the existing stock of small firms, entrepreneurship policy is more encompassing because it includes potential entrepreneurs. Entrepreneurship policy also has greater sensitivity to contextual conditions and framework that shape the decision-making process of entrepreneurs and potential entrepreneurs.

While small business policy is primarily concerned with one organizational level, the enterprise, entrepreneurship policy encompasses multiple levels of organization and analysis. These range from the individual to the enterprise level and focus on clusters or networks. The various perspectives might involve an industry or sectoral dimension, or a spatial dimension, such as a district, city, region or even an entire country. Just as each of these levels is an important target for policy, the interactions and linkages across these disparate levels are also important. In this sense, entrepreneurship policy tends to be more holistic than small business policy.

The second way of distinguishing entrepreneurship policy from traditional small business policy is that virtually every country has a governmental agency charged with promoting the viability of the small business sector. These ministries and agencies have by now developed a large arsenal of policy instruments to promote small business. However, no agencies exist to promote entrepreneurship. Part of the challenge of implementing entrepreneurship policy is this lack of agency-level institution. Rather, aspects relevant to entrepreneurship policy can be found across a broad spectrum of ministries, ranging from education to trade and immigration. Thus, while small businesses have agencies and ministries to protect their issues, no analogous agency exists for entrepreneurs.

Not only is entrepreneurship policy implemented by different ministries or agencies than those implementing either the traditional policy instruments constraining the freedom of firms to contract or those implementing traditional small business policy, but it involves a very different and distinct set of policy instruments.

Stevenson and Lundström (2005) meticulously classified the broad and diverse range of instruments which are being used around the globe to promote entrepreneurship. Examples of the emerging entrepreneurship policy abound. Still, the point to be emphasized here is not so much the efficacy of the policy, but rather the clearly stated goal – to promote the spillover of knowledge from universities for commercialization that will foster innovation and ultimately economic growth.

Not only are the instruments of entrepreneurship policy decidedly distinct from those traditionally used towards business and small business in particular, but the locus of such enabling policies is also different. The instruments constraining the freedom of firms to contract – antitrust, regulation and public ownership – were generally controlled and administered at the national level. By contrast, the instruments of entrepreneurship policy are generally applied at decentralized levels: state, city and local government.

As Stevenson and Lundström (2005) point out, entrepreneurship policy uses a wide variety of instruments ranging from changing regulation to taxes, immigration, education, as well as more direct instruments such as the provision of finance or training. If entrepreneurship policy can be viewed as the purposeful attempt to create an entrepreneurial society, entire institutions that were the cornerstone of the managed economy are being challenged and reconfigured in favor of the entrepreneurial society.

5 CONCLUSIONS

This chapter has explained and documented that entrepreneurship is not just central as a topic for the management of private business but also for public policy. As knowledge has become important and the era of the managed economy has receded, shifting to an entrepreneurial society has become a priority for public policy. Entrepreneurship policy is less about creating and promoting any particular type of individual, firm or industry but rather more about creating a society where entrepreneurship serves as the driving force for growth, employment creation and competitiveness in global markets.

An important qualification, however, is that by itself, public policy will never succeed or guarantee the creation of an entrepreneurial society. As Gordon Moore, who is 'widely regarded as one of Silicon Valley's founding fathers' (Bresnahan and Gambardella, 2004: 7) and Kevin Davis warn, the policy rush to generate an entrepreneurial society is fraught with dangers and ambiguities: 'The potential disaster lies in the fact that these static, descriptive efforts culminate in policy recommendations and analytical tomes that resemble recipes or magic potions such as combine liberal amounts of technology, entrepreneurs, capital, and sunshine; add one university; stir vigorously' (Moore and Davis, 2004: 9).

Entrepreneurship policy has emerged as a bona fide priority and strategy for public policy because it can provide a missing link to economic growth. Investments in new knowledge, such as R&D, universities and human capital may be necessary but not sufficient for generating economic growth. Rather, mechanisms may also be needed to generate the highest return possible to society, in terms of growth, jobs and international competitiveness, from the investments made to create that knowledge in the first place. Entrepreneurship can make a crucial contribution to economic growth by facilitating the spillover and commercialization of ideas and knowledge that otherwise might never have been transformed into innovative activity. Public policy has accordingly begun to place a priority on not just investments in knowledge, but also in creating entrepreneurship capital, to try to ensure that those costly investments in new knowledge actually result in what society desires – growth and jobs in a globalized economy.

REFERENCES

Arrow, K. (1962), 'Economic welfare and the allocation of resources for invention', in Richard R. Nelson (ed.), *The Rate and Direction of Inventive Activity*, Princeton, NJ: Princeton University Press, pp. 609–26.
Audretsch, David (1995), *Innovation and Industry Evolution*, Cambridge, MA: MIT Press.
Audretsch, David and M.P. Feldman (1996), 'R&D spillovers and the geography of innovation and production', *American Economic Review*, **86**, 630–40.
Audretsch, David and R. Thurik (2001), 'What's new about the new economy? Sources of growth in the managed and entrepreneurial economies', *Industrial and Corporate Change*, **19**, 795–821.
Audretsch, David B. (2007a), *The Entrepreneurial Society*, New York: Oxford University Press.
Audretsch, David B. (2007b,) 'Entrepreneurship capital and economic growth', *Oxford Review of Economic Policy*, **23**, 63–78.
Audretsch, David B. and Max Keilbach (2007), 'The theory of knowledge spillover entrepreneurship', *Journal of Management Studies*, **44** (7), 1242–54.
Audretsch, David B., Max Keilbach and Erik Lehmann (2006), *Entrepreneurship and Economic Growth*, New York: Oxford University Press.
Braunerhjelm, P., Z.J. Acs, D.B. Audretsch and B. Carlsson (2010), 'The missing link: knowledge diffusion and entrepreneurship in endogenous growth', *Small Business Economics: An Entrepreneurship Journal*, **34** (2), February, 105–25.
Bresnahan, T. and A. Gambardella (2004), *Building High-Tech Clusters: Silicon Valley and Beyond*, Cambridge: Cambridge University Press.
Caves, R. (1998), 'Industrial organization and new findings on the turnover and mobility of firms', *Journal of Economic Literature*, **36**, 1947–82.
Chandler, A. (1977), *The Visible Hand: The Managerial Revolution in American Business*, Cambridge: Belknap Press.
Chandler, A. (1990), *Scale and Scope: The Dynamics of Industrial Capitalism*, Cambridge: Harvard University Press.
Dertouzos, M., R. Lester and R. Solow (1989), *Made in America: Regaining the Productive Edge*, Cambridge: MIT Press.
Galbraith, John Kenneth (1958), *The Affluent Society*, 3rd edn 1976, Boston, MA: Houghton Mifflin.
Galbraith, John Kenneth (1979), *The New Industrial State*, Boston, MA: Houghton Mifflin. (First published 1967.)
Gilbert, Brett A., Patricia P. McDougall and David B. Audretsch (2008), 'Clusters, knowledge spillovers and new venture performance: an empirical examination', *Journal of Business Venturing*, **23** (4), 405–22.
Lucas, Robert (1993), 'Making a miracle', *Econometrica*, **61**, 251–72.
Moore, Gordon and S.E. Davis (2004), 'Learning the Silicon Valley way', in *Building High-Tech Clusters. Silicon Valley and Beyond*, Cambridge: Cambridge University Press, pp. 7–39.

Mowery, D. (2005), 'The Bayh-Dole Act and high-technology entrepreneurship in U.S. universities: chicken, egg, or something else?', paper presented at the Eller Centre Conference on 'Entrepreneurship Education and Technology Transfer', University of Arizona, 21–22 January.
Prodi, Romano (2002), 'For a new European entrepreneurship', public speech, Instituto de Empresa, Madrid.
Romer, P. (1986), 'Increasing returns and long-run growth', *Journal of Political Economy*, **94**, 1002–37.
Schumpeter, Joseph A. (1942), *Capitalism, Socialism and Democracy*, New York: Harper.
Stevenson, L. and A. Lundström (2005), *Entrepreneurship Policy. Theory and Practice*, International Studies in Entrepreneurship Series, vol. 9, New York: Springer.

14 Environment for entrepreneurship

Jean J. Obrecht

In mainstream thinking on entrepreneurship, the entrepreneur is the central figure. He is seen to be involved in a process of searching for new opportunities and creating new organizations. As a driving force of competition, he takes risks and strives for profits. His behaviour lies on pursuing self-interest and his environment is confined to markets. In a sociological perspective of entrepreneurship as a whole, this way of understanding entrepreneurship belongs to 'the supply-side perspective which focuses on the availability of suitable individuals to occupy entrepreneurial roles', whereas the demand-side would focus on 'the number and nature of the entrepreneurial roles that need to be filled' (Thornton, 1999). Since differences in entrepreneurial role patterns are linked to differences in entrepreneurial environments, the latter perspective requires enhanced attention as to the context in which entrepreneurship occurs.

1 PRELIMINARIES ON CONTEXTUALIZATION

In a world where, despite the globalization of markets, diversity as regards people and institutions combines with inequality as regards economic development levels, the examination of what contextualization means in the field of research on entrepreneurship is all the more necessary, unless we assimilate the entrepreneur to a 'rational fool' which is equivalent, according to Amartya Sen, to the state of a 'social moron' (Sen, 1977). Indeed, the understanding of the entrepreneurial environment requires appropriate analytical tools. These are to be looked for outside prevailing literature on entrepreneurship which, as recalled above, draws up a single role model grounded on Western utilitarianism and which, therefore, might not be endowed with worldwide applicability. The case of entrepreneurship as a remedy against poverty in particular is one of the biggest challenges of our times but development policies which would promote such entrepreneurialism regardless of the context are liable to produce 'islets of wealth in an ocean of misery'.

The consideration of contextual factors influencing entrepreneurial action has without doubt been given a large space in the last 40 years. The influence of culture on local business climate and thereby on business creation was one of the topics which researchers in small business economics examined throughout (Johannisson, 1984). Much work has been based on Gert Hofstede's celebrated model which emphasizes the importance of cultural values such as individualism and collectivism, the former giving individuals the necessary freedom for entrepreneurial action as opposed to the latter. But this dichotomized view has been blended by many findings pointing to the fact that these cultural characteristics may coexist in the same country (Morris et al. 1993); moreover, other findings refer to entrepreneurial activities as being influenced by both (Tiessen, 1997). The notion of a 'symbiotic relationship between entrepreneurship and culture'

(Morrison, 2000), while emphasizing the fact that entrepreneurs' behaviour is deep rooted in local cultures and traditions, refers also to the influence the entrepreneur may have on the evolution of local usual practices because the entrepreneurial process is not entirely confined within cultural norms. Through the concept of 'innovative milieu', the focus was put on the influence of technology on local development (Maillat and Kebir, 1999). The notion of 'entrepreneurial milieu' widened the space of influence to the whole range of factors depending on the location of the entrepreneur and his business, positive collective attitudes towards entrepreneurship being seen as the most significant (Gasse, 2003). The part of local institutions in the development of an 'entrepreneurial culture' has been given due consideration too; in the French literature on this topic, the word 'territory' soon came into use to point out a regional area as a socially organized structure hosting the promotion of the small business sector (Marchesnay and Fourcade, 1996).

While recognizing the importance of contextual factors, entrepreneurship provided a relevant and exciting setting to explore the issue of networks, along the lines of social networks analysis developed in sociology. In the 1980s, Howard Aldrich and Catherine Zimmer took a critical position on traditional approaches. They focused on 'entrepreneurship as embedded in a social context, channelled and facilitated or constrained and inhibited by people's positions in social networks' (Aldrich and Zimmer, 1986). In current literature on entrepreneurship and small business, the network metaphor was used by a number of researchers following the pioneering work of Bengt Johannisson to develop comprehensive models of how the entrepreneur operates the environment through his personal network. 'The personal network of the entrepreneur not only is an instrument by which he acquires environmental resources but also an instrument by which he performs his organizing mission' (Johannisson, 1987). More recently, while noticing that the conceptualization of 'embeddedness' and its operationalization remain underdeveloped, he outlined an enlarged network framework, focusing on small firms where 'the point of departure is individual exchange relationships as personal ties concerning economic and social concerns'. He distinguishes three layers of embeddedness. 'First order embeddedness concerns the localized business networks created by combining these dyadic relations. Second-order embeddedness is achieved when considering also the memberships of business persons in economic and social local institutions while third-order embeddedness concerns the special cases where these institutions bridge gaps between firms' (Johannisson, 2002). In newer research on small business creation, the quality of the 'local relational environment', as a bearing of social capital, has been put forward as a crucial success factor of start-ups (Plociniczak, 2002).

From a perspective of 'true' contextualization, apparently singular forms of entrepreneurship have been explored. In-depth understanding of indigenous entrepreneurship is shown to require a careful analysis of the entrepreneurial environment because the characterization of entrepreneurial action and goal attainment and the nature of goals are contingent also on the social and cultural context and on people's history (Peredo et al., 2004). Ethnic entrepreneurship which concerns immigrant individuals striving for a better life through small business creation, is also approached in terms of 'social embeddedness of the entrepreneurial venture' (Levy-Tadjine and Paturel, 2006) or in terms of 'discrimination' and 'marginalization' that are obviously connected with social structures (Ramangalahy et al., 2002). On the subject of indigenous entrepreneurship, 'community-based enterprise' is a good case as this form of entrepreneurship often emerges in regional areas or localities threatened by poverty. It is defined as 'a community acting corporately as both entrepreneur and enterprise in pursuit of the common good' (Peredo, 2003; 2006). In contexts where the recovery of a region is at stake, local development agencies or the people of a local parish and so on may take initiatives like searching for new opportunities or implementing networks that facilitate access to information and provide every kind of support to small businesses operating in that region. Obviously these 'collective practices of opportunities identification' which substitute for the firm's defaulting occur in particular contexts (Tremblay and Carrier, 2006). Because of the common interests at issue, they might be considered as a form of 'community entrepreneurship'. It is also admitted that contextual fragilities lie at the root of social entrepreneurship: not surprisingly, the increasing volume of literature on social entrepreneurs, that is, individuals who are offering their time and energy to address any social or economic problem of a group or community, expresses by itself the increasing number of fragile contexts. Last but not least, one may find in the prolific literature on female entrepreneurship arguments which link the entrepreneurial significance of gender to the cultural and social context, including the case of indigenous or ethnic women's entrepreneurship.

These studies which have in common that they stress the significance of the entrepreneurial environment, give clear indication of the complexity of the entrepreneurial roles worldwide which are not reducible to a single model. Based on his work in international entrepreneurship, Dana suggests that the causal variable behind enterprise is not an opportunity, but rather one's cultural perception of opportunity (Dana, 1995). Many findings show that the same statement could be applied to risk perception. Above all, evidence has been provided that 'serving local community needs' as the main goal of business strategies or 'seeing communal values and the notion of the common good as essential elements in venture creation' makes alternative forms of entrepreneurship, in many settings, the culturally appropriate response to the problems it is meant to address, that is, most of the times problems related to poverty (Curry, 2005; Peredo, 2003). These are only very few of a number of findings which show the variety of the entrepreneurial roles as they crop up in different contexts.

The entrepreneurial environment consequently emerges as a possible field of research of its own. The next section, supported by a selective survey of literature, brings together the constituents of a possible conceptual framework for a comprehensive understanding. By way of a short-cut view, some of the constituents may be in the following proposition: embedding structures generate social capital as an indispensable resource for action; owing to local social capital, the entrepreneurial environment is moulded by a set of proximity dynamics.

2 EMBEDDING STRUCTURES AND SOCIAL CAPITAL

The most relevant theoretical advances likely to support the elaboration of a conceptual framework come from the critical positions some outstanding sociologists have taken towards the methodological individualism of neoclassical economic theory. Whereas the concept of 'embeddedness' was forged by Karl Polanyi and used from a historical perspective as an argument against the 'market ideologists' (Polanyi, 1944), it made Mark Granovetter the most quoted scholar in respect of the idea that economic action is embedded in actual social relations rather in abstract markets. In Granovetter's words, 'actors do not behave or decide as atoms outside a social context, nor do they adhere slavishly to a script written for them by the particular intersection of social categories that they happen to occupy. Their attempts to purposive action are instead embedded in concrete, ongoing systems of social relations' (Granovetter, 1985). Throughout a vast literature, the embeddedness perspective has proven to be the unavoidable starting point of any endeavour to work out a contextualized approach of entrepreneurship.

Embedding via Embeddedness

Granovetter's specific contribution lies in the concept of 'structural embeddedness' which refers to 'the structure of the overall network of relations'. As a higher level of embeddedness it includes the lower level of 'relational embeddedness'. Whereas the former refers to the network structure of relationships between numbers of actors, the latter describes the dyadic relations between individuals with reference to the quality level of such personal links (Granovetter, 1990). The characterization of the entrepreneurial environment therefore has to address the social network structures that are embedding the entrepreneur's action.

In the abundant literature that Granovetter's conceptualization has given birth to, many other kinds of embeddedness have been added over time. Among the most familiar types are those identified by Sharon Zukin and Paul DiMaggio. Besides structural embeddedness, three other types approximating well-established, other conceptualizations are distinguished: cognitive, cultural and political (Zukin and Dimaggio, 1990). Indeed, 'cognitive embeddedness' refers to 'the ways in which the structured regularities of mental processes limit the exercise of economic reasoning'. This notion points at the actors' limited ability to make use of the sort of rationality required by neoclassical economics and meets the well-known bounded rationality approach of Herbert Simon. 'Cultural embeddedness' refers to 'the role of shared collective understandings in shaping economic strategies and goals' and conveys a sociological perspective that goes back to Max Weber. By 'political embeddedness' is meant 'the manner in which economic institutions and decisions are shaped by a struggle for power that involves economic actors and non market institutions'. This has been discussed by numerous scholars, among others by Amitai Etzioni who, in particular, argues for the need to balance freedom with morality, and community with autonomy.

In view of the rehabilitation of 'embeddedness paradigm's' original meaning and a clear articulation of its essentially social dimension with other spatiality related dimensions, German geographer Martin Hess proposed an interesting view on the fundamental categories of embeddedness (Hess, 2004). 'Societal embeddedness' considers 'the societal i.e. cultural, political etc. background or genetic code, influencing and shaping the action of individuals and collective actors within their respective societies and outside it'. It also 'reflects the business systems idea of an institutional and regulatory framework that affects and in part determinates an actor's behaviour'. As a distinct concept, 'network embeddedness' refers to 'the network of actors a person or organization is involved in'. It may be described as a relational aspect, the relationships of an individual or a firm with other actors, and as a structural aspect including both business agents and non-business agents, for example, government and non-government agents. Spatiality is not a precondition for network embeddedness which is the result of a dynamic embedding and disembedding process within or across spatial configurations. 'Territorial embeddedness' considers 'the extent to which an actor is anchored in particular territories or places. Economic actors become embedded in the sense that they absorb, and in some cases become constrained by, the economic activities and social dynamics that already exist in those places.'

From this reconceptualization of embeddedness one may also extrapolate a hierarchical vision of embedding structures. Territorial structures embody the spatially bounded receptacle of located activities. Network structures are organized relationships which get settled within the territorial structures and beyond. Societal structures, on account of their fluidity, permeate through every other structure. This pattern of embedding structures could show up as a useful first approximation of the entrepreneurial environment.

Network Ties: Strong versus Weak

Within the inferences one may draw from the distinction between high and low density networks, Mark Granovetter initiated a stimulating proposition concerning 'the strength of weak ties' (Granovetter, 1973). He argued that in social structures where networks with strong ties are prevalent, 'cliques' are liable to take form. Without weak ties between the high density networks, these structures are exposed to overall fragmentation. 'Social systems lacking in weak ties will be fragmented and incoherent. New ideas will spread slowly, scientific endeavours will be handicapped, and subgroups separated by race, ethnicity, geography or other characteristics will have difficulty reaching a *modus vivendi*.' The function of weak ties is thus to set a 'bridge' between more or less knitted networks. The 'cohesive power of weak ties' idea has been explored in Granovetter's work in conjunction with some crucial issues such as poverty.

> The heavy concentration of social energy in strong ties, he says, has the impact of fragmenting communities of the poor into encapsulated networks with poor connections between these units; individuals so encapsulated may then lose some of the advantages associated with the outreach of weak ties. This may be one more reason why poverty is self-perpetuating. (Granovetter, 1983)

The last statement together with the main argument might have some interest in connection with the viability of entrepreneurship as a means to overcome poverty in underdeveloped countries.

As an established paradigm in network research, Granovetter's weak ties hypothesis has been widely drawn on within the entrepreneurship literature and linked to network structures. Taking the entrepreneur's point of view, it was necessary to get a better understanding about the strong versus weak ties' respective utility and about their mechanisms of utilization in networking. Despite non-convergent empirical findings, the argument is now that the effectiveness of networks depends upon the presence of both strong and weak ties since they are equally likely to provide various resources, depending on the form of the ties and on the context.

Network Structure of Social Capital

In that abundant literature, the lasting work of Ronald Burt has become an inevitable reference. His structural approach leading to the concept of 'structural holes' (Burt, 1982; 1992) and his recent contributions on the 'network structure of social capital' (Burt, 2000; 2001), provide a valuable theoretical coherent background to our search for a conceptual framework of the entrepreneurial environment. The 'holes in social structure' resulting from 'weaker connections between groups' 'create a competitive advantage for an individual whose relationships span the holes'. This is due to the fact that 'structural holes separate nonredundant sources of information', that is, on either side of a structural hole different flows of information are circulating. 'Structural holes are thus an opportunity to broker the flow of information between people, and control the projects that bring together people from opposite sides of the hole.' The information and control benefits obtained by an individual across structural holes are the constituents of social capital.

Now, there are other authoritative approaches of social capital as those pioneered by Pierre Bourdieu (1980; 1986), James Coleman (1988; 1990), Robert Putnam (1993; 2000) and Nan Lin (1999; 2001). In Lin's views, social capital as a resource is prominent: it can be defined as 'resources embedded in a social structure which are accessed and/or mobilized in purposive actions'. These resources may be existing or be latent. Bourdieu also defines social capital as 'the aggregate of the actual or potential resources that are linked to a possession of a durable network of more or less institutionalized relationships of mutual acquaintance and recognition'. According to the French sociologist's ideological position however , these 'assets in networks' together with the other forms of capital serve mainly as a leverage that individuals who are supposed to be only motivated by pursuing self interest, manipulate in order to gain dominating positions.

Coleman sets a link between social capital as a collective asset and purposive individual actions. It is 'some aspect of a social structure . . . facilitating certain actions of individuals who are within the structure. Social capital is productive, making possible the achievements of certain ends'. In Coleman's views as well as in Lin's, however, social capital needs to be activated to be effective. Over and above this, he emphasizes the case of closed networks with strong internal connections: they create normative sanctioning mechanisms and, consequently, higher levels of trust, that is, possible sanctions make it less risky for individuals in the network to trust one another.

Along the same lines, Putnam maintains the focus on action leveraged by social structure. 'Social capital, he says, refers to features of social organisation, such as trust, norms and networks that can improve the efficiency of society by facilitating coordinated action'. Social capital gets its utmost significance as 'bridging capital' which refers to the value assigned to social networks between socially heterogeneous groups whereas 'bonding capital' refers to that of homogeneous groups of people; the latter may turn in forms of networks harmful to society. Thus, according to Coleman and Putnam, social capital as a distinct resource stands out as a possible leverage for collective action.

Owing to the contributions of these scholars, Ronald Burt presented an integrative view of social capital as a set of structural holes and network closure. The latter takes up Coleman's argument: networks with closure or dense networks are favourable for direct access to information and have, in particular, the trust advantage. Taking the two network mechanisms into account, Burt suggests that 'while brokerage across structural holes is the source of added value, closure can be critical to realizing the value buried in the structural holes'.

While gaining popularity is a rather 'elusive concept' (Fukuyama, 2000), social capital has also been identified by the World Bank as a crucial issue for overcoming poverty worldwide. In one of many reports, it is argued that 'social cohesion is critical for societies to prosper economically and for development to be sustainable' and that public policy should therefore promote 'cross-cutting ties among social groups' (Narayan, 1999). Within the perspective set by Robert Putnam, experts of the World Bank resumed the 'bonding' and 'bridging' concepts and added the notion of 'linking'. Bridging capital refers to ties that cut across different communities, groups or individuals, whereas linking capital refers to vertical connections that span differences in power and/or status. They also insist on the fact that bonding capital which refers to horizontal tight knit ties may be exclusionary and may stand in the way of cooperation and trust at the societal level.

3 LOCALNESS AND PROXIMITY DYNAMICS

The 'effectiveness' and 'responsiveness' of social capital, to use Robert Putnam's words, come to the fore in local environments. Social capital is a latent resource for action. To be effective, it has to be activated so that some density within social relationships is needed: proximity contributes to the development of strong ties by favouring face-to-face relations between actors. But, drawing on the preceding conceptualizations, one may assume that the strength of localness is not only determined by the density of interactions within the frontiers of a local environment. Since in the literature on entrepreneurship localness happens to be seen as a possible source of competitive advantage in the global economy and, moreover, in the literature on economic development as a requisite for sustainability, it makes sense to elaborate upon localness as a relevant and significant dimension of the entrepreneurial environment.

On that score, the theoretical corpus related to the 'economics of proximity' appears to be a rich vein where useful concepts could be dug out. At the crossroads of spatial and industrial economics, this new field of research has been growing since the beginning of the 1990s, first in France and later internationally. For scholars of economic geography and regional science the matter was to get a better understanding of the role of space in the coordination of economic activities. Coordination therefore is analysed by considering 'situated agents', meaning agents as they are located in a geographical space but also how they are embedded in a local system of relations conditioning their economic activities. As yet, proximity economics has enriched the traditional analysis of clusters by providing different proximity typologies and suggesting different measurement tools. In newer work on industrial districts, technology districts, local productive systems and so on, the role of proximity as a matter of competitive advantage has been discussed by some researchers. In a quite different domain, other scholars have tried to find new solutions for environmental issues where antagonistic interests often prevail, with the help of proximity analysis.

The interesting point in proximity economics is to suggest that localness is not just a question of spatial distance and that proximity is a multidimensional concept bringing new inputs into the discussion of local development issues. As pointed out by the French sociologist Michel Grossetti, 'economic activities are not necessarily always and equally dependant on social networks' (2006). The process of embedding occurs through personal relations and, since these are mainly local, goes his argument, this process explains by itself the whole range of proximity effects.

Anyway, in view of a contextualized approach of entrepreneurship, one could expect from proximity economics some support to enter localness into the entrepreneurial environment on a new footing.

Proximity Typologies

The rudimental distinction between 'geographic proximity' and 'organized proximity' (Torre and Zuindeau, 2009) may be the first entry. The geographical distance between individuals or organizations is, of course, the most appropriate and tractable indicator to catch on the concept of geographic proximity. But other indicators may be relevant too, such as access times depending on the state of infrastructures. Geographical proximity finally proceeds from 'the opinion the agents may have on the nature of the geographic distance' which separates them. Organized proximity deals with relationships and refers to 'the capacity of an organisation to make its members interact'. Any organization is in a position to facilitate interactions between its members and, a priori, makes them easier than those with outsiders. On the one hand, there is the adherence logic at work: individuals come close because they are interacting and because their interactions are facilitated by explicit or tacit behavioural rules or routines they follow. On the other hand, members of an organization may share a similar system of representations or beliefs and knowledge as well. The functioning of this social tie is mainly tacit and answers a similarity logic. The point is that such organized proximity is not necessarily correlated with geographic proximity and that it may evolve its own, given time.

A more detailed typology has been provided by Ron Boschma in analysing the role of proximity in the process of interactive learning and innovation. His main argument is that 'the importance of geographical proximity cannot be assessed in isolation, but should always be examined in relation to other dimensions of proximity that may provide alternative solution to the problem of coordination' (Boschma, 2005). For that purpose he suggests a rather comprehensive typology distinguishing five proximity dimensions: cognitive, organizational, social, institutional and geographical proximities.

'Cognitive proximity' means that agents who share the same knowledge base and expertise may learn from each other. The question at stake is not only the access to information in terms of rapidity and efficiency but also, and above all, the extension of cognitive possibilities. The focus is on the cognitive capabilities of individuals and organizations and their development, rather than on the intrinsic nature of knowledge such as tacit and codified knowledge. However, for several scholars, cognitive proximity has a more extensive meaning such as to refer to the relationship of people that belong to a community of practice and therefore communicate efficiently (Torre & Rallet, 2005).

'Organizational proximity' matters because it facilitates the exchange of knowledge. It refers to the fact that learning by interaction depends on the capacity to coordinate through organizational arrangements, the flows of knowledge coming from a variety of actors within and between organizations. Organizational proximity finally is contingent on the level of autonomy and the degree of control that can be exerted in those organizational arrangements.

'Social proximity', following Granovetter's initial concept of embeddedness, refers to the interpersonal links between individuals in so far as they are socially embedded and thereby involving trust based on friendship, kinship and experience. Social proximity does not exclude situations where individuals are sharing values, such as ethnic or religious values but those characteristics of cultural proximity are more significant at the macro level of society. In Boschma's typology, those values are part of institutional proximity

'Institutional proximity' indeed resumes an earlier distinction made by André Torre and Jean-Pierre Gilly and refers to the fact that individuals and organizations, first, share the same space of representations and beliefs, as already mentioned above, and, second, face the same incentives and constraints due to their institutional environment made of laws, formal and informal rules, cultural habits, language, and so on (Torre and Gilly, 2000), that is, the 'invisible institutions' (North, 1990). It meets also the concept of 'institutional thickness' which puts emphasis on the role of strong combinations of regional cultures and institutions as positive factors underlying local development (Amin and Thrift, 1993).

'Geographical proximity', as a consequence of being superseded by alternative proximities, refers only to the spatial distance between agents so that its analytical relevance depends upon its coupling with the other forms of proximity. According to Ron Boschma, 'geographical proximity per se is neither a necessary nor a sufficient condition for learning to take place' but it may 'facilitate inter-organisational learning'.

The effects of proximity, however, are not univocal. 'Not only too little', asserts Boschma, 'but also too much proximity may be detrimental to interactive learning and innovation.' Too little cognitive proximity, for instance, decreases the capacity of an agent to identify, interpret and exploit the knowledge possessed by another agent, whereas too much proximity of this kind may result in 'cognitive lock-in'. Too little organizational proximity goes along with a lack of control increasing the risk of opportunism; too much entails the risk of being locked in a specific exchange relation leading to a lack of flexibility. But there are mechanisms which may enhance control, solving the problem of too little proximity, while they prevent locking-in through greater autonomy, solving the problem of too much proximity.

The differentiated pattern of proximities also has been given attention by a group of French economists whose purpose was to explain the success versus the decline of clusters (Vicente et al., 2007). Assuming that interactions between agents are always sequential, the concept of mimetic behaviours or interactions which has been the subject of a growing literature in economics, helps to 'understand how firms converge more or less rapidly in their decision to locate close to each other (geographical proximity) and how this convergence process gives rise to other forms of proximity'. The main point is that 'according to the mimetic process of co-location, the nature of socio-economic proximities can be very different and has a strong influence on the stability and the performance of clusters'.

In everyday situations, of course, the different aspects of proximity are linked together in a dynamic process like that of 'localized learning' (Malmberg and Maskell, 2006). The concept of 'interactive learning as a localized process' outlines how local conditions and spatial proximity between actors enable the formation of distinctive cognitive repertoires and influence the generation and selection of skills, processes and products within a field of knowledge or activity. Localized learning helps explain why there is regional economic specialization, why similar and related firms tend to co-locate to form clusters, why both these phenomena reproduce over time.

The relevance of the different types of proximity has been discussed and there is still much more empirical investigating to do. This is especially important given that increasing globalization puts the significance of geographical proximity into question. So the issue is to find out which kind of proximity or which arrangement of different proximities can make up for the diminishing leverage of geographical proximity. This leads to the questioning of what may be called the 'strength of localness'.

Strength of Localness

Whenever it comes to local aspects of the entrepreneurial environment, the characterization of localness has to take into consideration the variety of ways proximity permeates this environment: one may postulate that the strength of localness a priori is related to proximity's variety and is contingent on an appropriate set of proximities. Arguments can easily be found in the extensive literature on small businesses' internationalization and sustainable local development, to take only a few but relevant topics that form a striking part of the globalization debate.

In the literature on *small businesses' internationalization*, the well documented vulnerability of small and medium-sized enterprises (SMEs), as regards their position in the global economy, makes a good case for the local network structures as a substitute resource (for example, Julien, 1994). It is argued that fragility which accompanies small size can be offset by a supportive environment provided by networks as 'organized systems of relationships' (Szarka, 1990). Evidence has shown that, instead of 'going it alone', SMEs may go abroad by joining local business networks, especially in many countries where local governmental agencies and/or local development bodies themselves play an increasing role in resilient environments. By helping to establish contacts, promoting know-how transfers, setting up reputation mechanisms that prevent opportunistic behaviour, and providing inputs like education or technology transfer services to network firms, these local organizations develop strong ties with the small firms' local network. The 'glocal' market strategy which has been defined as 'combining global business operations with small firm local cooperation' (Johannisson, 1994) became a loop-hole for small business owner-managers' survival and a favourite research field for academe.

The local network argument also got much support from the 'resource-based view of the firm' (Wernerfelt, 1984) which was successfully taken over in the literature on strategic management in different ways (for example, Barney, 1991; Hamel and Prahalad, 1990; Brouthers et al., 2008). As regards the internationalization issue, the sustainability of a competitive advantage on international markets was said to require resources endowed with the quality of being unique assets. Resources of that kind may precisely come from local network structures. This has been highlighted by researchers interested in the case of 'international-at-founding' which refers to the situation of a business organization that, from inception, seeks to derive 'significant competitive advantage from the use of resources and the sale of outputs in multiple countries' (Oviatt and McDougall, 1994).

Technology-based 'born globals' have particular stakes in local networking. Far from substituting international for local networks, technology-intensive firms which have achieved high levels of internationalization in fact also exhibit above-average levels of local networking with respect to research collaboration and intra-industry links. Internationalization therefore appears to be grounded or embedded in successful local networking and research and technology collaboration (Keeble et al., 1998). In the more common case of 'international-by-stage', SMEs are pursuing internationalization only after a steady development on domestic markets and then internationalizing their activities through a series of progressive stages (Cavusgil, 1984; Johanson and Vahlne, 1977). The market-oriented niche strategies which usually are within the reach of SMEs may then be strengthened by resource-based strategies engaging the local network structures in which they are embedded.

The 'glocalized' process of SMEs' internationalization is still stirring up much attention from many researchers involved in the 'small business cause'. Some of them recommend that SMEs' strategies abroad be strongly supported by an 'increasing territorialization of export strategies' based on 'nearness proximity' (Torres, 2002). This means a stronger articulation between small business strategies and local development choices made by the local administrative bodies: 'glocalisation displays a dialectical relation between International Management of Enterprises, especially small sized business, and International Management of Territories'. From the perspective of the knowledge-driven global economy, others would insist in particular upon the 'localized learning' argument (Malmberg and Maskell, 2006). The 'challenge is to uphold a viable environment for localized learning . . . Successful globalization means strengthening rather than weakening the conditions for localized learning'. This requires 'the development of distinct and valuable localized capabilities that promote and guide learning processes into particular trajectories'. These capabilities originate within the local social and institutional set-up. Localized learning supported by localized capabilities thereby sets localness at the foreground in a domain where, a priori, there are no boundaries: knowledge is supposed to be volatile. All together these views, it seems, consider local structures and processes as critical contributors to localness' strength on their own.

It should be noticed however that such an account of spatial relationships hardly conceals an 'overterritorialized concept of embeddedness' in the words of Martin Hess, which we have previously referred to. His revisiting of the seminal work of Karl Polanyi and Mark Granovetter, led him to critically engage with views, like those expressed in 'most work in economic geography . . . proposing local networks and localized social relationships as the spatial logic of embeddedness' (Hess, 2004). The SMEs' glocal case indeed seems to exclude 'societal embeddedness' as a possible contributor to the strength of localness. In the terminology of social capital theory, bridging capital apparently is a non-important matter. Now the success potential of local business networks is by some means or other correlated not only with the entrepreneurial culture inside a territory, but also with the acceptance level of entrepreneurship by society as a whole. The latter is shaped by common history and common aspirations, for instance, as regards the contribution of entrepreneurship to common wealth in a market economy. The current discussions on the social responsibility of entrepreneurs and on the ethical dimension of entrepreneurship are good examples of this issue. As such sorts of concerns are kept outside local business strategies and local social relationships, this situation of 'network closure' – due to defaulting extra-local linkages of a crucial kind – would limit the strength of localness to the detriment of the small business sector in the global economy. In the face of globalization, the strength of a local network structure finally may depend over time on the societal values of the whole set of actors playing their respective roles in a territorial network that would be involved in the process of internationalization.

In the debate on *sustainable local development*, localness is, of course, considered the true base for overall sustainable development. Sustainability in the practices of local development appeared to be a concern before the famous Brundtland Report, *Our Common Future*, of 1987 (United Nations World Commission on Environment and Development, 1987). This was due to a greater sensitivity to non-market issues of economic development together with a greater awareness of the fact that they can best be dealt with at the local level. New ways of thinking about economic development, new values, new expectations and new norms are spreading now. On that score the analysis of the entrepreneurial environment should give greatest attention to sustainable local development as a possible leverage of evolving societal values.

In a theoretical perspective, any emphasis on the importance of localness leads to views that are opposite to macroeconomic theory which for a long time has disdained localness as a 'no-man's land'. Stressing localness means that it is the specific local characteristics that give the impetus or set the brakes on development. Most of the theoretical work on sustainable local development assumes that the development a territory may bring depends on the way it shapes its functioning and organizing, that is, its institutional settings. Such a view could easily be theorized by integrating the previous conceptualizations of social capital and proximity into a comprehensive framework such as the one elaborated by French economist Valérie Angeon and others (Angeon and Callois, 2005; Angeon et al., 2006). They endeavour to show how articulation between social capital and proximity dynamics is fundamental to a proper understanding of the social determinants of territorial sustainable development dynamics. In short, 'social capital, to be activated in an efficient way, needs a supportive environment through specific dynamic relationships. It rests on some density of ties, which supposes that the actors are embedded, in a certain way, in proximity relations'. The territorial social capital which is involved in this process is an endogenous set of mental representations, values related to trust and norms that are linked to certain forms of proximity like 'organized proximity' and 'institutional proximity'. Although it can best be activated in a territorial context, extra-local linkages are supposed to prevent lock-in situations. The latter condition obviously addresses the 'bridging capital' argument or, to put it in another way, the 'not too much, not too little proximity' reasoning. The strength of localness seems to be grounded on a mix of 'societal embeddedness' and 'territorial embeddedness'.

In older theoretical work on community development such as that elaborated by Ken Wilkinson, the focus had been put in particular on the interaction process of individuals, groups and organizations. The community is seen as a dynamic interaction field: it emerges from the normal flow of interactions among actors in a locality. The interests that actors have determine in part the course of the community's social process. The shared interest in the welfare of their locality differentiates the community field from other local interaction: 'locality orientation is the hallmark of community action' (Wilkinson, 1991). In that 'community interaction field theory' which is supposed to apply especially to rural communities, focus is then put on the fact that the organization of the community's action, that is, linking and coordinating local resources for the benefit of the community, does not occur spontaneously. Community capacity building and community leadership are therefore critical questions. Any community development programme, for instance by promoting entrepreneurship through educational programmes, has to give careful attention to these constraints (Korsching and Allen, 2004). This emphasis on the organizational aspects of community development obviously brings it near to the newer approach of sustainable local development, as mentioned before.

Localness, however, is also a controversial subject that different ideologies related to economic development issues have seized upon for a long time. It is worthwhile to remind ourselves of the main points of these ideologies on account of the various ways localness may be perceived and used. In the past there have been many pleadings, in particular within the cooperative movement, in favour of a social economy that meets the needs and aspirations of people and a society that enables the human being to strengthen its individual and collective identity to counteract the pervasive process of what we call today globalization. The enterprises that make up this sector – cooperatives, mutual societies, associations as well as informal organizations – have proven their efficiency throughout history in Europe, Africa, India and Latin America. They are still considered 'the best means for sustainable local development' (Draperi, 2005). Localness via these collective forms of locality-based enterprises comes forth as bred in the nature of things regarding the functioning of social economy.

Localness more recently has been ascribed to critical qualities through the 'glocal vision' of economic development. Whereas at a first stage the debate on sustainable development put the focus on the global level, the think tanks on 'glocalization' now recommend a greater balance between local and global dimensions in the evolution of world's affairs (CERFE, 2003). To put it more precisely, the goal is

> both to establish a link between the benefits of the global dimension – in terms of technology, information and economics – and local realities, while, at the same time, establishing a bottom-up system for the governance of globalization, based on a greater equality in the distribution of the planet's resources and on an authentic social and cultural rebirth of disadvantaged populations.

Local realities are recognized on the account of the importance of cultural diversity and on the vigorous entrepreneurial spirit of local actors. Localness in that vision is conceived of as a means to give the best chances of success to the Western development pattern.

As a radical criticism of the neoliberal model of globalization, a 'post-development' approach has gained ground since the last decade, where 'localism' has been given the force of a general unquestionable principle. It strongly emphasizes the 'necessity to revive the local land' in view of 'getting out of development and economy and fighting against globalisation. What is at stake is to avoid the "glocal" argument being used as an alibi for pursuing the wasting of the social tissue' (Latouche, 2004). This implies 'building down our mindset in the realm of economics' and to rethink the issue in terms of 'sustainable decrease'. In this perspective, localness is valued for itself as a necessary and sufficient condition of sustainability at the societal level and for everyday living.

From a policy perspective, the significance of localness and the various ways it is claimed in economic development issues is best documented in numerous reports on 'community development' which have been released since the 1970s. In these documents, community is usually understood in geographical terms but it may also refer to common cultural heritage, language, language and beliefs or shared interests. In short, a threefold challenge local grassroots practices have to face should be noted: it involves capacity building, organizing collective action, and good governance.

The capacity-building challenge has to do with the variety of tangible and intangible resources that have to be mobilized within a territory and which altogether determine its potential for change. It also includes all that is brought to bear on a process to make it successful, such as commitment, motivation and leadership. Capacity building thus depends on dynamic processes involving individual and collective actors pursuing a common goal.

The organization of collective action relies either on a contractual process through which partners commit themselves to consulting, coordination and cooperation and/or on a participatory planning process which creates a long-term framework for decision-making and action. The organizational effectiveness of collective action also depends on maintaining momentum in such key areas like leadership and partnership.

The governance challenge addresses the question of how possible diverging interests may be harmonized with a view to realizing a common project. Divergences could bear on the individual interests within the private sector or be entailed by the differences between market economy and social economy. The challenge concerning the latter issue is all the more significant as 'social entrepreneurship' is considered by an increasing number of leading personalities such as Muhammad Yunus, the advocate of micro-finance and Nobel Price winner, as a robust basis for sustainable development. Institutions empowered to grant participatory processes of decision and action and to secure transparency that everyone may benefit from are generally seen as the best way to tide over the difficulties rooted in the everyday situations of contradictory interests.

Again localness, by the mere fact of proximity dynamics, is supposed to ensure the best context for coming through with each of the challenges local development practices have to meet. But the defenders of local sustainable development should also care about the strength of localness which not only depends on the 'institutional thickness' of a community, but also on institutional bridging: the latter may provide external resources of any kind and information on alternative ways of organizing or participating which might have been experienced elsewhere.

As an overall statement, one may say that localness of social capital makes every possible environment unique since there are no grounds for proximity dynamics to evolve the same way or in the same direction. The local environment's uniqueness is enhanced by the variety of possible 'externalities' influencing its strength. By way of comparison, localness appears as a prism, with several parallel sides refracting and splitting each one of the colours coming from its environment. The analysis of the entrepreneurial environment has to cope with this prismatic appearance of social capital and has to render an account of the whole spectrum of resources and values it conveys.

4 CONCLUDING REMARKS

There stands out a clear parallel between development theory and entrepreneurship theory. While for a long time the tendency to conceive of development as being essentially a homogenous mechanical process prevailed, the contingent nature of development and a possible range of development alternatives are increasingly being acknowledged. The English version of the social regulation theory as elaborated by Paul Hirst and Jonathan Zeitlin is one of the new approaches that places much more emphasis on human agency and recognizes the contingency of development. Within this theoretical framework, the global economy is analysed 'in terms of a series of modes of development based on combination of the currently ascendant regime of accumulation and a variety of modes of social regulation' (Hirst and Zeitlin, 1991). The regime of accumulation determines the overall possibilities for the global economy in terms of production and consumption levels whereas a mode of social regulation is 'a complex of institutions and norms which secure, at least for a certain period, the adjustment of individual agents and social groups to the overarching principle of the accumulation regime'. As emphasized in the French approach to the theory of social regulation, rules are liable to a continuous renewing through a process of negotiation that grounds social relationship (Reynaud, 1997); rules resulting from social interactions allow for communication, exchange, collaboration, contract and, even, conflict mechanisms.

The theoretical approach of entrepreneurship is evolving in a similar manner, although with some appreciable delay. Most of the literature on entrepreneurship keeps up with entrepreneurialism, that is, the ethnocentric Western approach which sticks to searching for the 'essence of entrepreneurship'. The recognition of alternative forms of entrepreneurship, however, makes its way through specialized research on topics such as indigenous entrepreneurship, community-based entrepreneurship and so on, as recalled above. The conception of entrepreneurship as a 'rhizome' should show the way forward. Based on this metaphor, Chris Steyaert suggests.

> to keep entrepreneurship as what it is: a fertile middle space, a little chaotic and unfocused arena, a heterotopic space for varied thinking, a space that can connect to many forms of theoretical thinking and where many thinkers can connect to, a true inter-discipline. In this spirit, this would require us, secondly, to alter our way of thinking of science into a so-called rhizomatic one. (Steyaert, 2005)

The demand-side approach of entrepreneurship without doubt takes up this spirit. It highlights the distinct yet intertwining features of the entrepreneurial environments whose understanding needs connections with other fields of theoretical thinking, as we have indicated. Also it makes clear that there is no single role set to be played by entrepreneurs in the global economy. Entrepreneurship as leverage for wealth in developed countries and entrepreneurship as a remedy against poverty in developing countries do not occur on the same stage: researchers have to give the utmost attention to the differences regarding social capital as they originate from the societal, network and territorial embedding structures because the relevance of a unique entrepreneurial role pattern is at stake. In addition, on account of the uniqueness of local environments resulting from the proximity dynamics, researchers should contemplate a widely differentiated role pattern as a new reasonable working hypothesis for studying entrepreneurs and their environment. Logically, and considering especially the sustainable local development issue, this leads to a questioning of the entrepreneurial capabilities that are needed in such a unique environment: societal capabilities would not be the least important when compared with personal and organizational capabilities (Obrecht, 2004). Finally, there are, of course, methodological questions to be settled about the most appropriate ways for studying the entrepreneurial environment and/or meeting the capability approach: not surprisingly there is increasing evidence about the resourcefulness of qualitative research as has been clearly indicated by a number of experts (for example, Dana and Dana, 2005).

REFERENCES

Aldrich, H. and C. Zimmer (1986), 'Entrepreneurship through social networks', in D. Sexton and R. Smilor (eds), *The Art and Science of Entrepreneurship*, New York: Ballinger, pp. 3–23.

Amin, A. and N. Thrift (1993), 'Globalization, institutional thickness and local prospects', *Revue d'Economie Régionale et Urbaine*, no. 3.

Angeon, V. and J.M. Callois (2005), 'Fondements théoriques du développement local: quels apports de la théorie du capital social et de l'économie de proximité?', *Economie et Institutions*, nos 6 and 7; 1er et 2è semestre, 18–46.

Angeon, V., P. Caron and S. Lardon (2006), 'Des liens sociaux à la construction d'un développement territorial durable: quel rôle de la proximité dans ce processus?', *Revue Développement Durable & Territoires*, July, available at: http://developpementdurable.revues.org/index2851.html, accessed 2006.

Barney, J. (1991), 'Firm resources and sustained competitive advantage', *Journal of Management*, **17** (1), 99–120.

Boschma, R. (2005), 'Proximity & innovation: a critical assessment', *Regional Studies*, **39** (1), 61–74.

Bourdieu, P. (1980), 'Le capital social: notes provisoires', *Actes de la Recherche en Sciences Sociales*, **30**, 2–6.

Bourdieu, P. (1986), 'The forms of capital', in J. Richardson (ed.), *Handbook of Theory and Research for the Sociology of Education*, New York: Greenwood Press, pp. 241–58.

Brouthers, K.D., L.E. Brouthers and S. Werner (2008), 'Resource-based advantages in an international context', *Journal of Management*, **34** (2), 189–217.

Burt, R.S. (1982), *Toward a Structural Theory of Action*, New York: Academic Press.

Burt, R.S. (1992), *Structural Holes*, Cambridge, MA: Harvard University Press.

Burt, R.S. (2000), 'The network structure of social capital', in R.I. Sutton and B.M. Staw (eds), *Research in Organizational Behaviour*, Greenwich, CT: JAI Press, pp. 345–423.

Burt, R.S. (2001), 'Structural holes versus network closure as social capital', in N. Lin, K.S. Cook and R.S. Burt (eds), *Social Capital: Theory and Research*, New York: Aldine de Gruyter, pp. 31–56.

Cavusgil, T.S. (1984), 'Differences among exporting firms based on their degree of internationalisation', *Journal of Business Research*, **12** (2), 195–208.

CERFE (Centro di Ricerca e Formazione in Roma) (2003), *Glocalization. Research Study and Policy Recommendations*, Rome: CERFE.

Coleman, J. (1988), 'Social capital in the creation of human capital', *American Journal of Sociology*, **94**, 95–120.

Coleman, J.S. (1990), *Foundations of Social Theory*, Cambridge, MA: Harvard University Press.

Curry, G. (2005), 'Doing business in Papua New Guinea: the social embeddedness of small business enterprises', *Journal of Small Business & Entrepreneurship*, **18** (2), 231–45.

Dana, L.P. (1995), 'Entrepreneurship in a remote sub-Arctic community: Nome, Alaska', *Entrepreneurship: Theory and Practice*, **20** (1), 55–72. Reprinted in Norris Krueger (ed.) (2002), *Entrepreneurship: Critical Perspectives on Business and Management*, vol. 4, London: Routledge, pp. 255–75.

Dana, L.P. and T.E. Dana (2005), 'Expanding the scope of methodologies used in entrepreneurship research', *International Journal of Entrepreneurship and Small Business*, **2** (1).

Draperi, J.F. (2005), *Rendre possible un autre monde: économie sociale, coopération et développement durable*, Montreuil, France: Presses de l'Economie Sociale.

Fukuyama, F. (2000), 'Social capital and civil society', IMF, working paper WP/00/74.

Gasse, Y. (2003), 'L'influence du milieu dans la création d'entreprises', *Organisations & Territoires*, **12** (2), 49–56.

Granovetter, M. (1973), 'The strength of weak ties', *American Journal of Sociology*, **78** (6), 1360–80.

Granovetter, M. (1983), 'The strength of weak ties: network theory revisited', *Sociological Theory*, **1**, 201–33.

Granovetter, M. (1985), 'Economic action and social structure: the problem of embeddedness', *American Journal of Sociology*, **91** (3), 481–510.

Granovetter, M. (1990), 'The old and the new economic sociology: a history and agenda', in R. Friedberg and A.F. Robertson (eds), *Beyond the Marketplace: Rethinking Economy and Society*, New York, Aldine, pp. 89–105.

Grossetti, M. (2006), 'Proximities and embedding effects', Fifth Proximity Congress, Bordeaux, June.

Hamel, G. and C.K. Prahalad (1990), 'The core competence of the corporation', *Harvard Business Review*, **68** (3), 79–91.
Hess, M. (2004), 'Spatial relationships? Towards a reconceptualization of embeddedness', *Progress in Human Geography*, **28** (2), 165–86.
Hirst, P. and J. Zeitlin (1991), 'Flexible specialization versus post-fordism theory, evidence and policy implications', *Economy and Society*, **20** (1), 5–9.
Johannisson, B. (1984), 'A cultural perspective on small business – local business climate', *International Small Business Journal*, **2** (2), 31–41.
Johannisson, B. (1987), 'Anarchists and organisers: entrepreneurs in a network perspective', *International Studies of Management and Organisation*, **17** (1).
Johannisson, B. (1994), 'Building a glocal strategy. Internationalizing small firms through local networking', in *Small Business and Its Contribution to Regional and International Development*, proceedings of the 39th ICSB World Conference, Strasbourg, June.
Johannisson, B. (2002), 'The institutional embeddedness of local inter-firm networks: a leverage for business creation', *Entrepreneurship & Regional Development*, **14** (4) 277–315.
Johanson, J. and J.E. Vahlne (1977), 'The internationalisation process of the firm. A model of knowledge development and increasing foreign market commitment', *Journal of International Business Studies*, first quarter, **8** (1), 23–32.
Julien, P.A. (1994), 'Globalisation de l'économie et PME', in *Small Business and Its Contribution to Regional and International Development*, proceedings of the 39th ICSB World Conference, Strasbourg, June.
Keeble, D., C. Lawson, H.L. Smith, B. Moore and F. Wilkinson (1998), 'Internationalisation processes, networking and local embeddedness in technology-intensive small firms', *Small Business Economics*, **11**, 327–42.
Korsching, P. and J. Allen (2004), 'Local entrepreneurship: a development model based on community interaction field theory', *Journal of the Community Development Society*, **35** (1).
Latouche, S. (2004), '*Survivre au développement*', Paris: Editions Mille et Une Nuits.
Levy-Tadjine, T. and R. Paturel (2006), 'Modéliser et singulariser le phénomène entrepreneurial' in L'internationalisation des PME et ses conséquences sur les stratégies entrepreneuriales', 8ème Congrès International Francophone en Entrepreneuriat et PME, HEG, Fribourg, October.
Lin, N. (1999), 'Building a network theory of social capital', *Connections*, **22** (1), 28–51.
Lin, N. (2001), *Social Capital. A Theory of Social Structure and Action*, Cambridge: Cambridge University Press.
Maillat, D. and L. Kebir (1999), 'Learning region et systèmes territoriaux de production', *Revue d'Economie Régionale et Urbaine*, **3**, 429–48.
Malmberg, A. and P. Maskell (2006), 'Localized learning – what it is and what it isn't', paper presented at the 5th Proximity Congress, Bordeaux, June.
Marchesnay, M. and C. Fourcade (1996), 'Rationalités des politiques de développement local et PME', Actes du 3ème Congrès International Francophone sur la PME, Université du Québec at Trois-Rivières, Canada, October.
Morris, M.H., D.L. Davis and J.F. Allen (1993), 'Fostering corporate entrepreneurship: cross-cultural comparison of the importance of individualism versus collectivism', *Journal of International Business Studies*, first quarter, **25** (1), 65–89.
Morrisson, A. (2000), 'Entrepreneurship: what triggers it?', *International Journal of Entrepreneurial Behaviour & Research*, **6** (2), 59–71.
Narayan, D. (1999), 'Bonds and bridges: social capital and poverty', World Bank working paper no. 2167.
North, D.C. (1990), *Institutions, Institutional Change and Economic Performance*, Cambridge: Cambridge University Press.
Obrecht, J.J. (2004), 'Entrepreneurial capabilities: a resource-based systemic approach to international entrepreneurship', in L.-P. Dana (ed.), *Handbook of Research on International Entrepreneurship*, Cheltenham, UK and Northampton, MA, USA: Edward Elgar Publishing, pp. 241–64.
Oviatt, B.M. and P.P. McDougall (1994), 'Toward a theory of international new ventures', *Journal of International Business Studies*, first quarter, **25** (1), 45–64.
Peredo, A.M. (2003), 'Emerging strategies against poverty: the road less travelled', *Journal of Management Inquiry*, **12** (2), 155–66.
Peredo, A.M. (2006), 'Toward a theory of community-based enterprise', *Academy of Management Review*, **31** (2), 309–28.
Peredo, A.M., R.B. Anderson, C.S. Galbraith, B. Honig and L.P. Dana (2004), 'Towards a theory of indigenous entrepreneurship', *International Journal of Entrepreneurship and Small Business*, **1** (1/2), 1–20.
Plociniczak, S. (2002), 'Création de petites enterprises, réseaux relationnels et capital social: une approche interactive entre l'acte entreprenant et l'environnement relationnel', in *PME et développement régional*, Colloque de l'Association de Science Régionale de Langue Française, Trois-Rivières, August.
Polanyi, K. (1944), *The Great Transformation. The Political and Economic Origins of our Time*, Boston, MA: Beacon Press.

Putnam, R. (1993), *Making Democracy Work*, Princeton, NJ: Princeton University Press.

Putnam, R. (2000), *Bowling Alone: The Collapse and Revival of American Community*, New York: Simon & Schuster.

Ramangalahy, C., T.V. Menzies, L.J. Filion, G. Brenner and M. Discarmel (2002), 'Entrepreneuriat ethnique et développement local: comparaisons des contributions des entrepreneurs ethniques au Canada: les Chinois, les Italiens, les Indiens Sikhs', XXXVIIIe Colloque Annuel de l'Association de Science Régionale de Langue Française, Université de Québec à Trois-Rivières.

Reynaud, J.D. (1997), *Les règles du jeu: l'action collective et la régulation sociale*, Paris: Armand Collin.

Sen, A. (1977), 'Rational fools: a critique of the behavioural foundation of economic theory', *Philosophy and Public Affairs*, **6** (4), 317–44.

Steyaert, C. (2005), 'Entrepreneurship: in between what?: on the frontier as a discourse of entrepreneurship research', *International Journal of Entrepreneurship and Small Business*, **2** (1), 2–16.

Szarka, J. (1990), 'Networking and small firms', *International Small Business Journal*, **8** (2), 10–12.

Thornton, P.H. (1999), 'The sociology of entrepreneurship', *Annual Review of Sociology*, **25**, 19–46.

Tiessen, J.M. (1997), 'Collectivism and entrepreneurship: a framework for international comparative research', *Journal of Business Venturing*, **12** (5), 367–84.

Torre, A. and J.P. Gilly (2000), 'On the analytical dimensions of proximity dynamics', *Regional Studies*, **34** (2), 169–80.

Torre, A. and A. Rallet (2005), 'Proximity and localization', *Regional Studies*, **39** (1), 47–60.

Torre, A. and B. Zuindeau (2009), 'Proximity economics and environment: assessment and prospects', *Journal of Environmental Planning and Management*, **52** (1), 1–24.

Torres, O. (2002), 'Face à la mondialisation, les PME doivent mettre du territoire et de la proximité dans leurs stratégies de glocalisation', 11ème Conférence Internationale de Management Stratégique, AIMS, Paris, June.

Tremblay, M. and C. Carrier (2006), 'Pratiques collectives d'identification d'opportunités: une étude exploratoire', in L'internationalisation des PME et ses conséquences sur les stratégies entrepreneuriales, 8ème Congrès International Francophone en Entreneuriat et PME, HEG, Fribourg, Suisse.

United Nations World Commission on Environment and Development (1987), *Our Common Future*, Oxford: Oxford University Press.

Vicente, J., Y. Dalla Pria and R. Suire (2007), 'The ambivalent role of mimetic behavior in proximity dynamics: evidence from the French "Silicon Sentier"', in J. Suriñach, R. Moreno and E. Vayá (eds), *Knowledge Externalities, Innovation Clusters and Regional Development*, Cheltenham, UK and Northampton, MA, USA: Edward Elgar Publishing.

Wernerfelt, B. (1984), 'A resource-based view of the firm', *Strategic Management Journal*, **5** (2), 171–80.

Wilkinson, K. (1991), *The Rural Community in America*. New York: Greenwood.

Zukin, S. and P. Dimaggio (1990), 'Introduction', in S. Zukin and P. DiMaggio (eds), *Structures of Capital: The Social Organization of the Economy*, Cambridge: Cambridge University Press.

15 Ethics and entrepreneurship

Alan E. Singer

1 INTRODUCTION

According to Sen (1997), the economic way of thinking downplays the role of ethics. Since most theories of entrepreneurship have adopted that 'way', a contribution from ethics might be of substance. There is considerable consensus amongst contemporary philosophers that the economic way is a story or a narrative that *mainly* tells, in this context, how an entrepreneurial society based on trade is ethically superior to a totalitarian hierarchy, or a society at war, or overrun by crime (compare Baumol, Chapter 6, this volume). The ethics story plainly overlaps with this, but it *mainly* tells how a caring and just society that upholds rights and humane ideals is even better. Simply put, the former is somewhat dismal while the latter is idealistic.

There is also a (meta)-story in which ethics is ultimately captured or eventually revealed by economic theory. This tells us for example that (i) illegal entrepreneurship is often unethical, although in some cases it can have an economic coordinating or liberating function, but also that (ii) ethics is already built into the activities of productive entrepreneurs. In addition, many of the latter individuals believe that they are already 'acting ethically' (doing good) simply by being entrepreneurial: crafting a synthesis, mobilizing resources and innovatively engaging stakeholders (for example, Brenkert, 2002; Christensen, 2008). Entrepreneurs are thus seen as role models demonstrating self-help, often providing an exit from poverty for themselves and their families or communities, in a world of undistributed riches. They are not ethically required to do any more. To the extent that society as a whole might be 'heavily indebted' to entrepreneurs collectively (compare Chapter 6, this volume), this viewpoint seems justified.

2 DUALISM

In accordance with the notion of creative-destruction, it is extremely common for any given entrepreneurial act to be perceived and narrated in diametrically opposing ways. Descriptions of entrepreneurial activity as productive versus destructive are a matter of strong contention. For example, many appreciate that entrepreneurs (in general) serve society and add to the common good because, or to the extent that, they create jobs, satisfy demand, create and share knowledge, facilitate cultural renewal, restore the environment, design ecologies, pay taxes, lobby to update outmoded laws, stabilize governments, act as role models, keep the dream alive, demonstrate mastery, encourage value-expression, engage in philanthropy, and so on.

Others, or the same persons at different times, conclude precisely the opposite. Entrepreneurs damage society and detract from the common good, because they (correspondingly and variously) create sweatshops, decrease local affordability, conceal or monopolize knowledge, destroy ancient cultures, damage the environment, destroy ecologies, avoid and evade tax, lobby at other's expense, support corrupt or oppressive regimes, frustrate others with unrealistic goals, create slaves, colonise the mind, cynically service an image, and so on.

There is an extensive multidisciplinary literature that elaborates these two contrasting stories, thereby richly informing the ethics–entrepreneurship relationship. It can be helpful to organize this material within a framework of dualism. Such a 'dualism' is comprised of several bi-polar *components*, such as shareholder versus stakeholder models of management (or variants of capitalism), exploitative versus compensatory responses to market failures, right versus left political leanings, ethics now versus later (that is, timing), to mention a few. These 'components' each then inform a collection of topical *themes* within entrepreneurship and ethics, such as poverty, environment, property rights, corruption, relations between businesses, governments and non-government organizations (NGOs), and so on. There are also several *spanning* themes in the dualism framework, each of which inform both 'poles' of the bi-polar components. These include intentionality, character, imagination and societal macro-trends. The remainder of this chapter briefly discusses a selection of the components and themes.

3 COMPONENTS

The set of human values can be (roughly) partitioned, with one sub-set (that is, one side of the dualism) associated with efficiency, craftsmanship and free exchange; the other 'side' with justice, care, avoidance of harm and protection of rights. Productive for-profit entrepreneurship plainly expresses the former sub-set, while social and eco-preneurship, by definition, give priority to the latter (for example, care, stewardship, restoration).

On the same side as the efficiency-related 'values' one finds the economic principle of utility maximization (exchange) and normative ethical egoism. On the other side, one finds utilitarianism (which resembles the multi-stakeholder model of strategic management) *and* deontological ethics. The title 'Kantian entrepreneur' plainly belongs to the authentically caring social or humanistic eco-entrepreneur, but not to the entrepreneurial designer of a corporate empire that is 'oligarchic, elitist non-democratic and exclusive' (Neilsen, 2002: 233). Some other complex moral and political theories span the dualism (see below). Contractarianism, for example, has agreements amongst free self-interested individuals at its core, which places it on the 'exchange and efficiency' side of the dualism; but there is also an emphasis on justice and the avoidance of some types of harm.

3.1 Stakeholders

A dialectical tension between a stakeholder model and shareholder model of enterprise has been widely recognized in the general literatures of strategy (for example, De Wit and Meyer, 2005) *and* in business ethics. Freeman (1999: 234) described the term 'stakeholder' as an 'obvious literary device, meant to call into question the (typical) emphasis on stockholders'. The answer to that question then seems to depend on time and place. For example, Jawahar and McLaughlin (2001) noted that most start-up entrepreneurs are concerned only with stockholders, creditors and customers; but this often changes later on, as other stakeholders are engaged. This dovetails with 'rags to riches' stories that begin with an exit from poverty and end with Carnegie-style altruistic philanthropy.

This shareholder versus stakeholder component of the dualism plays out somewhat differently under the several regional variants of capitalism. Investor-capitalism (Anglo-US) and crony-capitalism (almost everywhere) invite a lot of Freeman-type 'questioning'; although as Hendry (2001) noted, in these regions, the issue seems broadly settled in favour of shareholders. In continental Europe and Japan (and in US managerial capitalism up to about 1980) a somewhat different balance has perhaps been struck.

3.2 Market Failures

Entrepreneurial strategies for profit involve the deliberate exploitation (taking advantage) of several known limitations (imperfections, failures) of market-based systems. These limitations forge a gap between capitalist enterprise and overall conditions of human well-being. In this context, Sheperd and Levesque (2002: 152) commented that the entrepreneurial-process 'can be used to exploit stakeholders, for the personal gain of the entrepreneur'. Accordingly, Prakash Sethi (2003) prescribed that institutions should 'hold companies accountable' for a more equitable distribution of above-normal profits that were obtained by the 'exploitation of market power'. Heath (2006: 551) then claimed that 'the exploitation of one or another form of market imperfection' is what 'upsets people' and 'gives profit-seeking a bad name'.

Ethics in general emphasizes doing the right thing in the first place, rather than being held accountable for what is wrong. Accordingly, it tells how entrepreneurs might (i) voluntarily refrain from exploitation by exercising self-restraint or self-regulation, or (ii) proactively compensate for and mitigate the effects of others' exploitative behaviour (for example, Singer, 2007a, 2007b). In practice, this type of ethical-strategy requires partnerships with suitably reformed institutions (see below) as well as a clear explanation to stakeholders.

4 TOPICAL THEMES

The topical themes associated with ethical entrepreneurship include poverty, property and corruption. Each can be informed by the above bi-polar components, but also by the various spanning-themes within the dualism framework (compare section 5 in this chapter).

4.1 Poverty

While entrepreneurship sometimes functions as an exit route from poverty, the larger ethical issue concerns the prospects for the alleviation of global poverty through capitalist enterprise. A mainstream view sees that for-profit enterprises create wealth, but they do not have an interest in re-distribution, other than through the capital markets to other business enterprises. Prahalad and Hammond (2002) have narrated the story of a benevolent global capitalism-as-usual, in which bottom-of-pyramid (poverty) markets are duly financed with micro credit and 'served' with consumer goods; where women are honoured and where high-technology infrastructures spread rapidly through less developed countries (LDCs) due to the deliberate strategies of for-profit enterprise.

According to its critics, this story leaves out the many people in poverty who cannot self-sustain or, more pertinently, are effectively prevented by others from doing so. Bhensadia and Dana (2004), for example, saw 'a real danger' that the rural poor (in India) would be 'left out'. More generally it is apparent that entrepreneurs can destroy value for the local poor. This is exemplified by food exports from regions in famine. Accordingly, there are many (for example, Freeman, 1998) who believe that for-profit enterprise alone is not a complete solution to poverty. It is also necessary to have changes in peoples' attitude, agenda, mindset or political philosophy. This implies that entrepreneurs themselves ought to have dual or mixed motives, including the direct and deliberate reduction of poverty. This alternative 'story' of deliberate targeted assistance aligns closely with almost all ancient theological texts that tell of ways of *routinely* and quietly helping the unproductive poor, while remaining productive oneself.

4.2 Property

Baumol (Chapter 6, this volume) notes that entrepreneurial talent can be shifted away from war and crime by having 'rules against confiscation of private property and for patent protection'. The idea is that intellectual property laws help would-be warriors, criminals and the once-poor, to capture revenue, appropriate profit and secure a return on investment, through legitimate non-violent enterprise.

A more distinctively ethical account begins at the other end. It is first asked (rhetorically and idealistically) how social and environmental values can be 'taken care of through the institutions of property and consumption' (Freeman and Venkataraman, 2003: 3) commenting on (Derry, 2002). Then, with a good definition of property as 'the relationship between people with respect to things' (Munzer, 1990) it becomes obvious that the contemporary capitalist laws on property are placing power-relations (that is, market power and political capital) far ahead of 'relations' of care, social justice and humane ideals.

Strong intellectual property rights (IPR) regimes in particular (patents and digital copyrights) are often seen as highly unjust and uncaring (for example, Collier, 2000). They arguably also create an inefficient tragedy of the anti-commons (Heller and Eisenberg 1998). There is a serious concern that patents make poverty worse to the extent that they are discriminatory, favour corporate interests over citizen–user-consumers and directly reduce specific freedoms and capabilities. Indeed, patent protection of pharmaceuticals has been a distal cause of millions of deaths. Patents also treat human-designed life-forms as legal property, thereby violating several widely held ethical principles, including some pertaining to slavery.

Accordingly, ethical entrepreneurs would be cautious about the implementation of their property rights in general, but especially their own dependence upon IPR. Authentic eco-preneurs, social-entrepreneurs and craft-based innovators have already subordinated profit (that is, the accumulation of property rights by shareholders) to more idealistic motives. They might attempt to overcome the tradeoffs involved in IPR-dependency by adopting IPR-free strategies, such as hypercompetitive cannibalization, or revenue-capturing from auxiliary market offerings.

4.3 Codes and Corruption

In the international context, entrepreneurs frequently encounter implicit requests for facilitating-payments and bribes (for example, Transparency International, 2009). Laws, guidelines and codes of ethics that proscribe this (and other aspects of entrepreneurial conduct) are often viewed with cynicism and frustration. There is a widespread sense that they are impractical and that in any case, the language of 'ethics' is deployed only by power elites (for example, in codes of conduct) who are themselves profoundly corrupt. Put differently, 'ethics is for the weak', as Nietzsche explained.

Accordingly, in cases where codes are in place 'knowing when to break the rules appropriately may be a sign of real respect and understanding of them' (Molyneaux, 2003: 142). This is the type of knowledge that can help the entrepreneur in practice and that can sometimes be provided by moral theory. The Principle of Double Effect, for example, implies that a facilitating payment for an otherwise normal deal (like unloading fruit from a dock) might be excusable, provided that (i) the deal depends on it, (ii) there is no expectation of subsequent violations of human rights or pollution danger, and (iii) the entrepreneur is providing routine and continuing support for other institutions and NGO's that battle against corruption (Roy and Singer, 2006).

4.4 Partnerships

Many for-profit entrepreneurs routinely lobby for policies that are expected to benefit the enterprise even though they might detract from the common good (for example, Smith, 1776; Brooke-Hamilton and Hock, 1997; Oberman, 2004). Some go further by promulgating a self-serving ideology, thereby shifting the attitudes of citizens and electorates towards favouring such activities and neglecting humane ideals. Ethical entrepreneurs, in contrast, would (and do) attempt to shift public attitudes in the opposite direction. They look for good-faith institutional partners in this mission. They do not just comply or wait for 'pertinent changes in institutions' (Baumol, Chapter 6, this volume) but they choose instead to be proactive in this ethical-political arena.

5 SPANNING THEMES

Various spanning themes further inform both 'poles' of various components of the ethics–entrepreneurship dualism framework. Some examples are: intention, character, imagination, trends and synthesis, as follow.

5.1 Intention

The efficiency motives *and* the justice motives of an ethical entrepreneur are both subject to the classical constraints associated with free will. The problem of free will versus determinism (or deliberate versus emergent strategy) is theological and secular, social and economic. Many theological texts contain warnings to the effect, 'make your plans, they will fail', and most for-profit entrepreneurs do just that. In the Western secular tradition, Kant emphasized only the quality of intentions. To be ethical, these must involve genuine goodwill. Whether or not a project succeeds is then of less moral significance. In practical enterprise, however, this Kantian emphasis is typically reversed. Only good outcomes count in the public mind and in the bank. The individual entrepreneur then becomes a celebrity or an (accidental) hero, despite (or perhaps because of) the substantial amount of luck (and malfeasance) that might have been be involved.

5.2 Character and Wisdom

Virtue ethics is sometimes regarded as the most important ethical theory of business and management (for example, Solomon, 1992). It spans the dualism because excellent craftsmanship and efficiency, as well as an attitude of caring and a practical commitment to humane ideals, are all marks of good character. By implication, any ethical entrepreneur would nurture and display all of these traits.

Virtue ethics also consider (along with philosophical pragmatism and practical wisdom) that the choice of the right course of entrepreneurial action 'cannot be reduced to the application of a universal rule or principle' (Dunham et al., 2008: 10). Doubt is thus cast upon the value of seeking 'a few good moral principles' or codes to guide the entrepreneur (compare Soule, 2002). The virtuous or wise or ethical entrepreneur is variously seen (for example, Dunham et al., 2008; Singer and Doktor, 2008; Zeleny, 2005) to be one who (i) has a detailed understanding of all the relevant circumstances, (ii) selects and explicates good purposes, (iii) remains mindful of the personal and enterprise lifecycles, and (iv) prioritizes activities accordingly. (Pragmatists might then be quick to point out that such habits are also the proper mark of a good strategist.)

5.3 Synthesis and Imagination

Synthesis per se is a rather obvious dualism-spanning theme (for example DeWit and Meyer, 2005). Many definitions of entrepreneurship refer to a 'synthesis' of economic opportunity, or to an economic imagination (for example, Earl, 1983; Sarasvathy, 2002). Competitive advantage can then be described with reference to a synthesis of various strategy components, such as shareholder and stakeholder, compliance and choice, and so on. At the same time, philosophers (for example, Werhane, 1999) have prescribed the exercise of moral imagination or ethical imagination in business and social life; that is, the crafting of a more inclusive plan or narrative: one that exposes and overcomes false choices between 'poles' like efficiency and justice (for example, Kuttner, 1984).

It is perhaps worth mentioning at this point that the 'dualism' framework is itself a candidate for a new synthesis. The relationship between entrepreneurship and ethics has also been described as a correspondence (that is, of similar ideas, not opposites). The correspondence thesis (for example, Logsdon and Wood, 2002; Singer 1994) claims that many of the categories of meaning deployed in the discourse of strategy and enterprise are *also* ethical categories (for example, strategic responsiveness to local market tastes is also a form of caring, or ethics). The dualism framework, in contrast, re-cast categories as opposites. Thus we have a 'dualism of (dualism versus correspondence)' that can be further expanded recursively, whereupon it becomes evocative of Bateson's theory of ecology, or ecological understanding (compare Singer, 2002). This, in turn, constitutes the deep-structure of 'living enterprise' and eco-preneurship (for example, Hawken, 1993).

5.4 Moral Progress

Ever since the idea of dialectics was first articulated (by Plato, 428–348 BC) it has been associated with progress, but especially in the sciences of life and mind. Accordingly, this brief account concludes with a consideration of trends. One can quickly find reports that associate reductions in poverty (in various locations) with periods of enterprising economic activity. This is often taken to mean that enterprise alleviates poverty in general. However, one can also find reports to the contrary, implying that something different or extra is needed. Similar levels of ambiguity surround the related issue of the empirical link between corporate social performance and financial performance (compare Margolis and Walsh, 2003).

Looking forward, yet another significant ambiguity appears. Pessimists perceive a moral regression in society as a whole, while optimists envision gradual moral progress. Few of the latter attribute this progress to the spread of for-profit enterprise (as distinct from social and eco-entrepreneurship, or alternative political arrangements). On this point, Godlovitch (1999: 219) has pointed out that for-profit enterprise *culminates* in an infinity of material goods and information; but this is not a human condition that we can seriously recognize as ideal. Accordingly, he wrote, we only make moral progress to the extent that something else (ethical enterprise perhaps?) is chosen as our 'most important progressive venture' (ibid.).

6 CLASSIFICATION

It is impossible to identify any fully representative set of contributions to 'entrepreneurship and ethics'. However, the organizing framework outlined in this chapter (common themes, bi-polar components, spanning themes) enables the classification of relevant contributions according to the following *types*:

1. Capturing: ethical entrepreneurial behaviours are explained purely in terms of rational utility maximization, as in game theory.
2. Separating: concepts from *within* one side of the dualism are linked together. For example, efficiency is used to justify and explain the for-profit goals of an enterprise.
3. Spanning: one or more 'spanning themes' are explored. For example, the character and wisdom of entrepreneurs is considered, in relation to their social *and* economic concerns.
4. Synthesising: synergies or complementarities are discussed, involving both poles of selected bi-polar component(s). For example, win–win strategies are described.
5. Re-casting: a claim is made that some component of the framework has superior explanatory power. For example, market failures explain more than value conflicts.

7 CONCLUSION

The dualism framework and classification might facilitate further inquiry into ethics and entrepreneurship. The many sceptics who continue to believe that such inquiry is not needed, or that the role of ethics should be 'downplayed' in business practice, might be impressed by a turn-of-the-century survey (mentioned in Kapustkina et al., 2008) in which it was found that only 8 per cent of secondary school students (in a region of Russia, in 1999) regarded 'honest labour' to be a suitable way to gain economic wealth. Fifty-nine per cent responded that 'more suitable ways' included organized crime, while 81 per cent mentioned power.

REFERENCES

Bhensadia, R.R. and L.P. Dana (2004), 'Globalisation and rural poverty', *International Journal of Entrepreneurship & Innovative Management*, **4** (5), special issue on entrepreneurship and poverty.

Brenkert, G. (2002), 'Entrepreneurial ethics and the good society', *Business Ethics Quarterly*, Ruffin Series no. 3 on Ethics and Entrepreneurship, 5–44.

Brooke-Hamilton, J. and D. Hock (1997), 'Ethical standards for business lobbying: some practical suggestions', *Business Ethics Quarterly*, **7** (3), 117–30.

Christensen, S.L. (2008), 'Ethical entrepreneurs: a study of perceptions', *International Journal of Entrepreneurship and Small Business*, **6** (1), special issue on entrepreneurship and moral progress.

Collier, J. (2000), 'Globalisation and ethical global business', *Business Ethics: A European Review*, April, 71–6.

De Wit, B. and R. Meyer (2005), *Strategy Synthesis: Resolving Strategy Paradoxes to Create Competitive Advantage*, London: Thompson Learning.

Derry, R. (2002), 'Seeking a balance: a critical perspective on entrepreneurship and the good society', *Business Ethics Quarterly*, Ruffin Series no. 3 on Ethics and Entrepreneurship, 197–208.

Dunham, L., J. McVea and R.E. Freeman (2008), 'Entrepreneurial wisdom: integrating the ethical and strategic dimensions', *International Journal of Entrepreneurship and Small Business*, **5** (5), 8–19.

Earl, P. (1983), *The Economic Imagination*, Brighton: Wheatsheaf.

Freeman, R.E. (1998), 'Poverty and the politics of capitalism', *Business Ethics Quarterly*, 1, special issue, 31–5.

Freeman, R.E. (1999), 'Divergent stakeholder theory', *Academy of Management Review*, **24** (2), 233–6.

Freeman, R.E. and S. Venkataraman (2002), 'Introduction', *Business Ethics Quarterly*, Ruffin Series no. 3 on Ethics and Entrepreneurship, 1–3.

Godlovitch, S. (1999), 'Varieties of progress', in P.H. Werhane and A.E. Singer (eds), *Business Ethics in Theory & Practice*, Dordrecht: Kluwer.

Hawken, P. (1993), *The Ecology of Commerce*, London: Weidenfeld and Nicolson.

Heath, J. (2006), 'Business ethics without stakeholders', *Business Ethics Quarterly*, **16** (4), 533–57.

Heller, M.A. and R.S. Eisenberg (1998), 'Can patents deter innovation? The anti-commons in biomedical research', *Science*, **280**, 698–701.

Hendry, J. (2001), 'Missing the target: normative stakeholder theory and the corporate governance debate', *Business Ethics Quarterly*, **11** (1), 159–76.

Jawahar, I.M. and G.L. McLaughlin (2001), 'Towards a descriptive stakeholder theory: an organisational life cycle approach', *Academy of Management Review*, **26** (3), 397–414.

Kapustkina, E., M. Sinyutin and Y. Veselov (2008), 'Entrepreneurial trust in the St Petersburg region of Russia', *International Journal of Entrepreneurship*, **5** (5), 94–102.

Kuttner, R. (1984), *The Economic Illusion: False Choices Between Prosperity & Social Justice*, Boston: Houghton Mifflin.

Logsdon, J. and D. Wood (2002), 'Business citizenship: from domestic to global level of analysis', *Business Ethics Quarterly*, **12** (2), 155–87.

Margolis, J. and P. Walsh (2003), 'Misery loves companies: rethinking social initiatives by business', *Administrative Science Quarterly*, **48** (2), 268–306.

Molyneaux, D. (2003), 'Saints and CEO's: an historical experience of altruism, self-interest and compromise', *Business Ethics: A European Review*, **12** (2), 133–43.

Munzer, S.R. (1990), *A Theory of Property*, Cambridge: Cambridge University Press.

Neilsen, R.P. (2002), 'Business citizenship and United States "Investor Capitalism": a critical analysis', *Business Ethics Quarterly*, Ruffin Series no. 3 on Ethics and Entrepreneurship, 231–40.

Oberman, W. (2004), 'A framework for the ethical analysis of corporate political activity', *Business & Society Review*, **109** (2), 245–62.

Prahalad, C.K. and A. Hammond (2002), 'Serving the World's poor, profitably', *Harvard Business Review*, September, 48–57.

Prakash Sethi, S. (2003), 'Globalisation and the good corporation. A need for pro-active co-existence', *Journal of Business Ethics*, **43** (1), 21–31.

Roy (Achinto) and A.E. Singer (2006), 'Reducing corruption in international business: behavioural managerial and political approaches', *Journal of Economic & Social Policy*, **10** (2), 3–24.

Sarasvathy, D.S. (2002), 'Entrepreneurship as economics with imagination', *Business Ethics Quarterly*, Ruffin Series no. 3 Ethics and Entrepreneurship, 95–112.

Sen, A. (1997), 'Economics, business principles and moral sentiments', *Business Ethics Quarterly*, **7** (3), 5–15.

Sheperd, D. and M. Levesque (2002), 'Stakeholder value equilibration, disequilibrium and the entrepreneurial process', *Business Ethics Quarterly*, Ruffin Series no. 3 on Ethics and Entrepreneurship, 151–6.

Singer, A.E. (1994), 'Strategy as moral philosophy', *Strategic Management Journal*, **15**, 191–213.

Singer, A.E. (2002), 'Global business and the dialectic: towards an ecological understanding', *Human Systems Management*, **21** (4), 249–65.

Singer, A.E. (ed.) (2007a), *Business Ethics & Strategy*, vols 1 and 2, Aldershot: Ashgate.

Singer, A.E. (2007b), 'Global strategy and ethics: managing human systems and advancing humane ideals', *Business Ethics Quarterly*, **17** (2), 341–64.

Singer, A.E. and R. Doktor (2008), 'Entrepreneurship as wisdom', *International Journal of Entrepreneurship and Small Business*, **6** (1), 20–27.

Smith, A. (1776), *An Inquiry into the Nature and Causes of the Wealth of Nations*, London: W. Strahan and T. Cadell.

Solomon, R.C. (1992), *Ethics and Excellence: Cooperation and Integrity in Business*, Oxford: Oxford University Press.

Soule, E. (2002), 'Management moral strategies: in search of a few good principles', *Academy of Management Review*, **27** (1), 114–24.

Transparency International (2009), *Business Principles for Countering Bribery*, available at http://www.transparency.org, accessed October 2010.

Werhane, P.H. (1999), *Moral Imagination and Managerial Decision Making*, New York: Oxford University Press.

Zeleny, M. (2005), *Human Systems Management: Integrating Knowledge Management and Systems*, Hackensack, NJ and Singapore: World Scientific.

16 Ethnic minority entrepreneurship

Léo-Paul Dana and Michael Morris

Entrepreneurship and immigration represent two of the most significant global trends in these early years of the twenty-first century. Both are occurring at historically unprecedented levels throughout the world. Dana (2007b) made it clear that these are not unrelated trends. Research over the past 40 years has demonstrated that immigrants often create new ventures at a higher per capita rate than populations in general. Yet, current knowledge of the ways in which immigrants and other minorities create ventures, the types of ventures they create and the outcomes of those ventures remains limited. As such, it becomes less clear how much we can generalize about immigrant or minority group entrepreneurship.

Indeed there are important differences among immigrant groups. The Government of Canada found that per 1000 Filipino workers in Canada, 18 were self-employed; the same reported that per 1000 Greek workers in Canada, 124 were self-employed (Dana, 1991). How can such differences be explained?

Other differences are also apparent across immigrant groups. For instance, while immigrant entrepreneurs are often characterized as having been forced into entrepreneurship because of limited opportunities within a host country, research studies (see Dana, 2007b) have demonstrated that a wide range of motives drive their behaviour. Furthermore, countries differ significantly in the extent to which they actively encourage entrepreneurial behaviour among new arrivals. Similarly, while one might conclude that immigrants only create lifestyle or 'mom and pop' type ventures concentrated in the retail sector, research suggests that significant diversity exists in the types of ventures that are being created.

This chapter is a synthesis of the 48 perspectives on immigrant and minority entrepreneurship provided in Dana (2007b). As a kind of meta-analysis, we have attempted to capture the dominant themes, major arguments and key findings put forward by the outstanding collection of contributors. It is our contention that some important generalizations may be possible based on the patterns that emerge in this chapter. Toward this end, we have formulated an integrative model of factors that explains the emergence of an immigrant or ethnic venture. Implications are drawn from the model for theory building, entrepreneurial practice and public policy. A set of priorities are proposed for future research.

DEVELOPING A MODEL OF IMMIGRANT AND ETHNIC ENTREPRENEURSHIP

The 48 perspectives provided in Dana (2007b), when considered collectively, suggest there may be a common set of key variables that explain immigrant entrepreneurship. That is, there may be common aspects to the immigrant experience that override ethnic and cultural differences. Figure 16.1 illustrates our attempt to capture these key variables. It focuses on six key variables, each of which is summarized below.

1 The Immigrant

Entrepreneurship does not happen without entrepreneurs. While the literature has historically focused on the traits of these individuals, and more recently there has been considerable attention devoted to their cognitive styles, or how they think, the research in this volume has tended to emphasize the relevance of other considerations.

Especially important in this vein are motives, values and skills. Motivation to create a venture can generally be categorized into 'push' versus 'pull' factors. Entrepreneurs are pushed into entrepreneurship when they have limited access to meaningful employment opportunities within existing companies. The obstacles can range from overt labour market discrimination and communication barriers to skill shortcomings. The need to make a living and support one's family, absent opportunities with existing organizations, pushes the individual towards entrepreneurship. Similarly, having technical skills, but an inability to sell these in the labour market, pushes one to create a venture. Alternatively, recognition of opportunity and the desire to achieve a vision can pull an individual towards the entrepreneurial path. While it is generally assumed that immigrants are more pushed than pulled, we find ample evidence of immigrants driven by motives to build growth-oriented ventures and to create wealth.

Values play a role as well, especially when the immigrant has a value-set that is strongly tied to his or her ethnic background. Strong identification with one's ethnicity can lead to a preference to create ventures tied to the ethnic network or enclave, but also to a motivation to serve the ethnic community. Such values will often be manifested in the business practices of the entrepreneur, including employment practices, incurrence of debt and approach to customer service. Yet, there is also evidence that ethnic entrepreneurs share universal values that are unrelated to their ethnicity. Examples of such universal values include individualism, achievement, competitiveness, risk-taking and a strong work ethic. The very act of emigrating may be reflective of some of these so-called entrepreneurial values.

Also relevant in this realm is the relative size of what we might call the 'ethnic gap', or the extent of difference between the norms, values, customs, symbols and language of the host and home countries. Where this gap is larger, the immigrant is driven towards the ethnic network or enclave and towards entrepreneurship. Finally, while the role of other demographics are clear, these chapters do suggest that age and gender also represent significant considerations in the tendency to create ventures in new environments, and in the types of ventures created.

2 Host Country Factors

While a wide range of country factors affect levels of entrepreneurship in general (for example, taxes, mandated social benefits provided by companies, regulation), our interest is in the environmental elements that most influence immigrant entrepreneurship. Based on the range of work submitted to this volume, the role of the informal economy within the larger economy of the host country appears to be an especially

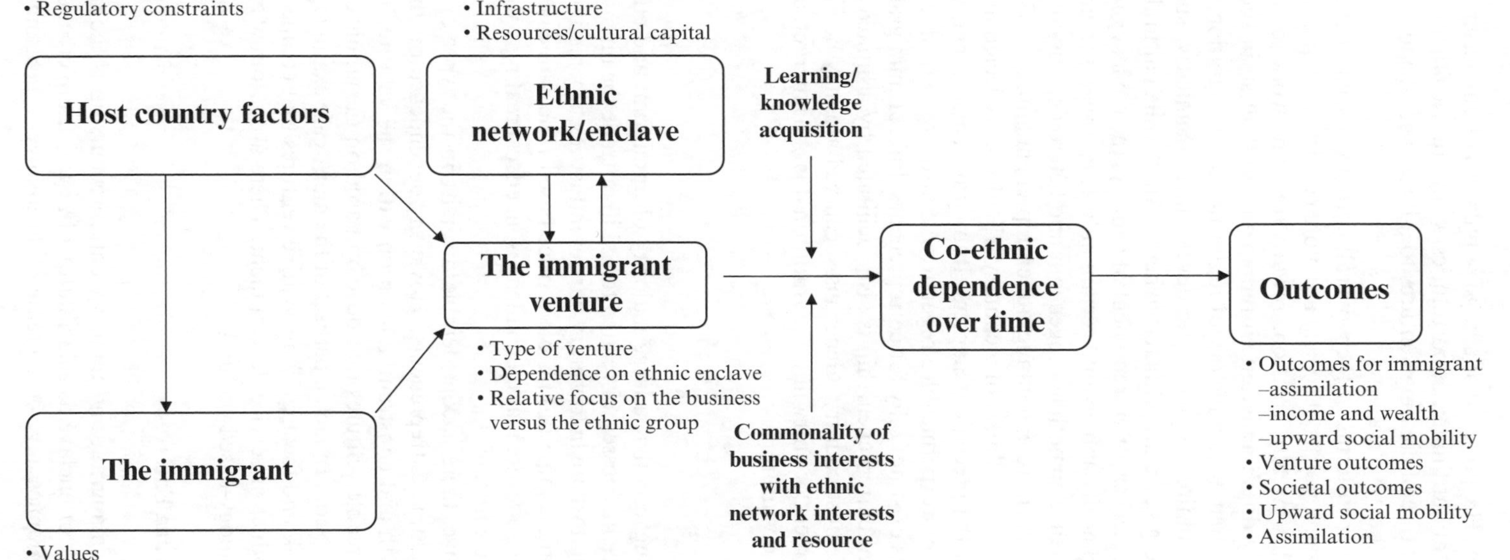
• Role of informal economy in larger economy
• Host country entrepreneurial culture
• Cultural heterogeneity
• Historical role of immigration
• Support programmes for entrepreneurs
• Welfare/social benefit system
• Permeability of markets
• Regulatory constraints
• Access to international ethnic network
• Homogeneity of ethnic group
• Cost of membership in network/enclave
• Reciprocity and trust
• Diversity of business types
• Extensiveness of network
• Crowding within enclave
• Infrastructure
• Resources/cultural capital
Host country factors
Ethnic network/enclave
Learning/ knowledge acquisition
The immigrant venture
Co-ethnic dependence over time
Outcomes
• Type of venture
• Dependence on ethnic enclave
• Relative focus on the business versus the ethnic group
Commonality of business interests with ethnic network interests and resource
• Outcomes for immigrant
–assimilation
–income and wealth
–upward social mobility
• Venture outcomes
• Societal outcomes
• Upward social mobility
• Assimilation
The immigrant
• Values
• Motives
• Ethnic gap (home versus new country)
• Age and gender
• Communication and networking skills
• Technical skills
• Linkage to ethnic businesses back home
Figure 16.1 Immigrant venture flowchart

salient consideration. The presence of a large population of unregistered businesses says something not only about limited opportunities within the 'legitimate' business sector, but also implies a culture of creating ventures to address needs, and a willingness of the government to look the other way.

Countries also differ in terms of their overall entrepreneurial orientation, where the basic cultural values and norms of society are more consistent with individual initiative, personal responsibility, wealth creation, reward for hard work, competitiveness and innovation. Not only does immigrant entrepreneurship flourish in such environments, but these countries often have a history of high rates of immigration, with immigrants making major contributions to economic development. Similarly, such countries will tend to demonstrate great cultural heterogeneity. And, while cultural heterogeneity is consistent with higher levels of entrepreneurial activity, the tendency for immigrants to cluster both geographically and around certain industries appears to occur regardless of this heterogeneity. Hence, in both homogeneous and heterogeneous countries, the ethnic network plays a significant role in immigrant entrepreneurship.

The entrepreneurial friendliness of a country will also be reflected in some other variables emphasized in the preceding chapters. Immigrant entrepreneurship is facilitated where markets are more permeable, regulatory constraints are limited, and specific support programmes exist not only for entrepreneurs, but for immigrant entrepreneurs. Ironically, immigrant entrepreneurship is also facilitated by a limited welfare or social benefit system in the host country. Generous social welfare may be more of a conduit either for unemployment or entry into the traditional labour market, as opposed to the creation of one's own venture.

3 The Venture

The evidence here suggests that a large majority of immigrant and ethnic ventures are either retail or service businesses, or related to a skill or trade the immigrant brings from their home country. Most are in low entry barrier industries, where differentiation of the business is difficult and competition is often price based. The ethnic network or enclave can serve to offset these severe market challenges, in effect creating a workable competitive space for the entrepreneur.

Yet, as noted above, there is considerable diversity in the types of ventures created by immigrant and ethnic entrepreneurs. However, dependence on the ethnic enclave may well limit growth and constrain innovation within the venture. This is not to say that there are not sizeable ventures that develop based on the ethnic enclave, but these appear to be the exception. In fact, a perusal of the many case examples provided within the pages of this book find few highly innovative ventures that compete on the basis on continuous new product or service development. There are also few examples of high-technology or technology-based ventures.

4 Ethnic Networks and Enclaves

A unique aspect of immigrant and minority entrepreneurship is the frequent presence of an ethnic network or enclave as a facilitator of new venture creation. In some contexts, entire sub-economies have been created that involve a given immigrant or ethnic group controlling all stages of the value chain. In other instances, the ethnic network is a source of resources and legitimization. In still other cases, the network extends to the immigrant's home country and/or is connected to a global diaspora. By viewing these ethnic networks and enclaves through the lens of different countries and ethnicities, we are better able to appreciate how they affect and interact with immigrant or ethnic entrepreneurs.

The critical importance of ethnic networks in affecting immigrant entrepreneurship is strongly supported in country after country. They are an invaluable source of a wide range of resources (money, suppliers, employees, customers, distributors) and generate what has been termed 'cultural capital'. Just as vital is the role of the network or enclave as a source of information and knowledge. They provide legitimacy and infrastructure, as well as the aforementioned competitive space within which the entrepreneur can survive in the early stages of the venture. And they can frequently provide connections to a larger international network.

Yet, ethnic networks differ based on some key characteristics. The relative homogeneity of the ethnic individuals within the network is a case in point. This homogeneity may contribute to levels of reciprocity and trust within the network or enclave. The greater the reciprocity and trust, the more engrained within the network a venture is likely to become over time. Another relevant characteristic is the extensiveness of the network. Extensiveness refers not simply to geographic scope, but to the diversity of the industries and business types represented within the network or enclave, the stages of the value chain within industries that are represented, the reach of the network or enclave into the non-profit and government sectors, and the related political activism of the network or enclave. Homogeneity, trust and extensiveness might also be expected to affect the cost of membership within the network or enclave, including resources (money, time, goods and services) that must be reinvested by the entrepreneur in the network over time. A related variable concerns the degree of 'crowding' within the network or enclave, particularly among ventures providing the same basic goods or services. Crowding undermines the relative returns to the entrepreneur from depending upon the network or enclave, and limits growth prospects. Yet, it can be an important incentive for ultimately lessening the venture's dependency on the ethnic network or enclave.

5 Co-ethnic Dependence over Time: Two Intervening Variables

The growth path followed by immigrant or ethnic ventures has not received sufficient attention from researchers. For instance, richer insights are needed regarding cross-national differences in the survival and growth rates between ventures started by immigrants or ethnic minorities and those in the mainstream economy, and the underlying reasons contributing to such differences. Further, we need to better understand the extent to which ethnicity affects strategic intent.

Again, the ethnic network plays a role. The studies here suggest that ethnic networks facilitate venture start-up and short-term growth, and may reduce failure rates, but might also either limit or have no effect on longer-term growth. Hence, dependency on the ethnic network, and the extent to which the entrepreneur views the venture as existing to serve the ethnic group, or views the ethnic group as a means of serving the venture, impact the firm's growth path.

Based on the work presented by the researchers in this volume, two key variables appear to impact the venture's co-dependence on the ethnic network or enclave, and the venture's ultimate growth path. The first concerns the amount of learning and knowledge acquisition that occurs over time. The more learning that is achieved by the entrepreneur and those working within his or her venture, the more growth occurs, while dependency on the ethnic network lessens. The network is initially the most critical source of information. The question is how much the entrepreneur identifies and utilizes new information sources over time, and how much he or she learns from ongoing experimentation with new products, markets, and internal business processes.

The second variable impacting the venture's growth path concerns the extent to which the core interests and needs of the venture coincide with the interests and resources of the ethnic network. Over time, commonalities in interests, needs and resources can often wane, especially as the ethnic network or enclave becomes more crowded. Emerging competitive practices within the industry can force the entrepreneur to develop new competencies in areas where the ethnic network has less to offer. The development of these competencies can, in turn, lead the entrepreneur to become less dependent on the ethnic enclave and to grow more aggressively. The dynamism of the ethnic network itself becomes an important consideration. More dynamic networks or enclaves can be expected to continually develop new capabilities and assets, fostered in part by the addition to the network of new but diverse immigrant or ethnic ventures. Less dynamic and more conservative networks will only limit the potential of the venture, and give rise to the entrepreneur diversifying away from co-ethnic dependency.

6 Outcomes

The immigrant and ethnic venture experience produces outcomes at three distinct but related levels. The first of these is for the immigrant or ethnic minority entrepreneur and his or her extended family. At this level, the most apparent outcome is income substitution and wealth generation. Yet, given the preponderance of survival and lifestyle ventures being created, wealth generation may be limited. Further, the considerable needs of the family combined with the need to invest in the ethnic community, may well constrain the amount of reinvestment into the business. Less clear is the extent to which these ventures represent stepping stones to employment in established companies within the mainstream economy. The opposite may often be the case, in that by focusing on the needs of the venture, the entrepreneur does not develop skills and experiences that are in demand within the labour market. The venture serves other purposes as well. One of these is upward social mobility for the entrepreneur, but even more so for the children of the entrepreneur.

An interesting issue concerns the impact of venture creation on the amount and rate of assimilation by the entrepreneur of the culture and norms of the host country. Ventures operating in relatively narrow niches and less dynamic markets may actually hinder the assimilation process. Heavy dependence on the ethnic network can also slow the assimilation process. A slow rate of assimilation can, in turn, limit the growth rate and directional path of the venture. This brings us to venture outcomes.

The financial performance of these ventures over time (that is, sales growth, profit growth, growth in numbers of non-family employees) would seem to be directly associated with the variables outlined in the model. Hence, ventures will perform better based on the motives and skills of the entrepreneur, the entrepreneurial friendliness of the host country, the type of venture created, the resources, extensiveness, crowdedness and dynamism of the ethnic network or enclave, the amount of learning by the entrepreneur over time, commonality of the business interests and needs with the interests and resources of the ethnic network, and co-ethnic dependence over time.

Finally, the perspectives provided in Dana (2007b) suggest that immigrant ventures can produce significant societal outcomes. National economic growth and vitality are chief among these outcomes. However, there is evidence to suggest that these ventures also contribute to a number of other quality-of-life dimensions. As these ventures are frequently started in poorer or more economically challenged neighbourhoods, they provide a source of neighbourhood stability. Further, by providing for the economic welfare of the immigrant's extended family, entrepreneurial ventures may serve as a deterrent to criminal and gang activity. In addition to any taxes paid, immigrant entrepreneurs frequently contribute in meaningful ways both to their communities and their ethnic networks. And, in the final analysis, these ventures add to the social, cultural and commercial fabric of society by adding diversity to communities, while also introducing new products and new business practices.

IMPLICATIONS

Five decades ago, Cochran (1960) focused on the role of cultural factors in economic growth. In 2000, the Human Genome Project claimed that race did not exist. Today, scientific teams study the genetic traits of ethnic groups. Are behaviour and ethnicity linked and if so, how and why, and does it matter?

The 49 chapters of Dana (2007b) all report on ethnic minorities and their respective entrepreneurial activities. As explained by Morris, 'An ethnic group is a distinct category of the population in a larger society whose culture is usually different from its own. The members of such a group are, or feel themselves, or are thought to be, bound together by common ties of race or nationality or culture' (1968: 167). Yet, 'Ethnic groups only persist as significant units if they imply marked difference in behaviour, *i.e.,* persisting cultural difference' (Barth, 1969: 15–16). In some cases, ethnic groups integrate into host societies, into which they have immigrated; in most cases they do not.

Where groups with unlike spheres of values coexist, the result is a pluralistic society. Barth (1963; 1966; 1967a; 1967b; 1981) is one who has placed great emphasis on the existence of different spheres of values. Central to his discussion is the notion of the entrepreneur as an essential broker, mediating boundary transfers in this situation of contacts between cultures. By being active in the transformation of a community, entrepreneurs are social agents of change.

The nature pluralism in a host society affects ethnic minority entrepreneurship. It is, therefore, useful to distinguish among (1) *melting pot* pluralism; (2) *structural* pluralism; and (3) *fragmented* pluralism:

1. When people, from different cultures, share activities in a secular mainstream arena, the expression of cultural differences tends to be limited to private life. Often,

employment is shared in a common sphere of life, while cuisine, customs, languages and religion are a domestic concern. This form of socio-economic pluralism is referred to as melting pot pluralism, and this is descriptive of the situation in the USA. Immigrant entrepreneurs thrive in such as scenario.

2. In contrast, structural pluralism involves a society with different cultures that do not share a secular mainstream arena. In such a case, there is minimal interaction across cultures. Rather, each ethnic group has its distinct institutions, and members of a given community have a lifestyle that is incompatible with that of people from other backgrounds. This type of pluralism is prevalent in the Muslim areas of China (Dana, 2007a) and in the Central Asian republics (Dana, 2002), where entrepreneurs often cater primarily (or only) to members of their own ethnic group.
3. Fragmented pluralism is an unstable state of socio-economic pluralism from which a society can shift toward 'ethnic cleansing'. With fragmented pluralism, distinct societies are *loosely* held together by a *weak* political unit, such as was the case with Yugoslav federalism (Dana, 2005), and each ethnic group lives a separate life. In this context, there is minimal interaction between competing ethnic groups.

TOWARDS FUTURE RESEARCH

Future research topics might include: the impact of the motives for migrating; host country factors such as the nature of pluralism; economic sectors of immigrant ventures; causal factors in patterns of growth among ethnic entrepreneurs; enclaves; and co-ethnic dependence over time. Also, more research would be welcome on the topic of ethnic networks, as pioneered by Aldrich and Zimmer (1986); on middlemen minorities, as pioneered by Bonacich (1973); and on social capital as discussed by Bates (1994). To what extent do immigrant entrepreneurs employ people from other ethnic communities? When do they cater to mainstream society? What might be the optimal strategy?

REFERENCES

Aldrich, H.E. and C. Zimmer (1986), 'Entrepreneurship through social networks', in D.L. Sexton and R.W. Smilor (eds), *The Art and Science of Entrepreneurship*, Chicago, IL: Upstart, pp. 3–20.

Barth, F. (ed.) (1963), *The Role of the Entrepreneur in Social Change in Northern Norway*, Bergen: Norwegian Universities' Press.

Barth, F. (1966), *Models of Social Organization*, London: Royal Anthropological Institute.

Barth, F. (1967a), 'Economic spheres in Darfur', in Raymond Firth (ed.), *Themes in Economic Anthropology*, London: Tavistock, pp. 149–74.

Barth, F. (1967b), 'On the study of social change', *American Anthropologist*, **69** (6), 661–9.

Barth, F. (1969), 'Introduction', in Fredrik Barth (ed.), *Ethnic Groups and Boundaries: The Organisation of Cultural Difference*, Oslo: Universitetsforlaget, pp. 9–38.

Barth, F. (1981), *Process and Form in Social Life*, London: Routledge and Kegan Paul.

Bates, T. (1994), 'Social resources generated by group support networks may not be beneficial to Asian immigrant-owned small businesses', *Social Forces*, **72** (3), 671–89.

Bonacich, E. (1973), 'A theory of middleman minorities', *American Sociological Review*, **38**(5), 583–94.

Cochran, T.C. (1960), 'Cultural factors in economic growth', *The Journal of Economic History*, **20** (4), 515–30.

Dana, L.P. (1991), 'Bring in more entrepreneurs', *Policy Options*, **12** (9), 18–19.

Dana, L.P. (2002), *When Economies Change Paths: Models of Transition in China, the Central Asian Republics,*

Myanmar, and the Nations of Former Indochine Française, Singapore, London and Hong Kong: World Scientific.

Dana, L.P. (2005), *When Economies Change Hands: A Survey of Entrepreneurship in the Emerging Markets of Europe from the Balkans to the Baltic States*, Binghamton: Haworth Press.

Dana, L.P (2007a) *Asian Models of Entrepreneurship – From the Indian Union and the Kingdom of Nepal to the Japanese Archipelago: Context, Policy and Practice*, Singapore and London: World Scientific.

Dana, L.P. (2007b), *Handbook of Research on Ethnic Minority Entrepreneurship: A Co-evolutionary View on Resource Management*, Cheltenham, UK and Northampton, MA, USA: Edward Elgar.

Morris, H.S (1968), 'Ethnic groups', in David L. Sills (ed.), *International Encyclopedia of the Social Sciences*, London and New York: Macmillan, vol. 5, pp. 167–72.

17 Evolution of entrepreneurship: toward stewardship-based economics

Raymond W. Y. Kao, Rowland R. Kao and Kenneth R. Kao

At the 1995 Entrepreneurship Conference held in Shanghai and jointly run by China's Fu-Dan University and Nanyang Technological University of Singapore, the senior author delivered an opening address in which he noted that entrepreneurship should be identified as a creative and innovative human activity that benefits both self-interest and the common good. A young attendee commented:

> In your address, you said that people in the drug-trafficking business are not entrepreneurs, but I think you are wrong. Drug trafficking is a business, and traffickers are just as much entrepreneurs as any other venture founders. They created the business, making money for themselves, and provide jobs for others. Why don't you consider them to be entrepreneurs?

The senior author responded: 'Well, I don't know about China, but in Singapore, a drug trafficker, if caught and found guilty as charged can be sentenced to death by hanging.'

Definitions are important. In this case, the difference in definition between what is considered to be an entrepreneur (in the questioner's mind) and what is considered a criminal (in Singaporean legislation) is literally the difference between life and death. Definitions are there to serve as a guide, in a learning environment, helping to communicate knowledge among those concerned. It is broadly agreed that laws are created on the basis of justice to govern the limits of human behaviour and business conducted. But the law does not define justice. To enforce and interpret justice in the law is the task of a person (usually a judge), or a group of persons, such as a jury. Similarly, a definition is created with a specific purpose in mind, and is intended to be used in practice. To uphold the intentions that lie behind a definition remains a human problem, for individuals to decide.

1 WHO IS AN ENTREPRENEUR?

It is slightly fanciful to say that the dinosaurs became extinct because they failed to be sufficiently entrepreneurial and adapt to a changing environment, but it is no less true that, in the absence of entrepreneurial spirit, we would either be extinct ourselves, or remain in a less 'innovative and creative society', as hunter-gatherers, just like our prehistoric ancestors. They certainly had no automobiles, computers, Internet, advanced medicine, cosmetic surgery or personal jets. These luxuries are the results of the entrepreneurial spirit in society, and can also be the reward of entrepreneurial action on the part of the individual. It is equally true that not all those who achieve these things are entrepreneurs. We are reminded of a now somewhat old – fashioned term – the 'American Dream'. Once upon a time the American dream referred to the right of every individual, by virtue

Table 17.1 Definitions of an entrepreneur

Richard Cantillon	1710	A self-employed person with uncertain returns
Abbe Nicollas	1767	A leader of men, a manager of resources, an innovator of ideas, including new scientific ideas, and a risk-taker
Jean-Baptiste Say	1801/1810	A coordinator of production with management talent
Joseph Schumpeter	1910	A creative innovator
Frank Knight	1921	A manager responsible for direction and control, who bears uncertainty
Edith Penrose	1959	A person with managerial capabilities separate from entrepreneurial capabilities, and able to identify opportunities and develop small enterprises
J.E. Stepanek	1960	A moderate risk-taker
D.C. McCelland	1961	A person with a high need for achievement
Robert E. Budner	1962	A person who has a high tolerance for ambiguity
Orvis F. Collins	1964	A person with a high need for autonomy
W.D. Litzinger	1965	Low need for support and conformity, leadership, decisiveness, determination, perseverance and integrity
J.B. Rotter	1976	Internal locus of control
Israel Kirzner	1979	An arbitrageur
J.A. Timmons	1985	'A'-type behaviour pattern

of their own talents, ambitions and hard work, to succeed. In short, America's pride was to be an entrepreneurial society. Unfortunately, now the fruits of that dream are viewed by too many to be the dream itself – a lottery winner, for example, is viewed by many as living the American Dream. Worse still, individuals can cheat and lie, manipulate the system, perhaps even commit murder to get what they want, in the name of the American Dream. In today's world of well-to-do countries, the desire for greater wealth is the main driver of many people's actions, and perhaps this is how entrepreneurship was spurred. In this case, the original meaning of the term has been lost – what is left is only a caricature of the original.

In Cantillon's words (1710; cited in Kao, 1995b: 69), an entrepreneur is someone who is 'self-employed with uncertain returns' characterized by the following:

1. An entrepreneur is a person.
2. The person is self-employed and assumed to operate in a self-created business venture.
3. The venture is in the exchange system.
4. The entrepreneur depends on the venture for his livelihood.

Based on Cantillon's definition (see also Table 17.1), the enterprise under a self-employed individual has a dual status: the enterprise is both an economic entity and a social entity. As an economic entity, the self-employed individual has the proprietary right to make decisions in allocating the 'uncertain returns' for him or herself. As a social entity, he or she is accountable as a steward for resources to see that all resource-providers will receive a fair share of return for their contribution, including the restoration of what was taken from nature and a fair share of the fruits of their labour.

Table 17.2 A comparison of identified entrepreneur attributes between the works of Hornaday and Gibb

Hornaday	Gibb
Self-confidence	Creativity
Perseverance, determination	Initiative
Energy, diligence	High achievement
Resourcefulness	Risk-taking (moderate)
Ability to take risks	Leadership
Need to achieve	Autonomy and independence
Creativity	Analytical ability
Initiative	Hard work
Flexibility	Good communication skills
Independence	
Foresight	
Dynamic leadership	
Ability to get along with people and take criticism	
Profit orientation	
Perceptiveness	
Optimism	

Source: Kao (1989: 7).

Entrepreneurial Attributes

The attribute of uncertainty signifies risk-taking. Cantillon's four elements listed above suggest that although an entrepreneur is a person, this person is in the centre of entrepreneurship knowledge. This definition, though almost 300 years old, by-and-large fits in well with the production functions of economic analysis that typically includes:

- factor of distribution – income or profit
- factor of exchange – income can only be generated from an exchange system under the market economy
- factors of production – the process of innovation and creation.

While an entrepreneur is generally perceived to be a risk-taker, this is of course only one attribute. Attempts to encompass the defining attributes of an entrepreneur are many (for example Table 17.2). However, such definitions are problematic; for example, there are questions about the relationship between an entrepreneur and his or her firm. In a firm, there can be others who have similar attributes as those of the owner/entrepreneur, with every management level having at least one decision-maker who makes at least some proprietary or stewardship decisions. They, like the owner/entrepreneur need to possess the ability to exercise characteristics such as confidence, creativity and innovative ability to assure a firm's success. There are, in fact, many known attributes of successful entrepreneurs. Hornaday's and Gibb's works are used here to highlight the essentials (Table 17.2).

The Entrepreneur and 'Income' or 'Profit' Distribution

Must all profit go to the proprietary decision-maker (owner) or is profit viewed as a residual for redistribution to all those who have made a contribution? A number of issues must be considered. Wages to workers must be paid first before 'income' – since the entrepreneur is self-employed, he or she would be the decision-maker to allocate resources (including human resources) according to his or her desires including, in particular, 'earned uncertain returns' or 'profit' which include appropriate remuneration to workers in the enterprise, traditionally providing a clear distinction between the entrepreneur and the non-entrepreneur. However, in accordance with Cantillon's definition, it is the matter of making proprietary decisions (traditionally ownership decision) that counts. This definition suggests that a self-employed person is the only entrepreneur, and that the distribution of uncertain income or profit is entirely at the discretion of the self-employed entrepreneur. However, this also raises a question: if an individual displays many or all of the attributes used to define an entrepreneur, but does not have decision-making powers over the distribution of uncertain income, does that mean that this person is not an entrepreneur? If that is so, then the attempts to define entrepreneur attributes are meaningless, since they are wholly dependent on a single (external) factor. On a broader scale, this issue is how socialism/communism takes the route to challenge the entrepreneur's decision.

2 ENTREPRENEURSHIP, ENTERPRISING CULTURE AND THE EVOLUTION OF ENTREPRENEURIAL THOUGHT

Like the awareness and definition of the entrepreneur, the knowledge-based discipline of *entrepreneurship* could be said to have started with Cantillon in 1710. Cantillon was followed by a number of writers who established new criteria forming the bases of new definitions of the discipline, though all these remain widely quoted (Table 17.3).

Cantillon's early, narrow definition based on a self-employed person with uncertain income, was considerably broadened by increasingly generic terms of reference. Menger

Table 17.3 Summary of entrepreneurship definitions

Contributor	Period	Contribution
Carl Menger	1871	Entrepreneurship involves obtaining information, calculation, an act of will and supervision
Joseph Schumpeter	1910	Entrepreneurship is in its essence the finding and promoting of new combination of productive factors
Harvey Leibenstein	1970	Entrepreneurship is the reduction of organizational inefficiency and the reversal of organizational entropy
Israel Kirzner	1975	The identification of market arbitrage opportunities
W. Ed. McMillan and Wayne A. Long	1990	Entrepreneurship is the building of growth organization
Howard H. Stevenson	1992	Entrepreneurship is the pursuit of opportunity beyond the resources currently under your control

(1871; cited in Kao, 1995a: 72) defined entrepreneurship as involving obtaining information, calculation, an act of will and supervision. Schumpeter's definition some 40 years later was in many ways the key to the modern conception and can be paraphrased as the making of different combinations and something that everyone participates in sometimes, but never all the time. This was followed by Timmons narrowing the definition to actions involving searching and sizing business opportunities. At the same time, a few others seemed focused on pushing entrepreneurship development including business development, enterprise development and growth.

Entrepreneurship is an all encompassing term covering all human creative and innovative endeavours, not just in profit-making commercial undertakings and not-for-profit organizations, but also any individual who has the urge to do something new and something different, first as motivation for self-interest, then as part of a group as whatever he or she does must be of benefit to others as well. This progression from individual to the group can been seen in the evolution of entrepreneurial thought as seen by the senior author over the past half century. In the 1960s, the emphasis was on 'independent business' and few people could even pronounce or spell 'entrepreneurship'. In the 1970s and 1980s, we saw the development of entrepreneurship as an academic discipline, with new chairs at universities and PhDs being offered. Finally, in the twenty-first century, the environment, poverty and the drain of resources drain have become ever more urgent issues. Social responsibility and concern for the common good drawn greater attention and action. Entrepreneurism has been seen increasingly as addressing these issues, and stewardship accountability applied to entrepreneurial undertakings.

This search for the meaning of entrepreneurship extends beyond its limited scope of small business commercial undertakings for the pursuit of profit making. Kathleen R. Allen (1989: 4) had the following description:

> Entrepreneurship is a mindset or a way of thinking that is opportunity focused, innovative, and growth oriented. Although entrepreneurship is most commonly thought of in conjunction with starting a business, the entrepreneurial mindset can be found within a large corporation , in socially responsible nonprofit organizations, and anywhere individuals and teams are desiring to differentiate themselves from the crowd and apply their passion and drive to executing a business opportunities.

It is certainly a notable effort to extend 'entrepreneurship' from the narrow confined means of just small business, to include all business undertakings, large or small. It should also be recognized, however, that entrepreneurs exist (creative and innovative individuals) in other organizations, such as not-for-profit organizations, governments, and so on. As a consequence, the definition of entrepreneurship needs to be welded together from three components. These are:

1. Wealth-creating and value-adding process.
2. Actions involved in wealth-creating and adding value to the process through venture formation and/or undertaking of entrepreneurial endeavours.
3. Wealth for the individual and value for society.

The definition emphasizes the importance of creating wealth and adding value. As well, it includes all such activities, and as such departs from Cantillon's self-employed

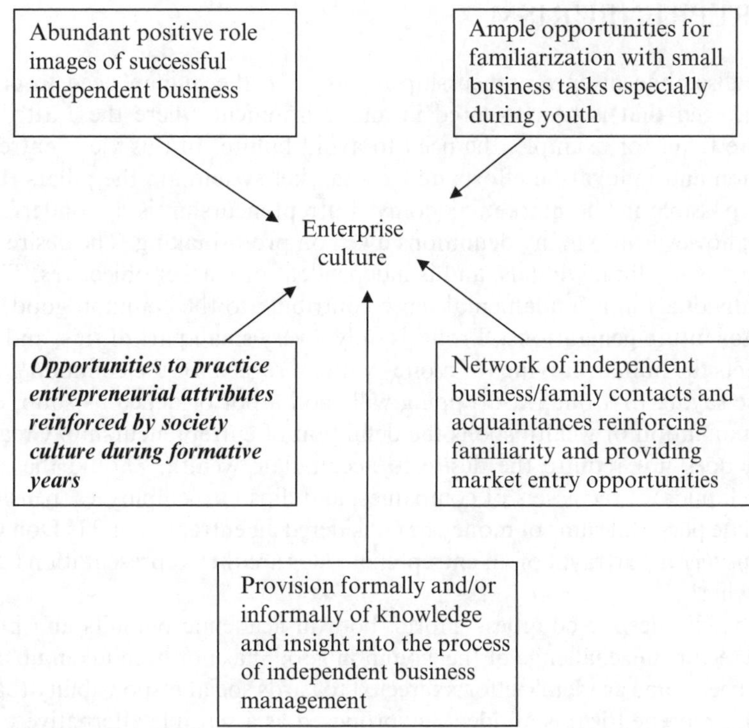

Source: Gibb (1987: 14).

Figure 17.1 Enterprise culture

individual. When the *Journal of Enterprising Culture* had its inaugural issue (1993), the editorial board decided to place the definition on the inside front cover with a refinement to include who is an entrepreneur in a two-part definition as follows:

> *To summarise*, entrepreneurship is 'The process of doing something new and something different for the purpose of creating wealth for the individual and adding value to society. An Entrepreneur is a person who undertakes a wealth-creating and value-adding process, through incubating ideas, assembling resources and making things happen'.

This broadening of the definition has led to a natural extension to consider not just entrepreneurship as a function of some individuals, but as a property of a collective and the identification of an enterprising culture. Enterprise or enterprising culture needs to be recognized in any organization, in order to sustain development and growth. It can be said that for a healthy enterprise culture, any organization is built on the academic discipline for research and learning. A.A. Gibb (1987) provided some useful guides for enterprise culture development, based on the cultivation of strong entrepreneur attributes within every individual in the organization (Figure 17.1).

These definitions led to a further refinement in the author's later work to replace 'adding value to society' with 'the common good'. This same definition led to the development of the doctrine of entrepreneurism.

3 ENTREPRENEURISM

The entire discipline of entrepreneurship is based on the human need to create and innovate, a need that is best fostered in an environment where these attributes are valued more than, for example, the need to avoid failure. In this view, entrepreneurship, creation and innovation efforts under a market system are the pillars that make everything possible in the market economy. Entrepreneurship is a wonderful human endeavour; however, too many definitions dwell on profit-making. The desire to create and innovate is in all individuals, and is independent of market objectives. The efforts of these individuals in a fundamental sense contribute to the common good, to make life better for future generations. 'Profit' is only a very small part of this, and unfortunately reflects the human craving for money with no regard for the common good. Like the Chinese saying that one rat dropping will spoil a pot of delicious soup, emphasis on the accumulation of wealth spoils the definition of entrepreneurship. Creation and innovation does not require the desire to accumulate wealth. Should the corporate raider who liquidates the assets of companies, and dips into employees' pension funds to accumulate personal sums of money be considered an entrepreneur? Is Don Corleone in *The Godfather* a portrayal of an entrepreneur? Or are they representations of the old Chinese saying?

Unfortunately, despite countless efforts, both in academic pursuits and practice in the private sector, the challenge of the 'common good' has not been taken up, although there have been some academic efforts directed towards social responsibility that should be noted. Entrepreneurism is an ideology proposed as a sensible alternative to capitalism, on the one hand, and socialism, on the other, the essence of it being based on the 'common good'. It is not just about making money, nor is it merely about starting up a venture or owning a small business – it is a way of life, applicable to all human economic activities. Living on a planet with finite resources, humanity is sustainable only if there is constant pursuit of innovation and creativity, not just for personal gain but also for the common good. It is also a philosophy, as it is based on the statement: 'To create and innovate is not a matter of choice, but necessity.'

The definition of entrepreneurship must include 'the common good'. Without this qualification, drug traffickers could easily justify their harmful trade by stating that they are 'job providers'. How does this compare to the Chinese soup analogy?

The notion of the common good can be seen in the following two sources:

1. From the *Second Vatican Council*: 'Factors that contribute to the common good and the overall conditions of life in society that allow the different groups and their members to be active in their own perfection more fully and more easily.'
2. From *Wikipedia*: 'The Common Good is a term that can refer to several different concepts. In the popular meaning, [it] describes a specific "good" that is shared and beneficial for all (or most) members of a given *community*. This is also how the common good is broadly defined in *philosophy*, *ethics*, and *political science*.'

The ancient Chinese scholar, Moen-Tzu, tells us that humans can be born good or bad. Those with good nature will do good for others, while the bad will take advantage of others. We are influenced by the examples of others, and can learn or be taught to be either good or bad. For those who were born bad, and those characterized as bad through influence by others can be taught and/or learn to be good.

A meaningful definition will serve as a guide for action, but action is still in the hands of people. For example, job creation is one of many benefits to society resulting from the initiation of a new venture. It is hardly a benefit to society however, to allow drug traffickers whose activity is aimed at making profit at the cost of human misery, to claim they are providing jobs. The idea of 'Constructive destruction' has been used by manufacturers of products that maximize the short term with a built-in obsolescense strategy that causes resource drain, creation of undue waste and contamination of the environment These are just a few negative repercussions that result when people have abused a sound concept for their own benefit, with no concern for the common good.

Reassessing the meaning of 'profit', it is more appropriate to advocate the use of residual to reduce harmful social injustice, avoiding unnecessary human conflict, still within the market system, to formulate an affordable means that will ease off human conflict. A definition of 'entrepreneurism' is therefore created on the premise that humans are driven by two fundamental desires: the desire to own and the desire to create. Ownership is not just the titular holding of property – physical, intellectual or otherwise – but the right to make decisions, or put another way, the right to free choice: the desire to create and desire to take that which is there, and to alter its form to suit our purpose, bringing into being something that did not exist before. However, it must be fully recognized that there is a world of difference between ownership and stewardship.

Entrepreneurism is all about making human proprietary decisions. Exercising ownership rights on the one hand, and assuring stewardship responsibilities on the other.

Entrepreneurism is an ideology in which an individual is a creative and innovative agent with the desire for ownership and the right to make proprietary decisions, with the common good to guide action. As a body of knowledge, it presupposes the involvement of three independent yet interrelated entities: the state, business entity and individuals.

1. The state: entrepreneurial government. Under entrepreneurism, the state is the infrastructure consisting of individuals committed to serving people for the common good that will facilitate their realization of economic freedom, their right to acquire ownership to harvest their labour, and their right and obligations to protect the environment.
2. The individual: entrepreneurial person.The individual is the centre of the economy, and as a stakeholder in any undertaking is responsible to him or herself. The individual views entrepreneurship and working as an entrepreneur as a way of life.
3. The business entity: entrepreneurial entity and entity entrepreneurial managers.

Entrepreneurship on the other hand is a process of doing something new (creative) and doing something different (innovative) for the purpose of creating wealth for the individual and adding value to society. Through entrepreneurship, the doctrine of entrepreneurism reigns over all economic endeavours. The entrepreneurial approach is applicable to business management in general, including the creation of new ventures, managing one's own business, business with family members, government and public institutions, charitable and not-or-profit organizations as well as professionals and professional organizations. It goes without saying that the entrepreneurial approach to corporate management is an integral part of entrepreneurial contemplation.

In addition to the instinctive entrepreneurial contemplation in individuals, government, organizations business and others, Entrepreneurism also puts forward the examination of accounting practice in matters of profit determination and cost recognition leading to the consideration of adopting 'residual' for measurement and as a basis for redistribution. Human effort, in particular, the redistribution of the fruits of labour, helps to relieve the tragedy of global poverty and environmental damage and the renewal of depleted resources where possible.

4 STEWARDSHIP-BASED ECONOMICS

Both capitalism and communism have their roots in Adam Smith's *Wealth of Nations* (1776). Capitalism can be viewed as a generalization of Schumpeter's notion of constructive destruction, in the sense that it emphasizes private property ownership without consideration for the common good. The pursuit of capital accumulation leads to aggregation beyond personal consumption requirements, exploitation of labour and exhaustion of non-renewable resources. The reliance on a market system to make adjustments itself would require waiting until there is a sub-system to make the 'invisible hand' to see human misery and desperate pleas to prevent environmental damage and the drain of resources. While innovation and creativity prompt new discoveries, better use of resources and the ability to harvest more for those who create and innovate, to advocate that 'profit' goes only to those who 'create business and anticipate uncertain returns' without taking into consideration of common good, would clearly push many people into the dark corner of poverty and lead our world towards disaster. While a capitalist society may stimulate the individual's desire for more (greed), the issue of unfair distribution of resources (wealth) would inevitably led to rebellion, and in this sense communism is a natural outgrowth from capitalism.

Communism, on the other hand, may have attracted many individuals concerned over the problem of 'distribution', but provides no clear incentive for the individual to create and innovate for his or her own personal benefit. Any system under the 'fair distribution' scheme is less than effective, and does not stimulate an individual's interest for common good.

Ownership-based economics has led to the rapid development and apparent universal success of the market economy. It is a system built on the deception of unlimited resource availability, ill-defined profit, and is misled by the idea that an 'invisible hand' alone can be an equitable system of distribution. While creating wealth for the few, it induces individuals and societies to continually grab for more and more. The undisciplined craving for more for the advantaged few, fuelled through the market system, creates poverty, damages environmental and human health, and drains limited resources which are not just for us, but for the future as well. As long as our economy's functionality is based on ownership, we will hardly see the end of these. It is neither feasible nor advisable to abolish the market system, however we must realize that the 'ownership' idea may be legal, but it has deceptively led us into a vicious circle of addiction out of which we may be unable to emerge.

While entrepreneurism serves as a guide based on creative and innovative nature, the real issue of 'ownership' challenge, is that it fundamentally is little more than a struggle for 'owning'. Indeed, the origin of human conflict throughout history is rooted in greed and forceful acquisition of ownership. In recent years, economic expansion has seen its share of unfairly acquiring ownership over resources by the fabrication of information to commit criminal activities ranging from cheating innocent investors in the market system to inflicting civil war in a foreign country.

Although Smith's idea of wealth in the market system was 'to create wealth for me and for you as well', the unfortunate reality in today's market economy is quite different from what Smith had in mind. This is what the market economy is: all justice is based on the matter of competition, based on the decision made by invisible hands. To some people this ownership-based system is 'the only system' for our ever-expanding economy. Therefore, we would have to accept that poverty is common, natural and inevitable, if:

1. Greed is the sole motivation to be rich.
2. The rich and powerful prefer to make the rich richer.
3. The political policy favours the rich.

There is no single sub-system within the market system to help ease the pressure on poverty. Religion, government policy and charitable organizations are all helpful, and significant efforts ease the pain. Bear in mind, both rich and poor are relative, and the only absolute is greed, an irrational desire for more. The fundamental problem is that while greed dictates that the 'sky is the limit', we have no idea what that limit is.

The depletion of non-renewable resources and erosion of environmental health available to present generations will mean there will be less for our descendants. Unless the creative and innovative efforts can restore what was once there for the future, we will have to expect that 'Humans landing on Mars' will be our only salvation. But how will this help to relieve the pressure on poverty, resources drain and environmental disaster?

Stewardship-based economics recognizes the importance of the market system. It is irreplaceable, but we cannot take advantage of the system merely to satisfy an individual's wants and greed at the expense of others' labour, limited resources and the freely provided living environment. We must realize that we are a part of the Earth, but we do not own it. We must exercise our right to make proprietary decisions, but we must also assume stewardship responsibility. While proprietary decision-making might give us a twofold approach to easing the pressure on both the human race and the opportunity to allocate resources for self-interest, it is necessary to accept the responsibility to ensure all decisions made are also for the common good. Stewardship economics acts as a signpost towards balancing the short-term need for survival with the long-term need for sustainable growth, and serves as a philosophical beacon that will guide individuals, particularly business leaders, toward actions in the interest of humanity.

As stewardship-based economics was developed from earlier work on entrepreneurship and entrepreneurism (Figure 17.2), it places a great deal of emphasis on acting now

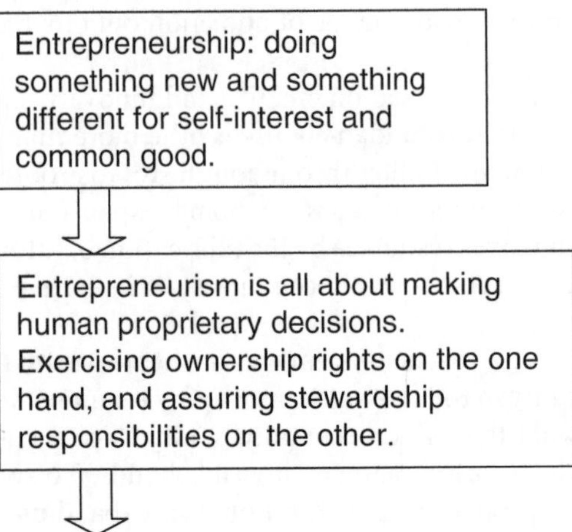

Stewardship-based economics: responsible stewardship for making resources allocation decisions, and educating others to act and think likewise. A broad knowledge-based discipline to overcome difficulties experienced by human beings through our past, of poverty, human conflicts, environmental damage and resources depletion.

Figure 17.2 Evolution: from entrepreneurship to stewardship-based economics

to be responsible stewards for making resources allocation decisions, as well as the need for education to consider a few key areas:

- We have only one Earth, and everything on it is meant for everyone. Some are strong, others may be weak, but everyone is entitled to his share of what Earth has to offer.
- The number of countries with their diversity of people, culture and background makes it difficult to generalize. Nonetheless, it is clear that no individual can live alone, and no one should take resources ruthlessly just for his personal use. The sharing of resources should be a way of life.
- Resources are finite. The challenge lies not in deciding who should or should not have them but, rather, in finding more sustainable and renewable resources through creation and innovation.
- As stewards, everyone has the right to make proprietary decisions while in control of the resources. Stewardship responsibility must, however, be exercised during decision-making, and there must be accountability for the consequences of actions taken based on any decision.

While entrepreneurship appeals to the individual's desire for advancement of personal wealth, it also includes consideration of the common good to allow entrepreneurial activities to work for both the individual now as well as for the future for humanity.

The common good idea could not fulfil its required action, unless every individual appreciates the reality of living and acting on the basis of stewardship responsibility and accountability, recognizing that we may be a part of the Earth, but we do not own it. It is on this that the shift from ownership-based economics and the early conception of entrepreneurship to stewardship-based economics and entrepreneurism is founded.

REFERENCES

Allen, K.R. (1989), *Launching New Ventures*, 4th edn, Boston, MA and New York: Houghton Mifflin.

Gibb, A.A. (1987), 'Enterprise culture, the meaning and implications for education and training', *Journal of European Industrial Training*, **11** (2), 14.

Kao, R.W.Y. (1989), *Entrepreneurship and Enterprise Development*, Toronto: Holt, Rinehart and Winston of Canada.

Kao, R.W.Y. (1995a), *Entrepreneurship: A Wealth-Creation and Value Adding Process*, Singapore: Prentice Hall Asia.

Kao, R.W.Y. (1995b), 'Entrepreneurship definitions', in *Entrepreneurship*, Englewood Cliffs, NJ: Simon & Schuster.

Smith, A. (1776), *An Inquiry into the Nature and Causes of the Wealth of Nations*, London: W. Strahan and T. Cadell.

18 Exit

*Karl Wennberg**

Much research has been devoted to look for characteristics that drive individuals towards engaging in entrepreneurship. Less attention has been given to the question of what makes people persist in or exit from entrepreneurship. However, recent years have seen an increasing focus on entrepreneurial exit in a number of specialized workshops and conferences, new research projects, and special issues in international journals. This chapter provides a stocktake on past exits, outlining the progress that research has made, together with some key problems in defining and investigating entrepreneurial exit. Conceptually, the chapter focuses on the level of analysis and different definitions of exit. Empirically, the chapter describes the streams of research suggesting that exit is either determined by the environment or the entrepreneur, together with a stream of research that emphasizes the connection between entry and exit as path-dependent processes. The chapter concludes by highlighting a number of unsolved issues and interesting pathways for future research on entrepreneurial exit.

Entrepreneurial exit is a multifaceted and multi-level phenomenon. It concerns both exit of entrepreneurial firms from the marketplace and exit of self-employed individuals from their entrepreneurial activities on the labor market. Empirical studies of these topics hold that entrepreneurs and new firms will be less likely to exit as they persist over time. Yet, few of these studies acknowledge that exit is multifaceted in that there are different types of entrepreneurial exit, such as liquidation, bankruptcy or sell-off of a firm. For example, closure rates are likely to be lower as firms' age and improve their performance, whereas sell-off rates increase with age but are less likely to be related to the firm's performance (Mitchell, 1994).

In studies of organizations and strategy, entrepreneurial exit has often been equated 'failure' as a fundamental performance measure of new organizations. Yet, recent studies show clear indications that exit from entrepreneurship is theoretically distinct from failure. Bates (2005) and Headd (2003) investigated the US Census Bureau's 1996 survey 'Characteristics of Busniess Owners' (CBO) which is based on a large representative sample of US businesses founded between 1989 and 1992. They found that about one-third of the discontinued business owners characterized their firms as successful at closure. Ucbasaran et al. (2005) surveyed a representative sample of 767 entrepreneurs in Great Britain and found that among the entrepreneurs that had closed down a business, more than a third considered their last business to be 'a success'. These studies indicate that, at least in the eyes of entrepreneurs, exit and failure are two distinct concepts. How, then, can we define the concept of entrepreneurial exit?

In order to define a phenomenon with clarity and precision, one needs to satisfy four conditions (Chopra, 2005). First, a clearly defined object must be present on which the phenomenon acts. Second, the boundaries of the phenomenon must be distinct; moreover, the gradations of boundaries must be apparent. Third, forces associated with the phenomenon – that affects or are affected by it – must be clear. Fourth, knowledge of the process by which the phenomenon unfolds must be clear. Looking at the accumulated knowledge on entrepreneurial exit on these dimensions, it becomes obvious that exit as a phenomenon needs better clarity and precision. The literature has made significant progress on the third and, to some extent, the fourth elements, identifying predictors and consequences of exit. Yet, knowledge of exit processes as they unfold are still few (an excellent exception is Burgelman, 1994). Research has also made little progress on the first and second elements. Although having looked at individual, firm and populations as the objects on which the phenomenon acts, research has failed to distinguish between the role of individual-level, firm-level and population-level elements of the exit decision. For example, if individual characteristics are ignored in a firm-level study, for very small firms the firm-level factors will often be highly correlated with the (unmeasured) actions and characteristics taken by entrepreneurs. A more important problem is that the conceptual boundaries of exit have not been clearly defined and discussed. This has hampered theoretical progress since much of the empirical efforts do not distinguish between exit, failure and closure. Before outlining the available evidence on exit, it is therefore necessary to discuss some conceptual and definitional issues of entrepreneurial exit.

LEVEL OF ANALYSIS AND MEASUREMENT OF EXIT

A key feature of entrepreneurship research is the intersection of individuals and organizations. Entrepreneurship is generally conceptualized as individuals pursuing entrepreneurial opportunities, often by the creation of new organizations. For new ventures, the firm may even be considered as 'an extension' of the founder (Chandler and Hanks, 1994). Yet, a problem in entrepreneurship research has been the lack of distinction between entrepreneurial failure and exit, that is, the difference between attempting to keep a business open but failing to do so, and the deliberate closure or successful sale of a business. Furthermore, exit operates on several levels of analysis: for example, the entrepreneur may exit (for instance, by selling and leaving the business) while the firm persists, signifying exit at the individual but not the firm level; or the entrepreneur may close the business but continue being an entrepreneur by starting a new business, that is through serial entrepreneurship.

A fundamental reason for the lack of research on entrepreneurial exit is probably that it is very difficult to measure in precise ways. Since the probability of exit is highest in the very early period of a new firm or the career of a self-employed person, studying entrepreneurial exit necessitates access to unbiased data-tracking firms or individuals from the very onset of their entrepreneurial activities. In the empirical literature on exit, it is apparent that exit rates vary greatly between different studies. One explanation is the fact that very small firms (Mata and Portugal, 1994) and very early attempts at self-employment (Arum and Muller, 2004) have much higher exit rates compared with larger firm or individuals which are more established in self-employment. It is therefore likely that some of the differences in exit rates are due to differences in measurement. Specifically, studies using register databases seem to exhibit higher exit rates than studies relying on survey data (see, for example, Aviad and Vertinsky, 2006, in Canada; Delmar et al., 2006, in Sweden; or Mata and Portugal, 1994, in Portugal). This indicates that many studies might be affected by reporting bias. Evans and Leighton (1989) noted that annual survey data as in their own study tends to under-report very short spells in self-employment. There are thus reasons to believe that the true exit rates, both of the firm level and on the individual level, might be much higher than the survey-based research has shown.

It should also be noted that predictors of exit often seem to differ between self-employed men and women (Arum and Muller, 2004), and between larger firms started and managed by men and women entrepreneurs (Kalleberg and Leicht, 1991). Since self-employed men, or firms started and managed by men, almost always make up a majority of the samples used in studies of entrepreneurial exit, analyses of pooled data with only an indicator variable for sex are therefore likely to be conflated by statistical associations evident only for men. Furthermore, empirical studies that have distinguished between exit by men and women entrepreneurs often find many fewer statistical relationships between theoretical variables and exit among women entrepreneurs, leading to poor explanatory power in these models. These facts have three important conclusions for research on entrepreneurial exit: (1) The theoretical predictors known to affect exit are based on samples dominated by men. Hence, we do not know if these theories matter for women entrepreneurs. (2) In order not to confuse statistical relationships, studies of entrepreneurial exit need to conduct separate analyses for men and for women. (3) the low explanatory powers of models of women's exit pattern indicate that current theoretical models are not good at explaining women entrepreneur's exit, and that much more research on this specific issue is needed.

ENTRY AND EXIT AS PATH-DEPENDENT PROCESSES

Many studies have found that initial conditions at the time of entrepreneurial entry are vital in shaping entrepreneurial exit. For an individual entrepreneur, the personal reasons and factors associated with entry into entrepreneurship are also often associated with both *if* and *how* the person eventually chooses to leave entrepreneurship (Taylor, 1999). For a new firm, the very factors present at the time of founding can influence the firm in long-lasting ways, regardless of whether the environmental conditions at time of founding subsequently change (Delmar et al., 2006). These firm-level factors can essentially be grouped into two different categories. The first category consists of resources at the time of founding, such as capital assets and entrepreneurial team members/employees. The second category consists of explicit goals and strategies for organizing and growing the firm. These two categories have been found to be the strongest types of predictors of exit. Studies of entrepreneurial exit have found that low probability of exit is strongly associated with a stronger resource base, both for the individual entrepreneur in terms of human capital and knowledge (Brüderl et al., 1992) and for the firm in terms of capital assets (Bates, 1990), product offerings (Kalleberg and Leicht, 1991) and number of employees (Delmar et al., 2006). Low exit rates are also associated with firms' growth strategies (Brüderl et al., 1992) and entrepreneurs' setting of specific goals with their ventures (Delmar and Shane, 2003; Kalleberg and Leicht, 1991). Goals and motivation at the time of founding affects both the likelihood of exit and how the exit process will evolve. That is, not all entrepreneurs have a clear goal of what they want to achieve with their venture. Some want to exploit a valuable invention or discovery. Some want freedom to decide how and when they work (Carter et al., 2003). These differences will affect how entrepreneurs' consider the possibility of exit as well as the relative attractiveness of different exit paths.

In this way, the progress of new firms and self-employed entrepreneurs follow a path-dependent process where initial conditions generally shape the paths by which firms and entrepreneurs subsequently evolve. Firm-level exit processes are path-dependent both in terms of initial goals and resource committed to the venture, as well as environmental conditions at the time of founding (Delmar et al., 2006). Individuals' self-employment is also path-dependent in that their process is shaped by the conditions by which the individual engage in entrepreneurship. For example, the exit rate for entrepreneurs who enter self-employment from unemployed or on a part-time basis is much higher than those that enter from employment (Taylor, 1999; Wennberg et al., 2006). In empirical research, it might be difficult to untangle the effect of such initial factors and how they interact with the entrepreneur or the entrepreneurial team. For example, firms started at times of economic prosperity, such as during the dot-com boom, often have more ambitious goals and are more likely to attract resources to their venture. Also on the individual level, the entrepreneurs' resources and knowledge are closely intertwined. Human capital factors have been found to be a strong predictor of both start-up capital and business survival, indicating that failure to control for entrepreneurs' human capital characteristics might lead research to overestimate the importance of capital (Bates, 1990).

IS EXIT DETERMINED BY THE ENVIRONMENT OR THE ENTREPRENEUR?

Various streams of literature has referred to individual-level, firm-level and population-level elements of the exit decision. In empirical studies, there are two predominant levels of analysis: the entrepreneur may exit while the firm persists, signifying exit at the individual but not the firm level; or the entrepreneur may close the firm but continue being an entrepreneur by starting a new firm. Yet, despite the preconception that 'new firms more often fail' in the organizational literature, new firms are not more likely to fail in unchartered markets than established firms engaging in this market. A study by Mitchell (1994) investigated 141 new entrepreneurial firms and 274 diversifying entrants in seven US medical product markets. He found that the new firms were no more likely than diversifying entrants to exit, but that they were less likely to sell their firm, *ceteris paribus*. This indication that entrepreneurs are less likely to sell their firm than diversifying entrants is interesting in that it suggest that entrepreneurs are attached to their ventures in excess of the economic value that can be earned from divesting them. Conversely, it is therefore also very likely that less profitable firms can subsist for many years, or as in van Witteloostuijn's model of organizational decline, 'Inefficient firms might outlast efficient rivals' (van Witteloostuijn, 1998: 501).

The issue of 'environment versus organizational factors' in entrepreneurial exit was investigated by Everett and Watson's (1998) study of 5196 Australian retail and service start-ups between 1960 and 1999. They found that environmental economic factors were associated with between 30 per cent and 50 per cent of small business exits, depending on which definition of exit is used. Excluding exit due to bankruptcy, which was negatively related to macroeconomic conditions, exit rates defined as (1) sell-off, (2) closure, (3) 'disbanding to prevent further losses' or (4) failure 'to make a go of it', were found to be positively associated with macroeconomic conditions. Everett and Watson interpreted this as a strengthening economy may trigger voluntary exits since entrepreneurship seeks to maximize the returns available to them on both their financial and human capital.

Perhaps the most conclusive evidence to date was provided by Gimeno et al. (1997) who followed 1547 US firms associated with the National Federation of Independent Businesses over the course of two to five years. They found that the exit of entrepreneurial firms was affected not only by individual-specific, firm-specific and environmental factors that simultaneously affected entrepreneurial income, but also by factors that did not affect income. They explained their findings by formulating a threshold model of entrepreneurial continuation, where a firm is terminated due to lack of performance below a critical level. This level, or threshold, is shaped by individuals' perceived value of economic and psychic returns associated with entrepreneurship. A key finding of the study was that exit is underspecificated as a dependent variable, that is, that there are several different types of exit decisions that might involve different theoretical explanations.

ARE THERE DIFFERENT *TYPES* OF EXIT?

The above studies provide some indications that delineating between different *types* of entrepreneurial exit could be an important area for future research. The dominating focus on 'survival' in the perspective on entrepreneurial exit inspired by organization theory reflects the implicit or explicit view that firms are frequently seen in the light of 'going concern' – that is, entities that try to prolong their existence. For incumbent firms with a multitude of stakeholders, such as large joint-stock corporations, this might not be an unreasonable assumption. Yet, for new independent firms run by one or a few entrepreneurs, the destiny of a firm is intimately linked to that of its owners(s). Headd (2003) investigated perceptual measures of success among the 12 185 firms in the 1996 'Characteristics of Business Owners' survey, a representative sample of all US firms started between 1989 and 1992. He found that after four years in business, half of all businesses had exited, however one-third of all exiting entrepreneurs considered their firm to be 'successful'. Headd also found that factors characterizing exiting firms such as lack of initial resources, started by a young entrepreneur, and so on, did not differ between what the entrepreneurs themselves perceived as 'successful' or 'unsuccessful' exits. A conclusion of the study was that searching for factors associated with firm exit is less meaningful since such a high proportion of exiting entrepreneurs seem to consider this a satisfactory outcome.[1] Another conclusion was that entrepreneurs' goals and time horizons at the onset of their firms are likely to diverge: some may want a lifestyle business, some are trying to build a high-growth firm that they can divest of in a few years, yet some other seek to avoid unemployment, and so on. This interpretation receives support from DeTienne and Cardon's (2006) study of exit strategies among 189 entrepreneurs in the US electrical measurement and surgical medical instruments industries. They found that older entrepreneurs were more likely and entrepreneurs with medical training were less likely to have an exit strategy, and that common human capital variables such as age, education and experience were related to which specific exit strategy (family succession, sale to individual, employee buy-out, initial public offering, liquidation) that the entrepreneurs envisioned. Another study by Wennberg et al. (2007) followed 1735 Swedish firms started in 1994 for nine years, finding that similar human capital variables were also associated with the eventual exit outcome (that is, sell-off, closure due to good performance, or closure due to poor performance).

DO EXIT RATES CHANGE OVER TIME?

The previously mentioned difficulties in measuring entrepreneurship from the time it is initiated, taken together with the studies suggesting there are types of exit that are systematically different, indicates two problems in summarizing and aligning the available evidence on entrepreneurial exit: if there is variation in the dependent variable that is not taken into account, and difficulties in measurement issues will cause most studies to sample on the dependent variable (that is, exclude most of the smallest/newest firms and self-employment attempts), it is not strange that prior research has been unable to align the various common predictors of exit into an overarching theoretical framework.

Some research has found a trend in that individual's exit rates seem to have increased during the past few decades. Meager and Bates (2004) found that over half of the 9356 persons they studied in the first to ninth waves of the British Household Panel Study had exited within three years, while Taylor (1999) used retrospective accounts from the same data and found that only one-third of the 769 persons that entered self-employment between 1979 and 1991 had exited within three years. Also, the patterns for men's exit seem to diverge greatly from those of women. In almost all studies, exit rates are significantly higher for women. This is a further indication that more research is needed on the exit processes of women entrepreneurs.

WHAT HAPPENS AFTER EXIT?

Entrepreneurship research has been discussing the importance of moving from solely discussing firm-level outcomes towards looking also at individual-level and societal-level outcomes (Venkataraman, 1997). Yet, to date there is a dearth of studies of societal-level outcomes of entrepreneurial exit. An important exception is Aviad and Vertinsky's (2006) investigation of manufacturing plants in 3908 local Canadian areas from 1983 to 1998. They found that the exit of older firms increases the entry rates of new firms, and that on average, new entrants were more productive. Also many questions related to individual-level outcome of exits remains to be answered. For example, Wennberg and Wiklund (2006) found in their study of 25 529 Swedish knowledge-intensive firms that 78 per cent of firms that were sold performed above the population average. They termed these seemingly successful sell-offs 'exit by success'. In the literature to date, there are still no investigations of the firm founders of such firms post sell-off. How is the financial net worth of these individuals compared with before they started their firms? And in subjective terms, do these individuals evaluate their sold firm as 'personal success' or 'personal failure' (Bates, 2005), and what are the factors associated with such evaluations?

NOTES

* I am grateful for comments from Miguel Amaral, Anders Landberg, and participants at the 2007 EM Lyon advanced entrepreneurship scholars retreat. All errors are mine alone.

1. An important objection to this interpretation would be that a large share of the successful exits might be due to entrepreneurs' post-exit rationalization of what were in fact unwanted outcomes.

REFERENCES

Arum, R. and W. Muller (2004), *The Re-Emergence of Self-Employment: A Comparative Study of Self-Employment Dynamics and Social Inequality*, Princeton, NJ: Princeton University Press.

Aviad, P.E. and I. Vertinsky (2006), 'Firm failures as a determinant of new entry: is there evidence of local creative destruction?', unpublished manuscript, Vancouver: University of British Columbia.

Bates, T. (1990), 'Entrepreneur human capital and small business longevity', *The Review of Economics and Statistics*, **72** (4), 551–9.

Bates, T. (2005), 'Analysis of young, small firms that have closed: delineating successful from unsuccessful closures', *Journal of Business Venturing*, **20** (3), 343–58.

Brüderl, J., P. Preisendörfer and R. Ziegler (1992), 'Survival chances of newly founded business organizations', *American Sociological Review*, **57** (2), 227–42.

Burgelman, R. (1994), 'Fading memories: a process theory of strategic business exit in dynamic environments', *Administrative Science Quarterly*, **39**, 24–56.

Carter, N.M., W.B. Gartner, K.G. Shaver and E.J. Gatewood (2003), 'The career reasons of nascent entrepreneurs', *Journal of Business Venturing*, **18** (1), 13–39.

Chandler, G.N. and S.H. Hanks (1994), 'Market attractiveness, resource-based capabilities, venture strategies, and venture performance', *Journal of Business Venturing*, **9**, 331–49.

Chopra, A. (2005), 'Survival', paper presented at the Academy of Management Conference, Hawaii, 5–10 August.

Delmar, F. and S. Shane (2003), 'Does business planning facilitate the development of new ventures?', *Strategic Management Journal*, **24**, 1165–85.

Delmar, F., K. Hellerstedt and K. Wennberg (2006), 'The evolution of firms created by the science and technology labor force in Sweden 1990–2000', in J. Ulhöi and P.R. Christensen (eds), *Managing Complexity and Change in SMEs: Frontiers in European Research*, Cheltenham, UK and Nothampton, MA, USA: Edward Elgar, pp. 69–102.

DeTienne, D. and M. Cardon (2006), 'Entrepreneurial exit strategies: the impact of general and specific human capital', paper presented at the Babson College Entrepreneurship Research Conference, Bloomington, Indiana, 8–10 June.

Evans, D.S., and L.S. Leighton (1989), 'Some empirical aspects of entrepreneurship', *The American Economic Review*, **79** (3), 519–35.

Everett, J. and J. Watson, (1998), 'Small business failures and external risk factors', *Small Business Economics*, **11** (4), 371.

Gimeno, J., T.B. Folta, A.C. Cooper and C.Y. Woo (1997), 'Survival of the fittest? Entrepreneurial human capital and the persistence of underperforming firms', *Administrative Science Quarterly*, **42** (4), 750–83.

Headd, B. (2003), 'Redefining business success: distinguishing between closure and failure', *Small Business Economics*, **21** (1), 51–61.

Kalleberg, A.L. and K.T. Leicht (1991), 'Gender and organizational performance: Determinants of small business survival and success', *Academy of Management Journal*, **34** (1), 136–61.

Mata, J. and P. Portugal (1994), 'Life duration of new firms', *The Journal of Industrial Economics*, **42** (3), 227.

Meager, N. P. Bates (2004), 'Self-employment in the United Kingdom during the 1980s and 1990s', in R. Arum and W. Muller (eds), *The Re-Emergence of Self-Employment: A Comparative Study of Self-Employment Dynamics and Social Inequality*, Princeton, NJ: Princeton University Press, pp. 135–69.

Mitchell, W. (1994), 'The dynamics of evolving markets: the effects of business sales and age on dissolutions and divestitures', *Administrative Science Quarterly*, **39** (4), 575–602.

Taylor, M.P. (1999), 'Survival of the fittest: an analysis of self-employment duration in Britain', *The Economic Journal*, **109** (March), 140–55.

Ucbasaran, D., D. Shepherd, P. Westhead and M.E. Wright (2005), 'Experiences of habitual entrepreneurs: business failure, overconfidence and "small wins"', paper presented at the Babson-Kauffman Entrepreneurship Conference, Babson College, Wellesley, 9–11 June.

Van Witteloostuijn, A. (1998), 'Bridging behavioral and economic theories of decline: organizational inertia, strategic competition, and chronic failure', *Management Science*, **44** (4), 501–19.
Venkataraman, S. (1997), 'The distinctive domain of entrepreneurship research: An editor's perspective', in J. Katz and R.H.S. Brockhaus (eds), *Advances in Entrepreneurship, Firm Emergence, and Growth*, Greenwich, CT: JAI Press. (vol. 3, pp. 119–38).
Wennberg, K. and J. Wiklund (2006), 'Entrepreneurial exit', paper presented at the Academy of Management Meeting, Atlanta, 11–16 August.
Wennberg, K., D. DeTienne, M. Cardon and J. Wiklund (2007), 'Human capital predictors of entrepreneurial exit paths', unpublished manuscript, Stockholm School of Economics.
Wennberg, K., T.B. Folta and F. Delmar (2006), 'A real options model of stepwise entry into self-employment', in A. Zacharakis (ed.), *Frontier of Entrepreneurship Research*, Babson Park, MA: Babson College, pp. 119–32.

19 Family business

Sascha Kraus and Rainer Harms

Family businesses are said to be the originating form of any business activity (Wakefield, 1995), dominating the economic landscape of most major economies in the world (Astrachan and Shanker, 2003; Heck and Stafford, 2001; Klein, 2000; Morck and Yeung, 2003; Shanker and Astrachan, 1996). More than two-thirds of all enterprises worldwide are said to be family-owned and/or managed (Gersick et al., 1997). The life-span of family businesses is however often relatively short, as only a limited number survive the transition to the second generation, and hardly one-third even into the third generation (Beckhard and Dyer, 1983; Neubauer and Lank, 1998; Paisner, 1999; Shanker and Astrachan, 1996). The Steinberg supermarkets, for example, were first launched in Canada in 1912, had great success under the leadership of Sam Steinberg (see Figure 19.1) but this family business disappeared in 1992.

Due to the high importance of family businesses, academia has finally begun to recognize their necessity as a research object (Chrisman et al. 2006). According to Dyer Jr (2003), the field of management studies has paid insufficient attention the family

Figure 19.1 Mr Sam Steinberg; photograph by Léo-Paul Dana

businesses' unique theoretical and practical problems so far. The interest in family business research has consequently grown significantly in recent years, leading to a distinctive legitimate and emerging field of study within entrepreneurship research, into which also the Academy of Management classifies this topic. The reason is that there is a large intersection between entrepreneurship and family business research (Fletcher, 2005). First, most family businesses are small and medium-sized enterprises (SMEs). Secondly, founders of family businesses are obviously entrepreneurs, having perceived an opportunity through the creation of a new firm (Aldrich and Cliff, 2003).

The underlying reasoning for particular research on family businesses is the question of whether they do really behave differently from non-family businesses, and if so, how and why they are different. Several researchers suggest that the family-form of organization holds essential advantages (Anderson and Reeb, 2003; McConaughy et al., 1998). Empirical studies, such as one among S&P 500 firms (Anderson and Reeb, 2003) show that firms being under the influence of the founding families outperform their counterparts. Especially in terms of corporate performance (such as size, growth, profitability, and so on), significant differences between family and non-family businesses could be identified (Gallo, 1995; McConaughy and Phillips, 1999).

DEFINING AND DESCRIBING FAMILY BUSINESSES

There is also no universal definition of what a 'family business' is yet. Westhead and Cowling (1998) have reviewed and analysed existing definitions of family businesses that have been used in previous research. They conclude that the problem is less differentiating between a firm that is clearly a family business and a firm that is clearly not, but rather the 'grey area' in between. The authors found, for example, that the ratio of family businesses varies dramatically depending on the definition used in the study. Accordingly, there are countless definitions of what a family business is out there.

For instance, researchers define a family business operationally by the components of a family's involvement in the business: ownership, management or business succession (Chrisman et al., 2003b). The definitions reach from 100 per cent ownership of shares to the majority of control (Chua et al., 1999), or they deal with the question of whether governance by the family is enough or management of the firm would be necessary. Some studies even consider a company a family business when the firm considers itself to be one (Westhead and Cowling, 1998). Shanker and Astrachan (1996) differentiate between a narrow and a broad definition of family businesses – in the former, the family is involved in the daily business, whereas in the latter, the family only sets the strategic direction for the firm. Accordingly, researchers have proposed a broad variety of combinations of the named components. When different definitions are applied, the percentage of family business in one sample can vary from 15 per cent to 80 per cent (Westhead et al., 1997).

Family business research has so far about four different *individual levels*:

1. the company founders (for example, Kelly et al., 2000; Kenyon-Rouvinez, 2001; Sorenson, 2000),

2. next-generation members (for example, Eckrich and Loughead, 1996; Goldberg, 1996; Stavrou, 1998),
3. women in family businesses (for example, Cole, 1997; Dumas, 1998; Fitzgerald and Muske, 2002; Poza and Messer, 2001), or
4. external managers within family businesses (for example, Mitchell et al., 1997).

Aditionally, at *group level*, popular research topics have been:

1. conflict within family businesses (for example, Boles, 1996; Drozdow, 1998; Habbershon and Astrachan, 1996; Kaye, 1996; Kellermanns and Eddleston, 2004; Sorenson, 1999), and
2. business succession (for example, Cadieux et al., 2002; Davis and Harveston, 1998; Harveston et al., 1997 ; Miller et al., 2003 ; Morris et al., 1997).

Owing to their dissatisfaction with existing definitions, several authors have shifted their approach to identify the 'essence' of a family business, for example, through the question of the family's influence in strategic decision-making (Davis and Tagiuri, 1989; Handler, 1989, Shanker and Astrachan, 1996). The idea behind is that the family could be the critical variable in family business research (Astrachan, 2003; Dyer Jr, 2003; Habbershon et al., 2003a; Rogoff and Heck, 2003; Zahra, 2003). Litz (1995), for instance, advocates that the essence of a family business is the family's purpose of retaining control over the company for more than the present generation. Habbershon et al. (2003a) introduced a new perspective called 'familiness' which describes unique, inseparable and synergistic resources and capabilities emerging from family involvement and interactions. Summarized, they say that the intersection of family and business lead to hardly duplicatable capabilities that make family business peculiarly suited to survival and growth (Habbershon and Williams, 1999; Habbershon et al., 2003b). If this familiness can be transferred from one generation to another as a heritage, this might be core of the family business concept (Baker and Wiseman, 1998; Kelly et al., 2000; Poza and Messer, 2001). Accordingly, an integrated definition of a family business could, for example, include:

1. familiness as described before,
2. control over the business for current and
3. next generations (Chrisman et al. 2003a; Habbershon et al. 2003b).

ADVANTAGES AND DISADVANTAGES OF FAMILY BUSINESSES

Mainly due to facts like long chief executive officer (CEO) tenures (typically more than 15 years) and concern for subsequent generations of the family, family businesses are more likely to take a long-term view when in making strategic investments (Le Breton-Miller and Miller, 2006). Family businesses, furthermore, tend toward sustaining strategy over a longer period of time (Ensley, 2006).

However, there are also several disadvantages connected with family businesses.

Family businesses have to deal with additional – namely, family – issues (Lester et al., 2006; Paisner, 1999), which might be resource-consuming. Besides, family businesses often experience slower growth as well as slower decision-making processes (Meyer and Zucker, 1989). Further, they are often more hesitant to invest in risky projects (Cabrera-Suárez et al., 2001; Gersick et al., 1997), and thus could miss opportunities. Also, family businesses are said to resist change and become fixated on maintaining the status quo (Kellermanns and Eddleston, 2006), and they are often regarded as being less innovative than their non-family counterparts (Gomez-Mejia et al., 2003).

GOALS OF FAMILY BUSINESSES

The majority of mainstream theories within business research consider economic reasoning, that is, wealth creation, as the major goal for any business organization. In family businesses, the situation could be different, and also non-economic goals play a major role in the decision-making processes of the firm (Olson et al., 2003; Stafford et al., 1999). The success of a family business would accordingly depend on effective management of the interface between the family and the business (Sharma, 2004).

Recognizing that family businesses almost always include family as well as business dimensions, the performance of family businesses will also most likely include both family and business dimensions (Mitchell et al., 2003). Understanding how the influence of a family might affect a business and its performance opens up interesting new avenues of research, as Chrisman et al. (2006) state.

If family businesses do have economic as well as non-economic goals, the measurement of the overall performance may be particularly difficult (Hienerth and Kessler, 2006). Besides, there is no heterogeneity within the group of family businesses.

Results of previous empirical studies indicate that family goals are often more important to the owners of family businesses than to the owners of non-family businesses, that is, financial goals might be traded against (non-financial) family goals (Lee and Rogoff, 1996). Although there have been prior studies about the goals of family businesses (Tagiuri and Davis, 1996), the driving forces behind these goals are still in their infancy. Altruism, fairness, justice and generosity have been investigated as some of these drivers for non-economic goals (Eaton et al., 2002; Lubatkin et al., 2002; Schulze et al., 2001). Nevertheless, goals of different family members can also be different, and vary over time, that is, an individual's life cycle, as Hoy (2006) calls it, which might also result in differences in power and status of family members.

When it comes to performance of family businesses, empirical studies such as that by Morck and Yeung (2003) conclude that it is worse than in non-family businesses owing to the family's desire for capital preservation, stability and risk aversion. Authors like Schulze et al. (2003) see potential for inefficiencies that will have a negative impact on profit when ownership is concentrated in the hands of a single family. They argue that the owner-managers' desire for family harmony and a tendency for altruistic behaviour towards family members, coupled with ineffective controls create inefficiencies that outweigh the positive effects of alignment of interests that comes with the concentration of ownership and management.

However, other authors see family businesses ahead in terms of performance, and claim this is through families being better stewards of firm resources due to less managerial opportunism within the company (Anderson and Reeb, 2003; Lester et al., 2006).

CONCLUSION

Both theoretical and empirical attempts to define 'family business' are still open for discussion, and the development of objective methods for separating family from non-family businesses is still in its infancy (Chrisman et al., 2003b).

Besides, 'very little attention has been paid to how family dynamics affect entrepreneurial processes' (Aldrich and Cliff, 2003: 574) so far. Furthermore, the extent of entrepreneurial behaviour within the organization tends to change over time (Kellermanns and Eddleston, 2006). The founders often become more conservative and risk-averse decision-makers because they fear losing family wealth (Sharma et al., 1997). The entrepreneurial impetus becomes diluted over time, and entrepreneurial practices become subsumed by other concerns (Fletcher, 2005).

Family businesses will continue to play an increasing greater role in world economies. Business schools and research institutions will recognize them as a serious career alternative for their students, and will thus have to provide them with direction and resources to pursuing opportunities there. Despite the progress made, especially in the twenty-first century, research on family businesses remains a new field which is trying to gain legitimacy within management studies and particularly entrepreneurship research, though much remains to be done (Chrisman et al., 2003b; Hoy, 2003).

REFERENCES

Aldrich, H. and J. Cliff (2003), 'The pervasive effects of family on entrepreneurship: toward a family embeddedness perspective', *Journal of Business Venturing*, **18** (5), 573–97.

Anderson, R. and D. Reeb (2003), 'Founding-family ownership and firm performance: evidence from S&P500', *Journal of Finance*, **58** (3), 1301–27.

Astrachan, J. (2003), 'The emergence of a field. Commentary on the special issue "The evolving family/entrepreneurship relationship"', *Journal of Business Venturing*, **18** (5), 567–72.

Astrachan, J. and M. Shanker (2003), 'Family businesses' contribution to the US economy: a closer look', *Family Business Review*, **16** (3), 211–9.

Baker, K. and K. Wiseman (1998), 'Leadership, legacy, and emotional process in family business', *Family Business Review*, **11** (3), 207–13.

Beckhard, R. and W. Dyer (1983), 'Managing change in the family firms – issues and strategies', *Sloan Management Review*, **24**, 59–65.

Boles, J. (1996), 'Influences of work-family conflict on job satisfaction, life satisfaction and quitting intentions among business owners: the case of family-operated businesses', *Family Business Review*, **9** (1), 61–74.

Cabrera-Suárez, K., P. De Saá-Pérez and D. Garcia-Almeida (2001), 'The succession process from a resource- and knowledge-based view of the family firm', *Family Business Review*, **14** (1), 37–46.

Cadieux, L., J. Lorrain and P. Hugron (2002), 'Succession in women owned family businesses: a case study', *Family Business Review*, **15** (1), 17–30.

Chrisman, J., J. Chua and R. Litz (2003a), 'A unified perspective of family firm performance: an extension and integration', *Journal of Business Venturing*, **18** (4), 467–72.

Chrisman, J.J, J.H. Chua and P. Sharma (2003b), 'Current trends and future directions in family business management studies: toward a theory of the family business', Coleman White Paper series, Nashville, TN: USASBE.

Chrisman, J.J., L.P. Steier and J.H. Chua (2006), 'Personalism, particularism, and the competitive behaviors and advantages of family firms: an introduction', *Entrepreneurship Theory and Practice*, **30** (3), 719–30.

Chua, J.H., J.J. Chrisman and P. Sharma (1999), 'Defining family business by behavior', *Entrepreneurship Theory and Practice*, **24**, 19–39.
Cole, P.M. (1997), 'Women in family business', *Family Business Review*, **10** (4), 353–71.
Davis, J. and R. Tagiuri (1989), 'The influence of life-stage on father–son work relationships in family companies', *Family Business Review*, **2** (1), 47–74.
Davis, P. and P. Harveston (1998), 'The influence of family on the family business succession process: a multi-generational perspective', *Entrepreneurship Theory and Practice*, **22** (3), 31–53.
Drozdow, N. (1998), 'What is continuity?', *Family Business Review*, **11** (4), 337–47.
Dumas, C. (1998), 'Women's pathways to participation and leadership in family-owned firms', *Family Business Review*, **11** (3), 219–28.
Dyer Jr, W. (2003), 'The family: the missing variable in organizational research', *Entrepreneurship Theory and Practice*, **27** (4), 401–16.
Eaton, C., L. Yuan and Z. Wu (2002), 'Reciprocal altruism and the theory of the family firm', Second Annual Conference on Theories of the Family Enterprise, University of Pennsylvania, Philadelphia, December.
Eckrich, C. and T. Loughead (1996), 'Effects of family business membership and psychological separation on the career development of late adolescents', *Family Business Review*, **9** (4), 369–86.
Ensley, M. (2006), 'Family businesses can out-compete: as long as they are willing to question the chosen path', *Entrepreneurship Theory and Practice*, **30** (6), 747–54.
Fitzgerald, M. and G. Muske (2002), 'Copreneurs: an exploration and comparison to other family businesses', *Family Business Review*, **15** (1), 1–16.
Fletcher, D. (2005), 'A family-embeddedness view of entrepreneurship', in M. Raffa and L. Iandoli (eds), *Entrepreneurship Competitiveness and Local Development – RENT XIX Proceedings*, Rome: Edizioni Scientifiche Italiane.
Gallo, M.A. (1995), 'The role of family business and its distinctive characteristic behavior in industrial activity', *Family Business Review*, **8** (2), 83–97.
Gersick, K., J. Davis, M. Hampton and I. Lansberg (1997), *Generation to Generation: Life Cycles of the Family Business*, Boston, MA: Harvard Business School Press.
Goldberg, S. (1996), 'Effective successors in family-owned businesses: significant elements', *Family Business Review*, **9** (2), 185–97.
Gomez-Mejia, L.R., M. Larraza-Kintana and M. Makri (2003), 'The determinants of executive compensation in family-controlled public corporations', *Academy of Management Journal*, **46** (2), 226–37.
Habbershon, T., M.L. Williams and I.C. MacMillan (2003a), 'Familiness: a unified systems perspective of family firm performance', *Journal of Business Venturing*, **18**, 451–65.
Habbershon, T.G. and J. Astrachan (1996), 'Perceptions are reality: how family meetings lead to collective action', *Family Business Review*, **10** (1), 37–52.
Habbershon, T.G. and M. Williams (1999), 'A resource-based framework for assessing the strategic advantages of family firms', *Family Business Review*, **12**, 1–25.
Habbershon, T.G., M. Williams and I. MacMillan (2003b), 'A unified systems perspective of family firm performance', *Journal of Business Venturing*, **18** (4), 451–65.
Handler, W. (1989), 'Methodological issues and considerations in studying family businesses', *Family Business Review*, **2** (3), 257–76.
Harveston, P., P. Davis and J. Lyden (1997), 'Succession planning in family business: the impact of owner gender', *Family Business Review*, **10** (4), 373–96.
Heck, R.K.Z. and K. Stafford (2001), 'The vital institution of family business: economic benefits hidden in plain sight', in G.K. McCann and N. Upton (eds), *Destroying Myths and Creating Value in Family Business*, Deland, FL: Stetson University Press, pp. 9–17.
Hienerth, C. and A. Kessler (2006), 'Measuring success in family businesses: the concept of configurational fit', *Family Business Review*, **19** (2), 115–34.
Hoy, F. (2003), 'Legitimizing family business scholarship in organizational research and education', *Entrepreneurship Theory and Practice*, **27** (4), 417–22.
Hoy, F. (2006), 'The complicating factor of life cycles in corporate venturing', *Entrepreneurship Theory and Practice*, **30** (6), 831–6.
Kaye, K. (1996), 'When the family business is a sickness', *Family Business Review*, **9** (4), 347–68.
Kellermanns, F.W. and K. Eddleston (2004), 'Feuding families: when conflict does a family firm good', *Entrepreneurship Theory and Practice*, **28** (3), 209–28.
Kellermanns, F.W. and K. Eddleston (2006), 'Corporate entrepreneurship in family firms: a family perspective', *Entrepreneurship Theory and Practice*, **30** (6), 809–30.
Kelly, L., N. Athanassiou and W. Crittenden (2000), 'Founder centrality and strategic behavior in family-owned firms', *Entrepreneurship Theory and Practice*, **25** (2), 27–42.
Kenyon-Rouvinez, D. (2001), 'Patterns in serial business families: theory building through global case studies', *Family Business Review*, **14** (3), 175–87.

Klein, S. (2000), 'Family businesses in Germany: significance and structure', *Family Business Review*, **13** (3), 157–81.
Le Breton-Miller, I. and D. Miller (2006), 'Why do some family businesses out-compete? Governance, long-term orientations, and sustainable capability', *Entrepreneurship Theory and Practice*, **30** (6), 731–46.
Lee, M. and E. Rogoff (1996), 'Comparison of small businesses with family participation versus small businesses without family participation: an investigation of differences in goals, attitudes, and family/business conflict', *Family Business Review*, **9** (4), 423–37.
Lester, R.H., A.A. Cannella and D. Miller (2006), 'Interorganizational familiness: how family firms use interlocking directorates to build community-level social capital', *Entrepreneurship Theory and Practice*, **30** (6), 755–76.
Litz, R.A. (1995), 'The family business: toward definitional clarity', *Family Business Review*, **8** (2), 71–81.
Lubatkin, M., Y. Ling and W. Schulze (2002), 'Fairness in family firms: lessons from agency and justice theory', Second Annual Conference on Theories of the Family Enterprise, University of Pennsylvania, Philadelphia, December.
McConaughy, D. and G. Phillips (1999), 'Founders versus descendants: the profitability, efficiency, growth characteristics and financing in large, public, founding-family-controlled firms', *Family Business Review*, **12** (2), 123–31.
McConaughy, D., M. Walker G. Henderson and C. Mishra (1998), 'Founding family controlled firms: efficiency and value', *Review of Financial Economics*, **7**, 1–19.
Meyer, M. and L. Zucker (1989), *Permanently Failing Organizations*, Newbury Park, CA: Sage.
Miller, D., L. Steier and I. Le Breton-Miller (2003), 'Lost in time: intergenerational succession, change, and failure in family business', *Journal of Business Venturing*, **18** (4), 513–31.
Mitchell, R., B. Agle and D. Wood (1997), 'Toward a theory of stakeholder identification and salience: defining the principle of who and what really counts', *Academy of Management Review*, **22**, 853–86.
Mitchell, R.K., E.A. Morse and P. Sharma (2003), 'The transacting cognitions of non-family employees in the family business setting', *Journal of Business Venturing*, **18** (4), 533–51.
Morck, R. and B. Yeung (2003), 'Agency problems in large family business groups', *Entrepreneurship Theory and Practice*, **27** (4), 367–82.
Morris, M., R. Williams, J. Allen and R. Avila (1997), 'Correlates of success in family business transitions', *Journal of Business Venturing*, **12**, 385–401.
Neubauer, F. and A. Lank (1998), *The Family Business: Its Governance for Sustainability*, London: Macmillan.
Olson, P., V. Zuiker, S. Danes, K. Stafford, R. Heck and K. Duncan (2003), 'Impact of family and business on family business sustainability', *Journal of Business Venturing*, **18** (5), 639–66.
Paisner, M. (1999), *Sustaining the Family Business*, Reading, MA: Perseus.
Poza, E. and T. Messer (2001), 'Spousal leadership and continuity in the family firm', *Family Business Review*, **14** (1), 25–36.
Rogoff, E.G. and R.K.Z. Heck (2003), 'Evolving research in entrepreneurship and family business: recognizing family as the oxygen that feeds the fire of entrepreneurship', *Journal of Business Venturing*, **18** (5), 559–66.
Schulze, W., M. Lubatkin and R. Dino (2003), 'Exploring the agency consequences of ownership dispersion among the directors of private family firms', *Academy of Management Journal*, **46** (2), 174–94.
Schulze, W., M. Lubatkin, R. Dino and A. Buchholtz (2001), 'Agency relationships in family firms: theory and evidence', *Organization Science*, **12**, 99–116.
Shanker, M.C. and J.H. Astrachan (1996), 'Myths and realities: family businesses' contribution to the US economy – a framework for assessing family business statistics', *Family Business Review*, **9** (2), 107–23.
Sharma, P. (2004), 'An overview of the field of family business studies: current status and directions for the future', *Family Business Review*, **17** (1), 1–36.
Sharma, P., J.J. Chrisman and J.H. Chua (1997), 'Strategic management of the family business: past research and future challenges', *Family Business Review*, **10** (1), 1–36.
Sorenson, R. (1999), 'Conflict management strategies used in successful family businesses', *Family Business Review*, **12** (4), 133–46.
Sorenson, R. (2000), 'The contribution of leadership style and practices to family and business success', *Family Business Review*, **13** (3), 183–200.
Stafford, K., K. Duncan, S. Danes and M. Winter (1999), 'A research model of sustainable family businesses', *Family Business Review*, **12** (3), 197–208.
Stavrou, E. (1998), 'A four factor model: a guide to planning next generation involvement in the family firm', *Family Business Review*, **11** (2), 135–42.
Tagiuri, R. and J.A. Davis (1996), 'Bivalent attributes on the family businesses', *Family Business Review*, **9** (2), 199–208.
Wakefield, M.W. (1995), *Antecedents of Conflict in Family Firms – An Empirical Study*, Lincoln, NB: University of Nebraska.

Westhead, P. and M. Cowling (1998), 'Family business research: the need for a methodological rethink', *Entrepreneurship: Theory and Practice*, **23** (1), 31–57.

Westhead, P., M. Cowling and D. Storey (1997), *The Management and Performance of Unquoted Family Companies in the United Kingdom*, Coventry: Centre for Small and Medium Sized Enterprises.

Zahra, S.A. (2003), 'International expansion of US manufacturing family businesses: the effect of ownership and involvement', *Journal of Business Venturing*, **18** (4), 495–512.

20 Feasibility of entrepreneurship

Yvon Gasse

A set of external factors, often independent of the individual, will influence entrepreneurship. Clearly, these factors interact with one another in order to create climates that are more or less favourable to business creation. It is also clear that these climates can change over time and that, to a certain extent, entrepreneurship in the past will impact on entrepreneurship in the future. Not only must the entrepreneur be aware of the desirability of the entrepreneurial act, but this act must also be reasonably feasible. Feasibility accordingly depends on a series of positive perceptions relating to the presence and accessibility of means and resources appropriate for the creation of a business. Some of these means may relate to the actual ability of the entrepreneur, but a number will relate more to the immediate environment. Here are a few of them.

PERCEPTIONS OF THE ENTREPRENEUR

A decision to create a business depends on the entrepreneur's perception of the risks and gratifications involved as well as on his or her knowledge of sources of financing and the individuals and organizations that could be of assistance and provide advice. Past entrepreneurship creates what could be called an entrepreneurial environment in which the potential entrepreneur is surrounded by examples and people familiar with the entrepreneurial process; often, in fact, entrepreneurship is seen in these environments as a recognized and valued way of life (Reynolds, 1997). The importance of perceptions among nascent entrepreneurs of the feasibility of a project to found a business has been shown by Diochon and her colleagues (Diochon et al., 2002), when they made a comparison with a control group of persons who did not intend to found a business. The results provided significant confirmation of the fact that nascent entrepreneurs view the feasibility of starting a business in a more positive light than other people.

ATTITUDES OF THE COMMUNITY

The attitude of the community to business people and entrepreneurship has an important impact on this decision. Unfortunately, this sociocultural dimension of the entrepreneurial process seems less tangible and more mysterious than the economic and psychological components. It is perhaps less obvious but it is just as fundamental.

Thus, the attitude towards investment in new technological businesses can change a great deal over time. In those areas where entrepreneurship is active, it is possible that the networks already exist and that it is relatively easy for a potential entrepreneur to make contact with lenders or promising investors. Successful entrepreneurs can bring prosperity to their region and also change perceptions of the risks and gratifications associated with lending to and investment in new businesses, especially in those cases where the community formally and visibly acknowledges the success of these entrepreneurs. The importance of formal and informal networks has been widely stressed in studies of nascent entrepreneurs (Diochon et al., 2001; Gasse et al., 2002a, 2002b).

GROUPINGS OF BUSINESSES

Location is also an important factor in the feasibility of a new business. It impacts not only on transportation costs but also, and above all, on the creation of groups (or clusters) of related businesses that purchase and sell their products from and to one another. It seems that the development of a cluster provides new businesses with many advantages, including a reservoir of qualified manpower and specialized suppliers (OECD, 1998; Porter, 1990). In the field of high technology, for example, it is sometimes essential to be able to work very closely with customers (Gasse, 2000). Another advantage is the creation among local accountants, bankers, lawyers and engineers of specific expertise focusing on the particular needs of small businesses with growth potential (Reynolds and Storey, 1993).

In its study of entrepreneurship, the Organisation for Economic Co-operation and Development (OECD, 1998) noted that groupings or 'poles' of businesses offer particular attractions for entrepreneurs. For example, thanks to the high specialization that these groupings make possible, an individual entrepreneur can launch a business focused on a specific aspect of a given area of activity, as this makes for fewer obstacles to the start-up of a new business. Furthermore, since groupings often include purchasers and vendors at different points in the production chain, pressure to innovate is strong and the conditions required for innovation are often present. Finally, many groupings display the great vertical mobility in the labour force; manual workers can launch their own businesses, partly thanks to the lack of constraints on vertical integration.

REFERENCES

Diochon, M., Y. Gasse, T.V. Menzies and D. Garand (2001), 'From conception to inception: initial findings from the Canadian study on entrepreneurial emergence', proceedings of the Administrative Sciences Association of Canada, London, Ontario, 27–29 May, pp. 41–51.

Diochon, M., Y. Gasse and T.V. Menzies (2002), 'Attitudes and entrepreneurial action: exploring the link', paper presented to the ASAC Conference, Winnipeg, Manitoba, May.

Gasse, Y. (2000), 'Les chercheurs-entrepreneurs canadiens: profil et entreprises', working paper, Centre d'Entrepreneuriat et de PME, Université Laval.

Gasse, Y., M. Diochon and T.V. Menzies (2002a), 'Canadian nascent entrepreneurs: the first two years of the project', proceedings of the 19th Conference of the Canadian Council, Halifax.

Gasse, Y., M. Diochon and T.V. Menzies (2002b), 'Les entrepreneurs naissants et la poursuite de leur projet d'entreprise: une étude longitudinale', Actes du 6ième Congrès International Francophone sur la PME, Montréal, HEC.

Organisation for Economic Co-operation and Development (OECD), (1998), *Stimuler l'Esprit d'Entreprise*, Paris: OECD.

Porter, M. (1990), *The Competitive Advantage of Nations*, New York: Free Press.

Reynolds, P. (1997), 'Who starts new firms?', *Small Business Economics*, **9** (1), 449–62.

Reynolds, P. and D. Storey (1993), 'Regional characteristics affecting small business formation', *ILE Notebook*, no. 18, OECD.

21 Geographic proximity in entrepreneurship

Udo Staber

It has become an axiom in research on entrepreneurship that certain key assets in the entrepreneurial process, such as knowledge, informal rules and creative potential, acquire value only in the context of interpersonal and interorganizational exchange. Accordingly, much research has focused on social networks as a basic unit of analysis and an important competitive entity in the entrepreneurial process (Thornton, 1999). Drawing on insights in economic geography (Dicken and Malmberg, 2001) and regional development (Polenske, 2004), the social network view of entrepreneurship has recently been extended to the level of the organizational community as the resource environment in which networks evolve and in which knowledge concerning available business opportunities, institution building and so forth is created and diffused. Such communities, which are variously referred to as business clusters, industrial districts, hot spots, learning regions, or entrepreneurial districts, tend to be spatially concentrated (Porter, 2000; Sorenson and Audia, 2000). Well-known examples of clusters include textiles in Northern Italy, software in Silicon Valley, advertising in London and new media in New York.

The argument that entrepreneurial networks evolve in a localized cluster of interdependent organizational populations marks an important step towards a more inclusive theory of entrepreneurship as a spatial phenomenon, to show that knowledge networks are not randomly distributed in space. Entrepreneurial activity occurs in clusters not merely because of the efficiency benefits of co-location, relative to the competitive pressures of location in densely populated areas. New organizations are founded more frequently in clusters also because these locations help entrepreneurs to accumulate knowledge, social connections, and social legitimacy (Stuart and Sorenson, 2003).

A growing number of both conceptual and empirical studies have elaborated on the idea that entrepreneurial activity takes place in a spatially defined social and institutional context. Many of these studies have drawn their basic insights from economics, focusing on positive externalities and knowledge spillover. Other studies have drawn on research in organization theory and strategic management, examining entrepreneurship with respect to local competitive processes (Baum and Haveman, 1997), functional interdependencies (Mezias and Kuperman, 2001), social cohesion (Anderson and Jack, 2002) and intermediary organizations like incubators and venture capital firms (Powell et al., 2002). On balance, these studies show that the basic entrepreneurial activities related to creating new knowledge, imitating the practices of others, and building new relationships are essentially a context-dependent social process (Low and Abrahamson, 1997), rooted in local social structures and traditions (Taylor and Leonard, 2002), and embedded in an institutional framework that provides supportive rules and norms (Sydow and Staber, 2002). However, the exact constellation of relevant variables, levels of analysis, place, and performance outcomes remains unclear, given the available evidence.

In this chapter, I review the findings from this research, organizing the work around accepted research areas and pointing out issues that are currently debated. I focus on discussions related to geographies of knowledge, social capital and institutions, noting that each of these areas is driven by theoretical perspectives in economics, sociology and institutionalism, respectively. The review suggests that the concept of geographic proximity is often (mis)used as a proxy measure of interorganizational cooperation and knowledge exchange. It needs to be unpacked to account for the partly competing and partly complementary interrelationships between knowledge, social capital, and institutions. While spatial proximity may in some cases be advantageous, it is neither a necessary nor a sufficient condition for effective entrepreneurship.

THE GEOGRAPHY OF KNOWLEDGE

Economists have long been interested in the role of knowledge as an engine of economic development. At the micro level, knowledge creation and transfer involves transaction costs that limit the efficiency of joint learning. To explain these limitations, economists frequently draw on the knowledge-based and resource-based views, describing the firm as a repository of routines and competencies that, if allowed to evolve freely, act as a source of competitive advantage (Nelson and Winter, 1982; Penrose, 1959). At the macro level, knowledge is seen as an important growth factor, explaining why some regional economies lag behind others in development (Suire et al., 2006). For economic geographers, the key question concerns the locational aspect of knowledge creation and transfer (Martin and Sunley, 2003).

The literature in this area reveals two lines of reasoning relevant to our understanding of entrepreneurship. One of these concerns the role of knowledge in the location decision of new firms, and the other concerns the relationship between knowledge and interorganizational learning and innovation. Following the early insights of Alfred Marshall (1920), many studies have documented the tendency of firms that use similar knowledge to co-locate, especially in knowledge-intensive industries such as biotechnology and advertising. The purported reason for this is that the public goods character of knowledge implies opportunities for spillover across organizational boundaries (Audretsch and Feldman, 1996). Once knowledge is created, it may spill over to benefit other firms able to observe and monitor its content and application potential. Proximity increases the availability of information and the incentive to attend to it (Porac et al., 1995). Thus, one would expect that geographic concentrations of innovative activity generate knowledge spillovers across technologically similar firms (Baptista, 1998).

Aharonson et al. (2007) studied entrepreneurs' location choices and the role of incumbents' technological capabilities as sources of potential spillovers in shaping these choices. They argued that opportunities for entrepreneurs to benefit from spillovers depended on the spatial distribution of research and development (R&D) activity, with more concentrated areas of activity representing more promising opportunities. Their findings supported the hypothesis that potential knowledge spillovers from firms existing in a cluster would attract entrepreneurs, relative to opportunities in distant locations. Other research has also shown that more concentrated areas of innovative activity tend to attract a disproportionate number of start-ups and generate a disproportionate share of innovative output (for a review, see Aharonson et al., 2007).

The second line of reasoning focuses on the effect of knowledge on learning and innovation through interorganizational interaction (Breschi and Lissoni, 2001). In order for knowledge held by a firm to be able to create new value, it has to be coordinated with knowledge held by other firms. The creation of new knowledge requires the transfer of knowledge from external sources, and therefore much new knowledge is created interactively. This is certainly true for entrepreneurship, seen as a process driven by the ability to identify and exploit new opportunities. Knowledge transfer is critical for small firms lacking the resources for expensive innovative efforts. Because much of the relevant information is held privately, awareness of opportunities and access to the necessary resources require connections to those individuals and firms that hold pertinent knowledge. Given their embeddedness in social structures, one would expect entrepreneurs to look for such knowledge first within the proximate organizational community. Entrepreneurs, so the argument goes, are subject to a social bias that confines their search for knowledge to the immediate community (Brökel and Binder, 2007).

The empirical evidence, however, does not strongly and consistently support the hypothesis that firms will cooperate more with others located in close proximity than with firms in distant locations. Some studies support the argument that knowledge exchange benefits are more likely to be obtained when entrepreneurs are located in close proximity, to the extent that proximity facilitates cognitive coordination and reduces opportunism among the exchange partners (Lorenzen and Foss, 2003). Bathelt (2005) attributed the stagnation of the Leipzig multimedia cluster partly to the lack of proximate social capital. Walker et al.'s (1997) study of biotechnology start-ups showed that clusters of densely connected partner firms were stronger sources of new alliances than more sparsely connected clusters. In a study of clusters in the Netherlands, proximity was shown to have a positive effect on a range of firm-level performance measures (Oerleman and Meeus, 2005).

Other studies, however, suggest that connections across cluster boundaries can be as important or even more important than collaboration that occurs locally (Boari et al., 2003). In many industries the spatial scale of effective interfirm collaboration has increased over time (Johnson et al., 2006), owing to improved communication technology and stronger (trans)national institutional regulation. Spatial proximity can also have negative effects. Research on textile clusters in Germany found that the competitive pressures of location in densely populated clusters overwhelm the spillover advantages of co-location (Staber, 2001). A study of the Boston biotechnology cluster showed that many new firms maintained effective partnerships across regional and national boundaries (Owen-Smith and Powell, 2004). A study of a footwear district in Italy found that co-location did not favour local networking (Boschma and Ter Wal, 2007). Firms with connections to organizations outside the cluster outperformed firms that were not well connected. Apparently, spatial proximity as such does not guarantee knowledge spillover or active resource exchange. While location in a cluster that is densely populated by other innovative firms may positively affect the likelihood of innovating, disadvantages may arise from the presence of non-innovative firms in a firm's own sector (Beaudry and Breschi, 2003).

THE GEOGRAPHY OF SOCIAL CAPITAL

Research on the geography of knowledge suggests that, if newly founded firms or existing firms locate too far from similar firms, they limit their access to knowledge spillovers and to other specialized resources such as skilled employees and research institutes. However, co-location risks expropriation of entrepreneurs' own knowledge. Hence, the question arises as to what factors might help to minimize this risk. One of these factors that has received considerable attention in the literature is social capital.

Social capital is often used as a catch-all term for those features of social interaction that support coordinated action (Portes, 1998). The central proposition is that the performance of entrepreneurs depends on the cluster's collective capacity for understanding business problems and taking appropriate action to solve them (Wolfe, 2002). Social capital is said to furnish the structures and processes required to accomplish that goal, and densely woven social networks are seen as the mechanism providing the necessary organizational integration. Entrepreneurs that are well embedded in local social networks are expected to have access to comparable market information, pursue similar strategies and therefore have deeper insight into each other's situations and strategies. A high level of mutual understanding facilitates trust building and interaction, which discourages ruinous rivalry and the opportunistic expropriation of other firms' knowledge. From a policy perspective, social capital is often seen as a source of regional competitive advantage (Tallman et al., 2004).

The idea of social capital as a critical element in the success of clusters agrees well with researchers interested in the social and institutional context in which entrepreneurship is expected to flourish. Social structures providing coherence and meaning are implicated in the many challenges that entrepreneurs face: learning about models for organization building, getting access to material resources, and building social legitimacy (Aldrich and Fiol, 1994). Managing these challenges requires supportive social resources and the appropriate network structures for gaining access to them (Krackhardt and Kilduff, 2002). Social capital is seen as a mechanism to meet these demands (Anderson and Jack, 2002).

The dominant approach in entrepreneurship research has been to view social capital as an instrumental resource, making possible the achievement of a variety of goals and supporting Putnam's (2000) propositions concerning the relationship between high levels of social capital within a region and the success of economic development projects. Optimistic statements concerning the benefits of social capital prevail in this literature. In some cases, one gets the impression that authors believe that it is sufficient to demonstrate the presence of high levels of social capital if one wants to argue that the cluster is successful and entrepreneurially dynamic. Some authors have gone so far as to formulate the benefits of social capital as a foregone conclusion or to discuss social capital as if it had positive performance implications, proposing, for example, that '[f]irms in communities with a large stock of social capital will, *of course, always* have a competitive advantage' (Maskell, 2000: 117, emphasis mine).

One may distinguish between three dimensions of social capital: structural, relational, and cognitive (Nahapiet and Ghoshal, 1998). The structural dimension denotes the configuration of connections between network members, such as density and multiplexity. The relational dimension indicates the properties of a particular relationship, such as trust, norms and obligations. The cognitive dimension of social capital refers to the schemes with which individuals interpret actions and events. These dimensions illustrate the essential demands on entrepreneurs: knowing the right partners, having access to their resources, forming a common set of expectations with respect to coordinated action, and developing a common scheme for interpreting these expectations.

The multidimensionality of social capital suggests the possibility that different dimensions have different effects in the entrepreneurial process. However, there is little systematic research that takes this multidimensionality into account, using an appropriate research design. Many entrepreneurship researchers have treated the dimensions of social capital interchangeably or assumed that they are positively correlated, based on the widely accepted premise that successful founders are embedded in a network of mostly close contacts, characterized by trust and consensus about the meaning of entrepreneurship. Some investigators have employed a global measure of social capital, calling it 'networking activity' or 'network quality' (for example, Chell and Baines, 2000), while others have focused on a processual dimension of social capital, such as communication (for example, Stanley and Helper, 2003). Others have equated social capital with network structure, such as relationship density (for example, Walker et al., 1997) or have taken a cognitive approach, viewing social capital as a set of strongly shared beliefs (for example, Heydebrand and Miron, 2002). Inconsistencies in the operationalization of the construct of social capital may be one reason why findings are often inconsistent.

Empirical studies suggest, for example, that the pay-offs of social capital are not uniform. Cooke et al. (2005) found different effects for regional social capital on small-firm innovation, depending on whether one considers business-related dimensions of social capital, such as trading relationships, or purely social dimensions, such as trust and commitment. Capello and Faggian (2005) showed that the effect of social capital on the innovativeness of cluster firms differed, depending on whether knowledge was diffused through local suppliers or through mobile local labour. Stanley and Helper (2003) distinguished between the extent of communication with stakeholders and the value of such communication. They found significant differences in the estimated effects of the extent and value of communication for fending off foreign competition, but not for productivity. Westlund and Nilsson (2005) showed that it made some difference for employment growth, but not for turnover growth, whether firms invested in the development of cooperative links with research and development agents, marketing agents or political bodies. A study of trust among individuals in an Italian entrepreneurial district demonstrated the importance of distinguishing between informal reputation-based and formal institution-based sources of trust, such as trade associations and research institutes (Dei Ottati, 2003).

The finding that social capital has differential effects should not come as a surprise, given what is known from research on social capital in intra-organizational networks. These studies have shown that not all contacts are alike, some are more useful than others, and their effects may interact with other factors (Hansen et al., 2005). Social capital also involves important trade-offs. While close contacts may facilitate access to scarce and sensitive information, they also contain the risk that they replicate old information that may not be useful in a new environment (Gargiulo and Benassi, 2000). Findings such as these suggest that research on entrepreneurial clusters should take a more fine-grained approach to social capital, differentiating between distinct dimensions and recognizing contingencies, trade-offs and path dependencies. However important social capital may be, social networks are not necessarily localized because there is nothing inherently spatial about networks (Boschma, 2005: 69).

THE GEOGRAPHY OF INSTITUTIONS

While the economic approach views clusters as an efficiency-motivated solution to the problem of entrepreneurship, driven mostly by actors' self-serving and calculative motives concerning knowledge creation and sharing, the institutionalist perspective turns on the social routines that describe (mature) networks as a more or less homogeneous organizational entity. And while sociological thinking focuses on social capital as the strategically most important of a cluster's resources, the institutionalist perspective is more concerned with those symbolic and normative aspects of clusters and cluster processes that cultivate collective sensibilities. The institutionalist view thus offers a qualitatively different logic than economic and sociological approaches, but arrives at essentially the same conclusions with respect to the importance of geographic proximity.

Institutions include the micro-level habits and rules that regulate interorganizational exchange as well as the macro-level organizational arrangements for supporting these habits and rules and for coordinating actions. As such, institutions provide constraining and enabling mechanisms for interactive learning and knowledge transfer. What matters, however, is not merely the presence of institutions providing material and informational resources (education, training, funding, and so on), but also a set of structures and processes to help stabilize expectations, share fine-grained knowledge, and induce network partners to engage in value-creation activities. Amin and Thrift (1994) refer to such structures and processes as 'institutional thickness'. An entrepreneurial network is said to be embedded in an institutionally thick environment if there are numerous institutions with a variety of competencies and resources on which network actors can draw, high levels of interaction among these institutions, collective structures that emerge as a result of this interaction and a mutual awareness of the necessity of developing common economic objectives and unified action. The central argument is that institutional processes, reflecting interaction, learning, power and flows of information and knowledge, are more important than the presence of institutional organizations per se.

The institutionalist perspective sees clusters as communities of firms and individuals who participate in the same meaning systems and are subject to common regulatory processes. These meaning systems tend to evolve toward stability and homogeneity, reducing uncertainty and creating a medium for joint problem-solving (Appold, 2005). Institutionalization means that cluster networks become more similar over time, overriding diversity in local environments (DiMaggio, 2001). Differences between clusters are explained by the fact that they operate in different institutional contexts with their own rationality criteria and historically grounded normative structures (Sydow and Staber, 2002). Differences in institutional mechanisms may be part of the explanation why clusters in the same industry often evolve along different trajectories. For example, one would expect radical industrial innovations to occur more often in clusters located in liberal markets than in coordinated market economies, to the extent that entrepreneurs align their strategies with the institutional framework in which they are embedded (Hall and Soskice, 2001).

The problem is that, while institutionalization helps to reduce current uncertainty, it also sacrifices the flexibility required for recognizing and responding to unfolding uncertainty. Institutional pressures may create restrictive blind spots, limiting the range of practices from which competitive advantage can emerge (Pouder and St. John, 1996).

Local entrepreneurial networks may be inward-looking, supported by institutional actors who react to environmental changes in an overly routinized and conservative way, especially when their own vested interests are threatened or they are formally obligated to support other actors in the local system. This may lead to cognitive and structural 'lock-in', hindering the development of innovations, as Grabher (1993) has shown for the Ruhr district in Germany. Isaksen (2003) explains the decline of the offshore engineering cluster in Norway partly as the outcome of a series of political decisions to develop region-specific routines that were successful initially, but later inhibited the search for alternative solutions under changed economic conditions. These and many other examples of institutional inertia point to a theoretical paradox in institutionalist reasoning. The same institutional forces that are hypothesized to support cluster integration in an uncertain environment may become a severely constraining factor when the same environment calls for a new strategy.

CONCLUSION

Regional clusters are a demanding context for research on entrepreneurship, one that is filled with multiple and partly competing theoretical perspectives, difficult-to-measure constructs, and inconsistent findings. The evidence from a large and growing number of empirical studies on the role of geographic entrepreneurship is largely mixed, leaving plenty of room for further research. For example, there are not many studies taking a strictly comparative approach that would enable investigators to test arguments about local context. A cluster's potential for increasing returns, institutional cohesion or social capital probably changes over time and across industries, affecting the location choices of entrepreneurs. One factor likely to influence the entrepreneurial process with respect to space is the complexity of knowledge underlying entrepreneurial activities. While simple knowledge diffuses fairly easily, highly complex and tacit knowledge tends to resist diffusion. It may be possible that clustering is facilitated when knowledge is mostly tacit and complex, making face-to-face exchange essential to knowledge flows across organizational boundaries. The analysis of these and other questions calls for a contingency perspective and research designs able to reveal contextual effects. Many authors seem to be aware of the limited generalizability of their findings, but they typically do not offer sufficient information about the setting under investigation to be able to make strong inferences about why and how context matters (for a summary of this research, see Staber, 2007).

Weak empirical evidence has not discouraged policy-makers from investing in building an entrepreneurial infrastructure that takes the positive effects of geographic clustering for granted. The basic proposition is that the exchange of entrepreneurial ideas and resources is more likely to be stimulated effectively in geographically concentrated settings that include a small number of important decision-makers, making low-cost investments and experiments possible. Public policy sees its primary role as one of creating institutional rules for pooling knowledge, supporting collaborative routines and turning social capital into a valuable public good (Belussi, 1999).

However, the results of studies examining the effectiveness of cluster-oriented public policy initiatives are mixed. Some studies suggest that public policy can help build local social capital only indirectly, by stimulating learning processes. The fact that these learning processes are ultimately controlled by the entrepreneurs themselves (Melander and Nordqvist, 2002) means that the outcomes of policy measures are largely unpredictable and difficult to trace back to policy-related features. It is, therefore, not clear whether the success of a given cluster is the result of policy-supported social capital, institution building or some other factor associated with macroeconomic change, demographic shifts and the like. Policy effects may also vary in duration. A study of an information and communications technology cluster in Washington, DC, showed that local government policies were influential only in the later stages of cluster development, after entrepreneurs had already set up the foundation for social capital (Feldman et al., 2005).

On balance, the available evidence suggests that it is premature to derive strong policy recommendations concerning the kinds of programme initiatives that should be devised, at whom they should be directed, and at what stage of cluster development they should be implemented. The potential for stimulating entrepreneurship on the basis of creating social capital in the region may be seriously overstated, not necessarily because theoretical arguments lack substance, but because the empirical tests of these arguments attempted so far have not produced conclusive evidence.

On the basis of the available research evidence, it seems premature to conclude that clustering always makes a significant difference in the performance of entrepreneurial firms, relative to the influence of other factors. The limited attention given in many studies to sampling issues, performance outcomes and generalization, coupled with the limited concern for the multidimensional nature of social capital, institutions and knowledge, may explain why the body of research to date has produced mostly inconclusive evidence. As a result, there are few, if any, empirically well-supported propositions. The mixed evidence on the role of geographic proximity in entrepreneurship is consistent with the lack of strong evidence for the commonplace argument that clustering confers competitive advantages to firms (for a critique, see Martin and Sunley, 2003; Staber, 1996). 'Much of the evidence seems to point to a reality in which industrial sectors are a lot less spatially localized than geographers and regional scientists might like to wish' (Malmberg and Power, 2005: 426). Based on the evidence, one cannot conclude that geographic clusters always provide entrepreneurs with favourable conditions that are not available elsewhere. The jury is still out on the conditions under which geographic proximity is essential for the entrepreneurial process.

REFERENCES

Aharonson, B., J. Baum and M. Feldman (2007), 'Desperately seeking spillovers? Increasing returns, social cohesion and the location of new entrants in geographic and technological space', *Industrial and Corporate Change*, **16** (1), 89–130.

Aldrich, H. and M. Fiol (1994), 'Fools rush in? The institutional context of industry creation', *Academy of Management Review*, **19** (4), 645–70.

Amin, A. and N. Thrift (1994), 'Living in the global', in A. Amin and N. Thrift (eds), *Globalization, Institutions and Regional Development in Europe*, Oxford: Oxford University Press, pp. 1–22.

Anderson, A. and S. Jack (2002), 'The articulation of social capital in entrepreneurial networks: a glue or a lubricant?', *Entrepreneurship and Regional Development*, **14** (3), 193–210.

Appold, S. (2005), 'Location patterns of US industrial research: mimetic isomorphism and the emergence of geographic charisma', *Regional Studies*, **39** (1), 17–39.

Audretsch, D. and M. Feldman (1996), 'R&D spillovers and the geography of innovation and production', *American Economic Review*, **86** (3), 630–40.
Baptista, R. (1998), 'Clusters, innovation and growth: a survey of the literature', in G. Swann, M. Prevezer and D. Stout (eds), *Dynamics of Industrial Clusters: International Comparisons in Computing and Biotechnology*, Oxford: Oxford University Press, pp. 13–51.
Bathelt, H. (2005), 'Cluster relations in the media industry: exploring the "distanced neighbour" paradox in Leipzig', *Regional Studies*, **39** (1), 105–27.
Baum, J. and H. Haveman (1997), 'Love thy neighbour? Differentiation and agglomeration in the Manhattan hotel industry, 1898–1990', *Administrative Science Quarterly*, **42** (2) 304–38.
Beaudry, C. and S. Breschi (2003), 'Are firms really more innovative in industrial districts?', *Economics of Innovation and New Technology*, **12** (4), 325–42.
Belussi, F. (1999), 'Policies for the development of knowledge-intensive local production systems', *Cambridge Journal of Economics*, **23** (6), 729–47.
Boari, C., V. Odorici and M. Zamarian (2003), 'Clusters and rivalry: does localization really matter?', *Scandinavian Journal of Management*, **19** (4), 467–89.
Boschma, R. (2005), 'Proximity and innovation: a critical assessment', *Regional Studies*, **39** (1), 61–74.
Boschma, R. and A. Ter Wal (2007), 'Knowledge networks and innovative performance in an industrial district: the case of a footwear district in the South of Italy', *Industry and Innovation*, **14** (2), 177–99.
Breschi, S. and F. Lissoni (2001), 'Knowledge spillovers and local innovation systems: a critical survey', *Industrial and Corporate Change*, **10** (4), 975–1005.
Brökel, T. and M. Binder (2007), 'The regional dimension of knowledge transfers: a behavioral approach', *Industry and Innovation*, **14** (2), 151–75.
Capello, R. and A. Faggian (2005), 'Collective learning and relational capital in local innovation processes', *Regional Studies*, **39** (1), 75–87.
Chell, E. and S. Baines (2000), 'Networking, entrepreneurship and microbusiness behaviour', *Entrepreneurship and Regional Development*, **12** (3), 195–215.
Cooke, P., N. Clifton and M. Oleaga (2005), 'Social capital, firm embeddedness, and regional development', *Regional Studies*, **39** (8), 1065–77.
Dei Ottati, G. (2003), 'Global competition and entrepreneurial behaviour in industrial districts', paper presented at the Conference on Clusters, Industrial Districts and Firms, Modena, 12–13 September.
Dicken, P. and A. Malmberg (2001), 'Firms in territories: a relational perspective', *Economic Geography*, **77** (4), 345–63.
DiMaggio, P. (ed.) (2001), *The Twenty-First-Century Firm: Changing Economic Organization in International Perspective*, Princeton, NJ: Princeton University Press.
Feldman, M., J. Francis and J. Bercovitz (2005), 'Creating a cluster while building a firm: entrepreneurs and the formation of industrial clusters', *Regional Studies*, **39** (1), 129–41.
Gargiulo, M. and M. Benassi (2000), 'Trapped in your own net? Network cohesion, structural holes, and the adaptation of social capital', *Organization Science*, **11** (2), 183–96.
Grabher, G. (1993), 'The weakness of strong ties: the lock-in of regional development in the Ruhr area', in G. Grabher (ed.), *The Embedded Firm*, London: Routledge, pp. 265–77.
Hall, P. and D. Soskice (eds) (2001), *Varieties of Capitalism: The Institutional Foundations of Comparative Advantage*, New York: Oxford University Press.
Hansen, M., M. Mors and B. Løvås (2005), 'Knowledge sharing in organizations: multiple networks, multiple phases', *Academy of Management Journal*, **48** (5), 776–93.
Heydebrand, W. and A. Miron (2002), 'Constructing innovativeness in new-media start-up firms', *Environment and Planning*, **34** (11), 1951–84.
Isaksen, A. (2003), 'Lock-in of regional clusters: the case of offshore engineering in the Oslo region', in D. Fornahl and T. Brenner (eds), *Cooperation, Networks and Institutions in Regional Innovation Systems*, Cheltenham, UK and Northampton, MA, USA: Edward Elgar, pp. 247–73.
Johnson, D., N. Siripong and A. Brown (2006), 'The demise of distance? The declining role of physical proximity for knowledge transmission', *Growth and Change*, **37** (1), 19–33.
Krackhardt, D. and M. Kilduff (2002), 'Structure, culture and Simmelian ties in entrepreneurial firms', *Social Networks*, **24** (3), 279–90.
Lorenzen, M. and N. Foss (2003), 'Cognitive coordination, institutions and clusters: an exploratory discussion', in D. Fornahl and T. Brenner (eds), *Cooperation, Networks and Institutions in Regional Innovation Systems*, Cheltenham, UK and Northampton, MA, USA: Edward Elgar, pp. 82–104.
Low, M. and E. Abrahamson (1997), 'Movements, bandwagons, and clones: industry evolution and the entrepreneurial process', *Journal of Business Venturing*, **12** (6), 435–57.
Malmberg, A. and D. Power (2005), '(How) do (firms in) clusters create knowledge?', *Industry and Innovation*, **12** (4), 409–31.

Marshall, A. (1920), *Principles of Economics*, London: Macmillan.
Martin, R. and P. Sunley (2003), 'Deconstructing clusters: chaotic concept or policy panacea?', *Journal of Economic Geography*, **3** (1), 5–35.
Maskell, P. (2000), 'Social capital and competitiveness', in S. Baron, J. Field and T. Schuller (eds), *Social Capital: Critical Perspectives*, Oxford: Oxford University Press, pp. 111–23.
Melander, A. and M. Nordqvist (2002), 'Investing in social capital', *International Studies of Management and Organization*, **31** (4), 89–108.
Mezias, S. and J. Kuperman (2001), 'The community dynamics of entrepreneurship: the birth of the American film industry, 1895–1929', *Journal of Business Venturing*, **16** (3), 209–33.
Nahapiet, J. and S. Ghoshal (1998), 'Social capital, intellectual capital, and the organizational advantage', *Academy of Management Review*, **23** (2), 242–66.
Nelson, R. and S. Winter (1982), *An Evolutionary Theory of Economic Change*. Cambridge: Belknap Press.
Oerleman, L. and M. Meeus (2005), 'Do organizational and spatial proximity impact on firm performance?', *Regional Studies*, **39** (1), 89–104.
Owen-Smith, J. and W. Powell (2004), 'Knowledge networks as channels and conduits: the effects of spillovers in the Boston biotechnology community', *Organization Science*, **15** (1), 5–21.
Penrose, E. (1959), *The Theory of the Growth of Firms*, New York: Wiley.
Polenske, K. (2004), 'Competition, collaboration and cooperation: an uneasy triangle in networks of firms and regions', *Regional Studies*, **38** (9), 1029–43.
Porac, J., H. Thomas, F. Wilson, D. Paton and A. Kanfer (1995), 'Rivalry and the industry model of Scottish knitwear producers', *Administrative Science Quarterly*, **40** (2), 203–27.
Porter, M. (2000), 'Location, competition, and economic development: local clusters in a global economy', *Economic Development Quarterly*, **14** (1), 15–34.
Portes, A. (1998), 'Social capital: its origins and applications in modern sociology', *Annual Review of Sociology*, **24**, 1–24.
Pouder, R. and C. St. John (1996), 'Hot spots and blind spots: geographical clusters of firms and innovation', *Academy of Management Review*, **21** (4), 1192–225.
Powell, W., B. Kogut, J. Bowie and L. Smith-Doerr (2002), 'The spatial clustering of science and capital: accounting for biotech firm-venture capital relationships', *Regional Studies*, **36** (3), 291–305.
Putnam, R. (2000), *Bowling Alone: The Collapse and Revival of American Community*, New York: Simon and Schuster.
Sorenson, O. and P. Audia (2000), 'The social structure of entrepreneurial activity: geographic concentration of footwear production in the United States, 1940–1989', *American Journal of Sociology*, **106** (2), 424–62.
Staber, U. (1996), 'Accounting for variations in the performance of industrial districts', *International Journal of Urban and Regional Research*, **20** (2), 299–316.
Staber, U. (2001), 'Spatial proximity and firm survival in a declining industrial district: the case of knitwear firms in Baden-Württemberg', *Regional Studies*, **35** (4), 329–41.
Staber, U. (2007), 'Contextualizing research on social capital in regional clusters', *International Journal of Urban and Regional Research*, **31** (3), 505–21.
Stanley, M. and S. Helper (2003), 'Industrial clusters, social capital, and international competition in the U.S. component manufacturing industry', paper presented at the Conference on Clusters, Industrial Districts and Firms, Modena, 12–13 September.
Stuart, T. and O. Sorenson (2003), 'The geography of opportunity: spatial heterogeneity in founding rates and the performance of biotechnology firms', *Research Policy*, **32** (2), 229–53.
Suire, R., J. Vicente and Y. Pria (2006), 'Why some clusters succeed whereas others decline? Modelling the ambivalent stability properties of clusters', Economics Working Paper Archive, 200619, Center for Research in Economics and Management, University of Rennes, University of Caen, and CNRS.
Sydow, J. and U. Staber (2002), 'The institutional embeddedness of project networks: The case of content production in German television', *Regional Studies*, **36** (3), 215–27.
Tallman, S., M. Jenkins, N. Henry and S. Pinch (2004), 'Knowledge, clusters, and competitive advantage', *Academy of Management Review*, **29** (2), 258–71.
Taylor, M. and S. Leonard (eds) (2002), *Embedded Enterprise and Social Capital*, Aldershot: Ashgate.
Thornton, P. (1999), 'The sociology of entrepreneurship', *Annual Review of Sociology*, **25**, 19–46.
Walker, G., B. Kogut and W. Shan (1997), 'Social capital, structural holes and the formation of an industry network', *Organization Science*, **8** (2), 109–25.
Westlund, H. and E. Nilsson (2005), 'Measuring enterprises' investment in social capital: a pilot study', *Regional Studies*, **39** (8), 1079–94.
Wolfe, D. (2002), 'Social capital and cluster development in learning regions', in J. Holbrook and D. Wolfe (eds), *Knowledge, Clusters and Regional Innovation*, Kingston: Queen's School of Policy Studies, pp. 11–38.

22 Global entrepreneurship and transnationalism[1]

Ivan H. Light

To an earlier generation of scholars, *diasporas* meant ethno-national communities scattered around the globe that nonetheless remained in continuous, long-term contact with one another as well as with their real or putative homeland (Armstrong, 1976; Cohen, 1997: 185). Their real or putative homeland constituted the hub of ethnic diasporas. The colonies scattered abroad represented the spokes. Thanks to their hub and spoke structure, diasporas linked distant continents such that ethnic minorities resident in any one place had strong social ties and cultural ties with co-ethnics in many others. Ethnic diasporas were commercially important, but they were not numerous. Diasporas were uncommon because most immigrants just assimilated into host societies within three generations. As a result, unless renewed by new migration, the spokes ceased to communicate with one another and with the hub. Before globalization, which began in about 1965 (Dicken, 1992), and arguably changed this arrangement, the world's international immigrants routinely assimilated to host societies in historically short order (Caliner, 2000). At a minimum, assimilation meant acquiring the language of one's new homeland and forgetting the language of one's ethnic origin. For immigrants, the road to assimilation went from monolingualism in a foreign language to bilingualism and back to monolingualism in a new language. In the USA, Canada, Australia and New Zealand assimilation meant that, whatever one's ethnic origins, one's grandchildren would become English monolinguals. Therefore, thanks to assimilation, international immigration routinely left no permanent ethnic colonies in place abroad as a permanent historical legacy. Diasporas were the exceptions to this generalization.

In the early twentieth century, diasporic communities initially attracted Max Weber's attention because of the remarkable commercial entrepreneurship they exhibited.[2] Weber termed this entrepreneurship 'pariah capitalism' because of the local unpopularity of the entrepreneurial minorities. Subsequent scholars agreed that diasporic ethnic communities displayed exceptional entrepreneurship, especially in international commerce (Cohen, 1971; Laguerre, 1998; Light et al., 1993: 38–43; Moallem, 1996). Entrepreneurial ethnic communities that operated around a diasporan structure earned the sobriquet 'middleman minorities' in the literature of social science (Bonacich, 1973; Kieval, 1997; Light and Gold, 2000: 6–8). *Middleman minorities* were non-assimilating ethnic minorities noteworthy for their abundant and persistent entrepreneurship wherever they lived. Among the middleman minorities, the Jews of Europe, the Hausa of Nigeria, the Sikhs of East Africa, the Chinese of South East Asia, the Armenians of the Near East and the Parsees of India were the most prominent, but there were others as well. Eschewing agriculture, middleman minorities were especially common in retail trade and international commerce. Indeed, the term 'middleman' reflected this specialization since the role of the middleman is to trade goods, not to manufacture or grow them.

The exceptional involvement of middleman minorities in international trade arose in part because of the ethno-religious oppression to which they were subjected, but also because of the unique ethnic resources they enjoyed (Light and Gold, 2000: 6–7).[3] Exploited and oppressed by host societies, which treated them as pariahs, middleman minorities turned to self-employment for self-defense amid the general absence of alternative earning options. This strategy increased their self-employment. However, the middleman minorities had also evolved over centuries distinct ethnic resources that facilitated commercial entrepreneurship. The middleman minorities were bilingual people, who bestrode international social networks of co ethnics. The also controlled and enjoyed superior business skills, which had worked their way over centuries into the cultural fabric of the community. These three characteristics of the entire group created serious natural advantages in trade promotion for individual group members (Collins, 1998: vol. 2, 398–99; Lever-Tracy et al., 1991: xi, 113). First, such people more easily notice the business opportunities that cultural frontiers generate than do mono-cultural stay-at-homes. Second, such people have the international social capital that supports international business (Fukuyama, 1995; Walton-Roberts and Hiebert, 1997; Wong, 1998: 95).[4] When they see a potential trading opportunity, they have the connections abroad to bring it to prompt fruition. Third, because they controlled superior business skills that they passed on through socialization to younger generations, middleman minorities produced many shrewd and effective business people. Taken together, these three characteristics (languages, networks, skills) supported and encouraged the entrepreneurship of group members to an outstanding degree, and the result was persistently high rates of self-employment among the middleman minorities.

Trading diasporas shipped commodities around the diaspora to continents that were, in terms of travel time, much more distant from one another than they are now and in historical epochs that did not have today's business-support electronics. In each diaspora site, co-ethnic merchants sold imported goods to locals. Middleman minority's specialization in international trade was a product of the diaspora's distinct advantages for this activity. The international disasporan structure conferred two well-known advantages to international traders recruited within each site. First, the ethno-linguistic homogeneity within diasporas supported the performance of the middleman minority's trading specialty. For example, an Armenian merchant in Lima could order rugs from an Armenian merchant in Istanbul in the Armenian language, thus surmounting the language problem that Turks and Peruvians encountered when they attempted to trade. The Armenians in Lima sold at retail in Spanish; the Armenians in Istanbul sold at retail in Turkish. To one another Armenian merchants spoke fluent and colloquial Armenian. Thanks to the Armenian diaspora, Turks and Peruvians could trade without having to learn one another's language.

Additionally, the social capital of diasporas permitted enforceable social trust among merchants, even over long distances. As a result, for example, Armenian merchants in Istanbul could ship rugs to Armenian merchants in Lima in confidence that invoices would be paid and that, if unpaid, informal community pressures could compel payment without recourse to litigation in Peruvian courts. Lacking equivalent social capital in the other country, Turks and Peruvians could not trade without the intercession of Armenians whose unique resource was their bilingualism and their international social capital.

Whatever initially caused a middleman diaspora, such as myths or projects of ultimate repatriation and redemption, once locked into international trading, middleman minorities had real economic motives to retain their cultural and social ties with their homeland. The mythos of repatriation and redemptive nationalism were cultural, but their consequence was real economic motives that acquired an independent influence of their own in the life of the community. After all, their diasporan livelihood depended upon their retaining the ability to speak the language of their ethnic homeland as well as their social capital there and in the diaspora. Hence, assimilation attacked their livelihood. If unable to speak Armenian, a sign of assimilation, an Armenian merchant in Lima could neither buy rugs in Istanbul through a co-ethnic intermediary nor feel confident that Armenian exporters there would offer him credit. Remaining ethnically Armenian was a prudent business policy under these circumstances, not just a sentimental attachment to an ancient culture and homeland. The point is not to reduce international ethnic solidarity to economic interest, but only to acknowledge the self-renewing support that economic interest gave to ideologically motivated non-assimilation. The culture promoted the business, and the business supported the culture.

TRANSNATIONALISM AND GLOBALIZATION

Unlike the older literature of middleman minorities, which addresses non-assimilating communities, the contemporary literature of transnationalism addresses novel processes that generate a transnational elite even within immigrant communities (Wong, 1997; Guarnizo and Diaz, 1999; Guarnizo et al., 1999; Landolt et al., 1999; Smart and Smart, 1998). In an influential paper, Schiller et al. (1992: 1–2) define *transnationalism* as 'processes by which immigrants build social fields that link together their country of origin and their country of settlement'. Immigrants who build such social fields they dub 'transmigrants'. *Transmigrants* are resident in at least two societies between which they shuttle frequently enough to remain active participants in both, but fully encapsulated (mono-cultural) participants in neither. Transmigrants acculturate, but they do not assimilate.[5] This cosmopolitan lifestyle enables transmigrants to form bi-cultural colonies that lodge within mono-cultural host societies. In this respect, contemporary transmigrants are resemble middleman minorities who also acculturated without assimilating. The single best and most accessible indicator of bi-cultural status is long-term maintenance of the transmigrants' complete fluency in the language of their homeland when coupled with complete fluency in the language of the host society (Portes and Hao, 1998). Native speaker fluency in two languages distinguishes transmigrants from immigrants, who lose their foreign language fluency within three generations.

Transnationalism arrives 'from above' when nation states give privileged access to entrepreneur immigrants, hoping thereby to stimulate economic growth (Wong, 2003). States award this privileged access when they set aside non-quota immigration priority to persons who pledge to start businesses or, at least, to invest in business in the host society. This increasingly common practice leavens immigrant populations with state-prioritized entrepreneurs, who were selected for admission precisely because of their existing business skills and financial capital. These entrepreneurs have class resources that their non-entrepreneur co-ethnics normally lack, but they nonetheless increase the percentage of self-employed within their immigrant group.

Transnationalism also arrives from below. Recent interest in transnationalism 'from below' (Chik, 2000; Lever-Tracy and Ip, 1996; Lie, 1995) identifies social processes that generate transmigrants from the immigrant population without recourse to the mechanism of state pre-selection that characterizes transnationalism from above. The literature of transnationalism from below has returned to many of the ideas that animated the middleman minorities literature as well First, transmigrants have diasporas just as did and do middleman minorities. However, because of transnationalism, it is argued, ethno-racial groups that were never middleman minorities can now have diasporas too. For example, Brazilians or Filipinos can have a diaspora such as was previously available only to middleman minorities like the Jews, Armenians, or Chinese (Gold, 1997: 410). In an era of globalization, diasporas are easier to maintain now than they were earlier, and much more numerous around the world in consequence (Cohen, 1997: 176).[6] Therefore, transnational studies examine groups that are *not* historic middleman minorities, but which have diasporas as well as, of course, classical middleman minorities. Haitians, Dominicans, Turks, Koreans, Colombians and Filipinos are exemplary transnational groups, who have never been middleman minorities. This novel combination of diaspora without a middleman minority's history would not have occurred in the past when middleman minorities virtually overlapped with disasporan minorities. In effect, if contemporary theorists of transnationalism are correct, diasporas are no longer reserved to middleman minorities so many more people can live in diasporas now than previously did so.

Second, contemporary transmigrants are bi-cultural just as are and were members of the classic middleman minorities. As a result, transmigrants enjoy some of the same advantages for international trade that middleman majorities enjoyed in the past. The spokes of the transmigrants' diaspora communicate with one another and with the diaspora's hub in the mother tongue while selling locally in the local vernacular. They can do this because and to the extent that transmigrants, like middleman minorities, retain their native-speaker fluency in the mother tongue over generations, for example, they do not assimilate. This is the advantage that Armenian merchants in Lima enjoyed when trading with Persia in the eighteenth century.

Third, like middleman minorities, contemporary transmigrants have international social capital that provides access to enforceable trust. International social capital hugely simplifies international trade. Enjoying international social capital, a Haitian transnational residing in New York City can buy and sell goods from a co-ethnic in Port-au-Prince in confidence that invoices will be paid or, if unpaid, can be informally collected without recourse to law. If Haitians simply assimilated, as do immigrants, that transnational merchant would lose the social networks that access Haitian business circles and underpin his or her creditworthiness. Because they shuttle frequently between Haiti and New York City, a lifestyle made possible by jet airplanes, and because they receive and send satellite messages from and to Haiti, a facility made possible by satellite communication, Haitians in New York City can retain social capital in Haitian business circles for protracted, even indefinite periods, thus retaining the advantages in international trade that international social capital permits. Should they assimilate, they would lose those advantages.

Given these similarities to middleman minorities, it is unsurprising that transmigrants from below display high entrepreneurship, especially in international trade (Portes, 2003). Some evidence reports that transmigrants are ten times more likely to become entrepreneurs than are co-ethnic immigrants. Portes et al. (2002) studied self-employment rates among immigrant Dominicans, Colombians and Salvadorans in five American cities. None of these ethno-racial groups is or was a middleman minority. Defining transnational entrepreneurs as those who went abroad for business twice a year or more, the authors found that only 5 per cent of each national-origin sample were transnational entrepreneurs, but 58 per cent of the self-employed were transmigrants. 'Transnational entrepreneurs represent a large proportion, often the majority, of the self-employed persons in immigrant communities' (Portes et al., 2002: 293). Better educated than co-ethnics, the transnational entrepreneurs also earned higher incomes than non-transnational co-ethnics. Transnationalism is even said to have affected middleman minorities. Ooka (2001) reports that 'ethnic social capital' did not increase the income of Chinese business owners in Toronto, but bridging social capital (connected to non-Chinese) did, as did class resources. Ethnic social capital would have been more characteristic of middleman minorities so its ineffectiveness here suggests a new kind of international business among the Chinese. Wong and Ng (2002: 509) also claim that Chinese transnational business represents a new form of Chinese business. Although still small business, like the Chinese business of the past, the new transnational Chinese business supposedly has a different modus operandi (Li, 1993; Yeung, 1999). The Chinese transnational business owners have more business associates in Asia than non-transnational Chinese entrepreneurs; they are also more likely to made use of Chinese business contacts, and more likely to target non-Chinese customers than are non-transnational Chinese entrepreneurs (552). The international traffic in prohibited drugs, sex commerce and immigrant smuggling offer additional illustrations of transnational business. The bilingualism and international social capital that confer success in legal industries also confer it in these illegal ones.[7]

Massey (et al., 1993: 446) observe that economic globalization 'creates cultural links between core capitalist countries and their hinterlands' and transnationalism is one of the ways globalization accomplishes this end. This line of thought eventuates in the hypothesis that transnationalism promotes international trade by multiplying the ethnic resources formerly restricted to middleman minorities. Transmigrants are a minority of the groups to which they belong whereas middleman minorities are whole groups, not just an elite. Middleman minorities enter business because of their underlying lifestyle, which makes business congenial to them; transmigrants more commonly adopt a cosmopolitan lifestyle in the interest of promoting their business. This lifestyle is an elite lifestyle. The past lingers. The era of transnationalism did not demolish middleman minorities. Middleman minorities did not vanish when transnational business elites appeared. However, if the theorists of transnationalism are correct, more people can have the key business-supporting resources now than could do so in the past when international commerce relied on middleman minorities. Therefore, more international trade is possible now. This attractive hypothesis already has some documentation to support it. The hypothesis links transnationalism and the expansion of world trade, which is the hallmark of globalization. Indeed, one could conclude that globalization requires transnationalism, which it also promotes. International trade requires international traders, and international traders are transmigrants. Hence, Silj and Cross (1999: 135) declare that transmigrant entrepreneurs no longer promote a 'second-rate form of capitalism' as Weber believed (Light and Gold, 2000: 6–7). Instead, transnational traders are 'the forefront of new economic ties'. If so, tranmigrant entrepreneurs arguably *caused* some of the last half century's increase in international trade (Kotkin, 1996). That is, because more people had access to the requisite skills, the world sprouted more international entrepreneurs, and more world trade ensued.

Strictly in its economic terms, *globalization* means the reduction of tariff and non-tariff barriers to trade, freer mobility of capital across international boundaries, international standardization of products, specifications, and legal codes as well as the migration of Third World workers, skilled and unskilled, to the developed countries (Hollifield, 1998–99; Sassen, 1994;). As globalization knits world markets, opportunities for trade increase as does the importance of international trade (Wolff and Pett, 2000: 35). World trade has increased substantially in the last generation, a result usually attributed to globalization. In the USA, the share of exports in national income rose from 4 per cent to 7 per cent between 1950 and 1990. The share of merchandise exports in the output of manufactured goods, a more revealing ratio, increased over the same period from 6 per cent to nearly 20 per cent (*The Economist*, 1997), and other countries have seen comparable changes. Exports now account for more than 20 per cent of US economic growth. Exports create more than 11 per cent of American jobs (Rondinelli et al., 1998: 75).

This abrupt growth of international trade *could not have relied* upon middleman minorities whose supply of international traders could not expand rapidly enough to match the growing need. Rather, it appears that even classic middleman minorities like the Jews and Chinese added transmigrant elites (from below + from above) to their existing population of middleman traders (Gold, 1997; Hamilton and Waters, 1997). Whether generated from above or from below, transmigrant elites utilized class resources of entrepreneurship, such as human and financial capital, more than the ethnic resources on which middleman minorities characteristically relied and continue to rely.[8] Similarly, hitherto non-trading immigrant communities began to produce international traders as an elite whose entrepreneurial resources derived from their class status rather than from the ethnic resources of traditional trading minorities. The joint result was expansion of the supply of persons qualified to undertake international business. Without this expansion, the growth of international commerce would be constrained by an inadequate supply of traders with the requisite entrepreneurial resources of social and cultural capital. Transnationalism arguably accomplished this historical task, outfitting more or less every immigrant group with its own cosmopolitan, bi-cultural and non-assimilating business elite, who had the resources to become international business owners and traders (Farrell, 1993). The result was a globalized world in which old-fashioned middleman minorities now shared international trade with new transnational elites rather than dominating it by themselves as they once had.

GLOBALIZATION AND ENGLISH LANGUAGE DOMINANCE

However, before pledging allegiance to this attractive hypothesis, we should examine the embeddedness of transnationalism in globalization, which is much bigger than just transnationalism. Globalization is changing the world in multiple ways, not just by way of transnational business elites. Kloosterman and Rath (2003: 7) and their colleagues have already drawn attention to possible increases in demand for immigrant entrepreneurs within the developed economies as a result of the transition to post-industrial economies in which small business has new advantages. Cultural globalization also generates demand in the developed countries for exotic food, merchandise and services (acupuncture, falafel, images of Buddha) that emanate from Third World countries and that immigrant entrepreneurs can readily provide (Light, 2004). In these cases, the impact of globalization tends generally to support and enhance the presence and viability of immigrant entrepreneurs abroad. But these positive effects, much celebrated though they are, may not end the story.

An additional and less studied effect of globalization on immigrant business occurs via the increasing international dominance of the English language in science, business, and government, a development that was not always welcomed (Crisafulli, 1996). English has not always been the world's dominant language. Globalization created the dominance of English since 1945 (Fishman, 1998–99; Fox, 2000; Phillipson, 1992). In effect, the contemporary dominance of English and transnational immigration are *both* effects of globalization. The dominance of the English language embeds transnational business elites in a world quite different from the one in which classic middleman minorities lived. Possibly that difference affects the trading advantages that transmigrants and middleman minorities enjoy.

We inhabit a globalized world in which English has almost become the universal second language of business people everywhere. In this world, bi-cultural transmigrants enjoy less linguistic advantage than classic middleman minorities earlier enjoyed before globalization. This reduction arises because so many non-immigrants have learned English as their second language. If, in an extreme and limiting case, all the inhabitants of the world's non-English-speaking countries achieved complete fluency in English, then anyone could trade with anyone elsewhere on the strength of their common second language, English. Immigrants would no longer need bi-cultural elites or middleman minorities to effectuate their international trade as they did when immigrants were monolinguals. Today the Japanese business travelers in Eastern Europe prefer to speak English to their Polish or Czech trading partners rather than having to learn Czech or Polish, and the Poles and Czechs reciprocate the preference. Thanks to the dominance of English, Japanese, Czechs and Poles now have this option. Returning to the illustration earlier used, we recall that Peruvians in Peru and Turks in Turkey patronized the Armenian diaspora because Peruvians did not speak Turkish and Turks did not speak Spanish. Lacking a common language, Turks and Peruvians needed to communicate through bi-cultural Armenians, one group of whom spoke Spanish and the other Turkish. Armenian intermediaries (middlemen) were indispensable in that world's rug business. In a fully globalized world, however, Turks speak English and Peruvians speak English. Therefore, Turks and Peruvians can communicate in English, and neither side needs Armenian middlemen any more just for the purpose of communication.

Of course, this thought-experiment relies upon a fully globalized world that does not yet exist. Nonetheless, the increasing dominance of the English language in world business does tend to move the world in that direction. In continental Europe today, half of the adult population claims to speak English. This unprecedented state of affairs means that the French and Germans, the Spanish and the Italians, or any other European combination can speak English to one another for purposes of international trade, reducing any need for either middleman minorities or transmigrants to interpret for them.

Middleman minorities translated business into Armenian from local vernaculars; transnational immigrant traders speak their native language plus the adopted language of their destination country. Both acquire trading advantages to the extent that everyone does not already speak English. If everyone speaks English, then neither middleman minorities nor bilingual transmigrants have any linguistic resource to exploit in commerce.

True, the European trading partners may not *trust* one another even though they communicate in English with other non-native speakers of English. To that extent, the Europeans would still need middleman minorities or the transmigrants whose international social capital stands surety for their business deals. Nonetheless, looking only at the linguistic indispensability, which the middleman minorities once exploited, we conclude that the dominance of English as a world language *reduces*, even if it does not yet extinguish, the linguistic advantage of both middleman minorities and of transmigrants today. If so, middleman minorities, like the Chinese, would have lost their trading advantage in intra-European trade, and would retain it only in the organization of trade between China and their current host country.

This point is speculative. However, evidence has already begun to build up behind other, trade-related economic effects of English dominance (Van Parijs, 2000). Examining the foreign trade of the USA and Canada in the 1980s, David Gould (1990; 1994) found that the volume and skill levels of immigrants increased the dollar volume of both American and Canadian exports to the immigrants' home countries without increasing imports from them. This discrepancy did not attend immigration from English-speaking countries. He explained the unexpected discrepancy by reference to transaction costs, arguing that immigrants enjoyed transactional advantages for exports, but not for imports. Light (2001) and Light et al. (2002) replicate Gould's basic finding on a comparable but slightly different American data-set. They too find that immigrants to the USA increased American exports to their home countries without increasing American imports *from* their home countries. However, this discrepancy does not attend immigration from English-speaking countries, which increased neither exports nor imports.

Light and his colleagues considered the possibility that transnational immigrants increased international trade more than non-transnational immigrants, but less than middleman minorities who, unlike transmigrants, have centuries of entrepreneurial culture on which to draw. Comparing the Chinese diaspora and the Spanish diaspora, they found that both diasporas increased American trade with overseas homelands net of control variables, but the size of the Chinese effect was twice the size of the Spanish effect. Moreover, a measure of fluency in English found that, net of control variables, high fluency in English increased immigrants' exports to their overseas homelands *without increasing* their imports from their homeland. This manipulation implied that English speaking countries *need the help* of non-English speaking immigrants to export goods to the immigrants' non-English speaking homelands because, partially thanks to globalization, English-speaking countries lack foreign language skills. Even in the world of globalized international commerce, an ancient rule of marketing still prevails: 'the merchant speaks the customer's language'. Nineteenth-century Armenians in Peru peddled rugs in Spanish. Today this ancient rule requires English-speaking countries to peddle their exports in languages other than English when they export to non-English speaking countries. Thanks to the dominance of English as a world business language, itself a product of globalization, the English-speaking countries have learned to rely on the rest of the world's fluency in English, thus relieving them of the necessity of learning foreign languages. Therefore, when they have to market their exports in non-English speaking countries, English-speaking countries rely upon the assistance of bi-cultural immigrants, who retain full fluency in foreign languages. Transmigrants have this capacity. Fully fluent in English, they are also fluent in the language of their homeland.

However, again thanks to the world dominance of English, the opposite situation does not apply. When exporting to English-speaking countries, non-English speaking countries enjoy a linguistic advantage. The exporters already speak English as a second language. Speaking English as their second language, the Spanish, the Koreans, the Chinese or the Swedes do not need the help of co-ethnic immigrants in the USA, Canada, Australia or New Zealand to market their exports to those English-speaking countries. As a result, Swedish or Spanish transmigrants residing abroad in English-speaking countries *cannot contribute* to the marketing effort of their homeland's companies in those English-speaking countries. This observation would explain why immigrants in the USA and Canada increase those countries' exports to the immigrants' overseas homelands without increasing their homelands' exports to the USA and Canada. They also explain or help to explain why immigrants from English speaking countries have *no effect* on the imports or exports of the USA and Canada to their homeland. Immigrants from English-speaking countries have no linguistic advantage in another English-speaking country.

It was correct to assert, as David Gould did, that cultural skills reduce the transaction costs of international commerce. However, Gould still thought of language as a trade friction, not a trade structure. Prior to globalization, when languages were more or less on an international standing of parity, with perhaps some superiority to French in the nineteenth century, one could conceptualize translation as a frictional cost of international business. Middleman minorities thrived in the shadow of that frictional cost. In the globalized world that is increasingly coming into existence, the global dominance of the English language is a global structure, not what economists call 'a friction.' This global linguistic structure affects international trade in new ways that require new theory. The theoretical heritage of middleman minorities, properly amended, offers the tools to accomplish this task.

CONCLUSION

Existing literature has correctly inferred that transmigrants from above and from below enjoy linguistic and social capital advantages that fit them advantageously for international commerce and entrepreneurship. On this view, transnationalism endows regional ethnic groups that were not historical middleman minorities and that do not inherit an ethnic culture of entrepreneurship with newly acquired class resources of entrepreneurship. As a result, those class resources of entrepreneurship are more common than they were previously among immigrants; hence, international trade can progress more rapidly than it did earlier. International trade requires international traders, and international traders require the resources of enforceable trust and bi-culturalism.

These inferences are correct as far as they go. However, missing from existing transnationalism literature, whether from above or from below, is any awareness that globalization reduces the utility of bilingual combinations that do not include English. Spanish to French competence is not useful when all French people and all Spanish people speak English. In this case, Spanish people can talk to French people in English, and vice versa, so what additional utility is conveyed by speaking French as well as Spanish? Globalization increasingly embeds world commerce, science, cinema and diplomacy in a dominant language, English. This dominant language creates a global linguistic *structure* where previously only linguistic *frictions* existed. There is every reason to suppose that economic consequences flow from the global dominance of English, and some recent evidence supports that hypothesis. Presumably the dominance of the English language embeds the world in a structure that transnationalism must subserve. Studying the manner in which transmigrants fit into this new language structure emerges as a future research path of consequence.

Both practical and theoretical issues are at stake. On the theoretical side, we learn that transmigrants are not just middleman minorities revived and many times multiplied. Even if they were, the world has changed in some ways advantageous to immigrant entrepreneurs and in some ways disadvantageous. Even if post-industrial economies and cultural globalization enhance demand for immigrant-owned business, as some authorities maintain, the linguistic effect of globalization diminish it. The global dominance of English reduces the advantage that bilingualism conveys in international trade, undermining transmigrants and middleman minorities alike. Both middleman minorities and transnational business elites exploit bilingualism for commercial advantage in international trade. Bilingualism is not their only resource; they also have enforceable social trust embedded in international networks. Nonetheless, the bilingualism has been a salient commercial advantage, which the increasing dominance of English tends to erode throughout the world. For this reason, extrapolating the dominance of English into the future, the long-term outlook for both transmigrants and middleman minorities, the modern and old-fashioned forms of international trade elites, is clouded.

On the practical side, the fourfold expansion of international trade since 1950, which is a defining feature of globalization, owes something to transnationalism in the functional sense of mutual affinity and support. Transmigrants made the expansion of globalization possible, and profited from the opportunities this expansion afforded. In effect, globalization and transnationalism co-produced one another. Moreover, in the context of the increasing dominance of the English language, the English-speaking countries derived peculiar and idiosyncratic advantages from transnational business migrants who increased their exports without increasing their imports! Because of this lop-sided advantage, the massive and dangerous balance of payments deficit of the USA was *reduced*, but not eliminated. This reduction performed a service to world trade, rendering it more secure than it otherwise would have been. Operating in tandem, transnational business elites and the dominance of the English language jointly reduced the vulnerability of the USA to the normal monetary corrections that attend large and protracted trade deficits. The same would obviously be true as well of other English-speaking countries, but since their international role is less pivotal than that of the world's super power, their trade deficits are comparably less important. Since that American balance of payments deficit has been many times identified as the endangered cornerstone of the global economy, whose collapse would pull down the whole global edifice, transnational business elites have proved a social adjunct of globalization in the last generation.

NOTES

1. An early version of this paper was presented at the European Science Foundation's 'Asian Immigrants and Entrepreneurs Conference' that was held at the Catholic University of Nijmegen, on 11 May 2001. Please direct all correspondence regarding this paper to light@soc.ucla.edu.
2. For an extended discussion, see Light and Karageorgis (1994).
3. The 2004 film *Ararat* offers Hollywood's attempt to deal with the oppression of Armenians, and their recourse to commercial entrepreneurship in self-protection.
4. 'Trust and cultural affinities facilitate involvement in transnational ethnic businesses. The moment of business encounter is not solely determined by formal rationalized rules, but also by the presence of cultural codes favoring the process of trust building in business transactions. In small-scale transnational entrepreneurial activities, culture can both promote and limit business opportunities. In this context, formal and rationalized market structures are subordinated to the economic culture of the social agents' (Moallem, 1996: 12).
5. To acculturate is to acquire the language and culture of a host society. To assimilate is to identify with the host society. Inter-marriage is the single most powerful indicator of assimilation.
6. 'Globalization has enhanced the practical, economic, and affective roles of diasporas, showing them to be particularly adaptive forms of social organization' (Cohen, 1997: 176).
7. The 2004 film *Maria Full of Grace* illustrates the operation of a drug smuggling ring around a Colombian diaspora.
8. The distinction between class and ethnic resources is discussed in Light and Karageorgis (1994).

REFERENCES

Armstrong, J.A. (1976), 'Mobilized and proletarian diasporas', *American Political Science Review*, **9**, 393–408.

Bonacich, Edna (1973), 'A theory of middleman minorities', *American Sociological Review*, **38**, 583–94.

Caliner, Geoffrey (2000), 'The language ability of U.S. immigrants: assimilation and cohort effects', *International Migration Review*, **34**, 158–82.

Chik, Frances (2000), 'Hong Kong Chinese immigrant women in business: the impact of transnational networks', paper presented at the Fifth Annual Metropolis Conference, Vancouver, 14 November.

Cohen, Abner (1971), 'Cultural strategies in the organization of trading diasporas', in Claude Meillassoux (ed.), *The Development of Indigenous Trade and Markets in West Africa*, London: Oxford University Press, pp. 266–84.

Cohen, Robin (1997), *Global Diasporas*, Seattle, USA: University of Washington Press.

Collins, Jock (1998), 'Cosmopolitan capitalism: ethnicity, gender and Australian entrepreneurs', vols 1 and 2, PhD dissertation, University of Wollongong.

Crisafulli, Edoardo (1996), 'La Diffusione dell'Inglese e l'Imperialismo Linguistico', *Rivista delle Lingue*, **5**, 20–23.

Dicken, Peter (1992), *Global Shift: The Internationalization of Economic Activity*, New York: Guilford Press.

Farrell, Christopher (1993), 'Shut out immigrants and trade may suffer', *Business Week*, 5 July, 82, 84.

Fishman, Joshua A. (1998–99), 'The new linguistic order', *Foreign Policy*, **28**, 26–40.

Fox, Justin (2000), 'The triumph of English', *Fortune*, **142**, 209ff.

Fukuyama, Francis (1995), 'Social capital and the global economy', *Foreign Affairs*, **74**, 89–103.

Gold, Steven (1997), 'Transnationalism and vocabularies of motive in international migration: the case of Israelis in the United States', *Sociological Perspectives*, **40**, 409–27.

Gould, David Michael (1990), 'Immigrant links to the home country: implications for trade, welfare, and factor returns', PhD dissertation, University of California, Los Angeles.

Gould, David M. (1994), 'Immigrant links to the home country: empirical implications for US bilateral trade flows', *Review of Economics and Statistics*, **76** (2), 302–16.

Guarnizo, Luis Eduardo and Luz Marina Diaz (1999), 'Transnational migration: a view from Colombia', *Ethnic and Racial Studies*, **22**, 397–421.

Guarnizo, Luis Eduardo, Arturo Ignacio Sanchez and Elizabeth M. Roach (1999), 'Mistrust, fragmented solidarity, and transnational migration: Colombians in New York City and Los Angeles', *Ethnic and Racial Studies*, **22**, 367–96.

Hamilton, Gary G. and Tony Waters (1997), 'Ethnicity and capitalist development: the changing role of the Chinese in Thailand', in Daniel Chirot and Anthony Reid (eds), *Essential Outsiders: Chinese and Jews in the Modern Transformation of Southeast Asia and Central Europe*, Seattle and London: University of Washington, pp. 258–84.

Hollifield, James F. (1998–99), 'Migration, trade, and the nation-state: the myth of globalization', *Journal of International Law and Foreign Affairs*, **3** (2), 595–636.
Kieval, Hillel J. (1997), 'Middleman minorities and blood: is there a natural economy of the ritual murder accusation in Europe?', in Daniel Chirot and Anthony Anthony Reid (eds), *Essential Outsiders: Chinese and Jews in the Modern Transformation of Southeast Asia and Central Europe*, Seattle and London: University of Washington Press, pp. 208–36.
Kloosterman, Robert, and Jan Rath (2003), 'Introduction', in Robert Kloosterman and Jan Rath (eds), *Immigrant Entrepreneurs: Venturing Abroad in the Age of Globalization*, Oxford: Berg, pp. 1–16.
Kotkin, Joel (1996), 'Cities of hope: thanks to global trade urban America's potential is revealed', *World Trade*, **9** (4), 24–30.
Laguerre, Michel (1998), 'Rotating credit associations and the diasporic economy', *Journal of Developmental Entrepreneurship*, **3**, 23–34.
Landolt, Patricia, Lilian Autler and Sonia Paires (1999), 'From Hermano Lejano to Hermano Mayor: the dialectics of Salvadoran transnationalism', *Ethnic and Racial Studies*, **22**, 290–315.
Lever-Tracy, Constance and David Ip (1996), 'Diaspora capitalism and the homeland: Australian Chinese networks into China', *Diaspora*, **5**, 239–71.
Lever-Tracy, Constance, David Ip, Jim Kitay, Irene Phillips and Noel Tracy (1991), *Asian Entrepreneurs in Australia*, Canberra: Australian Government Publishing Service.
Li, Peter S. (1993), 'Chinese investment and business in Canada: ethnic entrepreneurship reconsidered', *Pacific Affairs*, **66**, 219–43.
Lie, John (1995), 'From international migration to transnational diaspora', *Contemporary Sociology*, **24**, 303–6.
Light, Ivan (2001), 'Globalization, transnationalism and trade', *Asian and Pacific Migration Journal*, **10**, 53–79.
Light, Ivan (2004), 'The ethnic economy', in Neil Smelser and Richard Swedberg (eds), *The Handbook of Economic Sociology*, 2nd edn, New York: Russell Sage Foundation, pp. 650–77.
Light, Ivan and Steven J. Gold (2000), *Ethnic Economies*, San Diego, CA: Academic.
Light, Ivan, and Stavros Karageorgis (1994), 'The ethnic economy', in Neil Smelser and Richard Swedberg (eds), *Handbook of Economic Sociology*, New York: Russell Sage Foundation, pp. 647–71.
Light, Ivan, Parminder Bhachu and Stavros Karageorgis (1993), 'Migration networks and immigrant entrepreneurship', in Ivan Light and Parminder Bhachu (eds), *Immigration and Entrepreneurship*, New Brunswick, NJ: Transaction, pp. 25–50.
Light, Ivan, Min Zhou and Rebecca Kim (2002), 'Transnationalism and American exports in an English-speaking world', *International Migration Review*, **36**, 702–25.
Massey, Douglas S. Joaquin Arango, Graeme Hugo, Ali Kouaouci, Adela Pellegrino and J. Edward Taylor (1993), 'Theories of international migration: a review and appraisal', *Population and Development Review*, **19**, 431–66.
Moallem, Minoo (1996), 'Transnationalism, migrancy, and entrepreneurship', Beatrice M. Bain Research Group and Sociology Department, University of California, Berkeley.
Ooka, Emi (2001), 'Social capital and income attainment among Chinese immigrant entrepreneurs in Toronto', *Asian and Pacific Migration Journal*, **10**, 123–44.
Phillipson, Robert (1992), *Linguistic Imperialism*, Oxford: Oxford University.
Portes, Alejandro (2003), 'Conclusion: theoretical convergencies [*sic*] and empirical evidence in the study of immigrant transnationalism', *International Migration Review*, **37**, 874–92.
Portes, Alejandro and Lingxin Hao (1998), 'E pluribus unum: bilingualism and loss of language in the second generation', *Sociology of Education*,**71**, 269–94.
Portes, Alejandro, William J. Haller and Luis Eduardo Guarnizo (2002), 'Transnational entrepreneurs: an alternative form of immigrant economic adaptation', *American Sociological Review*, **67**, 278–98.
Rondinelli, Dennis A., James H. Johnson, Jr and John D. Kasarda (1998), 'The changing forces of urban economic development: globalization and city competitiveness in the 21st century', *Cityscape*, **3**, 71–105.
Sassen, Saskia (1994), 'Economic internationalization: the new migration in Japan and the United States', *Social Justice*, **21**, 62–82.
Schiller, Nina Glick, Linda Basch and Cristina Blanc-Szanton (1992), 'Transnationalism: a new analytic framework for understanding migration', in Nina Glick Schiller, Linda Basch, and Cristina (eds), *Towards a Transnational Perspective on Migration*, Annals of the New York Academy of Sciences, vol. 645, New York: New York Academy of Sciences, pp. 1–24.
Silj, Alessandro and Malcolm Cross (1999), *Ethnic Conflict and Migration in Europe*, Rome: Consiglio Italiano per le Scienze Sociali and Centre for European Migration and Ethnic Studies.
Smart, Alan, and Josephine Smart (1998), 'Transnational social networks and negotiated identities in interactions between Hong Kong and China', in Michael Peter Smith and Luis Eduardo Guarnizo (eds), *Transnationalism From Below*, New Brunswick, NJ: Transaction, pp. 103–29.
The Economist (1997), 'The world economy', 20 September.

Van Parijs, Philippe (2000), 'The ground floor of the world: on the socio-economic consequences of linguistic globalization', *International Political Science Review*, **21**, 217–33.
Walton-Roberts, Margaret and Daniel Hiebert (1997), 'Immigration, entrepreneurship, and the family: Indo-Canadian enterprise in the construction of Greater Vancouver', *Canadian Journal of Regional Science*, **20**, 119–40.
Wolff, James A. and Timothy L. Pett (2000), 'Internationalization of small firms: an examination of export competitive patterns, firm size, and export performance', *Journal of Small Business Management*, **38**, 34–47.
Wong, Bernard (1998), *Ethnicity and Entrepreneurship: The New Chinese Immigrants in the San Francisco Bay Area*, Boston, MA: Allyn and Bacon.
Wong, Lloyd L. (1997), 'Globalization and transnational migration', *International Sociology*, **12**, 329–51.
Wong, Lloyd L. (2003), 'Chinese business migration to Australia, Canada, and the United States: state policy and the global immigration marketplace', *Asian and Pacific Migration Journal*, **12**, 301–35.
Wong, Lloyd L. and Michele Ng (2002), 'The emergence of small transnational enterprise in Vancouver: the case of Chinese entrepreneur immigrants', *International Journal of Urban and Regional Research*, **26**, 508–30.
Yeung, Henry Wai-Chung (1999), 'The internationalization of ethnic Chinese business firms from Southeast Asia: strategies, processes and competitive advantage', *International Journal of Urban and Regional Research*, **23**, 103–27.

23 Historical context of entrepreneurship

Mark Casson

ECONOMIC THEORIES OF THE ENTREPRENEUR

The entrepreneur is a leading character in many accounts of economic growth. He appears in business biographies as a charismatic founder of a company; in industry studies as a prominent innovator, or a leading figure in a trade association or cartel; and in general economic histories as one of the hordes of self-employed small business owners who confer flexibility and dynamism on a market economy. Entrepreneurship is not confined to the private sector; it can also be discerned in personalities of people who establish progressive charitable trusts and reform government administration.

An adequate theory of entrepreneurship must address the following issues:

1. What does the introduction of the entrepreneur add to our understanding of economic behaviour? Do accounts of entrepreneurial behaviour supplement statistical evidence, or merely retell the same story through biographical anecdote?
2. Is entrepreneurship just a label for an area of ignorance? Does it – like 'culture' and 'institutions' – sometimes just denote residual causes of growth that cannot be properly measured?
3. Can anyone really know what goes on inside the mind of an entrepreneur? If not, what is the point of speculating about the subject?

The term 'entrepreneur' appears to have been introduced into economic theory by Richard Cantillon (1755), an Irish economist of French descent. According to Cantillon, the entrepreneur is a specialist in taking on risk. He 'insures' workers by buying their output for resale before consumers have indicated how much they are willing to pay for it. The workers receive an assured income (in the short run, at least), while the entrepreneur bears the risk caused by price fluctuations in consumer markets.

This idea was refined by the US economist Frank Knight (1921), who distinguished between risk, which is insurable, and uncertainty, which is not. Risk refers to recurrent events whose relative frequency is known from past experience, while uncertainty relates to unique events whose probability can only be subjectively estimated. Knight thought that most of the risks relating to production and marketing fall into the latter category. Since business owners cannot insure against these risks, they are left to bear them by themselves. Profit is a reward for bearing this uninsurable risk: it is the reward of the pure entrepreneur. With freedom of entry into industries, profits in one industry can exceed profits in another industry in the long run only if the uncertainties are greater in the more profitable industry – in other words, if the demands on entrepreneurship are greater in that industry.

Popular notions of entrepreneurship are based on the heroic vision put forward by Joseph A. Schumpeter (1934). The entrepreneur is visualized as someone who creates new industries and thereby precipitates major structural changes in the economy. The entrepreneur innovates by carrying out new combinations; he is not a pure inventor, because he adopts the inventions made by others, nor is he a financier, because he relies on bankers to fund his investments. The entrepreneur takes the crucial decision to commit resources to the exploitation of new ideas. An element of calculation is involved, but it is not pure calculation, because not all of the relevant factors can be accurately measured. He is motivated by profit, but not purely by profit: the other motivators include 'dream and the will to found a private kingdom'; the 'will to conquer: the impulse to fight, to prove oneself superior to others'; and the 'joy of creating'.

Schumpeter was concerned with the 'high level' kind of entrepreneurship that, historically, has led to the creation of railways, the development of the chemical industry, and the growth of integrated oil companies. His analysis left little room for the much more common, but no less important, 'low level' entrepreneurship carried on by small firms – in particular, by firms in the wholesale and retail trades. Alfred Marshall (1919) described the role of these firms in some detail, but omitted them from his formal analysis of supply and demand. Given the techniques that were available to him, Marshall could only model equilibrium situations, and so could not fit entrepreneurship into his analysis.

The essence of low-level entrepreneurship can be explained by the Austrian approach of Friedrich A. von Hayek (1937) and Israel M. Kirzner (1973). Entrepreneurs are middlemen who provide price quotations as an invitation to trade. While bureaucrats in a socialist economy have little incentive to discover prices for themselves, entrepreneurs in a market economy are motivated to do so by profit opportunities. They hope to profit by buying cheap and selling dear. In the long run, competition between entrepreneurs arbitrages away price differentials, but in the short run, such differentials, once discovered, generate a profit for the entrepreneur.

The difficulty with the Austrian approach is that it isolates the entrepreneur from the organization of routine activities which is so characteristic of a firm. It fits an individual dealer or speculator far better than it fits a small manufacturer, because the latter has to oversee an organization whereas the former does not. The link between the entrepreneur and the firm is considered in greater detail below.

JUDGEMENTAL DECISION-MAKING

The insights of these economists can be synthesized by identifying an entrepreneurial function that is common to all approaches. This is the exercise of judgement in decision-making (Casson, 1982). A middleman who buys before he knows the price at which he can resell must make a judgement about what the future price will be. An arbitrager must make a judgement about where price differentials are most likely to be found, in order to focus his price discovery effort on a suitable segment of the market. An innovator must assess whether a new product will prove attractive to consumers, or whether a new technology will really cut costs by as much as its inventor claims it will.

If information were freely available, and could be costlessly processed, then there would be no need for judgement. Every decision would be correctly taken and no mistakes would ever be made. But in practice information is costly. It is time-consuming to make and record observations. Human memory capacity is limited. Above all, communication is an expensive process. It follows that people do not have all the information they need when taking a decision.

When decision-makers cannot afford to collect all the information they need, they have to act under uncertainty. But the uncertainty faced by one person may be different from the uncertainty faced by another person. Sources of primary information are highly localized; for example, only people 'on the spot' can directly observe an event. Different people in different places will therefore have different perceptions of any given situation. They may therefore make different decisions. The nature of the decision therefore depends on the identity of the person who makes it. The entrepreneur matters because their judgement of a situation is potentially unique.

Not all information is reliable. The senses may be confused, but the biggest risk relates to information obtained from other people. The other person may be unreliable, or their message may be misunderstood. Alternatively, they may set out deliberately to mislead, so that they can extract more profit from their information for themselves. One person may check their information sources more carefully than another, and therefore stand less chance of being misled.

The interpretation of information may differ too. Different people may hold different theories about the way the environment works. As any social scientist knows, it is difficult to test conclusively between rival theories because of data limitations. Thus different theories may coexist, leading to different interpretations of similar evidence. In a business context, entrepreneurs may act differently on the basis of similar information because they interpret the situation in different ways.

If a situation recurs frequently, it is worthwhile investigating it carefully in order to find the theory that fits it best. This theory identifies which information is required to make the correct decision. Arrangements can be made to collect the information on a regular basis, so that it is always to hand when required. Whenever a decision needs to be made, this information is processed using an appropriate decision rule in order to arrive at a correct decision. If some information is very costly to collect, then its costs have to be traded off against its benefits to arrive at the correct decision rule. This rule does not guarantee the correct decision; but it is optimal in economic terms, in the sense that it trades off the risk of a mistake against the saving in information cost.

Once this optimal decision rule is known there is no further need for the entrepreneur. Everyone knows how the decision rule has been specified, and so no reward can be earned by those who take the decision properly.

Now consider the opposite case in which no such rule is available. This is likely to involve a novel situation. It either has no precedent, or is so unusual that it never pays to investigate it fully. Nobody knows the correct decision rule, and nobody systematically collects information on the situation. The more complex the situation, the more inadequate the theory is likely to be. There may be no theory at all, or there may be a range of rival theories which it is difficult to choose between. There may be no information, or a surfeit of information, because no one is quite sure what information is relevant and what is not. Matters are even worse if the decision has to be arrived at quickly – for example, because the situation is unstable, and will continue to deteriorate until something is done. This is the kind of situation that calls for the most intensive judgement. To improvise a decision quickly, people have to rely on the theories with which they are already familiar, and the information that they can retrieve from their memory. Differences in theories, combined with differences in memories, lead to differences in decisions. The people with the most relevant theories and the most comprehensive memories will tend to make the best decisions. These are the entrepreneurs – they possess the quality of judgement required to improvise a decision successfully when no agreed decision rule is available.

The greater the cost of a mistake, the greater the importance of finding the appropriate person to take the decision. The cost of a mistake depends upon the value of the resources involved, and the extent to which an erroneous decision can be reversed before it is too late. The greater the 'sunk costs' involved, the more important the quality of judgement becomes, and the more important it is that the decision is taken by a fully competent entrepreneur.

COMPLEXITY OF DECISIONS

To fully operationalize this theory, it is necessary to specify the nature of complexity. Complexity is best defined in terms of the size of the model that is required to represent the principal features of the situation. So far as entrepreneurship is concerned, the involvement of other 'major players' in the situation is a major source of complexity. Other firms are important players, whether as competitors or as potential partners in alliances. Government too is an important player, particularly in industries connected with defence, where it is a customer as well as the policy-maker. The greater the strategic skills of the other players, the more complex the situation becomes. International business issues are more complex than domestic issues because there are a larger number of skilful players involved.

Examples of judgemental decisions include the following:

- An opportunity to exploit a new technology has been identified and a quick decision is required in order to pre-empt a rival. The investment is irreversible – that is, the costs are sunk – so that a mistake cannot be corrected afterwards. The revenue stream is uncertain, and cannot be guaranteed by forward sales of output. Should the investment be undertaken right away?
- A new source of competition has just emerged from a firm in a newly industrializing country. Should the dominant firm in the industry cut its price, or can it rely upon its existing customers not to switch to the rival firm? Is the rival firm producing more cheaply because of low-cost labour and/or subsidies, about which nothing can be done, or is it using more efficient techniques which ought to be imitated?

THE SUPPLY OF GOOD JUDGEMENT

People differ in their quality of judgement. Some people have a personal comparative advantage in exercising judgement, and others do not. Those who own resources do not necessarily possess the quality of judgement needed to utilize them properly. Wealthy aristocrats, for example, do not necessarily make good businessmen. Economic efficiency requires that people with the best judgement are matched to the most judgemental decisions.

There are various reasons why people differ in their quality of judgement. Some people may be very observant, and notice things that others miss. Others may have strong powers of concentration, that enable them to process information more quickly than other people. Older people may have 'longer' memories, so that they can retrieve more information about similar situations that have arisen in the past. This is particularly useful in areas where theory is weak – for example, in understanding the motivations of other people. Some people may be more methodical than others, and better at checking information. For all these reasons, some people face lower information costs than other people. For a given expenditure of effort, they are more likely to arrive at a correct decision.

In a free society, people are allowed to decide for themselves whether their judgement is good. In choosing their occupations, people who are confident that their judgement is good will tend to gravitate to jobs that call for intensive use of judgement, while those who believe that their judgement is bad will gravitate to jobs where other people take decisions for them. On this view, entrepreneurs will *specialize* in taking judgemental decisions. Although everyone takes judgemental decisions from time to time – such as whether to marry, or change job, or move house – entrepreneurs specialize in taking these decisions on behalf of other people.

Not all entrepreneurs are successful. There is a strong bias in the historical literature towards successful entrepreneurs, for fairly obvious reasons: successful entrepreneurs make an impact on the national economy, they are inclined to self-promotion, and the enterprises they create survive long enough to leave good records. The successful entrepreneurs are those whose confidence in their judgement turns out to be well placed. For every high-profile success, however, there tend to be numerous failures. Small start-up businesses are notoriously prone to failure in the first two to three years. Failures are normally caused by over-confidence, though bad luck may also play its part. Luck is also a factor in business success, because ill-founded judgements may occasionally be validated by chance events. However, the proportion of luck to judgement in entrepreneurial success remains unknown.

Given the scarcity of entrepreneurship, the question naturally arises as to whether its supply can be increased, and if so how. For a given size of population, there are two main ways of increasing the overall supply of entrepreneurs. The first is to improve the quality of judgement in the population, and the second is to give people more confidence in the judgement that they have. The first approach raises the question of whether entrepreneurs are 'born' or 'made'. There is little evidence that entrepreneurship is inherited: the evidence on family firms suggests that sons usually display less initiative than the fathers they succeed. There is some support for the idea that entrepreneurial qualities are incubated in adversity. Fatalistic acceptance of poverty is certainly not an entrepreneurial characteristic, but determination to reverse an economic setback often seems to be (Brenner, 1983). The idea of 'proving oneself' in order to live down some humiliation may also be a factor, although the evidence is only anecdotal on this point. Many entrepreneurs claim to be 'self-made', but it is impossible to know whether, in making this claim, they are simply unwilling to give credit to parents, teachers and others who have helped them along their way.

The second approach suggests that people should be encouraged to become more self-confident, and to take greater risks. This attitude was characteristic of the 'enterprise culture' of the 1980s and 1990s (see below); the problem is that by encouraging people with poor judgements to make risky decisions, more resources may simply be wasted instead.

THE CONTRACTUAL POSITION OF THE ENTREPRENEUR

The preceding approach is based upon a functional definition of the entrepreneur: 'an entrepreneur is what an entrepreneur does', in other words. But how is an entrepreneur to be identified in practice; in particular, how can he be recognized in relation to the firm?

The principle of specialization outlined above provides the answer to this question. As Schumpeter emphasized, there are few roles that consist purely of taking judgemental decisions; most senior roles also involve some minor routine, as well as ritual activity such as making speeches. Specialization in entrepreneurship is not total, therefore, but a matter of degree. It follows that anyone who exercises judgement more than an average person is an entrepreneur to some degree.

In a market economy, specialization by entrepreneurs takes two main forms. In the first, the entrepreneur is an employee, and in the second they own a firm in which others invest. Looked at from the point of view of an entrepreneur, the problem is how to gain control of resources on a significant scale when personal means are modest. One method is to obtain a job that gives scope for the exercise of judgement over how the employer's resources are used; the other is to become self-employed, and borrow sufficient funds to buy the requisite resources.

THE REPUTATION OF THE ENTREPRENEUR

Some writers, such as Knight, claim that entrepreneurs are always owners and never employees. They argue that no one would ever trust someone else to take judgemental decisions on their behalf. The logic of this position, however, leads to Knight's bizarre conclusion that the shareholders in a large joint-stock companies are all entrepreneurs, however passive their role. The crucial judgement exercised by the shareholders concerns the appointment of a suitable manager to run the business; once he has been appointed, said Knight, his job would become routine.

Knight overlooked the fact that firms can offer managers both pecuniary and non-pecuniary rewards that are contingent on the performance of the firm: pecuniary rewards include promotions, bonus payments and stock options, while non-pecuniary rewards include status and recognition of achievement. These rewards can align the incentives of the shareholders and the employee-entrepreneur. The employee may not have a major investment at stake, but their reputation may be 'on the line' when they take a decision on their employer's behalf. Their reputation will affect their promotion prospects and their own self-esteem. They may therefore give just as much care and attention to decisions as if the resources were their own.

Not all entrepreneurs have a good reputation, however. There are two main aspects to reputation in business: honesty and competence. Honesty refers to the fact that an entrepreneur needs to be a faithful steward of other people's money. This not only means avoiding the temptations of fraud, but also a commitment to working hard even though others will be the main beneficiaries of the effort. Competence concerns effective handling of routine matters, but above all the quality of judgement.

Neither of these factors can be directly observed. Reputation must therefore be based on symptoms of these qualities. Where honesty is concerned, older family members may put their confidence in the filial duty of the younger generation. Members of a local community may rely upon the sense of shame that failure will bring to the entrepreneur. If the entrepreneur is believed to be a sincerely religious person, then they would be expected to feel very guilty if they behaved in a dishonourable way.

Matters are less clear where competence is concerned. An obvious indicator of competence is educational qualification: this should reveal whether the entrepreneur is intelligent, and whether they have worked hard at their studies. In fact, however, education seems to be a poor indicator of future entrepreneurial success. Examination performance may measure the ability to analyse abstractions, rather than the complex real world situations confronted by the entrepreneur. Schooling may reward conformity of belief, rather than the independent judgement by the entrepreneur; it places pupils in a subordinate role in a hierarchical organization, which is not conducive to an independent 'free spirit' who aspires to be their own boss.

Given the pragmatic nature of entrepreneurial activity, track record in business is an obvious basis for reputation. However, many entrepreneurs successfully re-enter business after failure, and some notable successes have only been achieved after a string of failures. It appears that many financial backers value the entrepreneur's previous experience for its own sake, independently of whether they were successful or not. People who fail lose some of their reputation – but not all of it: those who lack reputation most are those who have never tried it in the first place.

FINANCING ENTREPRENEURSHIP

An entrepreneur with a good reputation can borrow funds fairly easily. He can sell shares in his business to the public, or take loans from banks (or both). However, if he is raising large sums of money then he may need to subordinate himself to a board of directors by becoming the salaried manager of a firm in which he also owns shares; the existence of an active board reassures investors that if he should lose his reputation then he can be voted out of office.

By contrast, an entrepreneur who lacks reputation (or who has gained a bad reputation) must accumulate all the capital he requires for himself. However good his judgement, he cannot become an entrepreneur unless he has sufficient wealth. The resulting capital constraints can be alleviated in four main ways:

- *Inheritance*. The entrepreneur's parents or wealthy relatives may die while he is still young. Being the first son under primogeniture, and having elderly parents, is an advantage in this respect. Wealth can be augmented by strategic marriage too – for example, acquiring other people's inheritance from wealthy widows (except when their property is entailed).

- *By working and saving*. This is a slow method, but has the advantage that the entrepreneur may acquire useful skills while in employment, especially if he can obtain a responsible job. He may also make useful contacts with potential customers while in his job.
- *By starting on a very small scale and steadily reinvesting profits*. This method is also potentially slow but can be expedited if the initial venture is high risk. Thus a merchant may begin by smuggling, gun-running or piracy, and then become legitimate once sufficient capital has been accumulated to support a proper import-export business.
- *Other means*, including gambling and insurance fraud (for example, over-insuring warehouse contents and then committing arson).

The capital-constrained scenario is one that confronts many entrepreneurs from poor backgrounds. The factors identified above are therefore highly relevant to financing of growth of small businesses started by immigrant refugees and members of minority ethnic groups.

INFORMATION SYNTHESIS

Judgemental decisions normally require the synthesis of different types of information. A synthesis of information has commercial value only if it relates to a profit opportunity. If everyone recognizes the same opportunity at the same time then profits will be competed away. Thus a profitable synthesis needs to be unique.

There are two main ways in which a synthesis can be unique. The first is that the entrepreneur has different information from other people. For example, the entrepreneur may have access to the latest news, enabling him to act of the basis of information that other people do not yet possess. Alternatively, he may have effected a unique combination of information. While every item of information that he knows may also be known to someone else, no one possesses exactly the same combination of items.

The second possibility is that the entrepreneur can interpret information better than other people. He may have exactly the same information as other people, but he interprets it differently. This difference of interpretation arises because the entrepreneur brings different theories to bear on the subject. While these theories may be formal scientific theories, they are much more likely to be intuitive theories which the entrepreneur employs as a metaphor or heuristic device. Some of these theories may have been imbued from the culture in which the entrepreneur was brought up. Others may be generalizations that the entrepreneur has arrived at on the basis of his own personal experiences.

An entrepreneur who wishes to be the first to exploit the news must cultivate access to people who handle it prior to publication. Location in a major metropolis is a great advantage from this point of view. This is the place where travellers often call first when arriving from overseas; it is where journalists collect information for their stories, and where groups of people assemble to take important decisions – politicians in Parliament, business leaders at their headquarters, and so on. This explains why so much high-level entrepreneurial activity in any country is concentrated in the metropolis.

An entrepreneur who wishes to effect a unique synthesis from ordinary information needs to build a unique configuration of contacts. He requires a 'networking strategy', which involves joining suitable organizations, attending appropriate events, and generally obtaining introductions to the 'right people'. If he needs information about new inventions then he may socialize with scientists and engineers – for example, by sponsoring meetings of professional associations. To gain access to finance he may join organizations with a wealthy membership – for example, a sporting club, or the board of trustees of a charity. He needs to ensure that as far as possible other people do not replicate his pattern of contacts, for otherwise they may arrive at the same conclusions as himself where commercial opportunities are concerned. He therefore needs to belong to different organizations whose memberships do not otherwise overlap.

So far as the interpretation of information is concerned, some of the theories employed by the entrepreneur will be a cultural product, while others will have developed out of his experience. For a low-level entrepreneur, narrow experience of a specialized field may be of the greatest value, but for a high-level entrepreneur broad experience is likely to be most useful. The greater scale on which the high-level entrepreneur operates means that he must synthesize information not only from different functions areas – production, marketing, research and development (R&D), and so on – but from different countries and regions as well. He needs to be acquainted with the jargon of different professions, and with the languages of different countries too. It is therefore an advantage for him to have held different sorts of jobs, and to have lived and worked in different countries.

ENTREPRENEURIAL STRATEGY: PRE-EMPTING OPPORTUNITIES

Information has the properties of a 'public good' because it can easily diffuse to other people. An entrepreneur will therefore want to keep his information synthesis secret until he has pre-empted the profit opportunity. There are three main ways of pre-empting an opportunity, but not all of them are available in every case:

- *Patents, etc.* The simplest way is to obtain a legally enforceable monopoly: this may consist of a state charter, license or franchise, or a patent linked to the technology employed. This privilege will normally be valid for a fixed term, after which it may or may not be renewed.
- *Speculation and arbitrage.* In the absence of legal enforcement, the best alternative is to appropriate the profit from a speculative deal in some resource. This provides a basis for rapid capital gains; the entrepreneur can buy up the resources which appear undervalued in the light of his information, and then sell these resources on to others at higher prices once the information has entered the public domain. Commodity and currency traders appropriate profit in this way on a daily basis. The same strategy can be applied to land, mining rights, and the like: for example, buying up land that is used for agriculture and selling it off to a builder for housing.
- *Loyalty.* Where manufacturing and commerce are concerned, profit cannot usually be appropriated through a once-for-all transaction. The opportunity involves

creating a market for a type of product that did not previously exist, or making an existing product in a different way. It involves a succession of trades over a long period of time. The closest analogy to the speculative strategy is to tie in suppliers and customers using long-term contracts. This would prevent the suppliers and customers from switching to rival firms later on. These long-term contracts would capitalize the flow of future costs and benefits in the same way that the price of the speculative asset did before. The transactions costs associated with this strategy are likely to be high, however. Furthermore, once alerted to the situation, customers and suppliers will be reluctant to sign such contracts, since they will realize that they can get a better deal once competitors arrive on the scene. Under these conditions, the best strategy is to win the loyalty of their customers and suppliers, so that they are reluctant to switch to rivals when they appear. If rivals expect the clients to be loyal to the innovator, then this will discourage them from entering in the first place.

THE MARKET FOR ENTREPRENEURS

The demand for entrepreneurship, like the demand for any other factor of production, is a derived demand. Unlike more conventional factors of production, however, the demand for entrepreneurship derives not from the overall level of product demand, but rather from the volatility of such demand. If the pattern of product demand were completely stable, so that nothing ever changed, then every firm could repeat the same production plan from one period to the next without any difficulty. It is only because product demand changes that production decisions need to be reconsidered. Moreover, if product demand simply alternated between the same small number of states, the firm could prepare its plans in advance for each possible state, and simply implement the pre-specified plan appropriate to whichever of these states appeared. The demand for entrepreneurship arises from the fact that product demand is likely to enter new and unprecedented states for which no plan already exists, because it is uneconomic to devise in advance a plan for every conceivable state, since many conceivable states exist that may never actually occur.

It is not only the state of demand that is volatile in this way. In an open international economy, supply shocks are a regular occurrence. Then there are technology shocks arising from new inventions and discoveries, and cultural and institutional shocks which affect the contractual basis on which business is carried on. In general, the more volatile the environment, the greater the demand for entrepreneurs.

This means, in practical terms, that when volatility increases there will be an increase in the demand for entrepreneurs and a corresponding decline in the demand for substitutes, such as managers. This will normally be reflected in the formation of more small firms and the restructuring of large firms. The large firms may disappear through bankruptcy, or be split up through management buyout and 'asset-stripping'; alternatively, they may be reorganized in a more flexible form, as a coalition of internal entrepreneurs. Greater competition to hire entrepreneurial employees means that pay structures will tend to become more flexible, because it will no longer be possible to offer both entrepreneurial employees and non-entrepreneurial employees the same rates of pay.

GEOGRAPHICAL MOBILITY OF THE ENTREPRENEUR

It was noted above that everyone takes judgemental decisions from time to time. These decisions concern choice of occupation, where to live, and selection of partner – in business and marriage. People tend to be most mobile between the time that they leave school and the time that they settle down to pursue their main career. At this stage, entrepreneurs are more likely to move and non-entrepreneurs to stay. This is particularly true of people brought up in isolated rural areas where there are few opportunities for profit. Such areas tend to selectively lose their more entrepreneurial young people. Conversely, large cities tend to attract entrepreneurial young people. They offer greater profit opportunities, a wider choice of jobs, and access to large amounts of specialized information through clubs and societies that flourish there. Those who succeed in the city may well retire to the countryside, buying their way into the local gentry and acquiring positions of status – for example, becoming a magistrate. Some may retire to the area where they grew up, but envy of their success by those who remained behind may sometimes keep them away.

If entrepreneurs are prepared to move long distances, then they have a choice of political regimes under which to operate. The regimes that are most attractive to mobile entrepreneurs will have the following characteristics:

- private property, which is freely alienable, subject to certain minimal restrictions
- freedom of movement, and freedom to associate with business partners
- confidentiality of business information, especially regarding the relations with customers and suppliers
- protection of creative work through patents, copyright, design protection, and so on
- access to impartial courts which will enforce property rights and which have the competence to settle complex commercial claims
- a stable currency, based on a prudent control of the money supply
- democratic government, with sufficient balance of power between opposing interests to reduce the risks of draconian interventions in industry and commerce
- openness to immigration by entrepreneurs and skilled workers (and possibly other groups as well).

While the presence of such institutions may account for economic success, the converse also applies: the absence of such institutions may lead to poor performance. Their absence may explain the failure of many less-developed countries to commercialize and industrialize on a significant scale. Assuming that the leaders of these countries are seeking economic progress, their persistence in maintaining inappropriate institutional structures remains to be explained. One possibility is that their time horizons are very short and their motives are venal; their objective is to maximize the perks of holding political office for as long as they can cling to power. This approach appears quite common in countries where military dictators hold ultimate power. Another possibility is that the leader has misguided beliefs about the way that economies function. They overestimate the 'gains from raids' and underestimate the 'gains from trade', and therefore focus their attention on waging wars against neighbouring countries. They fail to appreciate that sources of information are highly decentralized, and therefore underestimate the value of competitive profit seeking, while overestimating the benefits of state control. A third possibility is that attitudes are so traditional and inward-looking that change of any kind is resisted, including change to a more entrepreneurial economy. Cultural attitudes may be so parochial that leaders are unaware, or unconcerned, about how far their country is lagging behind the most advanced economies.

OCCUPATIONAL MOBILITY OF THE ENTREPRENEUR

Young men who remain behind in a locality may well follow their father into the same line of business. Where father is an employee, they follow him 'into the works' or 'down the pit'. Father may even use his influence to get his son a job, even though the industry's long-term prospects may be poor. To those with narrow horizons and a parochial outlook, any long-standing local industry may appear secure. Those entrepreneurs who remain behind will reveal their qualities by getting jobs, or starting firms, in newer industries instead. The non-entrepreneurial workers may eventually join the ranks of the 'structurally unemployed'.

The same mechanism applies in a family firm (Church, 1993). 'One day all this will be yours', the father tells the son, and the son feels morally obliged to succeed his father, even though his interests lie elsewhere. A more entrepreneurial son might turn down the offer and set up his own business in a different industry, forcing the father to look outside the family for a successor – possibly with beneficial results for the firm.

Business owners who remain behind in a declining industry or region may join forces to lobby for protective tariffs or industrial subsidies. They harness organizations, such as trade associations, which were originally established to promote the provision of industry-specific 'public goods' like training, for collusive purposes. They attempt to maintain profit levels through (covert) price-fixing; to counter trade union power by bargaining collectively, and so on. A secretive and conspiratorial business culture develops, reflecting the entrepreneurial weaknesses of the business group.

HISTORICAL APPLICATIONS OF THE CONCEPT OF THE ENTREPRENEUR

Early academic writers on British economic and social history offered no systematic interpretation of the role of the entrepreneur, and employed the concept mainly as a descriptive device. The 'Victorian entrepreneur' was regarded more as a sociological than an economic phenomenon: a member of an upwardly mobile lower middle class, imbued with the bourgeois values of proprietary capitalism. The Victorians themselves seem to have been more impressed with their own engineering feats than their entrepreneurial achievements; thus it was the civil and mechanical engineers, rather than the railway promoters or the company secretaries, that were seen as the heroes of the Railway Revolution (Smiles, 1862). More generally, it was the creation of the Empire, rather than an entrepreneurial domestic economy, that was the main political preoccupation. Contemporary interest in Victorian entrepreneurship is more a reflection of a desire to recover something that has been lost than the continuation of a concern that the Victorians themselves expressed.

In the USA a powerful mythology developed around the 'rags to riches' entrepreneur (Sarachek, 1978). This was notable for sustaining a climate of optimism around small business start-up and playing down the very high risk of business failure. Where serious investigations were carried out (see, for example, Taussig, 1915) they highlighted the middle-class professional origins of many successful entrepreneurs. The large-scale entreprenurial exploits of the 'robber barons' of the late nineteeenth century were chiefly of interest to the 'muck-raking' press.

Schumpeter (1939) provided one if the earliest economic applications of entrepreneurial theory. He identified five main types of 'new combination' effected by entrepreneurs: new products, new processes of production, the development of new export markets, the discovery of new sources of war material supply, and the creation of new forms of institution – such as the cartel or trust. Schumpeter's classification fits well with the major forms of innovation that occurred in Europe during the 'Age of High Imperialism', 1870–1914. Schumpeter was also able to show that this schema fitted the earlier history of the Western economies, from the growth of Mediterranean trade during the Renaisssance down to the Industrial Revolution. Schumpeter also claimed that he could explain Kondratieff 'long waves' of 50–60 years duration by the periodic clustering of innovations since the Industrial Revolution. Unfortunately, however, the empirical basis of Schumpeter's speculations on long waves has not stood the test of time very well (see Solomou, 1987).

Pursuing the Schumpeterian theme, Hughes (1965) examined the influence of the 'vital few' in promoting economic growth. Hughes's approach is mainly biographical, emphasising the personality factor in entrepreneurship. The great value of his contribution lies in the fact that he recognizes the role of the entrepreneur in the public as well as the private sector, although he sees the public sector entrepreneur as heavily implicated in the growth of bureaucracy. The policy implication of Hughes's study would appear to be that people with entrepreneurial personalities need to be attracted into the private sector where, thanks to competitive markets, the incentives are better aligned with the long-run public interest.

A rather similar conclusion arises from Jones's (1981; 1988) studies of long-term world economic growth. Adopting an international comparative perspective, Jones argues that entrepreneurship is a natural feature of human behaviour which government can either encourage or suppress. Encouragement is provided by a regime of freedom under law, which allows people to carry out experiments in commercial and industrial organizations at their own expense. Suppression is effected by governments that fall into the hands of elites, who think they know best which experiments are socially desirable and which are not. They subsidize prestigious experiments out of taxes, and repress ordinary experiments because they are seen as either useless, immoral or politically subversive.

THE DEBATE ON BRITISH ENTREPRENEURIAL DECLINE

The most substantive recent discussion of entrepreneurship has focused on the alleged decline of entrepreneurship in Britain after 1870 (see, for example, Aldcroft, 1964;

Sandberg, 1981). This decline is seen as having both technological and cultural roots (Wiener, 1981). One of the major symptoms of failure is said to be lack of investment in key industries. It has been correctly pointed out, however, that good entrepreneurship does not always mean deciding to invest, for in many situations the correct decision is not to invest at all. Nor is innovation always an indicator of good entrepreneurship; it sometimes pays to let others make the first move, and to learn from their mistakes.

For the historian to know whether entrepreneurs should have invested more heavily in new technologies, it is necessary to develop a counter-factual scenario. This scenario will normally be based on what happened in other situations where such investment was undertaken, and the crucial question then becomes whether these situations were really similar to the original situation or not.

Even if it seemed, with the benefit of hindsight, that investment should have been undertaken, it may be asked whether a correct judgement could really have been made at the time, given the information that was then available. Were there other people arguing a sound case for investment, and were their opinions dismissed on spurious grounds? If not, then it may be more appropriate to ascribe the outcome to misfortune rather than entrepreneurial failure.

Finally, investment that seems worthwhile from a social point of view may not appear worthwhile from a private point of view. For example, if an innovator cannot capture profit from a successful innovation because imitation is too easy, then if the innovation is expensive each entrepreneur will wait for the others to make the first move. Conversely, an innovation may be profitable from a private point of view even though it is harmful from a social point of view – for example, because no charges are incurred for polluting the environment. This distinction between private and social returns is the basis of Baumol's (1990) distinction between 'productive' and 'unproductive' entrepreneurship.

The literature on entrepreneurial failure has touched upon all of these issues, but not in a systematic way. There is evidence that innovations made in other countries were ignored by some British entrepreneurs, despite British commentators urging that they should be imitated, while other innovations were adopted only with considerable delay. Some investments which might have been socially beneficial in maintaining employment in isolated reasons may have been rejected because the entrepreneurs concerned were fixing prices and restricting output. Overall, the debate remains inconclusive on whether more investments, made sooner, would have been more successful or not.

A satisfactory analysis of entrepreneurial decline needs to embed the issue within a wider perspective. There was significant emigration of entrepreneurial individuals, who left to colonize the growing Empire, and the London capital market played a major role in channelling resources to their overseas ventures. The great railway and mining entrepreneurs did not so much disappear, as transfer their skills overseas once the domestic railways system had matured, and traditional mining areas had begun to decline. Supplies of entrepreneurship are finite, and migration is a selective process. It is therefore hardly surprising that the limited group of less entrepreneurial businessmen who remained behind in Britain, and inherited family businesses, concentrated their efforts on managing their existing Imperial export trade, rather than pioneering new industries, in the manner of entrepreneurs in other countries that were attempting to 'catch up' with Britain. Moreover, in so far as there were deficiencies in UK technological innovation, these may have more to do with the limitation of the English university system than the quality of entrepreneurship per se – thus Scottish entrepreneurs were very active in high-technology shipbuilding throughout the period of 'decline'.

ENTERPRISE CULTURE

When there is a general perception in a society that volatility has increased, social and political attitudes may change as well. This is what appears to have happened in many Western industrial countries towards the end of the 1970s. Increasing awareness of global competition, and the failure of large-firm 'national champions' to respond effectively, led people to believe that future job-creation would come from small business. Recognizing the risks involved in small-firm start-up, the USA and the UK governments sought to reduce marginal tax rates in order to encourage risk-taking. Successful entrepreneurs became popular 'role models', creating a new set of myths about the 'rags to riches' entrepreneur. This 'enterprise culture' encouraged young people to make their careers in the private sector; recruitment to the public sector was discouraged through loss of status and pay restraint.

Considered as a historical phenomenon, the enterprise culture of the 1980s and 1990s was a natural reaction to some of the anti-entrepreneurial attitudes that had taken root in the West in the early post-war period. The growth of the Welfare State allowed public investment to 'crowd out' private investment, while the Cold War focused inventive activity on military projects. Productivity stagnated, while Keynesian full employment policy sustained unrealistic wage aspirations.

It should not be inferred, however, that the enterprise culture of the 1980s and 1990s was based on a correct understanding of the role of the entrepreneur. The highly competitive and materialistic form of individualism promoted by 'enterprise culture' did not accurately represent the dominant values of successful entrepreneurs of previous generations. For example, the Victorian railway entrepreneurs operated through social networks based in Britain's major provincial towns and cities. The limited amount of historical evidence that has been collected and analysed in a systematic way suggests that successful entrepreneurship is as much a cooperative endeavour, mediated by entrepreneurial networks, as a purely individualistic and competitive one.

REFERENCES

Aldcroft, Derek (1964), 'The entrepreneur and the British Economy, 1870–1914', *Economic History Review*, 2nd series, **17**, 113–34.

Baumol, William J. (1990), 'Entrepreneurship: productive, unproductive and destructive', *Journal of Political Economy*, **98** (5), 893–921.

Brenner, Reuven (1983), *History: The Human Gamble*, Chicago, IL: University of Chicago Press.

Cantillon, Richard (1755), *Essai sur la Nature du Commerce en Generale*, ed. Henry Higgs, London: Macmillan, 1931 edn.

Casson, Mark (1982), *The Entrepreneur: An Economic Theory*, Oxford: Martin Robertson.

Church, Roy (1993), 'The family firm in industrial capitalism: international perspectives on hypotheses and history', *Business History*, **35** (4), 17–43.

Hayek, Friedrich A. von (1937), Economics and knowledge', *Economica*, new series, **4**, 33–54.

Hughes, Jonathan R.T. (1965), *The Vital Few: The Entrepreneur & American Economic Progress*, New York: Oxford University Press.

Jones, Eric (1981), *The European Miracle*, Cambridge: Cambridge University Press.
Jones, Eric (1988), *Growth Recurring*, Oxford: Clarendon Press.
Kirzner, Israel M. (1973), *Competition and Entrepreneurship*, Chicago, IL: University of Chicago Press.
Knight, Frank H. (1921), *Risk, Uncertainty and Profit*, Boston, MA: Houghton Mifflin.
Marshall, Alfred (1919), *Industry and Trade*, London: Macmillan.
Sandberg, L.G. (1981), The entrepreneur and technological change, in R. Floud and D. McCloskey (eds), *The Economic History of Britain since 1700: 2. 1860 to the 1970s*, Cambridge: Cambridge University Press, pp. 99–120.
Sarachek, B. (1978), 'American entrepreneurs and the Horatio Alger myth', *Journal of Economic History*, **38**, 439–56.
Schumpeter, Joseph A. (1934), *The Theory of Economic Development*, trans. Redvers Opie, Cambridge, MA: Harvard University Press.
Schumpeter, Joseph A. (1939), *Business Cycles*, New York: McGraw-Hill.
Smiles, Samuel (1862), *Lives of the Engineers*, London: John Murray.
Solomou, Solomos (1987), *Phases of Economic Growth, 1850–1973*, Cambridge: Cambridge University Press.
Taussig, Frank W. (1915), *Inventors and Moneymakers*, New York: Macmillan.
Wiener, Martin J. (1981), *English Culture and the Decline of the Industrial Spirit*, Cambridge: Cambridge University Press.

24 Hotelier entrepreneur

Kirk Frith

A hotelier entrepreneur is an entrepreneur in the hotel business. Traditionally, an entrepreneur would own and operate one hotel. Conrad Nicholson Hilton (1887–1979) changed this when he created the world's first international hotel chain. This entry will focus on Hilton. The business career of Conrad Hilton was beset with obstacles, including both the First and the Second World Wars, the Great Depression as well as personal difficulties including the untimely death of his father and the break-up of his first marriage. However, despite the very difficult and often uncontrollable circumstances under which Conrad Hilton had to conduct his business activities, he revolutionized the hotel industry, first in the USA and later, using the resources so acquired, across the globe. Although Conrad Hilton was keen to buy and build hotels that had distinctive characters, he pioneered the process of standardization that ensured guests would have a familiar and comfortable stay no matter where they were in the world.

Conrad Hilton was born on 25 December 1887 in San Antonio, New Mexico Territory (now New Mexico). Born into a relatively prosperous immigrant family, Conrad Hilton was immersed in the business world from an early age. Conrad's father, August Hilton, had built and lost several fortunes in spectacular style but had managed to maintain his flagship enterprise, a large general store, which allowed him to build and live in a large and comfortable family home. In response to financial difficulties and under the direction of young Conrad, the Hilton's transformed their family home into a modest inn where, for $1 a night, travellers were given a good clean room and a large home-cooked meal.

In collaboration with his father, Conrad purchased his first hotel in 1919; the Mobley Hotel in Cisco, Texas. The hotel was an unassuming affair designed to service the Texas oil fields. Using the profits made at the Mobley Hotel, Conrad Hilton embarked on an aggressive purchasing strategy which saw him purchase a large number of hotels across Texas. In 1925, Conrad Hilton built and opened his first high-rise hotel, the Dallas Hilton (now the Hotel Indigo). However, the global economy was hit by the great depression at the end of the 1920s, causing a significant and sustained downturn in the hotel industry. The hotels of Conrad Hilton suffered as much as most with a lack of travellers resulting in reduced occupancy rates and declining levels of profitability. Within two years, creditors were threatening to foreclose and bankruptcy was becoming a probability as opposed to a possibility. It was around this time that Conrad Hilton came across a picture of New York's Waldorf-Astoria, built in 1931. Clipping the picture out of the magazine, Conrad Hilton wrote across it, 'the greatest of them all'. Conrad Hilton kept the picture close to him throughout the following years. The Waldorf-Astoria is featured in Figure 24.1.

Though many of Conrad Hilton's hotels were repossessed, his knowledge and expertise of the hotel industry ensured that he was retained as general manager. As the economy began to recover, Conrad Hilton was given and took the opportunity to

Figure 24.1 The Waldorf-Astoria; photograph by Léo-Paul Dana

purchase back the hotels he had lost during the depression. With increasing confidence in the United States economy, Conrad Hilton once again embarked on an aggressive purchasing campaign of hotels across Texas. In 1939, Conrad Hilton built and opened his first hotel outside of Texas, in Albuquerque, New Mexico. The first modern high-rise in New Mexico, this was Hilton's fourth hotel (see Figure 24.2).

In 1942, Conrad Hilton married Hollywood-star Zsa Zsa Gabor. In 1943, Hilton Hotels became the first coast-to-coast hotel chain in the USA. In 1946, the Hilton Hotels Corporation was formed, and became the first hotel chain to be listed on the New York Stock Exchange. The following year, Conrad Hilton formed the Hilton International Company – a name which quite clearly signalled Conrad Hilton's future business intentions.

The Hilton International Company opened its first hotel outside the USA, the Caribe Hilton in San Juan, Puerto Rico, in late 1949. In the same year, and 18 years after removing the photograph from a magazine, Conrad Hilton purchased the Waldorf-Astoria. Holding the picture throughout those many years helped give shape and substance to Conrad Hilton's ambition of being the leading hotelier in the world. This personal and career landmark was swiftly followed by the opening of the first overseas hotel, the Castellena Hotel, in Madrid, Spain. By focusing on the development of his portfolio of international hotels, Conrad Hilton was well poised to profit from the growth in international travel enabled by technological advances occurring in the civilian aviation

Figure 24.2 *Hilton's first hotel outside of Texas, renamed La Posada de Albuquerque in 1984 and reopened in 2009 as the Andaluz; photograph by Léo-Paul Dana*

industry. The following decade saw Conrad Hilton cement his reputation as the founder of the leading hotel brand in world. The aggressive purchasing strategy that had defined Conrad Hilton's early years as a hotelier continued throughout the 1950s and 1960s.

Conrad Hilton retired his presidency of Hilton Hotels Corporation towards the latter half of the 1960s, passing active control to his second son, Barron Hilton. At the time of his death, 3 January 1979, the Hilton Hotel Corporation owned 185 hotels in the USA and a further 75 in foreign countries.

25 Howard Hughes

Teresa E. Dana

Among the great entrepreneurs and philanthropists (see Acs and Dana, 2001, on entrepreneurship and philanthropy) of the twentieth century, Howard Robard Hughes was born in Texas in 1905 and lived until 1976. He was the only child of Howard Hughes Senior, who had patented the two-cone roller bit, an innovative tool that revolutionized oil drilling, and that was sold by his enterprise, the Hughes Tool Company. Howard Hughes, the son, became a film producer and industrialist. He also redefined the competitive environment for trans-Atlantic air travel, to the benefit of consumers as well as his airline. He was America's first billionaire (Hack, 2002). (See also Barlett and Steele, 1979; Dietrich and Thomas, 1972; Keats 1966; and Moore, 1984.)

In 1922 Howard's mother died from pregnancy complications. In 1925, he moved to California where he became a film producer the following year. In 1932, he founded the innovative Hughes Aircraft Company, the shares of which he later donated to the Howard Hughes Medical Institute. In 1939, he was awarded the Congressional Gold Medal in recognition of his achievements in advancing science.

Howard Hughes contributed to the development of the Boeing 307 Stratoliner (see Figure 25.1), the first commercial airliner to feature a pressurised cabin. Transcontinental & Western Air (TWA) – formed in 1930 when Transcontinental Air Transport merged with Western Air Express – would receive its first Boeing 307 in 1940. Meanwhile, Hughes had begun investing in the airline and by 1941 he had purchased controlling interest of the airline of which Charles Lindbergh (see Figure 25.2) was formerly President.

During his presidency, Lindbergh asked Douglas Aircraft, of Long Beach California, to design an aeroplane with transcontinental capabilities. This resulted in the DC-1 (see Figure 25.3), the bigger DC-2 (see Figure 25.4), and DC-3 Douglas Sleeper Transport (see Figure 25.5). By 1938, the DC-3 was carrying 95 per cent of United States air traffic.

Howard Hughes approached Lockheed to build an even better aeroplane, to replace the Boeing 307. The result was the Lockheed Constellation (see Figure 25.6), capable of flying across the Atlantic Ocean. TWA bought 40 of these.

During World War II, TWA flew 40 million miles for the United States military and Howard planned route expansions once the war would be over. When Pan American World Airways attempted to be the only US-based airline allowed to cross the Atlantic, Howard personally defended the right to have competition. He succeeded and in 1946 his Lockheed Constellations flew transatlantic for TWA, which he renamed Trans World Airlines.

In 1947 Howard flew his Spruce Goose, the largest aeroplane ever made of wood (Barton, 1982). In 1948, he gained control of a studio in Hollywood.

In 1961, Trans World Airlines retired its Lockheed 1649 Starliner (Figure 25.7) from the New York–Rome route, thus becoming the first airline to use only jet aircraft on international services. Among TWA's jets was the 615 mile-per-hour Convair 880

Figure 25.1 *TWA Boeing 307 Stratoliner; TWA photograph courtesy of Carl Barley, editor,* TWA Seniors Skyliner

Figure 25.2 *Charles A. Lindbergh at left, with Juan T. Trippe, founder of Pan American World Airways; photograph courtesy of Pan American World Airways*

Figure 25.3 *TWA Douglas DC-1 at Glendale, California; TWA photograph courtesy of Carl Barley, editor,* TWA Seniors Skyliner

Figure 25.4 *American Airlines Douglas DC-2; photograph courtesy of American Airlines*

Figure 25.5 *United Air Lines Douglas DC-3; photograph courtesy of United Airlines*

Figure 25.6 *TWA Lockheed Constellation 749; TWA photograph courtesy of Carl Barley, editor,* TWA Seniors Skyliner

Figure 25.7 *TWA Lockheed 1649 Starliner; TWA photograph courtesy of Carl Barley, editor,* TWA Seniors Skyliner

Figure 25.8 *Convair 880 formerly belonging to Elvis Presley; photograph by Léo-Paul Dana*

Figure 25.9 Republic Airlines Convair 580 turbo-prop; photograph by Léo-Paul Dana

Figure 25.10 NWA Airbus 319; photograph by Léo-Paul Dana

(Figure 25.8) an aeroplane type that broke many speed records and still holds some today.

In 1962, Trans World Airlines opened its Terminal 5 at New York's Idlewild Airport, renamed JFK the following year. In 1967, Trans World Airlines purchased Hilton International, operator of Hilton Hotels outside the USA (see separate entry on Hilton, Chapter 24 in this volume). In 1970, Hughes used profits from the sale of Trans World Airlines to purchase Air West and create Hughes Air West, later merged into Republic (see Figure 25.9) and subsequently engulfed by Northwest Orient, later NWA (see Figure 25.10). In 2008, Delta Air Lines announced its intention to absorb NWA, which it did in 2009.

REFERENCES

Acs, Zoltan J. and Léo-Paul Dana (2001), 'Two views of wealth creation', *Small Business Economics*, **16** (2), 63–74.

Barlett, Donald L. and James B. Steele (1979), *Empire: The Life, Legend, and Madness of Howard Hughes*, New York: W.W. Norton.

Barton, Charles (1982), *Howard Hughes and his Flying Boat*, Fallbrook, CA: Aero.

Dietrich, Noah and Bob Thomas (1972), *Howard: The Amazing Mr Hughes*, Greenwich, CT: Fawcett Publications.

Hack, Richard (2002), *Hughes: The Private Diaries, Memos and Letters: The Definitive Biography of the First American Billionaire*, Beverly Hills, CA: New Millennium Press.

Keats, John (1966), *Howard Hughes*, New York: Random House.

Moore, Terry (1984), *The Beauty and the Billionaire*, New York: Pocket Books.

26 The Hudson's Bay Company

Lynn Ferguson

Chartered on 2 May 1670, the Hudson's Bay Company (HBC) is the oldest incorporated joint-stock merchandising company in the English-speaking world. King Charles II approved the charter incorporating the group as 'The Governor and Company of Adventurers of England trading into the Hudson's Bay'.

These were the signatories of the Royal Charter – the original investors of the 'The Governor and Company of Adventurers of England trading into the Hudson's Bay':

1. *Prince Rupert* – Count Palatine of the Rhine, Duke of Bavaria and Cumberland, Earl of Holderness, the first Governor of 'Rupert's Land' and dear cousin to King Charles II.
2. *Sir George Carteret* – considered to be the wealthiest man in England at the time.
3. *Anthony Ashley Cooper*, Lord Ashley, Earl of Shaftesbury – recognized as the 'Father of modern Liberalism'.
4. *Christopher Monck*, 2nd Duke of Albemarle – Member of Parliament for Devonshire, Gentleman of the Bedchamber, Lord Lieutenant of Devon.
5. *Sir James Hayes* – Barrister-at-law and Member of Parliament.
6. *Sir Robert Vyner* – Prince of the Goldsmiths, Controller of the Mint, and Sheriff and Lord Mayor of London.
7. *Sir John Robinson* – an administrative wizard holding the positions of Committeeman of the East India Company, Court Assistant (chief lobbyist) for the Levant Company, Lord Lieutenant of the Tower of London, Member of the House of Commons, Colonel of the Green Regiment, preceded Sir Robert Vyner as the Lord Mayor of London and acted as the first Deputy Governor of the Hudson's Bay Company from 1670 to 1673.
8. *Sir William Craven*, Earl of Craven – had his estates seized by Oliver Cromwell for supporting King Charles II during his Continental exile. House of Stuart after King Charles II regained power. Held the positions of Privy Councillor, Tangier commissioner, Master of Trinity House, a Lord Proprietor of the Carolinas and a patentee of the Royal Fisheries Company.
9. *Sir Peter Colleton* – served a term as Governor of Barbados.
10. *Sir John Kirke* – the only adventurer with first-hand knowledge of the fur trade in America with an understanding and familiarity with both the European markets and the French goods and methods of trading. Publicized the Hudson's Bay beaver hats in England.
11. *Sir Paul Neele* – philosopher and founding member of the Royal Society.
12. *Sir Edward Hungerford* – Knight of the Bath, elected to the House of Commons.
13. *John Portman* – Hudson's Bay Company's first Treasurer, goldsmith and banker, treasurer of the Carolinas and New Providence (Bahamas) companies.
14. *Francis Millington* – Commissioner of Customs, draper and brewer.

15. *Sir John Griffith* – Professional soldier and Keeper at the Blockhouses of West Tilbury and Gravesend.
16. *William Pretyman* – held the title of King's Remembrancer of the First Fruits, and held a sinecure with the Treasury.
17. *John Fenn* – Paymaster of the Admiralty.
18. *Henry Bennet* Lord Arlington – Secretary of State, Keeper of the Privy Purse.

The Royal Charter stipulated several points of political and monetary significance for both the Crown and the investors including:

Structure – the structure of the company's authority was to be made up of a board of seven members, lead by the Governor (his cousin, Prince Rupert) and Deputy Governor.
Minerals – the right to utilize mineral deposits as they saw fit.
Land – extent of land covered by the Charter, namely, forty per cent of present-day Canadian boundaries.

The following is taken from original Royal Charter:

> . . . have, at their own great Cost and Charges, undertaken an Expedition for Hudson's Bay in the North-west Part of America, for the Discovery of a new Passage into the South Sea, and for the finding some Trade for Furs, Minerals, and other considerable Commodities, and by such their Undertaking, have already made such Discoveries as do encourage them to proceed further in Pursuance of their said Design, by means whereof there may probably arise very great Advantage to Us and Our Kingdom. AND WHEREAS the said Undertakers, for their further Encouragement in the said Design, have humbly besought Us to incorporate them, and grant unto them, and their Successors, the sole Trade and Commerce of all those Seas, Straits, Bays, Rivers, Lakes, Creeks, and Sounds, in whatsoever Latitude they shall be, that lie within the entrance of the Straits commonly called Hudson's Straits, together with all the Lands, Countries and Territories, upon the Coasts and Confines of the Seas, Straits, Bays, Lakes, Rivers, Creeks and Sounds, aforesaid, which are not now actually possessed by any of our Subjects, or by the Subjects of any other Christian Prince or State. (Royal Charter 1670)

THE COMPANY'S ENTREPRENEURSHIP

At one point, the Hudson's Bay Company owned much of Canada (Stefansson, 1908). Trading posts and stores, flying the company flag, opened at the junctions of rivers encompassing the Hudson Bay. Alliances were formed with bands of Cree traders living in the area. The blueprint for success, created by the company's original investors, was beginning to show a profit, for both the company and the indigenous people, but the European system of sovereignty and land holding was unfamiliar to the political systems of the indigenous groups, living in Rupert's Land. Aboriginal beliefs of land and ownership did not coincide with the European, possession and control, point of view.

The indigenous people knew their land, taught the Europeans how to build canoes for transportation, and showed them the best trails and canoe routes. Many Europeans would not have survived without the help of friendly aboriginal peoples. Dying of hunger and sickness the Huron and Algonquin helped them by providing food, and showing them how to boil spruce bark to cure scurvy. They showed the settlers how to live in the freezing climate, made mittens and leggings for them, and taught them how to snowshoe and toboggan, allowing them to travel in the winter.

The indigenous people were no strangers to hard work and offered their knowledge of the land and willingness to work to their new friends. The Cree, for instance, provided a connection between the trading posts by delivering the much anticipated mail. Since maps had not been drawn of the areas, and they knew the routes and trails, they were hired as guides. Maps of the routes were drawn in the sand, on birch bark, in the dirt, or in the snow.

The Iroquois, originally from the east, moved west with the fur trade, some travelled all the way to British Columbia. The Iroquois were thrifty, clever traders, but also proud warriors, which often got them into trouble with other aboriginal people.

Indigenous women were employed to prepare furs for transportation. The Europeans made money faster with these talented women, since the unit of currency, established by the European system, was based on a beaver pelt, cleaned, stretched and tanned. The 'Made Beaver' or 'MB' was traded at the Hudson's Bay posts for different European items. Other animal pelts, such as otter, squirrel or moose were quoted in MB equivalents. It was not remarkable for a European to be married to more than one native woman at that time. Times were changing and the places to trade pelts were becoming more competitive. More furs, more wives, different companies to trade with, meant more wealth.

COMPETITION

The Cree, Ojibwa, Montagnais, and Assiniboine would descend the Rupert, Moose, Albany or Eastmain Rivers to James Bay or down the Severn River or Hayes River to the west shore of Hudson Bay and know there was a Hudson's Bay Company outpost at each stop. Axes, kettles and other trade goods were more accessible as the trading posts grew in numbers. Native traders brought their trade goods far into the west, and each spring more canoes came downriver to the company posts. Competition was beginning to interfere with the company's profits, however. War with the French overflowed to the 'New World' where fierce wars saw France taking control of some of Britain's outposts. When the native people arrived at the outpost, they were met by the French, so they traded with whomever they could. The Treaty of Utrecht, in 1741, settled the unrest in Britain's favour, allowing Britain to regain control over their captured forts. After the Treaty, the competition took on a new faces, namely, the Northwest Company and the XY Company.

The North-West Company – formed by Simon McTavish, Isaac Todd and James McGill, after 1763 to exploit the North-West Territories not covered by the 1670 charter. In 1784 the North-West company gathered more investors and formalized its organization and name.

The XY Company – in 1798 some disgruntled members of the North-West Company organized the New North West Company, commonly known as the XY Company. The XY Company lasted until 1804 when they reconciled with the North West Company. In 1821 the British Parliament merged the North-West Company with the Hudson's Bay Company.

Competition was not only a problem with the Hudson's Bay; the aboriginal people had their competitions also. Wars between rival tribes were constant. The Huron, Susquehanne and the Seneca were literally wiped out, by the Iroquois, making the Iroquois the most powerful Eastern Nation.

EXPANSION

The Hudson's Bay Company expanded its holdings from Newfoundland (see Figure 26.1) to Vancouver Island and from the St. Lawrence to the Arctic. The popularity of their trading methods saw further expansion in the 1800s to the American Pacific Northwest, Alaska and Hawaii. There is a possibility that the Snake Country Expeditions reached as far south as Texas. In the 1920s there were HBC posts in the Russian Far East.

Through this expansion the Hudson's Bay Company encountered a large array of people by forming allies with other fur trade companies such as, the American Fur Company, the Russian American Company and Revillon Freres. In 1849 Britain granted the colony of Vancouver Island to the Hudson's Bay Company, to be developed as an agricultural community. Chief Factor James Douglas was appointed governor, in 1851. In, 1858, the existing colony of British Columbia, was formed out of New Caledonia. Sir James Douglas, governor of British Columbia, was ordered by the Crown to resign his commission with the company, beginning its independence from the Crown.

Figure 26.1 The Hudson's Bay Company in Newfoundland; photograph by Léo-Paul Dana

INDEPENDENCE

Success and adventure had attracted many Europeans to the 'New World', and by 1812 the company was obliged to provide supervision in the settlements. Up until now the company's chief concern was the fur trade, but the population was growing quickly and there was no other choice, but to take charge.

The International Financial Society bought controlling interest of the Hudson's Bay Company in 1863. Major changes were likely to happen in the not too distant future, because the majority of the new shareholders were more interested in real estate and the economic development of the West. Change also happened when the USA bought Alaska in 1867:

> The United States of America purchased Alaska from Russia in 1867, and within two years evicted Canadians from the Hudson Bay Company (HBC) post, Fort Yukon, that was built in 1846 on the Yukon River in Alaska . . . In 1870, the HBC ceded all interest in the Yukon Territory and Northwest Territories (NWT) to the Government of Canada . . . . Anderson, 2008: 185)

Under the terms of the agreement, the company received £300 000 and one-twentieth of the abundant areas for settlement. It also was able to keep title to the lands that already had trading establishments. The terms of the agreement strongly influenced company development after 1870. The amalgamation of Rupert's Land into the new Dominion of Canada meant that the HBC had to adapt as agricultural settlement. Retail stores began to appear in towns and cities across the prairies and British Columbia, leading to their slogan 'The Great Traders of the Great West'.

Trade and industry growth progressed quickly after 1870, as the amount of business with the settlers escalated. Originally, most of this activity was carried out at trading posts, but since the market was so much different than the trade with the native people, settlers accounts were separated. Retail and wholesale divisions eventually emerged, distinctly different from the fur trade outlets.

CHANGE

The company began opening department stores in 1912. The company became involved in the real estate market, selling farm lands and town lots. The retention of mineral rights, included with their properties, was the foundation of their ventures into the oil business. In 1926 it co-founded Hudson's Bay Oil and Gas.

Expansion across Canada continued for the company, from the 1960s to the early 1990s. Acquisition of companies such as: Morgan's, Freimans, Zellers, Simpsons (see Figure 26.2), Towers and Woodward's (see Figure 26.3), as shall be discussed below. The company even venturing so far as to acquire a mail-order liquor business during the Prohibition of the 1930s.

The Hudson's Bay Company took on the responsibility as shipping and purchasing agents for the governments of Romania, Belgium, Russia and France during the First World War. The 'French Government Business', business was so productive that a subordinate company, The Bay Steamship Company Ltd, was created to handle their fleet.

Figure 26.2 *Simpsons building in Montreal; photograph by Léo-Paul Dana*

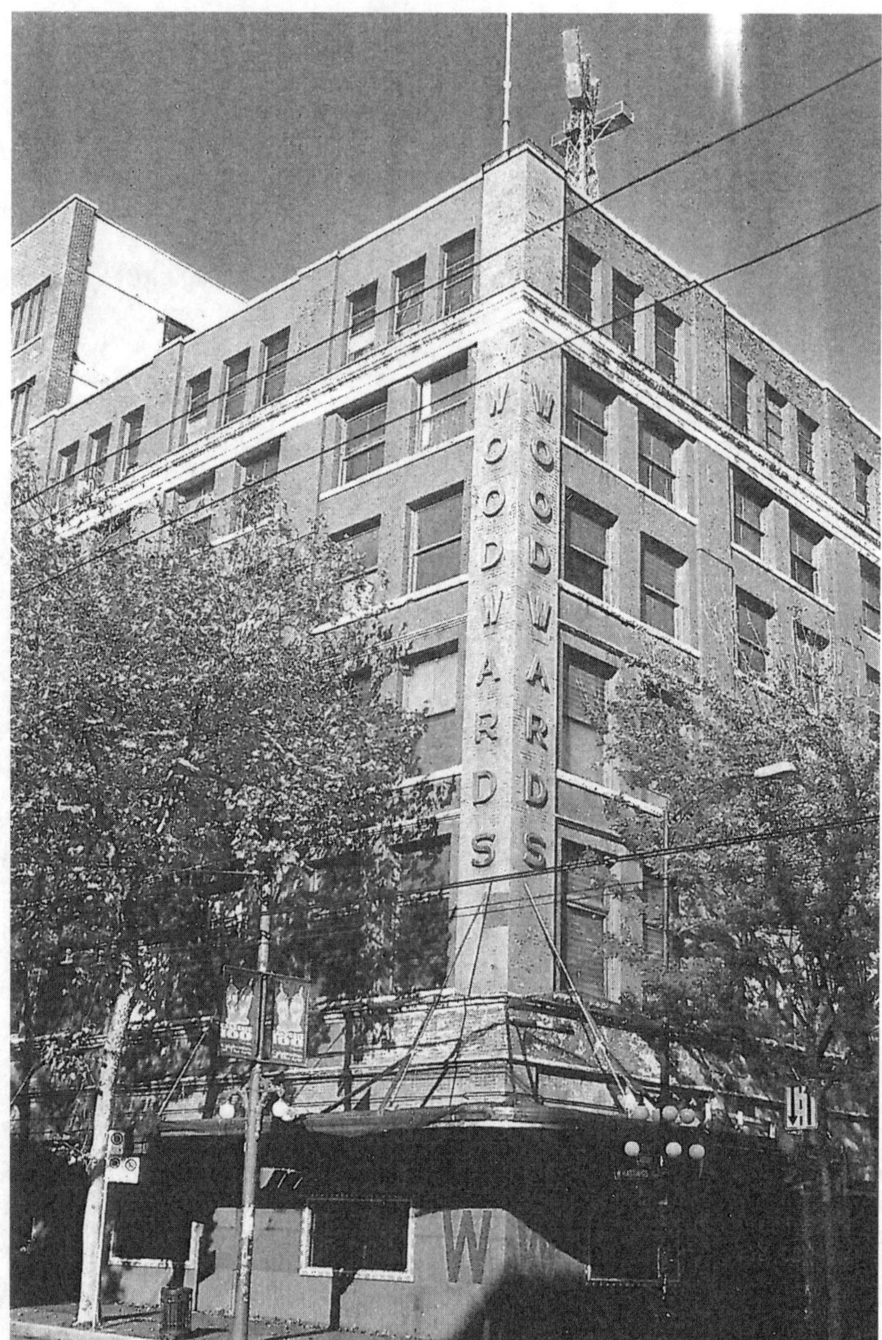

Figure 26.3 *This Woodwards was built in Vancouver in 1903 and the building was demolished in October 2006; photograph by Léo-Paul Dana*

Atypical businesses like frozen salmon companies, comic film productions and reindeer farming partnered with the company during the 1920s. The Hudson's Bay Company was spreading its wings, in a big way, all across Canada.

In 1960, the Hudson's Bay Company purchased the Henry Morgan department store in Montreal and renamed it La Baie, in 1972. Queen Elizabeth II granted a new charter to the company withdrawing most of the conditions of the original charter and officially transferring the company from the UK to Canada. Headquarters was established in Winnipeg, Manitoba, and later shifted to Toronto.

In 1978, the Hudson's Bay Company purchased the Zellers chain of stores. In 1979, the Hudson's Bay Company purchased the Simpson's chain of department stores. In 1987, the Hudson's Bay Company sold its Northern Stores. In 1998, the Hudson's Bay Company purchase Kmart Canada, formerly Kresge, and made these Zellers stores.

THE HUDSON'S BAY COMPANY TODAY

Real estate continues to be in the company veins. In 1973 it acquired control of Markborough Properties before branching it off in 1990 as an individual company. Also in 1973 the Hudson's Bay Company acquired 35 per cent of Siebens Oil and Gas, but disposed of it in 1979, only to buy controlling interest in Roxy Petroleum in 1980. In 1982 interest in HBOG was sold to Dome Petroleum.

Expansion was still primary for the Hudson's Bay Company in 1978, when, it purchased controlling interests in the Simpsons and Zellers retail chains. In the late 1970s a take over occurred between Canadian billionaire Kenneth Thomson and George Weston Limited fighting for control of the Hudson's Bay Company. Thomson eventually came out ahead obtaining a 75 per cent stake in a $400 million transaction.

In 1993 the Hudson's Bay Company purchased the bankrupt Woodwards Department Store chain and K-Mart Canada's stores followed in 1997, adding them to the Zellers division.

In 1997 the Thomson family sold the last of its shares, but in the superseding years they had sold off the company's interests in the oil and gas business, financial services and a distillery, along with other acquisitions, for approximately $550 million.

The Hudson's Bay Company leads its closest competitor, Sears, in terms of annual sales. In 2003, the Hudson's Bay Company published revenues of $7.4 billion and employed close to 70 000 employees working in 562 stores. The 7.4 billion in revenue for 2003 is broken down as follows: The Bay – 34.7 per cent; Zellers – 59.7 per cent; financial services from each store – 4.5 per cent; the rest of the revenue is divided up between Fields, and Home Outfitters. The company also reported $4.1 billion in total assets.

The Hudson's Bay Company permanently left the Canadian fur trade in January 1991, when it stopped selling fur coats, losing the estimated $350 million market. Today, the Hudson's Bay Company have retained their methods of trade through their stores and have now entered the computer age by offering online sales.

From its entrepreneurial roots, the Hudson's Bay Company has been an integral part of history for 340 years, and holds the distinction of being the longest operating corporation in Canada.

REFERENCES

Anderson, Erik (ed.) (2008), *Canada's Relationship with Inuit: A History of Policy and Program Development*, Ottawa: Minister of Indian Affairs and Northern Development.

Stefansson, V (1908), 'On the Mackenzie River', *Bulletin of the American Geographical Society*, **40** (3), 157–69.

27 Implicit theories of entrepreneurship

Jeffrey M. Pollack

Implicit theories that individuals hold about human characteristics have influence in numerous domains such as morality, personality, negotiation, leadership, intelligence, work and sports (for a review see Dweck and Leggett, 1988; Kray and Haselhuhn, 2007; Maurer et al., 2003). The idea that individuals differ in their belief systems and that these structures greatly influence attitudes and behavior is common to many perspectives on human behavior. For example, Piaget asserts that the development of meaning systems is as important as logical thinking in forming behavior (Piaget and Garcia, 1991). And, Kelly (1955: 8–9) suggests that each person sees the world through their own frame of reference or their own 'transparent template'. This social-cognitive approach is useful in an array of domains and would likely contribute to the study of entrepreneurship (Locke and Baum, 2007).

Specifically, Dweck's Implicit Theory Approach (ITA), which examines differences in goals, attributions, and motivational strategies stemming from a person's beliefs, may be a useful tool by which the literature on entrepreneurial motivation can be extended (Hong et al., 1999; Dweck and Leggett, 1988). For example, Dweck's ITA provides a framework for understanding a person's affect, cognition and behavior. The use of a social-cognitive approach within the field of entrepreneurship could prove promising for understanding goal-setting, achievement and responses to business setbacks for developing entrepreneurs (Dweck and Leggett, 1988).

Within the domain of entrepreneurship, a person can either hold an *entity implicit theory of entrepreneurship* (that is, entrepreneurs are 'born') or an *incremental implicit theory* (that is, entrepreneurs are 'made'). For instance, some individuals might believe more strongly in an *entity theory* adopting the idea that trying to change your entrepreneurial ability is like trying to change your natural eye and hair color (Pollack and Hawver, 2007), whereas some individuals might be more oriented towards an *incremental theory* believing that practice, hard work, effort, and persistence can change entrepreneurial ability (Pollack and Hawver, 2007).

A person's implicit theory of entrepreneurship, similar to other domains, will likely impact the propensity of an entrepreneur to be successful. People with entity and incremental meaning systems think, feel and act differently under similar situations. For example, two entrepreneurs who experience the same setback (for example, cost overruns, yearly losses) will react to the failure in accordance with their beliefs that guide the way they interpret their social world. A person more oriented towards an entity belief may react in maladaptive ways by expressing feelings of hopelessness, inadequacy and discouragement. In contrast, more incremental views can help buffer the potential downside of setbacks. For incremental theorists, failure has different meaning. It is an indication that more work or a different strategy is needed, rather than an indication that one lacks to ability to succeed. Thus, individuals with incremental beliefs should react with more positive coping strategies (for example, seeking the advice of a mentor, setting goals, working harder).

Locke and Baum observe that 'Nearly all entrepreneurs at some point in their careers will confront difficult obstacles (e.g., barriers to entry) or will have setbacks (e.g., a product that does not work as planned, cost overruns) or will even fail completely (and have to start over)' (2007: 102). How a person responds to the inevitable setbacks an entrepreneur encounters is a defining characteristic between entrepreneurs and non-entrepreneurs (Baum and Locke, 2004; Locke and Baum, 2007; Shaver and Scott, 1991; Shepherd, 2004). A person's implicit beliefs about the nature of entrepreneurial ability influence intentions in response to setbacks, establish the framework by which events are interpreted and this line of research, examining individual-level cognitive processes, may be particularly useful in understanding persistence in the face of challenges within the field of entrepreneurship (Baron, 1998; 2004).

REFERENCES

Baron, R. (1998), 'Cognitive mechanisms in entrepreneurship: why and when entrepreneurs think differently than other people', *Journal of Business Venturing*, **13** (4), 275–94.

Baron, R. (2004), 'Cognitive perspective: a valuable tool for answering entrepreneurship's basic "why" questions' *Journal of Business Venturing*, **19** (2), 221–39.

Baum, J.R. and E.A. Locke (2004), 'The relationship of entrepreneurial traits, skills and motivation to subsequent venture growth', *Journal of Applied Psychology*, **89**, 587–98.

Dweck, C.S. and E.L. Leggett (1988), 'A social-cognitive approach to motivation and personality', *Psychological Review*, **25**, 109–16.

Hong, Y., C. Chiu, C.S. Dweck, D. Lin and W. Wan (1999), 'Implicit theories, attributions, and coping: a meaning system approach', *Journal of Personality and Social Psychology*, **77**, 588–99.

Kelly, G.A. (1955), *The Psychology of Personal Constructs*, New York: W.W. Norton.

Kray, L.J. and M.P. Haselhuhn (2007), 'Implicit negation beliefs and performance: experimental and longitudinal evidence', *Journal of Personality and Social Psychology*, **93** (1), 49–64.

Locke, E.A. and J.R. Baum (2007), 'Entrepreneurial motivation' in J.R. Baum, M. Frese and R. Baron (eds), *The Psychology of Entrepreneurship*, Mahwah, NJ: Lawrence Erlbaum, pp. 93–112.

Maurer, T.J., K.A. Wrenn, H.R. Pierce, S.A. Tross and W.C. Collins (2003), 'Beliefs about "improvability" of career relevant skills: relevance to job/task analysis, competency modeling, and learning orientation', *Journal of Organizational Behavior*, **24** (1), 107–31.

Piaget, J. and R. Garcia (1991), *Toward a Logic of Meanings*, trans. P. Davidson and J.A. Easley Jr, Hillsdale, NJ: Erlbaum.

Pollack, J.M. and T.H. Hawver (2007), 'Predicting entrepreneurial success: a conceptual social-cognitive model', proceedings of the annual meetings of the Southern Management Association (SMA), Nashville, TN, November.

Shaver, K.G. and L.R. Scott (1991), 'Person, process, choice: the psychology of new venture creation', *Entrepreneurship Theory and Practice*, Winter, 23–45.

Shepherd, D.A. (2004), 'Educating entrepreneurship students about emotion and learning from failure', *Academy of Management Learning and Education*, **3** (3), 274–87.

28 Indigenous entrepreneurship as a function of cultural perceptions of opportunity

Léo-Paul Dana and Robert Brent Anderson

INTRODUCTION

Why do individuals from some nations have a greater propensity to engage in different forms of entrepreneurship, than do others who have unlike values? It appears that any given situation may present itself as an opportunity, or not, based on culturally influenced interpretation. Helander argued that 'the time is ripe for a new paradigm when looking at the issues of indigenous people' (1999: 26–27). Indeed, it is.

The leading scholars who contributed to Dana and Anderson (2007) discussed the contemporary economic activities of indigenous peoples from a variety of perspectives, including anthropology, business, development, education, entrepreneurship, ethnic studies, geography, management, sociology and subsistence. The editors could have assigned categories of analysis prior to data collection; instead, we wished to avoid imposing classifications in advance. Taking an emic approach, we opted to seek units of conceptualization by analysing the experiences of the people studied. Let us consider some inductive analysis, to identify patterns, themes that emerge from the data described in the collection.

OBSERVATIONS AND PATTERNS

1 Heterogeneity among Indigenous Peoples

There is rich heterogeneity among indigenous peoples; their respective values are far from identical. Even within one indigenous people, there can be significant differences, as explained, for example, by Helena Ruotsola's chapter in Dana and Anderson (2007). Some people are Dionysian, with emphasis on being. Others are Promethean, with emphasis on doing. Benedict wrote, 'Like most of the American Indians, except those of the Southwest pueblos, the tribes of the Northwest Coast were Dionysian' (1935: 175). More recently, Renshaw wrote:

> in order to understand the economy of the Chaco societies one must look beyond the external constraints that determine the Indian's economic situation and consider the system of values that underlies the economy. This system of values, with its emphasis on equality and personal autonomy, is, I believe, a defining feature of the Indians' sense of ethnic identity. An understanding of the Chaco societies' economic values, especially their conceptions of property . . . also helps shed light on their . . . preference for wage labor over other forms of production. (2002: 180)

Dana (2007: 152) explained that even one region reveals differences among unlike indigenous peoples, 'the Mina came to dominate to the exclusion of northern tribes, whom they treated as savages and excluded from significant positions'. In Dana and Anderson (2007), Nkongolo-Bakenda described the differing approaches to entrepreneurship among the Nande, Luba-Kasai and the Kumu in Northern Congo. Other authors bring out differences in a similar manner.

Olurode (2007) wrote that in Nigeria, the Yoruba regard work as the essence of creation; therefore, right from childhood, the young are socialized into a world of work. Older adults who fail to allocate roles to children may be regarded as permissive, as it is believed by the Yoruba that the only antidote against poverty is work. Work is not regarded as an ordeal but an integral part of social existence; in order to make it a routine, while work tasks are carried out, these may be interspersed with light entertainment, jokes, singing and dancing. Those who detest work are referred to as *ole* – the lazy ones – considered to be companions of thieves. Those who are wretched or poor because of failure to work or who display a positive attitude to work are undeserving of support.

We would like to emphasize, therefore, that there is not only one indigenous worldview about entrepreneurship. What we find that does tie indigenous approaches together is a special attachment to 'place' as the original inhabitant, that in most cases has been disrupted by relatively recent experience with colonization (military and/or economic) usually by the nations of the 'core'. And there is usually a related desire to reassert control over traditional territories and rebuild their communities with entrepreneurship and enterprise, shaped by history, culture[1] and values, often playing a prominent role in this process.

2 Incompatibility with Assumptions of Mainstream Theories

Cultural values of indigenous peoples are often incompatible with the basic assumptions of mainstream theories, which may be based on a different set of cultural values. As noted by Dana et al. (2005), entrepreneurship among the Inuit is different in form and substance from the commonly accepted model. This implies that when a person from an indigenous group starts a business, it may be difficult for people from unlike cultures to understand fully the causal variables and rationale behind attitudes toward enterprise. Renshaw, for instance, wrote, 'the system of tenure in the Indian colonies reflects the Indians' resistance to the idea of individual landholding, a resistance that is so strong that desire to hold individual title is taken as evidence that a person wants to adopt Paraguayan rather than Indian identity' (2002: 164). In Dana and Anderson (2007: 20), Wuttunee explained that what sets them apart are the personal values that they choose to bring to the workplace. Yet, as Hindle and Landsdowne indicated in Chapter 2 of Dana and Anderson (2007), 'entrepreneurship research has shown scant interest in values'. An exception is Dana (2006). Another exception is Chapter 9 in Dana and Anderson (2007), about Basuto culture in Lesotho, showing how cattle have an intrinsic value in this kingdom.

In Dana and Anderson (2007), Chapter 8 about the Maasai, Ndemo reported that results show that if it was their choice, they would rather retain their traditional economic system instead of integrating themselves with the rest of Kenya in a market economy. Chapter 9 of the same volume, about Basuto culture, showed how cultural values influence the definition of commodities and influences entrepreneurship accordingly. This confirms Dana (1995) who showed that aboriginal and non-aboriginal persons expressed fundamentally different concepts of self-employment; findings suggested that the causal variable behind entrepreneurship is *not* simply an opportunity, but rather one's *cultural perception of opportunity*.

Chapter 19 in Dana and Anderson (2007), by Rønning, explained that likewise the historical, natural and cultural landscape in which Sámi people live and undertake their reindeer herding business makes a strong contextual framework that itself has a conservative effect on change in the industry. While mainstream economics suggest that rationally one might choose to maximize profit, we learn from indigenous people that entrepreneurship has *non-economic* causal variables. The individual profit motive exists; however, there are also community needs and objectives.

Likewise, Degen's Chapter 10 in Dana and Anderson (2007: 115), noted that Bedouins persist in raising sheep, even at an economic loss, for 'maintenance of Bedouin traditional lifestyle'. Chapter 26 about the Namgis First Nation explained that some sales had an economic motivation, others a symbolic one. This supports the earlier findings of Lindsay, who stated 'indigenous entrepreneurship is more holistic than non-indigenous entrepreneurship; it focuses on both economic and non-economic objectives' (2005: 1).

3 Immediately Available Resources

Indigenous people are often close to nature and in some cases depend on immediately available resources, such as animals or fish; the Oroqen people, for instance, were hunter-gatherers until the 1980s. Chapter 14 of Dana and Anderson (2007) stated 'Ainu are self-employed fishermen, hunters and collectors by heritage'. As illustrated in Chapter 15 the Dhivehis also rely on immediately available resources. Sejersen, in Chapter 17 found the same among the Inuit of Greenland. Chapter 25 by William Simeone described the economy of the Athabaskan-speaking Han, based on hunting, fishing and gathering. Chapter 26 about the Namgis First Nation discussed the traditional reliance of the Kwakwaka'wakw economy, on immediately available resources. Likewise, Chapter 29, about Iqaluit illustrated the Inuit practice of relying on immediately available resources. Chapter 31 by Wall and Masayesva described how the Hopi relied strictly on precipitation and runoff water, along with hard work and prayer. This is consistent with earlier findings. About the Sámi people, Müller-Wille wrote, 'Original, indigenous land use was based on locally available renewable resources' (1987: 352). Renshaw described 'the lack of any perceived need for long-term planning, since the Indians of the Chaco assume that their needs can be met on a day-to-day basis' (2002: 157). Hukkinen et al. (2006) noted the goal of promoting reindeer herding *based on natural pastures (as opposed to feeding), which provides the herders with employment and income.* In contrast to mainstream societies, where firms have regular working hours, work in indigenous communities is *often irregular*, depending on animals, the weather or the tide.

4 Sustainability

Indigenous enterprise is often environmentally sustainable. As noted by Harris, 'Wastefulness is more a characteristic of a modern agribusiness than of traditional peasant economies. Under . . . automated feed-lot beef production in the United States, for example, cattle manure not only goes unused, but it is allowed to contaminate ground water over wide areas and contributes to the pollution of nearby lakes and streams' (1974: 31–2). Along the same theme, Morgan wrote, 'It is truly amazing that after fifty thousand years they have destroyed no forests, polluted no water, endangered no species, caused no contamination, and all the while they have received food and shelter. They have laughed a lot and cried very little' (1999: 111). While this may be an overstatement – there are certainly cases where indigenous populations have had a considerable impact on the environment – there are several chapters in our volume which illustrate sustainable activities often associated with traditional practises. For example, in Chapter 20 of Dana and Anderson (2007) Solveig Joks noted that Sámi reindeer herders utilized all parts of the slaughtered reindeer in an environmentally sustainable manner.

5 Kinship Ties

Social organization among indigenous people is often based on complex kinship ties, and not created in response to market needs. In Dana and Anderson (2007), Degen described the division of labour among self-employed Bedouins. Likewise, business activity and personal autonomy among the Sámi, are so intimately interwoven that it is difficult for the individual person to differentiate between business and household. In Chapter 11 of the same volume, Povoroznyuk also emphasized the importance of the family, and Ruotsola's Chapter 23 explained that Sámi reindeer owners employed their relatives. In Chapter 25, William Simeone explained that among the Athabaskan-speaking Han the distribution of resources was structured along kinship lines. Again, this is all consistent with earlier findings. Renshaw, for instance, explained, 'on the few occasions when individuals have tried to engage in commerce . . . stores have disappeared within a few weeks, since their owners have felt obliged to give credit to their kin and neighbors until the entire stock was used up' (2002: 179). Lindsay explained:

> the indigenous 'team' involved in new venture creation and development may involve not only the entrepreneur and the business' entrepreneurial team but also the entrepreneur's family, extended family, and/or the community. Thus, in indigenous businesses, there are more stakeholders involved than with non-indigenous businesses. For this reason, indigenous businesses can be regarded as more complex than non-indigenous businesses and this complexity needs to be reflected in defining entrepreneurship from an Indigenous perspective. (2005)

6 Markets and Internal Economic Activity

Much of the entrepreneurial activity conducted by indigenous people does not take place in the markets of the modern economy. Instead in some cases activities occur in the absence of exchange markets of any kind. They are internal subsistence activities. While in other cases there are markets but they are based on a traditional model, the bazaar, or they occur in the informal sector, outside the mainstream markets of the economy.

In certain cases there are no market transactions at all, but that is not to say there was no exchange. Wealth is created by individuals and within the community, but not through the creation and sale of goods and services for profit. That which is created is consumed or saved for personal use or exchanged through non-market cultural mechanisms such as the potlatch among the indigenous people of the northwest coast of Canada. Subsistence self-employment may take the form of farming (see Dana, 2006), hunting (see Kassam, 2005), or fishing, as described in Chapter 26 of Dana and Anderson (2007), about the Namgis First Nation. In Chapter 19 of Dana and Anderson (2007), Rønning explained that among the Sámi in Northern Europe, 'self-employment is the way of self-subsistence because it is the way to make a living'. Likewise, in this volume, Simeone's Chapter 25 discussed subsistence among the Athabaskan-speaking Han. The Inuit discussed in Chapter 29 were also involved in internal and informal activities. Chapter 33, about the Kuna, also discussed subsistence economic activities.

In instances where there are market transactions they often take place in the bazaar[2] and/or the informal sector. In contrast to mainstream society's firm-type organizations that are structured as aggregations of activities and tasks (with people being replaceable), each enterprise in the bazaar is organized according to roles and relationships that are central to recruitment, retention, promotion and purchasing. Prices in the bazaar are often negotiated, and the level of service quality reflects the relationship between the buyer and the seller. In this scenario, consumers do not necessarily seek the lowest price or the best quality. An individual may give business to another with whom a relationship has been established, to ensure that this person will reciprocate. Reciprocal preferential treatment reduces transaction costs. As discussed by Dana (2006), the bazaar is central to the Berber economy. As noted by Tayler, 'getting a job in Morocco, for Berbers and Arabs alike, frequently depends not on talent but on connections' (2005: 90).

The informal sector is important among indigenous peoples whose small firms rarely take on the qualities of large-scale entrepreneurship, because this would require an extensive infrastructure, for communications, information, transportation and capital (see Chapter 35 in Dana and Anderson 2007, about Bolivia, for instance). Without these, businesses are generally local. This was well explained by Naudé and Havenga in Chapter 5 of Dana and Anderson (2007). Informal economic activity can take the form of an impromptu stall or itinerant vending. Unrecorded cash sales circumvent taxation as well as regulation. The law is often bent, but authorities generally tolerate the sector. A relevant discussion from Dana (1992) was presented concisely by Chamard and Christie (1996). Johnson et al. (1998) discuss discretion in the sector. Kloosterman et al. (1998), noted that 'those who have poor access to the opportunities offered by the regular economy, are likely to be over-represented in the underground economy' (1998: 251). Often, regulatory barriers to entry and bureaucratic structures prompt small-scale enterprises to operate in the informal sector. Dana (1996) observed that municipalities in Mozambique have tried to discourage the informal sector. Likewise, Chapter 13 in Dana and Anderson (2007), noted the perceived privileged treatment of the untaxed shadow sector in Mongolia.

In contrast to firms in many mainstream societies, enterprise in the bazaar and in the informal sector often functions very well with limited inventory. This is evident, for example, among the indigenous people in Bolivia (chapter 35 in Dana and Anderson, 2007).

7 Propensity for Cooperation

Some communities have a propensity for cooperation in entrepreneurship. Chapter 2 (in Dana and Anderson, 2007: 14), by Hindle and Lansdowne mentioned the 'individuality versus collectivity paradox'. Wuttunee discussed community capitalism in Chapter 3 of the same book. The Sámi entrepreneurs discussed in this book are another example of a people who cooperate; although reindeer are owned individually, they are cared for communally. Ziker's Chapter 12, about indigenous people in Russia, stated that family/clan and communal/clan holdings had both an indigenous identity and a kinship element in their organisation. George Currie's Chapter 37 offers interesting insights into innovation to achieve non-monetary goals as well as monetary goals in Papua New Guinea.

In some communities, notably among the Maori in New Zealand and aboriginal people in Canada, ownership of land and more generally the package of indigenous rights (hunting, fishing, and so on) are held by the community and not the individual. An activity that draws on the capacity provided by these resources must be communal in nature, even if only to the extent that permission for an individual to use the land and/or exercise the right must be granted by the community.

Given the nature of reindeer herding, cooperation among Sámi has been and continues to be essential; reindeer herding neo-entrepreneurship *requires* a will to cooperate. In contrast, Chapter 30 of Dana and Anderson (2007), about the Mohawks suggests that these people *prefer* cooperative entrepreneurship built on alliances. In Chapter 34, Peredo discussed co-operatives and community-based enterprise in the context of Peru.

8 Culturally Influenced Opportunity Recognition

Opportunity recognition is culturally influenced, as are definitions of and the measurement of success. Mainstream society may give paramount importance to economic performance, growth in sales, growth in productivity, growth in profit, share value and growth in market share. So do many indigenous people and groups with many stating that their entrepreneurial ventures must be financially able to compete before they can deliver the other benefits often sought. In this respect, financial viability is not an end in itself, but rather a precondition necessary for the achievement the success sought; for example, respect for and preservation of traditional values and practices; reduction of poverty, improvement in living conditions, employment creation, and so on. Generally, value to society is not synonymous with value to a firm and monetary value is not necessarily social value. Similarly, it is useful to distinguish between shareholder value and stakeholder value. In addition, the social value of self-employment varies greatly. Chapter 9 (in Dana and Anderson, 2007), about Basuto culture and entrepreneurship explained how cattle are a measure of success among the indigenous people of Africa.

Thus, it can be said that *opportunity recognition is therefore culturally determined*, because different cultures have different goals and culturally specific needs. If person A wants to eat a fish and person B comes from a vegetarian culture, person B may not perceive an opportunity to go fishing as an opportunity having utility. Yet for person A, fishing is a means of attaining the goal of subsistence. The Cree people of the Lac La Ronge Cree Nation in northern Saskatchewan are developing a successful wild, organic mushroom harvesting and marketing operation. The processing, marketing and distribution methods are modern in every respect. But, the harvesting methods are not. Measured on purely economic terms, the return to harvesters is very low in relation to the hours invested. But these hours are 'on the land' and are highly valued for other than economic reasons. Indeed, the cash from the harvest is almost a bonus. So for this group harvesting wild mushrooms in a remote northern forest is a wonderful opportunity for entrepreneurship, while for others with different objectives it is not.

9 External Forces

Culturally determined opportunities for entrepreneurship are often disrupted by entities external to indigenous people. Crawford wrote:

> The State-Nation, a model invented in Europe, was exported around the world. It contributed to the marginalisation and even the exclusion of the languages and the cultures that could not acquire an official or national status in the states . . . However, there are languages and cultures that resisted this process of uniformity. Today, these . . . cultures are entitled to be respected and to exist. (2002: 60)

In Dana and Anderson (2007), Helena Ruotsola's Chapter 23 described suffering by the Komi people under Soviet rule. Likewise, Chapter 22 by Dana and Remes explained how the European Union is perceived as intervening with Sámi entrepreneurship. Also in this volume, Henry's Chapter 42 discussed interference by government in New Zealand. Interestingly, in both Canada and New Zealand the state is beginning to acknowledge that the best way to foster development among it indigenous people is to redress past wrongs by recognizing indigenous claims to land and resources, with these to form the basis for development by the indigenous people.

We suggest that the ability to produce wealth is more sustainable than the ability to sell resources. We believe that the ability to produce wealth is a function of skills and institutions. Welfare programmes likely reduce indigenous entrepreneurship and hinder macroeconomic development, given concomitant tax expansion.

10 Need versus Desire

Indigenous people are sometimes pulled to traditional forms of self-employment[3] but pushed to other money-earning activities, out of economic need. Ndemo's Chapter 8, in Dana and Anderson (2007), explained that virtually all those interviewed had livestock besides the business owned. Likewise, Chapter 9 about Basuto culture and entrepreneurship reported that indigenous people in Lesotho invest in cattle, even when their income comes from other sources. Degen's Chapter 10 noted that, while raising livestock is a desirable activity, many Bedouins have integrated into mainstream society, although 'as it is not socially acceptable, among the Bedouins, for women to work outside the house' (Dana and Anderson, 2007: 123). Chapter 22, by Teresa Dana and Liisa Remes, noted that Sámi people in Finland are sometimes pulled to traditional forms of self-employment but pushed to other money-earning activities, out of economic need. Likewise, Rønning wrote in Chapter 19, that many families partly rely on wages from external employment.

11 Emphasis on Community

Western-style, mainstream entrepreneurship is not for everybody, and should not be forced upon people with incompatible values. Indeed, some indigenous communities believe in elements of egalitarianism, sharing and communal activity. This was central to the discussion by Cajete, who wrote, 'Native people traditionally lived a kind of communal environmental ethics that stemmed from the broadest sense of kinship with all life' (2000: 95). Similarly, Renshaw wrote about 'a strongly held egalitarian ethic, an ethic that predisposes the Indians of the Chaco to view the accumulation of material possessions – beyond a certain, limited level – as a threat to the social order' (2002: 159). In Dana and Anderson (2007: 315) William Simeone's Chapter 25 about the Han discussed how sharing of resources is a 'hallmark of a subsistence economy and sharing was and continues to be a strong value of Han culture'. Also in Dana and Anderson (2007), Chapter 33 discussed the indigenous people of San Blas, in whose communities one finds minimal differences among household assets, and minimal variation in material circumstance; while some may explain this in terms of poverty, we believe that this is a function of a strong egalitarian ethic. In some cases it appears that the principles of equality provide a basis for identity. Thus, in some instances, Western business values conflict with traditional values. Along the same lines, Renshaw explained, 'In the traditional context, there appears to have been little or no possibility of an individual's accumulating property, let alone of using property as a means of acquiring prestige' (2002: 160). Of course, this contrasts sharply with the use of coppers among the Kwakwaka'wakw, discussed in Chapter 26 of Dana and Anderson (2007).

Egalitarianism may be said to lead to sharing and communal activities, which appear frequently in indigenous communities. Wenzel wrote about sharing among the Inuit, 'The result is an economy that, from Alaska to Greenland, optimizes social inclusiveness rather than the maximization of individual or family economic well-being' (2005, p. 1894). Renshaw described a similar situation among indigenous people in Paraguay, 'Commerce is an even more contradictory activity than either agriculture or stock raising, since it implies the deliberate negation of generosity, with market relations taking the place of sharing' (2002: 179). This is consistent with works by Bodenhorn (2000), Damas (1972), and Van de Velde (1956). In Dana and Anderson (2007), Chapter 9 explained how cattle in Lesotho are privately owned but may be used by others than the proprietor:

> Each owner of cattle is expected to lend his herd to other members of the community in order to plough their fields. Conversely, if an individual were to sell an ox for personal gain, this would be interpreted as hostile against society. Thus, such animals serve as a symbol of cultural identity and cultural regulation inhibits the convertibility of such property into property for consumption.

Also in this book, Curry (Chapter 37) discussed the context of economic decision-making, 'A villager returning home with a 1 kg carton of laundry detergent is likely to use only a very small proportion of the detergent himself before his supply is exhausted, because he would feel obligated to acquiesce to the demands of relatives for the remaining detergent after washing his own clothes'.

CONCLUSION

There is rich heterogeneity among indigenous peoples, and some of their cultural values are often incompatible with the basic assumptions of mainstream theories. Indigenous entrepreneurship often has non-economic explanatory variables. Some indigenous communities economies display elements of egalitarianism, sharing and communal activity. ndigenous entrepreneurship is usually environmentally sustainable; this often allows indigenous people to rely on immediately available resources, and consequently, work in indigenous communities is often irregular.

Social organization among indigenous peoples is often based on kinship ties, not necessarily created in response to market needs. Much entrepreneurial activity among indigenous people involves internal economic activity with no transaction, while transactions often take place in the bazaar and in the informal sector, where enterprises often have limited inventory.

Why do people from different cultures react in unlike ways, even when exposed to similar stimuli? It appears that what is an opportunity for some is less so for others. Individuals from different ethno-cultural backgrounds do not all become self-employed for the same reason, nor should they be expected to respond the same way to any stimulus. The perception of opportunity is culturally influenced, as is the measurement of success. We propose that entrepreneurship opportunity recognition and evaluation is therefore culturally determined; however, we note that culturally determined opportunities for entrepreneurship are often disrupted by entities external to indigenous people. Indigenous people are sometimes pulled to traditional forms of self-employment but pushed to other money-earning activities, out of economic need.

Perhaps it is appropriate for us, now, to remind our readers the words of Marlo Morgan, who wrote about her experience with indigenous people, 'They all agreed, automobiles were handy objects of transport. Being a slave to the payment of it, however. . . wasn't worth it, in their opinion. Besides they are never in a hurry . . . Maybe instead of calling this place the Outback, they should consider it the center of human concern' (1999: 106–7).

NOTES

1. Lindsay defined culture as 'the collective programming of the mind that distinguishes the members of one category of people from another . . . Culture influences attitudes and behavior, varies within and across nations and across ethnicities, and is strongly embedded in indigenous communities' (2005: 1–2).
2. For a detailed discussion of the bazaar, see Dana (2000).
3. King wrote, 'Without deer there is no culture' (2003: 133).

REFERENCES

Benedict, Ruth (1935), *Patterns of Culture*, London: George Routledge & Sons.

Bodenhorn, Barbara (2000), 'It is good to know who your relatives are but we were taught to share with everybody: shares and sharing among Iñupiaq households', in George W. Wenzel, Grete Hovelsrud-Broda and Nobuhiro Kishigami (eds), *The Social Economy of Sharing: Resource Allocation and Modern Hunter-Gatherers*, Osaka: National Museum of Ethnology, pp. 27–60.

Cajete, Gregory (2000), *Native Science: Natural Laws of Interdependence*, Sante Fe, New Mexico: Clear Light.

Chamard, John, and Michael Christie (1996), 'Entrepreneurship education programs: a change in paradigm is needed', *Entrepreneurship, Innovation, and Change*, **5** (3), 217–26.

Crawford, David (2002), 'Morocco's invisible Imazighen,' *Journal of North African Studies*, **7** (1), 53–70.

Damas, David (1972), 'Central Eskimo systems of food sharing', *Ethnology*, **11** (3), 220–40.

Dana, Léo-Paul (1992), 'Entrepreneurship, innovation and change in developing countries', *Entrepreneurship, Innovation, and Change*, **1** (2), 231–42.

Dana, Léo-Paul (1995), 'Entrepreneurship in a remote sub-Arctic community: Nome, Alaska', *Entrepreneurship: Theory and Practice*, **20** (1), 55–72. Reprinted in Norris Krueger (ed.) (2002), *Entrepreneurship: Critical Perspectives on Business and Management*, vol. 4, London: Routledge, pp. 255–75.

Dana, Léo-Paul (1996), 'Small business in Mozambique after the war', *Journal of Small Business Management*, **34** (4), 67–71.

Dana, Léo-Paul (2000), *Economies of the Eastern Mediterranean Region: Economic Miracles in the Making*, Singapore, London and Hong Kong: World Scientific.

Dana, Léo-Paul (2006), 'Business values among the *Imazighen*', *EuroMed Journal of Business*, **1** (2), 82–91.

Dana, Léo-Paul (2007), 'Promoting SMEs in Africa: some insights from an experiment in Ghana and Togo', *Journal of African Business* (The official publication of the International Academy of African Business and Development), **8** (2), 151–74.

Dana, Léo-Paul and Robert Brent Anderson (eds) (2007), *International Handbook of Research on Indigenous Entrepreneurship*, Cheltenham, UK and Northampton, MA, USA: Edward Elgar.

Dana, Léo-Paul, Teresa E. Dana, and Robert B. Anderson (2005), 'A theory-based empirical study of entrepreneurship in Iqaluit, Nunavut', *Journal of Small Business & Entrepreneurship*, **18** (2), 143–52.

Harris, Marvin (1974), *Cows, Pigs, Wars and Witches: The Riddles of Culture*, New York: Random House.

Helander, Elina (1999), 'Traditional Sámi knowledge', in Ludger Müller-Wille (ed.), *Human Environmental Interactions: Issues and Concerns in Upper Lapland, Finland*, Rovaniemi: Arctic Centre, University of Lapland, pp. 25–7.

Hukkinen, Jane, Hannu Heikkinen, Kaisa Raitio and Ludger Müller-Wille (2006), 'Dismantling the barriers to entrepreneurship in reindeer management in Finland', *Journal of International Entrepreneurship and Small Business*, **3** (6), 705–27.

Johnson, Simon, Daniel Kaufmann and Pablo Zoido-Lobaton (1998), 'Regulatory discretion and the unofficial economy', *American Economic Review*, **88** (2), 387–92.

Kassam, Karim-Aly (2005), 'Hunting, subsistence', in Mark Nuttall, *Encyclopedia of the Arctic*, New York: Routledge, pp. 899–901.

King, Alexander (2003), 'Without deer there is no culture, nothing', *Anthropology and Humanism*, **27** (2), 133–64.

Kloosterman, Robert, Joanne van der Leun, and Jan Rath (1998), 'Across the border: immigrants' economic opportunities, social capital and informal business activities', *Journal of Ethnic and Migration Studies*, **24** (2), 249–68.

Lindsay, Noel J. (2005), 'Toward a cultural model of indigenous entrepreneurial attitude', *Academy of Marketing Science Review*, **2005** (5), 1–18.

Morgan, Marlo (1999), *Mutant Message Down Under*, New York: HarperCollins.

Müller-Wille, Ludger (1987), 'Indigenous peoples, land-use conflicts, and economic development in circumpolar lands', *Arctic and Alpine Research*, **19** (4), 351–6.

Olurode, Lai (2007), 'Ifa, the deity of wisdom, and importance of work among the Yoruba people,' *Journal of Enterprising Communities: People and Places in the Global Economy*, **1** (2), 135–41.

Renshaw, John (2002), *The Indians of the Paraguayan Chaco: Identity & Economy*, Lincoln: University of Nebraska Press.

Tayler, Jeffrey (2005), 'Among the Berbers: a journey through Morocco's high Atlas Mountains', *National Geographic*, **207** (1), 78–97.

Van de Velde, Frans (1956), 'Rules for sharing the seals among the Arviligjuarmiut Eskimo', *Eskimo*, **41**, 3–6.

Wenzel, George (2005), 'Sharing', in Mark Nuttall (ed.), *Encyclopedia of the Arctic*, New York: Routledge, pp. 1891–94.

29 Interdependent innovation

Adam M. Kleinbaum

Interdependent innovation is the joint development and implementation of a new product or service by two or more product divisions of a multibusiness firm and is a valuable, but under-leveraged, source of corporate entrepreneurship (Kleinbaum and Tushman, 2007). The ability to actively create interdependence across divisional boundaries offers large firms the opportunity to reconfigure their assets, deploying resources into new product markets or combining resources in novel ways (Adner and Helfat, 2003; Burgelman and Doz, 2001; Peteraf, 1993) and, in doing so, allows them to purposefully explore new businesses and develop new strategies, improving their long-term profitability and adaptability. And yet, few organizations seize this opportunity successfully.

The reason for the persistent difficulty of interdependent innovation is an artifact of organization design: managers choose organizational structure to minimize the costs of coordinating across interdependent units (Thompson, 1967). As they do so, grouping decisions are based on a logic of maximizing the interdependencies within units and minimizing the interdependence between units, placing the most highly interdependent units, who have the greatest need to coordinate, into common divisions (Nadler and Tushman, 1997). As a consequence, divisions are explicitly designed to minimize interdependence between them, even when interdependent innovation offers substantial potential growth opportunity.

Historically, the literature focused almost exclusively on the roles played by formal structure and incentives in managing interdependent innovation. On the formal structure side, scholars have suggested that matrix designs or other formal structural overlays might enable interdependent innovation (for example, Clark and Wheelwright, 1992; Galbraith, 1973; 1994; Nadler and Tushman, 1997). Other scholars suggest incentive-based approaches (for example, Kaplan and Henderson, 2005; Prendergast, 1999), but even when incentives to collaborate can be well-specified, overall incentive programs are ineffective at promoting multiple, inconsistent goals at multiple levels of the organization, as is necessary to enable both exploitation of core, divisional resources and exploration of cross-divisional architectures (Ledford and Heneman, 2000; Simons, 2005).

More recently, scholars have viewed interdependent innovation through the lens of social structure (Kleinbaum and Tushman, 2007). Intraorganizational social networks provide an alternative way for individuals from disparate parts of the organization to collaborate across divisional boundaries and to facilitate the interdivisional coordination necessary to take these ideas and bring them into reality. Another benefit of network-based approaches to interdependent innovation is they require little or no changes to the formal structure – thus reducing the likelihood that focus on interdependent innovation will undermine the stand-alone performance of the core product lines.

To the extent that organizations can systematically promote individual network-based search for collaborative opportunities and can implement the resulting interdependent innovations, large, multibusiness firms can remain entrepreneurial. They can avoid losing valuable ideas to 'spinoffs' (for example, Klepper and Sleeper, 2005) and can avoid the stagnation and inertia that often follows success (Hannan and Freeman, 1984; Leonard-Barton, 1992).

REFERENCES

Adner, Ron, and Constance E. Helfat (2003), 'Corporate effects and dynamic managerial capabilities', *Strategic Management Journal*, **24**, 1011–25.

Burgelman, Robert A. and Yves L. Doz (2001), 'The power of strategic integration', *Sloan Management Review*, **42**, 28–38.

Clark, Kim B. and Steven C. Wheelwright (1992), 'Organizing and leading "heavyweight" development teams', *California Management Review*, **34**, 9–28.

Galbraith, Jay R. (1973), *Designing Complex Organizations*, Reading, MA: Addison-Wesley.

Galbraith, Jay R. (1994), *Competing with Flexible Lateral Organizations*, Reading, MA: Addison-Wesley.

Hannan, Michael T. and John Freeman (1984), 'Structural inertia and organizational change', *American Sociological Review*, **49**, 149–64.

Kaplan, Sarah and Rebecca Henderson (2005), 'Inertia and incentives: bridging organizational economics and organizational theory', *Organization Science*, **16**, 509–21.

Kleinbaum, Adam M. and Michael L. Tushman (2007), 'Building bridges: the social structure of interdependent innovation', *Strategic Entrepreneurship Journal*, **1**, 103–22.

Klepper, Steven and Sally Sleeper (2005), 'Entry by spinoffs', *Management Science*, **51**, 1291–306.

Ledford, Gerald E. and Robert L. Heneman (2000), 'Compensation: a troublesome lead system in organizational change', in Michael Beer and Nitin Nohria (eds), *Breaking the Code of Change*, Boston, MA: Harvard Business School Press, pp. 307–22.

Leonard-Barton, Dorothy (1992), 'Core capabilities and core rigidities: a paradox in managing new product development', *Strategic Management Journal*, **13**, 111–25.

Nadler, David and Michael L. Tushman (1997), *Competing by Design: The Power of Organizational Architecture*, New York: Oxford University Press.

Peteraf, Margaret A. (1993), 'The cornerstones of competitive advantage: a resource-based view', *Strategic Management Journal*, **14**, 179–91.

Prendergast, Canice (1999), 'The provision of incentives in firms', *Journal of Economic Literature*, **37**, 7–63.

Simons, Robert (2005), *Levers of Organization Design: How Managers Use Accountability Systems for Greater Performance and Commitment*, Boston, MA: Harvard Business School Press.

Thompson, James D. (1967), *Organizations in Action; Social Science Bases of Administrative Theory*, New Brunswick, NJ: Transaction.

30 Intermediated internationalization theory

Zoltan J. Acs and Siri Terjesen

This entry outlines Acs and Terjesen's (2008) theory of intermediated internationalization and offers suggestions for future research. Intermediated internationalization is 'the channeling of a venture's innovation through an existing multinational enterprise, located at home or abroad' (Acs and Terjesen, 2008: 1).

TWO PATHS TO INTERNATIONALIZATION: DIRECT AND INTERMEDIATED

International new ventures (INVs) are firms that, from their beginnings, pursue the use of resources and the sale of goods in multiple countries and are discussed by Ben Oviatt in this encyclopedia. When considering international markets for their goods and services, entrepreneurs face a variety of entry modes including export, license, joint venture, wholly owned subsidiary and greenfield investment. In the case of exporting, firms have two channel options: (1) export directly to customers abroad or (2) export indirectly through an intermediary (Peng and York, 2001). Direct exporting is a common path to internationalization and is well addressed in the extant literature.[1] The direct mode leads to the international new venture, however it is not always optimal given new venture's high trade barriers abroad, low levels of innovation, predominant focus on domestic niches and lack of necessary financial capital, information and ability to protect property rights abroad. Faced with these barriers, new ventures may choose the second path, intermediating their innovation through an established multinational enterprise. This process creates a feedback mechanism from new ventures to existing organizations, as new ventures become a part of existing multinationals' supply chains. Supply chain management takes place through formal and informal governance structures. The new venture's decision to pursue direct or intermediated paths to internationalization is based on an assessment of the costs of property rights protection, transactions and rent extraction.

Oviatt and McDougall (1994) employ two dimensions, coordination of value chain activities (few versus many) and number of countries involved (few versus many), to identify four types of international new ventures: export/import start-up, multinational trader, geographically focused start-up and global start-up. Acs and Terjesen (2008) suggest that for each case, there is also an intermediated form that is underexplored in the literature. For example, an export/import start-up with low levels of value chain activities and few countries could choose to go directly, or could pursue internationalization through an intermediary. See Figure 30.1 for the resulting matrix of eight cells.

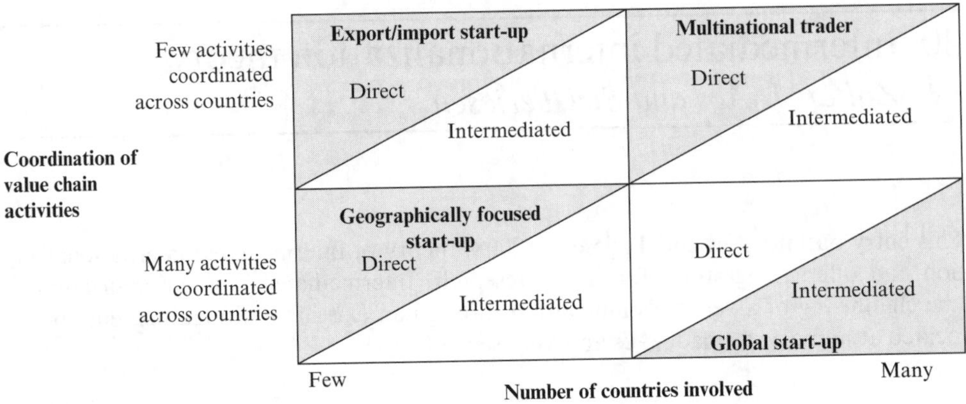

Note: Shading = optimal mode.

Source: Modified from Oviatt and McDougall (1994) in Acs and Terjesen (2008).

Figure 30.1 Two avenues to internationalization for each of four INV types

INTERMEDIATED INTERNATIONALIZATION: PHENOMENON

Entrepreneurial firms distinguish between the decision to exploit an opportunity and the decision to pursue overseas markets. The choice is a strategic one based on how best to maximize value. New ventures face higher barriers to foreign market entry than do large, established firms, and can meet this challenge by specializing in niche innovations and taking advantage of existing multinational enterprises' (MNEs') supply chains. The intermediation phenomenon is also driven by the compartmentalization of ventures, as Saxenian (2002: 184) describes:

> Today, independent enterprises produce all of the components that were once internalized within a single large corporation – from application software, operating systems and computers to microprocessors and other components. The final systems are in turn marketed and distributed by other independent enterprises. Within each of these horizontal segments again there is further specialization of production and a deepening social division of labor.

An emerging strand of research explores how entrepreneurial firms pursue indirect paths to internationalization (for example, Acs and Terjesen, 2008; Acs et al., 1997; Bell et al., 2003; Coviello and Munro, 1997; Hessels and Terjesen, 2008; Jones, 2001; Peng and York, 2001; Terjesen et al., 2008) using local and foreign intermediaries to sell their goods and services across national borders. Intermediaries include agents and distributors located at home or abroad (Burgel and Murray, 2000; Peng and York, 2001) and the local subsidiaries of MNEs (Terjesen et al., 2008). Export intermediaries play an important 'middleman' role in international trade, 'linking individuals and organizations that would otherwise not have been connected' (Peng and York, 2001: 328) and can help their clients overcome knowledge gaps, reduce uncertainties and to identify customers, sources of financing and distribution infrastructure (Balabanis, 2000). Intermediation is central to entrepreneurship: the term 'entrepreneur' stems from the French verb 'entreprendre' derived from 'entre' (between) and 'prendre' (to take) and has long been used to describe individuals who are 'in the middle' of business activities.

THE THEORY OF INTERMEDIATED INTERNATIONALIZATION

In developing a theory of intermediated internationalization, we start with theories of new venture creation. Entrepreneurial opportunities involve the discovery of novel means–ends relationships, through which new goods, services, resources and agency are created (Casson, 2003; Shane and Venkataraman, 2000). A key distinction between entrepreneurship and economics literatures is the existence of opportunities. In the entrepreneurship literature, opportunities are generally considered endogenous; however, in the economics literature, opportunities are endogenous and are more prevalent in certain industries such as high technology (Scherer, 1965). Innovations often come from third party firms or research institutions and *spillover* for application by other firms (Acs and Audretsch, 2005), although geographically bounded. The knowledge spillover theory of entrepreneurship (Acs et al., 2005) describes how the asymmetries between the agent possessing the knowledge and the incumbent organization's decision-making hierarchy leads to the gap in the valuation of this knowledge. Start-ups with access to such knowledge spillovers are more likely to be innovative: 'the revolutionary breakthroughs continue to come predominantly from small entrepreneurial enterprises, with large industry providing streams of incremental improvements that also add up to major contributions' (Baumol, 2004: 9). Thus, knowledge spills over from incumbent firms to individuals who endogenously create new firms, albeit geographically bounded. These knowledge spillovers must then be converted into innovative outputs which can then be internationally diffused.

Resource-constrained entrepreneurial firms with innovative products face a key decision in a world dominated by large, multinational enterprises. Entrepreneurs can choose to 'fight' giants by taking their innovations directly to international markets or they can 'dance' with giants by collaborating through indirect exports, becoming suppliers of foreign firms, becoming licencees/franchisees of foreign brands, becoming alliance partners of foreign direct investors and by investing and exiting through sell off- without leaving the home country (Peng, 2006).

There is a rich literature on internalization in international business. An MNE is 'a private institution devised to organize, through employment contracts, interdependencies between individuals located in more than one country' (Hennart, 2001: 127). Internalization theory describes how a MNE gains economic benefits by exploiting assets across international markets (Buckley and Casson, 1976) and will expand abroad (assuming is it already in another country) when it can organize interdependencies between agents located in different countries more efficiently in the firm than in open markets. Thus, according to internalization theory, the MNE has a firm specific asset with the potential for foreign exploitation and the choice of entry mode depends on the tradeoff between the costs of internally developing and absorbing local market knowledge versus the costs associated with accessing such resources from external actors. An MNE will organize interdependencies through hierarchy when it can do so more efficiently than markets. Three conditions must be met (Hennart, 2001: 136): (1) interdependent agents must be located in different countries, (2) the MNE must be the most efficient way to organize these interdependencies, and (3) given condition (2), the costs incurred by MNEs to organize these interdependencies are lower than the benefits of doing so. Dunning (1999: 28) describes how the boundaries of the firm are changing from hierarchy to alliance capitalism, suggesting that firms will increasingly pursue alternative governance strategies,

> for firms to benefit most from innovation-led production, the upgrading of consumer demand, and the imperatives of globalization, they need to engage in a network of cooperative agreements with other firms. This reflects the fact that economic activity is becoming more interdependent, and in order to exploit their core assets effectively, firms have to combine these with the core assets of other firms – or of public authorities. However, rather than enlarge their hierarchical influence, they prefer to establish cooperative relationships with other firms, namely, extend their soft boundaries. By so doing, they are able to improve and make better use of their own competencies, which, in turn, will help them sustain or push out further their market boundaries.

SYMBIOTIC RELATIONSHIP AND STRATEGIC CHOICE OF MNES AND NEW VENTURES

As described above, firms face two choices when internationalizing. Just as an MNE must consider a range of firm and country specific advantages when making the decision to pursue internalization (hierarchy) or use markets (licensing), an entrepreneurial venture has the same option. Due to the lack of resources, new ventures will pursue alternative governance structures even in the face of rent extraction. From the new venture's point of view, it must pursue some sort of internationalization strategy that relies on strategic alliances, technology licensing, and joint ventures.

Figure 30.2 depicts the symbiotic relationship between new ventures and MNEs. In the traditional model of internalization, an MNE has a firm specific asset with the potential for foreign exploitation. The choice is determined by the transaction costs of absorbing local knowledge versus the costs associated with assessing resources from external sources. A new venture also faces two options: it can internationalize on its own and forgo the costs of contracting and rent extraction or it can pursue an intermediated form of governance structure. These are shown by the arrows to the market and the governance boxes on the right. While both a new venture and an MNE can pursue market led internalization through exports and licensing, these market relationships do not involve direct governance relationships. However, what is not neutral ground is the intermediated internationalization box. Over the past two decades, a large literature has emerged in international management and strategy that suggests that networked forms of governance play an increasingly important role in international business for both new ventures and MNEs. In fact, alternative governance structures represent a form of international expansion that is increasingly common to both MNEs and INVs operating in a global economy. For example, Gomes-Casseres's (1999) study of the alliance strategies of small

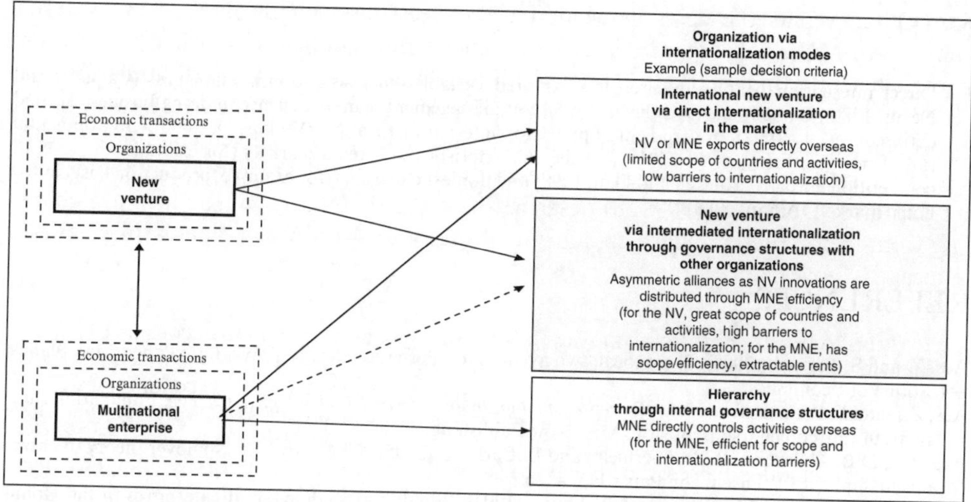

Source: Acs and Terjesen (2008).

Figure 30.2 INV and MNE symbiotic relationship under alliance capitalism

firms identifies a bimodal distribution of firms going overseas, however Kohn (1999) finds that indeed a large number of firms go overseas alone. These firms' pursue 'deep-niche' strategy and tend to be technology leaders and dominant players in their markets and to operate mostly in producer goods industries. Both studies suggest that both new ventures and MNEs rely on strategy as the source of how to expand internationally, particularly when technology is at stake.

FUTURE RESEARCH DIRECTIONS

Further research could pursue a number of directions. First, research could explore in what directions are firms evolving: Are there more direct, hierarchical or intermediated modes? Second, the propositions could be tested with a large dataset of new ventures across different industry and country contexts. Third, more fine-grained analyses of the decision to export directly or indirectly (or not at all) could prove promising. Key questions include: what is the process of decision making? How does the decision to pursue the indirect mode impact the decision to pursue the direct mode? What is the speed and growth trajectory of internationalizing firms? Fourth, further work in the area of new venture international entry modes has the potential to develop linkages between entrepreneurship and internationalization. A fifth promising stream of research would explore the regionalization of new ventures. Are INVs, in fact, mostly regional rather than international? Do new ventures select particular intermediaries based on the advantages they offer vis-à-vis a particular regions? Do MNEs seek new ventures that offer particular region specific, in addition to firm, industry and national advantages? Further research could take into account network perspectives, the role of institutional environments, economic geography, learning, managerial cognition and absorptive capacity.

NOTE

1. Direct internationalization research has explored variables such as product uniqueness (Cavusgil and Nevin, 1981), founder age (Westhead, 1995), top management team experience in doing business abroad (Eriksson et al., 1997), government support for internationalization (Wilkinson, 2006), environmental turbulence (Westhead et al., 2001), and the characteristics of foreign markets (for example, the level of competition abroad) (Thirkell and Dau, 1998) and domestic markets (for example, production costs in the home market) (Axinn, 1988).

REFERENCES

Acs, Z. and S. Terjesen (2008), 'Born local: two avenues to internationalization', Working Paper, Max Planck Institute of Economics.

Acs, Z.J. and D.B. Audretch (2005). *Entrepreneurship, Innovation and Technological Change*, Foundations and Trends in Entrepreneurship, Boston, MA: Now Publishing.

Acs, Z.J., D.B. Audretsch, P. Braunerhjelm and B. Carlsson (2005), 'The knowledge spillover theory of entrepreneurship', CEPR Discussion Paper No. 4326.

Acs, Z.J., R. Morck, J.M. Shaver and B. Yeung (1997), 'Small and medium sized enterprises in the global economy: a policy perspective', *Small Business Economics*, **9** (1), 7–20.

Axinn, C.N. (1988), 'Export performance: do managerial perceptions make a difference', *International Marketing Review*, **5**, 67–71.

Balabanis, G.I. (2000), 'Factors affecting export intermediaries' service offerings: the British example', *Journal of International Business Studies*, **31** (1), 83–99.

Baumol, W.J. (2004), 'Entrepreneurial enterprises, large established firms and other components of the free-market growth machine', *Small Business Economics*, **23** (1), 9–24.

Bell, J., R. McNaughton, S. Young and D. Crick (2003), 'Towards an integrative model of small firm internationalisation', *Journal of International Entrepreneurship*, **1**, 339–62.

Buckley, P.J. and M. Casson (1976), *The Future of the Multinational Enterprise*, London: Macmillan.

Burgel, O. and G.C. Murray (2000), 'The international market entry choices of start-up companies in high technology industries', *Journal of International Marketing*, **8** (2), 33–62.

Casson, M. (2003), 'Entrepreneurship, business culture and the theory of the firm', in Z. Acs and D. Audretsch (eds), *Handbook of Entrepreneurship Research*, Boston, MA and Dordrecht: Kluwer, pp. 223–46.

Cavusgil, S.T. and J.R. Nevin (1981), 'Internal determinants of export marketing behavior: an empirical investigation', *Journal of Marketing Research*, **18** (1), 114–19.

Coviello, N. and H. Munro, (1997), 'Network relationships and the internationalization process of small software firms', *International Business Review*, **6** (4), 361–86.

Dunning, J.H. (1999), 'Reconfiguring the boundaries of international business activity', in Z.J. Acs and B. Yeung (eds), *Small and Medium-Sized Enterprises in the Global Economy*, Ann Arbor, MI: University of Michigan Press, pp. 24–44.

Eriksson, K., J. Johanson, A. Majkgård and D.D. Sharma (1997), 'Experiential knowledge and cost in the internationalization process', *Journal of International Business Studies*, **28** (2), 337–60.

Gomes-Casseres, B. (1999), 'Alliance strategies fo small firms', in Z.J. Acs and B. Yeung (eds), *Small and Medium-Sized Enterprises in the Global Economy*, Ann Arbor, MI: University of Michigan Press, pp. 67–87.

Hennart, J.-F. (2001), 'Theories of the multinational enterprise', in A. Rugman and T. Brewer (eds), *Oxford Handbook of International Business*, Oxford: Oxford University Press, pp. 127–50.

Hessels, J. and S. Terjesen (2008), *Indirect Internationalization: A Development and Test of Two Theories*, Wellesley, MA: Babson.

Jones, M.V. (2001), 'First steps in internationalisation: concepts and evidence from a sample of small high technology firms', *Journal of International Management*, **7** (3), 191–210.

Kohn, T.O. (1999), 'Small firms as international players', in Z.J. Acs and B. Yeung (eds), *Small and Medium-Sized Enterprises in the Global Economy*, Ann Arbor, MI: University of Michigan Press, pp. 88–102.

Oviatt, B.M. and P.P. McDougall (1994), 'Toward a theory of international new ventures', *Journal of International Business Studies*, **25** (1), 45–64.

Peng, M.W. (2006), *Global Strategy*, Cincinnati, OH: Thomson South-Western.

Peng, M.W. and A.S. York (2001), 'Behind intermediary performance in export trade: transactions, agents and resources', *Journal of International Business Studies*, **32** (2), 327–46.

Saxenian, A. (2002), 'Transnational communities and the evolution of global production networks: the cases of Taiwan, China and India', *Industry and Innovation*, **9**, 183–202.

Scherer, F.M. (1965), 'Firm size, market structure, opportunity, and the output of patented inventions', *American Economic Review*, **55** (5), 1097–125.
Shane, S. and S. Venkataraman (2000), 'The promise of entrepreneurship as a field of research', *Academy of Management Journal*, **25** (1), 217–26.
Terjesen, S., C. O'Gorman and Z.J. Acs (2008), 'Intermediated mode of internationalization: new software ventures in Ireland and India', *Entrepreneurship & Regional Development*, **20**, 89–109.
Thirkell, P.C. and R. Dau (1998), 'Export performance: success determinants for New Zealand manufacturing exporters', *European Journal of Marketing*, **32** (9/10), 813–29.
Westhead, P. (1995), 'Exporting and non-exporting small firms in Great Britain', *International Journal of Entrepreneurial Behavior and Research*, **1** (2), 6–36.
Westhead, P., M. Wright and D. Ucbasaran (2001), 'The internationalisation of new and small firms: a resource-based view', *Journal of Business Venturing*, **16** (4), 333–58.
Wilkinson, T.J. (2006), 'Entrepreneurial climate and US state Foreign Trade Offices as predictors of export success', *Journal of Small Business Management*, **44** (1), 99–113.

31 International entrepreneurship

Benjamin M. Oviatt, Vladislav R. Maksimov and Patricia P. McDougall

DEFINITION

As its name suggests, international entrepreneurship combines international business and entrepreneurial behaviour. The international aspect of the phenomenon refers to the process of internationalization of firms as well as to the differences in firm behaviour based on national origin, while the entrepreneurial aspect refers to the act of tapping into new organizational opportunities. Oviatt and McDougall (2005: 540) offer the following formal definition: 'International entrepreneurship is the discovery, enactment, evaluation, and exploitation of opportunities – across national borders – to create future goods and services.'

The processes of discovery, enactment, evaluation and exploitation of opportunities are specific acts of a broader process that is commonly referred to as taking advantage of opportunities. Although general and simplified, the latter term is more practical and easily grasped in general discussions. At an intuitive level, taking advantage of opportunities could be equated to the act of exploitation. However, it is clear that opportunities have to first emerge and then be evaluated in order to be exploited. Opportunities can emerge either through an act of discovery or through enactment. Discovery is present when entrepreneurs find information about a potential business opportunity which is also readily available to others. Enactment is present when entrepreneurs create a business opportunity through a unique interaction with other people, sources of information, available knowledge through prior experiences, motivation to search for innovations, and other factors of their social environment.

The above definition of international entrepreneurship also allows for comparative studies of domestic entrepreneurs or organizations in different countries. For example, entrepreneurial actors in different countries could differ in the way they take advantage of business opportunities. Their behaviour can differ substantially because of the different institutional environment in each country (Busenitz et al., 2000). In this case, the phenomenon is international because of the international comparison of the actors, not the opportunity.

To summarize the implications of the definition of international entrepreneurship above and to explicate its meaning in practical terms, a few examples of the phenomenon are offered. The domain of international entrepreneurship includes the following:

1. A new venture is set up by an individual or a group of individuals to take advantage of an international business opportunity from inception or soon afterwards,
2. any existing venture crosses national borders to take advantage of opportunities to create future goods and services, or

3. a comparison of entrepreneurial ventures in different countries when those ventures take advantage of either domestic or international opportunities to create future goods or services.

HISTORY

While acts of international entrepreneurship have existed for centuries, the term is relatively new in the academic literature. According to Zahra and George (2002) it first appeared in an article by Morrow (1988), where he discussed the increased accessibility to once remote markets due to technological advances and increased cultural awareness. As the discipline has grown and been defined more accurately, it has become clear that certain aspects of international entrepreneurship had been discussed before 1988 in such areas as strategic management, international business and entrepreneurship (all being multidisciplinary themselves).

However, academic study in international entrepreneurship gained popularity in the 1990s with the recognition of and fascination with the international new venture. First, McDougall's (1989) empirical study comparing domestic and international new ventures provided rich insights into the differences between these two types of firms. Then, building on case studies of international new ventures developed by academics working independently around the globe and an interest in the popular business press in rapid internationalization, Oviatt and McDougall (1994) provided a theoretical base for the study of international new ventures. They defined such a venture 'as a business organization that, from inception, seeks to derive significant competitive advantage from the use of resources and the sale of outputs in multiple countries' (ibid.: 49). The available theories at that time could not explain the existence of international new ventures. For this reason, Oviatt and McDougall (1994) presented an integrative framework that explains an international new venture and describes it as one that owns certain valuable assets, uses alliances and network structures to control a relatively large percentage of vital assets, and has a unique resource that provides a sustainable advantage and is transferable to a foreign location.

Following this early focus on international new ventures, the field of international entrepreneurship broadened and went through a number of redefinitions to specify the array of phenomena hosted under the term. First, scholars recognized that international entrepreneurship should include corporate entrepreneurship – established firms which venture internationally – because such firms can also demonstrate entrepreneurial behaviour (Wright and Ricks, 1994; Zahra, 1993). This increased focus on entrepreneurial behaviour led scholars in the field to centre the definition around the set of entrepreneurial orientations – innovativeness, proactiveness and risk-taking – following Lumpkin and Dess (1996). As a result, the field expanded to include non-profit and government organizations in addition to business organizations (McDougall and Oviatt, 2000).

Second, as the definition of entrepreneurship itself evolved from a focus on entrepreneurial orientations to one on opportunities and individuals who take advantage of them (Shane and Venkataraman, 2000), so did the definition of international entrepreneurship. Zahra and George (2002) suggested that the definition should emphasize creative discovery and exploitation of international opportunities. More recently, Oviatt and McDougall (2005) expanded the definition to include discovery, enactment, evaluation and exploitation. Such a change in focus obviated the debate over how many dimensions of entrepreneurial orientations were important for definitional purposes.

Oviatt and McDougall (2005) formally recognized that international entrepreneurship includes comparisons of entrepreneurial behaviour across national borders. Such comparisons had been commonly agreed to be an integral part of the field since its infancy. As the authors put it: 'The comparison branch . . . has always been a part of the study of international entrepreneurship from the first special issue on the topic to appear in an academic journal (Hisrich, Honig-Haftel, McDougall and Oviatt, 1996) to the most recent comprehensive handbook on international entrepreneurship (Dana, 2004)'.

In summary, the current definition of international entrepreneurship focuses on opportunities, highlights entrepreneurial behaviour across national borders, permits both new venture formation and corporate venturing, includes non-profit and government organizations, and acknowledges cross-country comparisons of entrepreneurial behaviour.

MODELS OF INTERNATIONALIZATION

Until now, the discussion has focused mainly on the actors of international entrepreneurship – those who take advantage of international opportunities to create future goods and services. However, following Shane and Venkataraman's (2000: 218) definition of entrepreneurship, it is also important to examine how and with what effects these opportunities are taken advantage of. In this section, the two main models of how firms internationalize are described.

The first model is often referred to as the Uppsala Model or the process model of firm internationalization and is associated primarily with the work of Johanson and Vahlne (1977; 1990), who studied the initial internationalization activities of Swedish manufacturing firms. The authors explain that the process begins with an entry in a psychically close market and evolves over time through an interaction between foreign market knowledge and foreign market commitment. Initially, the commitment of the firm is low as indicated by such modes of entry as exporting or licensing, which require relatively few resources and could be terminated relatively quickly. However, over time firms gain experience, and hence their tacit knowledge about a foreign market increases. As a result, firms may decide to increase their foreign market commitment by forming alliances or making greenfield investments. As the managers of the firm feel more comfortable doing business in a particular foreign market, they can later decide to expand to a more psychically distant foreign market. The incremental pattern of taking advantage of international opportunities in the Uppsala Model, however, makes this process of internationalization less entrepreneurial than a process of accelerated internationalization.

Therefore, the second model that has emerged is a model of accelerated internationalization and is associated primarily with the work of Oviatt and McDougall (1994; 2005) and McDougall and Oviatt (2000). The process of rapid internationalization can reveal itself in a number of ways, for example, rapid initial entry into a foreign market after inception, fast accumulation of the number of foreign markets entered and/or a quick increase in the percentage of revenue coming from foreign sales. At the core, such processes are a result of taking advantage of international opportunities to create future goods and services relatively quickly. Such fast actions could be enabled by technological advances in transportation and communication or motivated by the fear of competitive action or retaliation. Further, the accumulation of foreign market knowledge, as well as the increase in knowledge intensity, has been reported to significantly improve the ability of firms to internationalize fast (Autio et al., 2000; McNaughton, 2001; 2003 Reuber and Fischer, 1997;). Similarly, certain characteristics of the entrepreneurial actor's network – tie strength, size, and density – are said to moderate positively the ability of firms to internationalize rapidly (Oviatt and McDougall, 2005).

IMPORTANCE OF INTERNATIONALIZATION SPEED

The accelerated model of internationalization has received substantial attention within the field of international entrepreneurship because of the potential for a counter-intuitive, positive relationship between internationalization speed and performance. Two empirical studies in this regard have had a substantial impact in the field. First, Autio et al. (2000) looked at the effects of early internationalization on subsequent growth. Their indication of a significant positive relationship has highlighted the existence of certain advantages of newness – in addition and counter to the widely accepted liabilities of newness (Stinchcombe, 1965). Second, Zahra et al. (2000) have related the international diversity and commitment of new venture firms to performance. Their study indicated that greater diversity and higher commitment entry modes lead to greater technological learning which, in turn, leads to better performance. Collectively, these studies suggest that the speed of internationalization is an important factor which should be paid greater attention to in future.

CURRENT STATE AND FUTURE DIRECTIONS

Academia has increasingly recognized the importance of international entrepreneurship. Special issues and forums have appeared in various journals, including *Entrepreneurship Theory & Practice* in 1996 and *Academy of Management Journal* in 2000. Other journals, such as *Journal of Business Venturing* and *Journal of International Business Studies* regularly publish articles in the area. The *Journal of International Entrepreneurship* was launched as interest in international entrepreneurship grew and is specifically devoted to its study. In 2004, an edited handbook of international entrepreneurship was published (Dana, 2004), while in 2007, an edited volume reviewing the field appeared (Oviatt and McDougall, 2007). The annual Academy of Management meeting has devoted specific sessions and forums to the topic, while other academic meetings focused specifically on international entrepreneurship take place on multiple continents. Overall, the academic interest in the field is strong and growing.

The domain of international entrepreneurship is rich in opportunity. As suggested by its definition, the field is broad and many interesting research questions can be explored.

Researchers can employ various existing theories from different fields, such as international business, entrepreneurship, strategic management, economics, psychology, finance, sociology, and so on. The rich, multidisciplinary nature of the field provides both an opportunity and a promise for an abundance of valuable and interesting research. It is well known that when insights from different domains are brought together, valuable new knowledge is often created.

Further, by its nature the field also encourages cooperation of researchers from multiple countries. A number of multi-country research teams have been utilized to work on international entrepreneurship projects and have resulted in excellent scholarly achievements. As with bringing insights from different domains together, bringing people with different backgrounds together can prove invaluable. Overall, the field provides opportunities not only for academic exploration, but also for individual learning and enrichment, which can later become an indispensable asset in conducting international entrepreneurship research.

REFERENCES

Autio, E., H.J. Sapienza and J.G. Almeida (2000), 'Effects of age at entry, knowledge intensity, and imitability on international growth', *Academy of Management Journal*, **43** (5), 909–24.

Busenitz, L.W., C. Gomez and J.W. Spencer (2000), 'Country institutional profiles: unlocking entrepreneurial phenomena', *Academy of Management Journal*, **43** (5), 994–1003.

Dana, L.-P. (2004), *Handbook of Research on International Entrepreneurship*, Cheltenham, UK and Northampton, MA, USA: Edward Elgar.

Hisrich, R.D., S. Honig-Haftel, P.P. McDougall and B.M. Oviatt (1996), 'International entrepreneurship: past, present, and future', *Entrepreneurship: Theory & Practice*, Summer, 5–7.

Johanson, J. and J.-E Vahlne (1977), 'The internationalization process of the firm – a model of knowledge development and increasing foreign market commitments', *Journal of International Business Studies*, **8** (1), 25–34.

Johanson, J. and J.-E. Vahlne (1990), 'The mechanism of internationalization', *International Marketing Review*, **7** (4), 11–24.

Lumpkin, G.T. and G.G. Dess, (1996), 'Clarifying the entrepreneurial orientation construct and linking it to performance', *Academy of Management Review*, **21**, 135–72.

McDougall, P.P. (1989), 'International versus domestic entrepreneurship: new venture strategic behavior and industry structure', *Journal of Business Venturing*, **4**, 387–99.

McDougall, P.P. and B.M. Oviatt, (2000), 'International entrepreneurship: the intersection of two research paths', *Academy of Management Journal*, **43**, 902–8.

McNaughton, R.B. (2001), 'The export mode decision-making process in small knowledge-intensive firms', *Market Intelligence and Planning*, **19**, 12–20.

McNaughton, R.B. (2003), 'The number of export markets that a firm serves: process models versus the born-global phenomenon', *Journal of International Entrepreneurship*, **1**, 297–311.

Morrow, J.F. (1988), 'International entrepreneurship: a new growth opportunity', *New Management*, **3**, 59–61.

Oviatt, B.M. and P.P. McDougall, (1994), 'Toward a theory of international new ventures', *Journal of International Business Studies*, **36** (1), 29–41.

Oviatt, B.M. and P.P. McDougall (2005), 'Defining international entrepreneurship and modeling the speed of internationalization', *Entrepreneurship: Theory & Practice*, **29** (5), 537–53.

Oviatt, B.M. and P.P. McDougall, (eds) (2007), *International Entrepreneurship*, Cheltenham, UK and Northampton, MA, USA: Edward Elgar.

Reuber, A.R. and E. Fischer (1997), 'The influence of the management team's international experience on the internationalization behavior of SMEs', *Journal of International Business Studies*, **28** (4), 807–25.

Shane, S. and S. Venkataraman (2000), 'The promise of entrepreneurship as a field of research', *Academy of Management Review*, **25**, 217–26.

Stinchcombe, A.L. (1965), 'Social structure and organizations', in J.G. March (ed.), *Handbook of Organizations*, Chicago, IL: Rand McNally, pp. 142–93.

Wright, R.W. and D.A. Ricks (1994), 'Trends in international business research: twenty-five years later', *Journal of International Business Studies*, **25**, 687–701.

Zahra, S.A. (1993), 'Conceptual model of entrepreneurship as firm behavior: a critique and extension', *Entrepreneurship: Theory & Practice*, **14** (4), 5–21.

Zahra, S.A. and G. George (2002), 'International entrepreneurship: the current status of the field and future research agenda', in M.A. Hitt, R.D. Ireland, D. Sexton and D.L. Camp (eds), *Strategic Leadership: Creating a New Mindset*, London: Blackwell, pp. 255–88.

Zahra, S.A., R.D. Ireland and M.A. Hitt (2000), 'International expansion by new venture firms: international diversity, mode of market entry, technological learning, and performance', *Academy of Management Journal*, **43** (5), 925–50.

32 Internationalization of European entrepreneurs

Léo-Paul Dana, Isa Welpe, Vanessa Ratten and Mary Han

This entry compares internationalization experiences in various European countries. Based on empirical studies conducted in 36 countries, we propose an extension of current theory with regard to small and medium-sized enterprise (SME) internationalization in Europe. We develop a process model to explain the moderating and mediating influences on SME internationalization in various economies in Europe.

So far, there have been many studies on the globalization strategies of large firms and multinational enterprises but until recently SMEs have been overlooked in the literature to date (Dana et al., 1999). Prior research on SMEs tends to concentrate on their impact on domestic economic growth and the few extant studies of SME internationalization are focused on the USA, Japan or on individual European countries. Comparative, regional research on SMEs in Europe is still emerging.

Europe is a unique agglomeration of countries within the world. Its countries are diverse in size, political background and economic development. Europe has both island economies and transition economies and its developed economies range from the very small (for example, Vatican City) to the very powerful (for example the UK). Moreover, Europe is influenced by the two major world trade networks, the European Union (EU) and the World Trade Organization (WTO) so there are many opportunities for foreign direct investment (FDI) and export. Indeed, the European Union (EU) is the world's second largest economy by gross domestic product (GDP) (see note to Table 32.1) and the third most populous region – it is an international trade powerhouse (World Bank, 2006). Studying the internationalization process of entrepreneurs and their SMEs in such a diverse and important region has the potential to shed light on the internationalization phenomenon of SMEs in other parts of the world as well as to test the fit and applicability of existing theories of internationalization to the diverse European context.

Secondly, extending the first reason, Japan, the USA and Europe form the world's largest trading blocs; however, only Europe is itself a bloc of many countries. As such, it offers unique insights into international business and entrepreneurship that have not yet been fully explored. Third, Europe is politically and socially diverse. Relatively small, highly educated, technologically advanced countries neighbour nations which have struggled with years of recession, reverse economic growth and war.

Based on the meta-analysis of 36 recent empirical studies on the internationalization of SMEs in Europe, we provide testable propositions of the internationalization of SMEs in (1) transitional economies, (2) developed economies and (3) island economies. Overall, our study contributes to the international entrepreneurship research and practice in several aspects. First, by unravelling the uniqueness of European international entrepreneurship we build understanding that will transfer to other parts of the world. Second,

Table 32.1 EU countries from richest to poorest[1]

Country	Population	Per capita gross national income
Luxembourg	474413	$61610
Ireland	4062235	$32930
Austria	8192880	$31800
Denmark	5450661	$31770
Belgium	10379067	$31530
United Kingdom	60609153	$31430
Netherlands	16491461	$31360
Sweden	9016596	
Finland	5231372	
France	60876136	$29460
Germany	82422299	$28170
Italy	58133509	$28120
Spain	40397842	$24750
Greece	10688058	
Cyprus	784301	
Slovenia	2010347	$20830
Portugal	10605870	$19240
Malta	400214	$18590
Czech Republic	10235455	$18420
Hungary	9981334	$15800
Slovakia	5439448	$14480
Estonia	1324333	$13630
Poland	38536869	$12730
Lithuania	3585906	$12690
Latvia	2274735	$11820

Notes:
1. Based on 2004 PPP GNP per capita in international dollars.
Boasting the world's second-largest economy by gross GDP and third-highest population, the EU is an international trade powerhouse. Based on World Bank Development Indicators published in July 2006, these are the 25 EU countries and their corresponding gross national product (GNP) per capita based on global purchasing power parity (PPP) in international dollars. Gross national product per capita, also referred to as gross national income, represents the total amount of money that a country's consumers spend on all goods and services in a year divided by that country's population.

our work fills a gap in the existing literature because it includes many European countries in their diversity, addresses the critical role of transitioning economies, and recognizes that Europe has been undergoing rapid change. Finally, our theoretical frameworks help to inform and depict these variables and the process of SME internationalization with supporting evidence from 36 European countries.

MODEL DEVELOPMENT

To develop our model, we categorize European countries into three major types: transition economies, market economies, and island economies.

Transition Economies

Transition economies exist in countries that have shifted from centralized political power to privatization (Kornai, 1999) and from central planning to market economics. They are sometimes called 'emerging market economies' (Gelb, 1999). Their economic growth is such that they already interact with advanced market economies (Svejnar, 2002). Eventually, these countries will compete with developed market economies, but they are not at this stage yet, they are in transition. Examples include Estonia, Poland, the Czech Republic, Hungry, Slovenia, Bulgaria and Slovakia.

Market Economies

Market economies exist in countries that generate rapid and sustainable rates of economic growth. They compete with other advanced market economies without any trade protection. Examples include Germany, France, the UK, Italy, Netherlands, Austria, Belgium, Denmark, Turkey, Switzerland and Finland.

Island Economies

Island economies exist in countries with self-sustained economies and can be separate geographically from other countries or be geographically next to another country. Examples include Malta, Andorra, Monaco and Liechtenstein.

INTERNATIONALIZATION OF SMES IN TRANSITION ECONOMIES

There are three issues, unique to transition economies, that have not yet been fully explained in the extant literature: (1) why have so many SMEs emerged in these countries in such a short time? (2) Why are they concurrently internationalizing at the same pace? (3) How does the internationalization of SMEs operate? We adopt a variable-theorizing and process-theorizing approach to explain the factors behind these interdependent issues. Figure 32.1 illustrates the process of SME internationalization in transition economies. We also propose four variables that might be contributing to this phenomenon.

The transition from central planning economies to market economies has been difficult. We have seen the collapse of the Soviet political and economic system in the late 1980s, the fall of the Berlin wall in 1989 and ongoing economic recession in Soviet Bloc countries. Yet, transition economies have progressed (Svejnar, 2002), evidenced by the rapid internationalization of SMEs. We argue that the microeconomic and macroeconomic openness of these countries is a mediating factor in this development.

Before abandoning central planning in the late 1980s, transition economies were characterized by poor economic growth, inefficient resource distribution, poor access to information about other market models and unclear government policy. Economic rigidity discouraged innovation, invention and efficient allocation of resources. The population lived in a state of fear and uncertainty and lacked the resources, capabilities and knowledge to make informed decisions. The rules of the central government planning

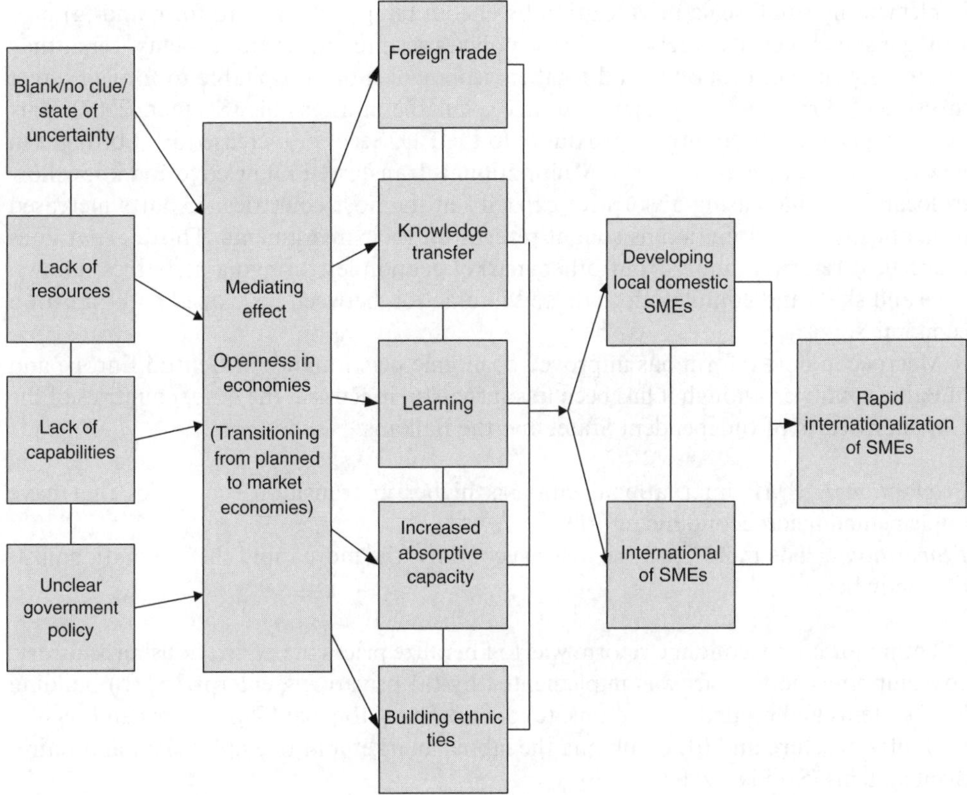

Figure 32.1 Internationalization of SMEs in transition economies

systems were unclear and opaque. Corruption undermined regulation and made foreign trade and investment risky. These conditions directly impacted domestic and international entrepreneurship.

MACROECONOMIC AND MICROECONOMIC REFORM

In the late 1980s, various Soviet Bloc policy-makers formulated strategies to open their economies via macroeconomic stabilization and microeconomic restructuring. These policies were adopted at different rates and to varying degrees by the transition economies. Hence, we see differences in the internationalization strategies of SMEs in these countries.

The major macroeconomic reforms included dismantling the communist system, abolishing the Council for Mutual Economic Assistance (CMEA), and encouraging price liberalization. Transition economies took several steps to operationalize these objectives including: (a) implementing restrictive fiscal and monetary policies, (b) managing wages, (c) fixing exchange rate, (d) reducing subsidies to state-owned enterprises, (e) breaking up the 'monobank' system to create new and independent banks, (f) implementing small-scale privatization by encouraging new firms to form and (g) providing a social security safety net. These policies resulted in several benefits. First, they created a political, economic and legal environment more hospitable to foreign direct investment. Privatization projects became available and feasible (Svejnar, 2002), particularly given these countries' proximity to the EU. Second, increased FDI brought in new learning from outside world. Multinationals transferred knowledge and know how to local firms, increasing absorptive capacity in the host countries. Exports increased dramatically as multinationals sought returns on their investments. Third, expatriates (ethic ties) returned home from other market economies, bringing resources, knowledge and skills and stimulating trade and interaction between developed and transition economies.

Macroeconomic reform has improved economic performance in Central Europe and in Baltic countries, though it has been less successful in Russia, the other countries of the Commonwealth of Independent States and the Balkans.

Proposition 1: SME internationalization is higher in transition economies that have implemented macroeconomic reform.
Proposition 2: The more open the macro economy, the more rapid the internationalization activities.

The major microeconomic reform was to liberalize prices in energy, housing and basic consumption goods. This was implemented by (a) privatizing enterprises, (b) building legal systems and related institutions, (c) developing viable banking systems and regulatory infrastructure and (d) regulating the labour market and unemployment and retirement systems (Svejnar, 2002).

Proposition 3: Domestic entrepreneurship is higher in transition economies that have implemented microeconomic reform.
Proposition 4: The more open the micro economy, the more rapid the domestic entrepreneurship activities.

HUNGARY: A SUCCESSFUL REFORMER

There are major obstacles to macroeconomic and microeconomic reform in transition countries. Success often depends on the ability of the government to control corruption and collect sufficient tax revenues to finance public programmes. However, implementing these reforms is critical to shifting from a centrally planned to an economy in which domestic entrepreneurs and foreign investors can exploit and explore new opportunities. The example of Hungary illustrates how domestic entrepreneurship and SME internationalization occurs concurrently and rapidly.

Hungry has a relatively strong track record of reform (see Table 32.2 and Box 32.1). It has built clear property rights, improved corporate governance, privatized most state-owned enterprises and substantially supported the creation of new and private firms (Svejnar, 2002). Macroeconomic stability and microeconomic institutional restructuring have helped the country increase its level of knowledge, information, resources, learning,

Table 32.2 Economic openness, internationalization and performance

Transition economy	Economic openness	Macro reforms	Micro reforms	Results
Poland	Medium	Foreign direct investment Rapidly privatize small enterprises Encourage creation of new firms	Firms remain state-owned, but run by independently appointed supervisory board	Slow internationalization
Hungry	High	Significant flow of foreign direct investment Substantially support creation of new firms Break up and privatize state-owned large enterprises into small firms	State-owned enterprises sold outright to outside owners	Fast internationalization Improved managerial skills More external revenues
Lithuania	Low	Foreign direct investment Encourage creation of new firms	Subsidized, management–employee buyout of state-owned firms	Fast internationalization Poor economic performance

and absorptive capacity. These characteristics have helped it generate new firms, accelerate economic growth and stimulate SMEs to internationalize. Thus, we propose:

Proposition 5: Transition economies are more likely to achieve superior performance in both domestic entrepreneurship and SME internationalization when they achieve macroeconomic and microeconomic openness.
Proposition 6: The more open the economy (macro and micro), the more likely that rapid domestic entrepreneurship and SME internationalization will occur.

INTERNATIONALIZATION OF SMES IN MARKET ECONOMIES

Extant literature suggests that resources are important criteria for internationalization (Zahra et al., 2005). We argue that the internationalization of SMEs in Europe is positively influenced by: (1) government policy, (2) membership of a cluster or network, (3) internal firm resources and capabilities and (4) the size of the domestic market. Small and medium-sized enterprises that leverage resources and capabilities, operate under favourable government policy regimes, and take advantage of networks and clusters, will derive greater performance benefits from internationalization. These factors will accelerate SME internationalization.

BOX 32.1 EAST-CENTRAL EUROPE GROWTH OUTPACES CORE EU 13 MARCH 2006

The release of final GDP growth numbers from the four largest EU accession countries – Czech, Hungary, Poland, and Slovakia – confirm these countries' rapid growth compared to the core EU. Consider:

Czech GDP growth soared to a stellar 6.9 per cent year on year (y/y) pace in quarter 4 2005 versus expectations for a 5.0 per cent increase. This boosted 2005 Czech GDP growth to 6.0 per cent – the biggest increase since the Czech Republic and Slovakia separated 13 years ago. Foreign trade remained the mainstay of growth, although domestic consumption and investment also contributed to the outturn.

Hungary's GDP growth eased to 4.3 per cent y/y in the third quarter from 4.5 per cent in the third quarter 2005. Strong manufacturing and construction sectors as well as robust exports remained the key drivers of Hungary's economic growth. January trade data showed Hungary's exports jumped 21.6 per cent y/y, the fastest pace in 19 months, following a 14.6 per cent increase in December. Imports, meanwhile, grew by 23.0 per cent y/y, up 9.1 per cent on the December growth which already represented a 19-month high.

Poland's GDP growth in 2005 was 3.5 per cent – not bad, but still very good considering the poor start at the beginning of last year. Economic activity in the country grew steadily in 2005, from 2.1 per cent y/y in quarter 1 to 2.8 per cent y/y in quarter 2, 3.7 per cent y/y in quarter 3 and 4.2 per cent y/y in quarter 4. Hence, much of this growth is expected to continue.

Source: EDC website, http://edc.ca, written by Jean-Louis Renaud.

Proposition 7: The internationalization of SMEs in Europe is driven by factors such as government policy, national economy, firm resources, membership of networks and clusters, market competition and industry sector.
Proposition 8: Firms in established economies in Europe that can leverage resources, join a cluster and operate under favourable government policies, will internationalize fastest and achieve higher performance benefits.

We draw on propositions 7, and 8 to develop a model for SME internationalization in market economies in Europe (Figure 32.2). This model helps to explain the importance of resources (R), networks (N), government policy (P) and size of the domestic market (S). The greater the intensity of R, N, P, and S, the greater the benefits for the internationalizing SME and the faster its speed of internationalization.

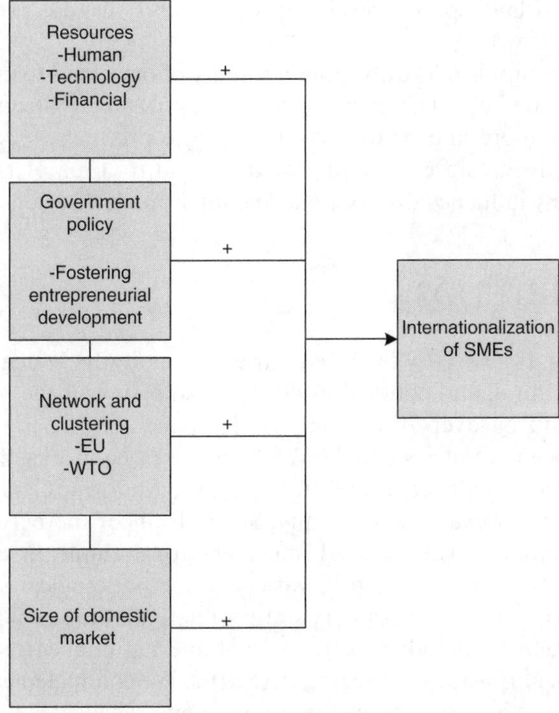

Figure 32.2 Internationalization of SMEs in developed economies

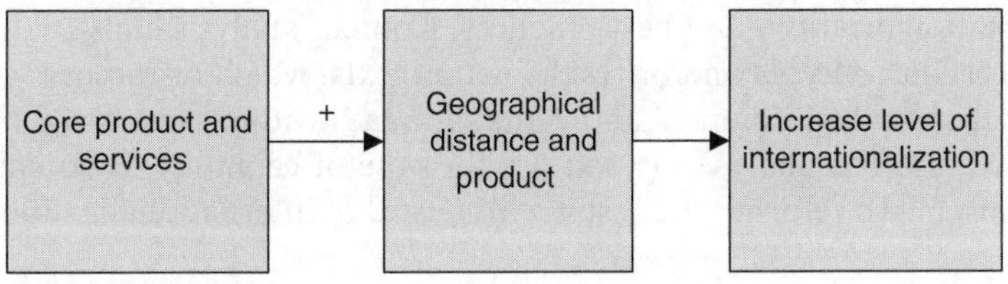

Figure 32.3 Internationalization of SMEs in island economies

INTERNATIONALIZATION OF SMES IN ISLAND ECONOMIES

Based on observation, we argue that there are two major factors that enhance the internationalization of SMEs in island economies: (1) the availability of island-specific core products, services and business processes and (2) the geographical location of the island (Figure 32.3). The former argument is consistent with the resource-based view that productivity (in this case, of the country) largely depends on available resources (Barney, 1991; Wernerfelt, 1984). The geographical location of the island also impacts domestic and international entrepreneurship. For example, the success of the tourism industry in Malta is largely due to the proximity of the island to other major market economies. Thus, we propose:

Proposition 9: Core island specific products, services and business processes are critical to island economic growth.
Proposition 10: Geographical location and proximity of the island to other major market economies significantly impact economic growth and internationalization.
Proposition 11: The more and better the island's core products, services and business process coupled with the close proximity of the island to a major network of market economies, positively influence the domestic and internationalization activities.

RESEARCH METHODS

Table 32.3 provides an overview of the countries in our study, which represent the different economic, cultural, and political spectrums existing in Europe. We have examined 36 studies conducted by over 70 researchers. They include, six island economies, 12 former East European countries and 18 West European countries. The sample is also well balanced between small economies (for example, Andorra, Cyprus, Liechtenstein) and large economies (for example, Germany, Spain, France) and between EU members (for example, Belgium, Italy) and non-EU members (for example, Belarus, Switzerland). The studies of our book make use of a variety of methodological approaches. Study data include secondary as well as primary sources and quantitative as well as qualitative research designs. Each study indicates the state of international entrepreneurship in the respective countries in Europe with regards to SMEs. We conducted content analysis on these empirical studies in order to achieve a more comprehensive understanding of the current phenomenon in Europe and to derive patterns and categories theme by theme. In other words, we analysed the completed reports to identify patterns, differences, inhibitors to internationalization, and best practices. Content analysis aims to determine the presence of certain concepts and/or results within texts, which researchers quantify and analyse and then make inferences about the messages within the texts. The categories which we have used to analyse the text are the type of economy, economic openness, macro reforms, micro reforms and result with regard to internationalization of SMEs.

FINDINGS

The propositions above will now be examined in terms of whether they were supported or not supported by the findings in our book Dana et al. (2008). Proposition 1 argues that SME internationalization is higher in transition economies that have implemented macroeconomic reform and this is supported by the research. Many new EU members from the former Soviet Union in Eastern Europe such as Latvia, Lithuania and Estonia have undergone significant macroeconomic reforms in order to achieve EU requirements. As part of the EU, these countries have higher SME internationalization rates than European countries that have not undergone macroeconomic reform. Turkey is an example of a non-EU member country that has low levels of macroeconomic reform being conducted that has resulted in a low SME internationalization rate.

Proposition 2 argues that the more open the macro economy, the more rapid the internationalization activities and the result is somewhat mixed in the research. Both

Table 32.3 Characteristics of countries in content analysis

Country	Population	EU membership	Type of country	Type of sample
European VCs	n.a.	n.a.	n.a.	Email survey of VC firms
Andorra	71 800	No	Island economy	Secondary data from a range of sources
Austria	8 037 400	Yes	Market economy	Qestionnaire survey of Austrian SMEs
Belarus	10 044 800	No	Transition economy	Statistical data from two surveys
Belgium	10 339 300	Yes	Market economy	Questionnaire data collected between 1991 and 1995
Bosnia	4 207 300	Potential candidate country	Transition economy	Case study of a medium-sized company in the food processing industry
Bulgaria	7 917 600	Acceding country	Transition economy	Secondary data from the reports about SME sector by the Agency for SMEs, Ministry of Economy, National Statistic Institute, Bulgarian National Bank
Croatia	4 397 400	Candidate country	Transition economy	Combination of primary and secondary data
Cyprus	935 400	Yes	Island economy	Extensive literature search and review and is largely a conceptual analysis
Denmark	5 387 300	Yes	Market economy	Mail and telephone survey
Estonia	1 268 300	Yes	Transition economy	Conceptual
Finland	5 215 100	Yes	Market economy	Secondary data, conceptual
Former Yugoslav Republic of Macedonia	2 114 500	Candidate Country	Transition economy	Secondary data
France	60 656 178	Yes	Market economy	Survey of high-technology firms
Germany	82 431 390	Yes	Market economy	1450 manufacturing firms
Greece	10 668 354	Yes	Market economy	In-depth case study
Hungary	10 006 835	Yes	Yes	2000 SMEs
Ireland	4 015 676	Yes	Market economy	405 Irish entrepreneurs in tourism enterprise
Israel	6 556 000	No	Market economy	Case studies
Italy	58 103 033	Yes	Market economy	Survey of medical firms

Table 32.3 (continued)

Country	Population	EU membership	Type of country	Type of sample
Latvia	2 290 237	Yes	Transition economy	Two samples: 1 survey by Central Statistical Bureau of Latvia 2 Latvian exports' survey
Liechtenstein	34 600	No	Island economy	Secondary data and survey
Lithuania	3 596 617	Yes	Transition economy	44 manufacturing SMEs
Malta	398 534	Yes	Island economy	Government data and case studies
Moldova	4 229 700	No	Transition economy	Secondary data analysis, qualitative data
Monaco	32 409	No	Island economy	Government data and case studies
Netherlands	16 258 300	Yes	Market economy	Survey data
Poland	38 635 144	Yes	Market economy	Surveys conducted on SMEs by Poland Scientific Research Committee
Portugal	10 566 212	Yes	Market economy	81 manufacturing SMEs
San Marino	28 400	No	Island economy	In-depth interviews
Slovenia	2 011 070	Yes	Transition economy	Government data
Spain	40 341 462	Yes	Market economy	Global entrepreneurship monitor data
Sweden	9 001 774	Yes	Market economy	In-depth case studies
Switzerland	7 376 000	No	Market economy	Survey
Turkey	69 660 559	Candidate country	Transition economy	98 private companies in Istanbul
Ukraine	47 425 336	No	Transition economy	Empirical data
Constituents of the United Kingdom:				
England	50 690 000	Yes	Market economy	SMEs in international trade partnerships
Scotland	5 116 900	Yes	Market economy	SMEs in international trade partnerships
Wales	2 958 876	Yes	Market economy	SMEs in international trade partnerships

Ireland and Scotland have open macro economies but have significantly different levels of internationalization activities. While Ireland has been very successful in developing businesses in the information technology (IT) field, Scotland has not developed its internationalization activities at the same rate

Proposition 3 states that domestic entrepreneurship is higher in transition economies that have implemented microeconomic reform and the result is supported in the research. The Ukraine government has successfully created state innovation agencies and technology parks that have been combined with microeconomic reforms such as the deregulation of state owned enterprises that have encouraged domestic entrepreneurship. Proposition 4 argues that the more open the micro economy, the more rapid the domestic entrepreneurship activities and this was supported by the research. Israel is an example of such a country that has an open micro economy and a very dynamic domestic economy that is highly focused on knowledge intensive industries such as biotechnology.

Proposition 5 states that transition economies are more likely to achieve superior performance in both domestic entrepreneurship and SME internationalization when they achieve macroeconomic and microeconomic openness and this was supported by the research. New EU members such as Poland have undergone a significant amount of microeconomic reform prior to entering the EU and have become more macroeconomically open as a result of becoming an EU member. However, because of the EU protectionist stance on farming, transition economies in Europe need to focus on competing on a global basis with more macroeconomics and microeconomic openness.

Proposition 6 argues that the more open the economy (macro and micro), the more likely that rapid domestic entrepreneurship and SME internationalization will occur and the result was mixed in this research. For example, Spain has a low SME internationalization rate with a high percentage of large multinationals that have decreased the SME internationalization rate. Proposition 7 states that internationalization of SMEs in Europe is driven by factors such as government policy, national economy, firms resources, membership of networks and clusters, market competition and industry sector, and this proposition is supported. These factors allow different countries in Europe including small and large population sized countries to focus on different aspects of their economy in which they are the most efficient. For example, the internationalization of SMEs in Germany is largely driven by the government policy focusing on international markets while Malta's government focuses on the development of networks and clusters that encourage collaboration in niche industries such as the craft industry.

Proposition 8 argues that firms in established economies in Europe that can leverage resources, join a cluster and operate under favorable government policies, will internationalize fastest and achieve higher performance benefits and the results were mixed in the research. Countries in Europe such as Ireland have higher internationalization rates than similar established economies such as Scotland, and Ireland's growth has largely been attributed to the predominance of technology firms. However, similar government policies in Scotland have yet to see comparable internationalization rates similar to that of Ireland. Proposition 9 states that core island-specific products, services and business processes are critical to island-economic growth and this proposition is supported in the research. Particularly in island economies that are focused on tourism such as Cyprus it is important that services are incorporated into measures of economic growth. Likewise, in Liechtenstein the growth of the financial service sector has greatly increased its growth rate.

Proposition 10 argues that geographic location and proximity of the island to other major market economies significantly impact economic growth and internationalization and this was supported by the research. Liechtenstein has benefited from being close geographically to Germany which has allowed for many German businesses to operate in Liechtenstein due to the favourable taxation laws. Similarly, Andorra while being close to Spain is further away from the other mainland European countries that have affected its economic growth rate. Proposition 11 states that the more and better the island's core products, services and business process coupled with the close proximity of the island to a major network of market economies, positively influence the domestic and internationalization activities and this was supported by the research. Monaco is a good example of an island economy that has achieved a high internationalization rate through utilizing its position close to France and focusing on high-technology industries.

IMPLICATIONS

Much of the existing research on international entrepreneurship takes the position that all transitional economies can be classified together. However, as the chapters of Dana et al. (2008) show, many transitional economies are at different stages of development that affect SME internationalization rates. For example, Eastern European transitional economies such as Estonia, Latvia and Lithuania that are now part of the EU have a macroeconomic environment that is conducive to entrepreneurship because of the stability of financial institutions. However, transitional economies such as Turkey and the Ukraine are at a different stage of development in their quest for EU membership. The conceptual models developed in this chapter also highlight the importance of island economies in Europe. Past research on international entrepreneurship in Europe has seemed to neglect the importance of island economies and the context of geography in developing different types of entrepreneurship. European countries located in the Mediterranean have typically had a craft-based entrepreneurship culture that fosters domestic entrepreneurship. However, despite the existence of island economies, there seems to lack an existence of theories to explain international entrepreneurship in island economies. The theoretical models developed in this chapter are an attempt to initiate a framework that can help to understand the role of geography, culture and market conditions in SME internationalization rates in Europe. Thus, it is important for international entrepreneurship theory to take into account these differences when building theory and take a wider stance on the use of terms such as transitional economies.

We propose a theoretical framework in which to understand the complexity of the SME internationalization process in Europe. For governmental organizations involved in developing future policy initiatives this chapter has provided a useful analysis of how transitional, island and developed economies in Europe undergo their SME internationalization efforts. As the majority of businesses in Europe are SMEs, it is particularly helpful for governments to learn and understand the internationalization process through examining how different factors such as resources and clusters impact on a country's development process. By pinpointing the most important factors that speed up the internationalization process of SMEs, governments can save money and develop more cost-efficient plans for helping SMEs achieve higher rates of market penetration.

For practitioners, this chapter is useful in providing examples and a discussion of SME internationalization processes in Europe. Managers can learn through experience and example about the best ways in which to foster internationalization whether it be through micro or macro policy initiatives. For future research, there needs to be further analysis on the different types of transitional economies and how they differ from island economies. Given the abundant diversity of economic systems in Europe, there is a plethora of research needed on SME internationalization efforts in Europe.

REFERENCES

Barney, J.B. (1991), 'Firm resources and sustained competitive advantage', *Journal of Management*, **17** (1), 99–120.

Dana, L., H. Etemad and R.W. Wright (1999), 'The theoretical foundations of international entrepreneurship', in Richard W. Wright, (ed.), *International Entrepreneurship: Globalization of Emerging Businesses*, Stamford, CN: JAI Press, pp. 3–22.

Dana, Léo-Paul, Isabell M. Welpe, Mary Han and Vanessa Ratten (2008), *Handbook of Research on European Business and Entrepreneurship: Towards a Theory of Internationalization*, Cheltenham, UK and Northampton, MA, USA: Edward Elgar.

Gelb, A. (1999), 'The end of transition?', in A. Brown (ed.), *When Is the Transition Over?*, Kalamazoo, MI: W.E. Upjohn Institute for Employment Research, pp. 39–49.

Kornai, J. (1999), 'Reforming the welfare state in postsocialist economies', in A. Brown (ed.), *When Is the Transition Over?* Kalamazoo, MI: W.E. Upjohn Institute for Employment Research, ch. 8.

Svejnar, J. (2002), 'Transition economies: performance and challenges', *Journal of Economic Perspectives*, **16** (1), 3–28.

Wernerfelt, B. (1984), 'A resource-based view of the firm', *Strategic Management Journal*, **5** (2), 171–80.

World Bank (2006), *World Bank Development Indicators*, New York: World Bank.

Zahra, S.A., J.S. Korri and J. Yu (2005) 'Cognition and international entrepreneurship: implications for research on international opportunity recognition and exploitation', *International Business Review*, **14**, 129–46.

33 Involuntary entrepreneurship

Teemu Kautonen, Simon Down, Friederike Welter, Kai Althoff, Jenni Palmroos, Susanne Kolb and Pekka Vainio

Involuntary entrepreneurship refers to the phenomenon of business enterprises replacing employment relationships with contracted self-employed workers as a result of vertical de-integration and outsourcing processes. An involuntary entrepreneur is an individual who has become self-employed even though he or she would prefer paid employment, and who is mainly self-employed in contractual terms but in practice is treated as an employee because of the way the contract is executed. Other terms used in this context include forced (Hakala, 2006; Palkkatyöläinen, 2007) and reluctant entrepreneurship (Boyle, 1994; Stanworth and Stanworth, 1997), false self-employment (Harvey, 2001), para-subordination (Perulli, 2003), employed self-employment (Paasch, 1990; Wank, 1988), hybrid self-employment (Bögenhold, 1987) and dependent self-employment (Böheim and Muehlberger, 2006).

Developments such as vertical de-integration, lean production and outsourcing in large firms as well as the introduction of new technologies allowing for a separation of work place and activity (Beck, 2000; Boyle, 1994; Harrison, 1994; Sennett, 1998) have given rise to growing political interest and concern regarding people being pushed into new forms of precarious self-employment. These new working arrangements are located somewhere in a grey area between employment and self-employment (Perulli, 2003; Schulze Buschoff, 2004). The employer's motive for such arrangements is to find more flexibility by avoiding the costs, obligations and responsibilities related to employment relationships. The employee, on the other hand, is often effectively 'forced' into becoming a subcontractor. Two streams of literature relate to this context: one addressing the negative 'push' motives behind the decision to start up in business and the other focusing on the legal and economic aspects of operating in the grey area between an employment relationship and self-employment. The main arguments and central policy questions of each stream are introduced in the following two sections. The expressions 'self-employed' and 'entrepreneurs' are used interchangeably to refer to individuals who are in business for themselves.

THE INVOLUNTARINESS OF ENTREPRENEURSHIP

The involuntariness in the employee's decision to become self-employed is related to a strong influence of 'push' factors (for the pull/push discussion see, for example, Brüderl et al., 1996; Granger et al., 1995; Mallon, 1998; Stanworth and Curran, 1973). Perhaps the most common 'push' factor is unemployment or its threat. This affects people in situations where work that used to be done in employment relationships is being outsourced. Here, former employees and other individuals are offered work but only if they do this as self-employed. These individuals would not become self-employed were it not for (the threat of) unemployment. However, involuntariness does not mean that the individuals were 'forced' into self-employment – it rather means that remaining in paid employment would have been their preference. Moreover, involuntariness has a dynamic dimension too. Previous studies point out that self-employment which began as a reluctant choice may evolve to a desirable alternative over time (Granger et al., 1995; Hinz and Jungbauer-Gans, 1999). Thus, the central empirical question in this context is whether the entrepreneur, at a given time, would be willing to give up self-employment if he or she could continue doing the same work in an employment relationship.

The central policy question concerns whether the involuntariness of self-employment has any consequences to the new entrepreneur personally or to the performance and development of his or her business. Examining the motives for starting up in business is an 'evergreen' issue in entrepreneurship research (for example, Blackburn, 2001; Davidsson, 1995). The aim of this research is to identify which 'types' of entrepreneurs are more successful in developing their venture and thus produce more positive externalities associated with entrepreneurship, such as job creation, increased potential for innovation and improvement of technological adaptability (for example, Ministerie van Economische Zaken, 2000; Parker, 2004; see also the opportunity/necessity discussion in the Global Entrepreneurship Monitor studies, for example, Reynolds et al., 2002). Thus, the discussion around whether entrepreneurship is push or pull-driven implicitly assumes that the motives for entering self-employment and subsequent business development are closely linked. For example, Amit et al. (1996: 2) suggest that 'the decision to start a new venture gives a strong basis for predicting the likely success'. In other words: the contribution of involuntary entrepreneurship to economic development is likely to be limited. This becomes apparent in most Global Entrepreneurship Monitor studies, which tend to judge necessity entrepreneurship (as opposed to opportunity entrepreneurship) as a negative factor as far as national growth and development are concerned (for example, Allen et al., 2006; Reynolds et al., 2002). Moreover, involuntary entrepreneurs have been found to have a lower job satisfaction and a higher level of stress and risk related to the personal unsuitability of self-employment compared to paid employment (Block and Wagner, 2006).

OPERATING IN THE 'GREY AREA' BETWEEN EMPLOYMENT AND SELF-EMPLOYMENT

The discussion on involuntary entrepreneurship is not limited to the motives, but it also includes the legal and economic aspects of precarious self-employment in the 'grey area' between employment relationships and self-employment. Following Dietrich (1999) and Schmidt and Schwerdtner (1999) the notion 'quasi self-employed' is used in the following to address the (quasi-)legal status of an individual who is mainly self-employed in contractual terms but in practice is treated as an employee because of the way the contract is executed. Typical characteristics associated with such working arrangements include not having employees, the initiative for self-employment and the business idea originating from the former employer, economic dependence on one client (often the former employer), and working under the authority of the client with little control over the time, place, and content of work (Böheim and Muehlberger, 2006; Harvey, 2001; Kautonen et al., 2007).

Depending on the political, legal and economic framework of the country in question, quasi self-employed individuals may face several disadvantages compared to being an employee or a 'real' entrepreneur. Compared to an employment relationship, such downsides include for example loss of trade union representation and the benefits of collective bargaining, loss of legal status and protection as an employee, a downgrade in social security status, and having to take care of one's own pension, sick and parental leave arrangements (Block and Wagner, 2006; Böheim and Muehlberger, 2006; Filion 2004; Parker, 2004). Since quasi self-employed are highly dependent on one client, they lack such independence as often associated with 'real' entrepreneurs. On the other hand, 'real' entrepreneurs – for example, industrial subcontractors – can also be economically dependent on one client, and since this dependence can guarantee a steady flow of business, it is not necessarily a negative factor. However, it becomes one if a company hires self-employed workers primarily in order to avoid the commitment involved in an employment relationship and to shift the risk of fluctuations in demand to the new self-employed, who as a result may experience periods of near unemployment (Böheim and Muehlberger, 2006). Also ambiguities regarding the legal status – whether their working arrangement is interpreted as employment or self-employment by tax or other authorities – may cause problems to the new entrepreneurs (see, for example, Harvey, 2001).

According to a recent investigation of involuntary entrepreneurship in Finland, Germany and the UK (Kautonen et al., 2007), the primary policy concern in terms of the legal position of the quasi self-employed appears to be the need to protect the interests of the individual, who as an involuntary entrepreneur is in a disadvantageous position compared to an employee. Interestingly, the disadvantages compared to 'real' entrepreneurs or the actual involuntariness of entrepreneurship seemed to be minor concerns. The central question in this context is how to correctly assess and legally classify (self-)employment and to distinguish one from the other (Perulli, 2003). By which criteria individual working arrangements are classified as employment, self-employment or something in between, and what rights and obligations such classifications involve, is a political matter that varies between countries and governments. The aforementioned cross-country examination of involuntary entrepreneurship revealed an unsurprising divergence between employers and trade unions on this issue (Kautonen et al., 2007). The employers are concerned about the possibility of rising labour costs through extensions of employment rights (and thus employer's obligations) to more of the atypical workforce, or the possible regulation of quasi self-employment harming 'voluntary' forms of inter-firm cooperation or business concepts such as franchising which in some respects may resemble quasi self-employment (Vainio, 2007). The trade unions, on the other hand, reject this and emphasize the confusion, short-sightedness and injustice involved in precarious working arrangements.

REFERENCES

Allen, I.E., N. Langowitz and M. Minniti (2006), *Global Entrepreneurship Monitor: 2006 Report on Women and Entrepreneurship*, Babson College and London Business School, available at: http://www.gemconsortium.org (accessed 16 August 2010).

Amit, R., K.R. MacCrimmon and J.M. Oesch (1996), 'The decision to start a new venture: values, beliefs, and alternatives', paper to the Babson College-Kauffman Foundation Entrepreneurship Research Conference, Seattle, June.

Beck, U. (2000), *The Brave New World of Work*, Cambridge: Polity.

Blackburn, R. (2001), 'Researching entrepreneurship and small firms: towards a new agenda?', keynote address to the RENT XV Conference, Turku, November.

Block, J. and M. Wagner (2006), 'Necessity and opportunity entrepreneurs in Germany: characteristics and earnings differentials', MPRA Paper No. 610.

Bögenhold, D. (1987), *Der Gründerboom: Realität und Mythos der neuen Selbständigkeit*, Frankfurt and New York: Campus.

Böheim, R. and U. Muehlberger (2006), 'Dependent forms of self-employment in the UK: identifying workers on the border between employment and self-employment', IZA Discussion Paper No. 1963.

Boyle, E. (1994), 'The rise of the reluctant entrepreneurs', *International Small Business Journal*, **12**, 63–9.

Brüderl, J., P. Preisendörfer and R. Ziegler (1996), *Der Erfolg neugegründeter Betriebe: eine empirische Studie zu den Chancen und Risiken von Unternehmensgründungen*, Berlin: Duncker & Humblot.

Davidsson, P. (1995), 'Determinants of entrepreneurial intentions', paper to the *RENT IX*, Pracenza, November.

Dietrich, H. (1999), '"Scheinselbständige" oder "Quasi-Firmen"? – Zwei Seiten einer Medaille', in D. Bögenhold and D. Schmidt (eds), *Eine neue Gründerzeit? Die Wiederentdeckung kleiner Unternehmen in Theorie und Praxis*, Amsterdam: Fakultas, pp. 71–98.

Filion, L.J. (2004), 'Two types of self-employed in Canada', in L.P. Dana (ed.), *Handbook of Research on International Entrepreneurship*, Cheltenham, UK and Northampton, MA, USA: Elgar, pp. 308–29.

Granger, B., J. Stanworth and C. Stanworth (1995), 'Self-employment career dynamics: the case of unemployment push in UK book publishing', *Work, Employment and Society*, **9**, 499–516.

Hakala, A. (2006), 'Yrittäjyys ei ole aina vapaaehtoinen valinta', *Uutispäivä Demari*, 18 May.

Harrison, B. (1994), 'The small firms myth', *California Management Review*, **36**, 142–58.

Harvey, M. (2001), *Undermining Construction: The Corrosive Effects of False Self-employment*, London: Institute of Employment Rights.

Hinz, T. and M. Jungbauer-Gans (1999), 'Starting a business after unemployment: characteristics and chances of success (empirical evidence from a regional German labour market), *Entrepreneurship and Regional Development*, **11**, 317–33.

Kautonen, T., S. Down, F. Welter, K. Althoff, J. Kantola, S. Kolb and P. Vainio (2007), 'Involuntary entrepreneurship as a public policy issue in selected European countries', paper to the ICSB 2007 World Conference, Turku, June.

Mallon, M. (1998), 'The portfolio career: pushed or pulled to it?', *Personnel Review*, **27**, 361–77.

Ministerie van Economische Zaken (MEK) (2000), *The Entrepreneurial Society: More Opportunities and Fewer Obstacles for Entrepreneurship*, Den Haag: MEK.

Paasch, U. (1990), 'Selbständig oder abhängig? Deregulierung von Arbeitsbedingungen per Statusdefinition', in J. Berger (ed.), *Kleinbetriebe im wirtschaftlichen Wandel*, Frankfurt and New York: Campus, pp. 129–58.

Palkkatyöläinen (2007), 'Pakkoyrittäjät: oman onnensa sepät', Palkkatyöläinen 1/2007, available at: http://www.palkkatyolainen.fi/pt2007/pt0107/p070131-a5.html (accessed 3 May 2007).

Parker, S.C. (2004), *The Economics of Self-Employment and Entrepreneurship*, Cambridge: Cambridge University Press.

Perulli, A. (2003), 'Economically dependent/quasi-subordinate (parasubordinate) employment: legal, social and economic aspects', study for the European Commission, Committee on Employment and Social Affairs, Brussels.

Reynolds, P., W.D. Bygrave, E. Autio, L.W. Cox and M. Hay (2002), *Global Entrepreneurship Monitor: 2002 Executive Report*, London: GEM.

Schmidt, B. and P. Schwerdtner (1999), *Scheinselbständigkeit. Arbeitsrecht – Sozialrecht*, Munich: Jehle-Rehm.

Schulze Buschoff, K. (2004), 'Neue Selbstständigkeit und wachsender Grenzbereich zwischen selbstständiger und abhängiger Erwerbsarbeit – Europäische Trends vor dem Hintergrund sozialpolitischer und arbeitsrechtlicher Entwicklungen', Discussion Paper 2004-108, Berlin: Wissenschaftszentrum Berlin für Sozialforschung.

Sennett, R. (1998), *The Corrosion of Character: The Personal Consequences of Work in the New Capitalism*, New York: Norton.

Stanworth, C. and J. Stanworth (1997), 'Reluctant entrepreneurs and their clients – the case of self-employed freelance workers in the British book publishing industry', *International Small Business Journal*, **16**, 58–73.
Stanworth, M.J.K and J. Curran (1973), *Management Motivation in the Smaller Business*, London: Gower Press.
Vainio, P. (2007), 'Vastentahtoisen yrittäjyyden oikeudellinen arviointi', in T. Kautonen (ed.), *Vastentahtoinen yrittäjyys. Työpoliittinen tutkimus 327*, Helsinki: Ministry of Labour, pp. 121–288.
Wank, R. (1988), *Arbirtnehmer und Subständinge*, Munich: Beck.

34 Islam and entrepreneurship

Wafica Ali Ghoul

INTRODUCTION

The number of Muslims worldwide was last estimated to be 1.6 billion, which represents about one-fifth of the world's population. The number of Muslims who currently live in the Western world (North America and Europe) is growing. There are around 7.5 million Muslims who currently live in the United States, 4 million live in Germany, 6 million in France, 3 million in Canada, and 1.8 million in the United Kingdom (Hassan and Carruthers 2007).

Muslim entrepreneurs around the globe have been increasingly seeking to set up enterprises that are consistent with Shari'ah law (Islamic principles of living), because they believe that these entities will enable them to achieve their economic goals while respecting and abiding by their religious beliefs.

Feldman (2008) had the following to say about Shari'ah:

> Shari'ah represents the idea that all human beings – and all human governments – are subject to justice under the law . . . The word 'Shari'ah' connotes a connection to the divine, a set of unchanging beliefs and principles that order life in accordance with God's will . . . Shari'ah is best understood as a kind of higher law, albeit one that includes some specific, worldly command.

Feldman goes on to say that '*a fourfold combination – the Koran, the path of the prophet as captured in the collections of reports, analogical reasoning and consensus – amounted to a basis for a legal system*' which is commonly known as Shari'ah.

A BRIEF OVERVIEW OF ISLAMIC ENTERPRISES

What are the Features that Distinguish Islamic Enterprises from their Conventional Counterparts?

What follows is a brief overview of the main distinguishing features of Islamic enterprises:

- One of the most distinct features of doing business within the Islamic framework is the prohibition of Riba (the earning or charging of interest); the word 'riba' is Arabic for 'growth', which means that Islam prohibits the growth of one's wealth through lending money to others and charging them interest as a compensation.

  In conventional enterprises the payment of interest is used to compensate lenders for their loss of liquidity, in addition to an inflation premium which makes up for a potential price increase, a default risk premium which is proportional to the credit risk of the borrower, and a maturity risk premium that increases with the life of the loan. Shari'ah prohibits the payment or receipt of interest because it can lead to an inequitable distribution of wealth, it does not promote productivity, and it can cause the exploitation of the poor and needy, besides the fact that usually there is no risk sharing in traditional lending.

- Money cannot be traded for money; all transactions should be based on real assets. This is intended to help society through the creation of jobs.
- One cannot sell what one does not own, which presents a problem for hedge funds that use short-sale as one of their main strategies for risk management.
- Speculative activities are forbidden because they are considered to be gambling or *gharar* (which means uncertainty or deceit in Arabic), and they involve taking risks which are intentional, avoidable and significant.
- Another distinct feature is the fact that Islam prohibits any vehicle or tool that promises a fixed rate of return because under Islamic principles all shareholders should be on an equal footing. Islam focuses instead on partnerships and risk-sharing. According to http://faraazm.tripod.com/id31.html 'The Islamic conception of abolishment of fixed interest rates does not mean that no remuneration is paid on capital. Profit-making is acceptable in Islamic society as long as these profits are not unrestricted or driven by the activities of a monopoly. Islam deems profit, rather than interest, to be closer to its sense of morality and equity because earning profits inherently involves sharing risks and rewards. Profit-making addresses the Islamic ideals of social justice because both the entrepreneur and the lender bear the risk of the investment.'

What are the Types of Enterprises which are Permissible in Islam?

Muslim entrepreneurs are allowed to establish companies, whose activities are *halal* (lawful) not *haram* (unlawful), and thus are not objectionable under Shari'ah 'Islamic law'. Business activities which are objectionable in Islam are those which involve:

- Money-lending and interest payment or receipt, thus conventional banks and insurance companies are *haram*.
- The production, distribution, and/or profiting from alcohol, pornography, tobacco, gambling, weapons, music, entertainment, processing pork meat or non-halal meat (Ghoul and Karam, 2007).
- Hotels and airlines which serve alcohol on their premises.
- In addition, restrictions are applied to certain financial ratios. Thus the Dow Jones Islamic Market Indices (DJIMI) apply the following screens to companies which pass the initial test Shari'ah compliance test:
  - 'Total debt divided by trailing 12-month average market capitalization must be less than 33%.
  - The sum of company's cash and interest-bearing securities divided by the trailing 12-month average market capitalization must be less than 33%.
  - Accounts receivable divided by the trailing 12-month average market capitalization must be less than 33%' (DJIMI, 1999).

Some enterprises have been rather lenient in their application of the Shari'ah compliance test. They have been taking the liberty to lower the restrictions on non-halal activities, as long as less than 5 per cent of their revenues are derived from such activities, with the condition that any profits from such activities shall be given to Islamic charities. This process is known as 'portfolio purification'. However, this is controversial and a subject of debate.

Typical businesses which generally comply with Shari'ah are those involved in technology, telecommunications, steel companies, engineering, transportation, health care, utilities, construction, as well as real estate.

FACTORS THAT HAVE CONTRIBUTED TO THE RISING INTEREST IN ISLAMIC ENTREPRENEURSHIP

Several factors have been contributing to the recent growing interest in setting up Islamic enterprises. These include:

- The recent surge in oil prices which has created excess liquidity in many parts of the Muslim world.
- The events of 11 September 2001 (9/11) in the USA, which led many Muslims to repatriate their money back home for fear of new Western regulations that resulted in increased scrutiny combined with a backlash against Muslims around the world, both real and perceived.
- The high population growth rate in Muslim countries, currently estimated to be 1.6 billion Muslims, means that the target audience for Muslim enterprises is significant and growing.
- The recent religious awakening of Muslims and their realization of the importance of compliance with Shari'ah rules and principles in their business dealings. According to Feldman (2008), 'In the Muslim world, on the other hand, the reputation of Shari'ah has undergone an extraordinary revival in recent years. A century ago, forward-looking Muslims thought of Shari'ah as outdated, in need of reform or maybe abandonment. Today, 66 percent of Egyptians, 60 percent of Pakistanis and 54 percent of Jordanians say that Shari'ah should be the only source of legislation in their countries'.
- High unemployment rates, internal conflicts, wars with neighboring countries, poverty, gender issues, as well as political oppression currently plague most of the Muslim countries. Consequently, the number of Muslims who are choosing to immigrate to the Western world (particularly North America and Europe) has been growing, which necessitates the establishment of Muslim enterprises in Muslim immigrant communities.
- There is an anticipated growth of interest by non-Muslim clients who have been seeking socially responsible and ethical products and services, which would contribute to sustaining the growth of Muslim enterprises (IIR Middle East, 2007).

FACTORS THAT ARE CURRENTLY IMPEDING THE EMERGENCE OF ISLAMIC ENTREPRENEURSHIP

Several factors present hurdles to the healthy growth of the Islamic enterprises, these include the current lack of standardized regulation, an unclear legal framework, different scholar's interpretations of the Shari'ah, and different levels of strictness.

Divergence Issues in Shari'ah Interpretation

A major hurdle that currently faces the growth of Islamic enterprises is that the Shari'ah scholars who belong to different sects of Islam have been issuing divergent interpretations of the teachings of the Holy Koran. This is an issue because it affects the marketability and tradability of Islamic products across the different Muslim countries.

According to Humayon Dar, managing Director of a London-based Shari'ah consultancy, the Dar Al Istithmar Institute, 'There are perhaps 150 [such scholars] worldwide who are involved with Islamic finance but only 20 are internationally recognized' (Tett, 2006: 1).

One might think that with a very small number of recognized Muslim Shari'ah scholars there would be a convergence of interpretations of Shari'ah; however, the cause of divergence of interpretations is the diversity of personal beliefs of scholars, not to mention diverse Islamic religious sects, regional, and cultural influences. This problem is compounded by the varying degrees of religious strictness among entrepreneurs and clients with whom they are dealing.

Interestingly, Sheikh Usmani argues that '*the interpretations of most aspects of Shari'ah are never disputed. For example, everyone agrees that interest is not allowed. It is when you address the alternatives to interest that some differences arise*' (Wigglesworth, 2007).

Deutsche Bank's Geert Bossuyt, Managing Director, Regional Head of Middle East Structuring argues that Shari'ah is inherently open to individual scholars' interpretation; he has reportedly said:

> Shari'ah itself has inherent flexibility and fewer constraints than is often assumed by the financial services industry. Fundamental research is the key to unlocking this inherent flexibility, thereby allowing this market to grow to its full potential . . . too often, 'innovation' is achieved by pushing the barriers and/or misusing fatwas by taking them out of their context. Innovation ideally should be the result of a well documented and fundamental discussion on Shari'ah. (MENAFN.COM, 2007)

Corporate Governance and Islamic Enterprises

Islamic enterprises have additional constraints imposed on them besides those dictated by generally expected good corporate governance practices, which conventional enterprises have to abide by. An Islamic enterprise has to operate within the framework of Islamic law known as Shari'ah, this requires respecting the fundamental values of Islamic Shari'ah which balance the interests of society and individuals. These values include fairness, non-exploitation of the poor, moral responsibility, accountability, and equity in financial dealings. Not surprisingly, most of the reported development efforts of Islamic governance models have been observed in the financial sector of Islamic business, which is what we focus on next.

A KPMG report (2006) pointed out the lack of a unified Islamic governance model by stating that 'demonstrating compliance with Shari'ah can be difficult as different institutions have different governance models by which they set, measure, and monitor their compliance. These varying governance models have added a level of operational risk for any Islamic financial institution.'

Two organizations have been spearheading the effort for setting standards for corporate governance at Islamic financial institutions, the IFSB and the AAOIFI. The Islamic Financial Services Board (IFSB) is based in Kuala Lumpur, it began operating in 2003; it is an international organization which has been issuing standards for the effective supervision and regulation of Islamic financial institutions.

The Accounting and Auditing Organization for Islamic Financial Institutions (AAOIFI), is based in Bahrain, it has been working on a set of standards which cover accounting, ethics, and Shari'ah compliance; it claims that its principles are followed by the majority of Islamic financial institutions.

Islamic corporate governance requires the establishment of operating procedures that guarantee that a Shari'ah Supervisory Board (SSB) certifies all products, transactions, and services in advance, as well as facilitating the continuous monitoring of the permissibility of existing offerings and practices.

Solé (2007) has defined Shari'ah non-compliance risk as 'the risk that the terms agreed in a contract do not effectively comply with Islamic jurisprudence and thus are not valid under Islamic law'. This is the risk that Islamic corporate governance practices aim to minimize, through the supervision, guidance, and continuous monitoring by Shari'ah scholars.

Besides being external auditors, the SSB scholars function as consumer advocates by ensuring that all the transactions conducted by Islamic financial institutions, as well as their products and service offerings are consistent with Shari'ah law, thus respecting the wishes of the Muslim believers who deal with such enterprises. It is very important that customers have full confidence in the independence, integrity, ability, and credibility of Shari'ah scholars who certify a product or service as being halal. However, these virtues have been the subject of a lot of debate and controversy lately.

Sheikh Yusuf Talal DeLorenzo, one of the best known Shari'ah scholars, compared the responsibilities of a Shari'ah supervisor to those of a financial auditor (DeLorenzo, 2000; emphasis added):

> the functions of a Shari'ah supervisor may be compared to those of an independent financial auditor, in the sense that regulatory compliance is ensured, Shari'ah supervisors have both religious and fiduciary responsibilities there is a need for *impartiality and independence*. In the same way that independent auditors are brought in to review the finances of a business, Shari'ah Supervisory Boards review compliance to Shari'ah precepts. Independent audits are understood as ways to gain and maintain the trust of investors and consumers. Independent Shari'ah supervision is the best way to gain and maintain the trust of Muslim investors and consumers.

Additionally, any defects in the products offered should be stated in the SSB report with recommendations for rectifying the defects.

Financing Islamic Enterprises

As with conventional small and medium enterprises, Islamic enterprises have to deal with the difficulty of access to capital, however, there is an additional hurdle which is that when capital is available it has to be compliant with Shari'ah.

According to Khan (2008) 'the growth and development of many Muslim owned small businesses is constrained as a result of the unavailability of Islamic financial services'. Next we present a simplified discussion of some Islamic finance vehicles commonly used by Islamic enterprises, these are financing vehicles which are considered to be halal substitutes to conventional vehicles:

1. *Murabaha: Cost-plus-mark-up financing.* Individual (A) who desires to buy a house for $100 000 approaches an Islamic bank (B), which buys the house, marks it up to $120 000 and sells the house to (A) at a cost plus a declared profit for deferred payments.
2. *Ijara: Lease-based products.* Individual (A) needs to use a machine (a productive asset) which costs half a million dollars, bank (B) buys the machine, and rents it out to (A), charging him rental payments, which is Ijara in Arabic. If (A) ends up buying the machine, the contract would be *Ijara-wa-Iqtana*, which means a lease with an option to buy (*Iqtana* is Arabic for ownership, *wa* means and).
3. *Bai-Salam: Advance purchase.* This is similar to a Forward or a Futures contract. In Arabic, the word *Bai* means sale, *Salam* is supposed to stand for delivery; it really should be *Tasleem* or handing over of commodities. Assume that merchant (A) wants to have suits manufactured by factory (B), (A) pays (B) in advance, and in return (B) charges (A) a lower price, thus splitting the profits with (B). This contract represents a transaction rather than a loan.
4. *Istisnaa: Progressive financing.* The word *Istisnaa* in Arabic means manufacturing, assume individual (A) wants to build a house, he approaches bank (B) which will pay the builders on behalf of individual (A) as the work progresses. This allows for deferral of payment as well as delivery.
5. *Musharakah: Company or partnership contract.* Two or more persons contribute to the financing as well as the management of the business, in equal or unequal proportions. *Musharakah* (which means sharing in Arabic), is an equity financing arrangement and partnership where profits are shared according to an agreed ratio, whereas the losses are shared in proportion to the capital/ investment of each partner.
6. *Mudarabah: Investment partnership.* The investor (*Rab al mal* which means provider of capital in Arabic), provides capital to the bank (the *Mudarib*, which means the one who is competing with investor for profit). The bank invests the money in halal activities. Profits are shared on a pre-agreed ratio, whereas losses are born by the investor only. A *Mudarabah* contract is very similar to a mutual fund because both pool money from many investors and invest it on their behalf, sharing in the profits but not the losses.
7. *Sukuks: Islamic bonds.* The word *Sukuk* is Arabic for a bond, that is, an indenture. Conventional bonds are used to borrow money for financing a project or an asset acquistion, they pay a fixed interest rate to bond holders semiannually. In Islamic finance, a *Sukuk* issuance is a method of financing that has to be backed by the

project's fixed assets. *Sukuks* give their owners a proportionate beneficial ownership in the underlying asset. Profits from the project are distributed to owners.

Islamic Enterprises and Risk Exposures

Various types of unique risk exposures plague Muslim economies and need to be managed.

- The prevalence of wars and conflicts in many Muslim countries raises the level of transaction, economic and translation risk exposures and necessitates the development of Shari'ah-compliant risk management products.
- The economies of many Muslim countries depend heavily on petrodollars; the price of oil has been very volatile, which creates significant risks.
- The phenomenon of the globalization of trade and finance means that most business deals and investments involve multiple countries and currencies.
- A less-discussed source of risk exposure is the impact of global warming on agriculture; it is creating additional hazards for farmers' crops world wide.
- After experiencing a boom for at least three years, stock markets in the Middle East are currently in a correction mode, the availability of risk management devices would attract additional local and foreign investors' interest.

RISK MANAGEMENT AND ISLAMIC SHARI'AH

Muslim entrepreneurs are not currently taking serious measures to protect themselves from various risks. Progress is being made mainly in developing instruments that protect against foreign exchange rate fluctuations (profit rate swaps) and stock price volatility (Islamic hedge funds and alternatives to options). However, a concern remains that some Muslim entrepreneurs and their clients will not be comfortable with using them. The Islamic finance industry is being criticized for synthesizing copycats of conventional financial derivative products.

Conventional risk management tools, such as derivatives, involve speculation which is equivalent to gambling. The holy Koran prohibits gambling by comparing its cost to its benefit: 'They ask you [O Muhammad] about wine and gambling. Say there is great sin (harm, *'ithm*) in them, and some benefit to mankind. However, their sin (harm, *'ithm*) outweighs their benefits' (2:219).

Kamali (1999: 199) defines *gharar* as follows:

> literally meaning fraud (*al-khid'a*), gharar in transactions has often been used in the sense of risk, uncertainty and hazard. In a contract of sale *gharar* often refers to uncertainty and ignorance of one or both of the parties over the substance or attributes of the object of sale, or of doubt over its existence at the time of contract. *Gharar* is, however, a broad concept and may carry different shades of meaning in relationship to different transactions.

El-Gamal (2001) cited Professor Mustafa Al-Zarqa who had the following definition of *gharar*: 'it is the sale of probable items whose existence or characteristics are not certain, due to the risky nature which makes the trade similar to gambling'.

Thus for a contract to be Shari'ah-compliant the object of the trade as well as the price has to be stated, which would eliminate ambiguities that are characteristic of *gharar*.

Examples of Halal Risk Management Tools

Profit-loss sharing account

This is the equivalent of a conventional money market hedge. If a Malaysian company owes a British company a payment of 105 British pounds in one year, it can buy 100 pounds today, deposit the pounds in an Islamic bank account, such as a *Mudarabah* account or a *Musharakah* account, such that in one year it can use 105 pounds to cover its liability, and only the amount above 105 is uncovered. Alternatively, if the account falls below 105, then the foreign currency exposure would be limited to the shortage.

Shari'ah-compliant non-derivative risk-management methods

- Invoicing payables and receivables in the same currency, as much as possible.
- Matching the levels of revenues and expenses in a foreign currency.
- Holding similar levels of assets and liabilities in each currency.
- Lagging and leading foreign currency payables payment strategies.
- Portfolio diversification, in terms of financial products, currencies, and projects.

ISLAM AND FEMALE ENTREPRENEURSHIP

Islam does not prohibit or frown upon women being entrepreneurs. In fact, the prophet Muhammad, peace be upon him, was married to a very wealthy and capable woman called Khadijah, peace be upon her, who helped him spread the message of Islam. According to Feldman (2008), there is an 'oversimplified assumption that Muslims want to use Shari'ah to reverse feminism and control women . . . Large numbers of [Muslim] women support the Islamists in general and the ideal of Shari'ah in particular'.

CONCLUSION

There are some critics who are of the opinion that by insisting on complying with Shari'ah law, to the letter, some Muslim entrepreneurs might be losing sight of the main objective of Islam, namely, fairness and social equity, as well as protecting the well being (physical and mental health) and providing for a decent living of mankind.

Husain (2007) reports Laldin, chairman of the Shari'ah advisory committee of HSBC Amanah Malaysia, to have said:

> scholars look at three basic areas when assessing the compliance of products: belief, legalilty and morality . . . products could fairly easily comply with Islamic law but it is more difficult to ascertain whether they comply with the morals of Islam. The price of a product may not be controversial from a legal perspective but if the product costs more than an equivalent conventional product, it may not fulfill Islam's moral obligations of fairness and social equity.

REFERENCES

DeLorenzo, Yusuf Talal (2000), 'Shari'ah supervision of Islamic mutual funds', 4th Annual Harvard Forum on Islamic Finance 3, 6 April, available at: http://www.failaka.com/downloads/Sharia%20Supervision%20of%20Funds%20-%20DeLorenzo20%202000.pdf (accessed 21 July 2009).

Dow Jones Islamic Market Indexes (DJIMI) (1999), http://djindexes.com/islamicmarket/?go=shariah-compliance (accessed 21 July 2009).

El-Gamal, Mahmoud A, (2001), 'An economic explication of the prohibition of gharar in classical Islamic jurisprudence', available at: http://www.ruf.rice.edu/~elgamal (accessed 21 July 2009).

Feldman, Noah (2008), 'The fall and rise of the Islamic state', available at: http://www.nytimes.com/2008/03/16/magazine/16Shariah-t.html (accessed 21 July 2009).

Ghoul, Wafica and Paul Karam (2007), 'MRI and SRI mutual funds: a comparison of Christian, Islamic (Morally Responsible Investing), and socially responsible investing (SRI) mutual funds', *Journal of Investing* (Summer), **16** (2), 96–103, available at: http://www.iijournals.com/JOI/default.asp?Page=2&ISS=23858&SID=686416 (accessed 21 July 2009).

Hassan, Nevinne and Stuart Carruthers (2007) 'Canada: Islamic financial services: overview and prospects for the Canadian marketplace', *Mondaq Business Briefing*, 11 May.

Husain, Ahmad Sanusi (2007) 'Islamic scholars call for "more attention to morals than law"', 27 June, available at: http://www.gifc.blogspot.com/search/label/Islamic%20finance (accessed 21 July 2009).

IIR Middle East (2007), 'Non-Muslims key to growth of Islamic finance', 19 February, available at: http://www.iirme.com/news_details.aspx?newsID=185 (accessed 21 July 2009).

Kamali, Mohammad Hashim (1999), 'Uncertainty and risk-taking (*gharar*) in Islamic law', *IIUM Law Journal*, **7** (2), 199, available at: http://www.iiu.edu.my/laws/journaltest.php (accessed 21 July 2009).

Khan, Ajaz Ahmed (2008), 'Islamic microfinance theory, policy and practice', February, available at: http://www.islamicrelief.com/submenu/policyandresearch/Islamic%20Microfinance%20-%20Theory,%20Policy%20&%20Practice.pdf (accessed 21 July 2009).

KPMG (2006), 'Making the transition from niche to mainstream Islamic banking and finance: a snapshot of the industry and its challenges today', available at: http://www.us.kpmg.com/microsite/FSLibraryDotCom/islamicfinance.aspx (accessed 21 July 2009).

Middle East and North Africa Financial Network (MENAFN.COM) (2007), 'Deutsche Bank publishes white paper to increase supply of Sharia compliant alternative investments', MENAFN.COM, 30 January.

Solé, Juan (2007), 'Islamic banking makes headway', IMF Monetary and Capital Markets Department, 19 September, available at: http://www.imf.org/external/pubs/ft/survey/so/2007/RES0919A.htm (accessed 21 July 2009).

Tett, Gillian (2006), 'Banks seek Islamic scholars versed in finance', *Financial Times*, 20 May, p. 1, available at: http://search.ft.com/search?queryText=banks+seek+islamic+scholars&ftsearchType=type_news

Wigglesworth, Robin (2007), 'Scholastic guidance', *Islamic Business and Finance*, Shari'ah section, **11**, 6 September, available at: http://www.cpifinancial.net/v2/Magazine (accessed 20 July 2009).

35 Learning business planning

P. Kyrö and M. Niemi

The objective of the constructive learning business planning (LBP) research project is to provide a novel application for learning business planning that considers learning as a process of innovative, opportunity recognition, development of individual readiness and abilities by adopting intelligent, human-like, non-linear soft computing.

The traditional business planning literature is somewhat normative, and, as Carrier (2005) argues, it neglects aspects of innovation and creativity. Some research findings indicate that there is actually only a tenuous relationship between business planning and performance (Karlsson, 2005) while others showing no significant relationship between these two (Carter et al., 1996; Delmar and Shane, 2004). Hindle (1997) suggests that the normative nature and linear logic of business planning easily leads to reductionism and inhibits an integrated approach to planning. It is therefore suggested that we indeed face a challenge to improve both the business planning models and our teaching practices.

In order to study how to overcome these problems and to advance this dialogue, we apply a *constructive problem-solving orientated research approach.* Lukka (2001) argues that the basic nature of the constructive research approach concerns problem-solving, which provides solutions as an outcome of the interplay between practice and theories. The constructive approach relies on heuristic innovations, thus differing from a decision-oriented approach to problem solving. This approach aims to solve a real-world problem by implementing a new construct, which, according to Lukka (2001), should contribute both practice and theories.

As a result we have developed a new, non-linear, five-phase, two-layer configuration model for an intelligent soft computing simulation tool of learning business planning. This simulation tool applies fuzzy linguistic variables, fuzzy rule sets and fuzzy reasoning. Thus we can differentiate the interface the learner experiences and the layer that technically transforms the complex data-handling processes. In this way we are able to apply computer modelling to more complicated phenomena than has previously been possible in linear models. This modelling offers an opportunity to advance traditional business planning models and their teaching. This should help potential entrepreneurs to understand how they can learn business competence, and can show them the essential relations within their business activities.

The leading partner of the LBP project is the Helsinki School of Economics (HSE). It is the largest and leading business school in Finland. The Helsinki School of Economics was awarded Association to Advance Collegiate Schools of Business (AACSB) accreditation in 2007. The Small Business Center at the Helsinki School of Economics (HSE) specializes in developing entrepreneurship and business abilities. Its offices are located in Helsinki, Mikkeli, St Petersburg and Tallinn. Its services are based on HSE core skills which have received many national and international quality awards. The HSE has received three times an award from the Ministry of Education for high-quality adult education. Other partners are the University of Tampere, the University of Helsinki and the BISC group at Berkley University of California.

REFERENCES

Carrier, C. (2005), 'Pedagogical challenges in entrepreneurship education', in P. Kyrö and C. Carrier, *The Dynamics of Learning Entrepreneurship in a Cross-cultural University Context*, Entrepreneurship Education Series 2/2005, Hämeenlinna: University of Tampere, Research Centre for Vocational and Professional Education.

Carter, N.M., W.B. Gartner and P.D. Reinolds (1996), 'Exploring start-up event sequences', *Journal of Business Venturing*, **11**, 151–66.

Delmar, F. and S. Shane (2004), 'Legimitating first: organizing activities and the survival of new ventures', *Journal of Business Venturing*, **19**, 385–410.

Hindle, K. (1997), *An Enhanced Paradigm of Entrepreneurial Business Planning*, Swinburne: Swinburne University of Technology.

Karlsson, T. (2005), 'Business plans in new ventures – an institutional perspective', JIBS Dissertation series, No. 030, Jönköping International Business School.

Lukka, K. (2001), 'The constructive research approach', available at: www.metodix.com (accessed 25 August 2010).

36 Mature-age entrepreneurship

Paull C. Weber and Michael T. Schaper

MATURE ENTREPRENEURS

Business researchers, policy-makers and practitioners have used many varied terms to describe those in self-employment who in their 'latter years' determine to own (or continue to own) and operate a business venture. Synonymous terms include:

- grey entrepreneurs (Weber and Schaper, 2004)
- senior entrepreneurs, or seniorpreneurs (Goldberg, 2000)
- golden entrepreneurs (Arkebauer, 1995)
- second career entrepreneurs (Baucus and Human, 1994)
- third age entrepreneurs ((Blackburn et al., 1998)
- elder entrepreneurs (De Bruin and Dupuis, 2003)
- mature small business owners (Weber, 2006).

While there has been a recent tendency to use the phrase 'grey entrepreneur', this has some negative connotations; accordingly, the term 'mature entrepreneur' or 'mature age entrepreneur' is preferred. The 'mature' terminology adopted also has resonance with the generational segmentation descriptions utilized by authors such as Still et al. (2004).

All of these terms are descriptors which recognize that there are significant behavioural, resource and motivational differences between older and younger entrepreneurs. These patterns begin to become noticeable somewhere between 45 and 55 years of age.

Studies that specifically look at mature entrepreneurs have only emerged in the past two decades (see, for example, Blackburn et al., 2000; Karoly and Zissimopoulos, 2004; Kean et al., 1993; Singh and DeNoble, 2003) Some studies have pointed out that the age of the business owner can have a direct impact on the business, as older individuals typically have lower levels of personal energy, but more commercial and life experience, more accumulated financial assets that can be used to fund the business venture, and access to a wider and longer-established network of personal contacts and supporters (Barclays Economic Reports, 2001; Blackburn et al., 1998; Carnegie UK Trust, 1993; Curran and Blackburn, 2001; Seymour, 2002). Other researchers have noted that mature entrepreneurs tend to have different work patterns (Quinn, 1996), personal values (Burroughs and Rindfleisch, 2002; King, 2002), attitudes towards self-employment (Curran and Blackburn 2001) and more limited alternative employment options (Platman, 2003) than younger entrepreneurs.

There is no given numerical point at which an entrepreneur can automatically be categorized as either mature-age or not. However, a point somewhere in the 50+ age bracket appears to be the most effective demarcation point. For example, age 55 is the minimum early retirement age for Australian workers (Senate Committee for Employment Workplace Relations and Education, 2003); age 50 is the youngest point in Britain at which individuals can access retirement entitlements (Blackburn et al., 1998); and other developed nations likewise have retirement points somewhere around this age point. Weber (2006) also found that differences between mature-age entrepreneurs and other younger owner-operators became more pronounced after the age of 55. By this point, the age-related characteristics and resources of the entrepreneur are likely to have become well-entrenched, and to have some practical bearing on the firm's activities.

Mature-age entrepreneurs do, however, share a number of characteristics in common with all other business venturers. They typically have majority or outright control of the enterprise, make most or all of the decisions, and remain one of the major influences in what it does and the strategies that it pursues.

In summary, mature entrepreneurs can typically be defined by reference to both age and the control they exert over the entrepreneurial business venture: *Mature Entrepreneurs (MEs) are over 55 years of age, own a business where they have close control of the business capital and are the principal decision-makers* (see Figure 36.1).

REFERENCES

Arkebauer, J.B. (1995), *Golden Entrepreneuring: The Mature Person's Guide to a Successful Business*, New York: McGraw-Hill.

Barclays Economic Reports (2001), *Third Age Entrepreneurs – Profiting from Experience*, London: Barclays PLC.

Baucus, D. and S.E. Human (1994), 'Second career entrepreneurs: a multiple case of entrepreneurial processes and antecedent variables', *Entrepreneurship Theory and Practice*, **19** (2), 41–71.

Blackburn, R., M. Hart and M. O'Reilly (2000), 'Entrepreneurship in the Third Age: new dawn or misplaced expectations?', proceedings of the 23rd ISBA National Small Firms Policy and Research Conference, Aberdeen University, pp. 1–17.

Blackburn, R., L. Mackintosh and J. North (1998), *Entrepreneurship in the Third Age*, Kingston: Kingston University Small Business Research Centre.

Burroughs, J.E. and A. Rindfleisch (2002), 'Materialism and well-being: a conflicting values perspective', *Journal of Consumer Research*, **29** (December), 348–70.

Carnegie UK Trust (1993), *Life, Work and Livelihood in the Third Age, The Carnegie Inquiry Into The Third Age*, Dumfermline: The Carnegie United Kingdom Trust.

Curran, J. and R. Blackburn (2001), 'Notes and issues, older people and the enterprise society: age and self-employment propensities', *Work, Employment & Society*, **15** (4), 889–902.

De Bruin, A and A. Dupuis (2003), *Entrepreneurship: New Perspectives in a Global Age*, Aldershot: Ashgate.

Goldberg, S. (2000), 'Business week: senior startups', *Business Week*, available at: www.kellogg.northwestern.edu/news/hits/000814bw.htm (accessed 26 March 2003).

Karoly, L.A. and J. Zissimopoulos (2004), 'Self-employment among older U.S. workers', *Monthly Labor Review*, **127** (7), 24–47.

Kean, R.C., S. Van Zandt and W. Maupin (1993), 'Successful ageing: the older entrepreneur', *Journal of Women & Aging*, **5** (1), 25–42.

King, S. (2002), 'Entrepreneurs measure of success: is it more than profits?', proceedings of the 47th World Conference of the International Council for Small Business (ICSB), SBANC University of Central Arkansas, 16–19 June, San Juan, Puerto Rico.

Platman, K. (2003), 'The self-designed career in later life: a study of older portfolio workers in the United Kingdom', *Ageing & Society*, **23** (3), 281–302.

Quinn, J. (1996), 'The role of bridge jobs in the retirement patterns of older Americans in the 1990's', proceedings of the International Association for Research in Income and Wealth Conference, Lillehammer, 16–23 August.

Senate Committee for Employment Workplace Relations and Education (2003), *Select Committee on Superannuation: Planning for Retirement*, Canberra: Senate Printing Unit.

Seymour, N. (2002), 'Starting up after 50', CELCEE Kauffmen Centre for Entrepreneurial Clearinghouse on Entrepreneurship Education, available at: http://www.celcee.edu/publications/digest/Dig02-05.html (accessed 25 February 2003).

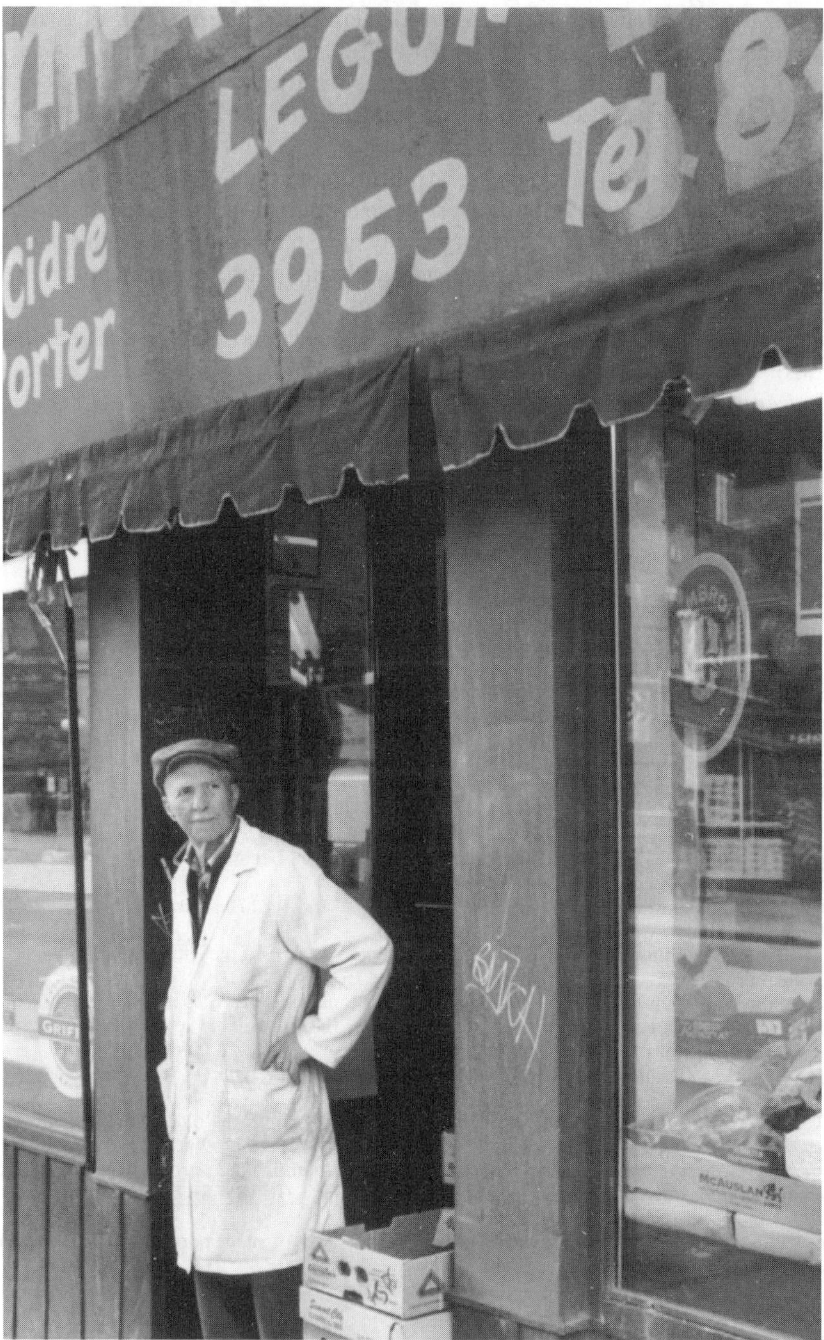

Figure 36.1 Simha is over 55 years of age, owns a business where he has close control of the business capital and is the principal decision-maker; photograph by Léo-Paul Dana

Singh, G. and A. DeNoble (2003), 'Early retirees as the next generation of entrepreneurs', *Entrepreneurship Theory and Practice*, **23** (3), 207–26.

Still, L.V., G.N. Soutar and E. Walker (2004), 'Generational differences in the start-up goals and later satisfaction of women small business proprietors', *Small Enterprise Research*, **12** (1), 71–9.

Weber, P. (2006), 'Understanding mature small business owners: success and age-related correlates of success within the Western Australian tourism industry', PhD thesis, School of Management, Curtin University of Technology, Australia.

Weber, P and M. Schaper (2004), 'Understanding the grey entrepreneur', *Journal of Enterprising Culture*, **12** (2), 147–64.

37 Pastoralism as a form of entrepreneurship

A. Allan Degen

Entrepreneurship is expressed in different ways by various societies (Dana, 1995). In this chapter I focus on entrepreneurship as it is practised by the Bedouin.

The word Bedouin is derived from the Arabic word *badawi*, man of the desert. Traditionally, Negev Bedouin depended on nomadic pastoralism for their lifestyle and livelihood. Sheep, goats and camels provided them with milk and milk products, wool and hair for weaving carpets and tents, and animals for traditional slaughter. Today, there are more than 150 000 Bedouin in the Negev Desert of southern Israel. About half of these Bedouin live in planned urban communities and half in rural, spontaneous, non-recognized settlements. Figure 37.1 shows a market at the predominantly Bedouin community of Rahat. Many of these Bedouin families raise some livestock, mainly sheep but also goats, camels and cattle. Figure 37.2 shows Awassi sheep and local goats being shepherded by Bedouin girls.

Changes since 1948 have turned the Bedouin pastoralists of pre-Israel times into marginal pastoralists today. Two important characteristics of current Bedouin pastoral activity in the Negev below the 220 mm isohyte are evident: (1) pastoralism can be

Figure 37.1 Rahat; photograph by A.A. Degen

Figure 37.2 *Awassi sheep and local goats being shepherded by Bedouin girls; photograph by A.A. Degen*

practised mainly on margins of other agricultural activities, on fallow and aftermath fields and in uncultivatable areas; and (2) that it has become a marginal occupation for the Bedouin population as only about 1000 families, or less than 10 per cent of the population, mainly rural Bedouin, derive their livelihood from raising sheep. The grazing sources under their control are insufficient to meet year-round flock maintenance yet flock movement to available grazing areas are strictly limited and regulations pertaining to their shepherding practices are costly.

In spite of these difficulties, the number of sheep has been increasing over the years, although the ratio of number of Bedouin to sheep has been decreasing. Officially, 200 000 sheep were registered with the Ministry of Agriculture's Veterinary Services in 2002, a number that has stayed relatively constant during the past few years. However, the ministry, which is responsible for compulsory vaccination of livestock, estimated that the actual number of sheep owned by Bedouin was in the vicinity of 300 000, as many sheep were not vaccinated and registered (Table 37.1). Furthermore, according to the Ministry, there were approximately 1500 registered flocks in 2002, with about half the flocks from urban and half from rural, non-recognized localities. According to the records of the *Statistical Yearbook of the Negev Bedouin* (1999; 2004), in 1998 and 2001, there were 1395 and 1281 registered flocks, of which 1186 (85 per cent) and 1063 (83 per cent), respectively, were owned by tribes from rural, non-recognized localities. The yearbook

Table 37.1 Number of sheep raised by the Bedouin and number of Bedouin in the Negev between 1932 and 2002 (numbers in thousands)

Year	1932	1955	1961	1974	1988	1997	2002
Sheep	100	60	70	130	140–250[a]	150–300[a]	200–300[a]
Bedouin	60	15	16–20	37[b]	69	104	129–159
Ratio	1.67	4.00	3.50–4.36	3.51	2.02–3.62	1.44–2.88	1.25–2.33

Notes:
[a] The lower value was registered with the Ministry of Agriculture; the higher value was estimated.
[b] 40 000 in 1976 (Shmueli, 1980); 37 000 was estimated in 1974.

lists the 1281 registered flocks according to flock size (number of head) with 75 per cent of the flocks falling between 50 and 250 head. There were 335 flocks between 50 to 100 head, 184 flocks of less than 50 head and three flocks greater than 650 head.

FLOCK MANAGEMENT

After the establishment of Israel, Bedouin pastoral practices can be regarded as a response adaptation to government restraints. Noy-Meir (1975) identified major Bedouin pastoral systems within the Negev determined by ecological conditions, flock movements and types of pasture, and the degree of feed supplementation. Bedouin practise the seasonal type in the semi-arid to arid Negev in that flocks are kept near the homestead in winter and are moved from the homestead for grazing in spring and summer.

Among Bedouin today, flocks are generally owned by household heads. However, this may not mean their outright possession, but rather as their responsibility for decision-making in management of the flock. Each household is usually related to others in a complex of alliances, obligations, reciprocal relations and clan obligations (Marx, 1974; personal data). Some members within (wives, children) and outside the household (married sons, relatives) may own some animals in the flock or corral them near the homestead and these are considered their property (Abu-Rabia, 1994; personal data). Furthermore, household heads often register some animals in the names of other family members and/or understate the number of animals in their flocks to the government veterinary authority. As a family-operated enterprise, wages are not paid (except where shepherds are hired) nor are expenses and income shared among family members.

Husbands decide when and where to graze the flock, when to corral the main flock at home and when to sell or buy sheep. Husbands are responsible for flock movement, either by foot or by truck, to distant pasture sources. They are also responsible for the everyday management of the flock such as providing drinking water (by either piped water or tractor-drawn water tanks). It should be noted, also, that there are cases where a woman (wife) is the sole owner of a flock, in particular in urban centres (Degen 2003).

In families living in rural settlements, usually unmarried daughters shepherded animals; wives and occasionally husbands and sons helped. However, as more girls are now attending school, since education is compulsory by Israeli law (Abu-Saad, 1996), the family labour force is being reduced. Of 24 families surveyed in 2003, children shepherded in only 14 flocks, wives in ten flocks and men in seven flocks (Stavi et al., 2006). Prior to 1999, shepherds from the administered territories were hired when needed at 130 dinars (1 dinar = US$1.3) per month plus meals. This practice has stopped due to security problems.

Each year, household heads apply to the Bedouin Affairs Department of the Ministry of Agriculture for grazing areas. Permits are issued only after sheep have received mandatory veterinary vaccinations against foot and mouth disease and rinderpest (at a cost of $0.70 per sheep and $0.40 per sheep, respectively), and ewe-lambs against brucellosis (no charge). Optional recommended treatments at present, but not required for a grazing permit, are against clostridium ($1.05 per sheep), pox ($0.40 per sheep) and parasites ($1.35 per sheep). The former two are administered by government veterinarians; the latter by the Bedouins themselves and/or private veterinarians. Vaccinated sheep are ear tagged with an identifying number, and only sheep with such tags can be moved within Israel. In fact, sheep without tags cannot be brought to markets for they can be confiscated. Consequently, veterinary care constitutes a compulsory and important expense in the flock management budget.

Grazing permits allow flock movement for about nine months during spring and summer, from approximately mid-February to October. The permits stipulate the designated areas and exact dates for grazing and payment for these sites is minimal and based on flock numbers. The grazing period is dependent on the condition and availability of pasture. In spring, these are usually lands in the control of the Jewish National Fund (mainly forests), the army and the Land Authority. Arrangements are also made to graze land under private control such as those of *kibbutzim* or *moshavim*. In these cases, fields are rented mainly for summer grazing and consist of cereal aftermath and winter fallowed fields that are weed infested. Bedouin are not able to graze their animals outside their permitted areas and must keep the flocks at the homestead for about three months during the late summer and autumn, during which time they are vaccinated. Black goats are restricted to the confines of the household because of the 'black goat' law passed in 1977 (grazing black goats were considered destructive).

Today, there are a number of problems in sheep management and marketing. First, the Palestinian West Bank is closed for security reasons much of the time, thus preventing buyers in the territories from entering Israel. This is a serious setback as these buyers purchased most of the Bedouin sheep in the past and brought them to the territories. Secondly, shepherds from the territories cannot be employed for, by law, they cannot remain overnight in Israel. Thirdly, outbreaks of contagious diseases such as foot and mouth occur frequently, which prevents animal movement and limits sales. These factors, together with frequent droughts, result in lower sheep prices and higher grain and fodder prices.

PRODUCTION AND ECONOMIC DETAILS

In a two-year study by Degen et al. (2000), six Negev Bedouin families averaged 130 breeding ewes per household, with a range from 61 to 176, and two to four rams. Sheep were mainly Awassi (see Figure 37.3), a fat-tailed breed common in the Middle East that is raised for meat, milk and wool. Most lambings occurred between November and

Figure 37.3 Awassi sheep; photograph by Léo-Paul Dana

March but continued sporadically throughout the year as rams grazed with the ewes. Of the ewes lambing, 2.5 per cent had twins and 130 ewes produced a total of 120 lambs of which 105 survived. Thus, the lambing rate over the two years was 0.93 with lamb mortality at 12.5 per cent.

Sheep mortality during the period was about 3.0 per cent. Of the surviving lambs, 68 (55–60 per cent) were sold at 3 to 5 months of age, which mainly covered expenses. Of the rest, 15 ewe-lambs were kept as replacements for ewes that either died, were sold or were slaughtered and 20 lambs were used as presents and for traditional slaughter. It was estimated that five to ten lambs were received as gifts or other reasons. In addition, about 10 lambs (at $136 per lamb) were expended for socio-economic reasons such as maintaining or establishing good relationships with people that might in the future act, among other things, as intermediaries on their behalf in obtaining grazing permits and other transactions necessary for managing their flocks. Sick animals were not slaughtered for home consumption but sold whenever possible. The income from sheep sales averaged US$9394, but the variation among the six individual households was considerable.

All families milked some sheep and goats for household use. However, only one family, owning 160 sheep, milked all the lactating ewes in one year of the two-year study. Labour shortage was given as the main reason for not milking by the other families. In the flock that was milked, ewes were milked once daily in the morning by two women: by two wives or by one of the wives and one of two daughters. Milk yield was approximately

20 kg per day over a two-month period between February and March, for a total of 1200 kg. The women processed the milk into yogurt (*laban*), butter (*samne*) and a hard, dry cheese (*afig*) which was stored for future consumption. It was estimated that 100 kg each of *samne* and of *afig* were made for home consumption, but occasionally some was given as presents and some was sold by the women. *Samne* sold for about $10.6 per kilo and *afig* for about $7.3 per kilo.

All sheep were hand-sheared prior to summer, yielding an average of 1.5 kg wool per sheep. Husbands, assisted by wives, children and/or shepherds, usually did the shearing, although wives and children often did the shearing as well. There was little demand for the wool and none was sold. In fact, much of the wool was discarded although some was used for blanket and pillow fillings. Almost no tents are made of wool and no wool weaving was observed during the study. Tents are made from burlap bags and carpets are hand-woven from colourful, synthetic material.

On average, expenses in raising sheep were US$7121 to US$7818 and constituted about 80 per cent of incomes from sheep. Most expenditure was on animal feed (60 per cent), followed by land rental (20 per cent), wages (8 per cent) and veterinary costs (7 per cent). In some households, expenses surpassed incomes from sheep raising; in the most favourable cases expenses were 55–60 per cent of incomes and in all other cases it was more than 67 per cent.

The average balance showed a yearly profit of US$1873. This does not take into account lambs used for social purposes and for home consumption. Net income varied from a loss of US$878 to a gain of US$5300. Within individual households, there were large yearly fluctuations. In fact, large fluctuations was the rule, rather than the exception, as was also found by Ginguld (1994) who studied nine Bedouin flocks over one year. The highest net income was realized not by the largest flock (176 sheep), but rather by an averaged sized flock (131 sheep). However, the lowest net income (negative balance) was realized by the owner of the smallest flock (81 sheep), although this owner was in the process of building up his flock.

Marketing

Bedouin must have access to grazing areas, supplementary feeds (straw, bran, hay, grains), seeds, agricultural contractors for cultivation, harvesting and transport in order to maintain their flocks and cultivate crops. They also must have outlets for their produce and access to retail markets for essential human foodstuffs. There are no official marketing channels such as those available for other agricultural enterprises in Israel (for example, milk, poultry, fruit and citrus marketing boards) for Bedouin livestock raisers. Furthermore, because Bedouin cultivate land below the 220 mm isohyte, they are not eligible for drought compensation.

Bedouin pastoralists, from roughly the mid-1950s, changed relatively quickly from an essentially subsistence and self-containing economy into the money-dependent market economy that exists today. Nearly all transactions take place on a purely cash and carry basis, that is, buying and selling depends on ready availability of cash money. The absence of any organized marketing venue and lack of any drought compensation effectively prevent the Bedouin from financial assistance such as credits and guaranteed prices. They are rarely able to negotiate bank loans or overdraft accounts. In addition, as

Bedouin buy their agricultural inputs individually, large processing mills and factories, as well as Israeli agricultural cooperatives (*kibbutzim* and *moshavim*) prefer to sell their products to large traders or through marketing boards.

Apart from the above sources and their own cultivated areas, inputs such as straw, hay and grains are purchased from large scale traders. Long-term relationships may be established with these traders as a means of financial assistance in the form of extended credit or even loans. For instance, inputs may be purchased on the basis of agreements to sell lambs, kids and mature stock to the traders in lieu of cash payment. Bran, an important feed input, is purchased directly from grain mills usually found in one of the seven Bedouin municipal localities.

Livestock are sold often from the households to other Bedouin, including members of the extended family, for traditional purposes such as religious holidays, weddings, births and circumcisions, and some to traders, often Palestinians. Prices of sheep increase considerably at holidays. Sheep are also sold at weekly morning markets (Kressel and Ben-David, 1995). A market is held at Beer Sheva on Thursday and smaller markets are held at the Bedouin localities of Tel Sheva on Friday and Rahat on Saturday. In the past, most buyers were traders from the Palestinian administered towns of Dahariyya, Hebron and Gaza. However, because of security reasons, very few if any traders from the administered territories attend these markets today.

CONCLUSIONS

In general, Bedouin today claim that raising sheep is non-profitable and that they are losing money in this enterprise (Degen et al., 2000). Furthermore, grazing restrictions are imposed upon the Bedouin and land conflicts are common. Why then do Bedouin persist in raising sheep for their livelihood today?

Of prime importance is the maintenance of their traditional lifestyle (Kressel, 2003). Economic difficulties and high unemployment in the wage labour market may also provide some of the answer. Retention of a flock may be a rational choice as a supplement for those Bedouin who are financially stressed, providing families with milk and other dairy products. Maintaining some sheep acts as a hedge against the risk of unemployment and, if sheep raising does become more profitable, it would be easy to start this enterprise (Dinero, 1996). Moreover, as pointed out by Ginguld et al. (1997), Bedouin have a decided advantage over other sectors in raising sheep, namely, cheap labour available in most households, cheap inputs in that marginal land is used and little investments in equipment. The future of most Bedouin would appear to be an integration into the Israel urban economy while attempting to maintain cultural traditions. Nonetheless, a relatively small but stable number of households will continue to practice agro-pastoralism as a means of livelihood.

REFERENCES

Abu-Rabia, A. (1994), *The Negev Bedouin and Livestock Rearing: Social, Economic and Political Aspects*, Oxford: Berg.

Abu-Saad, I. (1996), 'Provision of educational services and access to higher education among the Negev Bedouin Arabs in Israel', *Journal of Education Policy*, **11** (5), 527–41.

Dana, Léo-Paul (1995), 'Entrepreneurship in a remote sub-Arctic community: Nome, Alaska', *Entrepreneurship: Theory and Practice*, **20** (1), pp. 55–72. Reprinted in Norris Krueger (ed.) (2002), *Entrepreneurship: Critical Perspectives on Business and Management*, vol. 4, London: Routledge, pp. 255–75.

Degen, A.A. (2003), 'Roles of urbanized Negev Bedouin women within their households', *Nomadic Peoples*, **7** (2), 108–16.

Degen, A.A., R.W. Benjamin and J.C. Hoorweg (2000), 'Bedouin households and sheep production in the Negev Desert, Israel', *Nomadic Peoples*, **4** (1), 125–47.

Dinero, S.C. (1996), 'Resettlement and modernization in post-nomadic Bedouin society: the case of Segev Shalom, Israel', *The Journal of Planning Education and Research*, **15**, 105–16.

Ginguld, M. (1994), 'Managing herds and households: management practices and livelihood strategies of sheep-owning Bedouin households in the Negev Region of Israel', MA thesis, the Institute of Social Studies, The Hague, The Netherlands.

Ginguld, M., A. Perevolotsky and E.D. Ungar (1997), 'Living on the margins: livelihood strategies of Bedouin herd-owners in the northern Negev, Israel', *Human Ecology*, **25** (4), 567–89.

Kressel, G.M. (2003), *Let Shepherding Endure*, New York: State University of New York Press.

Kressel, G.M. and J. Ben-David (1995), 'The Bedouin market – corner stone for the founding of Be'er Sheva: Bedouin traditions about the development of the Negev capital in the Ottoman period', *Nomadic Peoples*, **36/37**, 119–44.

Marx, E. (1974), *The Bedouin Society in the Negev*, Tel Aviv: Reshavim (in Hebrew).

Noy-Meir, I. (1975), 'Primary and secondary production in sedentary and nomadic grazing systems in the semi-arid region: analysis and modeling', research report, Ford Foundation. Department of Botany, Hebrew University, Jerusalem.

Shmueli, A. (1980), 'The Bedouin of the land of Israel: settlement and changes', *Urban Ecology*, **4**, 253–86.

Statistical Yearbook of the Negev Bedouin (1999), Negev Development Authority, Ben Gurion University of the Negev, Beer Sheva.

Statistical Yearbook of the Negev Bedouin (2004), Negev Development Authority, Ben Gurion University of the Negev, Beer Sheva.

Stavi, I., G. Kressel, Y. Gutterman and A.A. Degen (2006), 'Flock use among Bedouin in "spontaneous" settlements in the Negev Desert, southern Israel', *Nomadic Peoples*, **10** (1), 53–69.

38 Process

Yvon Gasse

There is no universal model of the entrepreneurial process. However, it is possible to observe at least three recognized stages in the process: the idea, the project and the business, which are not only stages in development but also strategic moments in the life of an entrepreneur.

THE IDEA

The origins and sources of the idea are many and not always obvious. However, it is well known that 95 per cent of entrepreneurs work in fields in which they have experience, or at least a good knowledge, of the markets, the technologies or the industry. It also appears that 45 per cent of entrepreneurs have found their business idea in their previous employment (Gasse and D'Amours, 2000). More than 15 per cent of entrepreneurs have launched their businesses in areas linked to their hobbies and recreational pursuits as well as sports. The areas of study and training are also important sources of business ideas. Thus, it is above all the specific talents and knowledge of individuals that form the basis for business ideas.

However, not all good ideas are good business opportunities; ideas are useless unless they are used. An idea is a necessary prerequisite but not sufficient in itself for the creation of a business. Indeed, the business opportunity must be a feasible idea or concept that meets a need, adds value, is distinctive and involves suitable and appropriate marketing. Above all, it is the entrepreneurial and managerial skills that are crucial in converting an idea into a business opportunity and into a business; the idea must be personally and socially desirable.

THE PROJECT

While a large majority of people may have business ideas, barely 2 per cent of the population of Canada is actively involved in a business project (Gasse et al., 2002b). Once again, the reasons for developing a business project are both personal and are influenced by the community. Here, too, the projects must meet certain criteria in order to stand up to criticism. The feasibility of a business project will depend primarily on its potential for marketing, its projected profitability, its ability to reflect the major trends and the possibilities for managing it. In other words, only after certain checks and repeated tests can it reasonably be claimed that the business is firmly in place.

THE BUSINESS

Usually, a business is operational from the time it generates revenues; in the new economy, however, some businesses are considered to be operational even though they do not generate sales for long periods. In their study of nascent entrepreneurs, Gasse et al. (2002a) observed that after one year, only 34 per cent of the people working actively on a business project had in fact created an operational business; the others were either still involved in planning it (37 per cent), had temporarily shelved it (14 per cent) or had even completely abandoned it (15 per cent). The main reasons for not launching the business are either personal such as a lack of time or interest or related to business such as problems with financing or customers. Most of the businesses that are created can be found primarily in local services, retail and business services.

Communities are looking primarily for innovative businesses that are run by good citizens as well as being modern and satisfactory in terms of job creation and the wealth of the community. In order to achieve this, specific strategies for action that promote innovation and the development of people must be advocated. However, given the disappearance of borders and the great mobility of grey matter, the vast majority of communities and regions are often forced to compete with one another to encourage careers in entrepreneurship and to attract and keep entrepreneurs in their area.

REFERENCES

Gasse, Y. and D'Amours, A. (2000), *Profession: Entrepreneur*, Montréal: Les Éditions Transcontinentales.

Gasse, Y., M. Diochon and T.V. Menzies (2002a), 'Entrepreneurs naissants an Canada: la trame des deux premières années', proceedings of the 19th Canadian Council of Small Business and Entrepreneurship Annual Conference, Halifax Canada, 15 November.

Gasse, Y., M. Diochon and T.V. Menzies (2002b), 'Les entrepreneurs naissants et la poursuite de leur projet d'entreprise: une étude longitudinale', Actes du 6ième Congrès International Francophone de la PME, Montréal, 30 October.

39 A quantum-holographic approach to the psychophysiology of intuitive action

Raymond Trevor Bradley and Dana Tomasino

INTRODUCTION

Successful entrepreneurs are passionate, innovative risk-assessors whose actions are informed by accurate intuitions about future business opportunities. Often this intuitive foreknowledge involves perception of implicit information about non-local objects and/or events by the body's psychophysiological systems. A large body of experimental evidence has documented intuitive foreknowledge as a scientific fact, and studies using electrophysiological measures of autonomic nervous system activity have shown that such non-local intuition is related to the degree of emotional significance of the future event. Moreover, there is also solid experimental evidence that intentionally focused bio-emotional energy can have a subtle but significant (scientifically measurable) effect on non-local objects and events. Drawing on these findings and the principles of quantum holography, a theory of entrepreneurial intuitive action is described which shows how successful entrepreneurs not only use their *passionate attention* to intuitively locate a future business opportunity but can also influence its actualization into reality by their sustained *passionate intention*. It is their bio-emotional attunement to an order of energetically encoded quantum-holographic information beyond space/time that provides access to the rationality of implicit potentials and that sets them apart from other business actors. In short, attunement to this energetic domain of quantum-holographic information *in-forms* (gives shape to) creativity and entrepreneurship: it is the means by which future opportunities can be intuitively located and intentionally actualized into being.

As a key element in a healthy, thriving economy, successful entrepreneurs are innovators and risk-assessors who have extraordinarily accurate hunches about the locus of future opportunities (Mitchell et al., 2005; Shane and Venkataraman, 2000). Yet after more than a half-century of research (Baron, 2004), the explanation for entrepreneurial success still remains perplexingly elusive.

Early research to identify the personality traits and other individual characteristics that distinguish the entrepreneur yielded little success (Brockhaus and Horwitz, 1985; Gartner, 1986). Nowadays most scholars agree that what differentiates entrepreneurs from other actors in the economy is their behavior. But not only have definitive results from research on this question yet to be realized (Keh et al., 2002; Mitchell et al., 2002), but significant aspects of entrepreneurial behavior – such as creativity, intuition, and divergent thinking – have largely been studied from a cognitive perspective (Mitchell et al., 2005; Shane, 2000).

Cognitive approaches to understanding entrepreneurial behavior have emphasized the key question of opportunity recognition: that it is the *way* successful entrepreneurs process information to locate potential future business opportunities that distinguishes them from other business actors (Hahn and Chater, 1997; Larsen and Bundesen, 1996; Shane and Venkataraman, 2000). This has led to an effort to link various pattern recognition models with entrepreneurial decision-making behavior (Keh et al., 2002; Mitchell et al., 2002). And while there has been a growing recognition that entrepreneurs tend to be more intuitive and less logical/analytic in how they make decisions when responding to the temporal demands of competitive markets (Allinson and Hayes, 1996; La Pira and Gillin, 2006), typically such 'intuition' is thought to arise from unconscious, cognitive extrapolations of prior experience (Mitchell et al., 2005; Myers, 2002; Simon, 1987).

Certainly there is little doubt that information from prior experience – both conscious and unconscious knowledge – plays an important role in informing entrepreneurial intuition. Yet, as documented below, there is persuasive experimental evidence for another informational basis of intuitive decision and action. This is the tacit information about remote or future events that is encoded in the incoming energy wave fields of energy radiating from objects and which is processed and perceived by the body's psychophysiological systems (Marcer and Schempp, 1998; McCraty et al., 2004a; 2004b; Mitchell, 2000; Radin, 1997a). Moreover, this tacit information is not accessed by the dispassionate cognitive processing that underlies reason and logic. Rather, it is the entrepreneur's *passionate focus* on his mission in economic life that attunes his body's psychophysiological systems, by a process of energetic resonance, to intuitive information from non-local sources.

This work focuses on the *non-local* component of entrepreneurial behavior – that part of decision and action that is *not* based on reason or logic, or on memories or extrapolations from the past, but is based, instead, on accurate foreknowledge of the future. We draw on recent research on the psychophysiology of non-local communication and the principles of quantum holography to describe a theory that explains how – the processes by which – such entrepreneurial non-local intuitive action occurs (Bradley, 2006; 2007a).

The theory views intuition as a process of non-local communication by which energetically encoded information, normally outside of the range of conscious awareness, is immediately sensed and perceived by the body's psychophysiological systems (McCraty et al., 2004a). The theory explains how information about a future event is spectrally enfolded in the radiation of energy as an implicit field of information which exists as a domain apart from space and time. *Passionate attention* directed to the object of interest (such as a potential future business opportunity) attunes the bio-emotional energy of the body's psychophysiological systems – via energetic resonance – to the quantum level of the object, which contains quantum-holographic information about the object's future potential encoded in the radiation of energy from the object. The body's perception of such implicit information about the object's future is experienced by the entrepreneur as an intuition.

But successful entrepreneurs bring more than a passionate attentional focus to their quest for a new opportunity; they also direct *passionate intention* – in the form of a vision, a plan or a goal – to the object of interest (Roberts and King, 1996). It is postulated that the same processes of energetic resonance that enable perception of intuitive foreknowledge are also the means by which a passionate intentional focus can affect the object of interest's actualization from potential into economic reality.

By way of an overview of the theory, the energetic resonance between the entrepreneur's psychophysiological systems and the non-local object of interest establishes a two-way quantum-holographic communication channel between the percipient and the object. The incoming wave field of energy radiating from the object to the percipient contains quantum-level information about the object's future, which is experienced as intuition. The outgoing wave field of bio-emotional energy from the entrepreneur contains a quantum hologram encoding the entrepreneur's mental intention as energetic information, which is transmitted back through the communication channel to the non-local object. Part of the energy wave field containing the quantum hologram is absorbed by the object and the information it contains *in*-forms – *gives shape to* – the object's future organization and behavior.

These processes of energetic resonance are greatly amplified in groups and organizations with a coherent socio-emotional order. This strengthens the effects of non-local interaction which, in turn, enhances the entrepreneur's likelihood of locating and actualizing a future economic opportunity. In short, sustained passionate focus on the object of interest is what sets the entrepreneur apart from the ordinary business person: it provides entrée to the psychophysiological state-space or 'zone' from which intuitive foreknowledge is accessed and from which intention may effect, to some degree, actualization of an envisioned future (Tomasino, 2007).

INTUITION

The Concise Oxford Dictionary (Fowler and Fowler, 1964: 639) defines *intuition* as 'immediate apprehension by the mind without reasoning, immediate apprehension by a sense, and immediate insight'. Roberto Assagioli (1971: 27) observes that intuition is 'a synthetic function in the sense that it apprehends the totality of a given situation or psychological reality. It does not work from the part to the whole but apprehends a totality directly in its living existence'. Such intuitive experience is quite unlike that of normal cognitive awareness, in which the mind's contents are updated incrementally, as the sequences of sensory experience unfold (McCraty et al., 2004a).

Cognitive Perspective

The ability to quickly see both the whole and the key details of a situation is an important element of successful entrepreneurial behavior. It is by seeing the 'bigger picture' that entrepreneurs are able to integrate disparate information – about the environment, people, events and technology – into a holistic framework of meaning that provides the basis for decisive, and often effective, action (Mitton, 1989). It is, therefore, entirely appropriate to consider intuition, as just defined, as integral to entrepreneurial decision and action (La Pira and Gillin, 2006).

The dominant view among those who study intuition is that intuitive perception is largely the result of past experience – a function of the unconscious mind accessing existing information within the brain from prior experience (for example, Agor, 1984; Laughlin, 1997; Lieberman, 2000; Mitchell et al., 2005; 2007; Myers, 2002). For example, Simon's (1987) notion of intuition is the application of one's professional judgment to the situation; it is based on the accumulated knowledge and decision-making skill acquired by long experience of successes and failures in practice. This viewpoint stems from the common assumption in neuroscience that the mind is emergent from the brain, and therefore subject to the same physical constraints as all biological systems, in which time flows from the past to the future. Thus, awareness is thought to be restricted to perceptions of the present intermingled with memories of the past (McCraty et al., 2004a).

Drawing on the neuroscience conception of the human brain as a highly efficient and effective pattern-matching device (Pribram, 1971), a number of so-called 'pattern-recognition' models have been developed to show how fast, 'intuitive' decision and action by the entrepreneur can be understood purely in terms of cognitive processes in which the brain matches the patterns of existing opportunities facing the entrepreneur with stored templates in memory based on prior experience (Craig and Lindsay, 2001; Hahn and Chater, 1997; Larsen and Bundesen 1996). But there are also instances when accurate 'gut feelings' or 'intuitive insights' about distant or future – *non-local* – events are found to be scientifically valid and occur under controlled conditions that preclude information from past experience (see Radin, 1997a).

Non-local Perspective

These instances of non-local intuition involve communication of information from the non-local source to the percipient that appears to contradict the physical laws of causality and the constraints of space and time. Yet, as we will see, non-locality – the inherent inseparability or interconnectedness of everything in the universe at the quantum level – has been empirically verified and is now a widely accepted scientific truth in physics. This physical property of universal interconnectedness is one of the important foundations for the theory, described in the second half of this work.

Taking an information processing perspective, *non-local intuition* is viewed as a process by which implicit information normally outside the range of cognitive processes is sensed and perceived by the body's psychophysiological systems as certainty of knowledge or feeling (positive or negative) about the totality of some thing distant or yet to happen (McCraty et al., 2004a). This can be a material object or event, or a mental construct such as a thought or idea. Often the feeling of certainty is absolute – the intuition is experienced as beyond question or doubt – and the feeling can encompass positive emotions, such as love, appreciation and optimism, or negative emotions like dread or fear. Also, the experience of non-local intuition is not confined to cognitive perception, but involves the *entire* psychophysiological system, often manifesting through a wide range of emotional feelings and physiological changes experienced throughout the body. Indeed, it is this involvement of the entire psychophysiological system in processing intuitive perception that has enabled its detection and measurement in studies using electrophysiological instrumentation, as described next (McCraty et al., 2004a).

EVIDENCE

Aside from a series of pilot studies researching the efficacy of a new experimental protocol to measure non-local intuition in entrepreneurs (Bradley et al., 2008a; Gillin et al., 2007; La Pira and Gillin, 2006), involving researchers at the Australian Graduate

School of Entrepreneurship (AGSE) and the Institute of HeartMath (IHM), we know of no other empirical work on non-local intuition in entrepreneurs. Most work to date has used self-report cognitive measures on the use of 'intuition' in managerial decision making (Allinson and Hayes, 1996; Lieberman, 2000; Mitchell et al., 2002; 2005).

Fortunately, however, the fundamental question at issue here – accurate foreknowledge of the future – is a phenomenon that has been studied and consistently documented in rigorous scientific experiments for more than a century.[1] The key finding of this research is that individuals are able to receive and accurately perceive information from a distant source or about a future event, and that such intuitive perception *cannot* be explained by flaws in experimental design or research methods (including so-called 'experimenter effects'), statistical techniques, chance, or selective reporting of results. Moreover, this research shows that intuitive perception and the underlying psychophysiological processes involved are unlikely to be specific to any sub-population, such as entrepreneurs, but rather appear to be a general human ability (Radin, 1997a). Before moving to recent work, we want to emphasize the scientific significance of this large body of persuasive evidence. As Radin (1997a) reports, from meta-analyses of the results of the experiments involved, *the likelihood that an intuitive effect is true exceeds the certainty of measurement in experiments verifying quantum mechanics – the most accurate scientific description of reality* (see Penrose, 1989, or Nadeau and Kafatos, 1999).

The results of these studies question a commonly held view of intuition: that it is not registered by the five senses of normal perception (vision, audition, taste, smell, and touch), but, instead, is either a direct, unmediated interaction between the brain and a non-local source, or is the result of some subtle, extraordinary – even supernatural – sense or force which conveys accurate non-local information straight into the brain (Bernstein, 2005). Yet the interesting news from this research is *not* that of discovery of a new 'sixth sense' or of a new information pathway to non-local things. Rather, it is that known, familiar physiological structures are involved (*both* the brain and the heart), and that the body appears to process intuitive information in the *same* way it processes ordinary sensory input (McCraty et al., 2004b).

Recent Studies

The first studies showing evidence of changes in brain activity that preceded an unknown stimulus were conducted by Levin and Kennedy (1975). Warren et al. later found significant differences in event-related potentials (ERP)[2] between target and non-target stimuli presented during forced-choice precognition tasks (Warren et al., 1992a; 1992b). In a series of gambling studies, Don et al. extended these findings by showing that enhanced negativity in the ERPs was widely distributed across the scalp in response to future targets (Don et al., 1998; McDonough et al., 2002). Because the research subjects' overt guessing accuracy was no better than chance, these researchers concluded that the ERP effect was an indicator of 'unconscious precognition'.

Other studies broadened the focus beyond the brain and investigated whether the human autonomic nervous system (ANS) could unconsciously respond to randomly selected future emotional stimuli. With electrophysiological measures of skin conductance level (SCL) and of heart rate and blood volume, Radin (1997a; 1997b; 2004) used randomly selected emotionally arousing or calming photographs to evoke an emotional response, and found a significantly greater change in electrodermal activity around *5 seconds before* a future emotional picture than before a future calm picture. These results have since been replicated (for example, Bierman, 2000; Radin, 2004), and a follow-up study, using functional magnetic resonance imaging, found brain activation in regions near the amygdala (which handles the processing of strong emotions such as fear and rage) before the emotional pictures were shown, but not before the calm pictures (Bierman and Scholte, 2002).

A study, conducted by IHM (McCraty et al., 2004a, 2004b), augmented Radin's protocol by adding measures of brain response (EEG) and heart rhythm activity (ECG), and found that not only did *both* the brain and heart receive the pre-stimulus information some 4 to 5 seconds before a future emotional picture was randomly selected by the computer, but also that the *heart* appeared to receive this information *even before the brain* (see Figure 39.1). Moreover, based on classical psychophysiological interpretations of cardiac decelerations/accelerations in relation to the processing of sensory information, the data suggest that the heart responds to the unknown stimulus in the *same* way it does when a future stimulus is known. Overall, this study's findings suggest that intuitive perception is not a discrete function produced by a single part or system of the body alone – the brain – as previously thought. Rather, it appears that intuition is a system-wide process involving at least the brain, the ANS *and* the heart (and possibly other body systems), together, in the processing and decoding of energetically encoded information from non-local sources.

Entrepreneurs

The AGSE/IHM research team has found compelling evidence of a non-local intuitive response in a pilot study of a small sample (N = 8) of repeat entrepreneurs selected from the Cambridge Technopol (Gillin et al., 2007). The study was conducted to test the measurement efficacy of a new experimental protocol – the Roulette Experiment (McCraty and Atkinson, 2003). The protocol is based on a gambling paradigm and involves a computer-administered stimulus, in response to which the research subject is required to make an investment decision (a bet) before the computer randomly selects the outcome (win or lose). The experiment was repeated over 25 trials throughout which skin conductance and heart rhythm measurements were continuously recorded.

Results from an aggregate analysis of the data (see Figure 39.2) reveal that the heart receives pre-stimulus informational input some 6 to 7 seconds before the outcome of the investment choice is known. When analysed by individual, 'the physiological measures were able to detect intuitive perception of a future outcome in four of the eight entrepreneurs' (Gillin et al., 2007: 13). In a recently conducted IHM replication of the Roulette Experiment in a sample of non-entrepreneurs with many years of practice using emotional management techniques to enhance intuition, it was found that the heart received pre-stimulus informational input as much as *12 to 14 seconds prior* to the investment choice outcome (Bradley et al., 2008a). Compared to the 4 to 7 seconds length of the pre-stimulus period documented in prior research, this is potentially a very promising result, in that it suggests that regular practice of heart-based emotional management techniques may significantly enhance the psychophysiological systems' ability to detect intuitive information *even earlier* in the pre-stimulus period before the outcome event becomes known.

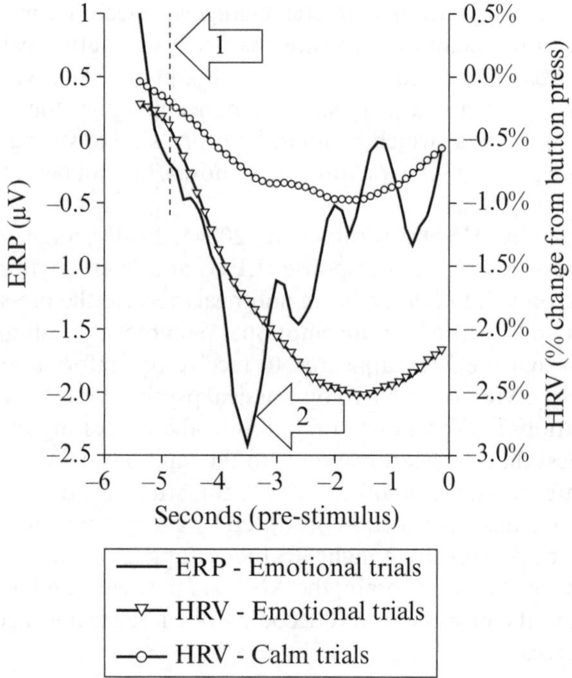

Source: © McCraty et al. (2004b), reprinted with permission.

Figure 39.1 Temporal dynamics of heart and brain pre-stimulus responses
This overlay plot shows the mean event-related potential (ERP) at FP2 and heart rate deceleration curves for the female subgroup (n = 15) in condition 1 during the pre-stimulus period. (The '0' time point denotes stimulus onset.) The heart rate deceleration curve for the emotional trials diverged from that of the calm trials (sharp downward shift) about 4.8 seconds prior to the stimulus (arrow 1), while the emotional trial ERP showed a sharp positive shift about 3.5 seconds prior to the stimulus (arrow 2). This positive shift in the ERP indicates when the brain 'knew' the nature of the future stimulus. The time difference between these two events suggests that the heart received the intuitive information about 1.3 seconds before the brain.

Overall, while these are preliminary results, which must await further confirmation, they are consistent with the studies reviewed above.

Collective intuition

In presenting one further piece of evidence of intuitive foreknowledge of a non-local event – only this time at the collective level – we transition from internal responses to non-local interaction measured by recording electrophysiological activity *within* the body, to external measures of the effect of bio-emotional arousal on physical devices placed *outside* and far away from the body.

The evidence comes from the Internet-based Global Consciousness Project (GCP)

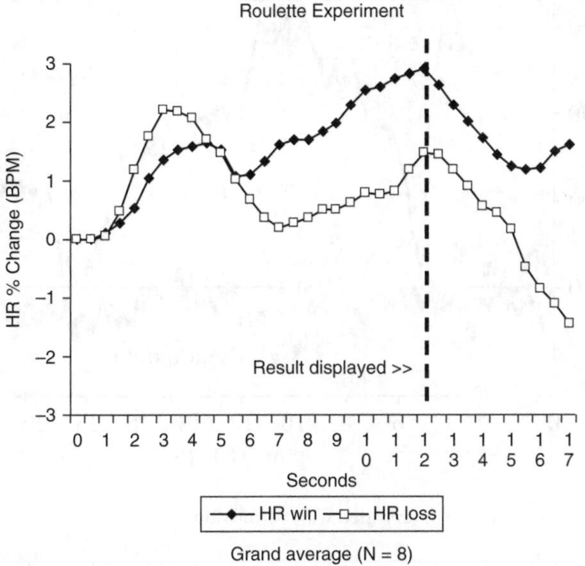

Source: © Gillin et al. (2007), reprinted with permission.

Figure 39.2 *Grand average of heart rhythm recordings in Roulette Experiment for repeat entrepreneurs during the post-bet and post-result period*

This figure presents the grand average of beat-to-beat change per minute in heart rate for 'wins' and 'losses' for all eight participants during the post-bet and post-result periods (the separation between the two time periods is shown by a dashed vertical line labeled 'Result displayed'). Clearly apparent is the separation between the win and loss curves in the mean heart rhythm patterns that begins at about 6 seconds prior to the outcome result being displayed.

which, since 1998, has been collecting the output continuously generated by random number generators (RNGs)[3] from more than 40 sites throughout the world to determine if there is a correlation between global events of mass consciousness (major occurrences that elicit a high level of emotionally charged attention from a large part of the world's population) and periods of non-random order generated by the RNGs (see Bancel and Nelson, 2008). Independent analyses of the RNG output in the hours *before* the terrorist attacks took place in the USA on the morning of 11 September 2001, suggest, as shown in Figure 39.3, that there was *implicit global foreknowledge of the impending terrorist attacks some three to four hours before the first plane crashed into the North Tower* of the World Trade Center at 8.45 a.m. (Nelson, 2002; Radin, 2002).[4] This anomalous pattern of RNG output could *not* be explained by artifacts such as electrical disturbances or high levels of mobile phone use.

Thus, as documented below, the energetic resonance of the bio-emotional energy generated by the body in processing precognitive energetic information about an impending future event appears to be amplified in social aggregations which share an emotionally charged interest (explicit or implicit) in the common event.

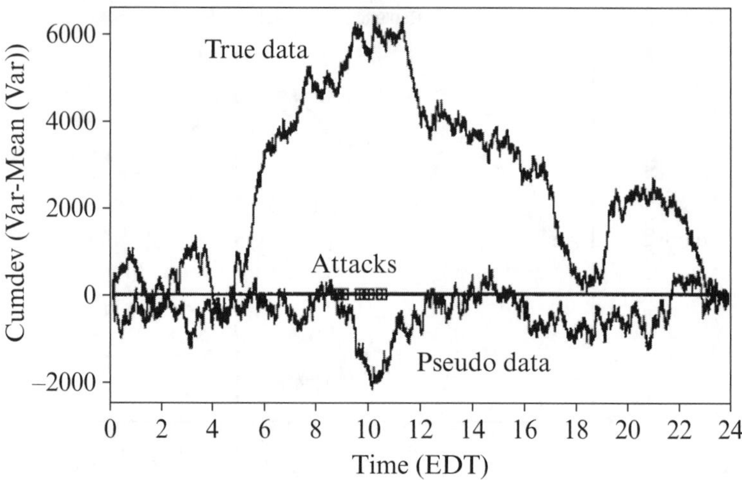

Source: From Nelson (2002), figure 3; reprinted with permission.

Figure 39.3 Cumulative deviation of variance across EGGs (RNGs) for each second on 11 September 2001

Times of the separate events in the terrorist attacks are marked with rectangles on the zero line. The curve labeled 'Pseudo data' shows a control calculation using a pseudo-random clone data-set for each day.

Empirical Generalizations

The consistent finding from the electrophysiological experiments discussed above is that the *body typically responds to a future emotionally arousing stimulus 4 to 7 seconds (and even as much as 12 to 14 seconds) prior to experiencing the stimulus*. This is well before the long-known half-second or so anticipatory pre-cortical priming of the brain that occurs prior to perception of a normal stimulus (Pribram, 1991). Thus, from review above, we can derive the following empirical inferences that an adequate theory of intuition must explain:

- Experiments involving information transmission between subjects in distant locations show that intuitive perception does not decrease over distance and is not affected by location.
- Experiments on precognition and presentiment show that intuitive foreknowledge is not limited by the normal causal relations of time.
- Experiments involving Faraday cages and steel wall shielding (see Radin, 1997a), show that electromagnetism cannot be the 'carrier wave' for intuitive communication between persons.
- Experiments on presentiment show that intuitive perception is related to the degree of emotionality of a non-local object or event.
- Recent experiments show that both the brain and the heart (and possibly other bodily systems) are involved in perception of intuitive foreknowledge, and also

that information from non-local sources appears to be processed in the same way as normal sensory input.

THEORY

Intuitive foreknowledge belongs to a class of consciousness phenomena that has eluded the light of scientific understanding and has long remained an enigma (Walach and Schmidt, 2005). While there is little scientific doubt about the existence of these phenomena, explaining *how* – the mechanisms and processes by which – such space/time-defying interaction occurs has not been possible until relatively recently. As Mitchell (2000: 299) states:

> It is likely that most, if not all, subtle, ephemeral and unexplained phenomena associated with subjective experience are connected, directly or indirectly, with the phenomenon of non-locality . . . Non-locality and the non-local quantum hologram provide the only testable mechanism discovered to date which offer a possible solution to the host of enigmatic observations and data associated with consciousness and such consciousness phenomena.

Three scientific developments have opened the door to rational explanation. The first is the discovery of the *hologram* – specifically, the principle of distributed organization by which information about an object is spectrally encoded throughout a field of potential energy by the radiating oscillations of energy waveforms (Gabor, 1948). In describing the theory of intuitive perception that follows, we draw on the principles of a special kind of holography – *quantum holography*, which we elaborate below.

The second is the empirical discovery of *non-locality* – that everything in the universe at the sub-atomic level is interconnected and inseparable. Modern science has found that non-local communication of information appears to be a fundamental property of both micro- and macro-scale physical and biological organization, and is likely due to the inherent interconnectedness of everything in the universe at the quantum level (Bohm and Hiley, 1993; Nadeau and Kafatos, 1999). Also known as quantum entanglement, non-locality was dramatically demonstrated in experiments in particle physics in the 1980s and 1990s. These experiments showed that it was impossible to break the connection between a pair of entangled sub-atomic particles (a photon pair) even when each particle was separated by enormous micro-scale distances; initially over meters (Aspect et al., 1982) and subsequently over kilometers (Tittel et al., 1998).

The third is the discovery of *quantum coherence* – that sub-atomic emissions from macro-scale objects are not random but exhibit coherence at the quantum level, reflective of an object's material organization and event history (Marcer, 1995; Schempp, 1992). At the molecular level, all matter absorbs and re-emits quanta of energy from and into an underlying field of quantum fluctuations called *zero point energy*. Instead of being random fluctuations, the emissions from complex matter exhibit quantum coherence reflective of the matter's material organization; these emissions also carry information non-locally about the event history of the matter's quantum states (Schempp, 1992). This suggests that all biomatter at all scales of organization is informationally connected by non-local quantum coherence and externally to the larger environment by its coherent quantum emissions (Mitchell, 2004: 155).

Coupling these developments in physics with the psychophysiological evidence reviewed above on the involvement of mental attention/intention and positive emotions in non-local interaction provides the key to the door of scientific understanding. This makes possible an explanation that is rational: an account that does not rest on unverifiable metaphysical processes or invoke divine or supernatural intervention; an account that is grounded in known sensory systems in the body and psychophysiological processes of information communication – one that does not require postulation of a yet-to-be-discovered sixth sense; and an account that is amenable to scientific verification.

Holographic Theory

The appeal of holographic theory (Gabor, 1948) is the explanatory power of its principle of distributed organization as the informational mechanism for non-local interaction – that information about the properties and organization of a whole (object or event) is spectrally encoded into oscillations of energy as an interference pattern and radiated throughout a field of potential energy to all points and locations. Because it is possible to retrieve information about the whole from *any* location within the field, holographic theory, with its basis in the linear mathematics of the Fourier transform function, has been postulated to provide a reversible physical mechanism by which intuitive information can be encoded, transmitted, received, decoded and perceived (for example, Laszlo, 2003; Mitchell, 2000; Tiller, 1999; 2004).[5]

To create a hologram requires two sets of waves – a set of object waves and a set of reference waves. The object wave is directed towards the object. It encodes intensity changes and phase-shifts reflecting the features of the object as the wave interacts with the object, and it is then emitted away from the object in all directions.[6] When a reference wave is directed back towards the emitted object wave, it interacts with the object wave and creates an interference pattern that records the phase-shifts of the object wave relative to the reference wave; these phase-shifts produce the apparent momentary freezing of the object's three-dimensional image in space-time. At the moment of conjunction, the instant the interference pattern is created, *both waves are spatially and temporally coherent* – an important point we build on in the theory below. Then they continue on radiating as separate waves. In short, it is the interference pattern that encodes the phase-shift information from which a three-dimensional image – a *holograph* – of the object can be reconstituted in space-time, via a Fourier transform function.[7]

Quantum holography

It is important to understand that there are two basic forms of holography (Pribram, 1991): *classical holography*, developed to understand the physics of *image* processing (Gabor, 1948); and *quantum holography*, developed to explain the physics of *information* transmission in signal processing (Gabor, 1946). By its nature, classical holography implies a deterministic order in which, by definition, human choice and free will are ruled out. Therefore, in describing the outlines of a general theory of non-local interaction, we will be aided by the principles of quantum holography (Pribram, 1991), since it provides

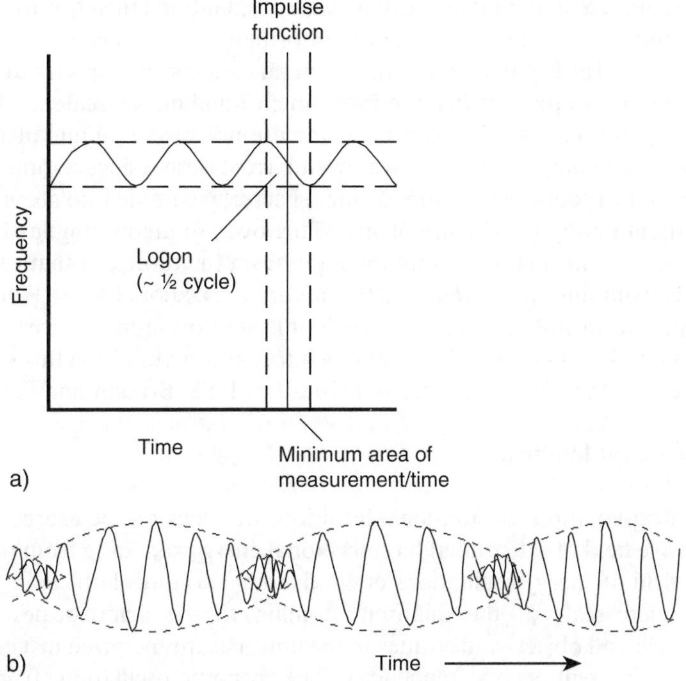

Source: © Bradley and Pribram (1998), reproduced with permission.

Figure 39.4 Gabor's elementary unit of energetic information – the logon

Figure 39.4a depicts an idealized graphical representation of a Hilbert Space showing a logon – an elementary unit of energetic information – in terms of Gabor's (1946) (energy) frequency and space/time limits of measurement. Figure 39.4b shows a representation of the overlap among a modularized series of logons.

the basis for a non-determinist kind of holographic organization (see Bradley, 2002; Bradley and Pribram, 1998).

Quantum holography is based on Gabor's (1946) energy-based unit of information, the *logon*, which he defines as *the minimum uncertainty with which a signal can be encoded as a pattern of energy oscillations across a waveband of frequencies*, as in the encoding and transmission of vocal utterances for telephonic communication.[8] Gabor was able to mathematically define the smallest area, in space and in time, within which a signal can be encoded in the oscillations of energy and still maintain fidelity for information communication (see Figure 39.4a). He called this area a *logon*, or a *quantum* of information (hence the term *quantum holography*; see Pribram, 1991: ch. 2), and showed that the signal that occupies this minimum area 'is the modulation product of a harmonic oscillation [of energy] of *any* frequency with a pulse in the form of a probability function' (Gabor, 1946: 435; our addition and emphasis). In mathematical terms, the logon is a sinusoidal module variably constrained by space-time coordinates – essentially a *space-time-constrained hologram* (see Bradley, 1998; Pribram, 1991).[9]

In relation to understanding non-local interactions, Gabor's theory provides the basis for an explanation. First, Gabor's concept of information – the encoding of information in energy oscillations at *any* frequency – is a general concept that applies to *all* energetic information communication, *both* in the four-dimensional macro-scale world and at the micro-scale of quantum reality. Second, logons are not discrete units of information, but overlap with each other and occur as a modularized series of space-time-constrained sinusoids in which the data in each module are spectrally enfolded, to some degree, into the data of adjoining logons (Figure 39.4b). This overlap among logons has a significant implication for information communication from the future, in that each logon, in Gabor's words, contains an '*overlap [with] the future*' (Gabor, 1946: 437; our addition and emphasis). This means, in effect, that each unit of information, by virtue of its spectral enfoldment with adjoining units, contains information about the future order energetically encoded in the unit that succeeds it (Bradley, 1998; Bradley and Pribram, 1998).

Explaining Non-local Intuition[10]

To develop an explanation for non-local intuition, we focus on the energetic resonance between the wave field of attentional bio-emotional energy radiating from the percipient and the wave field of energy oscillations emitted from a non-local object.

From the micro-scale of the quantum domain to the macro-scale of the four-dimensional world, all objects and entities in the universe are energized in a constant state of oscillation at different energy frequencies. The energetic oscillations from all objects generate energy wave fields that radiate outward and interact. As a wave field of *any* kind interacts with a physical object, a part of the wave is reflected directly from the object's surface while part of the wave's energy is absorbed, causing the object to become energized and emit another wave outward back towards the source of the initial wave. The interaction between these wave fields generates an interference pattern in which, at the moment of conjunction of the object and reference waves – the instant the interference pattern is created – *both waves are spatially and temporally coherent.* As a holograph, the interference pattern spectrally encodes phase-dependent information about the object's internal and external organization and also encodes its event history (Mitchell, 2000; Schempp, 1992). However, in order to decode the spectrally encoded information, a reference wave is required, and Marcer (1995) has established 'that *any* waves reverberating through the universe remain coherent with the waves at the source, and are thus sufficient to serve as the reference to decode the holographic information of *any* quantum hologram emanating from remote locations' (Mitchell, 2000: 302; our emphasis).

At the quantum level, the area of intersection in the interference pattern is a quantum hologram containing quantum level information reflecting this macro-scale process. Because the area of intersection involves an interaction between wave fronts, in which the radiation of energy in one wave front is modularized by the constraint of the wave front of radiating energy in the other, it is equivalent to Gabor's quantum or unit of energetic information, the logon (~ ½ cycle; Pribram, 1991). This means that the quantum hologram is essentially a logon, or a Gaussian-constrained hologram, in Pribram's (1991) terms. And since each logon contains non-local information about the future, then each quantum hologram also contains quantum level information about the future organization of the macro-scale object with which it is associated.

Marcer (1995: 153) has shown that the act of perception requires both an incoming wave field of sensory information about the object *and* an outgoing wave field of attentional energy, and that a relationship of '*phase-conjugate-adaptive-resonance*' must exist between the two wave fields in order to perceive an object in the macro-scale four-dimensional world. Phase-conjugate-adaptive-resonance is a process in which the incoming and outgoing wave fields are phase-conjoined by the percipient's act of attention, in that he or she tunes into and maintains 'vibratory resonance' with the object's energetic oscillations at the quantum level – that 'the perceived object and the percipient's perceptual system are locked in a resonant feedback loop' (Mitchell, 2000: 302).[11] Mitchell makes the important point that non-local quantum information can still be processed by the brain 'even in the absence' of space-time (electromagnetic) signals to establish the phase-conjugate-adaptive-resonance condition. All that is required is an 'icon', a symbol representing the object, which 'seems sufficient' for the brain to pay attention to the object and to thus establish phase-conjugate-adaptive-resonance with the quantum level of the object (Mitchell, 2000: 302).

It can be shown (see Figure 39.5a), that when two interpenetrating wave fields are radiating synchronized oscillations at the same energy frequency, the conjunction of individual waves creates a spatially and temporally coherent channel of interaction connecting the object source points of the two wave fields (Bradley et al., 2004). This channel is essentially a logon pathway for optimal information communication, and it is also generated in systems involving multiple objects with synchronized oscillations at the same energy frequency (see Bradley, 2006: fig. 8). But this does not generally hold for interaction between wave fields radiating energy oscillations at different or varying frequencies (see Figure 39.5b); in such cases effective communication is impeded by spatial and/or temporal incoherence in the pattern of interpenetration between the wave fields.

However, when wave fields at different energy frequencies oscillate in *harmonic resonance* (see Figure 39.6), a coherent channel of communication emerges from the radiation of synchronized oscillations across the wave fields. Thus when the set of wave fields constitutes a harmonic series – two waves, four waves, eight waves, and so forth, per cycle, with synchronized wave peaks and troughs across the series – oscillatory resonance creates a coherent channel of communication across the different frequencies of individual wave fields. This provides for a logon pathway of optimal non-local information communication across different scales of organization: from the quantum level micro-scale domain, to the four-dimensional macro-scale world, and vice versa. Since the overlap among logons means that information about future order is spectrally enfolded, this creates an information processing mechanism by which foreknowledge of the future is contained in the logon or non-local quantum hologram at hand.

When the dynamics of these interactions are considered, information communication at hyper-speeds emerges as a third wave field, radiating in all directions, from the point source of the interaction of wave fronts in the two wave fields, as described elsewhere (Bradley, 2006). This third wave field encodes the quantum holograms created by the interaction of the two original wave fields, and, as such, is a likely mechanism for non-local information communication at hyper-speeds. Moreover, when wave fields from different scales of organization are in harmonic interaction, an emergent oscillatory resonance is generated for non-local information communication within and between macro- and micro-scales of organization at hyper-speeds.

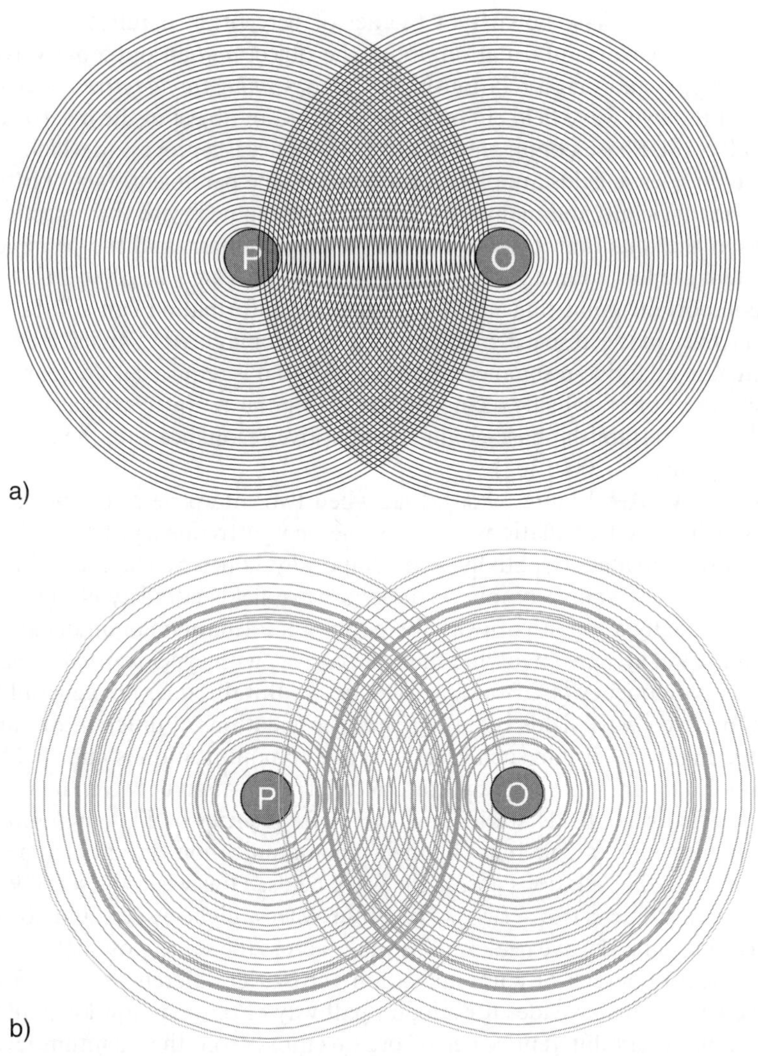

Source: © Bradley (2006), reproduced with permission.

Figure 39.5 *Emergence of coherent interaction channels in energy wave fields*
Figure 39.5a shows how a channel of coherent interaction is created between a percipient (P) and an object (O) when their two interpenetrating wave fields are radiating synchronized oscillations at the same energy frequency. This also holds for systems involving a percipient and multiple objects; coherent channels of interaction are created both between the percipient and each object and also among the objects themselves. However, this does not hold for interaction between wave fields radiating energy oscillations at different frequencies, as shown in Figure 39.5b; effective communication is blocked by an incoherent pattern of interpenetration between the two wave fields.

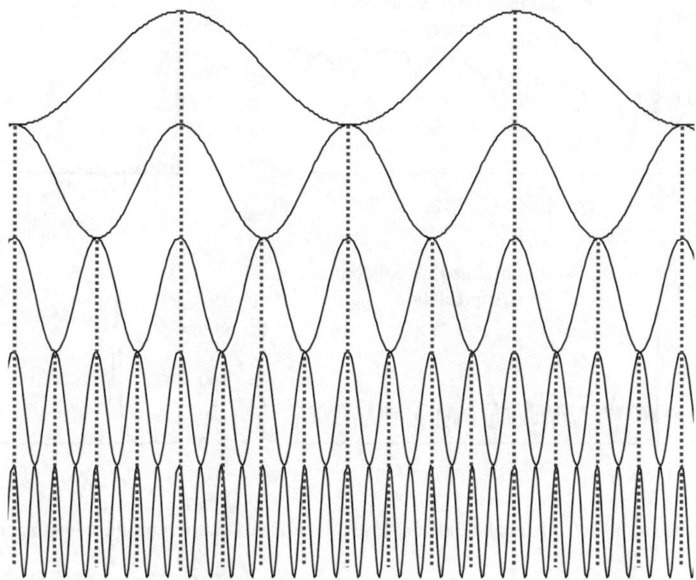

Source: © Bradley (2006), reproduced with permission.

Figure 39.6 Representation of harmonic resonance among energy wave fields across different scales of organization

This figure depicts a set of wave fields at different energy frequencies in a harmonic series – two waves, four waves, eight waves, and so forth, per cycle, with synchronized wave peaks and troughs across the series. Note how a coherent channel of resonance emerges from synchronized oscillations across the wave fields, depicted with a dashed vertical line in the figure.

Passion and the heart's role

As already noted, the act of conscious perception requires both an incoming wave field of sensory information about the object *and* an outgoing wave field of attentional bio-emotional energy. Based on recent research, it is clear that more than the brain is involved in the act of attention (see McCraty et al., 2006). The body's psychophysiological systems generate numerous fields of energy, at various frequencies, that radiate outwards from the body as wave fields in all directions. Of these, the heart generates the most powerful, rhythmic electromagnetic field. Not only does a massive deceleration in the heart's pattern of rhythmic activity occur at the moment of mental attention, which would generate a great change recorded in the outgoing wave field, but it is also clear from recent research that non-local perception is related to the percipient's degree of emotional arousal generated by an object. It is the individual's *passion* or 'rapt attention', as Radin (1997a) calls it – *the biological energy activated in the individual's emotional connection to the object of interest* – that generates the outgoing attentional wave directed to the object. And since it is well established that the heart's energetic pattern of activity reflects feelings and emotional experience (McCraty et

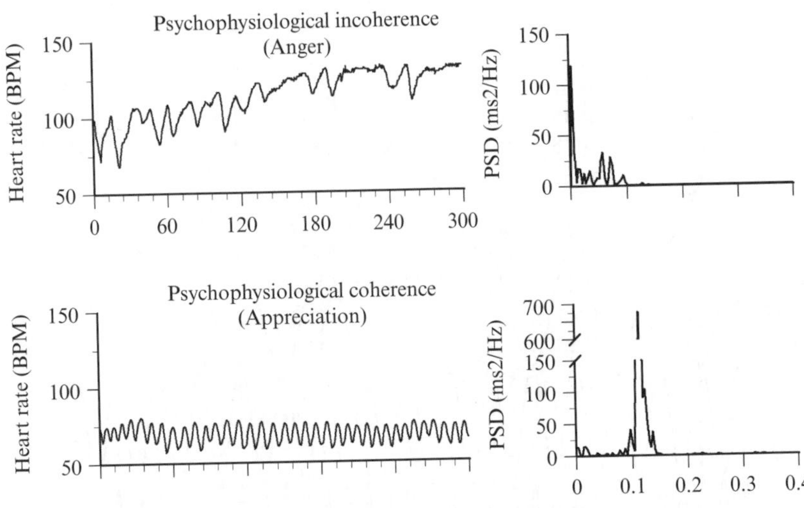

Source: Adapted from McCraty et al. (2006); © Institute of HeartMath, reproduced with permission.

Figure 39.7 *Typical heart rhythm patterns during two different psychophysiological modes – psychophysiological coherence and psychophysiological incoherence*

Negative emotions, like anger or frustration, generate a highly erratic pattern (incoherent) of beat-to-beat heart rhythm activity, whereas positive emotions, like appreciation or love, generate a highly ordered sine-wave-like pattern (coherent).

al., 2006; Tiller et al., 1996),[12] it is likely that the heart is instrumental in generating the outgoing wave of bio-emotional attentional energy directed to the object. In other words, *it is the energetically more powerful emotional component of attention and not just the mental (purely cognitive) element that is propelling the outgoing wave field of bio-emotional energy.*

The calming of extraneous thoughts and adoption of positive emotional interest involved in the act of 'paying attention to' distant locales or non-local objects establishes a relationship of phase-conjugate-adaptive-resonance with the quantum level of an object at the distant location. Research at the Institute of HeartMath (IHM) and elsewhere has found that attention is significantly enhanced when a focused, self-generated positive emotional state is sustained (McCraty, 2002; McCraty et al., 2006: 32–7). Maintenance of a positive emotional state induces a shift to a coherent order in the heart's beat-to-beat pattern of rhythmic activity (Figure 39.7), marking the movement to a global state of increased synchronization and harmony in psychophysiological processes, referred to as *psychophysiological coherence* (McCraty et al., 2006; Tomasino, 2007). Compare, in Figure 39.7, the coherent order of smooth, sine-wave-like waveforms generated by the heart's beat-to-beat pattern of rhythmic activity during a sustained positive emotional state such as appreciation or love, to the incoherent order of erratic, irregular waveforms produced in a negative emotional state like anger or frustration. Notably, the interpenetration between the outgoing coherent wave fields generated in

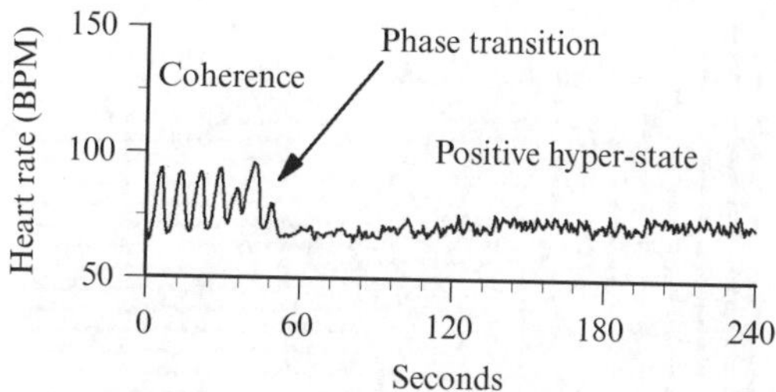

Source: From McCraty et al. (2006); © Institute of HeartMath, reproduced with permission.

Figure 39.8 Phase-shift to a positive hyper-state
This figure shows a typical example of the phase transition observed in a subject moving from the Psychophysiological Coherence mode to a positive hyper-state referred to as Emotional Quiescence. Note the abrupt change from the higher-amplitude sine-wave-like heart rhythm pattern distinguishing the Coherence mode to the much higher-frequency and lower-amplitude rhythm which marks the onset of the Emotional Quiescence positive hyper-state.

the state of psychophysiological coherence and the incoming wave fields of quantum coherence from objects and events outside the body creates an oscillatory channel of energetic resonance for information communication (see Figure 39.6a). In contrast, such communication is impeded when the body's psychophysiological systems are in a state of incoherence (as shown in Figure 39.6b above).

But there also is electrophysiological evidence of a 'deeper' internal state in which the body's psychophysiological systems seem optimally organized for connection to and communication with the non-local quantum world. In the example from an IHM study (McCraty et al., 2006) shown in Figure 39.8, an individual undergoes a phase transition from the state of psychophysiological coherence to enter *emotional quiescence* – a qualitatively different 'hyper-state' of emotional experience.[13] Notice how the lower-frequency, higher-amplitude, smooth, sine-wave-like pattern of heart rate variability for psychophysiological coherence rapidly transitions to the higher-frequency, lower-amplitude sine-wave-like pattern of emotional quiescence. Moreover, although the ECG spectra for emotional quiescence actually form a harmonic series (Figure 39.9), those for psychophysiological coherence (not shown) do not. It is thus postulated that while psychophysiological coherence provides a communication channel for intuitive perceptions that can inform day-to-day experience, the harmonic order of emotional quiescence is the channel, via *energetic resonance*, to a deeper connection to non-local quantum reality, whereby intuitive understanding – including spiritual insight – of oneself, others, and the tacit order of the universe is accessed.

To the degree that a coherent relationship of energetic resonance between the object and the percipient is maintained – that the object's quantum wave field and the attentional wave field of the percipient are locked in a resonant feedback loop – the individual's psychophysiological system (the brain, the heart and the body as a whole) can receive and process non-local information as quantum holograms. In essence, it is the continuous resonant feedback loop between the outgoing coherent wave fields of bio-emotional

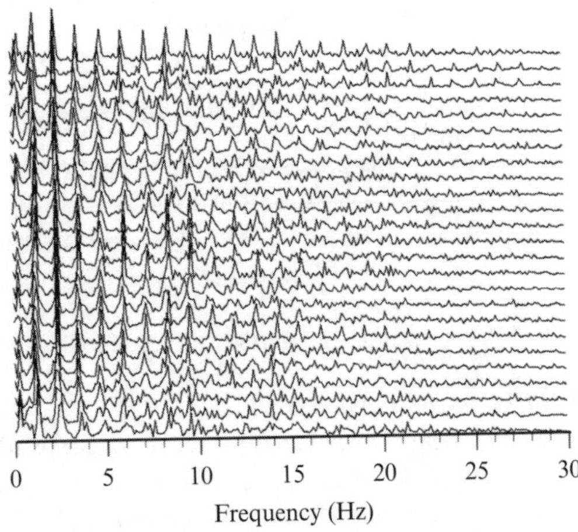

Source: From McCraty et al. (2006); © Institute of HeartMath, reproduced with permission.

Figure 39.9 *Waterfall plots of ECG spectra generated during emotional quiescence*
The figure shows the waterfall plot of ECG spectra from a subject generated while practicing the HeartMath 'Point Zero' technique. Categorized as a state of Emotional Quiescence, to emphasize the calm feeling of deep interconnection with everything around the percipient, the state is distinguished by a coherent structure of standing waves which form a harmonic series constant from spectrum to spectrum. This is due to the very low heart rate variability experienced in this mode.

energy generated by the body's psychophysiological systems and the incoming wave fields from objects that is the basis of non-local perception, in that the interaction between the two enables the body to receive and process quantum-holographic information about non-local objects and events spectrally encoded in the oscillatory radiation of energy.

One pathway of virtually instantaneous non-local information communication is at the quantum level through quantum coherence. Another pathway for information communication at hyper-speeds appears likely when a third emergent wave field is generated by the interaction between incoming and outgoing wave fields at the same frequency, or by harmonic resonance when wave fields of different frequencies interact, as described above. It is evident that the heart plays a significant role in the body's sensing and processing of the quantum holograms of non-local objects and events, in that the IHM study of intuition, as noted above, found that the heart receives information about future events *before* the brain (McCraty et al., 2004b). It is even possible that the pre-stimulus heart-generated change in afferent neural signals observed in this study is actually a signal to the brain about the incoming quantum-holographically encoded information about the intuitive event. Once received, such quantum-holographic information about distant objects is decoded and converted by the brain, through a reverse Fourier transform process, into mental imagery, feelings, and other sensations as described by Pribram (1991).

Non-local Agency

A secondary purpose of the theory developed here is to extend the account to include entrepreneurial non-local agency – the degree to which the entrepreneur's *passionate intentional focus* on the future object may influence its actualization into economic reality. This is a highly speculative proposition, in that we are unaware of any scientific evidence documenting this ability in entrepreneurs. However, there is a large body of rigorous experimental evidence showing that focused mental intention can exert a measurable effect on changing the future behavior of a physical object/system or a living organism/system (see Radin, 1997a: 128–56). Importantly, for the theory described below, there is evidence suggesting that a positive emotional state is involved as well.

Intention–matter effects

The idea that the mind can affect the physical universe is a fundamental postulate of quantum theory, wherein the observer's choice to conduct an experiment in a particular way determines what is actually observed. Thus, the observer's act of measuring the state of the quantum system causes the wave function of uncertainty (all possible states of the quantum system) to collapse to the certainty of the observed outcome. Of the three studies Radin (1997a) found in mainstream physics investigating this issue, one produced results exactly at chance and two produced positive results beyond chance.

Radin found hundreds of 'conceptually identical' dice tossing experiments and random number generator (RNG) experiments conducted over the last 60 years to test the proposition that the future outcomes produced by these physical systems could be influenced by mental intention.[14] In two meta-analyses that Radin conducted with colleagues, one on 148 dice tossing experiments (Radin and Ferrari, 1991) and the second on 832 RNG experiments (Nelson and Radin, 1987; Radin and Nelson, 1989), a small (~1.00% overall success margin), statistically significant result was found, with the odds against the involvement of chance calculated to be $>1^9$ to 1 and $>1^{12}$ to 1, respectively. This 1.00 percent overall success margin is consistent with results of an analysis of the entire database of RNG studies conducted at Princeton University's PEAR Laboratory, which by 1996 had conducted 1262 experiments involving 108 research subjects (Nelson et al., 1991).[15]

But there is also interesting evidence of a collective effect of '*coherent attention or emotional response*' to events of global import on the behavior of RNG output from the Global Consciousness Project (GCP) (Bancel and Nelson, 2008: 1, our emphasis). The GCP has been examining output from a worldwide network of RNGs[16] to test the hypothesis of a direct relationship between collective reaction to events of global interest (such as the 2000 Olympic Games Opening Ceremony) and the generation of non-random RNG output. Consistent with prior analysis (Radin, 2002), this hypothesis appears to be strongly confirmed by a recent study of 236 global events, which had a combined overall significance of $p < 3 \times 10^{-6}$ (Bancel and Nelson, 2008).

Overall, the results from hundreds of experiments conducted over the last 70 years or so have consistently documented a small but highly statistically significant mental/emotional effect on the future behavior of physical systems. This effect is 'not due to chance, selective reporting, poor experimental design, only a few individuals, or only a few experimenters' (Radin, 1997a: 144–5). Moreover, this intentional/emotional ability appears to be distributed throughout the general population. And consistent with the properties of non-locality, the experimental effects are not related to the distance between the research participant and the RNG, nor are they related to the timing of the subject's emotionally aroused intention (Nelson et al., 1984; 1991; Schmidt et al., 1986).

Intention–living system effects

Radin (1997a) located 131 published studies reporting the results of controlled experiments on the effects of non-local intention on living systems (including enzymes, cells, DNA, bacteria, plants, animals and humans), of which 56 had positive results with an overall odds against chance success rate of $>1^{12}$ to 1. Most experiments have been on the effects of non-local intention/emotion on the human autonomic nervous system (ANS) of remote percipients (for example, Braud, 1981; Braud and Schlitz, 1989, 1991). While a 5 percent success rate would be expected by chance, 57 percent of the experiments produced independent significant effects, with a combined odds against chance of 1^{14} to 1. In a subset of studies involving more than 400 trials, Braud and Schlitz (1991) measured the 'receiver's' electrodermal activity to record unconscious fluctuations in emotion, while a 'sender' at a remote location tried to arouse or calm the receiver purely by thinking about that person on a random schedule. Over the 400 sessions, the average effect size was ~53%,[17] with a combined odds against chance of $>1^{6}$ to 1.

Another set of experiments, conducted over a period of more than 80 years, test a 'receiver's' awareness of being watched by a 'sender' in a remote location. Today, these experiments involve monitoring the receiver's ANS activity while the sender stares at the receiver on a random schedule from a remote location over a one-way closed-circuit video system. Radin (1997a) conducted a meta-analysis of experiments conducted from 1913 to 1996, and found an overall effect of 63 percent, with odds against chance of $>3^{6}$ to 1.

Finally, from a series of pilot studies on the effects of heart-focused, positive emotional intention upon physical and biological systems (water, DNA, and human cells) *in vitro*, IHM has evidence connecting the transmission of a specific intention when in a state of psychophysiological coherence with measurable effects on the behavior of these systems (McCraty and Tomasino, 2003; Rein and McCraty, 1994).

Overall, there is persuasive experimental evidence showing that focused non-local intentional emotional energy has a subtle but measurable effect on the behavior of biological systems, including human psychophysiological systems. It is our belief that to the degree to which future studies both explicitly incorporate the emotional component of intention into the experimental protocol and also measure it, the observed effects of non-local intention will be significantly stronger.

Explaining non-local agency

The same multi-level psychophysiological and quantum-holographic processes of energetic resonance not only provide a channel for non-local intuition, but they are also the means by which entrepreneurial *passionate intention* may affect objects and events distant in space/time. We will now expand the theory of non-local intuition, described above, to sketch an understanding of how this occurs. In this account we focus on the quantum-holographically encoded mental intention in the wave field of bio-emotional energy radiated from the percipient to the object. In the same way, as noted above for intuition, we believe it is the individual's *passion – the biological energy activated in the individual's emotional connection to the object of interest* – that is propelling the outgoing wave field of intentional bio-emotional energy and driving the non-local effects.

We begin with the assumption that a thought or an intention is a distinct pattern of electrical activity in the brain, and that, as a unit of information, it is energetically encoded as a quantum hologram. The act of attention involves the generation of an outgoing wave field of bio-emotional energy from an individual directed towards the object of interest. And, insofar as this act includes an intentional disposition (for example, a preference, a desire, a goal, or a plan) this intention is recorded as implicit information spectrally encoded as a quantum hologram in the outgoing wave field. The more passion (focused emotional arousal) with which the intention is held, the greater the activation of the individual's bio-emotional energy, and, hence, the stronger the recording of the quantum hologram of intention in the outgoing wave field.

There are two pathways by which the quantum hologram of intention is transmitted to a non-local object. To the degree that the outgoing wave field of the intentional energy is coherent and attuned to the resonant frequency of the object, one pathway is created by the mechanism of energetic resonance between the individual's outgoing wave field and the incoming wave field of energy oscillations generated by the object. A second pathway is created when the wave field of intentional energy is organized as a harmonic series. This creates the potential for a multi-level channel across macro and micro scales of organization whereby the quantum hologram of intention is transmitted, via harmonic resonance, across wave fields at different energy frequencies to the quantum level of the object.

As the outgoing wave field interacts with the non-local object, the impact of each wave front reflects a part of the wave back from the object's surface towards the individual. However, part of the wave's energy is actually *absorbed* by the object. Since the record of the individual's intention is spectrally encoded and distributed throughout the entire outgoing wave field, the part that is absorbed by the object actually contains a quantum hologram of the individual's intention. Thus, as energetically encoded information, the quantum hologram of the individual's passionate intention can influence, via energetic resonance, the future potential of the object's material organization and behavior. And insofar as the outgoing wave field is organized as a harmonic series, the quantum hologram of intention is transmitted to the quantum level of the object, by means of harmonic resonance with the coherent wave field of quantum emissions from the object. Here, as energetically encoded information, the quantum hologram of intention can effect a subtle but significant change in the quantum organization of the object, thereby implicitly *in*-forming – literally, *giving shape to* – (Bohm and Hiley, 1993) the object's future macro-scale organization and behavior.

Social Amplification of Non-local Effects

In terms of the quantum-holographic theory of non-local interaction described here, the effects of both attentional and intentional emotional energy will be amplified and thus be significantly stronger when certain conditions are present in social groups and organizations. Such conditions are that the group has a membership boundary, an engaging shared collective purpose or ideology and, most importantly, that its members are bio-emotionally attuned to one another through a fully interconnected network of mutually reciprocated relations of positive affect, modulated by relations of social control, as described elsewhere (Bradley, 1987; 2003; Bradley and Pribram, 1998).

The harmonious group order that emerges from this bonding pattern generates a self-reinforcing collective field of coherent bio-emotional energy, which amplifies non-local interaction effects in much the same way that a signal of radio waves from distant stars and galaxies is amplified by an array of radio telescopes. By attuning all members to the same resonant socio-emotional frequency, the group generates a powerful collective receptive field of coherent bio-emotional energy through which implicit non-local information is accessed and amplified due to a stronger resonant feedback loop, both to the field of the group and to that of the individual member. For the individual group member, this eases the individual's shift to a state of psychophysiological coherence, which facilitates stronger access to non-local interaction. And to the degree to which the group collectively focuses passionate attention or passionate intention on a non-local object or event of common interest, the non-local effect is further amplified. Conversely, in socially incoherent groups, involving relations predominantly of negative affect due to disaffection or conflict, the wave field of collective energy is too disorganized for energetic resonance with the energy wave field from a non-local object. This impedes access to non-local information and also limits any intentional influence on the object's future (McCraty et al., 2004–05).

Empirical support for this expectation comes from the PEAR studies (Nelson et al., 1984; 1991) in which two people cooperate by focusing the same mental intention on the same RNG. These studies found that whereas same-sex pairs, irrespective of gender, produced an effect at chance level or slightly negative outcomes, mixed-sex pairs produced an amplification effect twice that of individuals. Of particular interest, is their finding that a bonded pair – a happily married couple or close family members – produce an amplification effect more than four times that of an individual. A similar amplification effect on RNG output has been found repeatedly in studies of social groups with a high degree of social coherence and a common emotionally intense focus, such as workshops and therapy groups (Radin, 1997a; Targ and Katra, 2000). There is also evidence from the Global Consciousness Project of the amplification of non-local effects in large human populations consciously or unconsciously emotionally connected to a global event, as mentioned above from the analysis of the RNG output associated with 236 events of worldwide mass interest (Bancel and Nelson, 2008). Together, these findings document a significantly enhanced amplification of the non-local effect of attentional and intentional emotional energy in coherent groups and large-scale social aggregations.[18]

CONCLUSION

Before concluding with some important implications, we present a summary of the theory from which we derive three hypotheses for empirical verification.

Recapitulation

Much of the present work to understand entrepreneurial intuition has adopted a cognitive perspective, in which intuition is viewed as based on information stored in the brain from prior experience. While these largely unconscious extrapolations play an important role in entrepreneurial decision and action, there are occasions when entrepreneurs have extraordinarily accurate intuitive hunches about future opportunities which cannot be explained by their past experience. Rather than presenting an opposing account of entrepreneurial intuition, our description of the psychophysiological and quantum-holographic processes by which intuitive foreknowledge of non-local events occurs is offered to complement the cognitive viewpoint and enlarge the understanding of how the future can be intuitively accessed and even shaped, to some degree.

Whereas the cognitive requirements of logic and reason demand *dispassion* as the entrepreneur considers alternatives and weighs outcomes and consequences in charting a 'rational' course of decision and action, intuitive access to non-local information about objects or events, whether distant in space or ahead in time, requires that the entrepreneur hold a sustained *passionate* focus on the object of interest. For both non-local intuition and non-local agency, the mental or purely cognitive component of attention or intention, respectively, is a necessary but not sufficient component to facilitate non-local interaction. Rather, and this is the important point we have tried to emphasize in this work, it is the more energetically powerful emotional component – *the biological energy aroused by the individual's passionate connection to the object of interest* – that is key.

Focused passionate attention directed to the object of interest (such as a future business opportunity) attunes the entrepreneur's psychophysiological systems to the quantum level of the object, which contains tacit, holographically encoded information about the object's future potential. Such emotional attunement – *phase coherence* – brings the outgoing wave field of attentional energy from the entrepreneur's psychophysiological systems into energetic resonance with the incoming wave field of energy from the object. The energetic resonance between the two wave fields of energy creates an optimal channel for communication of non-local information. The body's perception of such implicit information about the object's future is experienced by the entrepreneur as an intuition.

However, insofar as the entrepreneurial act of perception is more than interest in the object and involves a passionately held intention directed to the object as well, a quantum hologram containing the entrepreneur's energetically encoded mental/emotional intention is transmitted through the communication channel to the quantum level of the object. Once absorbed by the object, the quantum hologram of intention can produce subtle but significant effects on the non-local object's future organization and behavior. In this way, a sustained passionately held vision for the future, such as a plan or a goal, is communicated into the energy domain of potential and can be actualized into economic reality by the quantum hologram of the entrepreneur's passionate intention.

Constructing and maintaining a socially coherent group for the entrepreneur's business venture is optimal, in that the non-local interaction effects are amplified in a coherent group by a resonant feedback loop between the collective bio-emotional field of the group and that of the individual member.

The theory leads to three testable hypotheses:

1. The more coherent the passionate *attentional* interest directed to the object of interest, the greater the body's psychophysiological systems' access to the field of

quantum holographic non-local information, and, hence, the greater the entrepreneur's intuitive foreknowledge about the object of interest.
2. The more coherent the passionate *intentional* interest directed to the object of interest, the greater the body's psychophysiological systems' ability to communicate the quantum hologram of the entrepreneur's intention to the non-local object, and the more likely the effect on the object's future organization and behavior.
3. The more socio-emotionally coherent the group the entrepreneur builds for his or her business venture, the greater the amplification of non-local interaction effects and, hence, the greater the likelihood of intuitively locating a future business opportunity and intentionally actualizing it into economic reality.

Implications

A valid scientific account of non-local interaction has enormous implications for science and society (Radin, 1997a).

More specifically, for management science and economics, verification of intuitive foreknowledge in entrepreneurs will require an expanded concept of rational action. Instead of being confined to the wisdom of prior experience and the historicist logic of mean-ends schemas, the passionate attentional focus of these economic actors provides access to a source of information about the future – the potentials and possibilities spectrally enfolded in the incoming energy wave fields radiating from non-local objects. Sensed and processed in the body by the *same* psychophysiological systems as normal sensory input, this information is ontologically 'objective' (communicated from *real* non-local objects) and, therefore, provides a rational basis for intuitive decision and action. Moreover, by directing their passionately held intention to the object of interest, the outgoing wave fields of bio-emotional energy contain an enfolded quantum hologram of this intention which can influence, to some degree, its actualization into economic reality. Thus, the quantum-holographic principles and psychophysiological processes we have outlined here provide a plausible scientific basis for practices in management, sports, and all fields of human endeavor which emphasize envisioning the future as a means of influencing achievement of its actualization as reality. It is this rationality that is being tapped by genuine visionaries and prophets of the future (Bradley et al., 2008b). Such an expanded concept of rationality would profoundly alter the understanding of human consciousness and behavior in the social sciences as a whole.

There are important practical implications for management and entrepreneurship as well. There is now compelling evidence (Bradley et al., 2008a; McCraty et al., 2004b) that intuitive foreknowledge may be enhanced by regular practice of emotional management techniques that facilitate a shift to the psychophysiological coherence state, in which the body generates coherent energy wave fields, as described above. Indeed, this research suggests that such practice may significantly enhance the entrepreneur's psychophysiological systems' ability to detect intuitive information *even earlier* in the pre-stimulus period before the outcome event becomes known. Thus, it is likely that non-local intuition is a perceptual skill that can be developed or improved with positive emotion-based coherence-building techniques (Tomasino, 2007). This not only has the potential to improve the performance of entrepreneurs, managers, and experts – indeed decision makers in all social spheres – but also could significantly enrich navigation of life's path for all individuals.

Finally, at the most basic level of science, a revision of the fundamental laws of physics will be required in order to explain how non-local interactions defy space-time constraints and the temporal dynamics of cause and effect. This will spur development of a new psychophysics which will radically alter the understanding of human perception and consciousness. For humanity, this paradigm shift in science will ultimately transform our conception of reality itself, profoundly changing the way we view our potential and our relations to the world. This will open the door to a potent new era of possibility.

NOTES

1. See Radin (1997a) for the most definitive contemporary review of this research. Also see Bernstein (2005) and Walach and Schmidt (2005) for recent reviews.
2. Event-related potentials are voltage fluctuations that are associated in time with some physical, mental or emotional occurrence. These potentials can be recorded from the scalp and extracted from the ongoing electroencephalogram (EEG) by means of filtering and signal averaging.
3. The RNGs are hardware circuits that use inherent electronic noise to generate truly random bits. Each RNG is attached to a personal computer which collects 200 random bits per second and transmits packets of data over the Internet to a central server in Princeton, New Jersey, USA, for data archiving.
4. Scargle (2002) and May and Spootiswoode (2001) offer a different interpretation of the 11 September data.
5. There is compelling evidence that holographs are created by many living organisms in nature to process sensory information (Greguss, 1975). Studies have found that flies, fish, birds and mammals – including humans – all process sensory information about objects in their external environments holographically. Following Karl Pribram's (1971; 1991) pioneering work in developing a holographic theory to explain perception and memory in the brain, studies in humans have shown that chemical oscillations and cellular oscillations, and also of macro-scale oscillations of heart activity all strongly suggest that holographic-like processing not only exists at the neural level, but also at the cellular, molecular, and global levels of physiological function (see McCraty et al., 2006).
6. It should be noted that because photographs record the intensity changes and not the phase-shifts of the light waves bouncing off the object, only a two-dimensional image of the object can be recorded.
7. Research on the creation of holographs in nature, has shown that bats and dolphins actually create holograms by transmitting acoustical object waves and reference waves that radiate outwards into their environments and that are then reflected back to the animal for neural processing and translation into holographic images of objects in the environment (Greguss, 1975).
8. This is radically different from, although related to, the more commonly used concept of information, *reduction of uncertainty*, developed by Claude Shannon (1949), in which information is digitally encoded into a sequence of BITs (the BInary digiT – the smallest unit of information) to form a signal. Used in logical and computational systems, the uncertainty of the meaning of a signal is incrementally reduced by the successive addition of units of information, in much the same way that the resolution of the meaning of this sentence is increased with the addition of each word.
9. However, it should be noted, as Pribram (1991: ch. 2) points out, that a Gaussian or a rectangular function will also serve as the constraint to modularize the signal's encoding in energy.
10. While there is not space to review them here, there are three other recent theories of intuition (Mitchell, 2000; Rauscher and Targ, 2001; Tiller, 2004) which in different ways draw on certain principles and discoveries from classical and quantum physics to provide a physical means for explaining the space/time defying non-local communication of information involved in intuition. These theories are discussed in Bradley (2006; 2007a).
11. 'Marcer (1995) has proposed that . . . resonance requires a virtual path mathematically equal but opposite to the incoming sensory information about the object. Further, that it is the incoming space/time information (visual, acoustic, etc.), which decodes the information of the quantum hologram and establishes the condition of *pcar* [phase-conjugate-adaptive-resonance] so that accurate three dimensional perception is possible' (Mitchell, 2000: 297).
12. The research shows that information about a person's emotional state is communicated both throughout

the body *and* into the external environment via the heart's pattern of activity. The rhythmic patterns of beat-to-beat heart activity change significantly as we experience different emotions. In turn, these changes in the heart's beating patterns create corresponding changes in the structure spectra of the electromagnetic field radiated by the heart, as discussed in a moment (see McCraty et al., 2006).

13. The subjective experience of emotional quiescence is a state in which the intrusion of normal mental and emotional 'chatter' is reduced to a point of internal quietness, to be replaced by a profound feeling of peace and serenity and a heightened awareness of the movement of energy both within one's body and between oneself and other people; the feeling of being 'totally alive' and 'fully present' in the moment; the experience of an all-embracing, non-judgmental love (in the largest sense); and a sense of increased connectedness with one's higher self or spirit, and with 'the whole' (McCraty et al., 2006: 33–4, 37–43).
14. The early studies (1935–87) were dice-tossing experiments, whereas, since the 1990s researchers have conducted 'conceptually identical' experiments on the effect of mental intention on RNG output. An RNGs is a hardware circuit that uses inherent electronic noise to generate an output stream of truly random bits.
15. There is some compelling evidence that *more* than mental intention is involved. In a videotaped study of therapy sessions his Reichian bio-psychiatric practice, Blasband (2000) found a significant correlation between the direction of the shift in the output of an RNG unit he placed in his office and the valence of emotion spontaneously expressed by his patients.
16. As of January 2008, the GCP network comprised approximately 65 RNGs located throughout North and South America, Europe, Asia, Africa, Australia, New Zealand, and the Pacific Islands (Bancel and Nelson, 2008).
17. The 'average effect size' for these electrodermal studies is about 0.25 (effect sizes range from +1, absolute success in the predicted direction, to −1, absolute success in the opposite direction).
18. This is consistent with the conclusion of Nelson et al. (1998), who list group resonance in emotionally meaningful contexts, subjective and emotional contents, profound personal involvement, deeply engrossing communication, and spiritually engaging situations as conditions in which non-local intentional emotional effects are most likely.

REFERENCES

Agor, W. (1984), *Intuitive Management: Integrating Left and Right Brain Skills*, Englewood Cliffs, NJ: Prentice Hall.

Allinson, C.W. and J. Hayes (1996), 'The cognitive style index: a measure of intuition-analysis for organisational research', *Journal of Management Studies*, **33** (1), 119–35.

Aspect, A., P. Grangier and G. Roger (1982), 'Experimental realization of Einstein-Podolsky-Rosen-Bohm Gedankenexperiment: a new violation of Bell's inequalities', *Physical Review of Letters*, **49**, 91–4.

Assagioli, R. (1971), *Psychosynthesis*, New York: Viking.

Bancel, P. and R. Nelson (2008), 'The GCP experiment: design, analytical methods, Results', *Journal of Scientific Exploration*, **22** (3), 309–33.

Baron, R.E. (2004), 'Opportunity recognition: insights from a cognitive perspective', in J.E. Butler (ed.), *Opportunity and Entrepreneurial Behavior*, Greenwich, CT: Information Age Publishing, pp. 47–72.

Bernstein, P. (2005), 'Intuition: what science says (so far) about how and why intuition works', in R. Buccheri, A.C. Elitzur and M. Saniga (eds), *Endophysics, Time, Quantum and the Subjective*, Singapore: World Scientific.

Bierman, D.J. (2000), 'Anomalous baseline effects in mainstream emotion research using psychophysiological variables', *Proceedings of Presented Papers*, the 43rd Annual Convention of the Parapsychological Association, 17–20 August.

Bierman, D.J. and H.S. Scholte (2002), 'Anomalous anticipatory brain activation preceding exposure of emotional and neutral pictures', paper presented, Toward a Science of Consciousness IV, Tuscon, AZ, 4–8 April.

Blasband, R.A. (2000), 'The ordering of random events by emotional expression', *Journal of Scientific Exploration*, **14**, 195–216.

Bohm, D. and B.J. Hiley (1993), *The Undivided Universe*, London: Routledge.

Bradley, R.T. (1987), *Charisma and Social Structure: A Study of Love and Power, Wholeness and Transformation*, New York: Paragon Press.

Bradley, R.T. (1998), 'Values, agency, and the theory of quantum vacuum interaction', in K.H. Pribram, (ed.), *Brain and Values: Is a Biological Science of Values Possible*, Mahwah, NJ: Lawrence Erlbaum Associates, pp. 471–504.

Bradley, R.T. (2002), 'Dialogue, information, and psychosocial organization', in N.C. Roberts (ed.), *Transformative Power of Dialogue*, London: Elsevier, pp. 243–88.

Bradley, R.T. (2003), 'Love, power, mind, brain, and agency', in D. Loye (ed.), *The Great Adventure: Toward a Fully Human Theory of Evolution*, New York: SUNY Press, pp. 99–150.

Bradley, R.T. (2006), 'The psychophysiology of entrepreneurial intuition: a quantum-holographic theory', in M. Gillin (ed.), *Regional Frontiers of Entrepreneurship Research 2006*, Hawthorne: AGSE, Swinbourne University of Technology.

Bradley, R.T. (2007a), 'Psychophysiology of intuition: a quantum-holographic theory of non-local communication', *World Futures: The Journal of General Evolution*, **63** (2), 61–97.

Bradley, R.T. (2007b), 'The language of entrepreneurship: energetic information processing in entrepreneurial decision and action', in *Proceedings of the Fourth AGSE International Entrepreneurship Research Exchange Conference*, Australian Graduate School of Entrepreneurship, University of Technology Swinbourne, Brisbane, Australia.

Bradley, R.T. and K.H. Pribram (1998), 'Communication and stability in social collectives', *Journal of Social and Evolutionary Systems*, **21** (1), 29–81.

Bradley, R.T., M. Gillin and D. Tomasino (2008b), 'Transformational dynamics of entrepreneurial systems: the organizational basis of intuitive action', in M. Gillin (ed.), *Regional Frontiers of Entrepreneurship Research 2008*, Hawthorne: AGSE, Swinbourne University of Technology.

Bradley, R.T., R. McCraty and R. Rees (2004), 'Proposal concept for a study of highly effective and transformational teaching', unpublished manuscript, Institute of HeartMath, Boulder Creek, CA.

Bradley, R.T., R. McCraty, M. Atkinson and M. Gillin (2008a), 'Nonlocal intuition in entrepreneurs and non-entrepreneurs: an experimental comparison using electrophysiological measures', in M. Gillin (ed.), *Regional Frontiers of Entrepreneurship Research 2008*, Hawthorne: AGSE, Swinbourne University of Technology.

Braud, W.G. (1981), 'Psi performance and autonomic system activity', *Journal of the American Society for Psychical Research*, **75**, 1–35.

Braud, W.G. and M.J. Schlitz (1989), 'A methodology for the objective study of transpersonal imagery', *Journal of Scientific Exploration*, **3**, 43–63.

Braud, W.G. and M.J. Schlitz (1991), 'Consciousness interactions with remote biological systems: anomalous intentionality effects', *Subtle Energies*, **2** (1), 1–46.

Brockhaus, R.H. and P.S. Horwitz (1985), 'The psychology of the entrepreneur', in D.L. Sexton and R.W. Smilor (ed.), *The Art and Science of Entrepreneurship*, Cambridge, MA: Ballinger.

Craig, J. and N. Lindsay (2001), 'Quantifying "gut feeling" in the opportunity recognition process', in W. Bygrave (ed.), *Frontiers of Entrepreneurship Research*, Babson Park, MA: Babson College. 124–35.

Don, N.S., B.E. McDonough and C.A. Warren (1998), 'Event-related brain potential (ERP) indicators of unconscious psi: a replication using subjects unselected for psi', *Journal of Parapsychology*, **62**, 127–45.

Fowler, H.W. and F.G. Fowler (eds) (1964), *The Concise Oxford Dictionary*, Oxford: Oxford University Press.

Gabor, D. (1946), 'Theory of communication', *Journal of the Institute of Electrical Engineers*, **93**, 439–57.

Gabor, D. (1948), 'A new microscopic principle', *Nature*, **161**, 777–8.

Gartner. W.B. (1986), 'Who is the entrepreneur? Is the wrong question', *American Journal of Small Business*, Spring 11–32.

Gillin, M., F. LaPira, R. McCraty, R.T. Bradley, M. Atkinson, D. Simpson and P. Scicluna (2007), 'Before cognition: the active contribution of the heart/ANS to intuitive decision making as measured in repeat entrepreneurs in the Cambridge Technopol', in M. Gillin (ed.), *Regional Frontiers of Entrepreneurship Research 2008*, Hawthorne: AGSE, Swinbourne University of Technology.

Greguss, P. (1975), 'Holographic concept in nature', in P. Greguss (ed.), *Holography in Medicine: Proceeding of the International Symposium on Holography in Biomedical Science, New York, 1973*, Guildford, UK: IPC Science and Technology Press.

Hahn, U. and N. Chater (1997), *Concepts and Similarity*, Cambridge, MA: MIT Press.

Keh, T.H, D.M. Foo and C.B. Lim (2002), 'Opportunity evaluation under risky conditions: the cognitive processes of entrepreneurs', *Entrepreneurship: Theory and Practice*, Winter: 125–48.

La Pira, F. and M. Gillin (2006), 'Non-local intuition and the performance of serial entrepreneurs', *International Journal of Entrepreneurship and Small Business*, **3** (1), 17–35.

Larsen, A. and C. Bundesen (1996), 'A template matching pandemonium recognises unconstrained handwritten characters with high accuracy', *Memory and Cognition*, **24**, 136–43.

Laszlo, E. (2003), *The Connectivity Hypothesis: Foundations of an Integral Science of Quantum, Cosmos, Life, and Consciousness*, New York: SUNY Press.

Laughlin, C. (1997), 'The nature of intuition: a neuropsychological approach', in R. Davis-Floyd and P.S. Arvidson (eds), *Intuition: The Inside Story*, Routledge, London, pp. 19–37.

Levin, J. and J. Kennedy (1975), 'The relationship of slow cortical potentials to psi information in man', *Journal of Parapsychology*, **39**, 25–6.

Lieberman, M.D. (2000), 'Intuition: a social and cognitive neuroscience approach', *Psychological Bulletin*, **126** (1), 109–37.

Marcer, P. (1995), 'A proposal for a mathematical specification for evolution and the Psi field', *World Futures: The Journal of General Evolution*, **44** (2 & 3), 149–59.

Marcer, P. and W. Schempp (1998), 'The brain as a conscious system', *International Journal of General Systems*, **27**, 231–48.

May, E. and J. Spootiswoode (2001), 'Memorandum for the record, re: analysis of Global Consciousnesses Project's data near the 11 September 2001 events', available at http://noosphere.princeton.edu/papers/Sep1101.pdf (accessed 20 September 2006).

McCraty, R. (2002), 'Influence of cardiac afferent input on heart-brain synchronization and cognitive performance', *International Journal of Psychophysiology*, **45** (1–2), 72–3.

McCraty, R. and M. Atkinson (2003), 'Roulette experiment protocol', unpublished computer program, HeartMath Research Center, Institute of HeartMath, Boulder Creek, CA.

McCraty, R. and D. Tomasino (2003), 'Modulation of DNA conformational states by heart-focused intention', Boulder Creek, CA: HeartMath Research Center, Institute of HeartMath, Publication No. 03-008.

McCraty, R., M. Atkinson and R.T. Bradley (2004a), 'Electrophysiological evidence of intuition: part 1. The surprising role of the heart', *Journal of Alternative and Complementary Medicine*, **10** (1), 133–43.

McCraty, R., M. Atkinson and R.T. Bradley (2004b), 'Electrophysiological evidence of intuition: part 2. A system-wide process?', *Journal of Alternative and Complementary Medicine*, **10** (2), 325–36.

McCraty, R., M. Atkinson D. Tomasino and R.T. Bradley (2006), *The Coherent Heart: Heart–Brain Interactions, Psychophysiological Coherence, and the Emergence of System-Wide Order*, Boulder Creek, CA: Research Center, Institute of HeartMath.

McCraty, R., R.T. Bradley and D. Tomasino (2004–05), 'The resonant heart', *Shift: At the Frontiers of Consciousness*, **5**, 15–19.

McDonough, B.E., N.S. Don and C.A. Warren (2002), 'Differential event-related potentials to targets and decoys in a guessing task', *Journal of Scientific Exploration*, **16** (2), 187–206.

Mitchell, E. (2000), 'Nature's mind: the quantum hologram', *International Journal of Computing Anticipatory Systems*, **7**, 295–312.

Mitchell, E. (2004), 'Quantum holography: a basis for the interface between mind and matter', in P.G. Rosch and M.S. Markov (eds), *Bioelectromagnetic Medicine*, New York: Dekker, pp. 153–8.

Mitchell, J. R., P.N. Friga and R.K. Mitchell (2005), 'Untangling the intuition mess: intuition as a construct in entrepreneurship research', *Entrepreneurship Theory and Practice*, November, 653–79.

Mitchell, R.K., L. Busenitz, T. Lant, P. McDougall, E.A. Morse and B.J. Smith (2002), 'Toward a theory of entrepreneurial cognition: rethinking the people side of entrepreneurship research', *Entrepreneurship Theory and Practice*, Winter, 93–104.

Mitchell, R.K., L. Busenitz, Bird B. Lant, C.M. Gaglio, J.S. McMullen, A. Morse and J. Brock Smith (2007), 'The central question in entrepreneurial research', *Entrepreneurship Theory and Practice*, **31** (1), 1–27.

Mitton, D.G. (1989), 'The compleat entrepreneur', *Entrepreneurship Theory and Practice*, **13** (3), 9–19.

Myers, D.G. (2002), *Intuition: Its Powers and Perils*, New Haven, CT: Yale University Press.

Nadeau, R. and M. Kafatos (1999), *The Non-Local Universe: The New Physics and Matters of the Mind*, New York: Oxford University Press.

Nelson, R.D. (2002), 'Coherent consciousness and reduced randomness: correlations on September 11, 2001', *Journal of Scientific Exploration*, **16** (4), 549–70.

Nelson, R.D. and D.I. Radin (1987), 'When immovable objections meet irresistible evidence', *Behavioral and Brain Sciences*, **10**, 600–601.

Nelson, R.D., Y.H. Dobyns, B.J. Dunne and R.G. Jahn (1991), 'Analysis of variance of REG experiments: operator intention, secondary parameters, database structure', *Technical Note PEAR 91004*, PEAR, Princeton University.

Nelson, R.D., B.J. Dunne and R.G. Jahn (1984), 'An REG experiment with large database capability, III: operator related anomalies', *Technical Note PEAR 84003* (September), PEAR, Princeton University.

Nelson, R.D., R.G. Jahn, B.J. Dunne, Y.H. Dobyns and G.J. Bradish (1998), 'FieldREG II: Consciousness and Field Effect: Replications and Explorations', *Journal of Scientific Exploration*, **12** (3), 425–54.

Penrose, R., (1989), *The Emperor's New Mind: Concerning Computers, Minds, and the Laws of Physics*, Oxford: Oxford University Press.

Pribram, K.H. (1971), *Languages of the Brain: Experimental Paradoxes and Principles in Neuropsychology*, New York: Brandon House.

Pribram, K.H. (1991), *Brain and Perception: Holonomy and Structure in Figural Processing*, Hillsdale, NJ: Lawrence Erlbaum Associates.

Radin, D.I. (1997a), *The Conscious Universe: The Scientific Truth of Psychic Phenomena*, San Francisco, CA: HarperEdge.

Radin, D.I. (1997b), 'Unconscious perception of future emotions: an experiment in presentiment', *Journal of Scientific Exploration*, **11**, 163–80.

Radin, D.I. (2002), 'Exploring the relationship between random physical events and mass human attention: asking for whom the bell tolls', *Journal of Scientific Exploration*, **16** (4), 533–47.
Radin, D.I. (2004), 'Electrodermal presentiments of future emotions', *Journal of Scientific Exploration*, **18**, 253–73.
Radin, D.I. and D.C. Ferrari (1991), 'Effects of consciousness on the fall of dice: a meta-analysis', *Journal of Scientific Exploration*, **5** (3), 61–84.
Radin, D.I. and R.D. Nelson (1989), 'Evidence for consciousness-related anomalies in random physical systems', *Foundations of Physics*, **19**, 1499–514.
Rauscher, E. and R. Targ (2001), 'The speed of thought: investigation of a complex space-time metric to describe psychic phenomenon', *Journal of Scientific Exploration*, **15**, 331–54.
Rein, G. and R. McCraty (1994), 'Structural changes in water and DNA associated with new physiologically measurable states', *Journal of Scientific Exploration*, **8** (3), 438–9.
Roberts, N.C. and P.J. King (1996), *Transforming Public Policy: Dynamics of Policy Entrepreneurship and Innovation*, Jossey-Bass. San Francisco, CA.
Scargle, J.D. (2002), 'Was there evidence of global consciousness on September 11, 2001?', *Journal of Scientific Exploration*, **16** (4), 571–7.
Schempp, W. (1992), 'Quantum holography and neurocomputer architectures', *Journal of Mathematical Imaging and Vision*, **2**, 109–64.
Schmidt, H., R. Morris and L. Rudolph (1986), 'Channeling evidence for a PK effect to independent observers', *Journal of Parapsychology*, **50**, 1–16.
Shane, S. (2000), 'Prior knowledge, and the discovery of entrepreneurial opportunities', *Organization Science*, **11** (4), 448–69.
Shane, S. and S. Venkataraman (2000), 'The promise of entrepreneurship as a field of research', *Academy of Management Review*, **25** (1), 217–26.
Shannon, C.E. (1949), 'The mathematical theory of communication', in C.E. Shannon and W. Weaver, *The Mathematical Theory of Communication*, Urbana, IL: University of Illinois Press, pp. 3–91.
Simon, H.A. (1987), 'Making management decisions: the role of intuition and emotion', *Academey of Management Executive*, **1** (1), 57–65.
Targ, R. and J.E. Katra (2000), 'Remote viewing in a group setting, *Journal of Scientific Exploration*, **14**, 107–14.
Tiller, W. (1999), 'Towards a predictive model of subtle domain connections to the physical domain of reality: origins of wave-particle duality, electric-magnetic monopoles and the mirror principle', *Journal of Scientific Exploration*, **13** (1), 41–67.
Tiller, W. (2004), 'Subtle energies and their roles in bioelectromagnetic phenomena', in P.G. Rosch and M.S. Markov (eds), *Bioelectromagnetic Medicine*, New York: Dekker, pp. 159–92.
Tiller, W.A., R. McCraty and M. Atkinson (1996), 'Cardiac coherence: a new, noninvasive measure of autonomic nervous system order', *Alternative Therapies in Health and Medicine*, **2** (1), 52–65.
Tittel, W., J. Brendel, H. Zbinden and N. Gisin (1998), 'Violation of Bell inequalities by photons more than 10 km apart', *Physical Review of Letters*, **81**, 3563–6.
Tomasino, D. (2007), 'The psychophysiological basis of creativity and intuition: accessing "the zone" of entrepreneurship', *International Journal of Entrepreneurship and Small Business*, **4** (5), 528–42.
Walach, H. and S. Schmidt (2005), 'Repairing Plato's life boat with Ockham's razor: the important function of research in anomalies for consciousness studies', *Journal of Consciousness Studies*, **12** (2), 52–70.
Warren, C.A., B.E. McDonough and N.S. Don (1992a), 'Event-related brain potential changes in a psi task', *Journal of Parapsychology*, **56**, 1–30.
Warren, C.A., B.E. McDonough and N.S. Don (1992b), 'Partial replication of single event-related potential effects in a psi task', *Journal of Parapsychology*, **56**, 1–30.

40 Regional context of entrepreneurship

Dieter Bögenhold and Uwe Fachinger

1 INTRODUCTION

Many authors argue that looking at macro figures at a national level is often too empty and too vague because those figures hide diverse regional divergences. Instead, regional figures serve as more reliable indicators of socio-economic performance. These ideas are summarized by Michael Porter's formulation of 'microeconomics of prosperity' (Porter, 2000) which matches with thought on the core-periphery model as delivered by Krugman (1991) suggesting that economic progress is not universal and linear.

Those general comments concerning the adequate method of analysis are especially relevant with respect to the analysis of entrepreneurship as economic policy on national and even on international European Union (EU) level are aiming at reducing regional differences in living standards by fostering entrepreneurship (Henrekson and Roine, 2005). As a result, academic interest in entrepreneurship is certainly on the rise but unfortunately it is not always clear what the term covers concretely and where borderlines of entrepreneurship are compared to terms as innovation or self-employment (Bögenhold, 2004a; Stam, 2008). Not everything labelled entrepreneurship can be translated with the category of self-employment and, vice versa, not all self-employed people can be regarded as proper entrepreneurs. Too heterogeneous are standards of living, labour, biographies, expectations and aspirations of people (Brown et al., 2008; Knight and McKay, 2000; Ronen, 1989) and not all self-employed people match with the idea of an entrepreneur as permanent opportunity seeker and finder (Kirzner, 1973: Ch. 2). Many of them are close to low incomes and their existence is to be explained against a background of experienced or feared unemployment (Bögenhold and Fachinger, 2007; Bögenhold et al., 2001; Parker, 2004) and the intersections are manifolds (Budig, 2006).

This chapter will discuss the issue of self-employment in a framework which combines labour market research within a wider socio-economic context (Bögenhold 2004b) and compares the development at different regional levels in Germany. We are trying to shed some light on the forces which push self-employment, on how much regions matter, and whether a special level of self-employment is a proxy for higher wealth. Based on data for Germany our findings indicate that no convergence between specific ratios of self-employment and specific growth patterns exist at levels of regional units. Links between figures of economic prosperity and patterns of self-employment are contradictory and not linear. Evaluation of self-employment underlines the same conclusions some authors have drawn for entrepreneurship (Baumol, 1990). The functioning of capitalist economies is more complicated than public statements often suggest when they operate with a few sentences of beliefs in which entrepreneurship has a firm place. Multicomplex relations are ignored and it is suggested that the interplay is quite simple (Baumol, et al., 2007).

2 ENTREPRENEURSHIP, SELF-EMPLOYMENT AND INSTITUTIONAL CONTEXT

While following ideas introduced primarily by Schumpeter (1947; 1963) that economies always need 'fresh blood' out of social and economic innovations in order to keep the capitalist engine in motion, we partly agreed that entrepreneurship might be an appropriate instrument to 'transport' diverse forms of innovation. However, the conventional equation that entrepreneurship has to be translated by the labour market category of self-employment must be questioned theoretically and empirically. Self-employment is heterogeneous and has diverse elements, social logics and social path-dependencies leading to the fact that fractions of self-employment can be very constitutive as sources and agents of innovation but other fractions are simultaneously very non-entrepreneurial in a Schumpeterian sense of running enterprises in routines without ever having ideas of innovation. The last group is very often driven by needs to keep the firms running to secure life and income, and they are created out of diverse motives, frequently also against a background of unemployment.

The introduction of an *institutional* context to the debate on entrepreneurship, innovation and self-employment helps to foster a better understanding of many phenomena under discussion. The turn to an economy within an institutional context helps to realize a turn from an *economy in abstracto* to an *economy in concreto*. When talking entrepreneurship it must be related to real societies with concrete time-space coordinates. Arriving at real societies and economies we realize that theoretical scripts which are given through abstract models for capitalist development diverge from empirical findings.

When discussing links between entrepreneurship and the division of occupations and changes in the labour market the analytical category of 'self-employment' seems precise and adequate for operationalizing a quantifiable understanding of entrepreneurship. Self-employment as a labour market category can be numerically counted and individual fractions of the category can be compared with each other (Grilo and Thurik, 2005a; 2005b). However, referring to self-employment raises the difficulty that it usually serves as a kind of proxy for entrepreneurship but self-employment and entrepreneurship are never the same. Entrepreneurship covers only parts of the category of self-employment and the population of self-employed people includes people who can rarely be identified as entrepreneurial agents (Stam, 2008).

Entrepreneurship is treated as a policy instrument to introduce innovation in order to initiate positive effects for the economy and the labour market. Regarding the question of what innovation really means, it is necessary to operate with a wide understanding of the term 'innovation'. Having in mind the broad scenario of interpretations and applications of innovation we should take into account that no single pattern of innovations exists but diverse ways of innovations as formerly not known 'new combinations' (Schumpeter, 1963). Innovation research is an elementary part of the broader debate on stimulating economic growth. A long tradition exists in discussing how to implement further growth most appropriately. Competing approaches are still coexisting although recent debate is moving towards a so-called unified growth theory 'in which variations in the economic performance across countries and regions could be examined based on the effect of variations in educational, institutional, geographical, and cultural factors on the pace of the transition from stagnation to growth' (Galor, 2006: 284–5).

Many economic models try to come up as simple as possible in order to deduce core principles which can be applied to all situations. The institutional framing with specific socio-spatial-cultural characteristics including social, legal, demographic or regional specifica is often neglected in such models. Therefore, no relevant explanatory power is given to those characteristics and, as a consequence, the deduced policy measures are missing essential components. Thus, it should be no surprise that the success of economic policy with respect to reducing regional differences is deplorable. Engerman and Sokoloff (2005) express clearly that economic growth theories can be better formulated by a more sensitive understanding of institutions:

> Economists do not have a very good understanding of where institutions come from, or why societies have institutions that seem conducive to growth, while others are burdened by institutions less favorable for economic performance. Until they do, it will be quite difficult to specify the precise role of institutions in processes of growth. . . . what little we know about the evolution of institutions suggests caution about making strong claims about their relationship to growth . . . (Engerman and Sokoloff, 2005: 664).

The consequence for research on entrepreneurship is that not only the context of entrepreneurship has to be acknowledged but also its change in temporal sequences. Especially, historical analysis provides applications for entrepreneurship research. Baumol (1990) exemplifies this in his historical analysis of entrepreneurship and he expresses that entrepreneurship *as such* cannot always be equated with economic upswings and positive effects of innovations. He explains that 'entrepreneurs are always with us and always play *some* substantial role. But there are a variety of roles among which the entrepreneur's efforts can be reallocated, and some of those roles do not follow the constructive and innovative script that is conventionally attributed to that person' (Baumol, 1990: 894; original emphasis). An analytical look at the development over centuries indicates that frameworks of economies can vary considerably and that mentalities and further cultural dispositions change (Munro, 2006), which is an argument that specifications of space and time should be provided when talking about entrepreneurship (Bögenhold 1995). Comparing self-employment ratios and their dynamics internationally show considerable divergencies (Blanchflower, 2000; Göggel et al., 2007; Luber, 2003; Müller and Arum, 2004).

3 ENTREPRENEURSHIP, NETWORKS AND REGIONS

Network research (Nohria and Eccles, 1995; Scott, 2007; Stegbauer, 2008) increased a conceptual understanding that economic cycles are best interpreted as socially controlled and organized interaction processes of individual and corporate actors. Economic activities function along specific 'ties' of contacts which are organized according to specific social circles of communication. Organizational networks can be seen analogously to social networks. The difference is that organizational networks focus on interaction between organizations compared with ego-centred networks based on social action of human agents. Michael E. Porter (1990) argues that it is more reasonable to compare regions instead of referring to aggregate economies and their aggregate data. Regions are the core *subject* of socio-economic analysis. When talking about 'microeconomics of prosperity' (Porter, 2000) the term serves as a research programme. Nowadays discussion on growth and regional policies often claims the need to foster clusters, a discussion which is based upon a perspective spread by Porter (see Stern et al., 2000).

A big part of recent literature on innovation (see Kaiserfeld, 2005) is led by questions for adequate socio-economic contexts generating innovation. Social networks are explicitly treated as 'extra-market externality' (Westlund, 2006) and a direct link between 'networking' and 'entrepreneurial growth' is postulated (Johannisson, 2000). In the discussion, clusters as sources of innovation through cooperation has increased significantly (for a review see Karlsson, 2007), and the growth of *socio-economic* elements is simultaneously expressed within entrepreneurship literature. Looking at specific models of economic success and growth, we arrive at a matrix of specific combinations of information processing, product generation, opportunity and market finding and regional characteristics (Asheim and Coenen, 2005; Asheim et al., 2006), which are based upon issues of material and immaterial dimensions of production and organization (in the same direction see findings of Mugler et al. 2006).

To get an adequate understanding of growth patterns acknowledging the institutional context of entrepreneurship (Benneworth, 2004) implies the recognition of social factors being of strategic importance. These social factors include items such as language, mentalities, family structures, systems of basic and higher education, industrial relations, trust or knowledge. They constitute different societal regimes of production, which always have specific factors in divergent regional contexts. In that sense business historians explained it as 'cultural factors in economic growth' (Cochran, 1960) and Buchanan and Ellis (1955: 405) stated that 'the really fundamental problems of economic growth are non-economic'.

If one agrees with Buchanan and Ellis, one also has to agree with far-reaching consequences since non-economic factors have to be analysed and understood in order to explain economic growth. According to these ideas, Audretsch (2002) listed in his discussion of major factors several social *soft* factors as *key* factors influencing entrepreneurship beside catchwords such as finance and taxes. The most important of these soft factors are culture, networks and social capital. Finally, the focus of analytical observation must be narrowed down to local entities that are regional rather than national. Ideas about the microeconomics of prosperity (Porter, 2000) match with geographic thought as delivered by Krugman (1991). Looking at regions enables specific paths and path dependencies of economic and social development to be seen which allow analysis of regional prosperities within their own logics of evolution (Audretsch et al., 2008).

4 SELF-EMPLOYMENT IN REGIONAL DISTRIBUTION: LESSONS FROM EMPIRICAL INVESTIGATIONS IN GERMANY

Talking about links between regions, entrepreneurship, and growth and to get knowledge about what happened requires empirical data. Data are also needed which cover a broader timeframe because the development is a protracted process and reactions of people to political measure take time. The analysis is based upon German microcensus data from the Statistical Office Germany which are available for the period from 1989

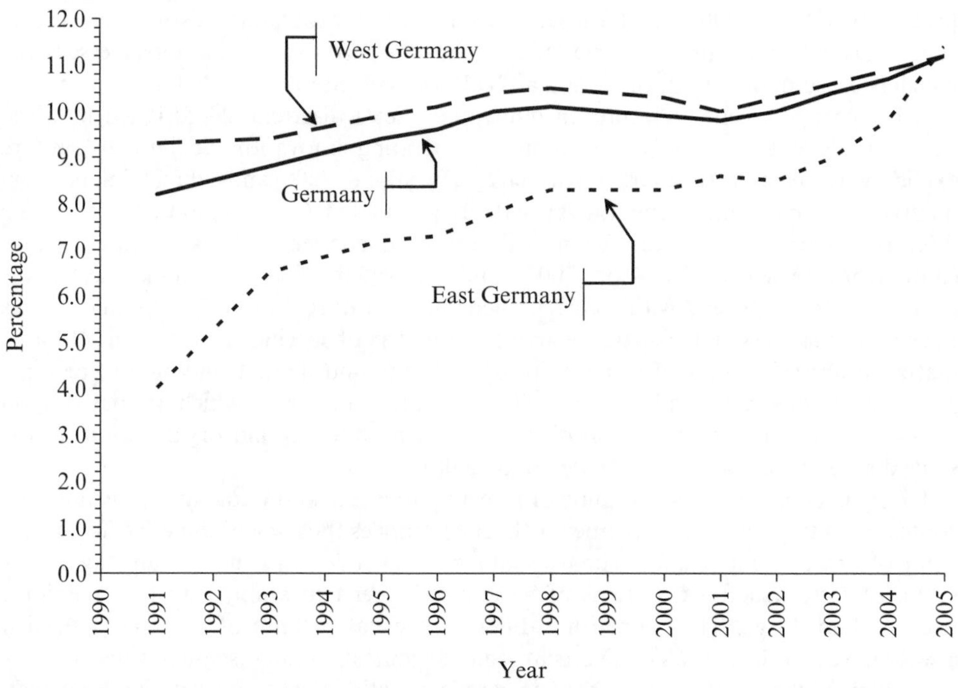

Source: Own calculations based on the scientific use files of the Microcensus of Federal Statistical Office Germany.

Figure 40.1 Self-employed people as percentage of labour force, 1989–2005

to 2005 (see, for a description of the data, http://www.gesis.org/en/services/data/official-microdata/microcensus/, accessed 25 January 2009). Those data are used to obtain further indications and specifications of the changes within the field of self-employment. Furthermore, we highlight some regional differences to demonstrate the relevance of spatial analysis. Our main interest is to ask for structural changes of self-employment by observing the period since 1991. The questions are (1) 'Do we find significant differences in the development between the two regions: West and East Germany?' and (2) 'Which differences can be located when asking for self-employment ratios in regional specifications?'

In Figure 40.1 the development of the self-employment rate in Germany is shown. Since the entry of the five states of the formerly GDR to the FRG – wrongly called the unification – the self-employment rate in East Germany increased and is now as high as in the old West German states. Overall, it seems as if an adjustment – fostered mainly by economic policy measures and by pressure groups – of East Germany to the standards of West Germany has taken place.

Figure 40.2 shows the development of the number of self-employed people in Germany, differentiated in two groups: the self-employed with and those without employees. This indicates that the development of self-employment is mainly due to the disproportionate increase of solo self-employment, whereas the self-employed people with employees

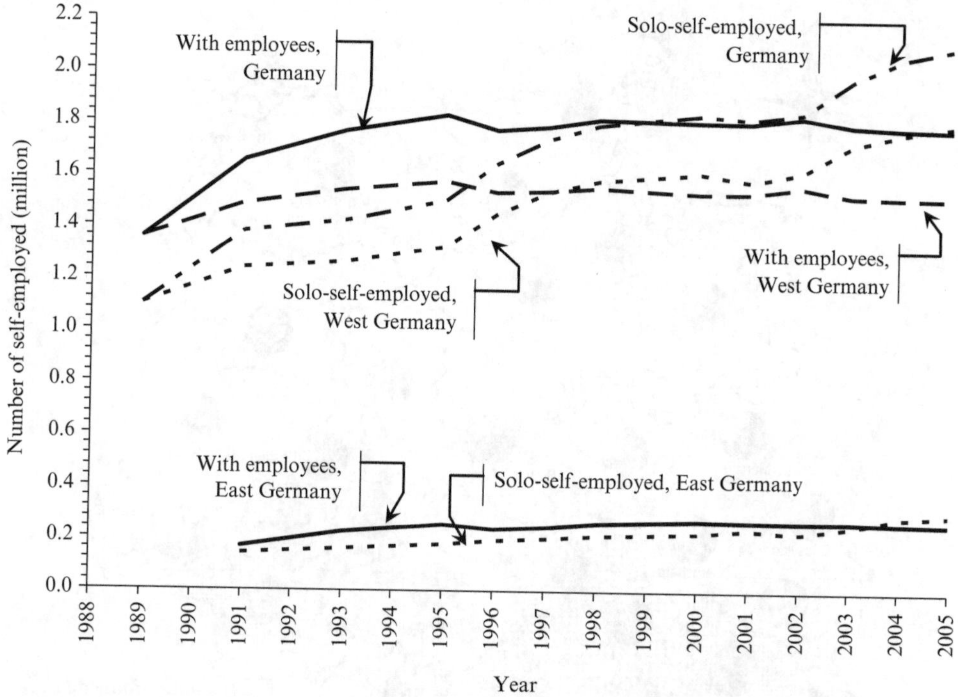

Source: Own calculations based on the scientific use files of the Microcensus of Federal Statistical Office Germany.

Figure 40.2 Self-employed people with and without employees

remain nearly at the same level (see, for Germany Block and Wagner, 2006; Bögenhold and Fachinger, 2007; for the UK Böheim and Muehlberger, 2006). Therefore, the political measures with which the government intended to reduce unemployment through promoting self-employment seem not to be reflected by the empirical data provided in these figures.

Where did this development lead to? Is it an overall 'harmonization' of self-employment, more or less equally 'distributed' over West and East Germany, or are there any regional differences hiding behind the figures?

To get an idea of the provisional result of the process in Figure 40.3 the regional distribution of self-employment is given.

Figure 40.3 shows an inconsistent picture and corroborates the argumentation of Porter (1990). There is a high self-employment rate in Saxony and in northern parts of Hesse, and a low rate in Brandenburg. Of note is also the fact that regions with high self-employment rates border on regions with a very low rates. This raises the question as to the reasons behind this pattern, which can only be answered by detailed comparative regional studies.

With respect to the economic sectors the situation turned out to be even more heterogeneous. There are regions with a low rate of self-employment in the tertiary sector, where the overall rate is also low – as for example in Schleswig-Holstein – and there are

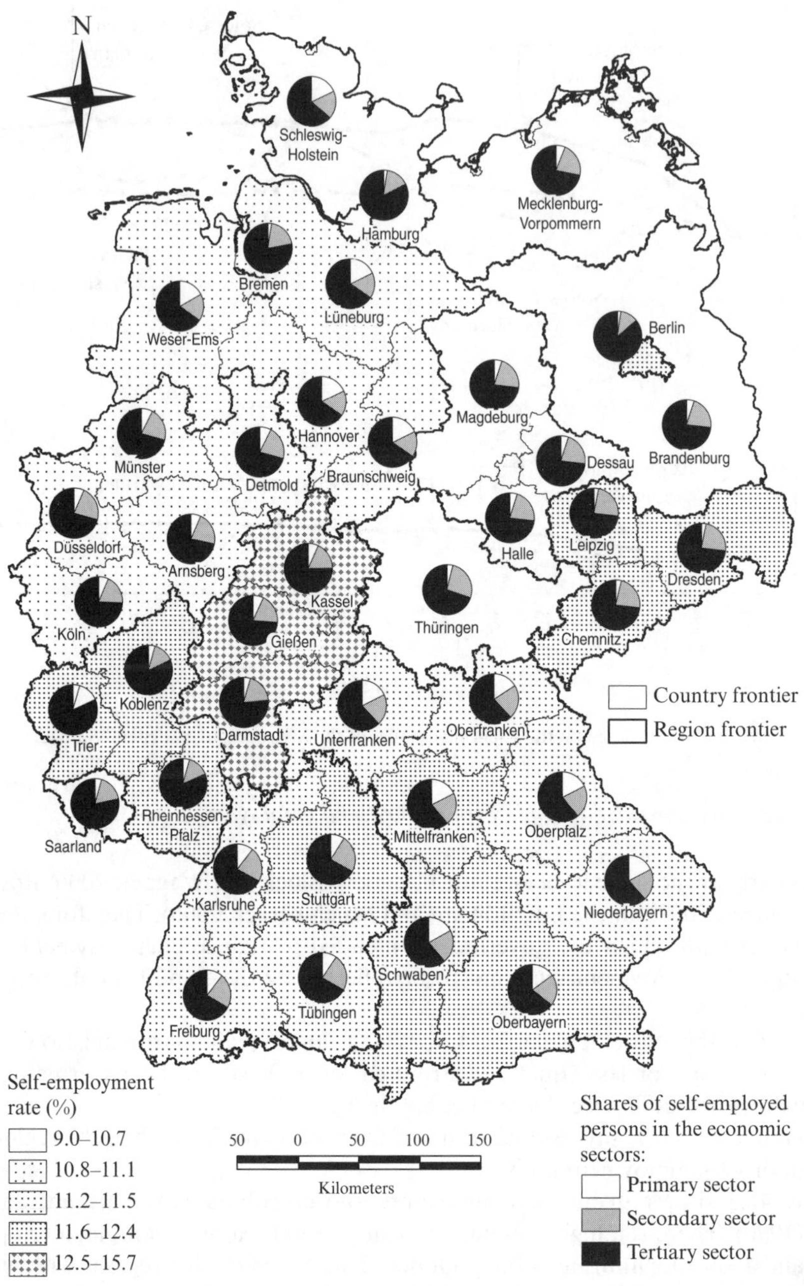

Source: Own calculations based on the scientific use file of the Microcensus of Federal Statistical Office Germany for the year 2005; we are grateful to Helmut Bäurle, who drew up the map.

Figure 40.3 Regional and sector specific self-employment rate, 2005

Table 40.1 Summary statistics of the regression

	Not standardized coefficients		Standardized coefficients	T	Significance
	B	Standard error	Beta		
Constant	16.331	.020		828 267	.000
Blossfeld's classification of occupation	.014	.000	.007	38 181	.000
Economic sectors	−1.671	.002	−.126	−700 333	.000
Wealth	.133	.001	.019	93 163	.000
Regions	−.126	.000	−.082	−449 936	.000
Counties	−.096	.001	−.024	−132 818	.000

R-square	corrected R-square	Standard error of estimation
.026	.026	6.91831

Source: Own calculations based on the scientific use file of the Microcensus of Federal Statistical Office Germany for the year 2005.

other regions with a high rate of self-employment in the tertiary sector and a high self-employment rate.

In general, the findings show that differences between regional levels cannot be reasonably explained simply according to the West–East scheme.

To complement the descriptive analysis, a linear regression was done with the county specific rate of self-employment as endogenous variable and economic sectors, Bundesländer (regions), counties, wealth,[1] and Blossfeld's classification of occupation as explanatory variables (for a description of the classification see http://www.gesis.org/en/research/programs-and-projects/official-microdata/blossfeld-s-occupational-classification//, accessed 25 January 2009 and, for its use, for example, Uunk et al., 2005). It turned out, that no linear relationship exists, as can be seen in Table 40.1.

5 CONCLUSION

Our analyses show that the social and economic process after the so-called German reunification proves to assimilate the ratios of self-employment in East Germany to that in West Germany. The gap between East and West German curves has increasingly shortened. However, differences between regional levels cannot be reasonably explained simply according to the East–West scheme but must better be interpreted in a *multi-complex* framework of intranational relations and different growth and labour market patterns within Germany (see Koetter and Wedow, 2008, for findings which are different but comparable). Attempts to explain variation primarily with German history of having post-communist and 'purely' capitalist parts in the country will fall too short.

We observe that the entire area of Germany is fragmented regarding the ratios of self-employment. At first glance, the heterogeneity has no clear and systematic logic of economic and social evolution. The link between entrepreneurship and growth (Audretsch and Thurik, 2001; Davidsson et al. 2006) is not linear and universal when looking at regional evidence. The variation in regional levels of self-employment ratios is contradictory relating to different sizes of metropolitan or rural regions and to different levels of economic prosperity. All possible explanations according to monocausal explanatory schemes can be countered with examples of regional development elsewhere.

Our findings serve as a first step to describing and explaining the development of self-employment with respect to the forces which push self-employment, on how much regions matter, and whether a special level of self-employment is a proxy for higher wealth. Much further research is needed to get to a state where we have a clear picture of a model for explaining self-employment development and for developing adequate economic policy measures. Also, information regarding further attributes of self-employed people, such as gender, age or educational level (Davidsson and Honig, 2003) or levels of social security (Sainsbury et al., 2006), could offer a deeper insight. Our results suggest that self-employment ratios on regional comparison are likely to be a dependent variable rather than an independent one. 'Understanding entrepreneurship' (Bjerke, 2007) implies getting better insight into diverse dynamics of entrepreneurship and trying to sort mechanisms into driving forces and effects.

The non-identity of entrepreneurship and self-employment has been discussed in the beginning of the chapter: not everything labelled entrepreneurship can be categorized as self-employment and, vice versa, not all self-employed people can be regarded as proper entrepreneurs. Celebrating a revival of entrepreneurship by indicating the increasing numbers of self-employed is not always serious since the explosion of solo self-employment has not much in common with a revival of entrepreneurship. These tendencies are better explained by global sectoral changes including labour market trends, secular processes towards tertiarization and the emergence of new professions which can be operated through freelanced activities or micro-firms.

NOTE

1. Wealth is measured as the median net income of households in the counties.

REFERENCES

Asheim, B. and L. Coenen (2005), 'Knowledge bases and regional innovation systems: comparing Nordic clusters', *Research Policy*, **34**, 1173–90.

Asheim, B., L. Coenen and J. Vang (2006), 'Face-to-face, buzz and knowledge bases: socio-spatial implications for learning, innovation and innovation policy', working paper, Universities of Lund, Aalborg and Oslo.

Audretsch, David B. (2002), '*Entrepreneurship: A Survey of the Literature. Research under Commission of the Commission of the European Union, Enterprise Directorate General*, Brussels: Commission of the European Union.

Audretsch, David B. (2007), *The Entrepreneurial Society*, Oxford: Oxford University Press.

Audretsch, D.B. and R. Thurik (2001), *Linking Entrepreneurship to Growth*, OECD Science, Technology, and Industry Working Papers 2001/2, Paris: OECD Publishing.

Audretsch, David B., Oliver Falck, Maryann P. Feldman and Stefan Heblich (2008), 'The lifecycle of regions', CEPR Discussion Paper 6757, Centre for Economic Policy Research.

Baumol, William J. (1990), 'Entrepreneurship: productive, unproductive, and destructive', *Journal of Political Economy*, **98** (5), 893–921.

Baumol, William J., Robert E. Litan and Carl J. Schramm (2007), *Good Capitalism, Bad Capitalism and the Economics of Growth and Prosperity*, New Haven, CT: Yale University Press.

Benneworth, P. (2004), 'In what sense "regional development"? Entrepreneurship, underdevelopment and strong tradition in the periphery', *Entrepreneurship and Regional Development*, **16**, 439–58.

Bjerke, Bjorn (2007), *Understanding Entrepreneurship*, Cheltenham, UK and Northampton, MA, USA: Edward Elgar.

Blanchflower, D.A. (2000), 'Self-employment in OECD countries', *Labour Economics*, **7**, 471–505.

Block, Joern H. and Marcus Wagner (2006), 'Necessity and opportunity entrepreneurs in Germany: characteristics and earnings differentials', MPRA Paper No. 610, Munich Personal RePEc Archive.

Bögenhold, Dieter (1995), 'Selbständige Erwerbsarbeit in sozial- und wirtschaftshistorischer Perspektive', in Jürgen Schmude (ed.), *Neue Unternehmen: Interdisziplinäre Beiträge zur Gründungsforschung*, Heidelberg: Physica Verlag, pp. 11–23.

Bögenhold, Dieter (2004a), 'Entrepreneurship: multiple meanings and consequences', *International Journal of Entrepreneurship and Innovation Management*, **4** (1), 3–10.

Bögenhold, Dieter (2004b), 'Creative destruction and human resources: a labor market perspective on firms and human actors', *Small Business Economics*, **22** (3–4), 165–77.

Bögenhold, Dieter and Uwe Fachinger (2007), 'Micro-firms and the margins of entrepreneurship: the restructuring of the labour market', *The International Journal of Entrepreneurship and Innovation*, **8**, 281–93.

Bögenhold, Dieter, Uwe Fachinger and Réne Leicht (2001), 'Entrepreneurship, self-employment, and wealth creation', *The International Journal of Entrepreneurship and Innovation*, **2**, 81–91.

Böheim, René and Ulrike Muehlberger (2006), 'Dependent forms of self-employment in the UK: identifying workers on the border between employment and self-employment', IZA Discussion Paper No. 1963, Institute for the Study of Labor.

Brown, Sarah, Lisa Farrell and Mark N. Harris (2008), 'Modelling the incidence of self-employment: individual and employment type heterogeneity', Sheffield Economic Research Paper Series SERP Number 2008010, University of Sheffield.

Buchanan, N.S. and H.S. Ellis (1955), *Approaches to Economic Development*, New York: Twentieth Century Fund.

Budig, Michelle J. (2006), 'Intersections on the road to self-employment: gender, family and occupational class', *Social Forces*, **84**, 2223–38.

Cochran, Thomas C. (1960), 'Cultural factors in economic growth', *Journal of Business History*, **20** (4), 515–30.

Davidsson, Per, and Benson Honig (2003), 'The role of social and human capital among nascent entrepreneurs', *Journal of Business Venturing*, **18** (3), 301–31.

Davidsson, Per, Frederic Delmar and Johan Wiklund (2006), 'Entrepreneurship as growth; growth as entrepreneurship', in Per Davidsson, Frederic Delmar and Johan Wiklund (eds), *Entrepreneurship and the Growth of Firms*, Cheltenham, UK and Northampton, MA, USA: Edward Elgar, pp. 21–37.

Engerman, Stanley and Kenneth L. Sokoloff (2005), 'Institutional and non-institutional explanations of economic differences', in Claude Menard and Mary M. Shirley (eds), *Handbook of Institutional Economics*, Berlin: Springer, pp. 639–65.

Galor, Oded (2006), 'From stagnation to growth: unified growth theory', in Philippe Aghion and Steven Durlauf (eds), *Handbook of Economic Growth*, Amsterdam: Elsevier, pp. 171–293.

Göggel, Kathrin, Johannes Gräb and Friedhelm Pfeiffer (2007), 'Selbständigkeit in Europa 1991–2003. Empirische Evidenz mit Länderdaten', *Jahrbücher für Nationalökonomie und Statistik*, **227**, 153–67.

Grilo, Isabel and Roy Thurik (2005a), 'Entrepreneurial engagement levels in the European Union', *International Journal of Entrepreneurship Education*, **3** (2), 143–68.

Grilo, Isabel and Roy Thurik (2005b), 'Latent and actual entrepreneurship in Europe and the US: some recent developments' *International Entrepreneurship and Management Journal*, **1** (1), 441–59.

Henrekson, Magnus and Jesper Roine (2005), 'Promoting entrepreneurship in the welfare state', working paper, Research Institute of Industrial Economics, IUI.

Johannisson, B. (2000), 'Networking and entrepreneurial growth', in D.L. Sexton and H. Landstrőm (eds), *Blackwell Handbook of Entrepreneurship*, Oxford: Blackwell, pp. 368–86.

Kaiserfeld, Thomas (2005), 'A review of theories of invention and innovation', working paper, Royal Institute of Technology Stockholm.

Karlsson, Charlie (2007), 'Clusters, functional regions and cluster policies', Working Paper 84, Jönköping, CESIS.

Kirzner, Israel (1973), *Competition and Entrepreneurship*, Chicago, IL: University of Chicago Press.

Knight, Genevieve and Stephen McKay (2000), 'Lifetime experiences of self-employment', Policy Studies Institute, Department of Social Security, Research Report 120, Leeds.
Koetter, Michael and Michael Wedow (2008), 'Does regional redistribution spur growth?', Economic Studies Discussion Paper 28, Deutsche Bundesbank.
Krugman, Paul (1991), *Geography and Trade*, Cambridge, MA: MIT Press.
Luber, Silvia (2003), *Berufliche Selbständigkeit im Wandel*, Frankfurt a.M.: Peter Lang.
Mugler, Josef, Matthias Fink and Stephan Loidl (2006), *Erhaltung und Schaffung von Arbeitsplätzen im ländlichen Raum*, Wien: Manz.
Müller, Walter and Richard Arum (2004), 'Self-employment dynamics in advanced economies', in Richard Arum and Walter Müller (eds), *The Reemergence of Self-Employment: A Comparative Study of Self-Employment Dynamics and Social Inequality*, Princeton, NJ: Princeton University Press, pp. 1–35.
Munro, John (2006), 'Entrepreneurship in early-modern Europe (1450–1750). An exploration of some unfashionable themes in economic history', Working Paper 30, Institute for Policy Analysis, University of Toronto.
Nohria, Nitin, and Robert G. Eccles (eds) (1995), *Networks and Organizations. Structure, Form, and Action*, Boston, MA: Harvard Business School Press.
Parker, Simon C. (2004), *The Economics of Self-Employment and Entrepreneurship*, Cambridge: Cambridge University Press.
Porter, Michael E. (1990), *The Competitive Advantage of Nations*, New York: Free Press.
Porter, Michael E. (2000), 'Attitudes, values, beliefs, and the microeconomics of prosperity', in Lawrence E. Harrison and Samuel P. Huntington (eds), *Culture Matters. How Values Shape Human Progress*, New York: Basic Books, pp. 14–27.
Ronen, Joshua (1989), 'The rise and decay of entrepreneurship: a different perspective', *The Journal of Behavioral Economics*, **18**, 167–84.
Sainsbury, Roy, Naomi Finch and Anne Corden (2006), 'Self-employment and retirement', University of York, Department for Work and Pensions, Research Report No. 395.
Schumpeter, Joseph A. (1947), *Capitalism, Socialism and Democracy*, London: Allen and Unwin.
Schumpeter, Joseph A. (1963), *The Theory of Economic Development*, New York and Oxford: Oxford University Press.
Scott, John (2007), *Social Network Analysis*, London: Sage.
Stam, Erik. (2008), 'Entrepreneurship and innovation policy', Jena Economic Research Paper, 006-2008, Friedrich Schiller University and the Max Planck Institute of Economics, Jena.
Stegbauer, Christian (2008), *Netzwerkanalyse und Netzwerktheorie. Ein neues Paradigma in den Sozialwissenschaften*, Wiesbaden: VS-Publishers.
Stern, Scott, Michael E. Porter and Jeffrey L. Furman (2000), 'The determinants of national innovative capacity', Working Paper 7876, National Bureau of Economic Research (NBER).
Uunk, Wilfred, Bogdan W. Mach and Karl Ulrich Mayer (2005), 'Job mobility in the former East and West Germany: the effects of state-socialism and labor market composition', *European Sociological Review*, **21** (4), 393–408.
Westlund, Hans (2006), 'The social capital of regional dynamics: a policy perspective', University of Tokyo, Working Paper F 423, Center for International Research on the Japanese Economy.

41 Religion as an explanatory variable for entrepreneurship*

Léo-Paul Dana[1]

People with unlike cultural beliefs and religious values have looked at entrepreneurship with varying degrees of legitimacy. The Greek philosopher Aristotle (384–322 BC), a student of Plato and teacher of Alexander the Great, viewed entrepreneurship as unnatural and therefore illegitimate (Aristotle, 1924). Becker (1956) explained that some cultures consider business an unholy occupation. Woodrum (1985) found participation in religious activities to be a predictor of entrepreneurial success among Americans of Japanese origin. Dana (1995a) and Lumpkin and Dess (1996) advocated that a small firm's orientation is grounded in the values of its entrepreneur.

Values and culture shape the environment for entrepreneurship as well as the entrepreneurial event. Aldrich (1979) noted that the environment could provide or withhold resources. From an anthropological perspective, Stewart (1991) suggested that the legitimisation of enterprise was a function of culture. From a sociological perspective, Reynolds (1991) confirmed the importance of non-economic factors such as the legitimacy of entrepreneurship, on entrepreneurial activity. Specht (1993) emphasized the importance of cultural acceptance. Cultural acceptance of entrepreneurship varies among people with different cultural values. Likewise, people from different religious backgrounds have unlike propensities to become entrepreneurs.

Farmer and Richman wrote:

> There is a close correlation of countries in terms of how deeply the Calvinist spirit has penetrated their economic and social behavior with real per capita income and level of economic development. Thus, in 1958, all fifteen countries of the world with per capita incomes of over $700 per year were those which had followed the Calvinist ethic extensively; and, with the possible exceptions of France and Belgium, all were quite extensively Protestant in religion. No country where the Calvinist ethic had deeply penetrated was not included in this list of most wealthy countries, while none of the extensively non-Calvinist nations had yet achieved such economic success. (1965: 157)

More recently, Enz et al. (1990) identified different value orientations among various communities and concluded that value orientation may be an important component in entrepreneurs. Some cultures simply value entrepreneurial activity more than do others and empirical evidence suggests that some religions are less conducive to entrepreneurship than are others.

The Government of Canada found that per 1000 Filipino workers in Canada, 18 were self-employed; the same reported that per 1000 Greek workers in Canada, 124 were self-employed (Dana, 1991). How can such differences be explained? Could it be that the Greek Orthodox religion inculcated certain values among members of one group? Indeed, the world view of Greek Orthodoxy fosters a work ethic and leadership style that may facilitate successful entrepreneurship.

Galbraith et al. (1997) examined differences and similarities in attitudes and cultural norms between two groups in the USA: Catholic Hispanic entrepreneurs and non-Hispanic entrepreneurs; this study hypothesized that the first group consisted of hybrid persona, combining aspects of the traditional notion of the entrepreneur while retaining important cultural characteristics of the Hispanic community. The authors found that successful Hispanic entrepreneurs were also leaders in their Hispanic community; business leaders were often leaders in the religious realm.

Studies that investigate entrepreneurship as if it were an isolated phenomenon – derived from the self and based on psychological traits of the entrepreneur – risk ignoring important causal variables arising from the environment, including the religious milieu. As suggested by Drakopoulou-Dodd and Anderson (2007) the dynamics of embeddedness and social conditioning should be attributed equal weight to the entrepreneur's individual agency.

Religions are depositories of wisdom and of values; furthermore, religious beliefs are intertwined with cultural values. Are prevailing religious beliefs explanatory variables for a propensity for, or indifference about, entrepreneurship? Empirical findings suggest a causal relationship.

Drakopoulou-Dodd and Gotsis (2007) provided a literature review addressing implications of religious convictions in business settings. Religious beliefs – and cultural values deriving from these – influence the social desirability of entrepreneurship and its nature as well. Drakopoulou-Dodd and Gotsis (2007) categorized individual outcomes of religious belief.

A religion does not necessarily directly promote or prohibit entrepreneurship. Rather, religions teach, promote and propagate cultural value systems within a given society. Value orientations in turn affect propensity toward entrepreneurial activity. For instance, Methodism accepts disparity between the rich and poor. The wealthy may be charitable, and it can be argued that acquisition of wealth is good in that it allows one to be philanthropic. Asa Chandler, the pharmacist who incorporated The Coca-Cola Company, was a devout Methodist and Sunday school teacher who believed that making money was a form of worship. During the following century, Prime Minister Margaret Thatcher (raised with strict Methodist values[2]) stated 'I believe in "Judaeo-Christian" values: indeed my whole political philosophy is based on them' (Thatcher, 1993: 509). She emphasized that her political party originated as a Christian party, concerned with the Church and the State in that order, and she stated that religion was the source of a nation's values.

Candland (2000) viewed faith as social capital and Brammer et al. (2007) found that religious individuals tend to hold broader conceptions concerning the social responsibility of businesses than non-religious individuals. Anderson et al. (2000) suggested that a reduction in church attendances cannot be taken as a direct consequence of a reduction in religiosity.

Regardless of whether a person is religious, it can be argued that one is influenced by cultural values propagated by religions. As suggested by Anderson et al. (2000), it seems reasonable, to assume that religion has an impact upon the legitimization of enterprise, despite secularization.

In this chapter, the author combines three decades of personal studies and a review of the literature to discuss ways in which religion shapes entrepreneurship. Blending a sociological understanding of values, with an anthropological interpretation of culture, it will be suggested that religion is a vehicle to perpetuate both values and culture, thus shaping various forms of entrepreneurship. It will be shown that: (1) various religions value entrepreneurship to different degrees; (2) different religions yield unlike patterns of entrepreneurship, possibly due to value differences (such as asceticism, frugality and thrift) but also due to specialization (sometimes resulting in a monopoly) and networks; (3) specialization along religious lines shapes entrepreneurship; (4) credit networks, employment networks, information networks and supply networks of co-religionists affect entrepreneurship; (5) religions provide opportunities for entrepreneurship; (6) religious beliefs may hamper entrepreneurial spirit; and (7) religions have built-in mechanisms for the perpetuation of values.

VALUES AND CULTURE

Feuerbach (1855) argued that religion included values produced by people in the course of their cultural development. Durkheim (1912) and Thomas and Znaniecki (1918) were among the pioneers who studied the concept of values. David Emile Durkheim, son of Rabbi Moise and Melanie Durkheim of Epinal, is well known for his work *The Elementary Forms of Religious Life* (Durkheim, 1912). In this, he identified a pattern of organization consistent within all human societies; for this pattern, he used the term 'structural functionalism'. In essence, his theory described society as being built upon order that incorporates interrelationship and balance among various parts of its constitution; he argued that construction and identity of any given society is based on shared norms and values as the basis of existence.

One of two major macro-sociological perspectives, functionalism conceives society as a system of interrelated parts in which no part can be understood in isolation from the whole. A change in any part is seen as leading to a degree of imbalance that changes other parts of the system and at times the system as a whole. Functionalism places a great emphasis on values in terms of the functions they perform in a sociocultural system. As such, it contrasts directly with the other major macro-sociological perspective, conflict theory.

Sociology as well as anthropology provided early definitions. From a sociological perspective, Thomas and Znaniecki interpreted a value as having an acquired social meaning and, consequently, 'is or may be an object of activity' (1918: 21). Clyde Kluckhohn provided an anthropological definition of culture as the total life way of a society; he emphasized each culture is formed by values that the people from that culture consider as being normal. He defined a value as, 'A conception, explicit or implicit, distinctive of an individual or characteristic of a group, of the desirable which influences the selection from available modes, means and ends of action' (1951: 395). Kluckhohn's theoretical development was published in two famous books, *Mirror for Man* (Kluckhohn, 1949) and *Culture: A Critical Review of Concepts and Definitions* (Kroeber and Kluckhohn, 1952).

Trying to put Clyde's theory into practice, Clyde's wife, Florence, studied indigenous Americans and co-authored with Fred L. Strodtbeck (Kluckhohn and Strodtbeck, 1961). These authors defined value orientations as:

> complex but definitely patterned (rank-ordered) principles, resulting from the transactional interplay of three analytically distinguishable elements of the evaluative process – the cognitive, the affective, and the directive elements – which give order and direction to the ever-flowing stream of human acts and thoughts as these relate to the solution of 'common human' problems. (Kluckhohn and Strodtbeck, 1961: 4)

They suggested that cultures can be classified according to five value orientations: time; humanity and the natural environment; relating to other people; motive for behaving; and the nature of human nature. During the same decade, Farmer and Richman suggested that religious beliefs 'usually have a direct and very significant bearing on the dominant view toward work and achievement' (1965: 157).

Shortly thereafter, Rokeach (1968) defined a value as 'a type of belief, centrally located within one's total belief system, about how one ought or ought not to behave, or about some end-state of existence worth or not worth attaining' (1968: 124). Rokeach (1968) considered two sets of values: terminal values and instrumental values. Terminal values are cultural goals to be attained and developed, while instrumental values are the means of achieving the desired goals. Rokeach (1973) provided a new rendition of values and value systems: 'A *value* is an enduring belief that a specific mode of conduct or end-state of existence is personally or socially preferable to an opposite or converse mode of conduct or end-state of existence. A *value system* is an enduring organization of beliefs concerning preferable modes of conduct or end-states of existence along a continuum of relative importance' (1973: 5; original emphasis).

Hiebert defined culture as 'the integrated system of learned behaviour patterns, ideas and products characteristic of a society' (1976: 25). Hofstede defined a value as: 'a broad tendency to prefer certain states of affairs over others' (2001: 5). Relying heavily on culture and values as key constructs, he stated, 'Values are held by individuals as well as by collectivities; culture presupposes a collectivity' (Hofstede, 2001: 5). Schwartz (1992) focused on a variety of values including: achievement; benevolence, conformity, hedonism, power security, self-direction and tradition. Some of these values may be influential in determining the social desirability of entrepreneurship and the nature of entrepreneurial activity.

FINDINGS

1 Various Religions Value Entrepreneurship to Different Degrees

Over the years, numerous empirical studies have reported on the influence of religion on the economy or, more specifically, that some religions are more represented than others in entrepreneurship and/or the small business sector. Classical social theorist Max Weber compared taxation figures in Baden, and reported an average of 589 marks per Catholic, 954 marks per Protestant and 4000 marks per Jew (Weber, 1904); he argued that while Protestantism stressed the development of economic security, Catholics believed that it was easier for a camel to fit through the eye of a needle than for a wealthy man to go to heaven.[3] Weber also studied how religion affected the emergence of entrepreneurship in India; he explained that the Jains, an ascetic religious sect, became a trading sect for purely ritualistic reasons, as only in trading could one practise *ahimsa*, the absolute prohibition of the killing of live things. In contrast, Theravadism, as practised in Laos, discourages entrepreneurial behaviour and noted that the result is a relative absence of Lao men in entrepreneurial activity (Dana, 1995b).

Shapero wrote, 'Some cultures that value entrepreneurship are the . . . Jains . . . Jews . . . Mennonites and Mormons' (1984: 26). Writing about Estonia after its independence from the Russian Empire, Liuhto noted, 'Another interesting detail from the statistics is the considerable share of the companies classified as Jewish' (1996: 319). Analysing the Middle East, after the Second World War, Sayigh (1952) found Christians and Jews to be the prominent entrepreneurs of Lebanon. Gadgil (1959) noted that Muslims, Christians and Jews were the chief traders of Kerala, in South India. Lasry (1982) noted the percentage of entrepreneurs among Sephardic Jewish immigrants in Montreal as being significantly higher (38 per cent) than among immigrants to Canada, in general. Jenkins (1984) showed that Protestants in Northern Ireland manipulated ethnicity in the realm of economic transactions, and thus dominated the economy in Northern Ireland. In Germany, Klandt found that a Protestant upbringing 'is more likely to lead to independent business activity than a Catholic upbringing' (1987: 31). In Britain, Quakers have been (Corley, 1998) and continue to be (Ackrill and Hannah, 2001) overrepresented in the realm of enterprise. In the USA, Kraybill and Bowman (2001) and Kraybill and Nolt (1995) identified a causal relationship between religion and self-employment among the Amish.

In a study of attitudes, Guiso et al. noted that 'with the exception of Buddhists, religious people of all denominations are more inclined to believe that poor people are lazy and lack will power' (2003: 228). Zingales suggested, 'Buddhism and Christianity seem most conducive to capitalism, and Islam the least' (2006: 228). He elaborated:

> Comparing the average response of different religious denominations we find that, other things being equal, Buddhism seems to promote the best attitudes towards the market system. Christian religions follow . . . Islam appears as the religion least conducive to capitalism. Muslims are very much against competition, against private property and less willing to trade off equality for incentives. (Zingales, 2006: 228–9)

In contrast, Badawi suggested:

> Islam preaches a holistic and comprehensive notion of development in this world and for the hereafter. It does not negate the pursuit of material development in this world . . . The teachings of Islam are also eminently suited to development in the modern, knowledge-based economy . . . Besides its emphasis on knowledge, Islam also enjoins a work ethic that equips the individual to excel in economic pursuits. (Badawi, 2006: 208)

Arslan (2000) tested whether Muslims exhibited some values that corresponded to those encouraged by the Protestant work ethic; using multivariate and univariate analysis of variance, the study found high Protestant work ethic scores among Turkish Sufis.

In a study of Mennonite entrepreneurs in Paraguay, it was found that the Mennonite religion:

> values asceticism, frugality and thrift, but not private property. Entrepreneurship takes a collective form and cooperatives are important economic vehicles, providing jobs for indigenous workers and markets for the produce of self-employed farmers. While Mennonite cooperatives

thrive here, Indian cooperatives modelled after them have not had the same levels of success. (Dana and Dana, 2007: 82)

In the words of Lewis, 'If a religion lays stress upon material values, upon thrift and productive investment, upon honesty in commercial relations, upon experimentation and risk-bearing . . . it will be helpful to growth, whereas in so far as it is hostile to these things, it tends to inhibit growth' (1955: 105).

2 Different Religions Yield Unlike Patterns of Entrepreneurship

A contemporary of Weber, Sombart (1911) observed that the economic centre of Europe shifted with the migration of Jews; he linked economic development in Europe to Jewish entrepreneurs.[4] Across the Atlantic, William Howard Taft, former president of the USA, suggested that Jews 'developed trade, poetry, philosophy, science and literature' (Taft, 1919: 7). Taft also gave examples of how Europeans prospered by means of Jews, who 'were forbidden to hold land. The nobility manufactured the liquor, and they were willing and anxious to have the Jews sell it, who thus, for lack of other occupation, became the innkeepers, the purveyors in the demoralizing liquor business' (Taft, 1919: 10).

In a landmark study comparing different religious groups in New York City, Glazer and Moynihan noted:

> Jews already constitute a majority of those engaged in many businesses . . . In the great banks, insurance companies, public utilities, railroads, and corporate head offices that are located in New York, and in the Wall Street law firms, few Jews are to be found . . . Obviously, in addition to discrimination, one must also reckon with taste and tradition among Jews, which may have had their origin in discrimination, but which may now lead a good number of Jews voluntarily to avoid huge bureaucratic organizations in favour of greater freedom in small companies, as independent entrepreneurs . . . (1963: 147–8)

Iyer noted:

> The case of Indian business communities is slightly different from the generalized pattern observed for the rest of Asia, especially in that such business communities have traditionally evolved within specific religions and castes. Moreover, the religion of the Indian merchant community, in contrast to the general strictures on wealth and profits as in other religions (including Asian religions, such as Confucianism), treats money as neutral and does not condemn wealth generation itself. This has important implications in the ways the Indian merchant community assimilates the contradictory objectives of wealth creation and frugality with religious piety that serves to enhance market reputation. (1999: 103)

Circumstance led Jews to become merchants in Alsace:

> Their religion prevented them from working on Saturday, and the Church forbade them labouring in their fields on Sundays. The Church also banned them from giving employment to Christians. In addition, experience taught the Jews that, in times of religious persecutions, it was more convenient to have moveable assets, such as gold, cattle and later diamonds, than to own immovables . . . By the fourteenth century, Jews no longer had a choice; under the Saxon civil code, *Meißener Rechtsbuch*, Jews were banned from owning land. Yet, in Alsace, this did not lead to urbanisation, because Jews were not allowed to live in the cities. Alsace remained part of the Holy German Empire until being acquired in 1648, by the Kingdom of France. At

> the time, the French army was facing a shortage of horses, and a lack of animal feed for the horses it had. The Jews of Alsace, with their experience in commerce, efficiently supplied the French with horses and with animal feed. The French offered protection to these people who supplied their army and this led to a mass immigration of Jews from central Europe, to Alsace. (Dana, 2006: 589).

Controlling for climate, geographic position and other factors, Baldacchino and Dana (2006) compared entrepreneurship in French St Martin with that in Dutch Sint Maarten, the latter more influenced by a Protestant work ethic. While two cultures share a little island, colonial influences have been different, and the entrepreneurship sector reflects this. While Dutch St Martin is home to prosperous traders, French St Martin is home to self-employed farmers.

3 Specialization along Religious Lines Shapes Entrepreneurship

In some cases, certain religious groups specialized in specific economic sectors. For two centuries, Quaker entrepreneurs including John Cadbury, Joseph Fry and the Rowntree family, dominated the chocolate industry across England. Cadbury flourished in Birmingham, Fry blossomed in Bristol and the Rowntrees prospered in York. John Cadbury expanded his business when he invited his brother Benjamin to join him, in 1847; employees were well cared for, in accordance with religious values.

During the mid-nineteenth century, Seventh-day Adventists in the USA – preaching vegetarian values – established the Western Health Reform Institute, later renamed the Battle Creek Sanitarium, in Battle Creek, Michigan. Aligned with the beliefs of Sylvester Graham (the minister who invented the Graham cracker[5]) patients were required to adhere to strict diets. The superintendent was a fervent Seventh-day Adventist, Dr John Harvey Kellogg, who with his brother William Keith Kellogg invented the modern breakfast cereal, in line with their religious beliefs. Kellogg's thus began with 44 employees in Battle Creek, Michigan. A patient, Charles William Post, founded a competing manufacturer and launched the first nationwide advertising campaign in the USA. In Australia and New Zealand, the Seventh-day Adventist Church also had connections to the cereal sector; important players included Grain Products and Sanitarium.

In Canada, meanwhile, Methodist entrepreneurs established large department stores. In 1869, Timothy Eaton opened a store introducing fixed prices and cash sales (as opposed to negotiated prices and credit sales) soon expanding into the Eaton's chain; he introduced the mail order catalogue to Canadians in 1884. Robert Simpson opened his first department store in 1872, and this also developed into a national chain of department stores. Norcliffe (2001) noted that Toronto's principal bicycle manufacturers, during the late nineteenth century, were owned by Methodists, including the Flavelle, Harris and Massey families.

Fishberg (1911) observed that Jews were concentrated in precarious occupations such as commerce; he suggested that Jews were 'ambitious and persevering, possessing an enormous amount of "push", which he cannot always bring into play while struggling against adverse circumstances' (1911: 531). Raphaël (1980) noted the clustering of Jews in the livestock trade in Alsace. Dana wrote:

> Still forbidden to own land, deprived of entry into universities, excluded from the guilds and not allowed to reside in cities, these people tended to be travelling merchants, linking the urban and rural economies. In September 1791, Jews were permitted to reside in the cities of Alsace, and this helped them expand their commercial networks . . . The fathers and elder brothers would carry their loads on backs. This included utensils, candles and soap, as well as animal hides, laces, string and used clothing. Wealthier merchants used man-powered pushcarts. The exceptions were those known as *Esselje'de* (donkey-Jews), as they would travel from one village to another with a donkey-drawn cart; they traded kitchenware and other household items, accepting rags and beehives as payment. Livestock merchants constituted a class of their own. Some had a horse-drawn wagon on which two calves could be transported. At the end of the nineteenth century, Jews had a monopoly in cattle dealing in areas of Baden, Bavaria, Hanover, Rhineland and Westphalia. Until the First World War, most independent cattle dealers in Germany (including Alsace) were Jewish. (2006: 590)

Based on oral testimonies of retired entrepreneurs and verified by means of triangulation, Dana (2006) provided an account of the livestock distribution system, which prevailed in Alsace, until the Second World War. In this region of traditional rivalry between French and Germans, the sector was dominated by Jewish entrepreneurs speaking *Jédich-Daitch*, serving as a middleman minority, and dealing between French-speakers and German-speakers, who did not trade with one another.

In their study of New York City, Glazer and Moynihan found more evidence of clustering:

> Merchandising, garment manufacturing, and entertainment maintain their importance, but to them has been added a sizable range of light manufacturing, and real estate and building. In the latter, especially, Jews play a prominent role . . . In the great office-building boom that has transformed Manhattan, most of the big builders have been Jews: Uris Brothers, Tishman, Erwin Wolfson, Rudin, Webb and Knapp (Zeckendorf) . . . The finest of the postwar office buildings, Seagram's, which is perhaps the most lavish and expensive in use of space and detail, was erected by a company headed by a Canadian Jewish communal leader, Samuel Bronfman . . . (Glazer and Moynihan, 1963: 151)

Hawley wrote, 'Amish entrepreneurs tend to cluster heavily in certain small business ventures. This phenomenon can best be described by order of the *Ordnung*, which requires that the Amish establish only those stores and small businesses that meet the product and service needs of the Amish community' (1995: 320). Dana explained,

> In order to maintain their values, the Amish try to avoid close contact with people who do not hold the same traditions. Furthermore, due to religious discrimination in the past, the Amish often exhibit a mistrust of outsiders. The primary motive of self-employment among the Amish is neither profit nor prestige, but rather the maintenance of cultural values, separately from mainstream society such as to emphasize humility over pride. (2007b: 142)

Such segregation, from mainstream society, helps the Amish retain social capital, and this supports Borjas (1992), who analysed ethnic capital and the value of isolation.

An ethnographic study of Morocco noted that some goods:

> were sold only by Jews while others were sold only by Muslims. Silversmiths were invariably Muslim, while goldsmiths were Jewish. Jews were also very active in the spice trade, and they specialised in the socio-economic function of distribution . . . Many Jews were peddlers, or suppliers to other vendors, inland. They served as Barthian middlemen. (Dana and Dana, 2008: 215)

4 Credit Networks, Employment Networks, Information Networks and Supply Networks of Co-religionists Affect Entrepreneurship

4.1 Credit networks

Credit is at times linked to marriage within the Jain community. Dundas (1992) discussed carefully regulated marriage alliances among Jains, and Laidlaw further explained that when a Jain 'family contracts a good marriage, its credit increases' (Laidlaw, 1995: 355). Iyer and Shapiro (1999) refer to credit networks among Korean and Chinese in the USA.

Juteau and Paré (1996), refer to credit networks of Jewish entrepreneurs in Canada. Likewise, Dana (2006) noted that Jewish cattle dealers relied heavily on other Jews for financing. Co-religionists provided finance when needed. 'A network of livestock merchants, across the region, facilitated the dissemination of knowledge and availability of finance among co-religionists. In the event of bankruptcy, an individual was given assistance by other merchants' (Dana, 2006: 594).

Discussing Jewish and Muslim entrepreneurs in Morocco, Dana and Dana noted that 'Merchandise was often purchased on credit, thereby requiring a relationship of trust between supplier and peddler' (2008: 215). Again, there was often dependence on co-religionists for finance.

In a study of Catholic Hispanics, Galbraith et al. (2004) suggested that a co-ethnic capital market appears to be the last dimension developed within an ethnic community.

4.2 Employment networks

Porter (1937) noted that entrepreneurs were giving preference to members of their immediate circle rather than giving equal opportunity to outsiders. Raistrick (1950) found Quakers to be clannish and nepotistic.

Kraybill and Nolt (1995) observed that Amish entrepreneurs gave preference in business to co-religionists. Dana's ethnographic study explained the reason behind this: 'While the Amish people believe that a community of voluntary believers is the context for life, the fundamental unit of Amish society and of their economy is the family . . . home-based enterprises allow family members to work together, reinforcing the Amish family unit' (2007b: 146).

Galbraith et al. (1997) found that successful Hispanic entrepreneurs, often holding important leadership roles in the local Catholic church, were actively finding employment for other recent immigrants.

Galbraith et al. (2003) and Stiles et al. (2007) suggested that Catholic Hispanic and Muslim Arab entrepreneurs are both dependent on co-ethnic business in their respective enclave, relying upon co-religionists for labour, especially at the start-up phase.

In Malaysia, Abdullah (1992) found that Muslim Malays expressed strong preference for employing Muslim candidates over non-Muslims. In a study of Turkish entrepreneurs, Altinay (2008) likewise found a strong relationship between the religion of an entrepreneur and recruitment.

4.3 Information networks

Apart from co-religionist networks that provide credit or preferential treatment for employees, information networks also appear in the literature and these are sometimes comprised of co-religionists. Boissevain and Grotenbreg observed: 'Hindustanis appear to have a larger network of relatives than do Chinese and Creole businessmen. Given the value they attach to family loyalty, this seems to indicate that Hindustanis have access to a wider information and support network' (1987: 117).

A co-religionist information network existed in Alsace: 'They managed the link between the rural and urban economies, providing cash for farmers and a source of meat for consumers. In addition, they spread information as required. If one farmer needed a bull, temporarily, for breeding purposes, a livestock merchant could source this need' (Dana, 2006: 590).

There were also individuals who specialized in information:

> Some Jews did not themselves deal with livestock, but served as brokers, or informers who simply sold information which would lead to transactions. These entrepreneurs were called *Schmüsser*, and their commission was referred to as *Sassergeld.* Operating informally, these individuals mingled with the villagers, identified needs and opportunities and then waited by the side of a road, knowing that livestock merchants would be passing by eventually. The *Schmüsser* then sold their information to livestock merchants. (The word they used for this activity was *vermassere*, literally meaning 'to inform.') In order to reduce time spent away from their own villages, the transient merchants preferred to pay for this market research, rather than to conduct this time-consuming task themselves. The *Schmüsser* thus formed an integral part of the business network. (Dana, 2006: 592–3)

Likewise in his study of 1200 Muslim entrepreneurs in London, Altinay (2008) found a strong relationship between religion and advice-seeking practices. One interviewee stated, 'If people from the same religion and the background do not help and support each other, who else would do so' (Altinay, 2008: 120). Altinay (2008) found that Muslims who practise[6] their religion rely more on advice from co-ethnics.

4.4 Supply networks

Juteau and Paré (1996) and Lee (1999) found co-ethnic suppliers were prevalent among Jewish entrepreneurs in Canada and in the USA, respectively. Lee (1999) noted that this provided access to lower wholesale costs, which could translate to lower retail costs and enhanced competitiveness.

Galbraith (2007) examined buyers and sellers among two groups: Catholic Hispanics and Muslim Arabs, within a US metropolitan area; he suggested that the perceived advantage of intra-enclave buying and selling lies in a sense of ethnic identification that comes primarily from a religion, either Catholic or Muslim, common to each enclave.

5 Religions Provide Opportunities for Entrepreneurship

Religious values may create needs, and these can sometimes be translated into opportunities for entrepreneurship. When Toronto observed a day of rest and streetcars were prohibited on Sundays while bicycles were permitted, bicycle manufacturers – mostly Methodists – made unprecedented sales (Armstrong and Nelles, 1977). In this case, the observation of religion helped entrepreneurs in the bicycle sector.

The production of religious products also provides opportunities for entrepreneurship. Orthodox icons, for instance, bring profits to dealers as well as to those who make the icons. Likewise, religious dietary requirements can yield profits to entrepreneurs catering to specific needs. Buddhism, Hinduism, Islam, Jainism and Judaism are among religions that have dietary restrictions, providing opportunities for entrepreneurs and even for airlines catering to such religious needs of observers; this is what Aldrich and Weidenmayer (1993) have referred to as 'demand side' entrepreneurship.

In Islam, some food is *halal* (meaning 'permissible' in Arabic), while some is prohibited. All fish with scales (that the Bible approves of as kosher) are *halal.* The Qur'an specifically disallows the consumption of all blood, the carcass of an animal that died on its own or that was killed by another animal, donkey meat, fanged predators and pork. Furthermore, the Hanafi School of Islam does not approve of the eating of shellfish, including clams, crabs, lobster and shrimp; observers also refrain from eating frogs. According to Minkus-McKenna (2007), 70 per cent of Muslims worldwide follow *halal* food standards, translating into an opportunity worth an annual US$580 billion. Many McDonald's outlets are serving *halal* food, in Australia, India, Indonesia, Malaysia, Pakistan, Singapore, South Africa and the UK. Others to serve *halal* food, at selected locations, include A&W, Burger King, Dunkin' Donuts, KFC and Pizza Hut.

The Judaeo-Christian Bible has even more sophisticated guidelines with regards to what may be eaten, and these are outlined in Genesis, and Leviticus and Deuteronomy. The King James Bible states, 'Ye shall therefore put difference between clean beasts and unclean, and between unclean fowls and clean: and ye shall not make your souls abominable by beast, or by fowl, or by any manner of living thing that creepeth on the ground, which I have separated from you as unclean' (Leviticus 20:25). Leviticus 3:17 prohibits observers from eating blood or fat. Leviticus 22:8 elaborates, 'That which dieth of itself, or is torn with beasts, he shall not eat to defile himself therewith: I am the LORD' (King James Bible). This is understood to mean that it is not kosher to eat food from animals that die themselves or that are killed by another animal. Leviticus also provides details as to what species the Bible allows observers to eat or not. It is not permitted to eat camel, 'he is unclean onto you' (Leviticus 11:4). The hare (Leviticus 11:6); pork (Leviticus 11:7); eagles (Leviticus 11:13); vultures (Leviticus 11:14); ravens (Leviticus 11:15); owls (Leviticus 11:16); cormorants (Leviticus 11:17); swans, pelican and eagles (Leviticus 11:18) are specified as not allowed. The same is true of the stork, the heron and the bat (Leviticus 11:19). Leviticus 11:29 states, 'These also shall be unclean unto you among the creeping things that creep upon the earth; the weasel, and the mouse, and the tortoise after his kind'. Leviticus 11:30 adds, 'And the ferret, and the chameleon, and the lizard, and the snail, and the mole'. It is not allowed to eat scavengers and predators; for this reason, observers refrain from eating catfish, clams, lobsters, oysters, and shrimp.

The result of biblical commandments specifying food laws is a lucrative niche market providing kosher products. Rosen (2008) noted that in North America alone kosher products are a US$14 billion a year business; she quoted Chaim Goldberg saying, 'There's no question that kosher is growing . . . As the world is getting more global, manufacturers . . . see kosher as a very easy way to market their product' (Rosen, 2008: 105). Based in Fair Haven, Newfoundland, Neptune Sea Products is a kosher-sanctioned secondary fish-processing plant; it produces 200 different products, including Cajun cod and wasabi salmon. According to Rosen (2008), sales for the first year of this new venture were estimated to top $2 million. Rosen interviewed the entrepreneur behind Neptune Sea Products and he explained, 'We only use fish that have fins and scales. . .The other main thing is, my employees can't bring in ham sandwiches for lunch' (Rosen, 2008: 106).

Fifteen minutes down the road from Neptune Sea Products is the Rodrigues Winery, a family business in Markland. This is the first winery in Newfoundland and the first kosher and sulphite-free winery in Canada, producing wines from local blueberries, cloudberries, cranberries, raspberries and strawberries. Exports are shipped as far away as Japan.

6 Religious Beliefs May Hamper Entrepreneurial Spirit

Buddhism emphasizes the afterlife, and it has been suggested that Buddhists are not focused on entrepreneurial activity (Cousins, 1996). This especially so among Theravada Buddhists. Lewis wrote, 'Where Theravada Buddhism is the backbone of social and cultural values . . . it may have a restraining effect on the accumulation of wealth and the rise of an entrepreneurial class' (1955: 105). Over half a century later, Theravada monks are still highly influential in Lao society.

As discussed by Dana (1995b), Theravada monks have traditionally had a great impact on the educational system in Laos; in former times, the only schools were in *wats*,[7] and they are still consulted on virtually all matters, thereby playing an important role in a diversity of spheres, ranging from private life to government policy. This is elaborated upon in detail in Dana (2007a). Central to Theravada beliefs is the ultimate goal to extinguish unsatisfied desires. Its doctrine focuses on aspects of existence, including *dukkha* (suffering from unsatisfied desire) and *anicca* (impermanence). Assuming that unsatisfied desires cause suffering, then suffering can be eliminated if its cause (desire) is eliminated. A respectable person, then, according to this ideology, should not work towards the satisfaction of materialistic desires, but should, rather, strive to eliminate the desire itself. A monk, for instance, is specifically prohibited by the religion, from tilling fields or raising animals.

Lao folk tales reinforce the belief that a male monk should not labour for material wealth; yet, the same folklore conditions women to accept a heavy burden in exchange for honour, protection and security. Even the Lao currency portrays agricultural work being done by women. Numerous Lao families who farm during the wet season become self-employed gold-diggers during the dry season. Prospectors camp along the Mekong River, especially in the region of Luang Prabang. The women do the heaviest work, digging for dirt and panning it in wooden trays. The men weigh the gold, up to 1 gram per day.

Writing about the former Kingdom of Moldavia, Dana (2005: 223) observed:

> Orthodoxy in this kingdom emphasized the respect of authority, along with the importance of guilt. A good Moldavian was expected to obey the religion and work the land. A non-mercantile culture did nothing to encourage the development of entrepreneurship. In 1812, when the kingdom lost Bessarabia to Russia, the tsar's feudal system continued to meet non-conformity with punishment.

Rafiq (1992) suggested that Islam constitutes a barrier to capital access, due to the religious prohibition on interest payments. Metcalf et al. (1996) concluded that Pakistanis were less successful than Indians in self-employment because they were Muslim.

Finally, a religion may encourage entrepreneurship in the broad sence but limit the sectors in which entrepreneurship takes place. Jainism encourages entrepreneurship in trade, but does not allow self-emplyment in agriculture (Iyer, 2004; Nevaskar, 1971).

Adherance to this religion thus limits avenues for self-employment, because of its strict pacifism (Iyer, 1999; Nevaskar, 1971).

7 Religions Have Built-in Mechanisms for the Perpetuation of Values

In Jain communities where business and family overlap, a merchant's family and community status is linked to optimal marriage (Bayly, 1983). Marriage takes place among co-religionists and within boundaries, and values are propagated from one generation to the next.

Dana noted co-religionist matchmaking that allowed the perpetuation of religious values:

> Travel was intrinsic to their livelihood and during business trips these frequent travellers would pray, and eat, with co-religionists, and sleep at their homes. The religious duty of allowing animals to rest on the Sabbath (from sunset on Friday until dusk on Saturday) made it impossible to travel with livestock during this time of rest. Therefore, business trips were often extended due to religious obligations, and considerable time was spent with the families of other merchants. During this time, matchmaking was a common occurrence, as the son of a merchant fancied the daughter of another. The co-religionists shared the same language, holidays, belief system and dietary restrictions. All this, in turn, reinforced social networking among this ethnic minority. (2006: 589)

Likewise, in a study of Amish entrepreneurship, Dana noted how values – as well as skills – are passed on from one generation to the next:

> From a very young age, Amish children develop a close relationship with their parents. Parents spend almost all of their time with their children, teaching them Amish cultural values. It is not from formal education in school, but rather from their parents that children learn to become self-sufficient in life. Amish boys normally learn a variety of skills on their father's farm. This typically includes cabinetry, carpentry, furniture-making and masonry . . . Most importantly for the Amish, each generation transmits cultural values to the next. This includes asceticism, frugality and thrift . . . Children thus become predisposed towards self-employment, as parents guide them along an almost pre-determined road in life. The young are not encouraged to explore such as to discover themselves, but rather to fit into Amish society, and to feel needed within it. Often, a son learns his trade from his father. Even when a son does not adopt the same profession as his father, it is practical to learn as many manual skills as possible. A son becomes the apprentice of his father at a very young age. Not only does a son learn how to work, but also more importantly according to Amish tradition, he is conditioned into accepting the Amish belief that work is healthy and enjoyable. (2007b: 148–9)

For the Amish – as is the case among some other religious groups – marrying outside the faith is shunned. 'If an Amish woman wants to marry an outsider, she must leave the community, unless he joins Amish society. A deterrent to her leaving is that she is unprepared for secular society, while a stumbling block in the attempt to become Amish is the dialect' (Dana, 2007b: 149).

Likewise, but to different degrees, intermarriage is discouraged by other religions. In a study of comparing Indian entrepreneurs in Singapore and their counterparts in the UK, Hamilton et al. (2008) found that in both countries, most respondents would *not* allow their children to marry outside the faith.

TOWARD THE FUTURE

In a study of mixed marriages and separation, Monahan and Kephart (1954) showed that Jewish families broke up less than non-Jewish ones. Presumably this allowed values to be reinforced and to be passed on from one generation to the next. As society becomes increasingly tolerant of mixed marriages, what will happen to values in the future?

Glazer and Moynihan (1963) found no evidence of convergence among different religions.

> Thus, a Jewish ethos and a Catholic ethos emerge: they are more strongly affected by a specific religious doctrine in the Catholic case than in the Jewish, but neither is purely the expression of the spirit of a religion . . . The important fact is that the differences in values and attitudes between the two groups do not, in general, become smaller with time. On the contrary: there is probably a wider gap between Jews and Catholics in New York today than in the days of Al Smith. (Glazer and Moynihan, 1963: 298–9)

Is this still true almost five decades later?

Linking entrepreneurship to values offers endless possibilities for future research, whether or not these values are promoted by a religion. Some of Rokeach's (1973) values may impact entrepreneurship, and empirical investigation of this could be present interesting research opportunities. Amish entrepreneurs value religion over prosperity, but might Rokeach's terminal value of a prosperous life lead to an entrepreneurial start-up? Could it be hypothesized that one who values freedom (independence, free choice), as per Rokeach (1973), might choose to become an entrepreneur?

Likewise, it could be empirically tested whether entrepreneurs exhibit some of Rokeach's (1973) instrumental values. Might there be a relationship between Rokeach's instrumental value of ambition (hard-working, aspiring) and successful entrepreneurship? Does entrepreneurship involve being broadminded (open-minded), capable (competent, effective), or courageous? Examining Rokeach's instrumental value of self-control, might this be linked to Weber's (1930) values of asceticism, frugality and thrift?

FINAL WORDS

Sociologist Max Weber suggested that asceticism, frugality and thrift (Weber, 1930) were values that encourage successful entrepreneurship; these are perhaps necessary but insufficient. I would add that *context* is important. Mennonites value asceticism, frugality and thrift, but Old Colony Mennonites have traditionally been *opposed to the concept of private property*. Hence, among Mennonites, individual entrepreneurs are not flagships of entrepreneurship; instead, entrepreneurial activities take a collective form, as described by Dana and Dana (2007). Indeed, different religions yield unlike patterns of entrepreneurship.

This chapter discussed several observable patterns: (1) various religions value entrepreneurship to different degrees; (2) different religions yield unlike patterns of entrepreneurship, possibly due to value differences (such as asceticism, frugality and thrift) but also due to specialization (sometimes resulting in a monopoly) and networks; (3) specialization along religious lines shapes entrepreneurship; (4) credit networks, employment networks, information networks, and supply networks of co-religionists affect entrepreneurship; (5) religions provide opportunities for entrepreneurship; (6) religious beliefs may hamper entrepreneurial spirit; and (7) religions have built-in mechanisms for the perpetuation of values.

Learning about religions, it is evident that each has a set of values. Respect must be paid to the distinctiveness and differences of all.

NOTES

* This paper is reprinted with permission from the *International Journal of Entrepreneurship & Innovation*, **10** (2), 2009, 87–99.

1. The author thanks Professor Ivan H. Light (UCLA) for interesting discussions leading to this chapter. The author also thanks the following for comments on preliminary drafts: Dr Garth Cant (University of Canterbury); Dr Sarah Drakopoulou-Dodd (Athens Laboratory of Business Administration Graduate Business School and Robert Gordon University); Professor Gopalkrishnan R. Iyer (Florida Atlantic University); and Professor Richard W. Wright (UCLA).
2. See Young (1991) and Young and Sloman (1986).
3. This is based on Matthew 19:23–4.
4. Rath and Kloosterman (2003) revisited this theme. They noted that 'The arrival of Jews from the Iberian Peninsula in the sixteenth century and later from Eastern Europe, and of Roman Catholics from Westphalia throughout the nineteenth century, greatly influenced the Dutch economic landscape as their business acumen enhanced the nation's economic and cultural wealth' (ibid.: 123–4).
5. Today, Grahams are manufactured by Nabisco and certified as Kosher by the Union of Orthodox Rabbis.
6. Altinay (2008) distinguished among religious Muslims and secular Muslims. Other studies have treated Muslims as a homogenous group, and did not distinguish between religious and non-practising individuals (see Basu and Altinay, 2002; Dana and Dana, 2008; Metcalf et al., 1996; Rafiq, 1992).
7. *Wats* are places of worship.

REFERENCES

Abdullah, Asma (1992), 'The influence of ethnic values on managerial practices in Malaysia', *Malaysian Management Review*, **27** (1), 3–18.

Ackrill, Margaret and Leslie Hannah (2001), *Barclay's: The Business of Banking 1690–1996*, Cambridge: Cambridge University Press.

Aldrich, Howard E. (1979), *Organizations and Environments*, Englewood Cliffs, NJ: Prentice Hall.

Aldrich, Howard E. and Gabriele Weidenmayer (1993), 'From traits to rates: an ecological perspective on organisational foundings', in Jerome Katz and Robert H. Brockhaus (eds), *Advances in Entrepreneurship, Firm Emergence and Growth*, Greenwich, CT: JAI Press, vol. 1, pp. 145–95.

Altinay, Levent (2008), 'The relationship between an entrepreneur's culture and the entrepreneurial behaviour of the firm', *Journal of Small Business and Enterprise Development*, **15** (1), 111–29.

Anderson, Alistair R., Sarah L Drakopoulou-Dodd and Michael G Scott (2000), 'Religion as an environmental influence on enterprise culture: the case of Britain in the 1980s', *International Journal of Entrepreneurial Behaviour & Research*, **6** (1), 5–20.

Aristotle (1924), 'The politics', (trans. B. Jowett), in Arthur Eli Monroe (ed.), *Early Economic Thought*, Cambridge, MA: Harvard University Press, pp. 3–29.

Armstrong, Christopher and H.V. Nelles (1977), *The Revenge of the Methodist Bicycle Company: Sunday Streetcars and Municipal Reform in Toronto, 1888–1897*, Toronto: Peter Martin Associates.

Arslan, Mahmut (2000), 'A cross-cultural comparison of British and Turkish managers in terms of protestant work ethic characteristics', *British Ethics: A European Review*, **9** (1), 13–19.

Badawi, Abdullah Ahmad (2006), 'Islam and development', *Global Agenda 2006*, Davos: World Economic Forum, pp. 208–9.

Baldacchino, Godfrey and Léo-Paul Dana (2006), 'The impact of public policy on entrepreneurship: a critical investigation of the Protestant ethic on a divided island Jurisdiction', *Journal of Small Business and Entrepreneurship*, **19** (4), 419–30.

Basu, Anuradha and Eser Altinay (2002), 'The interaction between culture and entrepreneurship in London's immigrant businesses', *International Small Business Journal*, **20** (4), 371–94.

Bayly, Christopher Alan (1983), *Rulers, Townsmen and Bazaars: North India in the Age of British Expansion, 1770–1870*, Cambridge: Cambridge University Press.

Becker, Howard (1956), *Man in Reciprocity*, New York: Praeger.

Boissevain, Jeremy and Hanneke Grotenbreg (1987), 'Ethnic enterprise in the Netherlands: the Surinamese of Amsterdam', in Robert Goffee and Richard Scase (eds), *Entrepreneurship in Asia: The Social Processes*, London: Croom Helm, pp. 105–30.

Borjas, George J. (1992), 'Ethnic capital and intergenerational mobility', *Quarterly Journal of Economics*, **107**, 123–50.

Brammer, S., Geoffrey Williams and John Zinkin (2007), 'Religion and attitudes to corporate social responsibility in a large cross-country sample', *Journal of Business Ethics*, **71** (3), 229–43.

Candland, Christopher (2000), 'Faith as social capital: religion and community development in Southern Asia', *Policy Sciences*, **33** (3-4), 355–74.

Corley, Thomas Anthony Buchanan, (1998), 'Changing Quakers attitudes to wealth, 1690–1950', in David J. Jeremy (ed.), *Religion, Business and Wealth in Modern Britain*, London: Routledge, pp. 137–50.

Cousins, Lance S. (1996), 'The dating of the historical Buddha: a review article', *Journal of the Royal Asiatic Society*, **6** (1), 57–63.

Dana, Léo-Paul (1991), 'Bring in more entrepreneurs', *Policy Options*, **12** (9), 18–19.

Dana, Léo-Paul (1995a), 'Entrepreneurship in a remote Sub-Arctic community: Nome, Alaska', *Entrepreneurship: Theory and Practice*, **20** (1), 55–72.

Dana, Léo-Paul (1995b), 'Small business in a non-entrepreneurial society: the case of the Lao People's Democratic Republic (Laos)', *Journal of Small Business Management*, **33** (3), 95–102.

Dana, Léo-Paul (2005), *When Economies Change Hands: A Survey of Entrepreneurship in the Emerging Markets of Europe from the Balkans to the Baltic States*, Binghamton, NY: International Business Press.

Dana, Léo-Paul (2006), 'A historical study of the traditional livestock merchants of Alsace', *British Food Journal*, **108** (7), 586–98.

Dana, Léo-Paul (2007a), *Asian Models of Entrepreneurship – From the Indian Union and the Kingdom of Nepal to the Japanese Archipelago: Context, Policy and Practice*, Singapore and London: World Scientific.

Dana, Léo-Paul (2007b), 'Humility-based economic development and entrepreneurship among the Amish', *Journal of Enterprising Communities: People and Places in the Global Economy*, **1** (2), 142–54.

Dana, Léo-Paul and Teresa E. Dana (2007), 'Collective entrepreneurship in a Mennonite community in Paraguay', *Latin American Business Review*, **8** (4), 82–96.

Dana, Léo-Paul and Teresa E. Dana (2008), 'Ethnicity & entrepreneurship in Morocco: a photo-ethnographic study', *International Journal of Business and Globalisation*, **2** (3), 209–26.

Drakopoulou-Dodd, Sarah and Alistair R. Anderson (2007), 'Mumpsimus and the Mything of the individualistic entrepreneur', *International Small Business Journal*, **25** (4), 341–60.

Drakopoulou-Dodd, Sarah and George Gotsis (2007), 'The interrelationships between entrepreneurship and religion', *International Journal of Entrepreneurship and Innovation*, **8** (2), 93–104.

Dundas, Paul (1992), *The Jains*, New York: Routledge.

Durkheim, Émile (1912), *Les formes élémentaires de la vie religieuse: Le système totémique en Australie*, Paris: Felix Alcan.

Enz, Cathy A., Marc J. Dollinger and Catherine M. Daily (1990), 'The value orientations of minority and non-minority small business owners', *Entrepreneurship, Theory and Practice*, **15** (1), 23–35.

Farmer, Richard N. and Barry M. Richman (1965), *Comparative Management and Economic Progress*, Homewood, IL: Richard D. Irwin.

Feuerbach, Ludwig (1855), *The Essence of Christianity*, trans. Marian Evans, New York: Calvin Blanchard.

Fishberg, Maurice (1911), *The Jews: A Study of Race and Environment*, London: Walter Scott.

Gadgil, Dhananjaya Ramchandra (1959), *Origins of the Modern Indian Business Class*, New York: Institute of Pacific Relations.

Galbraith, Craig Scott (2007), 'The impact of ethnic-religious identification on buyer–seller behaviour: a study of two enclaves', *International Journal of Business and Globalisation* **1** (1), 20–33.

Galbraith, Craig Scott, Donald R. Latam and Jacqueline Benitez Galbraith (1997), 'Entrepreneurship in the Hispanic community of the Southeastern United States', *Frontiers of Entrepreneurship Research*, Wellesley, MA: Babson College.

Galbraith, Craig Scott, Curt H. Stiles and Jacqueline Benitez-Bertheau (2004), 'The embryonic development of an ethnic neighbourhood: a longitudinal case study of entrepreneurial activity', in Curt H. Stiles and Craig Scott Galbraith (eds), *Ethnic Entrepreneurship: Structure and Process*, Oxford: Elsevier, pp. 95–112.

Galbraith, Craig Scott, Curt H. Stiles and Carlos Rodriguez (2003), 'Intra-enclave trade: Hispanic and Arab small businesses', *Journal of Small Business and Entrepreneurship*, **16** (3/4), 18–29.

Glazer, Nathan and Daniel Patrick Moynihan (1963), *Beyond the Melting Pot: The Negroes, Puerto Ricans, Italians and Irish of New York City*, Boston, MA: MIT.

Guiso, Luigi, Paola Sapienza and Luigi Zingales (2003), 'People's opium? Religion and economic attitudes', *Journal of Monetary Economics*, **50** (1), 225–82.

Hamilton, Robert T., Léo-Paul Dana and Camilla Benfell (2008), 'Changing cultures: an international study of migrant entrepreneurs', *Journal of Enterprising Culture*, **16** (1), 89–105.

Hawley, Jana M. (1995), 'Maintaining business while maintaining boundaries: an Amish woman's entrepreneurial experience', *Entrepreneurship, Innovation, and Change*, **4** (4), 315–28.

Hiebert, Paul G. (1976), *Cultural Anthropology*, Philadelphia, PA: J.B. Lippincott.

Hofstede, Geert (2001), *Culture's Consequences*, 2nd edn, Beverly Hills, CA: Sage.

Iyer, Gopalkrishnan R. (1999), 'The impact of religion and reputation in the organization of Indian merchant communities', *The Journal of Business & Industrial Marketing*, **14** (2), 102–17.

Iyer, Gopalkrishnan R. (2004), 'Ethnic business families', in Curt H. Stiles and Craig Scott Galbraith (eds), *Ethnic Entrepreneurship: Structure and Process*, Oxford: Elsevier, pp. 243–60.

Iyer, Gopalkrishnan R. and Jon M. Shapiro (1999), 'Ethnic entrepreneurial and marketing systems: implications for the global economy', *Journal of International Marketing*, **7** (4), 83–110.

Jenkins, Richard (1984), 'Ethnicity and the rise of capitalism in Ulster', in Robin Ward and Richard Jenkins (eds), *Ethnic Communities in Business: Strategies for Economic Survival*, Cambridge: Cambridge University Press, pp. 57–72.

Juteau, Danielle and Sylvie Paré (1996), 'L'entrepreneurship ethnique', *Interfaces*, **17** (1), 18–28.

Klandt, Heinz (1987), 'Trends in small business start-up in West Germany', in Robert Goffee and Richard Scase (eds), *Entrepreneurship in Europe: The Social Processes*, London: Croom Helm, pp. 26–38.

Kluckhohn, Clyde K. (1949), *Mirror for Man*, Toronto: Whittlesey House.

Kluckhohn, Clyde K. (1951), 'Values and value orientations in the theory of action: an exploration in definition and classification', in Talcott Parsons and Edward A. Shils (eds), *Toward a General Theory of Action*, Cambridge: Harvard University Press, pp. 388–443.

Kluckhohn, Florence R. and Fred L. Strodtbeck (1961), *Variations in Value Orientations*, Evanston, IL: Row, Peterson.

Kraybill, Donald B. and Carl F. Bowman (2001), *On the Backroad to Heaven: Old Order Hutterites, Mennonites, Amish, and Brethren*, Baltimore, MD: Johns Hopkins University Press.

Kraybill, Donald B. and Steven M. Nolt (1995), *Amish Enterprise*, Baltimore, MD: Johns Hopkins University Press.

Kroeber, Alfred Louis and Clyde K. Kluckhohn (1952), *Culture: A Critical Review of Concepts and Definitions*, Cambridge, MA: The Museum.

Laidlaw, James (1995), *Riches and Renunciation: Religion, Economy, and Society among the Jains*, Oxford: Clarendon.

Lasry, Jean-Claude (1982), 'Une Diaspora Francophone au Québec: Les Juifs Sépharades', *Questions de Culture*, **2**, 113–38.

Lee, Jennifer (1999), 'Retail niche domination among African-American, Jewish and Korean entrepreneurs', *American Behavioral Scientist*, **42** (9), 1398–417.

Lewis, W. Arthur (1955), *The Theory of Economic Growth*, Homewood, IL: Richard D. Irwin.

Liuhto, Kari (1996), 'The transformation of the enterprise sector in Estonia: a historical approach to contemporary transition', *Journal of Enterprising Culture*, **4** (3), 317–29.

Lumpkin, G.T. and Gregory G. Dess (1996), 'Clarifying the entrepreneurial orientation construct and linking it to performance', *Academy of Management Review*, **21** (1), 135–72.

Metcalf, Hilary, Tariq Modood and Satnam Virdee (1996), *Asian Self-employment: The Interaction of Culture and Economics in England*, London: Policy Studies Institute.

Minkus-McKenna, Dorothy (2007), 'The pursuit of halal', *Progressive Grocer*, **86**, December 17.

Monahan, Thomas P. and William M. Kephart (1954), 'Divorce and desertion by religions and mixed religious groups', *American Journal of Sociology*, **59** (5), 454–65.

Nevaskar, Balwant (1971), *Capitalists Without Capitalism: The Jains of India and the Quakers of the West*, Westport, CT: Greenwood.

Norcliffe, Glen (2001), *Ride to Modernity: The Bicycle in Canada 1869–1900*, Toronto: University of Toronto Press.

Porter, Kenneth Wiggens (1937), *The Jacksons and the Lees: Two Generations of Massachusetts Merchants, 1765–1844*, Cambridge, MA: Harvard University Press.

Rafiq, Mohammed (1992), 'Ethnicity and enterprise: a comparison of Muslim and non-Muslim owned Asian businesses in Britain', *New Community*, **19** (1), 43–60.

Raistrick, Arthur (1950), *Quakers in Science and Industry*, London: Bannisdale.

Raphaël, Freddy (1980), 'Les Juifs de la campagne alsacienne: les marchands de bestiaux', *Revue des Sciences Sociales de la France de l'Est*, **9**, 220–45.

Rath, Jan, and Robert Kloosterman (2003), 'The Netherlands: a Dutch treat', in Robert Kloosterman and Jan Rath (eds), *Immigrant Entrepreneurs: Venturing Abroad in the Age of Globalization*, Oxford: Berg, 123–46.
Reynolds, Paul D. (1991), 'Sociology and entrepreneurship: concepts and contributions', *Entrepreneurship Theory and Practice*, **16** (2), 47–70.
Rokeach, Milton (1968), *Beliefs, Attitudes, and Values*, San Francisco, CA: Jossey-Bass.
Rokeach, Milton (1973), *The Nature of Human Values*, New York: Free Press.
Rosen, Amy (2008), 'Kosher quality: a rabbi, a Newfoundlander and a fish walk into a bar . . . ', *enRoute*, November, 105–8.
Sayigh, Yezid A. (1952), *Entrepreneurs of Lebanon*, Cambridge, MA: Harvard University Press.
Schwartz, Shalom H. (1992), 'Universals in the content and structure of values: theoretical advances and empirical tests in 20 countries', in Mark P. Zanna (ed.), *Advances in Experimental Social Psychology*, Book 25, Orlando, FL: Academic Press, pp. 1–65.
Shapero, Albert (1984), 'The entrepreneurial event', in Calvin A. Kent (ed.), *The Environment for Entrepreneurship*, Lexington, MA: D.C. Heath, pp. 21–40.
Sombart, Werner (1911), *Die Juden und das Wirtschaftsleben*, Leipzig: Duncker und Humblot.
Specht, Pamela Hammers (1993), 'Munificence and carrying capacity of the environment and organizational carrying capacity', *Entrepreneurship: Theory and Practice*, **17** (2), 77–87.
Stewart, Alex (1991), 'A prospectus on the anthropology of entrepreneurship', *Entrepreneurship: Theory and Practice*, **16** (2), 71–91.
Stiles, Curt H., Carlos L. Rodriguez and Craig S. Galbraith (2007), 'The impact of ethnic-religious identification on buyer–seller behaviour: a study of two enclaves', *International Journal of Business and Globalisation*, **1** (1), 20–33.
Taft, William Howard (1919), 'The progressive world struggle of the Jews for civil equality', *National Geographic*, **36** (1), 1–16.
Thatcher, Margaret (1993), *The Downing Street Years*, London: HarperCollins.
Thomas, William Isaac and Florian W. Znaniecki (1918), *The Polish Peasant in Europe and America*, Boston, MA: Badger.
Weber, Max (1904) 'Die protestantische Ethik und der "Geist" des Kapitalismus. I. Das Problem', *Archiv für Sozialwissenschaft und Sozialpolitik*, **20** (1), 1–54.
Weber, Max (1930), *The Protestant Ethic and the Spirit of Capitalism*, trans. by Talcott Parsons, New York: Charles Scribner's Sons.
Woodrum, Eric M. (1985), 'Religion and economics among Japanese Americans: a Weberian study', *Social Forces*, **64**, 191–204.
Young, Hugo (1991), *One of Us*, London: Macmillan.
Young, Hugo and Anne Sloman (1986) *The Thatcher Phenomenon*, London: BBC.
Zingales, Luigi (2006), 'Gods and Mammon', *Global Agenda 2006*, Davos: World Economic Forum, pp. 228–9.

42 Rural entrepreneurship

Gerard McElwee and Andrew Atherton

This chapter defines the concept of a rural economy; it indicates what the drivers of success in a rural economy are and identifies the barriers confronting entrepreneurs in the rural environment and the strategies that can be used in order to overcome these barriers. It continues by considering some of the pressures on the rural environment in developed economies, before conceptualizing the rural entrepreneur and defining rural entrepreneurship.

The problem of definition is not confined to entrepreneurship for there also are issues of conceptualization when terms such as 'rural' or 'rurality' are used. Furthermore, Beedell and Rehman (2000) suggest that to understand the phenomenon necessitates understanding rural entrepreneurs' attitudes and motivation in an environmental/conservation awareness context.

For the purpose of this contribution rural businesses are defined as those occupied on a part or full time basis and engaged in a range of activities that are primarily dependent on the natural and physical resources of the rural environment as the main source of income and or utilize local labour to achieve business objectives. This definition includes tourism, food production and processing, for example (see Figure 42.1). It excludes those firms which do not contribute to a local economy and trade outside of the local(ized) area. The definition would also include social entrepreneurship (see separate entry in this volume).

Corman and Lussier (1996), suggest that the importance of adopting community, ethical and social responsibilities as a way of doing business is becoming increasingly necessary to the success of the rural business. Bryant (1989) discusses the role and importance of farm and non-farm entrepreneurs in the rural environment. He suggests that the notion of entrepreneur is freely applied within the agricultural sector and the entrepreneurs themselves are argued to be key decision-makers in the political, social and economical environment.

Farmers are, of course, particularly important as rural entrepreneurs as they attempt to construct sustainable rural livelihoods. This involves a shift away from agriculture's traditional 'core' activities by means of diversification with new on-farm activities or 'conversion' to adding value within the production chain. This raises the question of how the role of those enterprises that fall into the vast category of 'main-stream' farms within the process of rural development (van der Ploeg, 2000) can be conceptualized.

This entry explores the issue of how a rural economy can be analysed and, in particular, how an enterprising rural economy can be framed. The notion of an enterprising rural economy is important because entrepreneurship, as measured by indicators such as new firm formation rates, has been correlated with economic prosperity and growth. At a policy level, there is broad consensus that enterprise generates economic growth and vitality within an economy, and is fundamental to coping with and responding to broader changes in the organization and dynamics of economic activity and interaction (Bolton, 1971; DTI, 2001; EC, 2003; OECD, 1996).

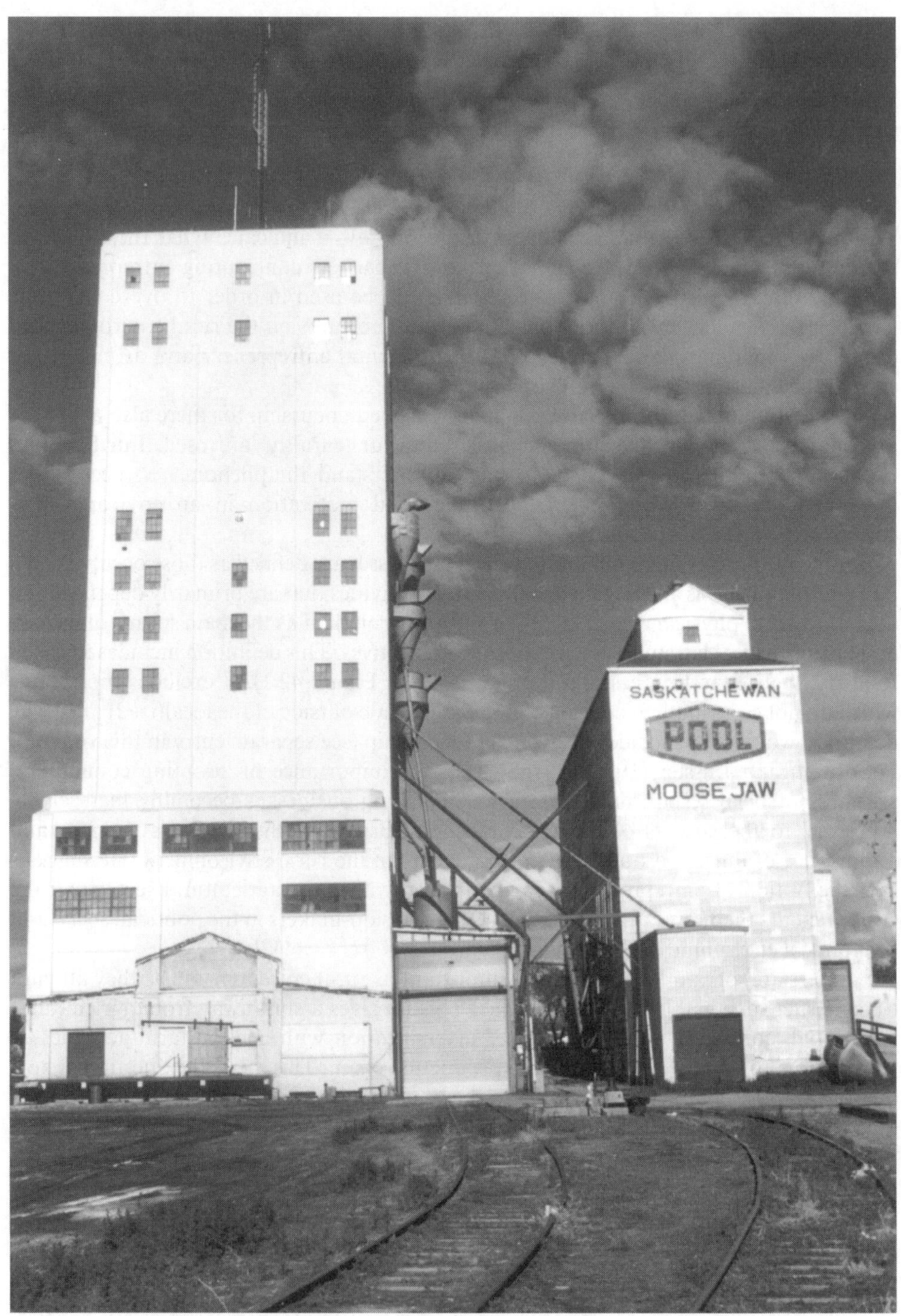

Figure 42.1 Rural enterprise in the prairies; photograph by Léo-Paul Dana

Increasing the entrepreneurial capacity and capability of rural areas has been identified as a means of addressing economic development constraints and under-performance in rural areas (Atherton and Hannon, 2006; Jordaan et al., 2003; Laukkanen and Niittykangas, 2003). This has led the Department of the Environment, Food and Rural Affairs (DEFRA) in the UK to initiate strategies for economic development in less prosperous rural areas in England, through enterprise development as well as other forms of intervention, the intention being to: 'reduce the gap in productivity between the least well performing quartile of rural areas and the English median by 2008, demonstrating progress by 2006, and improve the accessibility of services for people in rural areas' (DEFRA, 2005b: 7).

Similar initiatives, have occurred in many other economies. And yet there is little discussion of the notion of a rural enterprise economy, as a distinct concept and phenomenon. Although there have been broad descriptions and discussions of the 'enterprise economy' and an 'enterprise culture' as a whole (for example, Schram, 2004), these have typically taken the nation or region as the spatial unit of analysis, rather than differentiating between different types of geography, such as rural and urban. Where enterprise and entrepreneurship is explored in a rural context, studies have tended to focus on the dynamics and behaviours of individuals, often focusing on farmers, as, entrepreneurs within a rural setting (for example, Carter 1996, 1999; Kalantaridis and Bika, 2006a; 2006b; Kalantaridis and Labriandis, 2004; McElwee, 2006a; 2006b; 2008a; McElwee and Bosworth, 2010; Simmons and Kalantaridis, 1996).[1] Carter (1998), Carter and Rosa (1998), McNally (2001) and Borsch and Forsman (2001), argue that the methods used to analyse business entrepreneurs in other sectors can be applied to rural businesses such as farmers.

What appears to be missing from accounts of rural enterprise, therefore, is its spatial and socioeconomic context, that is, the locational characteristics and features of entrepreneurial activity within a rural context. This risks the emergence of a portrayal of rural enterprise as under-socialized because of a greater concern with individual agents than with the contextual structure within which entrepreneurs operate (Granovetter, 1985).

DRIVERS OF THE RURAL ENTERPRISE ECONOMY

A number of drivers of development in a rural regional and local economy have been identified and discussed in the literature. These are shown in Table 42.1.

The Organisation for Economic Co-operation and Development (OECD, 1996) suggests that less tangible factors are the reasons why rural areas with very similar characteristics, can exhibit differences in economic performance. According to DEFRA (2005a), rural areas can display significant strengths socially and economically. From this perspective, they are likely to have attractive housing, good labour relations, lower wages, lower rental and premises costs, and greater space for business expansion. The 'quality of life associated with living and working in a rural environment can have a positive impact on competitiveness because these attributes attract entrepreneurial incomers who energise business, political and cultural life, leading to positive developmental changes' (Agarwal et al., 2004: 6). As Maskell et al. suggest, 'some geographical environments are endowed with a structure as well as a culture which seem to be well suited for

Table 42.1 Drivers of rural success

Drivers	References
Employment and skills	HM Treasury (2001), Boddy et al. (2005)
Investment	HM Treasury (2001), Boddy et al. (2005)
Innovation	HM Treasury (2001)
Enterprise	HM Treasury (2001), Kupiainen et al. (2000)
Competition	HM Treasury (2001)
Economic capital	Falconer (2000), Poot et al. (2006), Agarwal et al. (2004)
Human capital	McElwee (2008b), Agarwal et al. (2004)
Social capital	Agarwal et al. (2004), Lowe and Talbot (2000), McElwee (2004)
Cultural capital	Agarwal et al. (2004)
Environmental capital	Agarwal et al. (2004)
Mobility	Maskell et al. (1998), Boddy et al. (2005)
Travel time and peripherality	Boddy et al. (2005)

dynamic and economically sound development of knowledge, while other environments can function as a barrier to entrepreneurship and change' (1998: 181).

Rural development, in summary, is influenced by multiple factors, and can be explained and analysed in different ways and from varying perspectives. Enterprise in the rural economy is clearly driven by rates of new venture formation, and there is a clear and well-established link between business start-up dynamics and local economic development. It is influenced by standard market factor inputs and dynamics, such as those used by HM Treasury to conceptualize and analyse economic growth and development; as stated in the Blue Book and Green Book frameworks for analysing the economy and assessing the impacts of intervention.

However, rural enterprise, and hence the development of the rural economy, is also a function of the cultural values and norms that hold within an area, and so is based on the behaviours and predispositions of individuals towards, or against, enterprise within a locality (Atherton, 2004). The intangible dimensions of the rural economy, society and specific community within which exchange and interaction occur, therefore define, describe and determine localized levels of entrepreneurial activity and potential. It is these implicit, contextualized and yet critical 'institutional' dimensions of local development and activity that determine localized patterns of enterprise, and broader socio-economic, development.

BARRIERS TO ENTERPRISE IN THE RURAL ECONOMY

This section identifies the barriers confronting entrepreneurs in the rural environment and the strategies that can be used in order to overcome these barriers (for example, change of strategic business direction, diversification, specialization or other strategies such as merger). A barrier can be defined as a phenomenon – political, social, economic, technical or personal – that places a restriction, either permanently or temporarily, on the potential of the individual to develop the business (McElwee, 2004).

Table 42.2 Barriers to the development of the enterprise

Barriers	References
Access to distribution channels	McElwee (2008b)
Capital requirements of entry	Gasson (1998), Rantamäki-Lahtinen (2002)
Economies of scale	Kupiainen (2000), McElwee and Bosworth (2010)
Geography and proximity to markets including labour markets	Maskell et al. (1998)
Skills/education	
Inward investment	OECD (1996)
Legislation and regulation	Falconer (2000), Poot et al. (2006), European Commission (1996)
Limited access to business support	Lowe and Talbot (2000), McElwee (2004)
Poor management skills	McElwee and Bosworth (2010)
Position on the 'experience curve'	McElwee (2006b)
Security	European Commission (1996)
Travel time and peripherality	Maskell et al. (1998)

Specific potential barriers to the development of the enterprise include those shown in Table 42.2. Barriers will differ for different enterprises depending on the personal and business characteristics of the individual entrepreneur and enterprise.

THE RURAL BUSINESS ENVIRONMENT

The rural business environment in developed economies is becoming increasingly complicated. The major trends described by McElwee (2006b) are:

- globalization of the market and the enlargement of the EU
- Common Agricultural Policy (CAP)-reform, including the decrease of market regulation measures and price subsidies
- changing consumer demands
- changes in the supply chain: scale increase of retailers and supermarkets and a growing demand for quality control and quality assurance
- changing environment and growing pressure on the rural area
- growing demand for non-agricultural functions and services
- climate changes
- increasing energy prices.

Descriptions of entrepreneurship emphasize opportunity recognition and realization (Stevenson and Jarillo, 1990; Timmons, 1999; Shane and Venkataraman, 2000), the acceptance of risk and failure, innovation and the creation of something new, and the role of networks and cooperation, and strategic thinking (Dana, 2004).

CONCEPTUALIZING THE RURAL ENTREPRENEUR

There are difficulties associated with defining the entrepreneur; indeed, as noted by Palich and Bagby (1995: 426), 'when tracing the development of this concept in the literature, it becomes clear that no one definition of the entrepreneur prevails'. Definitions have emphasized a broad range of activities the more well known of which include, uncertainty-bearing and the subcontractor who takes risks (Cantillon, 1755), coordination (Say, 1803), innovation (Schumpeter, 1934) and arbitrage. Defining rural entrepreneurs' entrepreneurial activity is perhaps even more complex as these entrepreneurs do not operate in similar business activities characterized by their urban counterparts.

Defining rural entrepreneurship is complex but in summary a rural entrepreneur is an individual who uses the resources of the regional economy; geographical, physical, topographical, labour, and so on in order to gain competitive advantage by trading in goods or services which ultimately generate social or economic capital for the rural environment in which the entrepreneur is located. This definition would exclude the entrepreneur who is located within a rural environment but who exclusively trades outside of the local economy, does not employ local labour or other resource nor utilize local business services nor contribute to regional rural value chains.

NOTE

1. See Niittykangas (1996), for a paper focusing on SMEs in a rural economic context as an exception to this tendency.

REFERENCES

Agarwal, S., P. Courtney, A. Errington, M. Moseley and S. Rahman (2004), 'Determinants of relative economic performance of rural areas', final research report prepared for DEFRA, July, University of Plymouth and Countryside and Community Research Unit.

Atherton, A. (2004), 'Unbundling enterprise and entrepreneurship: from perceptions and preconceptions to concept and practice', *International Journal of Entrepreneurship and Innovation*, **5** (2), 121–7.

Atherton, A. and P. Hannon (2006), 'Localised strategies for supporting incubation: strategies arising from a case of rural enterprise development', *Journal of Small Business and Enterprise Development*, **13** (1), 48–61.

Atkinson J. and J. Hurtsfield (2004), 'Small Business Service Annual Survey of small businesses: UK 2003', London, Small Business Service, available at: http://www.sbs.gov.uk/content/analytical/sbsannualsmesurvey2003.

Beedell, J. and T. Rehman (2000), 'Using social-psychology models to understand rural entrepreneurs' conservation behaviour', *Journal of Rural Studies*, **16** (1), 117–27.

Boddy, M., J. Hudson, A. Plumridge and D. Webber (2005), 'Meeting the productivity challenge', final report on a study carried out for the South West of England Development Agency, and summary report.

Bolton, J. (1971), *Small Firms – Report of the Committee of Inquiry on Small Firms*, Cmnd 4811, London: HMSO.

Borsch, G. and T. Forsman (2001), 'The competitive tools and capabilities of micro firms in the Nordic food sector. The food sector in transition – Nordic Research', proceedings of NJF seminar No. 313, June 2000 NILF, 2001 2.

Bryant, C. (1989), 'Entrepreneurs in the rural environment', *Journal of Rural Studies*, **5** (4), 337–48.

Cantillon, R. (1755) 'Essai sur la Nature du Commerce en General', available at: http://socserv.socsci.mcmaster.ca/~econ/ugcm/3113/cantillon/essay1.txt (accessed 6 April 2004).

Carter, S. (1996), 'The indigenous rural enterprise: characteristics and change in the British farm sector', *Entrepreneurship and Regional Development*, **8** (4), 345–58.

Carter, S. (1998), 'Portfolio entrepreneurship in the farm sector: indigenous growth in rural areas?', *Entrepreneurship and Regional Development*, **10** (1), 17–32.
Carter, S. (1999), 'Multiple business ownership in the farm sector: assessing the enterprise and employment contributions of farmers in Cambridgeshire', *Journal of Rural Studies*, **15** (4), 417–29.
Carter, S. and P. Rosa (1998), 'Indigenous rural firms: farm enterprises in the UK', *International Small Business Journal*, **16** (4), 15–27.
Corman, J. and R.N. Lussier (1996), *Small Business Management, a Planning Approach*, New York: Irwin/ McGraw-Hill.
Dana, L.P. (2004), *Handbook of Research on International Entrepreneurship*, Cheltenham, UK and Northampton, MA, USA: Edward Elgar.
Department for the Environment Food and Rural Affairs (DEFRA) (2005a), *Productivity in Rural England*, November, London: Rural Economics Unit, DEFRA.
Department for the Environment Food and Rural Affairs (DEFRA) (2005b), 'Agriculture in the United Kingdom', London.
Department of Trade and Industry (DTI) (2001), *Opportunity for All in a World of Change*, London: HMSO.
European Commission (EC) (1996), 'Introduction to electronic commerce', DGIII/F/6, available at: www.ispo.cec.be/ecommerce/whatis.html (accessed 23 February 1996).
European Commission (EC) (2003), Com Green Paper, *Entrepreneurship in Europe*, Brussels: European Commision.
Falconer, K. (2000), 'Farm-level constraints on agri-environmental scheme participation: a transactional perspective', *Journal of Rural Studies*, **16** (3), 379–94.
Gasson, R. (1998), 'Educational qualifications of UK farmers: a review', *Journal of Rural Studies*, **14** (4), 487–98.
Granovetter, M. (1985), 'Economic action and social structure: the problem of embeddedness', *American Journal of Sociology*, **91**, 481–93.
HM Treasury (2001), *Productivity in the United Kingdom: 3 – The Regional Dimension*, London: HM Treasury.
Jordaan, J., M. Alderson, I. Warren-Smith and M. Lehmann (2003), 'Enterprise development in rural communities: experiences and preliminary results on the use of an integrated demonstration and training business incubator in South Africa', 13th Global Conference on Internationalizing Entrepreneurship Education and Training, Grenoble, France, 8–10 September.
Kalantaridis, C. and Z. Bika (2006a), 'In-migrant entrepreneurship in rural England: beyond local embeddedness', *Entrepreneurship and Regional Development*, **18** (2), 109–31.
Kalantaridis, C. and Z. Bika (2006b), 'Local embeddedness and rural entrepreneurship: case-study evidence from Cumbria, England', *Environment and Planning*, **38** (8), 1561–79.
Kalantaridis, C. and L. Labriandis (2004), 'Rural entrepreneurs in Russia and the Ukraine: origins, motivations and institutional change', *Journal of Economic Issues*, **38** (3), 659–81.
Kupiainen, K. (2000), *Maaseudun pienyritysten menestyminen (Performance of Small Rural Enterprise)*, Agricultural Economics Research Institute, research reports, 239.
Laukkanen, M. and H. Niittykangas (2003), 'Local developers as virtual entrepreneurs: do difficult surroundings need initiating interventions?', *Entrepreneurship and Regional Development*, **15**, 309–31.
Lowe, P. and H. Talbot (2000), 'Providing advice and information in support of rural microbusinesses', Centre for Rural Economy Research Report University of Newcastle, Newcastle upon Tyne.
Maskell, P.H., I. Eskelinen, A. Hannibalsson, J. Malmberg and E. Vatne (1998), *Competitiveness, Localised Learning and Regional Development. Specialization and Prosperity in Small Open Economies*, London: Routledge.
McElwee, G. (2004), 'A segmentation framework for the farm sector', 3rd Rural Entrepreneurship Conference, University of Paisley, 28–29 October.
McElwee, G. (2006a), 'The entrepreneurial farmer: a Pandora's box', *Rural Enterprise and Management*, **2** (2), 23–42.
McElwee, G. (2006b), 'Farmer's as entrepreneurs: developing competitive skills', *Journal of Developmental Entrepreneurship*, **11** (3) 187–206.
McElwee, G. (2008a), 'The rural entrepreneur: problems of definition', *International Journal of Entrepreneurship and Small Business*, **6** (3), 320–21.
McElwee, G. (2008b), 'A taxonomy of entrepreneurial farmers', *International Journal of Entrepreneurship and Small Business*, **6** (3), 465–78.
McElwee, G. and G. Bosworth (2010), 'Exploring the strategic skills of farmers across a typology of farm diversification approaches', *Journal of Farm Management*, **13** (12), 819–38.
McNally, S. (2001), 'Farm diversification in England and Wales – what can we learn from the farm business survey', *Journal of Rural Studies*, **17** (2), 47–257.
Niittykangas, H. (1996), 'Enterprise development in different rural areas of Finland', *Entrepreneurship and Regional Development*, **8** (3), 245–62.

Organisation for Economic Co-operation and Development (OECD) (1996), *Territorial Indicators of Rural Development and Employment*, Paris: OECD.
Palich, L. and D. Bagby. (1995), 'Using cognitive theory to explain entrepreneurial risk-taking: challenging conventional wisdom', *Journal of Business Venturing*, **10**, 425–38.
Ploeg, J.D. van der (2000), 'Revitalizing agriculture: farming economically as starting ground for rural development', *Sociologia Ruralis*, **40**, 497–511.
Poot, E.H., A.J. Balk-Theuws, J.S. de Buck, C.J.M. Buurma, C.J. van der Lans and P.L. de Wolf (2006), 'Voorlopers en voortrekkers, ondernemerschap in netwerken – case plant', Netherlands: Wageningen University and Research Centre.
Rantamäki-Lahtinen, L. (2002), 'Finnish pluriactive farms – the common but unknown rural enterprises', in H.W. Tanvig (ed.), *Rurality, Rural Policy and Politics in a Nordic-Scottish Perspective*, Working Paper 1/02, Esbjerg: Danish Centre for Rural Research and Development.
Say, J.B. (1803), 'A treatise on political economy, or the production, distribution and consumption of wealth', available at: http://socserv.mcmaster.ca/econ/ugcm/3ll3/say/treatise.pdf (accessed 19 March 2006).
Schram, S. (2004), 'Building entrepreneurial economies', *Foreign Affairs*, July/August, 104–15.
Schumpeter, J. (1934), *The Theory of Economic Development: An Inquiry into Profits, Capital, Credit, Interest and the Business Cycle*, Cambridge, MA: Harvard University Press.
Shane, S. and S. Venkataraman (2000), 'The promise of entrepreneurship as a field of research', *Academy of Management Review*, **25** (1), 217–26.
Simmons C. and C. Kalantaridis (1996), 'Making garments in Southern Europe: entrepreneurship and labour in rural Greece', *Journal of Rural Studies*, **12** (2), 169–85.
Stevenson, H.H. and J.C. Jarillo (1990), 'A paradigm of entrepreneurship: entrepreneurial management', *Strategic Management Journal*, **11**, 17–27.
Timmons, J.A. (1999), *New Venture Creation; Entrepreneurship for the 21st Century*, 5th edn, Boston, MA: McGraw-Hill.

43 Schumpeter, creative destruction and entrepreneurship

Dieter Bögenhold

Following many years in which the political and scientific debate was fixed on large and very large firms, which were regarded as the guarantors and drivers of economic prosperity, of technical progress and of secure and growing employment, the tide began to turn, slowly but surely, at the beginning of the 1980s, with the result that more interest arose in self-employment and in small and medium-sized enterprises. The transformation which entrepreneurship underwent in the eyes of the public, especially in more critical social and economic circles, can be described as a change from demons to demiurges, who in Greek mythology were regarded as a kind of innovative creators of worlds (Bögenhold and Staber, 1994). Since then, we have been able to observe a multicoloured political alliance in favour of entrepreneurship. At the same time when unemployment had climbed into comparatively high figures which were unknown for the decades before, smaller economic units were increasingly seen as beacons of hope for economic and labour market policies.

Also, talking entrepreneurship has become very fashionable but the more one comes across the term the more one has to confess that no consensual understanding exists as to the meaning of the term. Entrepreneurship seems to be poorly defined and, furthermore, the concept is almost based on non-questioned assumptions. One has to differentiate what entrepreneurship is (and can be) and that the phenomenon is more complex in reality than public discourse sometimes suggests. Entrepreneurship has two sides at least (Boegenhold, 2004).

In public debate and within the public policy arena, we find an example of this dilemma in a report by the Organisation for Economic Co-operation and Development (OECD) entitled *Fostering Entrepreneurship*:

> Measuring the amount of entrepreneurship taking place in a country is difficult to do, in part because there is no consensus about what would be a reliable and practical set of indicators. Some emphasize the number of new firms starting up, while others consider turnover in the number of firms to be more important. Some would focus on small and medium sized enterprises (SMEs) where the owner(s) and manager(s) are the same. But others concentrate on the performance of fast-growing firms, whether new or well-established. Some associate entrepreneurship with the development of 'high-tech' industries. None of these approaches is able to provide a complete picture of the state of entrepreneurship; each one takes only one aspect of it. Nonetheless, while many large and well-established firms can be very entrepreneurial, measures of small and especially new firm development are more often used as indicators of entrepreneurial activity. (OECD, 1998: 11–12)

The list as suggested in the quotation by the OECD book is far from being complete: one may add several further interpretative contexts which are used in in combination with the term entrepreneurship. 'Female entrepreneurship' (Hughes, 2005), 'ethnic entrepreneurship' (Light and Rosenstein, 1995) or 'academic entrepreneurship' (Shane 2005) are some of them.

Many dashed hopes are also on the agenda, and we find not always convincing the empirical and theoretical vision of how prosperity, innovative behavior, the dynamics of ventures and the dynamics of employment and the issue of entrepreneurial activities interact both positively and negatively on international comparisons. Many economic policy statements about supposed positive causalities between growth, prosperity and self-employment and business start-ups fail when operating with only a few variables at the level of national economies (Baumol et al., 2007). Economic life is too complex to think of only in terms of labor, capital and technologies without acknowledging further 'soft dimensions' such as regional cultures including believe systems, human relations, demographic patterns and different network forms (Audretsch, 2007).

Looking at the subject of entrepreneurship, it is striking to see how arguments acquire a certain tenacity. Various interpretative issues surrounding the word 'entrepreneurship' are overlooked, and the use of the term is often based on selective associations. The nature of entrepreneurship has not only changed during the historical process of the last centuries (Baumol, 1990; Munro, 2006) but also the academic handling of entrepreneurship in the history of economic thought has been changed widely. Different approaches coexist and academic discussion on entrepreneurship is trying to develop typologies of different concepts. Already a brief look into selected pieces of the classics shows how disparate the contents of the meaning of entrepreneurship has been (Swedberg, 2000; Westhead and Wright, 2000; Shane, 2002).

Scanning the history of economic thought in the area of entrepreneurship shows that the contents of what is captured by the term entrepreneurship has also been changing and is far from being universally shared, so that competing and changing conceptions can be found. However, Joseph A. Schumpeter is most associated with the term entrepreneurship, and vice versa: when involved in talk about entrepreneurship, Schumpeter is among the first economists who comes to mind. Like no other author Schumpeter's work stands for the idea of an innovative entrepreneur so that the term entrepreneurship seems to serve very often only in a combination with Joseph A. Schumpeter. In fact, Schumpeter's *oeuvre* was much broader than this (Stolper, 1951). The discussed relevance of Schumpeter shows his thematical and systematical variety so that one has to agree with Deutsch (1956) who summarized Schumpeter's 'intellectual stature, his broad learning, and his analytic power': 'There have been few men in any generation who had so much to say on so many vital topics, and who said it with such clarity and freshness' (Deutsch, 1956, 41).

JOSEPH ALOIS SCHUMPETER

Schumpeter (1883–1950) is regarded as one of the most prominent economists of the twentieth century. Schumpeter was an Austrian economist who had professorships in Austria and Germany before joining the faculty at Harvard University in the early 1930s where he spent the rest of his career. He was born in the same year as John Meynard Keynes, which was also the year of death of Karl Marx. Marx was for Schumpeter and for many of his contemporaries a very important provider of headwords to get verified or falsified in his own discussion. Schumpeter not only wrote on the 'Communist Manifesto' (Schumpeter, 1949) but also his famous *Capitalism, Socialism, and Democracy* (1942 [1947]) proved to be a very long and substantial critical dialog with Marx's conception. Schumpeter and Keynes were both in their advanced scientific phases within the Department of Economics at Harvard University at the same time. Keynes is most associated with ideas of Keynesianism and many related works in the area of financial economics, whereas Schumpeter in broad circles of academic recognition is primarily identified with ideas of industrial dynamics and entrepreneurship, which comes up with elements of innovation. From a contemporary perspective Schumpeter was truly interdisciplinary and his many works span fields such as sociology, finance economics and politics (Harris, 1951), which is mirrored by the fact that many of his papers were distributed posthumously to separate academic subjects, for example, papers on economic theory (Schumpeter, 1952), papers on sociology (Schumpeter, 1953), papers on the history of economic thought and biographies (Schumpeter, 1954b), papers on economic policies (Schumpeter 1985), articles on socioeconomics (Schumpeter, 1987), 'political speeches' (Schumpeter 1992) and essays on daily politics (Schumpeter, 1993a).

Over a time span of nearly 50 years Schumpeter published series of articles and books. While John Maynard Keynes was regarded for several decades as the most eminent economist of the twentieth century, during the past 20 or 25 years those statements increased which tried to rank Schumpeter at the same level as Keynes (Giersch, 1984). Nevertheless, Schumpeter has found a firm place as one of the most important economists of the twentieth century. His ideas remain in vogue and an international Joseph A. Schumpeter Society was founded in the 1980s. The interest in his work is highlighted best by a series of books and essays shedding light on different aspects of his writings (among them are Heertje, 2006; McCraw, 2007; Reisman, 2004; Shionoya, 1997; Swedberg, 1991).

The originality of Schumpeter's research is his truly interdisciplinary scientific approach, referring to lessons of history, sociology, psychology and further disciplines, and he can be regarded as pioneer of a research tradition which is commonly called socioeconomics. Schumpeter not only practiced such inter- or trans-disciplinary 'putting together' which, of course, was even more common in his time than it is today, but he also argued theoretically in this direction: the extensive preface of Schumpeter's *History of Economic Analysis* (1954a) which was published four years after his death includes four separate chapters in which Schumpeter did systematic academic reflection on the nature and status of economics. When does theory gets the distinction of being 'pure theory'? Why do we need studies in the history of economic thought? What are the intersections between theory, statistics, and economic history about? Where are borders and overlaps between economics, philosophy, psychology, political economy and economic sociology? Which are general principles of scientific processes? Treating those questions which fall into the area of a science or sciences marks Schumpeter as representative of an academic procedure which did not fit with 'primitive economics' (Schumpeter, 1954a: 26), which has no cooperation with other disciplines and which are steadily working apart. When Schumpeter argues, for example, that 'we cannot afford . . . to neglect the developments of sociology' (Schumpeter, 1954a: 25) and especially not the 'fundamental field of economic sociology in which economists nor sociologists can get very far without treading on one another's toes' (Schumpeter, 1954a: 26) he demonstrates very well what he means by his so-called need for academic 'cross-fertilization'. Spiethoff said, that Schumpeter regarded himself as a 'gourmet' in issues of theory (Spiethoff, 1949–50: 291).

Reading related chapters by Schumpeter shows that his type of thought matches with ideas of so-called old and new institutionalism in economics. Schumpeter argues not only in favor of economic history that renders service to economic theory but also 'a sort of generalized or typified or stylized economic history' (Schumpeter, 1954a: 20) which includes institutions like private property or free contracting or government regulation. While modern economic theory is going to turn increasing attention towards issues of human behavior and motivation (Ackerlof, 2007), we can already find the related methodological script within Schumpeter's reflections:

> Economic analysis deals with the questions how people behave at any time and what the economic effects are they produce by so behaving; economic sociology deals with the question how they came to behave as they do. If we define human behavior widely enough so that it includes not only actions and motives and propensities but also the social institutions that are relevant to economic behavior. (Schumpeter, 1954a: 21)

We will be dealing with a much more real conceptualization of economic life.

CREATIVE DESTRUCTION

Schumpeter is not only known worldwide as a theorist of entrepreneurship but also for his view of an evolutionary economy, which is often summarized as never-ending process of 'creative destruction' (Harris, 1951). Creative destruction refers to the economic processes by which old systems, technology and thinking is destroyed by the new. The Schumpeterian view of the economy is not static in which economy is regarded as being in equilibrium, but is always newly 'in the making'. Economy is interpreted as a snapshot which balances developments of potential losses and new traits. Our lives have plenty of examples of such creative destruction where threats or deaths of traditional markets, firms or branches appear or, at least, where specific production lines lose their regional production ground, as for example wide parts of shipbuilding, coal mining or textile industries in Europe or North-America, whereas new fields of economic activities emerge simultaneously, such as tourism or leisure industries, microelectronic-related industries or biotechnology-driven production. Examples of creative destruction in the music industry would include the evolution from wax cylinders to vinyl records to compact discs and MP3 files. Schumpeter saw creative destruction as the essence and logical byproduct of capitalism.

The ambiguous expression of 'creative destruction' was first used in *Capitalism, Socialism, and Democracy* (Schumpeter, 1942). The book has a substantial chapter entitled 'Creative destruction' which deals with the modus operandi of competition. In opposition to the predominant economic thought of equilibrium theory, Schumpeter conceptualized economy being permanently in an evolving process of economic and social change, which is the reason that he is regarded as one of the pioneers of 'evolutionary economics' (Metcalfe, 1998).

Schumpeter frequently discussed parallels and divergences of his thought and

Marxism: he viewed capitalism as a 'form or method of economic change'. Creative destruction is a contradictory expression which seeks to highlight the fact that completion and inherent processes towards monopolistic and oligopolistic competition are only one part of the overall economic game. Too often simultaneous processes of the creation of new firms, new ideas and even new business leaders elsewhere in an economy are neglected. Deaths and births – both of business enterprises and individuals – are two sides of the same coin, and Schumpeter dubbed creative destruction as an essential fact about capitalism.

It was Schumpeter (1942 [1947]) who problematized this complicated interlocking 'up' and 'down' of economic development. As well as Marx, Schumpeter acknowledged the double-face of capitalism with its interplay of destruction and creativity, but Schumpeter stressed the dynamic process of industrial change much more than Marx ever did, and Schumpeter highlighted the open nature of the process:

> The essential point to grasp is that in dealing with capitalism we are dealing with an evolutionary process. It may seem strange that anyone can fail to see so obvious a fact which moreover was long ago emphasized by Karl Marx. Yet that fragmentary analysis which yields the bulk of our propositions about the functioning of modern capitalism persistently neglects it. . . . Capitalism . . . is by nature a form or method of economic change and not only never is but never can be stationary. And this evolutionary character of the capitalist process is not merely due to the fact that economic life goes on in a social and natural environment which changes and by its change alters the data of economic action. . . . This process of Creative Destruction is the essential fact about capitalism. It is what capitalism consists in and what every capitalist concern has got to live in. (Schumpeter, 1942 [1947]: 82–3)

Innovation is the steady new 'fresh blood' through new ideas and people who keep the 'capitalist machine' going. However, creativity is always combined with destruction elsewhere. When new products appear, consumer demands change, and existing production and related markets are rendered obsolete. In some cases entire communities are negatively impacted when the production of new products locates elsewhere. Labor historians and economists have long studied the fall-out from deindustrialization. There are, for example, cities and towns throughout European or American regions that are yet to recover from the economic decline associated with the closure of traditional industries.

INNOVATION AND ITS DYNAMICS

Creative destruction has to be seen in a wider context of innovation and entrepreneurship for which Schumpeter is so well known. Schumpeter is obvious for his intermediate positions. Edgar Salin, Swiss economist and prestigious professor at Heidelberg, wrote in his introduction to the first German translation of *Capitalism, Socialism, and Democracy* that Schumpeter would not match with any school, political party or general interpretative scheme (Salin, 1950: 1). Salin described Schumpeter as socialist but he added that no socialist will find his or her socialism within Schumpeter. According to Salin, Schumpeter's advantage is the clear pointing to failures and limitations of Marx's contributions but also the highlighting of Marx's strengthens and discoveries elsewhere. Capitalism could only be understood – according Marx and non-Marxist Schumpeter simultaneously – in its long-term development.

The process of industrial change – in Schumpeter's new – gives the basic crescendo which provides the music of the economy. However, the process has two faces. These two faces are, on the one hand, the achievements of capitalism, including the increases in living standards which fascinated Schumpeter principally. But those advantages act, on the other hand, simultaneously with an increase of monopolistic structures as gravedigger of capitalism, since they minimize the dynamics of innovation. Schumpeter's conclusion was clear but empirically wrong until now. He opened up the second part of *Capitalism, Socialism, and Democracy* with the rhetorical question 'Can capitalism survive?' and did not hesitate to answer 'No, in my opinion not' (Schumpeter, 1942 [1947]). So far, Schumpeter can be said to have underestimated the potential innovation sources of capitalism (Swedberg, 1992).

Innovation and technical progress are not external factors but belong to the economic system as internal factors. The crucial question is not what capitalism does with economic structures but how capitalism creates and destroys the own structures. Basic assumption of its dynamics is the existence of competition for innovation: companies always compete for new ways of innovation. Innovation is regarded as introducing a new combination of things which did not exist before or which were not done in that way before. Implementation of a new combination is the successful test on the market.

Innovations are commonly thought of as new inventions which will be further developed to new products but in Schumpeterian thought this interpretation is just one out of several cases of an innovation.[1] Producing means combining things, means or forces, innovative producing means to do it in a new way. Schumpeter spent some further detailed thought on the issues in his *Theory of Economic Development* which was Schumpeter's first book and was published in German in 1912.[2] The English version appeared only in 1934 (see here Schumpeter, 1963). He distinguished between five different matters of innovation:

I. The introduction of a *new good* – that is one with which consumers are not yet familiar – or a new quality of a good.
II. The introduction of a *new method of production*, that is one not yet tested by experience in the branch of manufacture concerned, which needs by no means be founded upon a discovery scientifically new, and can also exist in a new way of handling a commodity commercially.
III. The opening of a *new market*, that is a market into which the particular branch of manufacture of the country in question has not previously entered, whether or not this market has existed before.
IV. The conquest of a *new source of supply of raw materials* or half-manufactured goods, again irrespective of whether this source already exists or whether it has first to be created.
V. The carrying out of the *new organization* of any industry, like the creation of a monopoly (for example through trustification) or the breaking up of a monopoly position (Schumpeter, 1963: 66).

The strategically important question is who or what mechanism introduces the innovations into the business cycle? Schumpeter's answer is that often young companies come up with innovations and that basically *entrepreneurs* play the central role in installing and implementing innovations.

ENTREPRENEURS AND ENTREPRENEURSHIP

Entrepreneurs are treated as agents to introduce new inputs into the economy. Schumpeter defined an entrepreneur as a person who comes up with 'new combinations' (new goods, new methods of production, new markets, new sources of supply, new organizations of any industry or combinations between these items) which are commonly called innovation. The activity of entrepreneurs is fundamental for economic development.

Entrepreneurship is regarded as an institution which has to provide innovations. According to Schumpeter the economic function of entrepreneurship is to initiate and to continue the process of creative destruction as the 'permanent storm of capitalist development'. In this view entrepreneurs act as personifications of economically necessary functions of economic change.

Schumpeter's definition is remarkable since he considers only those economic actors to be entrepreneurs who create 'new combinations', and who take risks with credited capital. In this sense, being entrepreneurial is 'not a profession and as a rule not a lasting condition' (Schumpeter, 1963: 78). Being an entrepreneur is ultimately linked to the status of being innovative. It is not entrepreneural to continue to run a newly created enterprise in further routines and cycles. The Schumpeterian entrepreneur is portrayed by the related dynamics. Being an entrepreneur means being innovative and dynamic. Non-dynamic economic actors who run their (small) firms just in the way to maintain a market position or to defend the existing earnings are excluded by Schumpeter's definition since they are figures of a static economy. Those people in their economic and occupational routines do not take credit or accept risks at all and they are not concerned with creation of further ventures or an expansion of the company.

A further interesting point of Schumpeter's definition of entrepreneurship is that entrepreneurs are people being innovative independently, whether they are working on their own or being employed in companies and working for a salary or a wage.[3] In times when stock market companies gain further importance and dominance former romanticism of business adventurers is declining. The most important criterion, according to Schumpeter, is that entrepreneurs 'put things forward' and keep capitalism going.

MOTIVATION OF ENTREPRENEURS

Mainstream economics or 'primitive economics' (Schumpeter, 1954a: 26) is concerned only with economic functions of actors or institutions; it is not concerned with actors' motives and their modes of origin. In contrast to that conventional practice, Schumpeter asked for the rationality of actors and – in this case – of entrepreneurs. Why do they do what they do? Schumpeter points to the necessity to employ sociological and psychological arguments in order to provide a more grounded perspective (Schumpeter, 1993b). In doing this, Schumpeter follows an interdisciplinary practice which was not common in his time and which is also currently not used much. Schumpeter worked explicitly on the relationship of economics and psychology in his final book *History of Economic Analysis* (1954a) as we have already discussed in this chapter. But he started his career treating the same questions. In *The Theory of Economic Development* (1963), which was his first book, Schumpeter pointed to entrepreneurs' behavior: 'We shall finally try to round off our picture of the entrepreneur in the same manner in which we always, in science as well as in practical life, try to understand human behavior, viz. by analyzing the characteristic motives of his conduct' (Schumpeter, 1963: 90).[4]

Reading Schumpeter shows a principle criticism of the cultural system of capitalism, which is a kind of general civilization criticism and which is very similar to what we know already from Max Weber.[5] However, Schumpeter's point is not to leave the discussion at a level of dark diagnosis of recent cultural and economic times related to capitalism, but he tries to understand the *sense* of economic activities. When Schumpeter asks for the *meaning* of economic action, he discusses models of rationality. All his theorizing is against practices of utilitarianism and against basic assumptions of economic theorizing. In other words, Schumpeter proves to systematize arguments in favor of economics being oriented towards 'real life' which has now become popular under the flag of 'heterodox economics' (Lawson, 2006; Lee, 2004).

Schumpeter discusses and distinguishes three different complexes of motives which lead entrepreneurial activities:

1. 'First of all, there is the dream and the will to found a private kingdom, usually, though not necessarily, also a dynasty. The modern world really does not know any such positions, but what may be attained by industrial or commercial success is still the nearest approach to medieval lordship possible to modern man. Its fascination is specially strong for people who have no other chance of achieving social distinction.'
2. 'Then there is the will to conquer: the impulse to fight, to prove oneself superior to others, to succeed for the sake, not for the fruits of success, but of success itself. From this aspect, economic action becomes akin to sport – there are financial races, or rather boxing-matches. The financial result is a secondary consideration, or, at all events, mainly valued as an index of success and as a symptom of victory, the displaying of which very often is more important as a motive of large expenditure than the wish for the consumers' goods themselves.'
3. 'Finally, there is the joy of creating, of getting things done, or simply of exercising one's energy and ingenuity. This is akin to a ubiquitous motive, but nowhere else does it stand out as an independent factor of behavior with anything like the clearness with which it obtrudes itself in our case. Out type seeks out difficulties, changes in order to change, delights in ventures. This group of motives is the most distinctly anti-hedonist of the three' (Schumpeter, 1963: 93–4).

Schumpeter provides not only very important elements for a psychology of entrepreneurial activity but also of economy-related behavior. He clearly insists that motives as need for achievement and success can also be found in regular professions and that the financial motive is always present but never dominant:

> Only with the first groups of motives is private property as the result of entrepreneurial activity an essential factor in making it operative. With the other two it is not. Pecuniary gain is indeed a very accurate expression of success, especially of *relative* success, and from the standpoint of the man who strives for it, it has the additional advantage of being an objective fact and largely independent of the opinion of others. (Schumpeter, 1963: 94)

CONCLUSION

Discussing entrepreneurship implies dealing with a variety of semantic associations. Entrepreneurship serves to be a key word for diverse contexts and motivations. Schumpeter whose name is connected with discussion of entrepreneurship possibly more than anyone else in academic circles has a very specific understanding of what entrepreneurship is. For Schumpeter entrepreneurship is less related to ownership but more to control over means. Schumpeter stresses the dynamics aspects which lead to innovation and which emphasize the state of the economy further.

Capitalism exists always as a development with a fragile balance of 'coming' and 'going' of firms, entrepreneurs, goods, ideas, mentalities and ideologies. Although Schumpeter is often regarded as the academic hero of entrepreneurship and innovation, he was highly sceptical about the endogenous creativity of capitalism to achieve a balance between creativity and destruction over a longer period. So far, Schumpeter can be said to have underestimated the potential innovation sources of capitalism. And Schumpeter is cynical concerning the entrepreneur and the motivational background of related activities. The hero of capitalism loses a lot of the overwhelming sympathies he or she gains in conventional rhetorics. Schumpeter helps to understand dynamics of capitalism very well, his contribution towards entrepreneurship is still of relevance and an important part of textbooks, as are his socioeconomic thought and methodological reflections.

NOTES

1. See Braunerhjelm and Svensson (2006) for a discussion the asymmetry between invention and innovations.
2. Specialists in the history of economic thought are still in debate if the first publication date was 1911 or 1912. What is much more important is that the first edition is widely unknown and only a few single copies are available in European libraries. Current scholars reading the *Theory of Economic Development* in German refer to a reprint of the second edition while English readers refer to a reprint of the revised English translation published first in 1934. The English version is not identical to the second German edition (1926) while the German first edition differs in many parts substantially from the German second edition. For example, the first German edition had a final seventh chapter ('The holistic view on the economy') which was largely based on sociological thought.
3. As Schumpeter wrote: 'As it is the carrying out of new combinations that constitutes the entrepreneur, it is not necessary that he should be permanently connected with an individual firm; many 'financiers', 'promoters', and so forth are not, and still they may be entrepreneurs in our sense' (Schumpeter 1963: 75).
4. This point underlines very well Osterhammel's thesis that Schumpeter had developed the 'basic outlines' of his thinking until 1920 (Osterhammel, 1987: 107).
5. For convergences between Weber and Schumpeter see MacDonald (1965), Osterhammel (1987) and Collins (1986: 117 ff.).

REFERENCES

Ackerlof, George A. (2007), 'The missing motivation in macroeconomics', presidential address, prepared for the Conference of the American Economic Association, Chicago, 5–7 January.

Audretsch, David B. (2007), *The Entrepreneurial Society*, Oxford: Oxford University Press.

Baumol, William J. (1990), 'Entrepreneurship: productive, unproductive, and destructive', *Journal of Political Economy*, **98** (5), 893–921.

Baumol, William J., R.E. Litan, C.J. Schramm (2007), *Good Capitalism, Bad Capitalism and the Economics of Growth and Prosperity*, New Haven, CT: Yale University Press.

Bögenhold, Dieter (2004), 'Entrepreneurship: multiple meanings and consequences', *International Journal of Entrepreneurship and Innovation Management*, **4** (1), 3–10.
Bögenhold, Dieter and Udo Staber (1994), *Von Dämonen zu Demiurgen? Studien zur (Re-)Organisation des Unternehmertums in Marktwirtschaften*, Berlin: Akademie-Verlag.
Braunerhjelm, Pontus and Roger Svensson (2006), 'The inventor's role: was Schumpeter right?', paper presented at 'The Oslo Research Workshop 2006 on Entrepreneurship, Innovation and Innovation Policy', Norwegian School of Management, Oslo, 9–10 November.
Collins, Randall (1986), *Weberian Sociological Theory*, Cambridge: Cambridge University Press.
Deutsch, Karl W. (1956), 'Joseph Schumpeter as an analyst of sociology and economic history', *Journal of Economic History*, **16**, 41–56.
Giersch, Herbert (1984), 'The age of Schumpeter', *American Economic Review*, **74**, 103–9.
Harris, Seymour Edwin E. (ed.) (1951), *Schumpeter: Social Scientist*, Cambridge, MA: Harvard University Press.
Heertje, Arnold (2006), *Schumpeter on the Economics of Innovation and the Development of Capitalism*, Cheltenham, UK and Northampton, MA, USA: Edward Elgar.
Hughes, Karen D. (2005), *Female Enterprise in the New Economy*, Toronto: University of Toronto Press.
Lawson, Tony (2006), 'The nature of heterodox economics', *Cambridge Journal of Economics*, **30** (4), 483–505.
Lee, Frederic S. (2004), 'To be a heterodox economist: the contested landscape of American economics, 1960s and 1970s', *Journal of Economic Issues*, **38** (3), 747–63.
Light, Ivan and Carolyn Rosenstein (1995), *Race, Ethnicity, and Entrepreneurship in Urban America*, Hawthorne, CA: Aldine de Gruyter.
MacDonald, R. (1965), 'Schumpeter and Max Weber – central visions and social theories', *Quarterly Journal of Economics*, **80**, 373–96.
McCraw, Thomas K. (2007), *Prophet of Innovation: Joseph Schumpeter and Creative Destruction*, Cambridge, MA: Harvard University Press.
Metcalfe, J. Stanley (1998), *Evolutionary Economics and Creative Destruction*, London: Routledge.
Munro, John (2006), 'Entrepreneurship in early-modern Europe (1450–1750): an exploration of some unfashionable themes in economic history', University of Toronto, Institute for Policy Analysis, Working Paper No. 30.
Organisation for Economic Co-operation and Development (OECD) (1998), *Fostering Entrepreneurship*, Paris: OECD.
Osterhammel, Joachim (1987), 'Varieties of social economics: Joseph A. Schumpeter and Max Weber', in W. Mommsen and J. Osterhammel (eds), *Max Weber and His Contemporaries*, London: Allen and Unwin, pp. 106–20.
Reisman, David (2004), *Schumpeter's Market. Enterprise and Evolution*, Cheltenham, UK and Northampton, MA, USA: Edward Elgar.
Salin, Edgar (1950), German Introduction to *J.A. Schumpeter: Kapitalismus, Sozialismus und Demokratie*, München: Lehnen.
Schumpeter, Joseph A. (1942), *Capitalism, Socialism, and Democracy*, London: Allen and Unwin, 2nd edn 1947.
Schumpeter, Joseph A. (1949), 'The Communist Manifesto in economics and sociology', *Journal of Political Economy*, **57** (3), 199–212
Schumpeter, Joseph A. (1952), *Aufsätze zur ökonomischen Theorie*, Tübingen: J.C.B. Mohr.
Schumpeter, Joseph A. (1953), *Aufsätze zur Soziologie*, Tübingen: J.C.B. Mohr.
Schumpeter, Joseph A. (1954a), *History of Economic Analysis*, Oxford and New York: Oxford University Press.
Schumpeter, Joseph A. (1954b), *Dogmenhistorische und biographische Aufsätze*, Tübingen: J.C.B. Mohr.
Schumpeter, Joseph A. (1963), *The Theory of Economic Development*, New York and Oxford: Oxford University Press.
Schumpeter, Joseph A. (1985), *Aufsätze zur Wirtschaftspolitik*, eds W.F. Stolper and C. Seidl, Tübingen: J.C.B. Mohr.
Schumpeter, Joseph A. (1987), *Beiträge zur Sozialökonomik*, Wien: Böhlau.
Schumpeter, Joseph A. (1992), *Politische Reden*, eds C. Seidl and W.F. Stolper, Tübingen: J.C.B. Mohr.
Schumpeter, Joseph A. (1993a), *Aufsätze zur Tagespolitik: Ökonomie und Psychologie des Unternehmers*, eds C. Seidl and W.F. Stolper, Tübingen: J.C.B. Mohr.
Schumpeter, J.A. (1993b): Ökonomie und Psychologie des Unternehmers (orig 1929), in J.A. Schumpeter, *Aufsätze zur Tagespolitik: Ökonomie und Psychologie des Unternehmers*, eds C. Seidl and W.F. Stolper, Tübingen, J.C.B. Mohr, pp. 193–204.
Shane, Scott (ed.) (2002), *The Foundations of Entrepreneurship*, 2 vols, Cheltenham, UK and Northampton, MA, USA: Edward Elgar.
Shane, Scott (2005), *Academic Entrepreneurship: University Spinoffs and Wealth Creation*, Cheltenham, UK and Northampton, MA, USA: Edward Elgar.

Shionoya, Yuichi (1997), *Schumpeter and the Idea of Social Science: A Metatheoretical Study*, Cambridge: Cambridge University Press.
Spiethoff, A. (1949–50), 'Joseph Schumpeter in memoriam', *Kyklos*, **3–4**, 289–93.
Stolper, Wolfgang F. (1951), 'Reflections on Schumpeter's writings', *The Review of Economics and Statistics*, **33** (2), 170–77.
Swedberg, Richard (ed.) (1991), *Joseph A. Schumpeter. The Economics and Sociology of Capitalism*, Princeton, NJ: Princeton University Press.
Swedberg, R. (1992a), 'Can capitalism survive? Schumpeter's answer and its relevance for new institutional economics', *Archive Europeene Sociologique*, **33**, 350–80.
Swedberg, Richard (ed.) (2000), *Entrepreneurship. The Social Science View*, Oxford, Oxford University Press.
Westhead, Paul and Mike Wright (eds) (2000), *Advances in Entrepreneurship*, vol. 1, Cheltenham, UK and Northampton, MA, USA: Edward Elgar.

44 Self-efficacy

Jeffrey M. Pollack

Entrepreneurial self-efficacy (ESE) can be defined as how confident a person feels about their ability to accomplish the tasks that make a person a successful entrepreneur (for a review see Chen et al. 1998; Wilson et al. 2007). Entrepreneurs take on many different tasks such as starting a new business, finding investors, hiring employees, engaging customers, performing market analyses, and dealing with governmental regulations and rules (Locke and Baum, 2007). The ability of an entrepreneur to accomplish these tasks effectively relates directly to the performance of a business over time (for example, Gist, 1987; Stajkovic and Luthans, 1998).

Research, in general, supports the perspective that entrepreneurial self-efficacy plays a role in the ability of an entrepreneur to succeed. Data show a link between ESE and the emergence of an entrepreneur, as well as entrepreneurial success (for example, Bird, 1988; Boyd and Vozikis, 1994; Chen et al., 1998; De Noble et al. 1999; Jung 2001; Zhao et al. 2005). Evidence also shows that high entrepreneurial self-efficacy may be very important in the early stages of business creation (Baron and Markman, 2005; Chen et al., 1998; Tierney and Farmer, 2002).

Common measures of entrepreneurial self-efficacy seek to assess competencies across five areas: innovation, risk-taking, marketing, management and financial control (Chen et al., 1998; Locke and Baum, 2007). It is important to note that entrepreneurial self-efficacy is a separate and distinct concept from self-esteem. Self-esteem describes a more general sense of confidence. Self-efficacy is much more task-dependent (Bandura, 1997). Entrepreneurial self-efficacy, then, relates to a person's specific confidence about being able to meet the demands of the role that an entrepreneur undertakes (Bandura, 1982; Chen et al., 1998; Wilson et al., 2007).

Entrepreneurial self-efficacy has been studied in both leaders of companies as well as employees within companies (Bandura and Locke, 2003; Baum et al., 2001), and in laboratory experiments (for example, Audia et al., 2000). Findings show that individuals high in entrepreneurial self-efficacy are more likely to persevere at tasks that are difficult (Locke and Baum, 2007) and this fact has important implications for the study and practice of entrepreneurship. Specifically, this social-cognitive approach to the study of entrepreneurship has been overlooked and 'has important applications to the field of entrepreneurship' (Locke and Baum, 2007: 94). These inquiries into the individual-level cognitive processing of entrepreneurs could prove a fruitful line of research (Baron, 1998).

REFERENCES

Audia, P., E.A. Locke and K.G. Smith (2000), 'The paradox of success: an archival and a laboratory study of strategic persistence following a radical environmental change', *Academy of Management Journal*, **43**, 837–53.

Bandura, A. (1982), 'Self-efficacy mechanism in human agency', *American Psychologist*, **37**, 747–55.

Bandura, A. (1997), *Self-efficacy: The Exercise of Control*, New York: Henry Holt.

Bandura, A. and E.A. Locke (2003), 'Negative self-efficacy and goal effects revisited', *Journal of Applied Psychology*, **88**, 87–99.

Baron, R. (1998), 'Cognitive mechanisms in entrepreneurship: why and when entrepreneurs think differently than other people', *Journal of Business Venturing*, **13**, 275–94.

Baron, R.A. and G.D. Markman (2005), 'Toward a process view of entrepreneurship: the changing impact of individual level variables across phases of new venture development', in M.A. Rahim, R.T. Golembiewski and K.D., MacKenzie (eds), *Current Topics in Management*, vol. 9, New Brunswick, NJ: Transaction, pp. 45–64.

Baum, J.R., E.A. Locke and K.G. Smith (2001), 'A multidimensional model of venture growth', *Academy of Management Journal*, **44**, 292–303.

Bird, B. (1988), 'Implementing entrepreneurial ideas: the case for intention', *Academy of Management Review*, **13**, 442–53.

Boyd, N.G. and G.S. Vozikis (1994), 'The influences of self-efficacy on the development of entrepreneurial intentions and actions', *Entrepreneurship Theory and Practice*, **18**, 63–90.

Chen, C.C., P.G. Greene and A. Crick (1998), 'Does entrepreneurial self-efficacy distinguish entrepreneurs from managers?', *Journal of Business Venturing*, **13**, 295–316.

De Noble, A., D. Jung and S. Ehrlich (1999), 'Entrepreneurial self-efficacy: the development of a measure and its relationship to entrepreneurial action', in R.D. Reynolds, W.D. Bygrave, S. Manigart, C.M. Mason, G.D. Meyer, H.J. Sapienza and K.G. Shaver (eds), *Frontiers of Entrepreneurship Research*, Waltham, MA: P&R Publication, pp. 73–87.

Gist, M. (1987), 'Self-efficacy: implications for organizational behavior and human resource management', *Academy of Management Journal*, **12**, 472–85.

Jung, D.L., S.B. Ehrlich, A. De Noble and K.B. Baik (2001), 'Entrepreneurial self-efficacy and its relationship to entrepreneurial action: a comparative study between the US and Korea', *Journal of Applied Psychology*, **6** (1), 41–53.

Locke, E.A. and J.R. Baum (2007), 'Entrepreneurial motivation', in J.R. Baum, M. Frese and R. Baron (eds), *The Psychology of Entrepreneurship*, Mahwah, NJ: Lawrence Erlbaum, pp. 93–112.

Stajkovic, A.D. and F. Luthans (1998), 'Self-efficacy and work-related performance: a meta-analysis', *Psychological Bulletin*, **124**, 240–61.

Tierney, P. and S.M. Farmer (2002), 'Creative self-efficacy: potential antecedents and its relationship to creative performance', *Academy of Management Journal*, **45**, 1137–48.

Wilson, F., J. Kickul and D. Marlino (2007), 'Gender, entrepreneurial self-efficacy, and entrepreneurial career intentions: implications for entrepreneurship education', *Entrepreneurship Theory and Practice*, May, 387–406.

Zhao, H., S.E. Siebert and G.E. Hills (2005), 'The mediating role of self-efficacy in the development of entrepreneurial intentions', *Journal of Applied Psychology*, **90** (6), 1265–72.

45 Signalling

Uschi Backes-Gellner and Arndt Werner

Start-ups and their respective market partners are faced with severe problems of asymmetric information due to their lack of prior production history and reputation. *Entrepreneurial signalling* (for example, via education or patenting) can help entrepreneurs to signal their true abilities to relevant market partners like banks, new customers or prospective employees. Reversing Spence (1973), who argues that workers signal unobservable productivity to an employer by acquiring an educational degree, the idea of entrepreneurial signalling is that, likewise, entrepreneurs, who are assumed to be fully aware of their own productivity potential, signal unobservable entrepreneurial productivity by observable characteristics to potential employees, or lenders, customers, and so on. Since the market partners of entrepreneurs cannot readily observe the quality of their venture, they have an incentive to approximate that information via reliable entrepreneurial signals.

According to Spence (1973) educational degrees have to meet two additional criteria to become valid as a signal separating high-quality from low-quality employees. In the original model, where employees signal their unobserved productivity, the degree first must be closely related to the type of productive capability employers are looking for in filling a particular job vacancy (for example, if a company is looking for a creative and trendy hairdresser it might not be best to hire someone with a PhD just because he has the highest educational degree among the applicants). Secondly, in order to guarantee a separating equilibrium, the cost to the employee of obtaining the degree must be strongly negatively correlated with the employee's hidden productivity. Thirdly, the educational degree has to be observable to the respective market partner. Only if these three conditions are met will a separating equilibrium be established. Embedding Spence's original model in the entrepreneurial context, the question is, which signals are likely to meet these two conditions?

The role of signals for entrepreneurs has rarely been analysed in depth, despite some early mentions in the economics literature. In the late 1970s there was a first discussion on how the educational degrees of employees compared with entrepreneurs could be used to test the educational screening hypothesis (Lazear, 1977; Wolpin, 1977). Wolpin argues that entrepreneurs should have lower levels of education if schooling is merely a signal, because there is no need for entrepreneurs, who are by definition self-employed, to signal. Lazear, on the other hand, argues that educational signals might not be irrelevant for entrepreneurs because customers may use their credentials as a signal in assessing product quality. However, this argument was never systematically followed up in entrepreneurship research until Backes-Gellner and Werner (2007). Backes-Gellner and Werner (2007) study entrepreneurial signalling via education and patenting in the case of innovative start-ups. The authors argue that especially for innovative product or business processes, there is no experience and no benchmark on which to build. Outside financiers of an innovative start-up, for example, have no relevant data about production facilities, processes or product markets to use as benchmarks in evaluating a proposed business plan. The value of an innovative project is therefore difficult to judge, even for the most experienced of creditors. Accordingly, the asymmetric information gap between the founder of an innovative start-up and the creditor is likely to be extraordinarily large, potentially causing problems like credit rationing. Creditors may ration credit, finance only a fraction of assets and operations, claim high collateral or shorten the length of their loans. Furthermore, other stakeholders may find investments in an innovative start-up particularly risky, given the lack of history, reliable benchmarks and prior reputation. Employees may be reluctant to accept a job at such a company, that is, to invest in company-specific knowledge if the risk of failure is too high or totally unknown. Suppliers may be hesitant to grant trade credit, and customers may be cautious about ordering products of possibly unacceptable quality or products that may not be delivered in due course. Taken together, founders of start-ups who find a way to overcome the initial problem of asymmetric information in the relevant markets by signalling their above average quality are likely to run their new venture more successfully. Using a unique data-set of more than 700 German start-ups collected in 1998/99 Backes-Gellner and Werner (2007) show that innovative entrepreneurs signal their quality especially by means of certain characteristics of their educational history. In particular, they can show that potential employees use an entrepreneur's university degree as a quality signal when deciding whether to accept a job at an innovative start-up. They also show that banks – who have more information on the educational history of their potential credit-takers than employees have on their potential bosses – use a more precise indicator, namely, the actual length of study in relation to a standard length, as a quality signal when deciding to provide credit to an innovative founder. Furthermore, the authors show that innovative founders holding a patent have less difficulty obtaining credit than innovative founders without patents.

Although there may be various ways for innovative entrepreneurs with above average quality to overcome informational problems in the beginning of a new venture's life cycle (for example, through screening mechanisms), these instruments are no complete substitutes for educational signals. Innovative entrepreneurs use entrepreneurial signalling via education successfully to overcome crucial information problems. However, since the situation is different for traditional start-ups, where potential creditors or employees can draw upon prior start-up experience and business history to evaluate the risk of a particular start-up, the same educational 'signals' do not work to signal the quality of a traditional start-up.

REFERENCES

Backes-Gellner, U. and A. Werner (2007), 'Entrepreneurial signaling via education: a success factor in innovative start-ups', *Small Business Economics*, **29**, 173–90.

Lazear, E.P. (1977), 'Academic achievement and job performance: Note', *American Economic Review*, **67**, 252–4.

Spence, M. (1973), 'Job market signaling', *Quarterly Journal of Economics*, **87**, 355–74.

Wolpin, K.I. (1977), 'Education and screening', *American Economic Review*, **67**, 949–58.

46 Simulation games

Christian Lendner and Jutta Huebscher

ENTREPRENEURSHIP SIMULATION GAMES

Entrepreneurship education requires teaching methods that try to assimilate the complexity of real business. A simulation game can be defined as a dynamic model of the real entrepreneurial process in which a balanced number of decision variables require strategic integration of several subunits such as marketing or new venture finance for organizational start-up performance (Keys and Wolfe, 1990). The game is a teaching method which provides first-hand multiple experiences of management interdependencies and competition in one common marketplace. Participants allocate virtual resources and have to follow the rules of the specific virtual market framework in their decision-making process (Klabbers, 1999). This concrete experience and its outcome are observed and reflected on by the participants in an iterative process with immediate feedback. Games are designed specifically to eliminate some of the complexity and accelerate the frame of action of the long-run planning situation in order to mirror the whole entrepreneurial process (see Keys and Wolfe, 1990). Simulation games are all quite similar in that they require input from the students who must first process the information. Then participants are confronted with a certain outcome of their decisions, both in absolute terms of profit, loss, liquidity status or market share, and in relation to other virtual competitors. The models of the games are usually designed to show the general principles of management interdependencies and strategy and to teach students not to focus too much on tactical decisions based on revelations of the short-term financial statement. Games differ, however, in the credibility of their scenario, in the appropriateness of their sophistication level, in their technical reliability and in their entrepreneurial content. Entrepreneurship simulation games as opposed to business simulation games should include opportunity recognition, business plan writing or venture financing issues.

After a lengthy period of disagreement among scholars about the possibilities of entrepreneurial training, the general opinion is now that entrepreneurs can indeed be trained – at least to some extent (see, for example, Ronstadt, 1990: 69; Solomon and Fernald, 1991; Timmons, 1990: 165). Getting students to experience entrepreneurial behavior during a simulation game is a teaching approach based on constructivist learning theory (Piaget, 1950). According to the theory, students have to gain knowledge by gathering their own experience. The role of the teacher is limited to facilitating the active learning-by-doing process of the students. Ideally, this learning should also include a double-loop learning process (see Argyris and Schön, 1996), that is, students are encouraged to rethink concepts that have proven inadequate.

Simulation games are an intrinsically motivating teaching method (see Gee, 2003), for problem-oriented learning in an authentic context. In line with the constructivist learning theory, the decision-making process of the participants is characterized by trial and error, which supports the development of logical thinking and problem-solving skills (see, for example, Whitebread, 1997). But these are generally desirable characteristics of teaching methods. For the needs of future entrepreneurs especially, it creates a 'mistake-friendly' environment for understanding, selecting and appropriately using a set of key business skills. Venture evaluation and its deeper integrated understanding are an integral part of the simulation game seminar. Participating entrepreneurs or students are, moreover, forced to apply otherwise inert knowledge acquired in more or less theoretical classes (see Kriz and Hense, 2004). This facilitates retention, understanding and further active use of that knowledge. Learning without reflection is therefore replaced by critical thinking. This is all the more important, as start-up reality requires decision-making under uncertainty. The necessary ambiguity tolerance can be sensitized towards this and also expanded in a simulation game.

From the theoretical perspective, the objective of the course is not only the procurement of new knowledge about start-up strategies, marketing and finance issues, but also to foster a deeper understanding of change processes themselves. It could be rated that a simulation game seminar had been successful if the participants had not only contextualized their existing knowledge so that they had developed a feeling for when and where to use it (see Bransford et al. 2000), but also if they had gained an impression about the interdependencies of management decisions of the competitors and their probabilities for dynamic change. Further learning objectives include logical thinking in the processing of information, problem-solving and team-building experience. Finally, a very important general teaching objective is the sensitization and motivation for topics in entrepreneurship. Simulations can be used for gaining deeper insight into the subject as well as for a motivating 'crash course' on basic entrepreneurial issues. Non-business students, especially, can thereby be sensitized to the whole topic of entrepreneurship. Simulations can be organized as a one-weekend block-seminar so that they find easy acceptance in non-business school disciplines of universities too. For the most part, teaching objectives are similar for participants with a business or a non-business background, even though the importance of the different objectives varies among the different groups.

A review of the empirical literature on the subject shows that simulation games are more than just a game, they indeed have a positive pedagogical effect. Lendner and Huebscher (2007) show that learning effects of simulation game seminars are especially valued by entrepreneurs as opposed to students. But the evidence on specific entrepreneurship learning effects, such as knowledge gains in finance, business planning or other entrepreneurial decision-making related issues, remains scarce and offers a rich field for further research in entrepreneurship education.

REFERENCES

Argyris, C. and D. Schön (1996), *Organizational Learning II: Theory, Method, and Practice*, Reading, MA: Addison-Wesley.

Bransford, J.D., A.L. Brown and R.R. Cocking (2000), *How People Learn: Brain, Mind, Experience, and School*, Washington, DC: National Academy Press.

Gee, J.P. (2003), *What Video Games Have to Teach Us about Learning and Literacy*, New York: Palgrave Macmillan.

Keys, B. and J. Wolfe (1990), 'The role of management games and simulations in education and research', *Journal of Management*, **16**, 307–36.

Klabbers, J.H.G. (1999), 'Three easy pieces', in D. Saunders and J. Severn (eds), *The International Simulation & Gaming Research Yearbook*, vol. 7, London: Kogan Page, 16–33.
Kriz, W. and J. Hense (2004), 'Evaluation of the EU-project "SIMGAME" in business education', in International Simulation and Gaming Association (ed.), *Bridging the Gap: Transforming Knowledge into Action Through Gaming and Simulation*, Munich: SAGSAGA, pp. 352–63.
Lendner, C. and J. Huebscher (2007), 'Business simulation games with entrepreneurs and students – an empirical evaluation', paper presented at IntEnt Conference in Gdansk, 8–11 July.
Piaget, J. (1950), *The Psychology of Intelligence*, New York: Routledge.
Ronstadt, R. (1990), 'The educated entrepreneurs: a new era of entrepreneurial education evolves', in C.A. Kent (ed.), *Entrepreneurship Education*, New York: Quorum Books, pp. 69–88.
Solomon, G.T. and L.W. Fernald (1991), 'Trends in small business management and entrepreneurship education in the United States', *Entrepreneurship Theory and Practice*, **15** (3), 25–39.
Timmons, J. (1990), *New Venture Creation: Entrepreneurship in the 1990s*, Homewood, IL: Irwin.
Whitebread, D. (1997), 'Developing children's problem-solving: the educational uses of adventure games', in A. McFarlane (ed.), *Information Technology and Authentic Learning*, London: Routledge, pp. 13–37.

47 Small island entrepreneurship*

Godfrey Baldacchino

Most definitions of entrepreneurs tells us nothing about how difficult or easy it may be for such an entrepreneur to develop in a particular geographical, regional, socio-economic or cultural context. Nor does it tell us whether the act of being an entrepreneur renders this activity exceptional, habitual or anywhere in between the members of a particular social group. Are entrepreneurial skills really scarce by definition? And can the experience, nature and overall challenges of entrepreneurship be somehow patterned in terms of geographical context?

DAUNTING CONTEXT

Island entrepreneurship relates to the practice of 'doing business' on, and by, island societies. These communities have to contend with the various implications of their islandness: limited land area and finite resources; limited domestic markets and client bases; physical isolation; and local consumption patterns that prefer imports from the metropole to locally made commodities. A powerful local mercantile elite would also often peddle low-risk mercantilism (meaning wholesale and retail trade with low local productive value added) or otherwise engage in service activities which do not suffer as badly from scale economies (Baldacchino, 1995; 1998). Even where island territories have good quality and competitive products, there may be difficulties in sourcing effective research and development capability, skilled human resources, suitable terms for financing and/or appropriate technology. And there may be important differences even on one island (Baldacchino and Dana, 2006; Dana and Dana, 2000).

A global knowledge economy context continues to raise the stakes. As the world heads inexorably towards becoming a network of prosperous city-regions (Ohmae, 2001), there is even less scope for places and firms to try and survive as 'islands' of productive activity. It therefore comes as no surprise that research on island entrepreneurs is often heavily laced with pessimism (Fairbairn, 1988; Saffu, 2003).

Note that the above observations apply generally to all island societies, but more significantly so with decreasing size of the resident island population, and irrespective of whether these islands are listed as having developed or developing economies. Indeed, smaller size and geographic isolation are readily viewed as sources of economic vulnerability which adversely affect economic growth and firm performance (Bertram, 2004). Remoteness and peripherality are seen to compound the problems.

The challenges claimed to be faced by entrepreneurs based in island territories are, to say the least, daunting. The size of the domestic market is small and, in the case of archipelagos, also fragmented and dispersed; there are high transport costs, especially handling, freight and insurance expenses, partly because of a tendency towards oligopoly and imperfect competition; there is an inability to achieve and exploit economies of scale in the local market: as a result, costs such as health, energy, education and public administration, tend to be higher per capita, thus requiring higher tax revenues per capita; with isolation, significant transport costs come into play in order to access distant alternative markets or to source raw material; there are often limited linkages to the local economy, which may tend to be signficantly dependent on, and biased towards, the production of a single crop, product or service (such as bananas, copra, sugar, tourism or offshore finance); there may be a lack of skilled labour power or expertise which, where available, is likely to move away in search of better returns on investment and larger markets; and there may be a dearth of effective and competitive support and infrastructural services, such as telecommunications and venture capital (Armstrong et al., 1993; Baker, 1992; Dolman, 1985; Doumenge, 1985; Encontre, 1999; Fisher and Encontre, 1998; Payne, 1987). Finally, the more common strategy and attitude among islanders appear to favour *intra*preneurship, where individuals seek to become innovative and creative *within* the confines and protection of an existing, public or private organization (Baldacchino and Fairbairn, 2006). Michael Porter has gone so far as to refer to an industry cluster which becomes gripped by complacency and an inward focus as *insular*, probably on the assumption that 'islands are closed and inward looking systems' (Porter, 1998: 171–2).

PROSPECTS

What then are the prospects for fostering entrepreneurship and business development in (especially small) islands? One major theme in the literature is the importance of good economic management and the creation of an enabling policy and a sound institutional environment conducive to business investment and enterprise (Easterly and Kraay, 2000). The focus here is primarily macro and institutional, looking at what governments and arm's-length supporting agencies (including banks, development corporations, vocational colleges, universities and non-governmental organizations) can do to generate 'capacity building' and 'resilience', facilitating a more business and entrepreneur-friendly environment (Briguglio et al., 2006). This strand seems to have taken over the more fatalistic assessment of the island condition as inherently and chronically vulnerable, particularly as it affects small island developing states (SIDS) (Commonwealth Consultative Group, 1985; Harden, 1985). Structural vulnerability would therefore only be usefully addressed via concessionary, bilateral or multilateral arrangements struck mainly with metropolitan powers, rather than by any endogenous policy initiatives by island governments (Briguglio, 1995). The economic challenges facing islands are so widely acknowledged that a number of international and regional organizations – including the United Nations (via its SIDS programme), the European Union (which recognizes that 'island regions', among others, suffer from 'structural handicaps') and the Commonwealth Secretariat (Atkins et al., 2000; Charles, 1997; Wignaraja et al., 2004) – remain in general agreement that small territories, especially small island regions, share a set of characteristics which pose specific development challenges. These characteristics are fairly similar to those borne by peripheral rural areas which lose out from agglomeration economics and demographics (Polèse and Shearmur, 2002) or by remote, land-locked or mountainous regions (Srinivasan, 1986).

A MORE OPTIMISTIC TACK

Regretfully, such mainstream economic wisdom discounts the strategic opportunism that characterizes many islanders the world over. This involves behaviour grounded in economies of scope (and not of scale); and the flexible and opportunist operation in monetized, non-monetized, public/formal *and* intermediate/informal economies, both local and foreign, for overall economic gain (Baldacchino, 2000). This typically involves both employment and self-employment. The life-histories of the inhabitants of small islands, where meticulously documented, reveal a complex juggling of such antinomies. Thus, both Isaac Caines, from the Caribbean island of St Kitts (profiled in Richardson, 1983) and Kawagl, from the Melanesian South Pacific (profiled in Brookfield, 1972), demonstrate an uncanny skill repertoire in the economies and temporalities of scope which include entrepreneurship, but also flexible specialization, public sector employment and stints abroad (see also Brookfield, 1975; Carnegie, 1987; Comitas, 1973). Island entrepreneurship remains surprisingly alive and well: in spite of the pessimistic scenario described earlier, even export-oriented, locally owned, technologically innovative firms can be found to operate in many small island territories. (Baldacchino, 2005a; 2005b; 2005c; Baldacchino and Fairbairn, 2006).

Moreover, islands do offer specific advantages to competitive business platforms. These attractions include lower occupancy costs, a more stable and loyal workforce, and reduced labour costs (Greenwood and McCarthy, 2000).

RESEARCH INSIGHTS

While there remains much to be learned about the nature of island entrepreneurship, a series of case studies, in both developed and developing economy contexts, provide some valuable insights. The wide-ranging population of island entrepreneurs is ambitious. They view their involvement in business as a means of providing cash income for themselves and their families, an opportunity to be in control of their own lives, acquire some prestige, extend influence and, even, as a means of winning political office. Interestingly, overall, the accumulation of wealth for its own sake did not figure prominently as a motivating factor.

Most island entrepreneurs operating in traditional economic sectors (such as food or natural product processing) are mature individuals, typically over the age of 40, who were widely respected in their community, with strong family ties and social responsibilities (Hailey, 1988). In contrast, those engaged in more technology or knowledge intensive products (such as computer software), tended to be young and generally well educated. Practically all had work experience overseas, had studied at a technical institution or university before returning home, or had been employed with an international company, thus bringing along with them savings, know-how, business and client contacts that would prove crucial to the motivation to start, and maintain, a successful business. Others had benefited from a period of paid employment locally, either in another business or government service. For others, informal trading has served as an entrepreneurial training ground and a means of maintaining traditional skills, as in the case of handicrafts (Dunlop, 1999; Finney, 1971; Punnett and Morisson, 2006). With a few exceptions, all had drawn upon financial and labour resources from their own savings and of their extended families to start, and eventually upgrade, their business. The few who source bank loans do so by securing them against personal guarantees. Many are 'poor innovators but good imitators' in the type of business established (Ritterbush, 1988). An example is the common tendency to copy those businesses, perceived to be successful, a practice that invariably led to overcrowding and business failure (for example, Prasad and Raj, 2006).

Being small and based on a peripheral island does not appear to present disadvantages in exploiting the opportunities presented by the growth of modern information and communication technologies. The Internet has witnessed and spawned a completely new range of services and software. The latter are, in a sense, manufactures since they are tangible and can be bought and sold via operations that are distinct from those involving their actual production. Still their virtual nature, their relative weightlessness and high portability remove any disadvantages that firms on small islands might have to bear in relation to transportation costs.

Indeed, managing to identify and maintain clients abroad is always a challenge, and all the more so to firms located in relatively remote island locations. This condition may oblige specific tactical measures. Working in cosmopolitan centres, and with multinational firms, helps one to connect with regional or global markets and to nurture and plug into useful contacts and cutting-edge technologies that can prove crucial for business survival. However, the lure of the island is strong. Central to the 'quality of island life' is its rich 'social capital', defined as 'networks, together with shared norms, values and understandings that facilitate co-operation within and among groups' (Baldacchino, 2005d: 24; Groome Wynne, 2007; Helliwell, 2003). This is in sharp contrast to the frenetic, stress-laden and competitive environment of the city and can be strong enough to draw would-be entrepreneurs back to their island, and to encourage others to immigrate. It is the ability to become 'glocal' (Robertson, 1995) – combining the desirability of the island milieu with the necessity to be globally competitive – that is a major, but not impossible, challenge. Both island *roots* and off-island *routes* need to be privileged. This detail cannot be stressed enough: many island-based entrepreneurs are convinced that they are likely to enjoy larger turnovers if their businesses had been located in metropolitan areas: but they remain determined to keep their firm located 'on the island' because of the 'quality of life' factor.

Branding and customer loyalty are important considerations. Many small island firms trade products with substantial local raw material input and so can benefit handsomely by associating their product with what their home island stands for. It is vital for such small firms to support, and 'piggy back' on, the branding exercise that their governments, marketing agents and the advertising industry advance (Baldacchino, 2010). Here, the 'lure of the island' has a captivating and enduring appeal, especially among consumers in the industrialized world, meaning that islands stand out as tourism destinations and tourists stand out as customers for island products (Baum, 1997; Lockhart, 1997; Royle, 2001). Moreover, the association means that any off-island competition for similar products is skilfully avoided: a pepper sauce from Trinidad is not just *any* pepper sauce; it is by definition protected from international competition. The same can be said for coconut soap from Fiji (Baldacchino, 1999), preserves from Prince Edward Island (Baldacchino, 2002) or bottled water from Iceland.

The human resources required to develop and maintain up-market products cannot be short of professional. Many island firms explain that their employees (which include family members) while all 'craft trained' in-house, have been sourced mainly from suitable post-secondary institutions and include a number of graduates. Many have been trained or sent on work experiences off island. Many are bilingual or trilingual, with English recognized as a key international language. Some employees have benefited from apprenticeships with international firms. Above average salaries and lean hierarchies keep staff turnover at extremely low levels, reward staff investment in higher education and recognize the scarcity of skilled, specialized yet flexible labour in small, island-based, labour markets.

Women have so far played a peripheral role in the business life of many island economies. Prevailing sociocultural norms may dictate that the women's role is first and foremost concerned with the performance of domestic chores and child-rearing and, not uncommonly, that business activities are the domain of males (Fairbairn-Dunlop, 2001; Hailey, 1988). Women may also be handicapped by the property rights systems prevailing in some countries which deprive them of the right to own assets that can be mortgaged to raise funds for business and other purposes (Novaczek and Stuart, 2006). Women have been most active in informal trading and in selected areas of the formal economy such as handicrafts, restaurants and dressmaking. Nonetheless, there are cases of women who have achieved outstanding success as entrepreneurs and who deserve to be showcased. The late Aggie Grey, of Samoa, is the founder of what is now the largest hotel/resort complex in Samoa (http://www.aggiegreys.com/). Wilma Malcolmson, who runs Shetland Designer, manages an operation with 30 outworkers that produce a well-branded luxury garment line, based in the Shetland Islands of Scotland (www.shetland-designer.co.uk/). Katrin Olafsdottir, is the managing director of Lysi, a very successful fish-based, health product manufacturer in Iceland (www.lysi.is/is/english/; Baldacchino and Vella Bonnici, 2006).

Islanders face, in varying degree, complex challenges in relation to entrepreneurship and business development, many of which are contoured by their idiosyncratic geographical predicament. However, the evidence speaks of success stories that provide hope and serve as encouraging examples to others. The entrepreneurial experiences of islanders the world over offer limited but tangible examples of business success, even if deductive, macro-driven, analyses may suggest that such is hardly possible to attain.

NOTE

* This chapter was originally published as Godfrey Baldacchino and Te'o I.J. Fairbairn (2006), 'Entrepreneurship and small business development in small islands', *Journal of Small Business and Entrepreneurship*, **19** (4), 331–40. Thanks to Bob Anderson for permission to reproduce.

REFERENCES

Armstrong, H., G. Johnes, J. Johnes and A. Macbean (1993), 'The role of transport costs as a determinant of price level differentials between the Isle of Man and the United Kingdom, 1989', *World Development*, **21** (2), 311–18.

Atkins, J.P., S. Mazzi and C.D. Easter (2000), *A Commonwealth Vulnerability Index for Developing Countries: The Position of Small States*, London: Commonwealth Secretariat.
Baker, R.A. (1992), *Public Administration in Small and Island States*, Westport, CT: Kumarian Press.
Baldacchino, G. (1995), 'Labour formation in small developing states: a conceptual review', *Compare*, **25** (3), 263–78.
Baldacchino, G. (1998), 'The other way round: manufacturing as an extension of services in small states', *Asia Pacific Viewpoint*, **39** (3), 267–79.
Baldacchino, G. (1999), 'Small business in small island nations: a case study from Fiji', *Journal of Small Business Management*, **37** (4), 80–4.
Baldacchino, G. (2000), 'The challenge of hypothermia: a six-proposition manifesto for small island territories', *The Round Table: Commonwealth Journal for International Affairs*, (353), 65–79.
Baldacchino, G. (2002), 'A taste of small island success: a case from Prince Edward Island', *Journal of Small Business Management*, **40** (3), 254–9.
Baldacchino, G. (2005a), 'Successful small sale manufacturing from small islands: comparing firms benefiting from local raw material input', *Journal of Small Business and Entrepreneurship*, **18** (1), 21–38.
Baldacchino, G. (2005b), 'Successful small-scale manufacturing from Malta: a comparative assessment across five European island regions', *Bank of Valletta Review (Malta)*, (31) Spring, 17–31.
Baldacchino, G. (2005c), 'Island entrepreneurs: insights from exceptionally successful knowledge-driven SMEs from five European island territories', *Journal of Enterprising Culture*, **13** (2), 145–70.
Baldacchino, G. (2005d), 'The contribution of "social capital" to economic growth: lessons from island jurisdictions', *The Round Table: Commonwealth Journal for International Affairs*, **94** (1), 31–46.
Baldacchino, G. (2010), 'Island brands and "the Island" as a brand: insights from immigrant entrepreneurs on Prince Edward Island', *International Journal of Entrepreneurship and Small Business*, **9** (4), 378–93.
Baldacchino, G. and L.P. Dana (2006), 'The impact of public policy on entrepreneurship: a critical investigation of the Protestant ethic on a divided island jurisdiction', *Journal of Small Business and Entrepreneurship*, **19** (4), 419–30.
Baldacchino, G. and T.I.J. Fairbairn (eds) (2006), Special issue: 'Entrepreneurship and small business development in small islands', *Journal of Small Business and Entrepreneurship*, **19** (4).
Baldacchino, G. and J. Vella Bonnici (2006), *Small Business from Small Islands: Real Stories of Real People: A Training Manual*, Malta: Malta Enterprise.
Baum, T.G. (1997), 'The fascination of islands: a tourist perspective', in D.G. Lockhart and D. Drakakis-Smith (eds), *Island Tourism: Trends and Prospects*, London: Pinter, pp. 21–35.
Bertram, G. (2004), 'On the convergence of small island economies with their metropolitan patrons', *World Development*, **32** (2), 343–64.
Briguglio, L. (1995), 'Small island developing states and their vulnerabilities', *World Development*, **23** (9), 1615–32.
Briguglio, L., G. Cordina and E.J. Kisanga (eds) (2006), *Building the Economic Resilience of Small States*, Malta and London: Islands and Small States Institute and Commonwealth Secretariat.
Brookfield, H.C. (1972), *Colonialism, Development and Independence: The Case of the Melanesian Islands in the South Pacific*, Cambridge: Cambridge University Press.
Brookfield, H.C. (1975), '*Multum in Parvo*: questions about diversity and diversification in small developing countries', in P. Selwyn (ed.), *Development Policy in Small Countries*, London: Croom Helm in association with Institute of Development Studies, pp. 54–76.
Carnegie, C.V. (1987), 'A social psychology of Caribbean migrations: strategic flexibility in the West Indies', in B.B. Leine (ed.), *The Caribbean Exodus*, New York: Praeger, pp. 32–43.
Charles, E. (1997), *A Future for Small States: Overcoming Vulnerability*, London: Commonwealth Secretariat.
Comitas, L. (1973), 'Occupational multiplicity in rural Jamaica', in L. Comitas and D. Lowenthal (eds), *Work and Family Life: West Indian Perspectives*, New York: Anchor Press, pp. 157–73.
Commonwealth Consultative Group (1985), *Vulnerability: Small States in the Global Society*, London: Commonwealth Secretariat.
Dana, L.P. and T.E. Dana (2000), 'Taking sides on the island of Cyprus', *Journal of Small Business Management*, **38** (2), 80–87.
Dolman, A.J. (1985), 'Paradise lost? The past performance and future prospects of small island developing countries', in E.C. Dommen and P.L. Hein (eds), *States, Microstates and Islands*, London: Croom Helm, pp. 40–69.
Doumenge, F. (1985), 'The viability of small, inter-tropical islands', in E.C. Dommen and P.L. Hein (eds), *States, Microstates and Islands*, London: Croom Helm, pp. 70–118.
Dunlop, E.R. (1999), 'Pisinisi laititi: Samoan women and the informal sector', unpublished master's thesis, Massey University, Palmerston North.
Easterly, W. and A.C. Kraay (2000), 'Small states, small problems? Income, growth and volatility in small states', *World Development*, **28** (11), 2013–27.

Encontre, P. (1999), 'The vulnerability and resilience of small island developing states in the context of globalization', *Natural Resources Forum*, **23** (2), 261–70.

Fairbairn, T.I.J. (ed.) (1988), *Island Entrepreneurs: Problems and Performances in the Pacific*, Honolulu: The East-West Center, University of Hawaii Press.

Fairbairn-Dunlop, P. (2001), 'Women and the privatization of the coconut oil mill, Samoa', *Pacific Economic Bulletin*, **16** (1), 64–75.

Finney, B.R. (1971), *Big-Men, Half-Men and Trader Chiefs: Entrepreneurial Styles in New Guinea and Polynesia*, Working Paper No. 12, Honolulu: Technology and Development Institute, The East-West Center.

Fischer, G. and P. Encontre (1998), 'The economic disadvantages of island developing countries: problems of smallness, remoteness and economies of scale', in G. Baldacchino and R. Greenwood (eds), *Competing Strategies of Economic Development for Small Islands*, Charlottetown: Institute of Island Studies, University of Prince Edward Island, pp. 69–87.

Greenwood, R. and S. McCarthy (2000) 'Manufacturing development on the North Atlantic Rim', in G. Baldacchino and D. Milne (eds), *Lessons from the Political Economy of Small Islands: The Resourcefulness of Jurisdiction*, Basingstoke: Macmillan, pp. 172–92.

Groome Wynne, B. (2007), 'Social capital and social economy in sub-national island jurisdictions', *Island Studies Journal*, **2** (1), 115–32.

Hailey, J.M. (1988), 'Fijian entrepreneurs: indigenous business in Fiji', in T.I.J. Fairbairn (ed.), *Island Entrepreneurs: Problems and Performances in the Pacific*, The East-West Center, University of Hawaii Press, Honolulu: pp. 35–53.

Harden, S. (1985), *Small is Dangerous: Microstates in a Macro World*, London: Frances Pinter.

Helliwell, J.L. (2003), 'Maintaining social ties: social capital in the global information age', *Policy Options*, **24** (8), 9–15.

Lockhart, D.G. (1997), 'Islands and tourism: an overview', in D.G. Lockhart and D. Drakakis-Smith (eds), *Island Tourism: Trends and Prospects*, London: Pinter, pp. xiii–xv.

Novaczek, I. and E.K. Stuart (2006), 'The contribution of women entrepreneurs to the local economy in small islands: sea-plant based micro-enterprise in Fiji and Vanuatu', *Journal of Small Business and Entrepreneurship*, **19** (4), 367–80.

Ohmae, K. (2001), *The Invisible Continent: Four Strategic Imperatives of the New Economy*, New York: Harper Business.

Payne, T. (1987), 'Economic issues', in C. Clarke and T. Payne (eds), *Politics, Security and Development in Small States*, London: Allen and Unwin, pp. 50–62.

Polèse, M. and R. Shearmur (2002), *The Periphery in the Knowledge Economy*, Montreal: INRS.

Porter, M.E. (1998), *The Competitive Advantage of Nations*, New York: Free Press.

Prasad, N. and S. Raj (2006), 'The perils of unmanaged export growth: the case of Kava in Fiji', *Journal of Small Business and Entrepreneurship*, **19** (4), 381–94.

Punnett, B.J. and A. Morisson (2006), 'Niche markets and small Caribbean producers: a match made in heaven?', *Journal of Small Business and Entrepreneurship*, **19** (4), 341–54.

Richardson, B.C. (1983), *Caribbean Migrants: Environment and Human Survival on St Kitts and Nevis*, Knoxville, TN: University of Tennessee Press.

Ritterbush, S.D. (1988), 'Entrepreneurship in an ascribed status society: the Kingdom of Tonga', in T.I.J. Fairbairn (ed.), *Island Entrepreneurs: Problems and Performances in the Pacific*, Honolulu: The East-West Center, University of Hawaii Press, pp. 157–64.

Robertson, R. (1995), 'Glocalization: time-space and homogeneity-heterogeneity', in M. Featherstone, S. Lash and R. Robertson (eds), *Global Modernities*, London: Sage, pp. 25–44.

Royle, S.A. (2001), *A Geography of Islands: Small Island Insularity*, London: Routledge.

Saffu, K. (2003), 'The role and impact of culture on South Pacific Island entrepreneurs', *International Journal of Entrepreneurial Behaviour and Research*, **9** (2), 55–73.

Srinivasan, T.N. (1986), 'The costs and benefits of being a small, remote, island, landlocked or ministate economy', *Research Observer*, **1**, 205–18.

Wignaraja, G., M. Lezama and D. Joiner (2004), *Small States in Transition: From Vulnerability to Competitiveness*, London: Commonwealth Secretariat.

48 Social entrepreneurship

Ana Maria Peredo

The concept of 'social entrepreneurship' has attracted considerable attention in the past decade or more, though arguably the phenomenon to which it applies has been with us for a very long time. The term appears with notable and increasing frequency in scholarly books and articles as well as the popular press. 'Social entrepreneurship' has become conspicuous in the vocabulary of governmental public policy in the UK and elsewhere. It is promoted by influential and wealthy foundations, and prominently featured in the curriculum of highly ranked business schools with numerous professorships in the subject.

A PROPOSED DEFINITION

The concept of 'social entrepreneurship' applies the notion of entrepreneurial intervention, drawn from the world of business economics, to attempts at addressing social problems. Social entrepreneurs, then, 'are one species in the genus entrepreneur' (Dees, 1998: 2). They are people who act 'entrepreneurially' in pursuit of social value.

This much is obvious and agreed upon by those who use the concept and those who study the phenomenon it represents. But there is considerable variety in the more detailed understanding of both what it is to be entrepreneurial, and what it is to be *socially* entrepreneurial (Peredo and McLean, 2006; Tan et al., 2005). We propose the following elaboration of the concept, and argue below for its plausibility: social entrepreneurship is an activity aimed primarily at the creation of social value over and above the usual positive externalities of profit-seeking business. It involves alertness to the need for social good and the means to create it, as well as innovation, willingness to bear risk, and resourcefulness in the face of scarce assets.

WHAT MAKES SOCIAL ENTREPRENEURSHIP *ENTREPRENEURIAL*?

There is no scholarly consensus among business scholars on what it is that entrepreneurs do when they are being entrepreneurial (Venkataraman, 1997). Notwithstanding the debate that continues on this subject (see, for example, Brenkert, 2002; Shane and Venkataraman, 2000), a survey of the literature suggests the following list of characteristics to be included in a reasonably 'developed' understanding of entrepreneurship. First, and obviously, entrepreneurs attempt to create new value. Second, they show a capacity to recognize and exploit opportunities to create that value (Kirzner, 1973). Third, they exhibit a degree of innovation in attempting to produce it (Schumpeter, 1934). Fourth, they are willing to bear risk in the process of value creation (Knight, 1921). Fifth, they are resourceful in the sense that they recognize or value resources not recognized by others (Kirzner, 1997).

There is no attempt to specify the elements in this 'definition' with great precision, and the ways in which they might be combined, even the degree to which all must be present, should be understood flexibly. The real world of value creation is varied and untidy and a proper understanding of entrepreneurship must reflect that fact.

Two elements are deliberately omitted from the above list of characteristics. First, it is not assumed that entrepreneurs necessarily launch or operate organizations, though they frequently do. There is a common use of 'entrepreneur' simply to designate someone who sets up and/or operates a small business (Barber, 1998: 467). But if we are paying attention to the specific contributions to value creation represented in the developed concept of 'entrepreneurship', there are good reasons for saying that not all businesses or start-ups are entrepreneurial (Carland et al., 1984), and not all entrepreneurs launch new organizations (Shane and Venkataraman, 2000). Second, this definition should not be taken to include the widespread assumption that entrepreneurship is normally exercised by individuals. It has been pointed out (Peredo, 2003; Peredo and Chrisman, 2006; Peterson, 1988) that entrepreneurship is at home in relatively 'collectivist' cultures; and Thompson (2002) has reminded us that social entrepreneurship in particular may well be an activity carried out by a group, with its members dividing and sharing roles as in a performance.

WHAT MAKES SOCIAL ENTREPRENEURSHIP *SOCIAL*?

The value social entrepreneurs aim to create and amplify is social value beyond the positive externalities such as employment and income that profit-seeking ventures normally produce. There is, however, a range of opinion concerning the place that social aims must occupy in social entrepreneurs' goal structure. Closely related to that issue is the question of how compatible social entrepreneurship is with profit-seeking on the part of the entrepreneur.

At one extreme are those who would require that social entrepreneurs be driven exclusively by social goals. Accordingly, there is a considerable body of literature (for example, Dees et al., 2002) that locates the concept of social entrepreneurship in the world of not-for-profit (NFP) undertakings. Many of these will be activities that receive income in the course of their operation – in fact there is a subgroup who would confine the idea of social enterprise entirely to income-generating operations, but it seems arbitrary to rule out those who inventively and resourcefully pursue a social good without engaging in any form of exchange. On this 'NFP' view, however, any income generated in the course of social entrepreneurship must be strictly reserved for achieving the social purpose in view, accepting that providing a living for the social entrepreneur and/or the employees of a social enterprise, if one is formed, may be among the legitimate means to that end.

There are good reasons, however, not to confine the notion of social entrepreneurship to NFP activities. Perhaps the most salient is that it is hard to see how crossing the border between NFP and for-profit operations disqualifies an entrepreneur as social. Margaret Cossette, for instance, used a grant of $4000 to turn a small public-sector programme into an NFP enterprise providing home care for rural seniors in a small US county which needed an alternative to nursing home care (Boschee, 1995). Most would consider Cossette to have been a social entrepreneur. When Medicaid money became available that allowed her to fund more clients, Cossette lacked the capital she needed to support the increased demand. Since her NFP status disqualified her for bank credit, Cossette transformed her venture, Missouri Home Care, into a for-profit organization. She secured her loan, expanded her service many times over, and turned her business into a multimillion dollar enterprise serving several thousand clients. Assuming that Cossette's activities qualified as social entrepreneurship before they become profitable, it is hard to see how they lose that status when profit-seeking became an added feature.

Cases like this (for others, see Peredo and McLean, 2006: 61) suggest that profit-seeking undertakings may indeed be instances of social entrepreneurship. But, assuming the social entrepreneur aims at producing social value, how strong a commitment to making money is allowed in addition? The well-known ice-cream franchise, 'Ben and Jerry's', combined profit-seeking with social activism from its founding in 1978. In 1985, the company's founders endowed the 'Ben and Jerry's Foundation' to support community-oriented projects, and continued to fund the foundation with 7.5 per cent of the company's annual pre-tax profits. Are Ben and Jerry social entrepreneurs?

It is important to draw a distinction between the social entrepreneur and the founder and/or operator of a social enterprise. Most commentators on social enterprises see them as NFP organizations engaged in revenue generation and aimed at a social cause while operating with business disciplines (see, for example, Alter, 2004), It was argued above that there is no reason to limit the activity of social entrepreneurship to NFP ventures. On the other hand, even if Ben and Jerry's fails to qualify as a social enterprise, it seems hard to deny that their innovative approaches to social improvement (for example, its 'PartnerShop' programme, which Unilever retained after acquiring the company in 2000) amount to social entrepreneurship.

It must be admitted that a good deal of the literature on social entrepreneurship links it explicitly with the creation and/or operation of social enterprises, just as the study of business entrepreneurship has often focused on the development and running of business firms. But in both cases it seems important to insist (as pointed out above) that value-seeking activity, which is alert to opportunity, innovative, risk-bearing and resourceful, need not lead to the formation of a new organization. The creation of a social enterprise is only one possible expression of social entrepreneurship. Another may be to introduce a new initiative within the structure of an existing organization – public, for-profit or NFP. Yet another is to initiate a completely informal but highly innovative and resourceful arrangement whereby something usually wasted is turned into a resource for the poor. And still another may be the intentional pursuit of a social good by means which are chosen in part because they are highly profitable. Each of these may be, in its own way, entrepreneurial and highly productive of social good.

POTENTIAL AND CONCERNS

A consequence of the above argument is the recognition that there have been social entrepreneurs throughout history, though the label and public attention given to the phenomenon date only from the 1970s. The phenomenon itself, with its goal of creating new social value, is clearly of huge potential benefit to a society. Plainly, the activity of social entrepreneurs, and the work of social enterprises (as mentioned, the two are often run together), are especially important where societies have been unwilling or unable to provide the institutions for delivery of such social goods as health care, education and employment. This function is especially crucial in addressing the problems in so-called 'developing' countries, where cycles of social deprivation entrench the poverty that afflicts their citizens. But the role of the social entrepreneur has also become highlighted in many 'developed' countries with the retreat from government-led, publicly supported welfare networks, and a consequent shift of responsibility to independent agents within civil society and the community at large. Societies may depend increasingly on alert, inventive, risk-taking and resourceful persons and groups who are socially motivated and work towards the creation and distribution of social goods.

Some worries about social entrepreneurship arise from the increasing attention paid to the concept and the label. To some eyes, it is a reflection of that ideological shift that focuses increasingly on the individual and admires both the discipline of market interaction and the sound business practices that are supposedly fostered by that discipline. The very concept of entrepreneurship, drawn from the world of business and economics, adds weight to the sense that it is business activity and market forces that should be counted on to provide all of a society's goods, including social goods. Those who distrust this outlook may be concerned that the concept of 'social entrepreneurship' brings with it echoes of a dangerous ideology.

Allied with this may be the concern that promoting the idea of social entrepreneurship as a means of addressing social problems in the 'developing' world risks reinforcing and advancing a narrow, culturally conditioned notion of entrepreneurship: the heroic individual using business methods to bring help to people by encouraging them to adopt mainstream 'western' entrepreneurial approaches. Creative and resourceful means of addressing the needs of underprivileged peoples are needed now more than ever, but there may be cautions that we must take care in promoting their occurrence not to underwrite an alien and finally unhelpful form of social change.

REFERENCES

Alter, S.K. (2004), *Social Enterprise Typology*, Washington, DC: Virtue Ventures LLC, available at: www.virtueventures.com/setypology.pdf (accessed 5 February 2008).

Barber, K. (ed.) (1998), *The Canadian Oxford Dictionary*, Toronto, Oxford and New York: Oxford University Press.

Boschee, J. (1995), 'Social entrepreneurship', *Across the Board*, **32** (3), 20–23.

Brenkert, G.G. (2002), 'Entrepreneurship, ethics and the good society', in R.E. Freeman and S. Venkataraman (eds), *Ruffin Series in Business Ethics No. 3: Ethics and the Entrepreneur*, Charlottesville, VA: Ruffin Publishing, pp. 5–43.

Carland, J.W., F. Hoy, W.R. Boulton and J.A.C. Carland (1984), 'Differentiating entrepreneurs from small business owners: a conceptualization', *Academy of Management Review*, **9** (2), 354–9.

Dees, J.G. (1998), 'The meaning of "social entrepreneurship"', available at: http://www.gsb.stanford.edu/csi/SEDefinition.html (accessed 8 February 2008).

Dees, J.G., J. Emerson and P. Economy (2002), 'Editor's introduction', in J.G. Dees, J. Emerson and P. Economy (eds), *Strategic Tools for Social Entrepreneurs: Enhancing the Performance of Your Enterprising Nonprofit*, New York: John Wiley and Sons.

Kirzner, I.M. (1973), *Competition and Entrepreneurship*, Chicago, IL: University of Chicago Press.
Kirzner, I.M. (1997), 'Entrepreneurial discovery and the competitive market process: an Austrian approach', *Journal of Economic Literature*, **35**, 60–85.
Knight, F.H. (1921), *Risk, Uncertainty and Profit*, Boston, MA and New York: Houghton Mifflin.
Peredo, A.M. (2003), 'Emerging strategies against poverty: the road less traveled', *Journal of Management Inquiry*, **12** (2), 155–66.
Peredo, A.M. and J.J. Chrisman (2006), 'Toward a theory of community-based enterprise', *Academy of Management Review*, **31** (2), 309–28.
Peredo, A.M. and M. McLean (2006), 'Social entrepreneurship: a critical review of the concept', *Journal of World Business*, **41** (1), 56–65.
Peterson, R. (1988), 'Understanding and encouraging entrepreneurship internationally', *Journal of Small Business Management*, **26** (2), 1–8.
Schumpeter, J. (1934), *Capitalism, Socialism and Democracy*, New York: Harper and Row.
Shane, S. and S. Venkataraman (2000), 'The promise of entrepreneurship as a field of research', *Academy of Management Review*, **25** (1), 217–26.
Tan, W.-L., J. Williams and T.-M. Tan (2005), 'Defining the "social" in "social entrepreneurship": altruism and entrepreneurship', *International Entrepreneurship and Management Journal*, **1**, 353–65.
Thompson, J.L. (2002), 'The world of the social entrepreneur', *International Journal of Public Sector Management*, **15** (5), 412–31.
Venkataraman, S. (1997), 'The distinctive domain of entrepreneurship research: an editor's perspective', in J. Katz and R. Brockhaus (eds), *Advances in Entrepreneurship, Firm Emergence, and Growth,* vol. 3, Greenwich, CT: JAI Press, pp. 119–38.

49 Strategy and entrepreneurship

Robert T. Hamilton

In Chapter 6 in this volume, Professor William Baumol explains why the entrepreneur was superfluous for the development of the neoclassical theory of the firm. In another place he has likened this to Shakespeare's *Hamlet* without the character of the Prince of Denmark (Baumol, 1968). The influence of microeconomics on the development of mainstream strategic management has also helped to ensure that entrepreneurship and strategy have developed, thus far, as largely distinct constructs. They do however intersect, particularly with regard to the nature and source of opportunities. In this short review of the relationships between entrepreneurship and strategy, we adopt a similar starting point, namely, mainstream microeconomics, and show how its assumption of rational decision-making has underpinned a static model of competition and strategies that appear to have no place for entrepreneurs or entrepreneurship. We then contrast the traditional or 'classical' line of strategy development (Whittington, 1993) with that deriving from the Austrian School (Jacobson, 1992) in which the entrepreneur has a key role in an ongoing competitive process. This leads into a discussion of the common ground between entrepreneurship and strategy, namely, the critical role of opportunities to each construct. The chapter then develops an overview of entrepreneurship and strategy in two contexts: small owner-controlled firms and large corporations striving to become more entrepreneurial. At its conclusion the chapter notes the recent emergence of the field of 'strategic entrepreneurship', a development that clearly acknowledges a convergence of entrepreneurship and strategy.

SOME DEFINITIONS

The concepts of entrepreneurship and strategy have been around for hundreds of years. Entrepreneurship is generally traced back to the eighteenth-century writings of Cantillon (1931), while strategy derives from the military strategems of ancient China (Sun Tzu, 1971) which continue to have modern-day relevance (for example, Gagliardi, 2003; McNeilly, 1996). To adopt the definition of Shane and Venkataraman (2000: 218), entrepreneurship is about 'how, by whom, and with what effects opportunities to create future goods and services are discovered, evaluated, and exploited'. This definition does seem to have gained some general acceptance by those in the field and is sufficient for our purposes. A key aspect, which we develop later, is the emphasis placed on the nature and source of 'opportunities'. These are fundamental to the nature of entrepreneurship and also critical to the development of any strategy. Without some set of feasible opportunities, the whole apparatus of strategy and strategic management has nowhere to go. Also, looking ahead in this chapter, the answer to the 'by whom' in Shane and Venkataraman's definition is not limited to the independent founder entrepreneur and does extend to those trying to infuse entrepreneurship into large organizations owned by others.

There are also many modern definitions of strategy. In essence they can be reduced to the answers that an individual or organization has devised to four questions: where are we now? How did we get here? Where would we like to be? How do we get there? In more formal language, one popular textbook defines strategy as 'the direction and scope of an organisation over the long term, which achieves advantage in a changing environment through its configuration of resources and competences with the aim of fulfilling stakeholder expectations' (Johnson et al., 2005: 9). More succinctly, Hill et al. (2007: 4) describe a strategy as 'an action an organisation takes to attain one or more of its goals'. These definitions convey the sense of a deliberate strategy based on a heavily analytical process that, following Hill et al., (2007: 7), that will 'build on the organisation's strengths so as to exploit opportunities and counter threats, and to correct the organisation's weaknesses'. Some strategies, or parts thereof, may not be deliberate however. Strategy can also emerge (Mintzberg and McGugh, 1985) as the organization strives to mould itself through time by constantly adapting its resources to the opportunities perceived in its changing environment. However, the notion of perceived opportunity remains central to strategy, whether deliberate or emergent.

STATIC MODELS OF COMPETITION: STRATEGY MINUS ENTREPRENEURSHIP

Those in the strategy field have long recognized the important influence of microeconomics to their understanding of market structure and the conduct and performance of firms. Yet, as Baumol has pointed out, much of modern microeconomics denied any role to the entrepreneur as the agent of innovation and risk-taking (for example, see Minkes and Foxall, 1980). The main reason for this is the assumption that all markets already exist and everyone involved in a market has all the information necessary to lead that market to equilibrium. While the sharing of full information among the market players is necessary for it to get to equilibrium, this also undermines the incentive to innovate or develop any other unilateral strategy. As soon as any innovation was attempted, perfectly informed imitators would ensure that no abnormal level of profit would be earned from that strategy. In this neoclassical world of instantly clearing markets, the only way for a firm to sustain a level of profit that is higher than its competitors' is for the firm in question to exercise a degree of market power, or monopoly control, over all or part of the market.

The power of the monopolist is such that it can raise prices to customers and maintain the level of additional profits that arise. Other firms may have the information about what is going on but they are unable to influence the situation. This powerlessness may stem from natural sources when the size of the market cannot sustain more than one efficient provider. Where there might be space in the market for other suppliers, the monopolist can prevent them from entering by means such as setting market prices at levels that new entrants could not match and/or erecting other barriers to entry, for example, maintaining a high level of advertising intensity (annual advertising expenditure per dollar of sales), which new entrants would need to counter. This analysis leads to the conclusion that exceptional profit can only derive from the wielding of market power due to a firm's market dominance. The analysis of the nature and consequences of market power, and indeed market structures in general, falls within the academic ambit of industrial organization economics, or IO. If industry structure determines firm profitability, then it should come as no surprise that a large body of the 'classical' strategy literature (Whittington, 1993: 13–17) is devoted to trying to affect industry structure – to the benefit of the strategizing firm.

This view of strategy puts the chief executive officer (CEO) as the lead strategist, capable of unboundedly rational decision-making, informed by a confidence that variables and settings from the past will be a reliable guide to future strategy. Opportunities are assumed to emerge as part of the analytical process: 'The object of external analysis is to identify strategic *opportunities* and *threats* in the organisation's operating environment' (Hill et al., 2007: 7, first emphasis added). So, sufficient opportunities are assumed to be waiting 'out there' in the environment waiting to be uncovered. As Alvarez and Barney (2007) put it, opportunities are just like mountains waiting to be discovered and climbed. Strategy is a means-ends process in which those opportunities that play the key role in mobilizing resources can be specified by systematic analysis. But not all opportunities will present themselves in the timely manner required by the strategy process. Entrepreneurship focuses on the nature and supply of these opportunities, including those that are not 'out there' and need to be created by a process of effectuation (Sarasvathy, 2001), the antithesis of traditional means-ends strategic analysis.

The best-known guide to this form of strategy is in the early work of Michael Porter, and in particular his well-known 1980 book on competitive strategy (Porter, 1980). In the period leading up to publication of this book, Porter published extensively in the IO literature on different facets of the relationship between industry structure and the conduct and performance of firms. In this treatise, he inverts the focus to explain how firms can influence the structure of their industries in order to gain a profit advantage. Porter invites strategizing firms to analyse their industries in terms of five forces that define the profit potential of the industry: ease of entry; degree of rivalry; threat of substitutes; power of suppliers; and power of buyers. After weighing up the threats and the opportunities represented by these forces, the strategist chooses from Porter's trichotomy of competitive strategies to position the firm for superior performance. Three basic positions were set out: lowest cost producer; differentiation; and focus. A firm could become the lowest cost producer subject to delivering product or service quality that was commensurate with that provided by competitors. Firm size is a relevant consideration here since unit costs can be influenced heavily by both economies of scale and the learning curve, the inverse relationship between unit cost and the cumulative volume produced. Differentiation has to be such as to justify the premium price and a profit margin that exceeds the margins obtained by lower cost but less differentiated players. The focus strategy invites firms to adopt either lowest cost or differentiation but within a narrow segment of a market. The focus strategies are more accessible by smaller firms who may be able to dominate a part of a market to an extent that would not be possible in the total market. Thus we have a mainstream prescriptive strategy that is analytic, rational, cast in a traditional IO/market structure framework and hence largely devoid of entrepreneurship. The caveat of 'largely' in the previous sentence acknowledges that, in his 1991 contribution to a dynamic theory of strategy, Michael Porter was clearly aware of the need for competitive strategy to avoid the stasis of the microeconomics that formed the backdrop to his earlier work:

> a theory [of strategy] must provide latitude to the firm not only to choose among well-defined options but to create new ones. The firm cannot be seen only as having the ability to shift the constraints but as having the ability to shift the constraints through creative strategy choices, other innovative activity, and the assembly of skills and other needed capabilities. (Porter, 1991: 110)

In these words, Porter comes very close to articulating the role of entrepreneurship in strategy but he leaves open the question of the extent to which the environment, creative decision-making, and plain luck determine the flow of new opportunities. The strategy literature has generally assumed that opportunities already exist among known products and markets and that an analytical process will discover these. Opportunities are then developed as mutually exclusive options and evaluated in terms of feasibility, suitability and acceptability. Resources are allocated accordingly and the process recurs in response to unacceptable levels of performance or as part of the strategy-making cycle of the firm.

It is appropriate here – at the risk of some digression – to defer to the seminal contribution of Penrose (1968) to both entrepreneurship and strategy from a resources standpoint. For Edith Penrose, a firm's growth path over time is the resultant of an interaction between its available resource base, including entrepreneurship, and a set of opportunities that is perceived. The intersection of these is what Penrose termed the firm's 'productive opportunity' (Penrose, 1968: 31–3). The point here is that some person must decide finally when sufficient and appropriate resources are available and to which productive opportunity they are to be applied. Thus, the Penrosian growth firm is one that did confine resources and strategy through active entrepreneurship. Penrose's insights may have been ahead of their time and it has to be noted that they have been criticized on a number of grounds including the assumed availability of worthwhile growth opportunities and, anathema to microeconomic theory, the absence of any limit to the size of a firm (see Marris, 1999).

The value of analysing firms in terms of resources rather than products was re-engaged in the much cited Wernerfelt (1984), although the modern debate on resources as the primary basis for strategy stems from Barney (1991). Barney argued that the sustainability of any competitive position depended on the resource-based advantages possessed by the firm as a result of imperfections in the factor markets. In other words, while the positioning school gave emphasis to opportunities and threats from beyond the firm, the resource-based view leads us to focus on the strengths and weaknesses that are internal to the firm. Strategy is now derived from the leveraging of a resource base rather than the judicious picking of a market position that aligns with the firm's value chain, although Porter (1991: 108) was quick to point out that this stress on resources must complement the positioning approach rather seek to replace it. If however the resource-base necessary to challenge the incumbent players can be acquired easily, developed, or simply copied, then in time the superior level of profit will attract entrants whose activity will erode profits. Resources such as reputation, systems and culture will each be difficult to acquire, develop or copy and so will endure. In contrast, just relying on the latest technology is likely to be much less effective because other firms can also obtain access to this technology. Generally, the more complex and less visible a resource base, the higher will be its rent-earning capacity (Rumelt, 2005) and hence the more enduring will be the higher rate of profit.

The main challenges to devising a formal strategy through positioning or resource-leverage are the constant competitive challenges that come from ever more frequent shifts in technology; changes in the institutional rules that regulate (or, more often, deregulate) the conduct of business; and continued globalization, a process that greatly expands the set of competitors. The shifts in technology help to reduce the span of product life cycles and fuel an increased intensity of competition, aptly labelled hyper-competition by D'Aveni (1994). It is this accentuation of the competitive process that requires us to look at an alternative framework for strategy, one which does appear to have a pivotal role for entrepreneurs as the creators of future goods and services. In their interesting paper on the sources of competitive advantage in such 'high velocity' markets, Eisenhardt and Sull (2001) use the example of Yahoo! to support their contention that the sources of competitive advantage in such markets does not derive from either an attractive industry position or unique, valuable resources – Yahoo! had neither. It is instead the flow of opportunities that dominates strategy: 'In traditional strategy, advantage comes from exploiting resources or stable market positions. In strategy as simple rules, by contrast, advantage comes from successfully seizing fleeting opportunities' (Eisenhardt and Sull, 2001: 108).

DYNAMIC COMPETITION: STRATEGY PLUS ENTREPRENEURSHIP

Under static competitive rules, market equilibria are attained because market information is assumed to be distributed symmetrically, that is, everyone has access to all the information needed to ensure stable equilibria. The essence of dynamic competition as developed by the Austrian School is that the distribution of information is asymmetric, with different people being privy to different bits of information and able to act entrepreneurially to exploit such discrepancies (Kirzner, 1973). New opportunities will be perceived by those most alert to them while remaining invisible to others. So, those who are the first to move to exploit viable information advantages can make superior profits but, having made themselves visible to many, the competition will soon appear. Hence the constant search for the next opportunity – from travel, through new technology, international comparisons or changes to regulations – to make superior profits for a time. Here there is no presumption of sustained competitive advantage, even where this appears to be based on scarce resources. It may be the case that a strong resource base and elements of secrecy will help extend periods of superior profit but, ultimately, all such advantages are seen as transitory to be competed away by replication or substitution. The essence of strategy is now the flexible and proactive quest for new opportunities – the entrepreneurial role now becomes centre stage and, to reuse Baumol's allegory, the Prince of Denmark is back in *Hamlet*.

Casson (2005) takes this a stage further by pointing out that both the neoclassical and the Kirznerian models of markets are restricted in their treatment of entrepreneurs by the shared implicit assumption that all possible markets, that is, all possible goods and services already exist. Casson defines his entrepreneurs as those individuals who specialize in judgemental decision-making based on differential access to information; subjective perceptions of the risk associated with new opportunities; and sufficient optimism to pursue opportunities that others would shun. These entrepreneurs do not have to start a new firm or be self-employed: they are just as likely to be employed in large organizations. The dynamism in this theory of entrepreneurship comes from the continuous volatility in the economic environment and the repercussions of this on the value of information over time:

> At any given time, the system as a whole and the individual firm in particular, is subjected simultaneously to shocks of many different types. Entrepreneurs establish organisations that identify and then monitor key sources of volatility. They maintain social networks that channel selected information to key decision-makers in these organisations. Entrepreneurial organisations are located at nodes on social information networks. Information from these diverse sources converges on these nodes, and it is there, in the headquarters of entrepreneurial firms, that the information is synthesised prior to investment decisions being made. (Casson, 2005: 335)

It is possible for this model of dynamic competition to tend towards an equilibrium as all useful pieces of asymmetric information are utilized, but external shocks and the processes of 'creative destruction' as articulated by Joseph Schumpeter ensure that this does not happen or, if it does, then it will not persist for long. Schumpeter developed his theory of economic momentum around the incidence of radical innovation led by entrepreneurs. Indeed, to a considerable extent it was Schumpeter who resurrected the entrepreneur and brought the role back into the model. He saw entrepreneurs as people with a set of special aptitudes that were not common in the population. Their role, was 'to reform or revolutionize the pattern of production by producing a new commodity or producing an old one in a new way, by opening up a source of supply of materials or a new outlet for products, by reorganizing an industry and so on' (Schumpeter, 1942: 132).

This dynamic model has no more than a transitory role for market power or market structure in determining the profitability of firms (Hill and Deeds, 1996). Indeed, it seeks to account for the structure of industries as the outcome of the performance of successful entrepreneurs rather than something that is determined by the economics of supply and demand. The growth to world prominence of companies such as Yahoo!, Ford, Amazon.com, Microsoft and Starbucks has little to do with the technological economics of their respective industries but much to do with the individuals who built these companies (see Bhide, 2000). The strategic priority is constant adaptation and innovation – better to create change than become its victim. Strategic planning and prediction of strategic outcomes do not apply here because the environment in which individuals and companies have to act is too dynamic. To return to Eisenhardt and Sull (2001), the strategy is to be positioned for maximum exposure to new opportunities, with the capability (or simple rules) to act on the best of these for the short time that they are available.

The foregoing discussion was intended to give an insight into entrepreneurship and strategy from two opposing perspectives affording very different roles for the entrepreneur. We now turn to how entrepreneurship and strategy coexist in two topical contexts: the small entrepreneur-controlled firm and the large corporation seeking to become more entrepreneurial.

SMALL ENTREPRENEUR-CONTROLLED FIRMS

This section draws on the comprehensive discussion in Bhide (2000). Most entrepreneurial small firms start off very small with a capital base determined by how much friends and family have been able to pledge in support of the founder. Innovation, and in particular the radical innovation that Schumpeter had in mind as the province of the entrepreneur, is unlikely to be apparent. Indeed, most new businesses are attracted into those existing industries that are easy to enter and offer low uncertainty. These are, however, the industries where competition from other small firms also trying to gain a foothold is such that even survival is problematic. Indeed, the more successful start-ups are often to be found in niche markets exhibiting considerable uncertainty, from which stems at least the prospect of very high (as well as very low) returns to founders. However, although we can observe some degree of replication in the product or service provision, new firms will have different resource endowments and so the challenge facing the founder is that of effectuating an acceptable future state (Sarasvathy, 2001). To the extent that they have any scarce and hard-to-copy resource, this is likely to be confined to the talent, energy and enthusiasm of the founder. Hence, what is likely to differentiate early-stage businesses is the effectiveness and zeal with which a fairly mundane strategy of replication is implemented by the founder (Bhide, 2000: 49).

The role of strategy and the use of strategic management tools (Wood and Joyce, 2003) become apparent in the small minority of firms that have an objective to grow well beyond their size at start-up. This requires some form of strategy that can guide the investment of time and of money over time. The strategy is geared towards what Bhide (2000: 211) describes as an audacious vision of how they want their firm to look in the future. This is vital if for no other reason than it attracts and retains key resource providers such as initial employees, key suppliers and early customers. Growth at a rate that is far beyond the capacity of the small firm to fund from internal sources will also expose the founder to the risks of using large amounts of external funds to invest in the assets needed to achieve the vision. This quantum of funding will be far beyond what has been raised thus far through bootstrapping and hence the founder needs to be able to tolerate the additional amount of risk involved. It is at this juncture that our audacious entrepreneurs begins to conform to the critical role so famously assigned to them by Joseph Schumpeter (1942: 132): 'To act with confidence beyond the range of familiar beacons and to overcome that resistance requires aptitudes that are present in only a small fraction of the population.'

So, it is the pursuit of an audacious vision that stimulates strategy development in the growing small firm. At the same time, behaviour shifts away from the effectuation that drove the bootstrapped start-up and towards the causal form of means-end thinking traditionally associate with strategic management (Where are we now? How did we get here? Where would we like to be? How do we get there?). Nevertheless, as Bhide (2000: 209) points out, it will always be the case that the ambition and capability of individual entrepreneurs will have a significant impact on the longevity and growth of a firm. This is especially worth remembering when we note that the vision may take many years to achieve and that, during this time, the growth path is unlikely to be always smooth and positive. There will be setbacks over which the firm has no control (Garnsey and Hefferman, 2005; Vinnell and Hamilton, 1999) and it is the resolve and determination of the entrepreneur that will dictate the success or otherwise of any strategy. In such situations, entrepreneurship and strategy are intertwined. Exceptional entrepreneurs build exceptional companies and it is the size and success of these businesses that is the cause rather than the consequence of the market structures in which they operate.

LARGE CORPORATIONS

In the writings of Joseph Schumpeter we can read of his concerns that the rapid growth of the large joint-stock companies would be at the expense of the archetypal small entrepreneurial venture. His expectation was that the onus for innovation would increasingly fall on the large bureaucratic and perhaps risk-averse large companies, and that the entrepreneurial seedbed would be lost. This seedbed was indeed under some threat in the major developed economies through into the middle of the century but, since the late 1960s, there has been a marked revival in new and small firm activity (Wennekers and Thurik, 1999). In large part this has been fostered by changes in technology and consumer preferences. However, as noted previously, it is the rapid shifts in technology, coupled with the multiple threats that come from deregulation and the globalization of manufacturing and distribution, that conspire to create the hyper-competitive environments that can swamp even the largest companies. So, to survive in this world of constant change and uncertainty, large corporations, even exceptional ones, need to become entrepreneurial. They need to cultivate within themselves the individuals who are proactive; who can identify opportunities; who can innovate and take risks (Morris et al., 1994), that is, (corporate) entrepreneurs!

If we accept that these large corporates will have in place a strategy that is geared to achieving ends and that entrepreneurship is about imagination and creating beginnings, then we can see why Venkataraman and Sarasvathy (2001) regard the creative process in established firms as the nexus of entrepreneurship and strategy. It is at this point that the constructs of entrepreneurship and strategy intersect, with entrepreneurship providing the frame of reference for opportunities and strategy the rules that will, more often than not, ensure that the best opportunities are exploited before they disappear.

It is a little unclear when academic interest in so-called corporate entrepreneurship began to develop. While Minkes and Foxall (1980: 295) makes reference to 'entrepreneurial behaviour in large enterprises', it was probably Rosabeth Moss Kanter's (1983) book that laid the foundation. While there is some evidence that corporate entrepreneurship or 'intrapreneurship' (Pinchot, 1985) is positively related to the growth and profitability of the organization (for example, Antoncic and Hisrich, 2001), there are also warnings that this is a very expensive and often unsuccessful strategy (McGrath and Keil, 2007). Nevertheless, its adoption by so many large companies does suggest that they are looking to embrace entrepreneurship rather than market power or position as the basis for their future profits.

While there are several different manifestations of corporate entrepreneurship, such as corporate venturing and strategic renewal, there is not space here to develop each of these. Instead we focus on the more general notion of 'intrapreneurship', defined as 'the process in which innovative products or processes are developed by creating an intrapreneurial culture within an organisation' (Kirby, 2003: 299–300), and while we do relate this to large organizations, there is also evidence that intrapreneurship can work in small businesses (Carrier, 1996).

Intrapreneurs are strong-willed individuals, caricatured as those more likely to seek forgiveness rather than approval. They can be difficult to manage on a one-to-one basis, and in striving to innovate they will be intolerant of any bureaucratic obstacles placed in their path (see Kirby, 2003: 310).

Since the intrapreneur is an employee, he or she will not have the same degree of personal autonomy and the traditional independent entrepreneur. Intrapreneurs also have to discover, fund, develop and test their ideas through the internal approval systems, often a political process that does not encumber independent entrepreneurs. Both culture and strategy are essential conditions for intrapreneurial activity. They need a culture that, among other things, empowers them to act on their own initiative; values the innovation and change that they cause; and enables people to experiment without the fear of failing (see Burns, 2005: 117–19). The strategy that accommodates this form of entrepreneurship is one that: accepts the environment is no longer either certain or controllable; offers flexibility to harness innovation and change; and which operates on strategic goals such as resources devoted to innovation and new product launches (rather than historic measures of return on assets). This stems essentially from the Austrian view of the world, bringing together entrepreneurship – creating new concepts and opportunities – with strategy, those rules and filters that give relevance and coherence in pursuit of a shared vision.

THE FUTURE – 'STRATEGIC ENTREPRENEURSHIP'

The two separate constructs that have been woven through this chapter each have a long history and a nexus at the point where new opportunities are generated. Although foreshadowed by Porter (1991), very recent developments have seen the formal combination of entrepreneurship and strategy into 'strategic entrepreneurship', destined to become an important new area of integrative study. In practical terms, strategic entrepreneurship is concerned with how firms allocate their scarce resources so that they can have both the strategy to exploit current competitive advantages and the entrepreneurship to explore for future opportunities (Ireland and Webb, 2007). At the end of 2007, a new academic journal (*Strategic Entrepreneurship Journal*) was launched and positioned 'to fill the gap that exists, and to expand and develop the natural relationship that exists between strategic management and entrepreneurship' (Schendel and Hitt, 2007: 1).

While the scope of this new journal is much wider and deeper than can be covered in an chapter such as this, it seems appropriate to conclude here with some of the *questions* raised by its editors (Schendel and Hitt, 2007: 2–3) in order to drive home the pivotal position of opportunities in this convergence of entrepreneurship and strategy: *What and who creates opportunities? How do individuals and groups identify opportunity? How are opportunities exploited by individuals and/or organizations? Does uncertainty create opportunities? How does environmental uncertainty present entrepreneurial opportunities? How is strategy formation integrated with entrepreneurship to create value?* In the years ahead, as researchers develop answers to these and related questions, so the fields of entrepreneurship and of strategy will grow together with a synergy that would not be possible from separate development.

REFERENCES

Alvarez, S.A. and J.B. Barney (2007), 'Discovery and creation: alternative theories of entrepreneurial action', *Strategic Entrepreneurship Journal*, **1** (1–2), 11–26.

Antoncic, B. and R.D. Hisrich (2001), 'Intrapreneurship construct refinement and cross-cultural validation', *Journal of Business Venturing*, **16** (5), 495–527.

Barney, J. (1991), 'Firm resources and sustained competitive advantage', *Journal of Management*, **17** (1), 99–120.

Baumol, W.J. (1968), 'Entrepreneurship in economic theory', *American Economic Review*, **5** (2), 64–71.

Bhide, A.V. (2000), *The Origin and Evolution of New Businesses*, New York: Oxford University Press.

Burns, P. (2005), *Corporate Entrepreneurship: Building an Entrepreneurial Organisation*, Basingstoke: Palgrave Macmillan.

Cantillon, R. (1931), *Essai sur la nature de commerce en general*, H. Higgs (ed.), London: Macmillan. (First published in French in 1775.)

Carrier, C. (1996), 'Intrapreneurship in small businesses: an exploratory study', *Entrepreneurship Theory and Practice*, **21** (1), 5–18.

Casson, M. (2005), 'Entrepreneurship and the theory of the firm', *Journal of Economic Behaviour & Organisation*, **58** (2), 327–48.

D'Aveni, R.A., with R. Gunther (1994), *Hyper-competition – Managing the Dynamics of Strategic Maneuvering*, New York: Free Press.

Eisenhardt, K.M. and D.N. Sull (2001), 'Strategy as simple rules', *Harvard Business Review*, **79** (1), 107–16.

Gagliardi, G. (2003), *Sun Tzu's The Art of War plus The Art of Management*, Seattle, WA: Clearbridge Publications.

Garnsey, E. and P. Hefferman (2005), 'Growth setbacks in new firms', *Futures*, **37** (7), 675–97.

Hill, C.W. and D.L. Deeds (1996), 'The importance of industry structure for the determination of firm profitability: a neo-Austrian view', *Journal of Management Studies*, **33** (4), 429–51.

Hill, C.W., G.R. Jones, P. Galvin and A. Haidar (2007), *Strategic Management – an Integrated Approach*, 2nd Australasian edn, Milton, QLD: Wiley & Sons.

Ireland, R.D. and J.W. Webb (2007), 'Strategic entrepreneurship: creating competitive advantage through streams of innovation', *Business Horizons*, **50** (1), 49–59.

Jacobson, R. (1992), 'The "Austrian" School of Strategy', *The Academy of Management Review*, **17** (4), 782–807.

Johnson, G., K. Scholes and R. Whittington (2005), *Exploring Corporate Strategy – Text and Cases*, 7th edn, Harlow: Pearson Education.

Kanter, R.M. (1983), *The Change Masters – Corporate Entrepreneurs at Work*, New York: Simon and Schuster.

Kirby, D.A. (2003), *Entrepreneurship*, Maidenhead: McGraw-Hill.

Kirzner, I.M. (1973), *Competition and Entrepreneurship*, Chicago, IL: University of Chicago Press.

Marris, R. (1999), 'Edith Penrose and economics', *Contributions to Political Economy*, **18** (1), 47–65.

McGrath, R. and T. Keil (2007), 'The value captor's process: getting the most out of your new business ventures', *Harvard Business Review*, **85** (5), 128–36.

McNeilly, M. (1996), *Sun Tzu and the Art of Business*, New York: Oxford University Press.

Minkes, A.L. and G.R. Foxall (1980), 'Entrepreneurship, strategy, and organisation: individual and organization in the behaviour of the firm', *Strategic Management Journal*, **1** (4), 295–301.

Mintzberg, H. and A. McGugh (1985), 'Strategy formation in an adhocracy', *Administrative Science Quarterly*, **30** (2), 160–97.

Morris, M.H., D.L. Davis and J.W. Allen (1994), 'Fostering corporate entrepreneurship', *Journal of International Business Studies*, **25** (1), 65–89.

Penrose, E. (1968), *The Theory of the Growth of The Firm*, 4th impression, Oxford: Basil Blackwell. First published in 1959.

Pinchot, G. (1985), *Intrapreneuring: Why You Don't Have to Leave the Corporation to Become an Entrepreneur*, New York: Harper and Row.

Porter, M.E. (1980), *Competitive Strategy – Techniques for Analyzing Industries and Competitors*, New York: Free Press.

Porter, M.E. (1991), 'Towards a dynamic theory of strategy', *Strategic Management Journal*, **12**, 95–117.

Rumelt, R. (2005), 'Theory, strategy, and entrepreneurship', in S.A. Alvarez, R. Agarwal and O. Sorenson (eds), *Handbook of Entrepreneurship Research*, New York: Springer, pp. 11–32.

Sarasvathy, S.D. (2001), 'Causation and effectuation: toward a theoretical shift from economic inevitability to entrepreneurial contingency', *Academy of Management Review*, **26** (2), 243–63.

Schendel, D. and M.A. Hitt (2007), 'Comments from the editors', *Strategic Entrepreneurship Journal*, **1** (1-2), 1–6.

Schumpeter, J.A. (1942), *Capitalism, Socialism and Democracy*, New York: Harper.

Shane, S. and S. Venkataraman (2000), 'The promise of entrepreneurship as a field of research', *Academy of Management Review*, **25** (1), 217–26.

Sun Tzu (1971), *The Art of War*, London: Oxford University Press.

Venkataraman, S. and S.D. Sarasvathy (2001), 'Strategy and entrepreneurship: outlines of an untold story', in M.A. Hitt, R.E. Freeman, J.S. Harrison (eds), *The Blackwell Handbook of Strategic Management*, Oxford: Blackwell. pp. 650–668. (Also Darden Business School Working Paper No. 01-06.)

Vinnell, R. and R.T. Hamilton (1999), 'A historical perspective on small firm development', *Entrepreneurship Theory and Practice*, **23** (4), 5–18.

Wennekers, S. and R. Thurik (1999), 'Linking entrepreneurship with economic growth', *Small Business Economics*, **13** (1), 27–55.

Wernerfelt, B. (1984), 'A resource-based view of the firm', *Strategic Management Journal*, **5** (2), 171–80.

Whittington, R. (1993), *What Is Strategy – and Does It Matter*? London: Routledge.

Wood, A. and P. Joyce (2003), 'Owner-managers and the practice of strategic management', *International Small Business Journal*, **21** (2), 181–95.

50 Teams

Leon Schjoedt and Sascha Kraus

The concept of entrepreneurial teams (ETs) has not been adequately defined in the literature (Birley and Stockley, 2000), unlike top management teams (Hambrick, 2007; O'Reilly et al., 1993). The existing literature on entrepreneurial teams contains numerous different definitions of entrepreneurial teams. These definitions share one thing in common: the ET consists of, at least, two individuals. However, this quantitative approach disregards qualitative aspects, especially the difference between the concepts of groups and teams. The literature on groups shows that the concept of teams is something different from the concept of groups (Katzenbach and Smith, 2003). Also, the literature on top management teams recognizes this difference between groups and teams. For example, Hambrick (1994) points out how the top management team is not a team per se, but a group of people with management responsibilities. To better define the ET, the concept of groups needs to be considered. A group is defined as, 'two or more individuals, interacting and interdependent, who have come together to achieve particular objectives' (Robbins and Judge, 2008: 123). Furthermore, Cohen and Bailey (1997) note that a group also shares the outcomes. These researchers also note that for a group to be considered a group, the group members must see themselves as a social unit. This shows that teams are special groups in which members are more closely connected and stand up for one another, and are characterized by engagement and commitment (Katzenbach and Smith, 2003). Thus, a team is more than a group. The ET is more than a group because it involves a *shared commitment* to the new venture according to Cooper and Daily (1997). These scholars stop short of defining what constitutes a shared commitment. Katzenbach and Smith (2003) propose that what must be shared by the ET is accountability. Kamm and Nurick (1993) note that the shared commitment of the ET is established when two or more people formally establish a new venture in which they share ownership. The shared commitment seems to be towards the ET as a whole and the performance of the new venture. Additionally, Eisenhardt and Schoonhoven (1990) note the ET is a group of people holding executive positions during the founding process of a new venture. Building on these perspectives, the following definition of ET is proposed:

> An entrepreneurial team consists of two or more persons who have an interest, both financial and otherwise, in and commitment to a venture's future and success; whose work is interdependent in the pursuit of common goals and venture success; who are accountable to the entrepreneurial team and for the venture; who are considered to be at the executive level with executive responsibility in the early phases of the venture, including founding and pre-start up; and who are seen as a social entity by themselves and by others.

This definition emphasizes that interdependent tasks are coordinated in the pursuit of common goals, such as the creation of a new venture. This does not mean that tasks have to be performed by all team members (Katzenbach, 1997). It means that tasks can be performed by individuals in the ET, in subgroups of the ET (and with others outside the ET), or by the entire ET, but the tasks all contribute to the common goals of the ET and the future success of the venture. Thus, it is the tasks that are interdependent. Furthermore, the definition suggests that the ET should be seen by themselves and by others as a social entity. This means the ET is not formed based on titles or otherwise, but is formed based on a shared commitment to each other as participants in the ET, to the ET as an entity, and to the venture and its performance. Thus, the definition has an inherent link between the ET, its shared commitment, and the performance of the venture. In other words, the shared commitment will show itself in the extent to which the ET accomplishes its goals, which constitutes the definition of team performance (Devine and Philips, 2001)

Research has shown that teams start a significant number of new ventures, or a team is created within the first years of start up (Aldrich et al., 2002; Kamm et al., 1990; Watson et al., 1995). Researchers have established that there is a strong association between venture success and team-created ventures (for example, Birley and Stockley, 2000; Cooper and Bruno, 1977; Eisenhardt and Schoonhoven, 1990). Compared to new ventures founded by individuals, new ventures created by teams have more economic, cultural and social capital. As a consequence, they are better equipped when starting and developing new ventures (Lechler and Gemünden, 2003; West, 2007). Also, research on top management teams shows the executive team has greater influence on organizational performance than an individual executive (Hambrick and Mason, 1984; O'Reilly et al., 1993). Additionally, in today's an economic environment – characterized by increasing complexity and uncertainty – an entrepreneurial team seems to be better suited to manage the uncertainties and vicissitudes associated with new venture creation (Chowdhury, 2005). Therefore, the team composition of the team is a critical determinant of organizational performance (Glick et al., 1993; Hambrick, 1994). Further, venture capital firms rarely consider venture proposals from individual entrepreneurs, but favor proposals from entrepreneurial teams because team-based ventures, overall, have a better performance record (Baum and Silverman, 2004; Kamm et al., 1990; Timmons and Spinelli, 1999). As this shows and as Cooper and Daily (1997) phrase it, 'Entrepreneurial teams are at the heart of any new venture' (1997: 144).

Despite the importance of the entrepreneurial team, most of the extant entrepreneurship literature has focused on the individual entrepreneur (Watson et al., 1995), and only limited research has focused on the ET. This is illustrated by Birley and Stockley (2000) noting that the concept of entrepreneurial teams has not been adequately defined and by Foo et al. (2006) pointing out that the ET has been neglected in the literature. However, there are some notable exceptions. These notable exceptions show that a relationship between the ET and venture performance exist (for example, Amason et al., 2006; Ensley and Pearce, 2001; Foo et al., 2006; Francis and Sandberg, 2000; Vyakarnam et al., 1999). Despite these works, additional research on the determinants of ET performance is needed. This chapter contributes to the entrepreneurship literature by presenting a reformulated literature-based definition of entrepreneurial teams and by modelling how factors influence ET performance and, in turn, venture performance. In short, this chapter is intended to stimulate future research to fill the gap in the literature on entrepreneurial teams.

The entrepreneurial team interprets and responds to the external environment, as well as manages the venture internally. Consequently, the ET has a dual and complex function. This complexity is furthered by the fact that venture creation is a novel and unstructured task (Amason et al., 2006; Jackson, 1992; O'Reilly et al., 1993). Further adding to this complexity is the lack of operating history, non-developed scanning capabilities, and so on because there is no precedence to rely upon (Cooper et al., 1994). These aspects require that the ET needs heterogeneity in its human resources, for example, knowledge, skills, and abilities, as well as homogeneity to be able to function together and to be effective in managing the venture and in responding to the external environment.

The external environment has a direct influence on venture performance (Birley and Stockley, 2000). Eisenhardt and Schoonhoven (1990) found that a venture's present and founding environments had a significant influence on venture performance. These researchers found that a growth market provides the combination of present market size and rapid increases in demand that facilitates venture growth due to the abundance of resources that could be generated in this kind of environment. Notably, Eisenhardt and Schoonhoven (1990) also found that the effects of the founding environment did not fade but grew over time.

In addition to the direct effect the environment has on venture performance, the environment also indirectly affects venture performance via the ET. The type of external environment – stable or turbulent – influences venture performance indirectly through how the ET responds to the environment. In stable environments, a heterogeneous ET will experience lower venture performance because the need for communication is greater in a heterogeneous ET, and fast responses in the stable environment are essential (Murray, 1989). In turbulent environments, a heterogeneous ET will have superior performance because the heterogeneous ET makes more comprehensive decisions by considering more options for action (Glick et al., 1993). As this shows, it is how the ET responds to the environment that influences venture performance. This indirect influence of the environment on venture performance is further illustrated by Rumelt's (1991) comment that venture performance is business-level specific, not industry-level specific. Thus, for the ET to succeed, in the novel and unstructured task of venture creation and in its dual and complex function (Cooper et al., 1994; Jackson, 1992; O'Reilly et al., 1993), requires an ET with heterogenetic knowledge, skills and abilities. While the ET needs to be heterogeneous, it also needs to be homogeneous for it to function. Thus, heterogeneity and homogeneity of the ET affects how capable the ET is in responding to the environment, which, in turn, influence venture performance. In short, the environment influences venture performance directly and indirectly through the ET composition.

ENTREPRENEURIAL TEAM COMPOSITION

The ET composition refers to the collective characteristics of its members (for example, Bantel and Jackson 1989; Levine and Moreland 1990). Cooper and Daily (1997) suggest that an ET is most effective if the knowledge, skills and abilities of the ET are balanced. The situation facing the ET may be considered weak as venture creation a novel and discontinuous action (Cooper et al., 1994; Jackson, 1992; O'Reilly et al., 1993). For situations that include novel problems, or exist in a turbulent environment, heterogeneous team composition leads to superior team performance (Filley et al., 1976; Hambrick and

Mason, 1984), whereas, homogeneous teams are more efficient in dealing with routine tasks (Filley et al., 1976). This illustrates that ET composition is an important predictor of ET and, in turn, venture performance (Ensley and Pearce, 2001; Francis and Sandberg, 2000; Hackman, 1987; Stewart, 2006).

Individuals' characteristics form the basis for a heterogeneous ET. The individual characteristics, typically, used in entrepreneurship research consist of surface-level (or demographic) characteristics, such as tenure, age, functional experience, educational background and race (for example, Bantel and Jackson, 1989; Pelled et al., 1999). Even though surface-level characteristics are frequently used to assess ET heterogeneity, some surface-level characteristics have not been positively associated with ET or venture performance. For example, race has not been shown to have a significant impact on performance, but aspects related to race may limit the probability for a successful venture, such as a limited network in an entrepreneurial environment or in an industry (Cooper et al., 1994). Also, entrepreneurs having parents who were entrepreneurs has not been associated with successful ventures, but has been associated with ventures that experience marginal survival (Cooper et al., 1994). Other surface-level characteristics that had non-significant relationships with performance include: previous held management level of ET members, whether the ET member had experience in not-for-profit organizations or had not been in the labor force (Cooper et al., 1994). This leaves only two surface-level characteristics that have been shown to significantly influence ET and venture performance: educational background and industry experience.

Despite the fact that ET research has, largely, focused on surface-level characteristics, it is only a part of ET heterogeneity as illustrated by research which linked surface-level characteristics and organizational performance via unmeasured deep-level psychological constructs (for example, cognitive style or risk aversion; Eisenhardt and Schoonhoven, 1990; Hambrick and D'Aveni, 1992). This practice of assuming that surface-level characteristics are proxies for psychological constructs is unfortunate as researchers have shown the effect of surface-level heterogeneity is reduced over time as the ET engages in problem-solving and decision-making (for example, Glick et al. 1993; Harrison et al., 1998; 2002). Whereas the effect of heterogeneity based on deep-level characteristics (for example, personality, values and attitudes) is sustainable (Harrison et al., 1998; 2002). As surface-level heterogeneity is independent of deep-level heterogeneity, deep-level characteristics cannot be approximated from surface-level characteristics. Furthermore, scholars have suggested that deep-level characteristics have stronger effect on ET performance (Harrison et al., 1998; 2002; Hollenbeck et al., 2004). The use of surface-level characteristics may have been based on ease of use and collection (Bantel and Jackson, 1989; Carpenter et al., 2004; Hambrick, 1994). Thus, deep-level characteristics need to be examined separately when exploring the *black box* of the ET (Birley and Stockley, 2000).

Over time as the ET engages in problem-solving and decision-making, the effect of heterogenic surface-level characteristics decreases (Glick et al., 1993; Harrison et al., 1998; 2002). This may be beneficial to ET and venture performance as the ET develops and as tasks become routine which are handled more efficiently by a homogeneous ET. However, need for a heterogeneous ET may still exist as the heterogeneous ET makes more effective decisions because it considers more options in the decision-making process (for example, Eisenhardt and Schoonhoven 1990). Thus, as time erases surface-level characteristics, the need for deep-level characteristics still exist. For that reason, changes in ET composition may be desired to maintain, both surface- and deep-level, heterogeneity and homogeneity for effective and efficient ET performance. Scholars suggest that two pitfalls of ETs are the failure to consider the ET composition will change over time and the lack of mechanisms to adjust the ET to maintain an appropriate level of heterogeneity and homogeneity in order to stimulate constructive conflict while still being able to function (Amason, 1996; Kamm and Nurick, 1993; Timmons and Spinelli, 1999).

Both constructive and destructive conflicts arise from heterogeneity. This implies that heterogeneity should be limited. However, homogeneity, based on both surface- and deep-level characteristics, has consequences that may impair the ET and venture performance. Without (constructive) conflict, the ET may experience *groupthink* (Janis, 1972). An ET that suffers from groupthink unknowingly limits the range of options considered and limits information processing (Eisenhardt and Schoonhoven, 1990; Finkelstein and Hambrick, 1990). Despite this aversion of ET homogeneity, some homogeneity must exist for the ET to be able to function. It is too much homogeneity that is the issue. Heterogeneity leads to conflict; and conflict takes time, making the ET slower and less efficient in responding to the environment or other challenges (Hambrick et al., 1996; O'Reilly et al., 1993). Yet, several researchers have emphasized that heterogeneity is vital to ET and venture performance (Bantel and Jackson, 1989; Cooper and Daily, 1997; Eisenhardt and Schoonhoven, 1990; Hambrick et al., 1996). This is because through constructive conflict, the ET develops more comprehensive decisions based on richer information and different perceptions, gains a better understanding of the problems and develops more options for action (Eisenhardt et al., 1997). This requires that destructive or affective conflict (that is, personal attacks) and power and politics are limited as these consume time and make the ET less effective and efficient (Amason and Sapienza, 1997; Hambrick et al., 1996; Jehn, 1995; Pelled et al., 1999).

Changes in the environment or in the venture's development may require the ET to shift the distribution of power within the ET, permanently or temporarily. Power is the capacity to influence others (Robbins and Judge, 2008). A shift in the distribution of power within the ET may run contrary to the motivations of some ET members who may desire power for the sake of power (Timmons and Spinelli, 1999). These individuals will seek to concentrate power through the means of political behavior (that is, restricting information). Political behaviors are self-serving activities that are not required as part of one's organizational role (Robbins and Judge, 2008). For example, as an individual pursues a political goal of achieving power by restricting information or intentionally misleading the ET, the ET and venture performance will be negatively impacted as the ET cannot consider the necessary information for effective decision making. Thus, political behaviors in the ET reduce the shared commitment, as well as ET and venture performance.

Conflict is not the cause of politics, but the concentration of power is the cause of politics (Eisenhardt and Bourgeois, 1988). Conflict over venture goals or other important issues pertaining to the venture provides the ET with opportunity to communicate ET member expectations, decide on common goals that all ET members will work for, establish a shared commitment, and make more comprehensive decision-making by considering more perceptions, information, and alternatives (for example, Eisenhardt et al., 1997; Eisenhardt and Schoonhoven, 1990; Finkelstein and Hambrick, 1990). This way, communication may enhance ET and venture performance (Watson et al., 1995; Cohen and Bailey, 1997). However, disagreement over these issues and, especially, lack of communication to resolve these issues within the ET may lead, directly, to lower venture performance (West and Meyer, 1998). Continued communication rich in nature, such as face-to-face communication, leads to ET integration, more comprehensive decision-making, and facilitates coordination of interdependent tasks, which, in turn, results in better ET and venture performance (Glick et al., 1993; Hambrick, 1994).

The need for communication to 'iron out' differences in perspectives of the world (paradigms), interpretations and expectations for the venture and ET participation depends on the degree of heterogeneity within the ET. For example, as the ET communicates and becomes a socially integrated unit that reacts faster and is more flexible, efficient and effective because the ET, through its developed problem-solving skills and communicated aspirations, may allocate time and energy to where it will have the most impact (Smith et al., 1994). While ET homogeneity benefits the speed of decision-making, it comes at the cost of actions of less magnitude compared to a heterogeneous ET (Hambrick, 1994; Hambrick et al., 1996). This suggests that ET heterogeneity–homogeneity is a double-edged sword (Hambrick et al., 1996; Milliken and Martins, 1996). Thus, ET composition is a key determinant of ET and venture performance.

The purpose of this chapter was to contribute to the entrepreneurship literature by presenting a more comprehensive literature-based definition of entrepreneurial teams than what currently exists in the literature and to stimulate future research by discussing how the external environment, ET composition, conflict, power and politics, and communication influence ET and venture performance. Common to the five issues pertaining to the ET discussed in this chapter is that they illustrate how important an appropriate balance between heterogeneity and homogeneity is for ET and venture performance. Perhaps most importantly, the contribution of the collective considerations made in this chapter is that future ET research should seek to identify what is an appropriate balance between heterogeneity and homogeneity in the surface- and deep-level characteristics needed for an ET to stimulate constructive conflict, while avoiding destructive conflict and political behavior.

REFERENCES

Aldrich, H.E., N.M. Carter and M. Ruef (2002), 'With very little help from their friends: gender and relational composition of startup teams', in W.D. Bygrave (ed.), *Frontiers of Entrepreneurship*, Wellesley, MA: Babson College, pp. 156–69.

Amason, A. (1996), 'Distinguishing the effects of functional and dysfunctional conflict on strategic decision making: resolving a paradox for top management teams', *Academy of Management Journal*, **39** (1), 123–48.

Amason, A.C. and H.J. Sapienza (1997), 'The effects of top management team size and interaction norms on cognitive and affective conflict', *Journal of Management*, **23** (4), 495–517.

Amason, A.C., R.C. Shrader and G.H. Tompson (2006), 'Newness and novelty: relating top management team composition to new venture performance', *Journal of Business Venturing*, **21** (1), 125–48.

Bantel, K. and S. Jackson (1989), 'Top management and innovation in banking: does the composition of the top team make a difference?', *Strategic Management Journal*, **10**, 107–24.

Baum, J.A.C. and B.S. Silverman (2004), 'Picking winners or building them? Alliance, intellectual, and human capital as selection criteria in venture financing and performance of biotechnology startups', *Journal of Business Venturing*, **19** (3), 411–36.

Birley, S. and S. Stockley (2000), 'Entrepreneurial teams and venture growth', in D.L. Sexton (eds), *The Blackwell Handbook of Entrepreneurship*, Oxford: Blackwell Business, pp. 287–307.

Carpenter, M.A., M.A. Gelekanycz and W.G. Sanders (2004), 'Upper echelons research revisited: antecedents, elements, and consequences of top management team composition', *Journal of Management*, **30** (6), 749–78.

Chowdhury, S. (2005), 'Demographic diversity for building an effective entrepreneurial team: is it important?', *Journal of Business Venturing*, **6** (20), 727–46.
Cohen, S.G. and D.E. Bailey (1997), 'What makes teams work: group effectiveness research from the shop floor of the executive suite', *Journal of Management*, **23** (3), 239–90.
Cooper, A.C. and A.V. Bruno (1977), 'Success among high-technology firms', *Business Horizons*, **20** (2), 16–22.
Cooper, A.C. and C.M. Daily (1997), 'Entrepreneurial teams', in D.L. Sexton and R.W. Smilor (eds), *Entrepreneurship 2000*, Chicago, IL: Upstart, pp. 127–50.
Cooper, R.G., F.J. Gimeno-Gascon and C.C. Woo (1994), 'Initial human and financial capital as predictors of new venture performance', *Journal of Business Venturing*, **9** (5), 371–95.
Devine, D.J. and J.L. Philips (2001), 'Do smarter teams do better: a meta-analysis of cognitive ability and team performance', *Small Group Research*, **32** (5), 507–33.
Eisenhardt, K.M. and L.J. Bourgeois (1988), 'Politics of strategic decision-making in high-velocity environments: toward a midrange theory', *Academy of Management Journal*, **31** (4), 737–70.
Eisenhardt, K.M. and C.B. Schoonhoven (1990), 'Organizational growth – linking founding team, strategy, environment, and growth among U.S. semiconductor ventures, 1978–1988', *Administrative Science Quarterly*, **35** (3), 504–29.
Eisenhardt, K.M., J.L. Kahwajy and L.J. Bourgeois (1997), 'How management teams can have a good fight', *Harvard Business Review*, **75** (4), 77–85.
Ensley, M.D. and C.L. Pearce (2001), 'Shared cognition in top management teams – implications for new venture performance', *Journal of Organizational Behavior*, **22** (2), 145–60.
Filley, A.C., R.J. House and S. Kerr (1976), *Managerial Process and Organizational Behavior*, Glenview, IL: Scott Foresman.
Finkelstein, S. and D.C. Hambrick (1990), 'Top management team tenure and organizational outcomes: the moderating role of managerial discretion', *Administrative Science Quarterly* (35), 484–503.
Foo, M.D., H.P. Sin and L.P. Yiong (2006), 'Effects of team inputs and intrateam processes on perceptions of team viability and member satisfaction in nascent ventures', *Strategic Management Journal*, **27** (4), 389–99.
Francis, D.H. and W.R. Sandberg (2000), 'Friendship within entrepreneurial teams and its association with team and performance', *Entrepreneurship: Theory and Practice*, **25** (5), 5–25.
Glick, W.H., C.C. Miller and G.P. Huber (1993), 'The impact of upper-echelon diversity on organizational performance', in G.P. Huber and W.H. Glick (eds), *Organizational Change and Redesign: Ideas for Insights for Improving Performance*, New York: Oxford University Press, pp.176–214.
Hackman, J.R. (1987), 'The design of work team', in J.W. Lorsh (ed.), *Handbook of Organizational Behavior*, Englewood Cliffs, NJ: Prentice-Hall, pp. 315–42.
Hambrick, D.C. (1994), 'Top management groups: a conceptual integration and reconsideration of the "team" label', *Research in Organizational Behavior*, **16** 171–214.
Hambrick, D.C. (2007), 'Upper echelons theory: an update', *Academy of Management Review*, **32** (2), 334–43.
Hambrick, D.C. and R.A. D'Aveni (1992), 'Top team deterioration as part of the downward spiral of large corporate bankruptcies', *Management Science*, **38**, 1445–66.
Hambrick, D.C. and P.A. Mason (1984), 'Upper echelons: the organization as a reflection of its top managers', *Academy of Management Review*, **9**, 193–206.
Hambrick, D.C., T.S. Cho and M. Chen (1996), 'The influence of top management team heterogeneity on firms' competitive moves', *Administrative Science Quarterly*, **41**, 659–84.
Harrison, D., A.P. Kenneth, H.J. Gavin and A.T. Florey (2002), 'Time, teams and task performance: changing effects of surface- and deep-level diversity on group functioning', *Academy of Management Journal*, **45** (5), 1029–45.
Harrison, D.A., K.H. Price and M.P. Bell (1998), 'Beyond rational demography: time and the effects of surface- and deep-level diversity on work group cohesion', *Academy of Management Journal*, **41** (1), 96–107.
Hollenbeck, J.R., D.S. Derue and R. Guzzo (2004), 'Bridging the gap between I/O research and HR practice: improving team composition, team training, and team task design', *Human Resource Management*, **43** (4), 353–66.
Jackson, S.E. (1992), 'Consequences of group composition for the interpersonal dynamics of strategic issue processing', *Advances in Strategic Management*, **8**, 345–82.
Janis, I.L. (1972), *Victims of Groupthink: Psychological Studies of Foreign Policy Decisions and Fiascoes*, Boston, MA: Houghton Mifflin.
Jehn, K.A. (1995), 'A multimethod examination of the benefits and detriments of intragroup conflict', *Administrative Science Quarterly*, **40**, 256–82.
Kamm, J.B. and A.J. Nurick (1993), 'The stages of team venture formation: a decision-making model', *Entrepreneurship: Theory and Practice*, **17** (2), 17–28.
Kamm, J.B., J.C. Shuman, J.A. Seeger and A.J. Nurick (1990), 'Entrepreneurial teams in new venture creation: a research agenda', *Entrepreneurship Theory and Practice*, **14** (4), 7–17.
Katzenbach, J.R. (1997), 'The myth of the top management team', *Harvard Business Review*, **75** (6), 82–91.

Katzenbach, J.R. and D.K. Smith (2003), *Teams – Der Schlüssel zur Hochleistungsorganisation*, Frankfurt and Wien: Ueberreuther.
Lechler, T. and H.G. Gemünden (2003), *Gründerteams – Chancen und Risiken für den Unternehmenserfolg*, Heidelberg and New York: Physica.
Levine, J.M. and R.L. Moreland (1990), 'Progress in small group research', *Annual Review of Psychology*, **41** (1), 585–635.
Milliken, F.J. and L.L. Martins (1996), 'Searching for common threads: understanding the multiple effects of diversity in organizational groups', *Academy of Management Review*, **21** (2), 402–34.
Murray, A.I. (1989), 'Top management group heterogeneity and firm performance', *Strategic Management Journal*, **10** (special issue), 125–41.
O'Reilly, C.A., R.C. Snyder and J.N. Boothe (1993), 'Effects of executive team demography on organizational change', in G.P. Huber and W.H. Glick (eds), *Organizational Change and Redesign: Ideas for Insights for Improving Performance*, New York: Oxford University Press, pp. 147–75.
Pelled, L.H., K.M. Eisenhardt and K.R. Xin (1999), 'Exploring the black box – an analysis of work group diversity, conflict and performance', *Administrative Science Quarterly*, **44**, 1–28.
Robbins, S.P. and J.A. Judge (2008), *Essentials of Organizational Behavior*, Upper-Saddle River, NJ: Pearson.
Rumelt, R.P. (1991), 'How much does industry matter?', *Strategic Management Journal*, **2**, 167–85.
Smith, K.G., K.A. Smith, J.D. Olian, H.P. Sims Jr, D.P. O'Bannon and J.A. Scully (1994), 'Top management team demography and process: the role of social integration and communication', *Administrative Science Quarterly*, **39** (3), 412–38.
Stewart, G.L. (2006), 'A meta-analytic review of relationships between team design features and team performance', *Journal of Management*, **32**, 29–54.
Timmons, J.A. and S. Spinelli (1999), *New Venture Creation: Entrepreneurship for the 21st Century*, New York: McGraw-Hill.
Vyakarnam, S., R. Jacobs and J. Handelberg (1999), 'Exploring the formation of entrepreneurial teams: the key to rapid growth business?', *Journal of Small Business and Enterprise Development*, **6** (2), 153–65.
Watson, W.E., L.D. Ponthieu and J.W. Critelli (1995), 'Team interpersonal process effectiveness in venture partnerships and its connection to perceived success', *Journal of Business Venturing*, **10** (5), 393–411.
West, G.P. and G.D. Meyer (1998), 'To agree or not to agree? Consensus and performance in new ventures', *Journal of Business Venturing*, **13** (5), 395–422.
West, P.G. (2007), 'Collective cognition: when entrepreneurial teams, not individuals, make decisions', *Entrepreneurship Theory and Practice*, **31** (1), 77–102.

51 Ten percenters: fast-growth middle-market firms in Britain

David Storey

FOREWORD

By Peter Morgan, Partner, Deloitte & Touche

This is the third part in our series of 'Ten Percenters' reports jointly contributed by Professor David Storey and Deloitte & Touche.

Professor Storey has examined middle market companies – with a turnover of between £5 million and £100 million – which have grown rapidly since the early 1990s. Since such rapid growth firms constitute about one in ten of all companies in this size they are referred to as 'ten percenters'.

This report probes into what makes these ten percenters tick. It investigates my analogy of a boat moving swiftly down the river: for this to happen there are two strategies – one is to have a capable crew and the other is to have the boat backed by a strong current.

Professor Storey finds that it is demand within the marketplace which is the factor most crucial to the ten percenter. He provides a fascinating insight into the variety of 'market niches' which ten percenters occupy. However, what makes this report interesting is that while there is almost a uniformity of focus upon growing niche markets – the elements of the 'current' in the boating analogy – there is much greater diversity in the internal organization of these firms. In short the 'crew' appear to be organized and managed in a variety of ways.

In my view and that of Professor Storey, the report raises the fundamental question of exactly what constitutes management skills in rapidly growing small and medium-sized enterprises (SMEs). If management skills are the ability to spot and develop a market opportunity then ten percenters have them in abundance. If it is about formal procedures, then a remarkable number of ten percenters are currently not 'well managed' and would never wish to be so.

KEY FINDINGS

This report has investigated, through face-to-face interviews with those owning/managing ten percenters, the factors underlying their success. We have focused in particular on two factors which appear to be key to their ability to grow rapidly: their ability to select and develop their marketplaces and how internally they organize and manage the business.

Our conclusions are clear. When we observe ten percenters at close quarters we see that almost all of them are in buoyant marketplaces, most frequently in particular niches which are experiencing rapid growth, and where they have sought to differentiate themselves from the competition in a variety of different ways. In a number of instances they have been 'sucked' along by large enterprises purchasing their output or by the sheer buoyancy of demand in their niche. Some have always been in that niche and have grown with its development, whereas others have seen the opportunity and switched to the niche or created the niche in the first place. Many of these niches have been created by the development of information technology, but by no means are ten percenters exclusively found in the high-technology sectors such as software houses and electronics manufacturers. In this sample of 46 companies only five would be described as high technology.

However, the presence of the niche is only a necessary condition; to be successful on the scale of these ten percenters requires something else. That something else, which again seems to characterize virtually all these firms, is an understanding of what the customer requires and a determination, almost regardless of cost, to satisfy that requirement. Almost always the requirement is perceived as 'quality'. Interpretation of quality varies markedly from market to market – sometimes it is reliability, other times it is the introduction of new products and sometimes it is design. However, it is almost never price and price alone. The skill seems to be to isolate and identify a market niche and provide something which is not provided by competitors. It is this which means that the price is but one of the factors influencing customer choice, rather than being the exclusive factor.

A Kaleidoscope of Cultures

The above paragraph illustrates a remarkable homogeneity of approach to customers. This is in almost complete contrast to the ways in which these businesses are internally organized. While some companies are managed in a highly formal and structured way, placing emphasis upon teams, training, specification of objectives and monitoring, others eschew such practices. For them, their success depends upon being 'light on their feet' and 'faster than the competition'. Being 'well managed' is equated to a slow-moving dinosaur. The culture is informal, entrepreneurial; the management style is aggressive, dynamic and leader-orientated. These businesses describe their own internal culture as being relaxed, informal, 'shirt sleeves', 'hands on', 'laid back', 'fun'. However, we have an almost equal number which are highly professionally run, divisionalized, devolved and training-based. This diversity of approach and internal organization reflects a virtual kaleidoscope of cultures.

All this raises the question of exactly what constitutes managerial skills. Venture capitalists making decisions about growing businesses in which they choose to invest, place considerable emphasis upon the quality of formal management. Our observation from this research is that if formal management is the ability to spot and develop a market opportunity, then almost all ten percenters are well managed. If, however, management is about formal procedures, about controls, appraisals, training, market research, job descriptions and meetings, then there are a significant proportion of the UK's ten percenters which do not qualify as being at all well managed.

Having conducted the research we feel it points to the need to re-appraise exactly what constitutes good management particularly as regards smaller high-growth companies. If it is good performance which is sought, our research suggests that the premier quality is the ability to identify and satisfy the market, that is, to locate the boat in the fast-moving current. Of course, it is important to ensure that the 'crew' pull in broadly the same direction but there appears to be a striking diversity of methods by which this can be achieved – by no means always according to the management textbooks.

BACKGROUND

In 1996 we produced 'The ten percenters: fast growing SMEs in Great Britain'. Using the ICC/One Source UK companies database we found there were 7203 companies as:

- limited
- non-subsidiaries
- with a turnover of between £5 million and £100 million.
- with at least four years of records.

Of these, 708 or 9.8 per cent generated growth in turnover of at least 30 per cent per annum over each of the previous four years. It is these 9.8 per cent of businesses which achieved rapid growth which are referred to as the 'ten percenters'.

The first report examined the financial and performance characteristics of the ten percenters in comparison with the remainder of companies. It showed ten percenters were more likely to be:

- established in the 1980s and early 1990s, rather than being longer-established businesses
- located in London and the South East rather than, for example, the East Midlands
- concentrated in sectors such as the manufacture of office machinery and data-processing equipment or business and recreational services.

The second report showed the results of telephone interviews with a sample of 156 out of the original 708 firms identified as ten percenters in the 1996 study. It found that, among ten percenters, those which grew particularly rapidly were characterized as:

- being in buoyant niche markets
- focusing particularly heavily upon customer service
- focusing upon quality rather than price.

We were less able to link performance to indications of good managerial practice such as:

- training
- customer satisfaction monitoring
- profit sharing schemes
- innovation.

Peter Morgan in his foreword to the second report observed:

> Using a boating analogy, there are two strategies (for making the boat go faster) – one is to have a capable crew and the other is to have the boat backed by a strong current. Our observation is that the Ten Percenters place more emphasis upon locating the boat correctly in the current than on the quality of the crew.

This chapter seeks to investigate this somewhat controversial statement. In the analogy we view the market as reflecting the 'current' and the 'crew' as reflecting the organizational tightness and managerial formality of the business.

THIS RESEARCH

While the second 'Ten Percenters' report covered a wide range of issues, we now focus much more tightly upon:

- sectors and markets
- strategy
- management of people
- company culture.

Whereas the second report utilized telephone interviews with 156 firms, this report is compiled from in-depth conversations with (normally) one senior director of the business. These conversations took between one and three hours and were tape-recorded. Such conversations were undertaken on a face-to-face basis with 46 ten percenters and constitute the raw material for this report.

SECTORS AND MARKETS

The first 'Ten Percenters' report demonstrated that fast-growing medium-size companies were found in a wide variety of sectors. While they were more concentrated in some sectors than in others, identifying fast-growth companies by focusing upon a narrow range of specific sectors would miss the vast bulk of ten percenters.

The second report identified three key findings relating to markets:

- Exceptional ten percenters have invariably increased their market share as well as having benefited from a growing market.
- Firms reporting increased market share are also much more likely to report rapid profit growth.
- Those firms selling in the USA are less likely to report fast growth in profits than those selling into Germany/France.

This research serves to highlight the difference between sectors and markets. The former are classifications, generally for statistical purposes, of aggregating firms. Markets, however, reflect the sales and purchasing patterns of particular, often small, groups of buyers and sellers. An illustration of a sector might be food manufacturing, within which sales may be growing no faster than in manufacturing as a whole. However, within that sector there are highly buoyant marketplaces which contain significant numbers of ten percenters.

A second illustration might be a firm, the market for whose services is driven by the information technology revolution. Such a firm might specialize in the laying of electrical cabling, and so gets classified sectorally as being in the construction sector. Equally, firms in the retailing and distribution of computer software and hardware are classified sectorally as distributors, and so are classified as being in the same sectors as those distributing products where demand is significantly less buoyant. It should be clear that sectors and marketplaces are therefore very different.

Our task in this section is to examine the nature of marketplaces served by ten percenters, recognizing that these may be spread over a wide variety of sectors.

Expanding

Almost every ten percenter is selling into a marketplace which is experiencing significant expansion. We have only two instances of ten percenters achieving their growth by substantially increasing their market share in a declining marketplace. This is a most important finding since it implies that a necessary – but clearly not sufficient – condition of being a ten percenter is being located in a growing marketplace.

Niches

Approximately three-quarters of ten percenters are in highly specific niches. Some occupy a number of niches, often in separate companies within the group, and in some instances the niches are more clearly defined than in others. Very few occupy wide marketplaces and compete directly with large enterprises. Of those which do not occupy niches, the biggest concentration is among those distributing/retailing computer and information technology (IT)-related products and services. Here, we assume, the market is so buoyant that the requirement for a niche is minimal.

Almost all respondents recognize the importance of the niche. They seek to both differentiate their product/service within the niche and to defend it:

> We don't want to be over-successful in capturing the market. We want to be a minor irritant to the multinationals rather than make them so sick that they react . . . There is always money in a niche, rather than following everybody else. If you have something nobody else has – and you have 100% or 50% of it – that's how you make money. (Retailer and wholesaler)

What is most striking is that many of these niches exist because of a whole range of special circumstances. The skill which we observe among ten percenters is to identify the niche and then ensure that customer needs are met in full.

Seven illustrations of these special circumstances include:

- changing tastes and social change
- growth of own labels
- outsourcing

- preferred supplier relationships
- local circumstances
- new technologies
- legislation.

Changing tastes and social change

A number of ten percenters have grown on the basis of changing tastes and the subsequent creation of new marketplaces. These are most familiar in the case of firms with new technologies, but there are many less obvious, yet in aggregate probably more important, changes which create market opportunities. One retailer said:

> The market for pet food has increased dramatically over the last ten years, everybody used to feed pets with scraps but now they want to give them proper cat and dog food . . . People have more money and are willing to spend more on their pets and think nothing of spending £14 on a bag of dog food whereas years ago that was too much. (Retailer)

Another illustration is the growth of single person households. This has influenced the demand for food, so that a number of foodstuffs which previously were produced in family packs are now produced in individual packs to satisfy the demands of individuals living on their own.

A third example is the considerable growth in travel and leisure activities. There are several firms in these sectors which have grown, partly on the back of overall growth in these sectors, but almost all of them have sought to specialize. Travel agents which are ten percenters, have all chosen to specialize geographically, or in producing 'customized' leisure or business travel packages.

Own labels

At least five firms are 'ten percenters' because of the retail power of supermarkets, which are seeking to develop 'own labels'. One respondent said:

> The market's changed in that the multiples have made strategic decisions to build their own label business and squeeze out the brands. They have introduced two-tier brands, they have a very good quality copy of the brand and are also trying to compete with the discounters. So the market's changed for us – there has been a greater emphasis on own label which has helped us to develop the business . . . It's not going to disappear, it's here to stay, because it's now too profitable for the supermarkets . . . I can only see it increasing into other product lines. (Food manufacturer)

The role of the supermarkets has been to identify, very often small, enterprises serving a local market but producing a high-quality product, and to offer to take not only the whole of the firm's current output, but generally substantially more. Supermarkets, therefore, are like a giant vacuum cleaner sucking up a few hand-picked suppliers capable of satisfying their stringent quality requirements. While margins may be thin on this type of work, the sheer scale of the orders adds considerably to the profitability of the supermarket supplier.

Outsourcing and preferred supplier relationships

A not dissimilar development is the growth of outsourcing. Many large enterprises now seek to outsource many of their services, stimulating a demand for organizations able to supply individuals with skills in information technology, provision of secretarial services, and so on.

A second type of growth for ten percenters is the trend among giant enterprises towards having a small number of 'preferred suppliers'. These suppliers are normally required to undertake quite a wide range of activities. To become a preferred supplier requires them to obtain this expertise, often achieved by purchasing other companies. As in the case of the supermarkets, giant enterprises provide a powerful incentive for some small firms to become substantially larger over a short period of time.

Local circumstances

Buoyant niche markets can exist because of special local circumstances. Examples include house builders in geographical areas which are less prone to cyclical downturns. Other instances include the growth of a transport firm that expanded to satisfy a special large local business.

New technologies

The most obvious example of the development of new markets within the last ten years has been the growth of the information technology industry. Not surprisingly, firms in this sector are well represented among ten percenters but, as noted earlier, they do not always appear in the most obvious 'sectors'. Of course there are software houses which produce specialized computer programs, but almost as interesting is the presence among ten percenters of firms stimulated by information technology, but in conventional 'sectors'. For example, ten percenters selling computer equipment and software are found in the distribution sector; firms installing cabling to enable data transmission to take place are found in the construction sector. Those using IT for producing labels for retail outlets are in the printing industry.

Furthermore, ten percenters in highly conventional industries have often obtained a huge competitive boost from installing new IT systems. One manufacturer said:

> Four years ago our IT department was someone working in a farmhouse in Hereford and one other person . . . now we have 15 direct staff and four subcontractors . . . We used to have manual books and tickets for each customer . . . now we have an autoplan system and we are working on shop floor data capture with our bar code swiping. (Manufacturer)

Indeed the embracing of new technologies, even by those outside the IT sector is a characteristic of ten percenters which we will discuss in more detail later on.

Legislation

Governments can be vitally important, often unintentionally, in creating new marketplaces. One example is health and safety legislation, a cause of considerable irritation to many ten percenters, but which has often acted to exclude competition. Food legislation in particular means that only those firms fully capable of compliance can remain in the marketplace. Firms may need to grow, often to a considerable size, in order to make it fully economic to comply with the legislation. In this respect some legislation can foster growth.

In another context a security company clearly recognized the role of government:

> The Thatcher government in the mid '80s made it clear to businesses that they were responsible for their own security and for looking after their own assets. Many businesses have been reliant on the police for crime prevention advice, but a market opportunity opened up when large businesses realised that things could not go on as they had in the past. (Services firm)

Finally, an IT specialist company which grew rapidly, focused on providing specialist programs and services to what were formerly public utilities. Since the UK was a world leader in privatization, and was followed by many other countries, this created a marketplace for this firm to sell its expertise.

The central point here is that ten percenters are heavily concentrated in these special niche markets where there is clearly considerable opportunity to grow. What is also observable is that these reflect not single changes in the economy but a wide and diverse set of developments each of which facilitates the growth of a small number of ten percenters. These are not macroeconomic developments affecting large numbers of enterprises, but instead a diverse range of special changes going on within the economy reflecting changes in tastes, the ability of firms themselves to be innovative, and efforts by larger enterprises to become competitive in world marketplaces.

Although it is not true in all instances, in many cases there is a huge market 'suck' factor which pulls these ten percenters along. Sometimes, as in the case of software, it is the enormous growth in the market as a whole and the opportunity which this provides even for smaller players. In other cases it is the key role played by major businesses which have 'nurtured' hand-picked ten percenters which have made the transition into middle-sized companies. Clearly this is apparent in the growth of supermarkets, but it is also apparent elsewhere, most notably in the development of outsourcing. Obtaining the goodwill and then the associated orders of a multinational was as vital for the security firm as was becoming a preferred supplier for the engineering firm.

Competitive

It might be expected that these marketplaces would all be highly competitive and in the majority of cases they are. In some marketplaces the competition is clearly fierce, but in others this is less the case. For example, in several of the buoyant markets supply seems unable to keep pace with demand as one respondent said, 'I think there is room for all of us at the moment' (Retailer), and another said, 'The market is competitive, but with so few suppliers it isn't cut-throat' (Manufacturer).

We also observe that markets in which competition seems to be most fierce, or is perceived as being most fierce, are those where the niches are widest. The more that ten percenters are able to both narrow the niche, yet still ensure that demand is buoyant, the less competitive is the marketplace.

The ability of ten percenters to achieve this over a long period of time must be open to question but, in the vast majority of the cases which we have examined, those firms have achieved exceptional rates of growth in sales over a five or six-year period. It certainly suggests these markets are far from transitory.

Cyclical

In the majority of cases these marketplaces are not particularly susceptible to macro-economic and other changes. However, in some instances there is a strong sensitivity to the economy. Illustrations of this are reflected in the comments of the recruitment company:

> Firms in our sector seem to feel the economic cycles incredibly strongly. At the moment we are having a surge out of all proportion to economic growth in the country as a whole. Then, as soon as there is a slow down, we will go through a bad period out of all proportion. During the last recession recruitment companies were closing down left, right and centre. (Services firm)

Exporters

Almost two-thirds of the ten percenters export to some extent, but only about half are significant exporters. Those which do, vary the dependence they have upon the export market. The majority of firms focus heavily upon Europe, rather than wider export markets. Their experiences in selling overseas are worth reporting. Two general lessons emerge:

- To be successful in Europe it is necessary to clearly differentiate the product from one European country to another and ideally to give the impression of being a French company when selling in France or a German company when selling in Germany.
- The American market is generally much more competitive than the European market. United States consumers are vastly more demanding as well as nationalistic, bordering upon jingoistic.

The following quotations reflect the above observations:

> The US is difficult because it is very, very big. The market works differently from the UK in terms of who you sell into and the customers are particularly demanding in terms of quality and price. (Manufacturer)

> The UK doesn't understand service . . . we should look at the US as an example to follow. (IT services firm)

> We have had our own particular problems in Germany, similar to many British companies. Germany is most peculiar. It's a fragmented market and Germans like German things. So, if you can make yourself look like a German company they are much more likely to come back to you than if they think you are British company. (Manufacturer)

> Europe is not necessarily an easier market than the United States. I'd say this is because of the different cultures we experience throughout Europe. I mean what's good for France is not necessarily good for Germany or Holland etc. Each country has its own different culture. (Manufacturer)

> The US market is highly competitive because it's a front line for any software developments, so that's quite challenging for us. (Software house)

> Europe is again different; it's made up of different languages, different cultures, different markets within countries. In Germany we have to operate or manage the whole of Eastern

> Europe via Germany as other people do. It can be difficult to sell to the French. Any whiff of the fact that you are not a French company can put their backs up. (Manufacturer)

Information technology firms find the USA particularly challenging. The market is enormous and buoyant but even ten percenters have found it extremely difficult to become well established. The strategies which they have adopted include the formation of alliances and seeking to appear as US companies – such as obtaining quotes on NASDAQ. Several felt that even the lack of an American accent on the telephone was a major hindrance. One said: 'We behave like an American company, as far as we report in dollars, we have a US presence, we are listed in American etc.' (Software house)

How Did They Get There?

Many ten percenters recognize that they arrived in their chosen marketplace through either good luck or having particular specialist knowledge which happened to be in high demand, or through trial and error. The role of luck in arriving in the marketplace should not be underestimated; indeed it is not underestimated by a number of the respondents:

> It was a big opportunity at the time, although I didn't identify it in such a clear fashion. I happened to get into the market before it was established. (Software company)

> To be fair we've been very fortunate. (Haulage contractor)

To imply an element of good fortune in identifying the niche does not, of course, imply a lack of awareness on the part of the business or its owners in exploiting that niche. In other words, although there may be a chance element in being within the niche, the skill of the ten percenters is to exploit the niche significantly better than the competition.

Perhaps this is most accurately reflected in a senior director talking about his business:

> If you listen to our Chairman he will say we were lucky, we were there at the right place at the right time and took advantage of the right technology. But I think we were clever enough to recognize that we had to use the latest techniques and we have a combination of highly capable technologies with highly capable businessmen, sometimes in the same skin. (Software House)

How, then, did ten percenters seek to develop their businesses? It is to the issue of strategy that we now turn.

STRATEGY

In the second 'Ten Percenters' report we found:

- Ten percenters regarded themselves as significantly better than their competitors in the area of customer service, understanding customer needs and quality of product or service.
- Among ten percenters, those performing most spectacularly were likely to view themselves as having a better understand of customer needs.

- Ten percenters do not seek to compete primarily in the areas of low selling prices or access to credit.

We now examine these areas in more detail. In particular, we seek to identify those strategies which ten percenters have used both to develop and to defend the niche markets which they occupy.

Quality

Almost all ten percenters view 'quality' as either their key comparative advantage, or at least a major comparative advantage which they have over their rivals. Only three firms did not view 'quality' as a key comparative advantage.

The term 'quality', however, means different things in different contexts. For example, a recruitment agency viewed its 'quality' as identical to its 'ethics': 'We operate an extremely high ethical standard and focus entirely on quality which makes us, from a pure business sense, relatively inefficient at times, but I think it has paid dividends in establishing the brand that we have' (Services firm).

On the other hand the notion of 'quality' employed by the engineering firm is much more associated with a formal quality standard such as ISO9000. It is also about an attitude of ensuring that the informal – almost measurable – quality is maintained:

> Product quality comes down to your quality department and you having somebody there who is prepared to stand up and say 'No, I'm not letting this go out the building in that state' . . . Here there is a constant conflict between production and quality and that is inevitable. The quality manager is looked upon as the prima donna of the industry, a bit like restaurants where the chef is the prima donna and there is a very good reason for it because he signs the release note to say the product meets the standard. In that respect he is the most important and has to be very strong willed – too damned strong willed sometimes! (Manufacturer)

However, for businesses in the service sector in particular, very different notions of quality exist. For example, for the electrical maintenance firm, the 'quality' which they provide is the guarantee that the customer could talk, 24 hours, to a technical specialist – not simply someone who took messages – who is able to help them in the event of a breakdown. In the case of a haulage firm, 'quality' was a guaranteed reliability of delivery. In other instances 'quality' meant a business which was run within the law. In some cases people would use phrases such as 'there's so many cowboys out there' – implying that a quality business was merely one which was not run by cowboys.

In almost all instances the notion of quality is clearly linked to satisfying the requirements of the customer. A total emphasis in almost all these businesses is the requirement of the customer. Ten percenters clearly recognize that the effort to retain customers is a fraction of that of obtaining new customers. While the nature of 'quality' differs from one business to another, the emphasis which is placed upon it is, for virtually all ten percenters, paramount.

Innovation

About half of ten percenters claim to be innovative, to the extent that it is a factor which significantly influences their competitiveness. Furthermore, where they are innovative, they view this as their key competitive advantage over their rivals.

The nature of that innovation varies considerably and it is *not* exclusively found in high-technology firms. For example, several food manufacturers were continually seeking to develop new products. One said: 'We have developed a revolutionary technology and are putting a huge amount of effort and energy into our research and development, building up highly advanced laboratories and licensing our technology to major companies around the world' (Manufacturer). In other instances the innovation is the fact that the service is not provided by anyone else: 'We've created our own niche by providing products and services which are not provided by any other participants in the marketplace. The skill in this case was identifying a service which was required but which was not being supplied anywhere else' (Services company).

It should be noted that innovation can take place in a wide variety of contexts. For example, a travel agent attributed its growth to a movement away from low-margin, high-volume activity, towards being the innovator in terms of assembling a tailored package of holidays to specific countries. Another had introduced a revolutionary comprehensive ticket system which they had developed in-house, and which was generating huge interest from both customers and larger travel agents.

In other cases innovation is more conventional such as the software firms which are seeking to continually update and develop new packages in an innovative marketplace. Here the key issue is to ensure that the customer returns to buy the next version of the updated software.

Innovation also relates to process rather than to product innovation. There are a striking number of ten percenters that have spent heavily on new IT systems which they are convinced will provide them with a huge competitive advantage over their rivals. One firm said:

> We are currently putting together a datafile with information on all distributors' products, stock, price and availability. We'll pool the data and maintain it. We've had three full-time people working on this project for a year and the file will be updated two or three times a day. Since 40 per cent of sales time is taken up with collecting information for a quote, this computer system will provide massive savings in producing efficient quotes. (Distribution company)

Price

As we found in our earlier work, almost none of these firms attribute their success in the marketplace to having, primarily, a price-based strategy. In about one-third of cases firms say price plays virtually no role and, so, for two-thirds of the firms price plays some, but very rarely indeed, a significant role.

The firms placing more emphasis upon price are those likely to be selling to a large powerful purchaser, rather than to a wide range of purchasers or to the general public. Even this generalization, however, is not appropriate in all instances with, for example, one general public retailer attributing its success to low prices.

In essence most ten percenters view competitiveness as a package in which price plays a role, but rarely the key or sole role. Indeed the skill of the business is to seek to identify a niche; the strength of that niche is reflected in the absence of price competition within that marketplace.

The special chemicals manufacturer summed it up best: 'It's not particularly price sensitive. There's no business in the world where price doesn't matter and buyers are getting tough, but yes, you don't have to be the cheapest if you've got the quality' (Manufacturer).

Other Differentiation Strategies

As noted above we can consider differentiation strategies as the 'mirror image' of price. The firms which are most successful at differentiating are those having to rely least upon price to give them their comparable advantage within the niche. We also noted that quality – in the widest sense – is the prime differentiation strategy and that innovation is also frequently used.

However there are a number of other strategies which are employed either as an alternative, or as a complement to, the innovation/quality approach. Several firms referred to the emphasis which they place upon marketing skills:

> We have been a seriously focused marketing company. A lot of investment has been put into marketing. That's why we are as successful as we are domestically in the UK, and around the world. We have invested heavily in marketing to get where we are now and will continue to do so. It's a very important part of the company's budget and our profile. (Software house)

At its most extreme, ten percenters seek to, and in one case have achieved, a major 'brand image'. One has achieved a brand which is in the top 100 world's most recognized brands and so clearly their logo is fiercely protected. But even at more modest levels, several ten percenters seek to develop brand recognition within their niche.

A second differentiation strategy has been the development of alliances:

> We look for areas in the marketplace where we can have something which is either unique or where we can build a partnership. We have actually built a partnership with 'X' which provides us with a way of growing the business in which they are prepared to help fund the project. It gives off extra business in other product lines and builds a relationship to guarantee to take our production from the new plant for up to five years. (Food manufacturer)

A third differentiation strategy is to focus upon ethical issues. As noted earlier some firms seem merely to regard their own firm as ethical because it is not run by a cowboy. Others however employ a rather tighter definition, emphasizing ethics in terms of a particular approach:

> We never do anything that would come back and bite you later on; stay whiter than white. There are so many opportunities when you have a growing business to take the view that it would be alright to sweep it under the carpet. If we had done that as a business we wouldn't have had a clean bill of health. We've never had anything that's come out of the woodwork that has made people worry. (Construction company)

Acquisition

About one-third of ten percenters plan to acquire businesses as a key element in their growth strategy. In addition, a small number seek to achieve organic growth by the development of new outlets.

Of the remainder, some have made an explicit decision not to continue their historically high growth rates and therefore the acquisition of new businesses is not a priority. Others have themselves been acquired and have therefore lost the power to acquire new businesses. Hence, it is only a minority of ten percenters who are seeking to grow in the future, that have the power to acquire but are seeking to achieve that growth purely organically.

Fairly typical is the following: 'I think our main challenge is to identify good acquisition targets. . .that will fit in with our existing businesses and which are available at the right price' (Manufacturer).

Although it would be unwise to view this as statistically significant, two of the ten percenters which have placed the greatest emphasis upon acquisition are in markets which are either exhibiting minimal growth or where uncertainty is considerable. One said: 'The market was actually declining as it's very mature. We achieved organic growth by making private businesses sweat that bit harder. The rest was growth through acquisition, it worked out at about 50:50' (Manufacturing company).

Another major acquirer is in the leisure market. It is constantly seeking to acquire new businesses because of the uncertainty and fast moving character of this marketplace.

In general, however, most ten percenters do not have a prime focus on acquisition, although several have made them in the last five years. Where these have been made they reflect a combination of hearing, often by chance on the grapevine, about a business and reorganizing so that it fits with the overall development of the core activity of their own enterprises.

Implementing Strategy

Strategy seeks to define and implement the competitive advantages of individual enterprises. When asked about these competitive advantages firms generally referred to the items identified above, most notably quality, innovation, service and marketing skills.

In addition, some others referred to the internal way in which the business was organised and, in particular, their ability to make decisions significantly more quickly than their larger rivals. The latter were characterized as rather cumbersome and bureaucratic compared with ten percenters which were 'quick on their feet'.

Two other notable comparative advantages referred to by businesses were the purchasing skills of the key entrepreneur. In one case these purchasing skills related to land acquisition for housing and in another the ability to purchase raw materials at favourable rates.

Another internal organizational advantage possessed by ten percenters was their information systems which enabled them to make not only better, but also quicker decisions.

Finally, but vitally important to many ten percenters, was attitude. It is clear that many are driven by hungry entrepreneurs and are characterized by aggressive selling. One said:

> Why we are so successful is intensity of management. We sell because we keep knocking on their doors and bothering them to death. If it means we have to be cheaper, then we're cheaper. If it means we have to provide better service then we make sure we do that. We've never given up the chase yet. We haven't won them all, but we're still chasing. (Printing company)

MANAGEMENT OF PEOPLE

This section identifies a number of characteristics of good 'textbook' or 'formal' management. The extent to which ten percenters achieve and implement these 'textbook' criteria are then assessed. Finally, a highly subjective formal management score for each firm is provided.

In short we are trying to provide the reader with a picture of the 'quality' of the management in these enterprises, in terms of formal management structure.

Training

In our previous work we found that approximately three-quarters of ten percenters provided some formal training. However, in the current survey we have examined this in more detail and feel that the 75 per cent figure may be an overestimate of the scale of workforce training.

Among our case studies, there are very few ten percenters which place staff training at the forefront of their activities. The spectrum of training usage is very wide indeed. For example, the following firms might be classified as providers of training even though they could hardly be regarded as a training-led organization. 'We've got an old chap that goes around looking at a bit of training and operations and does the job for us' (Retailer). Other ten percenters were even less training orientated: 'Not a lot is done it has to be said. Apprentices go on day release courses, but as far as everybody else is concerned we learn on the job' (Manufacturer).

It is also important to distinguish between workforce training and that of the management and directors of the business. It is clear that the more senior the individual the less likely they were to be in receipt of recent training. One managing director, after describing the training activity in his business, announced with clear pleasure: 'I'm even going on a half day course myself next month. . .if nothing else gets in the way' (Manufacturer).

There are also major sectoral differences. For example, in the software industry, and those using IT intensively, the key issue is to ensure that the IT professionals are highly aware of all new developments. Training and development are therefore at the forefront in these companies and, to some extent, this percolates through to the top management, who are more likely to devote time to training than those in more 'traditional' sectors. Nevertheless, the key point remains that the more senior people are less likely to be in receipt of training.

What is also interesting is that a number of the ten percenters which currently provide some training recognize this has begun only fairly recently. It also seems that in a number of cases it was a response to growth, rather than a cause of growth. Several companies referred to now having reached a scale at which it was important to 'get ourselves organized' and in this context the role of Investors in People (IIP) was important. This will be discussed later in more detail.

Training expenditure was also clearly influenced by the state of the business cycle so currently, when there are major labour shortages in many industries, training budgets are higher, as are profits. An engineering firm said:

> Training has always been dictated by profit. In a good year you're going to make more of it, in a bad year it's going to be the first thing you cut . . . I do take the long-term view; but I'm also realistic and it's easier to cut out a training programme than it is sending ourselves to see a customer. (Manufacturer)

No more than one in six ten percenters give a consistently high priority to training throughout the organization, even though well over half of them recognized that their people were their main asset. There are, perhaps, only three exemplars out of the 46 firms. One of these said:

> We take a lot of people without a background in our area so there are three stages in their development. The first stage is 'Step to Success', which is a fairly structured six months of their time in the firm in which they learn all the skills they need to do their job well. Then they go onto the career ladder. The second course is 'Management is Fun'. There's a lot of in-house training throughout provided by our small training department. Step three is the 'Freedom Initiative' in which everyone is given a chance to think about their career and how the company is run. We want the people with a bit of gumption to come through and even if they ruffle a few feathers when they initially state an opinion, we want them to present themselves as being ready for promotion. (Recruitment agency)

But this is definitely a minority response – most ten percenters either undertake no training at all or have only recently implemented changes in this direction, often as a 'we can't go on doing it this way' type of response to pressures. In perhaps up to half of all cases respondents make reference to having implanted changes during the past 12 months, employing consultants, training managers, human resource professionals, implementing or considering Investors in People.

Investors in People

Only four ten percenters have implemented Investors in People throughout the organization. Others have at least demonstrated an awareness of IIP but found their procedures were so short of the mark that they are unlikely to continue.

> We looked at Investors in People and we had a survey about a year ago which revealed considerable shortcomings in our training, which is inevitable because we didn't have any formal training programmes . . . we probably owe it to staff to give them a bit of formalized training, getting them to NVQs etc, which we shall be doing. Whether we go for IIP or not I don't know. If we do we've got a lot of things that we don't particularly think we need to do, like appraisals and that sort of stuff. (Retailer)

Objectives and Job Descriptions

A central function of Investors in People is to encourage the definition of aims and objectives at both a corporate and individual level, leading to definitions of job descriptions. The extent to which this takes place currently within ten percenters is very mixed. Less than two-thirds of firms clearly specify objectives for all managers throughout the organization. The spectrum of this ranges from on the one hand:

> All our senior managers are set objectives on a six-monthly basis. We had a major restructuring two years ago, a minor restructuring a year ago and are probably about to head into another restructuring. We are constantly redefining. It's a very fast moving market. (Services Company)

Or:

> The company has business objectives. It's broken down into sales and marketing objectives all the way down to the bottom guy. So where does he fit into that picture? If you don't have a mission statement at the top and you don't have objectives for the guy down the bottom, then it's a waste of time. (Manufacturer)

For other ten percenters a very different approach is adopted:

> The objectives and accountabilities of senior managers are ongoing. Any redefinitions happen frequently at informal meetings, normally in the local Indian restaurant. (Manufacturer)

Or:

> The objectives and accountabilities of senior managers are not written down. This is an entrepreneurial company and I wouldn't have ever recruited anyone who didn't know that their responsibility was to drive the company forward. (Retailer)

Another Ten Percenter, when asked about defining objectives and accountabilities said:

> That's an interesting question . . . I suppose not at all; it's an ongoing process. In a company like ours it doesn't work like that but it goes on all the time, but I suppose we don't do it formally, because everything is moving so fast. If we came to a standstill I suppose we might formalize it then. (Distributor)

This encapsulates the view of many ten percenters that their comparative advantage is being 'light on their feet'. The specification of objectives and the provision of job descriptions would be a self-imposed bureaucratic burden which would destroy, rather than enhance, their competitiveness.

In short, while some companies have clearly defined objectives and job descriptions which stem from this, it is not a dominant characteristic of ten percenters. Many feel that to do this would lose the flexibility which provides them with their comparative advantage. Probably the majority, however, are now either moving towards greater formality in this respect or already have such systems in place. Nevertheless the variation in practice is extremely wide.

Appraisals and Feedback

Ten percenters were questioned about the extent to which managers were provided with appraisals and formal feedback. Clearly if appraisals exist then there will be feedback, but a number of ten percenters indicated that, although formal appraisals did not take place, there were many opportunities for informal feedback. Overall, less than half the ten percenters had formal appraisals and feedback. Very few of these involved top management, and none had 360° appraisals involving the owner.

Among those emphasizing the informality of feedback one said: 'There is a strong subculture in any small society like this and if there are pockets of dissatisfaction it gets to us very quickly and my senior colleagues are very sensitive to this and we address it. We don't have committees dealing with these issues' (Manufacturer). Another said:

> I've been in companies where you have formal appraisals every six months, you set your objectives, you talk about what you've achieved. Nothing like that here. In this sort of environment if you've not done something then you get a rocket off Ray. 'Why hasn't it been done? I'd have thought you'd have sorted that out by now.' (Services company)

Use of Non-Executive Directors (NEDs)

Virtually two-thirds of ten percenters use NEDs. Two firms anticipate using them shortly and the remainder do not use them and have no plans to do so.

Of those using NEDs, opinions on their value are very mixed. Views are negative, particularly where NEDSs are 'imposed' by outside venture capitalists, or where they are viewed as 'pals' of the chairman. However, the negative comments do not only relate to these instances. One respondent said: 'I would really love to say "Yes it was really useful and beneficial". Unfortunately when you work in a business on a day-to-day basis as all the management do, the NED was an irritant because he comes and asks questions and we've got to answer them' (Manufacturer). Another said: 'We've had a problem with non-execs. You can't sack one without telling the market, so you've got to be very careful. I've seen too many of my friends get stitched up by non-execs, going to lunch, having a bottle of wine and telling stories out of school. You've got to be wary.' (Manufacturer)

However in other instances NEDs play a clearly positive role in 'going behind the scenes to smooth things over . . . which can be useful because they don't have an axe to grind with anybody', while others perform a useful specialist function in exercising a marketing or financial negotiation role. One said:

> When we're having discussions with our bankers, having a very senior ex-banker on the board is very useful, particularly interpreting some of the things that we may be getting from the banks etc . . . non execs also chair important committees such as the Audit Committee, the Remuneration Committee and bring a special perspective to this. (Services company)

Two other reservations about NEDs coming from a minority of firms were related to the choice of individuals. In several instances the NEDs were not truly 'external' individuals, but close family – often spouses or sons. This, it is felt, does not provide the independence of view expected from NEDs. A second reservation relates to the choice of outsiders. In several instances reference was made to the choice of 'X' as being one of the chairman's 'cronies', 'drinking partners', 'school friends', and so on. Again, it suggests that the independence of view which NEDs are expected to provide is not always expressed.

While more ten percenters have NEDs than do not, there is a striking diversity of opinions on their value. On balance, there may be more taking the positive view, but this is far from unanimous.

Management Score

In our efforts to summarize the formal management of ten percenters we have specifically examined formal management according to 11 indices:

- extent of meetings
- job descriptions
- use of market research
- training
- IIP
- defining objectives
- use of non-executive directors
- financial control
- succession plan
- feedback
- appraisals.

Using each of these 11 indicators for each company, we have produced a (highly subjective) score to reflect management formality. In the extreme case, totally informal firms would score zero and those which are highly structured would score ten.

The management scores generated demonstrate one key point. This is the extreme diversity among the ways in which these businesses are managed. While there are no businesses scoring zero, 1 or 2, there are a remarkable number where the businesses are managed in a fairly informal manner. Conversely, there are a number of businesses, broadly of a similar size, exhibiting similar growth rates and being of similar age and ownership structure, which are very much more formalized. It is this diversity of practice which is most striking.

Those who run their businesses informally (that is, have low scores) argue that the introduction of additional formality would undermine the entrepreneurial spirit and customer focus of their business. Yet it is clear that businesses which are equally customer focused and growing at similar rates do have much more formalized procedures.

It is clear that the achievement of rapid growth rates is, by no means, the exclusive prerogative of tightly organized and 'well-managed' businesses. In short, we conclude that the style, tightness and formal managerial procedures, among ten percenters, is not obviously related to firm performance. This is in stark contrast to our earlier findings on markets, where clear preconditions for being a ten percenter were market growth, customer focus, differentiation and quality.

COMPANY CULTURE

All respondents were asked about the 'culture' of their business. Four dimensions of culture are shown below:

Team → Autocratic
Relaxed → Aggressive
Formalized → Informal
Frantic → Analytic

The first is the extent to which the business is characterized by a team, or by an autocratic culture. Businesses which are classified towards the autocratic end of the scale are those where respondents described culture as being 'leader dominated', 'top down', 'paternalistic', 'entrepreneur dominated', 'people watching', and so on. This contrasts with businesses which are team dominated such as those who refer to the need to 'create an ownership culture', 'develop a team', 'ensure workers are interested', 'employ the best people', 'training based'.

- When businesses are classified according to this dimension, significantly more appear to be autocratic than team based.

The second dimension is the extent to which company culture varies from 'relaxed' to 'aggressive'. Illustrations of aggressive culture include phrases such as 'motivated', 'dynamic', 'to be the best', 'hard graft', and so on. This contrasts with businesses where the culture is more relaxed where phrases such as 'laid back', 'don't overwork', 'laissez-faire', 'typical software company' abound.

- On balance, there appear to be broadly similar numbers of firms viewing their company culture as being 'relaxed', compared with those viewing it as being 'aggressive'.

The third dimension is the extent to which the company culture reflects formality. Again at the opposite ends of the spectrum we have businesses which view themselves as highly informal. They place great emphasis upon informality and attempting to minimize bureaucracy. Many of these are businesses which view themselves as typical family businesses. They therefore see decisions being made by the family in informal circumstances, rather than through formal meetings. This contrasts with more formalized companies who are clearly divisionalized and devolved, and often financially led.

- Overall ten percenters appear to be characterized more by informal than formal cultural dimensions.

The fourth dimension of culture identified can be considered as the activity index. Some businesses' activities are very clearly frantic, constantly seeking to satisfy customer demands, facing consistent new challenges and often undergoing organizational re-structurings. This contrasts with others which seem to have a more analytical, even reflective, approach to business. Such firms are highly selective about the markets they enter and the customers they seek to serve.

- On balance ten percenters seem to be more characterized as being at the 'frantic', rather than the 'analytic' end of this spectrum.

In conclusion, there is clearly a diversity of business cultures among ten percenters. Overall however the business cultures seem to be characterized by autocracy, informality and activity, rather than by team-working, formality and analysis.

APPENDIX 1: PRIME SECTOR OF COMPANIES

1. Scientific instruments manufacturer
2. Distribution and retail
3. Staff recruitment
4. Food manufacturer
5. Housebuilder
6. Precision engineering
7. Food manufacturer
8. Software house
9. Travel agent
10. Electrical equipment manufacturer
11. Retailer (software)
12. Financial services
13. Food manufacturer
14. Software house
15. Distribution
16. Travel agent
17. Housebuilder
18. Food manufacturer
19. Haulage
20. Construction
21. Transport
22. Leisure
23. Security
24. Leather manufacturing
25. Mechanical engineering
26. Distribution
27. Distribution (computers)
28. Leisure
29. Distribution (computers)
30. Staff recruitment
31. Travel agent
32. Retailer and wholesaler
33. Software house
34. Travel and holidays
35. IT services
36. Electronic systems manufacturer
37. Retail and rental
38. Distribution
39. Metal manufacturer
40. Mechanical and electrical maintenance
41. Printing
42. Distribution
43. Distribution
44. Shopfitters
45. Furniture manufacturer
46. Chemicals manufacturer

APPENDIX 2: BROAD SECTORAL COMPOSITION

Manufacturing	16
Retail and distribution	11
Construction	3
Software	4
Other services	12
Total number of companies interviewed	46

52 Territorial entrepreneurship

Pierre-André Julien

INTRODUCTION

The study of entrepreneurship can be limited to the actions of the entrepreneurs during the start-up or transformation of their enterprises as have done a good number of studies on the subject. But, proceeding in this manner is to some extent to put ourselves in a positivist cause-and-effect approach. However, it cannot provide all of the answers such as those that would explain why there are localities or regions where a great number of enterprises are created that include long-lived innovative firms that grow rapidly, while others nearby with roughly the same resources and structures stagnate, and may even decline.

In order to account for these territorial entrepreneurial differences, then, we must dig further by taking into account the entrepreneur's background and his use of models that help orient his actions and get back to the traits theory already strongly criticized, when these are vague, not independent of the industrial sector in which the industry evolves, and change as the firm develops. We must also take into account at the second level the obstacles or advantages of the milieu and the networks that may or may not support the creation and transformation of enterprises. But, to better understand local or regional differences in entrepreneurship, we must go to a third level of analysis, involving the collective behaviour that the well-known economist Alfred Marshall at the close of the nineteenth century, called 'the industrial atmosphere' (Marshall, 1919), and which the specialists in entrepreneurship designate as the 'entrepreneurial culture', that is the socio-economic rules, conventions and ideologies, or again the dynamic complicities favouring the multiplication of new ideas, thereby increasing resources needed for their implementation and systematically supporting the action of entrepreneurs in their efforts to create and develop enterprises. We find ourselves in a constructivist approach that values complex and direct observation by taking into account the players' behaviour, including their intuition and their emotions, the development and the exchange of resources in complex networks, in particular rich information, and thus the multiplication of 'ideas in the air', or, finally, opportunities to be taken to innovate and grow.

To understand more deeply this entrepreneurship view, both in theory and in practice, we must discuss the five socio-economic actors that explain the type of territorial entrepreneurship and, then, integrate the three factors favouring the enterprise's distinction and then the dynamism of the territory. Thirdly, we define the mechanism that permits this collective process, explaining the difference between local or regional entrepreneurship, to close this short analysis with a metaphor to understand more easily this complexity.

THE FIVE ACTORS OF THE COLLECTIVE NATURE OF ENTREPRENEURSHIP

Let us start this short analysis by discussing the principal social players or socio-economic actors in entrepreneurship: the entrepreneur, his organization and the milieu that may or may not favour their actions. The *entrepreneur*, founder of the enterprise, is for a time the cornerstone of its development. His antecedents include various aptitudes occasioned by his family environment, the space for the socialization and transmission of values and habitus, by his acquaintances and by the acquisition of knowledge, whether in school or with his contacts in his work environment. It is there that he will find the models and different dynamisms and opportunities.

The second player is the *organization* (or the enterprise), constituting first the extension of the entrepreneur and his capacity to marshal resources, and then the implementation of his effort at appropriating market space. The organization parts from these gradually as the internal and external stakeholders, if not the external proprietors (stockholders), take on more significance. The organization becomes a system of social relations, or even a field of interest, but especially a combination of 'rare and inimitable' resources and skills such as interdisciplinary personnel of the enterprise and other complementary resources provided by upstream or downstream firms with which it negotiates and which, in particular combination, ensures its distinctiveness and hence its competitiveness with respect to the market.

The third player, the most directly social, is the *milieu* that constitutes a collection of local players based on knowledge and shared know-how. It consists of various institutions such as schools to train future employees, organizations offering development assistance or entrepreneurial clubs, an industrial structure diversified or complementary, and various partnership relations between the enterprises of goods and services. It constitutes a more or less dynamic place in the development of endogenous entrepreneurship, a reservoir of various resources (manpower, financing, infrastructure, but also model firms to imitate), a capacity to mobilize one's resources and, finally, meeting places (in particular, cafés, bars and restaurants) well organized between the players and with the outside. It could also be a place of conformism, curbing or blocking initiatives as well as dynamism. In short, it is a reducer of uncertainty and ambiguity, facilitating or not the research of opportunities, the multiplication and the distinction of firms and their development.

In particular, the milieu is a creator of *social capital* that can stimulate change in enterprises. This cannot only facilitate research, accessibility and mobilization of various resources (specialized manpower, preferred location, angel capital, and so on) at a preferential price, but generates reputation, an essential element in starting up an enterprise, and thus the ingredients of confidence (direct or indirect, through recommendation) to support the share, while weak experience cannot guarantee loans and a supply of various resources such as raw materials and second-hand equipment.

The milieu is concerned with the rules or norms, explicit or tacit, involving the legal, political and economic spheres, the *conventions* and even the ideology affecting the regional dynamism or the entrepreneurial culture. The entrepreneurial culture is this spirit shared in a region that gives recognition to and stimulates the creation of enterprises, changes and entrepreneurship.

To these three main actors, we must add time and the *environment*, which every entrepreneur must take into account. For example, it is generally easier to create an enterprise during buoyant demand than in a recession. Similarly, time may be a key if a given activity or innovation precedes the competition, as the word opportunity (*timeliness*) reminds us. Time and the environment create the industrial atmosphere where the entrepreneurial culture is transformed so as to multiply the complex resources, support the projects, and generate the enthusiasm thereby winning over the minds of a great number if not most of the entrepreneurs; on the other hand, an environment of suspicion and vituperation can block just about all initiatives.

THE THREE FACTORS TO STIMULATE ENTREPRENEURSHIP

The first factor which facilitates entrepreneurship is the presence of *rich information* shared by a great number of individuals, that is, information most often complex, cumulative and tacit that can be transformed into opportunity and innovation and which apprises us of various available resources for profiting from them. Rich information is the essential element in the transformation of organizations. It allows us to stay up to date with change, and even to get ahead of it through innovation.

The sharing of this rich information is greatly facilitated by *networks*. Networks are essentially disseminators and amplifiers of information for the enterprises. Their role is to obtain, sort out and adapt rich information for their members. They are like spider webs or meshed nets (as the saying goes: a *net* which *works*) made up of dozens of collaborators or players who are relatively knowledgeable on the needs of the interlocutor and thus make it possible to grasp and retain this rich information, letting pass current information of little or no interest. This information serves not only to learn more rapidly and more easily about various resources, but in seizing opportunities before others do. A dynamic milieu with strong social capital stimulates the exchange of information through the multiplication and enrichment of its networks, particularly if they are linked to other weak-signal networks or outside the region, with information that is not easy to understand owing to lack of trust and inattention, different from the usual representation and newer, but also sources of innovation.

Innovation, especially if it is global or diffuse (if it is concerned with all or most of the elements in the chain of values and with the product while leading the upstream and downstream firms), is the basis of the firms' distinctiveness to support their development and growth, whether for a convenience store or for a high-technology enterprise.

THE LOCAL OR REGIONAL ENTREPRENEURIAL MECHANISM

The presence of a particularly dynamic social capital, generated by the milieu and stimulated by effective networks, favours various forms of cooperation or complicity. These last facilitate obtaining and sharing various resources, among which are quality labour, advanced services, dynamic counsel and, finally, rich information provided by privileged links to organizations for economic valorization or for research and development, and

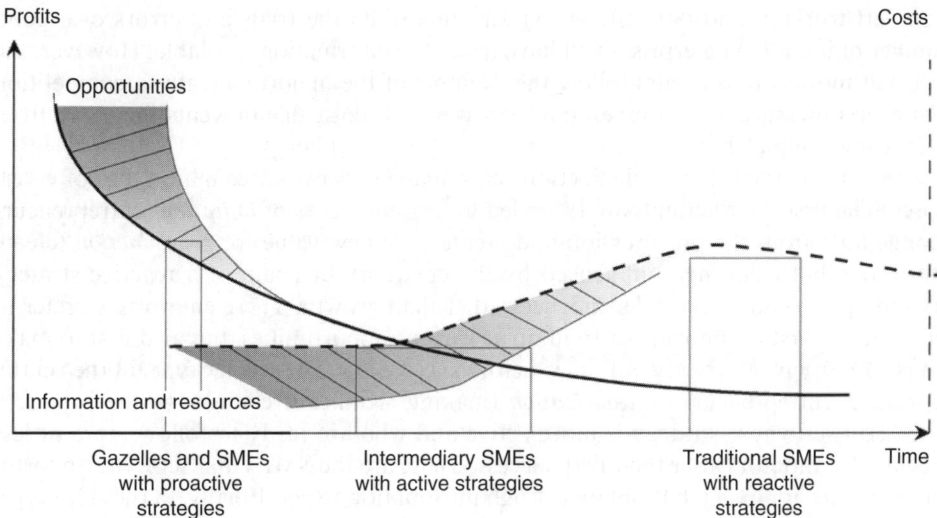

Figure 52.1 The impact of networking on profits and the cost of an opportunity or innovation, and on the share of proactive or high-growth firms within a region

innovation. All this makes possible the multiplication of the enterprises among which many set themselves apart on the markets as a result of renewed innovation, in particular the high-growth enterprises (the *gazelles*) that in turn stimulate other enterprises, through imitation if not emulation and new capacities of consultants, to create a particularly worthy circle increasing employment in the region.

Figure 52.1 provides a simplified view of this operation of the role of the milieu, networks and entrepreneurial culture and then the dynamic complicity. This two-dimensional figure shows a first curve on the left that represents the various business opportunities and a second curve on the right that is concerned with the necessary resources, in particular the informational resources for evaluating their cost/benefits. The first curve clearly indicates that it is generally very profitable to be first to seize new market opportunities or those derived from innovation. They can even be the condition for survival of certain firms. But the profits decrease as other entrepreneurs in turn seize some of these opportunities or innovations and reproduce them, since competition exerts a downward pressure on prices. This curve, then, decreases from left to right.

However, these new opportunities are uncertain; there are no guarantees that these meet the needs of the market or that the complementary elements satisfying them can be added rapidly. To diminish this uncertainty, the entrepreneur must resort to backup resources that will allow the advantages and the costs of each of these opportunities to be evaluated or which make it possible to bring these innovations to market. In other words, if being first to manufacture and sell a certain product can be highly profitable, the risks of making a mistake are high.

In order to limit this risk, more information must be obtained as well as assurances of complementary resources, which is costly. The second curve then begins by climbing from left to right, and dips after a certain time when the trials and errors of a good number of imitating enterprises will have made the information available. However, the fact that more entrepreneurs follow the example of the majority creates a competition that exerts pressure on resources and increases their cost; this prevents the curve from decreasing completely.

These two curves allow a distinction to be made between three main types of enterprises. The first, on the right, are those led by entrepreneurs of *imitation* (entrepreneurs change little from the previous job and create little new value) or *reproduction* (create little value but is strongly influenced by the creation), or again of a reactive strategy favouring continuity and independence rather than growth. These enterprises prefer to let others be first to innovate or to jump at various opportunities, but also first to make a mistake or have to try several times before succeeding. The second type, in the centre, represents entrepreneurs of *valorization* (making significant changes to the product), or enterprises whose strategy is more active and who are ready to follow more or less quickly the initiators after their first success. These are the SMEs that seize the opportunities with a certain lag, but obtain enough information to act. Finally, in the third type, on the left, we see entrepreneurs, the *adventurers* (great change on himself and value) or at least the firms having a proactive strategy and most likely to grow rapidly by grasping the opportunities and by innovating regularly. This last type includes the *gazelles*, which develop by quickly accepting challenges.

Normally, any territory generally has less than 10 per cent proactive enterprises, about 20 per cent active and nearly 70 per cent reactive (or *defensive* according to the typology of Miles and Snow). Evidently, the first risk a great deal; they often act intuitively and with little information. In some ways they are gambling on the future, hoping to win at least two out of three times, the second gain compensating for the loss. These are the enterprises that place the spirit of adventure before prudence and long analyses. The second try to seize opportunities early enough to draw superior benefits from them, but take the time to find enough information to lessen their mistakes or diminish the risk that they take. Finally, the reactive ones try to win every time by adopting an innovation only when it has proven itself in exchange for smaller gains than those of the trailblazers and innovators. It is the important presence of the first enterprises, in particular the gazelles, that best explains regional dynamism. But, how can local or regional networking or the multiplication of complicity and entrepreneurial culture facilitate their proliferation?

The answer can be seen in the rather large difference between the two curves at the start, a difference that decreases gradually in going towards the right (Figure 52.1). In the opportunities curve, it is networking, particularly that of the weak-signal networks, that causes the curve to be higher because it multiplies the information on the new opportunities for the enterprises on the look-out. But, these networks also provide at lower cost all sorts of information on the best ways of seizing these opportunities or to better adapt innovation to the market by offering as needed various resources at minimal cost, thanks to the available social capital. This is what is indicated by the widening of the information and resources curve at the origin.

Thus, the general effect of networking is first to help the proactive firms take even more chances (or more risk) with the market. In supplying them generously with ideas, information and resources, it allows these enterprises to succeed three out of four times, if not four out of five. With the help of the milieu, and thus of social capital, networking then encourages the firms to become gazelles even faster. This support, as much in the multiplication of ideas as in the increase of information to better utilize them, urges in this way active enterprises to move to the left in Figure 52.1, which increases accordingly the number of gazelles. This results in some regions having up to 15 to 20 per cent of these enterprises, which transforms the entire territorial dynamism.

In short, these networks develop a dynamic industrial atmosphere based on conventions and complicities, favouring new ideas and the sharing of various resources or links with external resources, and bridges with national and international markets. The enthusiasm spreads through the region, stimulating everybody. These networks end up creating spatial economies that compensate for the weakness in the economies of scale of small firms or completes those already existing, rendering the enterprises and the territory more competitive in order to ensure their development; unless, as observed in certain conservative regions, the milieu restricts all enthusiasm favouring instead ensured employment, for example, in the civil service, or discourages the entrepreneurs by placing all sorts of obstacles in the way of the establishment and development of the enterprises.

CONCLUSION

We can use the metaphor of well-known detective novels to understand the collective process of a dynamic entrepreneurship in a local or regional territory as in criminal matters. For example, if, like Colombo, one is able to recognize the direct causes of an isolated crime, when criminality increases in a community, or various forms of gangsterism occurs, this somewhat simple approach proves inadequate. Even the perspicacity of Sherlock Holmes or the intuition of Maigret, who created complex links which include the history of the criminal as well as the victim and the influence of their surroundings, are no longer sufficient. We must be able to reflect in the same way as William of Baskerville who *In the Name of the Rose* understood that the crimes committed by the monks of the Melk Monastery in the fourteenth century were related to a power struggle between the Pope and the Emperor and, ultimately, to a search for the truth. On the other hand, in their novels, Arthur Conan Doyle and Georges Simenon demonstrate that the success and the genius of Sherlock Holmes or Maigret cannot be explained without considering, in the first instance, the extremely entrepreneurial atmosphere of England in the late nineteenth century or, in the second, the work of hundreds if not thousands of policemen to complete the great detective task.

When we speak of criminality in a region, we cannot limit ourselves solely to the drives of the isolated petty or hardened criminals. On the contrary, we can consider that all societies can give rise to the marginal and the violent in greater or fewer numbers. In the case of widespread criminality, we must take into account the social disparities and exclusions. But, to leave it at that would lead us to believe that criminality per inhabitant would be greater in India, for example, where the religious caste system unofficially favours this exclusion, than in the USA where criminality is particularly high. It is then necessary to go to another level, that of the importance of permissiveness (particularly with arms in circulation) in the society and of the collective social delinquency. Likewise, a society like that in Russia, which for a long time had to operate in parallel with the highly centralized official system and use bribes, denunciations, as well as turning a blind eye, has much difficulty in curbing gangsterism. The developing economies that have witnessed the growth of relatively generalized systems of corruption have great difficulty in curbing crime that is an extension of this behaviour. It is all connected in a society.

In the same sense, we cannot describe enterprise multiplication by limiting ourselves to the simple analysis of some entrepreneurs' behaviour. The skills picked up during their childhood and adolescence and the one or more familiar models, as well as the idea of 'in the air' start-ups, the weight and dynamism of those directly involved like the family and, finally, the availability of nearby resources, have an important role to play even if many entrepreneurs, when asked, tend to attribute everything to their doggedness. Unless one wishes to limit himself to a positivist, or even neo-positivist, approach believing that everything can be explained by the existence of a prior order for a product or by a few exceptional individuals who take advantage of it; in the same way that in ancient history events were only explained by the king's behaviour, which was refuted in modern history. When we speak of multiple creations or territorial entrepreneurship, not only must we take into account the milieu, and thus the social capital and the dynamic complicity that it creates to systematically favour development, but we must integrate the shared conventions or the entrepreneurial culture that does or does not stimulate creation.

In other words, the entrepreneurs in one region, whatever their qualities, have a greater chance of succeeding if they can find all sorts of resources like good transportation and warehouses to receive their raw materials and expedite their products, like angel capital and banks to support their investments, like intermediaries such as proactive wholesalers, but also like all sorts of private and public organizations to sustain the innovation or the modernization of their production system and their development on both national and international markets, and especially like a shared willingness to succeed and back one another up. To understand this, a simple interpretationist approach (subjectivist) is not enough; as we have said, we need to reconstruct the complex reality in accordance with what we call a constructivist approach taking into account not only some of what is real, but also the wishes and the ways of doing things of the economic players.

Like every development process, entrepreneurship is simply the collective history of human beings (within a separate territory) seeking their own identity in order to find out who they are, and then seeking recognition for what they do (the noble results of their work through creation and innovation). And the entrepreneurs in question share this experience with all the members of their firms, their networks and their milieu.

REFERENCE

Marshall, A. (1919), *Industry and Trade*, 3rd edn, London: Macmillan.

53 Third-world entrepreneurship*

Peter Kilby

With but one exception, economists have conceptualized the task of the entrepreneur in the Third World as being no different than that in advanced economies. The sole exception is Everett Hagen. In his 1962 volume *On the Theory of Social Change: How Economic Growth Begins*, Hagen conceptualized the entrepreneur as a creative problem-solver interested in things in the practical and technological realm. His starting point is not a fully developed market economy, but a traditional economy in the Third World setting.

Deciding what to produce and how to do it, bearing risk, making judgments about men and things, being ever alert to price discrepancies, perceiving the possibility of a new combination and carrying it – such are the activities assigned to the entrepreneur, along with a supporting set of aptitudes, skills and psychological dispositions. With respect to the native populations of most developing countries, this conceptualization has not proved fruitful. Policies to promote entrepreneurship, in accord with the Knightian power to provide guarantees, have focused on the provision of finance. But experience has shown that the operational constraint has not been a shortage of risk capital, the problem has not been a shortage of entrepreneurial ventures. Rather the problem has been that, when established, these ventures fail to grow and fail to survive over the longer run.

Clearly, whether in an underdeveloped country or in an advanced market economy, the activities of the businessperson will, *inter alia*, everywhere entail – to greater or lesser degree – perceiving and pursuing apparent opportunity, mobilizing the necessary resources, making consequential judgments about uncertain outcomes, bearing the risk of loss those judgments bring and, as he or she pursues their venture, doing some things in a new way. And in both the advanced and the underdeveloped economy the growth of gross domestic product (GDP) is going to be powered by the engine of capital accumulation and advances in total factor productivity. Yet, it is the argument of this chapter, the entrepreneurial elements necessary to fuel this process differ. Specifically, what is requisite to success in 'Lagos' in terms of the mix of psychological propensities outlined by Smith, Knight and Schumpeter and in terms of the mix of concrete activities to be performed will bear only a partial resemblance to that which is observed in 'Chicago' or 'Osaka'.

I

The first step in setting out the precise nature of this Third World entrepreneurial task is to identify the structural circumstances that give rise to it. There are three. First, entrepreneurial activity is primarily directed towards import substitution. Second, in most instances there is a pre-existent technology shelf that the entrepreneur draws from.

Third, relative to their overseas industrial counterparts, these entrepreneurs face pervasive short-term uncertainties with regard to the supply of production inputs, uncertainties that directly impact the daily operation of the enterprise. Taken together these structural circumstances imply a significant shift in the balance of skills and activities that are called for.

Taking the last first, we begin with that structural feature in underdeveloped economies that is everywhere evident to the pedestrian observer, yet in its myriad manifestations is the most difficult to codify. It is the day-to-day *volatility of the market environment* in which the firm operates. Of the several sources of this volatility we shall label the first the problem of *imperfect factor inputs*. By this we mean there is often a mismatch between the quality of factor inputs required by a given technical process vis-à-vis those inputs that are actually available. A cause of downed or damaged equipment, electrical voltage is a good case. Many electric motors and control mechanisms are designed to tolerate a 5 to 7 per cent variation; surges or drop-offs of 15 to 30 per cent shut them down. Volatility is also present in raw material specifications in terms of such attributes as grade, moisture-content and foreign matter. For silica sand, cotton lint, kiln-dried lumber and cocoa beans, shortfall from the required standard not infrequently occurs because of poor quality control regimes or opportunistic adulteration by anonymous intermediaries. And then there is mismatch of labor skills. This finds its origins in the massive expansion in school enrollments that occurred after the end of colonialism. Because the supply of teachers is inelastic in the short run, formal teacher qualifications had to be reduced. Budgetary pressure on salaries, that came with this expansion, further weakened the quality of the recruitment pool. The circle was closed a decade later when adherence to external examination standards was terminated. A steep decline in formal skills in many countries has been the result, along with a rise in uncertainty as to what meaning an employer should attach to a given educational certification. All of these *factor imperfections* have implications for the entrepreneur's unit cost and product quality.

A second source of high volatility in the business environment comes from the normal range of *economic shocks*. There are external shocks to the firm's cost and level of demand that are present in almost all low-income agrarian economies. Agriculture looms large and farm output is subject to unforeseen drought, floods and outbreak of plant disease. Raw material prices and disposable income of the firm's customers are also directly impacted by shocks in the international sector – a shift in export prices, unexpected capital flows. And mention should be made of the turbulence that comes from the political domain. Some portion of these – electoral campaigns, urban strikes, ethnic conflict, even coups – might be said to be 'normal' to developing polities. Their most common impact is to result in the firm's temporary closure. Yet, significant as the productivity-depressing events are, in many countries far more volatility is needlessly added to the business environment by man-made *policy shocks*.

Policy shocks occur in varying degree in perhaps two-thirds of the countries in the developing world. Derivative from poor economic management, they are most prevalent in Africa and least in Southeast Asia. Badly designed policy or incompetent implementation of good policy handicaps the entrepreneur in one or more of the following ways: directing investment via price distortions into activities that may not add to GDP, raising the price of production inputs, and through irregular supply of infrastructural services causing stoppages in the firm's production. Again, electricity is a good example. A policy that provides the resources for a rapid expansion of generating capacity but skimps on financial provision for low-profile maintenance and rehabilitation leads to breakdown. The frequency of power interruption – reaching 3 to 6 hours *per day* in much of Africa – is worsened by lax implementation of existing maintenance regimes. Staff are recruited but little trained and lightly monitored, funds are diverted, supervision from the top is sporadic. As each firm protects itself by purchasing its standby generating plant, economies of scale vanish and the cost of power rises fourfold. A similar pattern of public breakdown and high-cost private provision holds for police protection respecting theft and armed robbery, destruction of property and personal security. Many firms cannot rely on the public water system and must drill their own bore holes. As for transport, poorly maintained roads raise delivery times, increase the frequency of vehicle breakdown and shorten their life. Finally, ill-designed policies in the domain of foreign trade – import quotas abruptly imposed and lifted, tariffs, customs administration, official and parallel foreign exchange markets – create far-reaching volatility for the price of what the entrepreneur sells and for the availability and cost of tradable inputs.

Such are the three sources of volatility the Third World entrepreneur faces, making his task both more difficult and more subject to supply-side uncertainties. The difficulty is augmented in that in wrestling with his numerous challenges, our Lagos entrepreneur has fewer specialist suppliers, management consulting firms and engineering services that he can draw on in the marketplace – or among his own employees – to help him solve his problems. Particularly when dealing with public officials – on foreign exchange permits, on utility connections, on standards certification, on import customs, on municipal regulations – the weakness in 'rules-based behavior' means that the entrepreneur is further taxed to invest in and rely upon personal ties to get things done. The lower the rung on the development ladder occupied by the economy, the greater the entrepreneur's burden in all these regards.

Happily, when we leave supply-side problems the second and third structural features of the late developing economy operate in the opposite direction, namely, to reduce and to simplify the demands placed upon the entrepreneur in other domains. The principal arena of investment activity is import replacement. In opposition to the classic view, rather than perceiving an unexploited market opportunity and bearing the demand-side risk in attempting to meet it, a huge array of market opportunities in the third world have been pre-identified and certified risk-free. Virtually every market that the local entrepreneur might serve has been mapped out and tested by imported products of every style, quality and cost. The extent of the market and its geographic distribution is known. Protected by tariff and quota, the entrepreneur's risks, while they are great, are primarily limited to the previously enumerated operational problems on the production side.

The third structural feature, also linked to 'being late', is the existence of an extensive technology backlog. This eases the burden in the initiation of new enterprises. No Schumpeterian innovation is required: for every would-be entrepreneur, off-the-shelf embodied technology is available in one form or another. Should one or more firms in the industry already be in place, the dominant modality is that of the departing skilled employee. Samuel Slater's famous 1789 exit from Arkwright & Strutt to bring the cotton textile industry to America, was followed by the less widely known spawning of some 30 additional cotton-spinning firms in the Blackstone Valley by former employees trained in Slater's own mills. And so it is in the Third World today. For virgin undertakings there is another modality. Knowledge as to choice of technology, equipment selection and installation is available through a variety of channels. Among them are the vast resources of the Internet, factory visits abroad, sales representatives of the major equipment suppliers, short-term training of key engineering staff at the supplier's home facility, turnkey used plant purchases, service agreements and joint-venture technical partnerships. In sum, to acquire production technology and to start up operation does not in itself present insurmountable difficulty.

II

As we have seen, entrepreneurial activities in the manufacturing sector takes place for the most part in the context of import-substitution. In contrast to the more advanced semi-industrialized countries – the erstwhile newly industrializing countries (NICs) – in the early-stage industrializing economies we observe import replacement of products and basic production technologies that can be characterized as 'mature'. Ongoing collaboration with a foreign firm is rare, beyond the initial six-months or a year at start-up, As for competition in the home market, it typically does not entail significant product differentiation, extensive advertising or sophisticated marketing strategies; after-sales servicing is minimal. Thus, the major element in the final price is the manufacturing cost. The central task of the entrepreneur is minimizing this magnitude and doing so within a difficult environment.

We can bring together the major elements of the import-substitution process – international cost differentials, the role of natural protection provided by transportation costs, tariff subsidies and the activities of the entrepreneur – in two diagrams. At this stage the exposition is set out in terms of an idealized, frictionless economy. In sections IV and V we add greater realism and consider a variety of factors that may thwart the process.

We take as our example light motorcycles. In Figure 53.1 Japan is shown as the most competitive supplier to Nigeria. The ex-factory price in Japan is \$750. With packaging and conveyance to a Japanese port, its free-on-board (FOB) price is \$780. Ocean freight, and insurance bring the Nigerian cost, insurance and freight (CIF) import price to \$1030, shown in panel (b). This is the price a local manufacturer must meet. But as shown by the potential average cost curve, the 27 per cent subsidy from natural protection is not sufficient to cover the anticipated cost of production. In panel (c) a 70 per cent tariff (T) is granted – bringing total protection to 97 per cent[1] – and profitable production is achieved. Consumption of motorbikes has fallen from 75 to 53. We have *commercial success* combined with a reduced real GDP. 'Nominal' entrepreneurial services are being rendered.

To achieve *economic success* the entrepreneur must bring costs down. The histograms in Figure 53.2 describe the desired path. From an initial cost-price at N_1 of \$1740, unit cost is brought down to the world CIF price (N_2) at \$1030, at which point the resources in the venture are just covering their opportunity cost and the entrepreneurial endeavor no longer represents a subtraction from GDP. 'Real' entrepreneurial services are now being rendered. Finally at N_3, Nigeria's comparative advantage of abundant labor is realized and the ex-factory price falls below that of Japan. Not only is the rate of return

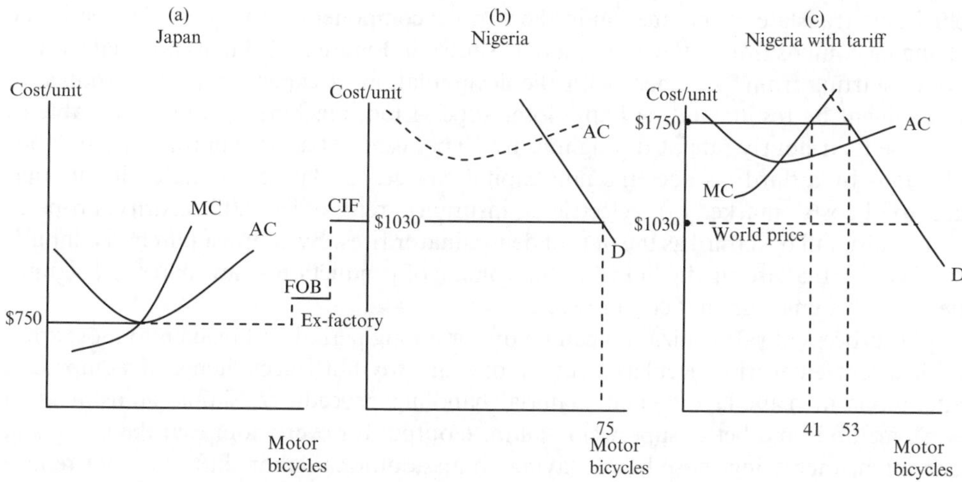

Notes: Ex-factory = $750; FOB = $780; CIF = $1030 = world price; CIF + T = $1750; Natural protection = $280 (27%); Tariff protection (T) = $720 (70%).

Figure 53.1 Entrepreneurship: replacing imports

now very high, but also with the door to exports open, the stage is set for entrepreneurial success on a vast scale.

How are these costs in Nigeria minimized, how is productivity increased? It is not mainly by investing in new technology or more advanced capital equipment. Rather it is by increasing the rate of materials-to-product throughput (MTPT) within the existing facilities. How potential throughput gains, that exist by virtue of raising organizational

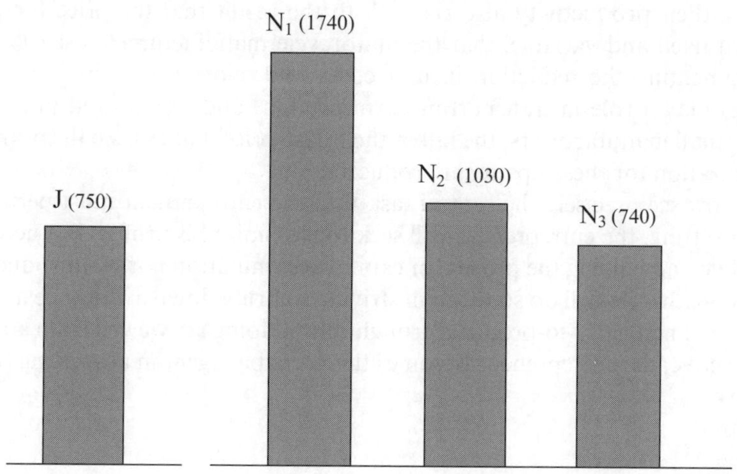

Notes: J: Japan; N_1: Nigeria – initial AC > world price; N_2: Nigeria – AC = world price; N_3: Nigeria – AC < world price.

Figure 53.2 Entrepreneurship: from nominal to real

efficiency, translate into reduction in the various components of unit cost is seen in the changing composition of the unit cost bars shown in Figure 53.2. Let us postulate a situation, starting from N_1, where with the accumulation of experience, the introduction of payment by results and perhaps closer supervision, machine operatives are able to increase their hourly rate of throughput by 50 per cent. At a first approximation, labor cost falls by a third, as does the unit capital charge, 'r'. Those purchased inputs that are 'fixed costs', marked (a) – electricity, insurance, rent, office staff, security, property taxes – also fall by a third as the output denominator rises. By contrast purchased inputs, marked (b), that are rigidly linked to the volume of production – raw materials, components, packaging – are not compressible.

This process of rationalization can go on for a long period and reach into most areas of business enterprise. Replacement of one or two bottleneck items of equipment, alterations in plant layout, new material handling procedures, simple adjustment in work methods and better supervision all raise output for every hour that the plant is in operation. Increasing those hours, laying on an additional labor shift, does not reduce unit labor cost, but it does so for capital and fixed-cost purchased inputs. And within a given shift there is often further lost time that can be captured, raising the productivity of all three inputs. Repeated visits to the factory floor typically disclose downed machines or other work stoppage that can be cut to a minimum by introducing planned maintenance regimes, holding spare parts inventories, and closer supervision of work methods. Unrelated to the continuity and pace of production, application of the same principles of management coordination and control can shrink materials wastage, prevent significant leakage to pilferage and theft, and insure uniformity in product quality; all of which reduce the cost of a standard unit of output.

Yet this is not the end of our story. The price of purchased inputs is in significant measure a function of productivity in supplier firms. As entrepreneurs in other firms similarly strive to minimize costs by raising utilization rates and lifting the pace of throughput, their productivity also rises. With the result that the price for purchased inputs, both fixed and variable, that the motorcycle manufacturer must pay now falls, further augmenting the reduction in unit cost. And, closing the circle, to the extent motorcycles play a role in transporting farm produce and inputs, and provide similar services to small manufacturers, the fall in their cost-price makes a small contribution to cost-minimization for these upstream producers.

We can now see precisely the central task that the entrepreneur must perform. As in every other setting, the entrepreneur will seek to maximize his profits. But he will not do so primarily by advancing the process of capital accumulation nor by introducing major innovation. Rather he will do so through striving to bring down average cost, striving to raise the rate of materials-to-product throughput. In doing so, viewed from an economy-wide perspective, the entrepreneur becomes the principal agent in advancing total factor productivity.

III

We can deploy our cost histograms in a heuristic fashion to capture the effects of a variety of phenomena. Indeed, as will soon become evident, the unit cost histogram is

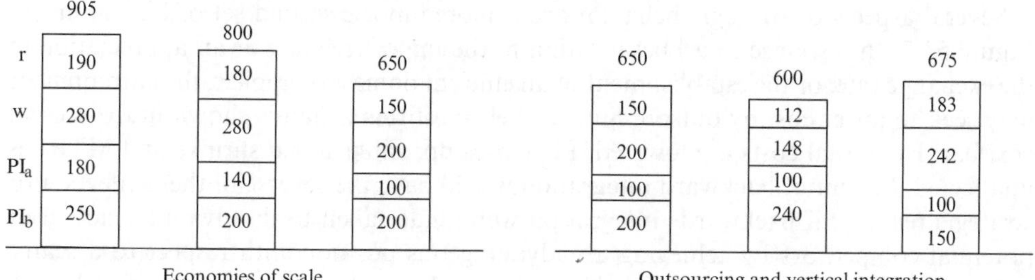

Notes: r: capital rental (interest foregone, obsolescence, risk premium); w: wages; PI_a: purchased inputs invariant to level of output; PI_b: purchased inputs that vary with output.

Figure 53.3 Economies of scale, outsourcing, and vertical integration (at 100 per cent efficiency)

capable of capturing the effects of all the factors that influence entrepreneurial performance. In this section we will examine the influence of economies of scale, of outsourcing and of vertical integration. We continue for a while longer to invoke the assumptions of a benign external environment and perfect operational efficiency.

Starting with the issue of scale, once the original risks of manufacture and consumer acceptance have been surmounted, entrepreneurs more often than not undertake to expand their productive facilities. This is done to increase sales and to improve competitiveness by gaining economies of scale. As to the latter, we can distinguish two groups of causal factors that reduce unit costs as the scale of production is enlarged. The first group includes the familiar items of spreading certain fixed costs in PI_a over a larger output, reaping pecuniary economies associated with bulk purchasing, and shifting from regional to national advertising. These cost reductions are unconnected with the pace of MTPT. This also holds for the pure scale effect ('the 0.6 rule') – the geometric relation of surface area to volume – wherein the capacity of buildings, storage vessels and continuous-process installations rises proportionately more rapidly than the materials required in their construction. Extra engineering costs may dilute this effect. The impact of these economies is depicted in the second cost bar of panel '(a)' in Figure 53.3, where unit cost of the motorcycle is reduced from the $900 shown earlier as N_3 to $800, for a savings of $100.

There are two additional scale factors that have their effect on cost by raising the MTPT. At higher levels of output it may be feasible to move to a more productive machine, or set off machines, of different design but subject to a high minimum threshold ('lumpiness'). This may also open the way for a better organization of plant layout and work flow. Either of these factors will raise MTPT. When both occur together the impact on MTPT is likely to be sizable. While the more rapid MTPT will augment labor productivity on a one-to-one basis, it typically will not do so for capital. This is because the embodied technology in the larger unit often entails a higher capital-intensity. The effect of adding these two factors to the first group of indirect factors adds another $150 in cost savings. These combined powerful scale effects are depicted in the third histogram. The $650 unit cost will be our starting point in section IV when we move to a more realistic set of descriptive assumptions.

Several aspects of strategic behavior are explored in the second set of histograms in Figure 53.3. In response to a liberalization in the import regime, or an appreciation in the exchange rate, or the establishment of an efficient domestic supplier, the entrepreneur may seek to lower cost by outsourcing. The effect of this action is shown in the second cost bar. Here total costs are lowered, PI_b jumps up, value added shrinks and MTPT is unaffected. Pursuit of backward integration would have the reverse of these effects. For strategic reasons, if backwards integration were undertaken to disadvantage actual or potential competitors by achieving an advantageous position with respect to a scarce input, such an action might well *raise* unit cost. This is shown in the third cost bar. A decision to extend credit to wholesale distributors might be done for the same reason, and with the same cost result. But such non-price cost-increasing stratagems are likely to be tempered owing to the fact that the ultimate weapon in the entrepreneur's arsenal and the one most critical for his survival is the capability to dig down to an average cost below that of all his competitors. Strategic behavior and economic efficiency meet.

IV

We now place our apparatus in a real-world setting. Here we encounter all the previously discussed natural volatility, factor input imperfections, public policy failures and internal organizational shortfalls that drag down productivity and raise unit costs. Some insights into the relative importance of each of these factors is afforded by the fact that the gross measure of MTPT – the rate of materials to finished product over the course of one year – can be broken down into three parts. The first is the average number of hours per week that the facility is in operation relative to maximum sustainable capacity, as judged by the entrepreneur. This is the well-known measure of 'capacity utilization', and almost all countries collect and publish numbers reporting 'capacity utilization in the manufacturing sector'. The second element affecting MTPT is duration of stoppages that occur in any given work shift. The final element is the *pace* of MTPT when production is actually under way.

Most of the factors controlling the level of capacity utilization are connected to maladroit economic policies. Starting with *the level of demand* for the firm's products, the number of shifts that are operated will be adversely affected by a slow-growing or stagnant GDP, by import-floods derivative from corrupt quota violation and by competition coming from smuggled goods.[2] Shifts are also lost to strikes, electoral campaigns and the other forms of public disorder mentioned earlier. But the most common causes of low capacity utilization is the inadequate *flow of production inputs*. On the one hand, foreign exchange shortages concomitant with an over-valued exchange rate constrict the supply of materials, components and spare parts available to the firm coming from abroad; on the other hand, the limited capacity of the banking system to provide short-term finance to cover normal working capital needs slows down the flow of all inputs. The litany is completed with the frequent breakdowns in the flow of public infrastructure inputs, in terms of port facilities, telecommunications, road transport and – most importantly – electricity.

Because we know average capacity utilization in the manufacturing sectors of Nigeria and Japan – and they are quite representative – we can roughly estimate the diminished

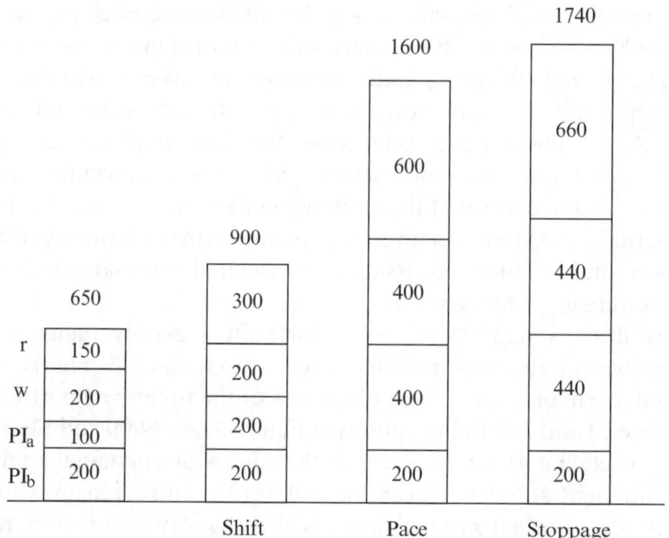

Notes: r: capital rental (interest foregone, obsolescence, risk premium); w: wages; PI_a: purchased inputs invariant to level of output; PI_b: purchased inputs that vary with output.

Figure 53.4 Average cost in a volatile environment and operational inefficiency

productivity and increased unit cost imposed by infrastructural and policy implementation mal-performance in Nigeria. In Japan – which sets the MTPT standard from which the \$650 ideal minimum cost is derived – utilization has ranged from 78 to 86 per cent; in Nigeria comparable numbers are 30 to 40 per cent.[3] Because reduction in the number of shifts worked does not affect labor productivity, the cost increases – a doubling – are limited to capital (r) and fixed-cost purchased inputs (PI_a). Thus, looking at the first and second histograms in Figure 53.4, we may say that policy-induced distortions in the Nigerian economic environment serve to raise production costs by more than a third.

Given the potency of these external factors in retarding the performance of the firm, it is not surprising that most development economists give little attention to the entrepreneurship question. They hold that problems of entrepreneurial performance do not spring from any supply shortage of the requisite services but rather flow from distorted economic incentives, defective regulatory environment, constrained availability of complementary inputs and incomplete information – more or less what our capacity utilization measure is capturing. While their data distinguish between 'foreign' and 'domestic', they do not identify the entrepreneurial direction of domestic firms by native-born, resident alien minority, state enterprise or joint venture. Nor are they likely to see statistics on the internal performance of the firm as is revealed in the *pace* of MTPT and the *stoppage rate* reported in the final two histograms of Figure 53.4.

Unlike our capacity utilization measure, which is a sector-wide average reflecting for the most part a common set of environmental conditions that every firm must deal with, our measures of MTPT pace and stoppage rate apply uniquely to firms directed by native entrepreneurs. With respect to pace, the average rate of throughput in these firms is typically one-third to one-half of best practice applicable to our \$650 benchmark.[4] Applying the more favorable figure of one-half, we see that the labor charge per motorcycle rises from \$200 to \$400 vis-à-vis our benchmark. More punishing is the fourfold increase in the capital charge and PI_a both handicapped by the earlier shift-related penalty. As reported in the third histogram, the total cost of manufacturing the motorcycle now has risen to \$1600. As for the stoppage rate, which we place at 10 per cent, its impact on MTPT is to lift costs for all categories, save PI_b by the same percentage amount. While pace is entirely under the control of the entrepreneur's management, stoppage is a function of both internal and external factors. Among the former are poorly trained workers, slack supervision, and maintenance issues; the principal external causes of short-term shutdown are power surges and cut-offs.

We can now draw several conclusions. First, in a poorly managed low-income economy, the native entrepreneur operates under a severe handicap in the running of his business. Second, even allowing for the roughness of the three-part partitioning, a comparison of the second and fourth histograms in Figure 53.4 – \$900 and \$1740 respectively vis-à-vis the \$650 benchmark – makes it clear that short-falls in managerial organization are a major component of this handicap. Indeed, for the entrepreneur who performs no better than average, the organizational factor is likely to play a more important role than the distorted market environment. It is here that a shortage in the supply of requisite entrepreneurial services makes itself manifest.

V

The final histogram of \$1740 returns us to our starting point in Figure 53.1, and now, in the language of the poet, 'we know the place for the first time'.[5] The task of the entrepreneur is simply to do what must be done to drive down that average cost figure below \$1030. We know that to achieve this cost-minimization objective he must raise his gross MTPT to a higher level. He does this by strengthening and extending his access to a steady flow of inputs coming from the foreign trade sector, from domestic suppliers, from public utilities and from financial institutions. Enlarging these transactions lifts the ceiling on capacity utilization. Elements in the perpetual search for alternative ways around the obstacles in the environment are likely to include building inventories to cushion supply interruptions, finding ways to substitute domestic for imported inputs, and diversifying into product lines subject to a different set of capacity constraints yet still within the core competence of the existing managerial organization.

The second avenue open to the entrepreneur to drive down average cost lies within his firm when production is under way. It is to institute those 'industrial engineering' initiatives, described earlier, that will maximize pace and minimize stoppage. These initiatives are supported by and take place within a larger managerial organization that sets objectives, plans the activities necessary to achieve those objectives, provides for their execution, and through control systems monitors outcomes, assesses feedback and sets in motion corrective action. While these systems of coordination and control must be in place and be well designed, more critical is the commitment and motivation of the firm's employees as they execute their tasks. Applying to all but the highest level of management, problems in this area seem to be responsible for much of the low rate of MTPT reported in Figure 53.4.

There are two aspects to the problem. One is the temptation facing every native entrepreneur to pursue a low-wage policy. With a queue of job applicants outside the factory gate, and the absence of public expectations as to employment conditions that apply to alien minority firms and multinational corporations, the entrepreneur can minimize his wage bill and reduce his administrative overhead by choosing the low-wage option. Thus one observes in many, perhaps a majority, of firms modest levels of pay, little in-house training, few if any formal promotion pathways, minimal health and retirement benefits, no job security and high labor turnover. Given the low level of commitment to the firm and to one's task that such conditions produce, attentiveness to the presence of substandard materials, to non-optimal work methods, to signs of equipment duress, to minor defects in product quality – attentiveness to these and other aspects of the work milieu is understandably low. A second factor, unconnected to the wage policy but contributing to low levels of employee initiative, is a reluctance of many entrepreneurs to delegate authority.[6] This has its greatest impact on top management and department heads, but tends to dampen spontaneous cooperative behavior and information transmittal at all levels.

If we have managed to identify what the entrepreneur's task is in early-stage developing countries, and if our orders of magnitude with respect to the contributing causes of low productivity are correct, are any new policy insights uncovered? Clearly the orthodox position on the importance of a stable macroeconomy, an open trade regime, regulatory reform and a limited but high-quality infrastructure is confirmed by our analysis of capacity utilization. While a well-functioning banking system is essential for the provision of working capital finance, we would downplay the importance of dedicated long-term risk-capital lending facilities. Rather pride of place should be given to training and demonstration missions in the area of production management and labor management. Such training, short term and often industry-specific, has been well provided in years long past by ILO Productivity Centers. Such centers or local graduate business schools are the obvious vehicles for providing such assistance. Finally, the delegation of authority issue would seem to be best approached through corporate governance. Elements of reform are likely to be enlarged boards of directors, more professional non-family members, representation of a variety of stakeholders and greater transparency. However, given that ownership is typically concentrated in the hands of the entrepreneur and his family, it is a difficult business and no simple enactments have yet been identified.

NOTES

* This is an initial draft of a chapter being prepared for the forthcoming volume *Entrepreneurship: Organizing for Development*. This research was supported by a generous grant from Wesleyan University.

1. If the manufacture of motorcycles in Nigeria utilizes materials bearing a tax of less than 70 per cent, the effective subsidy is larger.
2. When lack of demand is related to the poor quality of the firm's product – and thereby reducing the number of shifts – the culprit is the entrepreneur rather than government policy. Government policy is equally not at fault when low GDP growth is caused by adverse movements in the terms of trade or weather-related agricultural setbacks.
3. Both here and with respect to the two other elements of the MTPT, there is great dispersion around the

mean. Among the factors that determines the firm's place above or below that mark is the quality of the entrepreneur's performance.
4. Based on the author's field observations over several decades in manufacturing firms in East and West Africa and several Asian countries. Similar productivity differentials have been uncovered by econometric studies, matched inter-firm productivity comparisons, and a variety of management surveys.
5. 'And the end of all our exploring will be to arrive where we have started and know the place for the first time' (T.S. Eliot, 1943, p. 39).
6. Collectivist societies are characterized by a patriarchical social organization and 'high power distance'. Those in authority are reluctant to delegate power, even when the good of the organization may call for it. Evidence that this phenomenon has played a major role in firm mortality in West Africa is summarized in the author's 'The heffalump revisited' (Kilby, 2003).

REFERENCES

Eliot, T.S. (1943), 'Little Gidding', *Four Quartets*, New York: Harcourt, Brace and Company.
Hagen, E. (1962), *On the Theory of Social Change: How Economic Growth Begins*, Homewood, IL: Dorsey Press.
Kilby, P. (2003), 'The heffalump revisited', *Journal of International Entrepreneurship*, **1**, 13–29.

54 Trust and entrepreneurship

Friederike Welter

INTRODUCING THE CONCEPT OF TRUST

Trust has gained attention in entrepreneurship research over the past decade because of its influence on reducing transaction costs and risks involved with entrepreneurship. However, the concept has proved difficult to define. Most definitions build on the following elements: reciprocity, expectations and trustworthiness (Höhmann and Malieva, 2005). Reciprocity is required for trust as it signals to trustor and trustee that the trust they extend to each other will be given back. In this regard, trust is a result of expectations towards others. In other words, I expect an unknown person to act in my own interest or at least to take my interests into account although I cannot be sure about the final outcome of my decision; I just hope not to be disappointed, which can be based on my interpretation of signals sent by the other party. In this regard, trust involves a 'leap of faith' (Möllering, 2006) which is required to create familiarity between partners. It is here that trustworthiness comes in: individuals can signal that they are worthy of trust, thus reducing the initial 'leap of faith' and encouraging trusting behaviour. Trustworthiness is reflected in, for example, recommendations of other, trusted and known parties, reputations, previous behaviour and a general willingness not to cheat on others (Nooteboom, 2002).

UNDERSTANDING TRUST IN ENTREPRENEURSHIP

Trust can be differentiated into personal and institutional trust. Trust has been shown to play a role in networks and for network emergence (Anderson and Jack, 2002; Neergaard and Ulhoi, 2006), for credit relations of small firms (Howorth and Moro, 2006), to help new entrepreneurs in gaining legitimacy (Aldrich, 2000; Jenssen, 2001) and to start their business (Liao and Welsch, 2005), and to generally assist in business relations and cooperation (Chadarova, 2007), in particular also across borders (Wallace et al., 1999; Welter and Smallbone, 2008). Most entrepreneurship research has focused on the role of personal trust for entrepreneurial behaviour, often studying trust indirectly (for a review see Welter et al., 2004a). Personal trust may arise from the characteristics of a group such as an ethnic or kinship group, but it also occurs in bilateral (business) relationships, often longstanding ones, where persons have got to know each other (Williamson, 1993). In both cases, they know or assume that the partner/friend will not behave in a way detrimental to the relationship, even without written rules. Such relationships are therefore governed by norms, values and codes of conduct inherent in a business environment and/or wider society.

Research has also focused on the role of institutional trust for entrepreneurship (Welter and Smallbone, 2006). Institutional trust reflects trust into institutions, drawing attention to the fact that only people can trust; things, technical systems and institutions cannot (Höhmann and Malieva, 2005). Where trust into institutions is high, individuals are confident that they can rely on binding rules, regulations, laws and norms, which assists them when setting up business relationships with unfamiliar business partners, as they are able to draw on a shared understanding of the rules governing their mutual behaviour. Moreover, in case a business partner cheats, entrepreneurs are able to make use of legal regulations and go to court. Here, institutional trust is based on legal safeguards and sanctions in case the relationship fails; and it is essential for the efficient operation of a market economy, as the scope of trust extends beyond the number of people that are known personally.

In this regard, trust fulfils a role as a sanctioning mechanism, thus complementing the regulations and norms existing in economies and societies. Trust lowers transaction costs through providing information and a means to enforce contracts, so that the possibility of opportunistic behaviour diminishes. Moreover, personal trust complements institutional trust in those cases in which an individual does not want to rely merely on institutional arrangements (Granovetter, 1985).

On the other hand, research on trust in hostile and turbulent environments points out the role of trust in substituting for a deficient business and societal environment, where norms, rules and values are either absent or no longer functioning (well). This applies, for example, to economies that are in the process of transformation from centrally planned to market-based systems. Here, formal institutions that are essential for large-scale and sustainable development of private sector businesses are either non-existent or inadequately focused on the needs of entrepreneurs. This results in institutional distrust (Raiser, 1999; Rose-Ackerman, 2001), which is re-enforced by 'heritage' from the socialist period when individuals had strong mutual ties with family and friends, but mistrusted public institutions (Raiser et al., 2001). In such a situation, personal trust is required and simultaneously substitutes for missing and deficient institutions such as weakly specified legal regulations and inadequate law enforcement. Examples refer to a heavy reliance on networking in order to mobilize resources, and to cope with highly bureaucratic structures (Ledeneva, 1998; Smallbone and Welter 2001).

However, relations between personal and institutional trust are complex: personal trust is context-bound, but to a lesser extent than institutional trust, which requires a functioning institutional structure of the society. Williamson (1993: 476) therefore stated that 'transactions that are viable in an institutional environment that provides strong safeguards may be nonviable in institutional environments that are weak'.

Trust is either strong or weak. If an individual (the trustor) assumes that most people are reliable and well intentioned, that in case of negative experiences laws and regulations will be available, and that active and extensive cooperation can bring considerable advantages, trust is strong (Höhmann and Malieva, 2005). In this regard, some research focusing on trust environments has attempted to identify low- and high-trust countries (Fukuyama, 1995), where trust is seen as fostering the economic development and general performance of economies.

Trust also has dark sides. This is reflected in, for example, an over-embeddedness of entrepreneurial actions in social relations which in turn might restrict the development of entrepreneurship in the long run exactly because of its emphasis on personal trust in the form of strong ties for doing business (Zahra et al., 2006). Moreover, where institutional trust does not exist or is low, because rules are not implemented properly and leave room for discretionary decisions, individuals frequently are forced to resort to bribery in order to reduce risk and uncertainty in business relations (Möllering and Stache, 2007), which in turn contribute to a vicious circle as institutional trust cannot develop.

BUILDING TRUST

Surprisingly few studies so far have concentrated on how trust in entrepreneurship is built (and destroyed). This might partly be due to the fact, that empirically it would need a longitudinal research approach. Trust, including institutional trust, is triggered on a personal level, by, for example, personal contacts or recommendations through 'trusted' (known and familiar) entrepreneurs and customers, the reputation of one partner, or positive experiences with partners over time as a result of repeated exchanges. Positive experiences enhance trust-building, while negative experiences with one partner could result in an overall mistrusting attitude towards new partners. Trust-building is facilitated, where entrepreneurs can draw on a common background or common experiences. For example, research on trust in entrepreneurship across Western and Eastern Europe has demonstrated that entrepreneurs mainly rely on either recommendations from trusted persons or previous business experiences when selecting new business partners; regardless of whether they operate in Western or Eastern Europe (Höhmann and Welter, 2005; Welter et al., 2004b).

Where such a shared background is missing, individuals often revert to stereotyping in order to make the initial leap of faith, as stereotyping allows them to cope with unfamiliar situations and persons (Welter et al., 2008). Luhmann (2000: 95) refers to this process as 'familiarity breeding unfamiliarity', where symbols help to reintroduce the unfamiliar into an otherwise known and trusted world.

Regional and sectoral factors additionally facilitate trust-building so entrepreneurs are able to draw on shared rules and conventions (Welter, 2005). Examples include the long-distance trade relations in medieval Europe where trust-based relationships between unknown partners were rendered possible through a variety of 'pre-modern' institutions, such as guilds or merchant courts (Greif, 1993). This so-called traders' coalition relied on trust-based reputation mechanisms: agents gained reputations as honest persons based on their past behaviour, while merchants rewarded this reputation through repeated business (Greif, 1989). Close mutual supervision and control, as well as community penalties and the benefits coming with the membership of this particular group played a major role in preventing agents from cheating, thus assisting in building trust (Greif, 1993). Similar mechanisms are also known from Italian districts (for example, Dei Ottati, 2005), where the local 'code of fair behaviour' creates a specific trust milieu within a region and for the firms settled in the district. Other modern examples of organizational commonalities refer to common sectoral 'cultures' in the banking industry, which are, for example, documented in a specific dress code. All these examples indicate a role for sector-specific influences in building trust.

Nooteboom (2002) distinguishes three major stages of building trust: control in the absence of trust; assessing trustworthiness and developing tolerance levels of trust; and widenening these tolerance levels. In the control stage, partners either proceed step by step, or install safeguards based on their own interests, because there is no genuine basis for trust. In the second phase, knowledge and experience allows partners to assess their trustworthiness. By setting tolerance levels for trust, they create some scope for trusting each other, without giving up the control option. Tolerance levels are widened in the third stage, as a result of shared cognitive frames. These three stages may overlap and are not required to occur sequentially. The process of trust-building draws attention to the complex nature of the trust phenomenon, emphasizing its duality as pointed out by Möllering (2005: 283): 'trust and control each assume the existence of the other, refer to each other and create each other, but remain irreducible to each other'. Research on cross-border entrepreneurship illustrates this, showing that during the process of building trust, personal relations can substitute for formal control mechanisms, but trust also develops simultaneously from controlling partners and starting to socialize with them, indicating the 'daily life' embeddedness of trust in entrepreneurial actions (Welter and Smallbone, 2008).

Overall, trust-building is an upward spiral with self-reinforcing and recursive relationships between the different stages, and it is a time-consuming process. Negative experiences leave individuals disappointed. This results in or increases cognitive distance between partners, thus further impeding trust building, because it hinders the 'leap of faith' required for trust-building.

OUTLOOK

Trust is a conditional phenomenon, depending on contexts, situations and cognitions. Regarding the context- and process-dimensions of the trust phenomenon, this poses conceptual and empirical challenges for entrepreneurship research. Empirically, the operationalization of the various facets of trust poses a challenge, along with adequate methods for researching trust. Trust is very much socially constructed; it also is partly habitual behaviour. Both render 'objective' measurements difficult, especially in cross-cultural studies, and this also poses the question of how to adequately ask for trust. Ideally, the phenomenon of trust-building needs to be studied longitudinally.

Conceptually, the question remains as to whether it is genuine trust or more of a 'calculated risk' (Williamson, 1993) playing a role for entrepreneurship. As apparent in the dual nature of trust, it is both trust and control which are needed. For future research on trust and entrepreneurship research, it is therefore of interest to explore this duality and the consequences for entrepreneurial activities, in particular for their development potential, in more depth.

REFERENCES

Aldrich, H. (2000), 'Entrepreneurial strategies in new organizational populations', in R. Swedberg (ed.), *Entrepreneurship: The Social Science View*, Oxford: University Press, pp. 211–28.

Anderson, A.R. and S.L. Jack (2002), 'The articulation of social capital in entrepreneurial networks: a glue or a lubricant?', *Entrepreneurship & Regional Development*, **14**, 193–210.

Chadarova, T. (2007), 'Business relations as trusting relations: the case of Bulgarian small businesses', in K. Roth (ed.), *Social Networks and Social Trust in the Transformation Countries*, Freiburger Sozialanthropologische Studien 15, Münster: Lit, pp. 276–302.

Dei Ottati, G. (2005), 'Global competition and entrepreneurial behaviour in industrial districts: trust relations in an Italian industrial district', in H.-H. Höhmann, and F. Welter (eds), *Trust and Entrepeneurship: A West–East Perspective*, Cheltenham, UK and Northampton, MA, USA: Edward Elgar, pp. 255–71.

Fukuyama, F. (1995), *Trust – The Social Virtues and the Creation of Prosperity*, New York: Free Press.

Granovetter, M. (1985), 'Economic action and social structure: the problem of embeddedness', *American Journal of Sociology*, **28** (1), 1–22.

Greif, A. (1989), 'Reputation and coalitions in medieval trade: evidence on the Maghribi traders', *Journal of Economic History*, **49** (4), 857–82.

Greif, A. (1993), 'Contract enforceability and economic institutions in early trade: the Maghribi traders' coalition', *American Economic Review*, **83** (3), 525–48.

Höhmann, H.-H. and E.Malieva (2005), 'The concept of trust: some notes on definitions, forms and sources', in H.-H. Höhmann and F. Welter (eds), *Trust and Entrepreneurship: An East–West Perspective*, Cheltenham, UK and Northampton, MA, USA: Edward Elgar, pp. 7–23.

Höhmann, H.-H., and F. Welter (eds) (2005), *Trust and Entrepreneurship: A West–East Perspective*, Cheltenham, UK and Northampton, MA USA: Edward Elgar.

Howorth, C. and A. Moro (2006), 'Trust within entrepreneur bank relationships: insights from Italy', *Entrepreneurship Theory and Practice*, **30** (4), 495–517.

Jenssen, J.I. (2001), 'Social networks, resources and entrepreneurship', *Entrepreneurship and Innovation*, **2** (2), 103–9.

Ledeneva, A.V. (1998), *Russia's Economy of Favours: Blat, Networking and Informal Exchange*, Cambridge: Cambridge University Press.

Liao, J., and H. Welsch (2005), 'Roles of social capital in venture creation: key dimensions and research implications', *Journal of Small Business Management*, **43** (4), 345–62.

Luhmann, N. (2000), 'Familiarity, confidence, trust: problems and alternatives', in Gambetta, D. (ed.), *Trust: Making and Breaking Cooperative Relations*, Department of Sociology, University of Oxford, pp. 94–107, available at: http://www.cogsci.ed.ac.uk/~rnp/papers/jcscw/trust/luhmann94-107.pdf (accessed 11 May 2008).

Möllering, G. (2005), 'The trust/control duality: an integrative perspective on positive expectations of others', *International Sociology*, **20** (3), 283–305.

Möllering, G. (2006), *Trust: Reason, Routine, Reflexivity*, Amsterdam: Elsevier.

Möllering, G. and F. Stache (2007), *German–Ukrainian Business Relationships: Trust Development in the Face of Institutional Uncertainty and Cultural Differences*, MPIfG Discussion Paper 07/11, Cologne: MPIfG.

Neergaard, H. and J.P. Ulhoi (2006), 'Government agency and trust in the formation and transformation of interorganizational entrepreneurial networks', *Entrepreneurship Theory and Practice*, **30** (4), 519–39.

Nooteboom, B. (2002), *Trust: Forms, Foundations, Functions, Failures and Figures*, Cheltenham, UK Northampton, MA, USA: Edward Elgar.

Raiser M. (1999), 'Trust in transition', EBRD Working Paper, 39, London: EBRD.

Raiser, M., C. Haerpfer, T. Nowotny and C. Wallace (2001), 'Social capital in transition: a first look at the evidence', EBRD Working Paper, 61, London: EBRD.

Rose-Ackerman, S. (2001), 'Trust and honesty in post-socialist societies', *Kyklos*, **54** (fasc. 2/3), 415–44.

Smallbone, D. and F. Welter (2001), 'The distinctiveness of entrepreneurship in transition economies', *Small Business Economics*, **16** (4), 249–62.

Wallace, C., in association with O. Shmulyar and V. Bedzir (1999), 'Investing in social capital: the case of small-scale, cross-border traders in post-communist Central Europe', *International Journal of Urban and Regional Research*, **23** (4), 751–70.

Welter, F. (2005), 'Culture versus branch? Looking at trust and entrepreneurial behaviour from a cultural and sectoral perspective', in H.-H. Höhmann, and F. Welter (eds), *Trust and Entrepeneurship: A West–East Perspective*, Cheltenham, UK and Northampton, MA, USA: Edward Elgar, pp. 24–38.

Welter, F. and D. Smallbone (2006), 'Exploring the role of trust in entrepreneurial activity', *Entrepreneurship Theory and Practice*, **30** (4), 465–75.

Welter, F. and D. Smallbone (2008), 'Entrepreneurship in a cross border context: the example of transition countries', paper presented to ICSB World Conference, Halifax, June.

Welter, F., T. Kautonen and M. Stoycheva (2004a), 'Trust in enterprise development, business relationships and business environment – a literature review', in H.-H. Höhmann and F. Welter (eds), *Entrepreneurial Strategies and Trust: Structure and Evolution of Entrepreneurial Behavioural Patterns in 'Low Trust' and 'High Trust' Environments of East and West Europe, Part 1: A Review*, Arbeitspapiere und Materialien, 54, Bremen: Forschungsstelle Osteuropa, pp. 13–25.

Welter, F., T. Kautonen, A. Chepurenko, E. Malieva and U. Venesaar (2004b), 'Trust environments and entrepreneurial behavior – exploratory evidence from Estonia, Germany and Russia', *Journal of Enterprising Culture*, **12** (4), 327—49.

Welter, F., N. Veleva and S. Kolb (2008), 'Trust and learning in cross-border partnerships in an enlarged Europe', Deliverable 15 of the CBCED project, Siegen: University of Siegen.
Williamson, O.E. (1993), 'Calculativeness, trust and economic organization', *Journal of Law and Economics*, **36**, 453–86.
Zahra, S., R.I. Yavuz and D. Ucbasaran (2006), 'How much do you trust me? The dark side of relational trust in new business creation in established companies', *Entrepreneurship Theory and Practice*, **30** (4), 541–59.

55 Venture capital

Jeffrey M. Pollack and Thomas H. Hawver

Venture capital (VC) represents a financing option for entrepreneurs whereby funds are provided by an investor, to a recipient, as either seed money, start-up funds or expansion funding to start, or grow, a business (Jeng and Wells, 2000). Generally, a firm providing venture capital is a privately owned company representing the interests of multiple individual wealthy investors with the primary purpose of maximizing return on investment over time (Burton and Scherschmidt, 2004; de Bettignies and Brander, 2007). Though an award of VC funding is difficult to achieve, funds from venture capitalists are especially desirable for entrepreneurs due to the relative flexibility of the equity finance structure and available repayment options. We describe, briefly, the history of venture capital, the similarities and differences between alternative funding options, as well as the procurement process for entrepreneurs.

Since 1977, bank lending has remained fairly constant while VC investments are 100 times larger in 2001 than they were in 1997 (Ueda, 2002). An organization called American Research and Development, founded in Massachusetts in 1946, is considered to be the first modern venture capital company, and since then VC firms have specialized in matching investment capital with ventures that are screened and deemed worthy of investment (Allen, 1969; Jeng and Wells, 2000). In general, the venture capital process is described as having five main steps: (1) deal origination, (2) deal screening, (3) deal evaluation, (4) deal structuring and (5) post-investment activities (Tyebjee and Bruno, 1984). Due to the growth in VC funding, and the involved process of both receiving and utilizing VC funding, it is no surprise that academic interest in the domain of venture capitalism has grown considerably in recent years.

The activities, investments, structure and impact of VC firms across countries, industries, as well as between firm stages is well documented within the literature on venture capital (for example, Jeng and Wells, 2000; Pintado et al., 2007; Sheu and Lin, 2007). Additionally, much empirical evidence examines the actual impact of VC funding by comparing, over time, firms that receive VC funding with firms that do not receive VC funding (for a review see Brau et al., 2004). Extant research, ultimately, is not conclusive regarding the overall impact of VC funding. Research exists to support, as well as to refute, the conclusion that the investment of VC funding improves financial viability and survival of a firm over time (Brau et al., 2004).

Business ventures have several financing options available to them when seeking capital. These options often include (1) family and friends, (2) bank loans, (3) angels, and (4) venture capital (Pintado et al., 2007; Van Auken, 2001). Venture capital is distinct from these alternative financing options in important ways. Personal funds, or funds from family and friends are often quite limited and are generally exhausted on business expenses during the early stages of the investment-seeking process. Bank loans provide an alternative to using personal, family or friend's funds, but there are important differences between bank funding and VC funding.

Similar to VC firms, banks do evaluate new ventures and the risks that are associated with supplying capital. However, bank loans can be very small and VC firm investments typically start at very large amounts (Gompers and Lerner, 2006). Additionally, banks are often viewed as passive investors who focus on the financial health of the venture and receive a fixed return on their investment. Venture capital firms, however, are active investors. Venture capital firms often gain a level of ownership of the venture through equity financing and they actively participate in the management of the venture in an attempt to earn a return greater than that of a fixed loan (Gompers et al., 1998). In this process VC firms generally provide guidance and expertise to the recipient of the capital investment. This large amount of capital, time and energy that VC firms invest, though appealing to new ventures endeavoring to grow, make VC funding more difficult to obtain than bank loans.

'Angels', wealthy individuals who funds start-ups out of their own funds, represent another alternative funding option for entrepreneurs (Gompers, 1994). The scope of 'angel' financing is limited by the wealth of these individuals and this option is not a readily available, or generally viable, source for large amounts of capital (Jeng and Wells, 2000).

The process of procuring VC funding is an exhaustive endeavor with limited chances of success. First, the entrepreneur must have an idea or an existing venture that appeals to a VC firm. The entrepreneur has two options available to them when seeking VC capital (Schwienbacher, 2007). The first is to find a VC firm that is interested in the idea before a venture is created. This option alleviates the entrepreneur from wasting the effort on an idea that will not receive funding. The second option is to spend the time and effort on creating the venture and then seeking the investment of a VC firm to expand and grow.

If interest has been gained from a VC firm in a new venture, the new venture will be vetted thoroughly by the VC firm while negotiations take place. When negotiating with a bank for a loan the entrepreneur may not be compelled to share all the pertinent information regarding the venture. When negotiating with a VC firm there is rarely a case of asymmetric information between the entrepreneur and VC firm (that is, transparency theory, signaling theory; Ueda, 2004). The VC firm will consider the attractiveness of the opportunity (for example market size, technology, competition), the top management team, and the terms of the investment contract (Kaplan and Stromberg, 2001) during their negotiations with the entrepreneur. If the VC firm determines that the criteria for investing in the new venture are satisfactory, capital will likely be provided to the new venture.

As bank loans are provided with respective interest rates, VC financing comes with a price that some entrepreneurs may view as distasteful. If an entrepreneur attains financing from a VC firm, that entrepreneur is likely giving the VC firm a predetermined amount of ownership of the venture and, therefore, a portion of the control of the venture. Venture capital firms are sometimes allowed such rights as allocation of cash flow, voting, board and other control rights (Kaplan and Stromberg, 2001). However, while some control may be surrendered, VC financing can have benefits for a new venture as well. Venture capital firms will often provide assistance in fund-raising, strategic analysis and management recruiting (Gorman and Sahlman, 1989), all working for the goal of growing the venture.

While attaining venture capital for an entrepreneur can be, and usually is, a challenging task, the growth of VC firms in the past 30 years shows the importance of venture capital as a potential source of new venture funding. Distinct from other sources of funding such as banks and angel investors, venture capital financing provides entrepreneurs with an opportunity to develop their venture in ways that those other sources do not. However, as with most other sources of funding, there are risks and rewards associated with venture capital, for both the VC firm and the entrepreneur; control of the venture is surrendered for capital funding and strategic guidance. While the research related to the impact of VC funding is not conclusive, the growth of the firms indicates that it is a source of funding for entrepreneurial ventures that is likely to exist for years to come.

REFERENCES

Allen, L. (1969), 'Venture capital financing – an innovation', *Journal of Small Business Management*, **7**, 3–14.

Brau, J.C., R.A. Brown and J.S. Osteryoung (2004), 'Do venture capitalists add value to small manufacturing firms? An empirical analysis of venture and nonventure capital-backed initial public offerings', *Journal of Small Business Management*, **42**, 78–92.

Burton, J. and R. Scherschmidt (2004), 'First-time venture fund raising: challenges and best practices', *The Journal of Private Equity*, **8**, 9–21.

De Bettignies, J.E. and J.A. Brander (2007), 'Financing entrepreneurship: bank finance versus venture capital', *Journal of Business Venturing*, **22**, 808–32.

Gompers, P.A. (1994), 'The rise and fall of venture capital', *Business and Economic History*, **23**, 1–26.

Gompers, P.A. and J. Lerner, (2006), *The Venture Capital Cycle*, Cambridge, MA: MIT Press.

Gompers, P.A., J. Lerner, M.M. Blair and T. Hellmann (1998), 'What drives venture capital fundraising?', *Brookings Papers on Economic Activity (Microeconomics)*, 149–204.

Gorman, M. and W.A. Sahlman (1989), 'What do venture capitalists do?', *Journal of Business Venturing*, **4**, 231–48.

Jeng, L.A. and P.C.Wells (2000), 'The determinants of venture capital funding: evidence across countries', *Journal of Corporate Finance*, **6**, 241–89.

Kaplan, S.N. and P. Stromberg (2001), 'Venture capitalists as pricipals: contracting, screening, and monitoring', *The American Economic Review*, **91**, 426–30.

Pintado, T.R., D.G.P. de Lema and H.E. Van Auken (2007), 'Venture capital in Spain by stage of development', *Journal of Small Business Management*, **45**, 68–88.

Schwienbacher, A. (2007), 'A theoretical analysis of optimal financing strategies for different types of capital-constrained entrepreneurs', *Journal of Business Venturing*, **22**, 753–81.

Sheu, D.F. and H.S. Lin (2007), 'Impact of venture capital on board composition and ownership structure of companies: an empirical study', *International Journal of Management*, **24**, 573–620.

Tyebjee, T.T. and A.V. Bruno (1984), 'A model of venture capitalist investment activity', *Management Science*, **30**, 1051–66.

Ueda, M. (2002), 'Banks versus venture capital', paper presented at the CEPR, June, Discussion Paper No. 3411, available at: http://ssrn.com/abstract=321068.

Ueda, M. (2004), 'Banks versus venture capital: project evaluation, screening, and expropriation', *The Journal of Finance*, **59**, 601–22.

Van Auken, H.E. (2001), 'Financing small technology-based companies: the relationship between familiarity with capital and the ability to price and negotiate investment', *Journal of Small Business Management*, **39**, 240–58.

Index

Titles of publications are in *italics*.